THE LANAHAN READINGS

in the

American Polity

FOURTH EDITION

THE LANAHAN READINGS

in the

American Polity

FOURTH EDITION

—

Ann G. Serow
Kingswood-Oxford School
Central Connecticut State University

Everett C. Ladd

LANAHAN PUBLISHERS, INC.

Baltimore

The text of this book was composed in Bembo with display type set in Garamond.
Composition by Bytheway Publishing Services.
Manufacturing by Victor Graphics, Inc.

ISBN-10   1-930398-09-3
ISBN-13   978-1-930398-09-2

LANAHAN PUBLISHERS, INC.
324 Hawthorne Road
Baltimore, MD 21210-2303
1-866-345-1949 TOLL FREE
WWW.LANAHAN PUBLISHERS.COM

6 7 8 9 0

To Our Students

CONTENTS

PART TWO

The Constitution
and American Democracy

PART THREE

Separation of Powers

PART FOUR

Federalism

PART FIVE

Congress

PART SIX

The Presidency

PART SEVEN

The Executive Branch

PART EIGHT

The Judiciary

Contents

PART ELEVEN

Interest Groups

PART TWELVE
Voting and Elections

PART THIRTEEN

Political Parties

PART FOURTEEN

The Media

PART FIFTEEN

Political Economy and Public Welfare

PART SIXTEEN

America in a Changed World

PREFACE

The first edition of *The LANAHAN READINGS IN THE AMER-ICAN POLITY* began a happy new collaboration of the editors with LANAHAN PUBLISHERS, INC., and Donald W. Fusting, who founded this new publishing company in 1995. During the previous decade, we had worked closely and confidently with Don on two earlier versions of this book, *The American Polity Reader*, and we were pleased that the association would continue—in fact, quite pleased as it turned out: the third edition of *The LANAHAN READINGS* was assigned in nearly four hundred schools.

Launching another new edition of an established volume is still a big step. What matters to students using the volume, however, is what's between the covers. Here, readers of the new fourth edition will find in large measure both fundamental continuity in basic design and big changes in specific readings.

There's good reason for continuity. This book is designed to help undergraduates who are taking the basic American government course better understand their country's political system by providing essential readings on American ideas, constitutional system, core political institutions, public opinion, political competition, and policy debates. All of these readings have in fact shown exceptional continuity over time because they reflect the views and values of a society that is strikingly similar now at the beginning of the twenty-first century to what it was when the United States was founded in the late eighteenth century.

At first glance, this proposition might seem surprising. After all, in some regards the America we now inhabit differs greatly from that of George Washington, James Madison, and Thomas Jefferson. They traveled either on foot or, quite literally, by horsepower; we travel faster and more comfortably in automobiles and jet planes. They could communicate only face to face or through the written word; we have now gone beyond the telephone to the Internet. The average life expectancy in their day was thirty-three years; in ours, seventy-five—and so on is the process of change across so many of the physical dimensions of life.

But in social and political values, Americans in 1776 and now, in the twenty-first century, are similar people. That's true because America's founding brought the nation to modernity so abruptly and completely. It was a profound break from the aristocratic past that dominated European life—as indeed life in countries all around the world. The great French social commentator, Alexis de Tocqueville, grasped this fact more fully perhaps than anyone else and wrote what is still the most insightful book on American society, *Democracy in America* (Volume I, 1835 and Volume II, 1839). "The emigrants who colonized America at the beginning of the seventeenth century," Tocqueville wrote, "in some way separated the principle of democracy from all those other principles against which they contended when living in the heart of the old European societies, and transplanted that principle only on the shores of the New World." He did not study America, Tocqueville went on, "just to satisfy curiosity, however legitimate; I sought there lessons from which we might profit. . . . I accept that [democratic] revolution as an accomplished fact, or a fact that soon will be accomplished, and I selected of all the peoples experiencing it that nation in which it has come to the fullest and most peaceful completion. . . . I admit that I saw in America more than America; it was the shape of democracy itself which I sought, its inclinations, character, prejudices, and passions."

Now, over 170 years after Tocqueville wrote, America remains a democratic nation and an intensely individualist society—the latter encompassing much of what he understood when he used the term "democracy." This broad continuity in social values and social structure goes far to explain the institutional continuities we find in The LANAHAN READINGS.

The world of American politics keeps changing, nonetheless. Students need readings on the country's political institutions and its political competition that present the American polity in a fresh, contemporary form. So for the fourth edition of The LANAHAN READINGS IN THE AMERICAN POLITY, we have replaced over a quarter of the selections. Among the many new readings:

Sarah Binder, Barbara Sinclair, Michele Swers, and Katherine Tate tell us in their essays about the reasons for gridlock, the use of the Senate filibuster, what women bring to Congress, and the Congressional Black Caucus, respectively.

Kenneth Mayer, Larry Gerston and Terry Christensen, in their articles, and the Supreme Court in *Kelo v. City of New London* try to sort out presidential power and the executive order, the power of citizens to recall an elected official, and the power of local government to condemn property for the public good.

Charles Ogletree takes us back and revisits the meaning of "with all deliberate speed" in *Brown II*, while John García and Craig Rimmerman separately bring us up-to-date on Latino politics and gay and lesbian political achievements.

John White looks at the entire electorate and tries to measure the gap in our differing views of culture and morality while Donald Kettl grapples with post-9/11 USA PATRIOT Act and citizens' concerns with security and liberty.

Writing on the 2004 election, William Eggers and James Ceaser and Andrew Busch, in their articles comment on using the Internet in campaigns and seizing the "527" campaign finance loophole by the Swift Boat Veterans for Truth, respectively.

From case studies and personal experience, Sharon Hays looks back on the successes and failures of 1990s welfare reform.

Lastly, Joseph Nye considers soft power in the context of a nation's huge economic and military power while Chalmers Johnson reminds us of the possible and sometimes unintentional results of a nation's foreign policy.

To guide readers through these and all other selections, a brief description of each article appears in brackets below its listing in the table of contents. To help orient students, we continue to provide brief introductions to each article. In doing so, we can offer some political, and occasionally, historical and cultural background to the selections. To help students further, we again continue the process of writing footnotes not to dredge up obscure and unnecessary information, but to make clear those words, phrases, and allusions that students need defined or explained in order to understand the particular reading.

As with the first edition, Ann Serow has written the *Instructor's Guide and Quiz Book*. This ancillary gives instructors an ample amount of questions with which to test their students on each of the readings, and also, some further ideas on how the selections can be used. For example, there are a number of readings that can be set up in a point-counterpoint arrangement for instructors who might want to include this approach in their classroom.

Returning to our opening comments, we have been engaged in this project for nearly twenty years. We believe that the continuity of having the same team, author/editor and publishing editor, has helped keep the goals of the book in focus: This is a book for students of American government and the list of selections was made, and revised, for them. They, too, have contributed heavily to the reader-making process by their in-class comments. The selections can truly be said to have been class-tested. For this, we again dedicate The LANAHAN READINGS to these willing and observant participants, our students.

AGS

NOTE OF ACKNOWLEDGMENT   Much appreciation goes to our young political scientist-proofreaders for their many hours of assistance: Mary Gordon, Eliza Cassella, Samuel Bellingrath, Alissa Nulsen, Terance Trammell, Lauren Eicher, Christopher Hildebrand, Jaymin Mehta, Eleanor Brush, Zachary Cain, Bomani Brown, Miriam Ebo, and Constantino Portal.

The Lanahan Readings

in the

American Polity

FOURTH EDITION

PART ONE

American Ideology

I

ALEXIS DE TOCQUEVILLE

From *Democracy in America*

In May of 1831, a fancily-dressed, young French aristocrat arrived in the United States to begin his "scientific" study of a new social and political phenomenon, American democracy. After nine months of traveling across the new nation, interviewing numerous Americans from all walks of life, Alexis de Tocqueville returned to France to write Democracy in America, *the single best source with which to begin our exploration of American government and politics. Tocqueville saw the United States as a unique nation. From the start, Americans were all equal. Some were richer and others were poorer, but all who were not indentured or enslaved had an equal opportunity from the start. This clearly was not the case in any other nineteenth-century nation. To the young visitor, this idea of equality was America's identifying mark, a most cherished, if elusive, national virtue.*

AFTER THE BIRTH of a human being his early years are obscurely spent in the toils or pleasures of childhood. As he grows up the world receives him, when his manhood begins, and he enters into contact with his fellows. He is then studied for the first time, and it is imagined that the germ of the vices and the virtues of his maturer years is then formed.

This, if I am not mistaken, is a great error. We must begin higher up; we must watch the infant in his mother's arms; we must see the first images which the external world casts upon the dark mirror of his mind; the first occurrences which he witnesses; we must hear the first words which awaken the sleeping powers of thought, and stand by his earliest efforts, if we would understand the prejudices, the habits, and the passions which will rule his life. The entire man is, so to speak, to be seen in the cradle of the child.

The growth of nations presents something analogous to this: they all bear some marks of their origin; and the circumstances which accompanied their birth and contributed to their rise affect the whole term of their being.

If we were able to go back to the elements of states, and to examine the oldest monuments of their history, I doubt not that we should discover in them the primal cause of the prejudices, the habits, the ruling passions,

and, in short, of all that constitutes what is called the national character:
we should there find the explanation of certain customs which now seem
at variance with the prevailing manners; of such laws as conflict with
established principles; and of such incoherent opinions as are here and
there to be met with in society, like those fragments of broken chains
which we sometimes see hanging from the vault of an edifice, and supporting nothing. This might explain the destinies of certain nations which
seem borne on by an unknown force to ends of which they themselves
are ignorant. But hitherto facts have been wanting to researches of this
kind: the spirit of inquiry has only come upon communities in their latter
days; and when they at length contemplated their origin, time had already
obscured it, or ignorance and pride adorned it with truth-concealing
fables.

America is the only country in which it has been possible to witness
the natural and tranquil growth of society, and where the influence exercised on the future condition of states by their origin is clearly distinguish-
able. . . .

America, consequently, exhibits in the broad light of day the phenomena which the ignorance or rudeness of earlier ages conceals from our
researches. Near enough to the time when the states of America were
founded, to be accurately acquainted with their elements, and sufficiently
removed from that period to judge of some of their results, the men of
our own day seem destined to see further than their predecessors into
the series of human events. Providence has given us a torch which our
forefathers did not possess, and has allowed us to discern fundamental
causes in the history of the world which the obscurity of the past concealed
from them.

If we carefully examine the social and political state of America, after
having studied its history, we shall remain perfectly convinced that not
an opinion, not a custom, not a law, I may even say not an event, is upon
record which the origin of that people will not explain. The readers of
this book will find the germ of all that is to follow in the present chapter,
and the key to almost the whole work.

The emigrants who came at different periods to occupy the territory
now covered by the American Union, differed from each other in many
respects; their aim was not the same, and they governed themselves on
different principles.

These men had, however, certain features in common, and they were
all placed in an analogous situation. The tie of language is perhaps the
strongest and the most durable that can unite mankind. All the emigrants
spoke the same tongue; they were all offsets from the same people. Born

in a country which had been agitated for centuries by the struggles of faction, and in which all parties had been obliged in their turn to place themselves under the protection of the laws, their political education had been perfected in this rude school, and they were more conversant with the notions of right, and the principles of true freedom, than the greater part of their European contemporaries. At the period of the first emigrations, the parish system, that fruitful germ of free institutions, was deeply rooted in the habits of the English; and with it the doctrine of the sovereignty of the people. . . .

Another remark, to which we shall hereafter have occasion to recur, is applicable not only to the English, but to . . . all the Europeans who successively established themselves in the New World. All these European colonies contained the elements, if not the development, of a complete democracy. Two causes led to this result. It may safely be advanced that on leaving the mother country the emigrants had in general no notion of superiority one over another. The happy and the powerful do not go into exile, and there are no surer guaranties of equality among men than poverty and misfortune. It happened, however, on several occasions, that persons of rank were driven to America by political and religious quarrels. Laws were made to establish a gradation of ranks; but it was soon found that the soil of America was opposed to a territorial aristocracy. To bring that refractory land into cultivation, the constant and interested exertions of the owner himself were necessary; and when the ground was prepared, its produce was found to be insufficient to enrich a master and a farmer at the same time. The land was then naturally broken up into small portions, which the proprietor cultivated for himself. Land is the basis of an aristocracy, which clings to the soil that supports it; for it is not by privileges alone, nor by birth, but by landed property handed down from generation to generation, that an aristocracy is constituted. A nation may present immense fortunes and extreme wretchedness; but unless those fortunes are territorial there is no true aristocracy, but simply the class of the rich and that of the poor. . . .

In virtue of the law of partible inheritance, the death of every proprietor brings about a kind of revolution in the property; not only do his possessions change hands, but their very nature is altered; since they are parcelled into shares, which become smaller and smaller at each division. This is the direct and, as it were, the physical effect of the law. It follows, then, that in countries where equality of inheritance is established by law, property, and especially landed property, must have a tendency to perpetual diminuation. . . .

. . . But the law of equal division exercises its influence not merely upon the property itself, but it affects the minds of the heirs, and brings their passions into play. These indirect consequences tend powerfully to the destruction of large fortunes, and especially of large domains. . . .

Great landed estates which have once been divided never come together again; for the small proprietor draws from his land a better revenue, in proportion, than the large owner does from his; and of course he sells it at a higher rate. The calculations of gain, therefore, which decide the rich man to sell his domain, will still more powerfully influence him against buying small estates to unite them into a large one.

What is called family-pride is often founded upon an illusion of self-love. A man wishes to perpetuate and immortalize himself, as it were, in his great-grandchildren. Where the *esprit de famille* ceases to act, individual selfishness comes into play. When the idea of family becomes vague, indeterminate, and uncertain, a man thinks of his present convenience; he provides for the establishment of his succeeding generation, and no more.

Either a man gives up the idea of perpetuating his family, or at any rate, he seeks to accomplish it by other means than that of a landed estate. . . .

I do not mean that there is any deficiency of wealthy individuals in the United States; I know of no country, indeed, where the love of money has taken stronger hold on the affections of men, and where a profounder contempt is expressed for the theory of the permanent equality of property. But wealth circulates with inconceivable rapidity, and experience shows that it is rare to find two succeeding generations in the full enjoyment of it. . . .

. . . The social condition of the Americans is eminently democratic; this was its character at the foundation of the Colonies, and it is still more strongly marked at the present day. . . .

America, then, exhibits in her social state an extraordinary phenomenon. Men are there seen on a greater equality in point of fortune and intellect, or, in other words, more equal in their strength, than in any other country of the world, or in any age of which history has preserved the remembrance.

The political consequences of such a social condition as this are easily deducible.

It is impossible to believe that equality will not eventually find its way into the political world as it does everywhere else. To conceive of men remaining for ever unequal upon a single point, yet equal on all others, is impossible; they must come in the end to be equal upon all. . . .

2

JAMES BRYCE

From *The American Commonwealth*

The Englishman James Bryce visited the United States in the 1880s, during the so-called Gilded Age. His topic in this excerpt is equality in America. Equality can be measured in several different ways, he says, by money, knowledge, position, and status. The first three measures of equality point up the obvious differences among the American people. But wealthy or poor, educated or not, highly-positioned or lowly, Bryce concludes, Americans regard one another as fundamentally equal as human beings. A fellow citizen may be more famous or more accomplished or more successful, "but it is not a reason for . . . treating him as if he were porcelain and yourself only earthenware." Is Bryce on target over one hundred years later? What has happened to the idea of equality in America in the post-porcelain, post-earthenware age?

————

THE UNITED STATES are deemed all the world over to be preeminently the land of equality. This was the first feature which struck Europeans when they began, after the peace of 1815 had left them time to look beyond the Atlantic, to feel curious about the phenomena of a new society. This was the great theme of Tocqueville's description, and the starting point of his speculations; this has been the most constant boast of the Americans themselves, who have believed their liberty more complete than that of any other people, because equality has been more fully blended with it. Yet some philosophers say that equality is impossible, and others, who express themselves more precisely, insist that distinctions of rank are so inevitable, that however you try to expunge them, they are sure to reappear. Before we discuss this question, let us see in what senses the word is used.

First there is legal equality, including both what one may call passive or private equality, i.e. the equal possession of civil private rights by all inhabitants, and active or public equality, the equal possession by all of rights to a share in the government, such as the electoral franchise and eligibility to public office. Both kinds of political equality exist in America, in the amplest measure, and may be dismissed from the present discussion.

Next there is the equality of material conditions, that is, of wealth, and all that wealth gives; there is the equality of education and intelligence: there is the equality of social status or rank: and there is (what comes near to, but is not exactly the same as, this last) the equality of estimation, i.e. of the value which men set upon one another, whatever be the elements that come into this value, whether wealth, or education, or official rank, or social rank, or any other species of excellence. In how many and which of these senses of the word does equality exist in the United States?

Not as regards material conditions. Till about the middle of last century there were no great fortunes in America, few large fortunes, no poverty. Now there is some poverty (though only in a few places can it be called pauperism), many large fortunes, and a greater number of gigantic fortunes than in any other country in the world. . . .

As respects education, the profusion of superior as well as elementary schools tends to raise the mass to a somewhat higher point than in Europe, while the stimulus of life being keener and the habit of reading more general, the number of persons one finds on the same general level of brightness, keenness, and a superficially competent knowledge of common facts, whether in science, history, geography, or literature, is extremely large. This general level tends to rise. But the level of exceptional attainment in that still relatively small though increasing class who have studied at the best native universities or in Europe, and who pursue learning and science either as a profession or as a source of pleasure, rises faster than does the general level of the multitude, so that in this regard also it appears that equality has diminished and will diminish further.

So far we have been on comparatively smooth and easy ground. Equality of wealth is a concrete thing; equality of intellectual possession and resource is a thing which can be perceived and gauged. Of social equality, of distinctions of standing and estimation in private life, it is far more difficult to speak, and in what follows I speak with some hesitation.

One thing, and perhaps one thing only, may be asserted with confidence. There is no rank in America, that is to say, no external and recognized stamp, marking one man as entitled to any social privileges, or to deference and respect from others. No man is entitled to think himself better than his fellows, or to expect any exceptional consideration to be shown by them to him. Except in the national capital, there is no such thing as a recognized order of precedence, either on public occasions or at a private party, save that yielded to a few official persons, such as the governor and chief judges of a State within that State, as well as to the President and Vice-President, the Speaker of the House, the Federal senators, the judges of the Supreme Federal Court, and the members of the President's cabinet everywhere through the Union. In fact, the idea of a regular "rule of precedence" displeases the Americans. . . .

The fault which Americans are most frequently accused of is the worship of wealth. The amazing fuss which is made about very rich men, the descriptions of their doings, the speculation as to their intentions, the gossip about their private life, lend colour to the reproach. He who builds up a huge fortune, especially if he does it suddenly, is no doubt a sort of hero, because an enormous number of men have the same ambition. Having done best what millions are trying to do, he is discussed, admired, and envied in the same way as the captain of a cricket eleven is at an English school, or the stroke of the university boat at Oxford or Cambridge. If he be a great financier, or the owner of a great railroad or a great newspaper, he exercises vast power, and is therefore well worth courting by those who desire his help or would avert his enmity. Admitting all this, it may seem a paradox to observe that a millionaire has a better and easier social career open to him in England than in America. Nevertheless there is a sense in which this is true. In America, if his private character be bad, if he be mean, or openly immoral, or personally vulgar, or dishonest, the best society may keep its doors closed against him. In England great wealth, skilfully employed, will more readily force these doors to open. For in England great wealth can, by using the appropriate methods, practically buy rank from those who bestow it; or by obliging persons whose position enables them to command fashionable society, can induce them to stand sponsors for the upstart, and force him into society, a thing which no person in America has the power of doing. To effect such a stroke in England the rich man must of course have stopped short of positive frauds, that is, of such frauds as could be proved in court. But he may be still distrusted and disliked by the *élite* of the commercial world, he may be vulgar and ill-educated, and indeed have nothing to recommend him except his wealth and his willingness to spend it in providing amusement for fashionable people. All this will not prevent him from becoming a baronet, or possibly a peer, and thereby acquiring a position of assured dignity which he can transmit to his offspring. The existence of a system of artificial rank enables a stamp to be given to base metal in Europe which cannot be given in a thoroughly republican country. The feeling of the American public towards the very rich is, so far as a stranger can judge, one of curiosity and wonder rather than of respect. There is less snobbishness shown towards them than in England. They are admired as a famous runner or jockey is admired, and the talents they have shown, say, in railroad management or in finance, are felt to reflect lustre on the nation. But they do not necessarily receive either flattery or social deference, and sometimes, where it can be alleged that they have won their wealth as the leading spirits in monopolistic combinations, they are made targets for attack, though they may have done nothing more than what other business men have attempted, with less ability and less success.

The persons to whom official rank gives importance are very few indeed, being for the nation at large only about one hundred persons at the top of the Federal Government, and in each State less than a dozen of its highest State functionaries. For these State functionaries, indeed, the respect shown is extremely scanty, and much more official than personal. A high Federal officer, a senator, or justice of the Supreme Court, or cabinet minister, is conspicuous while he holds his place, and is of course a personage in any private society he may enter; but less so than a corresponding official would be in Europe. A simple member of the House of Representatives is nobody. Even men of the highest official rank do not give themselves airs on the score of their position. Long ago, in Washington, I was taken to be presented to the then head of the United States army, a great soldier whose fame all the world knows. We found him standing at a desk in a bare room in the War Department, at work with one clerk. While he was talking to us the door of the room was pushed open, and there appeared the figure of a Western sight-seer belonging to what Europeans would call the lower middle class, followed by his wife and sister, who were "doing" Washington. Perceiving that the room was occupied they began to retreat, but the Commander-in-chief called them back. "Walk-in, ladies," he said. 'You can look around. You won't disturb me; make yourselves at home." . . .

Perhaps the best way of explaining how some of the differences above mentioned, in wealth or official position or intellectual eminence, affect social equality is by reverting to what was called, a few pages back, equality of estimation—the idea which men form of other men as compared with themselves. It is in this that the real sense of equality comes out. In America men hold others to be at bottom exactly the same as themselves. If a man is enormously rich, or if he is a great orator, like Daniel Webster or Henry Ward Beecher, or a great soldier like Ulysses S. Grant, or a great writer like R. W. Emerson, or President, so much the better for him. He is an object of interest, perhaps of admiration, possibly even of reverence. But he is deemed to be still of the same flesh and blood as other men. The admiration felt for him may be a reason for going to see him and longing to shake hands with him, a longing frequent in America. But it is not a reason for bowing down to him, or addressing him in deferential terms, or treating him as if he were porcelain and yourself only earthenware.

3

LOUIS HARTZ

From *The Liberal Tradition in America*

Scholar Louis Hartz has used Alexis de Tocqueville's idea that Americans were "born equal" as a take-off point for his complicated philosophical analysis of the American political tradition. Citing the ideas of John Locke, Edmund Burke, and Jeremy Bentham, Hartz points to the many paradoxes evident in American thought: "pragmatism and absolutism, historicism and rationalism, optimism and pessimism, materialism and idealism, individualism and conformism." Underlying all these paradoxes is the ultimate one. Hartz argues that America, in many ways the most revolutionary nation in the world, never really had a revolution to attain the goal of equality. This paradox places the United States in a "strange relationship" with the nations that seek to emulate America's success.

THE ANALYSIS which this book contains is based on what might be called the storybook truth about American history: that America was settled by men who fled from the feudal and clerical oppressions of the Old World. If there is anything in this view, as old as the national folklore itself, then the outstanding thing about the American community in Western history ought to be the nonexistence of those oppressions, or since the reaction against them was in the broadest sense liberal, that the American community is a liberal community. We are confronted, as it were, with a kind of inverted Trotskyite law of combined development, America skipping the feudal stage of history as Russia presumably skipped the liberal stage. . . . One of the central characteristics of a nonfeudal society is that it lacks a genuine revolutionary tradition, the tradition which in Europe has been linked with the Puritan and French revolutions: that it is "born equal," as Tocqueville said. . . .

Surely, then, it is a remarkable force: this fixed, dogmatic liberalism of a liberal way of life. It is the secret root from which have sprung many of the most puzzling of American cultural phenomena. . . .

At bottom it is riddled with paradox. Here is a Lockian doctrine which in the West as a whole is the symbol of rationalism, yet in America the devotion to it has been so irrational that it has not even been recognized for what it is: liberalism. There has never been a "liberal movement" or a real "liberal party" in America: we have only had the American Way of Life, a nationalist articulation of Locke which usually does not know that Locke himself is involved; and we did not even get that until after the Civil War when the Whigs of the nation, deserting the Hamiltonian tradition, saw the capital that could be made out of it. This is why even critics who have noticed America's moral unity have usually missed its substance. Ironically, "liberalism" is a stranger in the land of its greatest realization and fulfillment. But this is not all. Here is a doctrine which everywhere in the West has been a glorious symbol of individual liberty, yet in America its compulsive power has been so great that it has posed a threat to liberty itself. Actually Locke has a hidden conformitarian germ to begin with, since natural law tells equal people equal things, but when this germ is fed by the explosive power of modern nationalism, it mushrooms into something pretty remarkable. One can reasonably wonder about the liberty one finds in Burke.

I believe that this is the basic ethical problem of a liberal society: not the danger of the majority which has been its conscious fear, but the danger of unanimity, which has slumbered unconsciously behind it: the "tyranny of opinion" that Tocqueville saw unfolding. . . . When Tocqueville wrote that the "great advantage" of the American lay in the fact that he did not have "to endure a democratic revolution," he advanced what was surely one of his most fundamental insights into American life. However, while many of his observations have been remembered but not followed up, this one has scarcely even been remembered. Perhaps it is because, fearing revolution in the present, we like to think of it in the past, and we are reluctant to concede that its romance has been missing from our lives. Perhaps it is because the plain evidence of the American revolution of 1776, especially the evidence of its social impact that our newer historians have collected, has made the comment of Tocqueville seem thoroughly enigmatic. But in the last analysis, of course, the question of its validity is a question of perspective. Tocqueville was writing with the great revolutions of Europe in mind, and from that point of view the outstanding thing about the American effort of 1776 was bound to be, not the freedom to which it led, but the established feudal structure it did not have to destroy. . . .

Thus the fact that the Americans did not have to endure a "democratic revolution" deeply conditioned their outlook on people elsewhere who did; and by helping to thwart the crusading spirit in them, it gave to the wild enthusiasms of Europe an appearance not only of analytic error but of unrequited love. Symbols of a world revolution, the Americans were not in truth world revolutionaries. There is no use complaining about the confusions implicit in this position, as Woodrow Wilson used to complain when he said that we had "no business" permitting the French to get the wrong impression about the American revolution. On both sides the reactions that arose were well-nigh inevitable. But one cannot help wondering about something else: the satisfying use to which our folklore has been able to put the incongruity of America's revolutionary role. For if the "contamination" that Jefferson feared, and that found its classic expression in Washington's Farewell Address, has been a part of the American myth, so has the "round the world" significance of the shots that were fired at Concord. We have been able to dream of ourselves as emancipators of the world at the very moment that we have withdrawn from it. We have been able to see ourselves as saviors at the very moment that we have been isolationists. Here, surely, is one of the great American luxuries that the twentieth century has destroyed. . . . When the Americans celebrated the uniqueness of their own society, they were on the track of a personal insight of the profoundest importance. For the nonfeudal world in which they lived shaped every aspect of their social thought: it gave them a frame of mind that cannot be found anywhere else in the eighteenth century, or in the wider history of modern revolutions. . . . The issue of history itself is deeply involved here. On this score, inevitably, the fact that the revolutionaries of 1776 had inherited the freest society in the world shaped their thinking in an intricate way. It gave them, in the first place, an appearance of outright conservatism. . . . The past had been good to the Americans, and they knew it. . . .

Actually, the form of America's traditionalism was one thing, its content quite another. Colonial history had not been the slow and glacial record of development that Bonald and Maistre loved to talk about.* On the contrary, since the first sailing of the *Mayflower*, it had been a story of new beginnings, daring enterprises, and explicitly stated principles— it breathed, in other words, the spirit of Bentham himself. The result was that the traditionalism of the Americans, like a pure freak of logic, often bore amazing marks of antihistorical rationalism. The clearest case of this undoubtedly is to be found in the revolutionary constitutions of 1776, which evoked, as Franklin reported, the "rapture" of European liberals everywhere. In America, of course, the concept of a written constitution, including many of the mechanical devices it embodied, was the endproduct of a chain of historical experience that went back to the Mayflower

*Louis Bonald and Joseph de Maistre were prominent French conservative political theorists of the early nineteenth century. Both were inveterate enemies of the radical and rationalistic ideas associated with the French Revolution. They were leading figures in the European Reaction.—EDS.

Compact and the Plantation Covenants of the New England towns: it
was the essence of political traditionalism. But in Europe just the reverse
was true. The concept was the darling of the rationalists—a symbol of
the emancipated mind at work. . . .

But how then are we to describe these baffling Americans? Were they
rationalists or were they traditionalists? The truth is, they were neither,
which is perhaps another way of saying that they were both. For the war
between Burke and Bentham on the score of tradition, which made a
great deal of sense in a society where men had lived in the shadow of
feudal institutions, made comparatively little sense in a society where for
years they had been creating new states, planning new settlements, and,
as Jefferson said, literally building new lives.* In such a society a strange
dialectic was fated to appear, which would somehow unite the antagonistic
components of the European mind; the past became a continuous future,
and the God of the traditionalists sanctioned the very arrogance of the
men who defied Him.

This shattering of the time categories of Europe, this Hegelian-like
revolution in historic perspective, goes far to explain one of the enduring
secrets of the American character: a capacity to combine rock-ribbed
traditionalism with high inventiveness, ancestor worship with ardent optimism. Most critics have seized upon one or the other of these aspects of
the American mind, finding it impossible to conceive how both can go
together. That is why the insight of Gunnar Myrdal is a very distinguished
one when he writes: "America is . . . conservative. . . . But the principles
conserved are liberal and some, indeed, are radical." Radicalism and conservatism have been twisted entirely out of shape by the liberal flow of
American history. . . .

What I have been doing here is fairly evident: I have been interpreting
the social thought of the American revolution in terms of the social goals
it did not need to achieve. Given the usual approach, this may seem like a
perverse inversion of the reasonable course of things; but in a world where
the "canon and feudal law" are missing, how else are we to understand
the philosophy of a liberal revolution? The remarkable thing about the
"spirit of 1776," as we have seen, is not that it sought emancipation but
that it sought it in a sober temper; not that it opposed power but that it
opposed it ruthlessly and continuously; not that it looked forward to the

---

*Edmund Burke, an eighteenth-century English political theorist, is perhaps the most artful
defender of tradition in the history of political theory. Jeremy Bentham, an English theorist
of the late eighteenth and early nineteenth centuries, was as rationalistic as Burke was
traditionalistic. While Burke generally saw virtues in inherited institutions, Bentham generally advocated their reform.—EDS.

future but that it worshiped the past as well. Even these perspectives, however, are only part of the story, misleading in themselves. The "free air" of American life, as John Jay once happily put it, penetrated to deeper levels of the American mind, twisting it in strange ways, producing a set of results fundamental to everything else in American thought. The clue to these results lies in the following fact: the Americans, though models to all the world of the middle class way of life, lacked the passionate middle class consciousness which saturated the liberal thought of Europe. . . .

But this is not all. If the position of the colonial Americans saved them from many of the class obsessions of Europe, it did something else as well: it inspired them with a peculiar sense of community that Europe had never known. . . . Amid the "free air" of American life, something new appeared: men began to be held together, not by the knowledge that they were different parts of a corporate whole, but by the knowledge that they were similar participants in a uniform way of life—by that "pleasing uniformity of decent competence" which Crèvecoeur loved so much. The Americans themselves were not unaware of this. When Peter Thacher proudly announced that "simplicity of manners" was the mark of the revolutionary colonists, what was he saying if not that the norms of a single class in Europe were enough to sustain virtually a whole society in America? Richard Hildreth, writing after the leveling impact of the Jacksonian revolution had made this point far more obvious, put his finger directly on it. He denounced feudal Europe, where "half a dozen different codes of morals," often in flagrant contradiction with one another, flourished "in the same community," and celebrated the fact that America was producing "one code, moral standard, by which the actions of all are to be judged. . . . " Hildreth knew that America was a marvelous mixture of many peoples and many religions, but he also knew that it was characterized by something more marvelous even than that: the power of the liberal norm to penetrate them all.

Now a sense of community based on a sense of uniformity is a deceptive thing. It looks individualistic, and in part it actually is. It cannot tolerate internal relationships of disparity, and hence can easily inspire the kind of advice that Professor Nettels once imagined a colonial farmer giving his son: "Remember that you are as good as any man—and also that you are no better." But in another sense it is profoundly anti-individualistic, because the common standard is its very essence, and deviations from that standard inspire it with an irrational fright. The man who is as good as his neighbors is in a tough spot when he confronts all of his neighbors combined. Thus William Graham Sumner looked at the other side of

Professor Nettels's colonial coin and did not like what he saw: "public opinion" was an "impervious mistress. . . . Mrs. Grundy held powerful sway and Gossip was her prime minister."

Here we have the "tyranny of the majority" that Tocqueville later described in American life; here too we have the deeper paradox out of which it was destined to appear. Freedom in the fullest sense implies both variety and equality. . . . At the bottom of the American experience of freedom, not in antagonism to it but as a constituent element of it, there has always lain the inarticulate premise of conformity. . . . American political thought, as we have seen, is a veritable maze of polar contradictions, winding in and out of each other hopelessly: pragmatism and absolutism, historicism and rationalism, optimism and pessimism, materialism and idealism, individualism and conformism. But, after all, the human mind works by polar contradictions; and when we have evolved an interpretation of it which leads cleanly in a single direction, we may be sure that we have missed a lot. The task of the cultural analyst is not to discover simplicity, or even to discover unity, for simplicity and unity do not exist, but to drive a wedge of rationality through the pathetic indecisions of social thought. In the American case that wedge is not hard to find. . . .

It is this business of destruction and creation which goes to the heart of the problem. For the point of departure of great revolutionary thought everywhere else in the world has been the effort to build a new society on the ruins of an old one, and this is an experience America has never had. We are reminded again of Tocqueville's statement: the Americans are "born equal."

That statement, especially in light of the strange relationship which the revolutionary Americans had with their admirers abroad, raises an obvious question. Can a people that is born equal ever understand peoples elsewhere that have become so? Can it ever lead them? . . . America's experience of being born equal has put it in a strange relationship to the rest of the world.

4

THEDA SKOCPOL

From *Diminished Democracy*

Alexis de Tocqueville's observations about America, based on his visit here in 1831, provide the starting point for Theda Skocpol's modern analysis of groups and associations. Tocqueville saw associations as the way that Americans most effectively participate in civic life. Skocpol acknowledges the continuing importance of groups in providing input, but she uncovers a significant difference in the composition of groups today. No longer are groups made up of grassroots members. Rather, groups have become increasingly "professionalized": led by experts, assisted by trained staff, funded by new money-raising techniques. The participation and involvement of average people—the heart of Tocqueville's view of the vitality of American group life—no longer exists as it once did. The events of September 11, 2001, Skocpol notes, could have reinvigorated associational life in the United States, but it didn't happen that way.

————

. . . . FROM THE 1800S THROUGH THE 1950S AND 1960S, U.S. civic life was dominated by a mixture of business associations . . . plus many kinds of representatively governed membership associations. . . . Since the 1960s, however, the ranks of professionally run groups . . . have swelled, especially groups other than business associations. Groups dispersing contributions from the wealthy; professionally run citizens' associations; and professionally managed advocacy groups for the poor and vulnerable—all of these types have expanded their presence on the U.S. civic scene. At the same time, representatively governed voluntary federations have ceased to proliferate, and their dues-paying memberships have contracted.

A new civic America has thus taken shape since the 1960s, as professionally managed advocacy groups and institutions have moved to the fore, while representatively governed, nation-spanning voluntary membership federations—especially those with popular or cross-class memberships—have lost clout in national public affairs and faded from the everyday lives of most Americans. Why all of this happened is the question I take up in the next chapter. We cannot fully rejoin ongoing debates about the vitality of U.S. democracy until we have gained a better understanding of the convergent forces that propelled and shaped the recent great transformation from membership to management in American civic life. . . .

After more than a century of civic life rooted in nation-spanning membership federations, *why* did America's associational universe change so sharply in the late twentieth century? Much hand-wringing over civic decline has concerned the individual choices of masses of Americans: Are people, especially youngsters, sitting in front of television and computer screens at home rather than voting and going out to community events and club meetings? Were the adults of the World War II generation unusually civically engaged, so that their passing from the scene brings an inevitable if unfortunate decline in participation? The answers to both questions may be yes, as Robert D. Putnam hypothesizes. But to attribute the sudden shifts in civic organizing between the 1960s and the 1990s merely to gradual processes of generational replacement is not entirely plausible and says far too little about the institutional and social causes at work.

The great civic transformation of our time happened too abruptly to be attributable primarily to incremental processes of generational replacement. And this attribution misses what we most need to understand. After all, contemporary Americans are not simply joining old associations less frequently than their forebears did. They are also organizing to an extraordinary degree, and engaging public affairs in very new ways.

Social capital theorists examine all forms of social connectedness at once, lumping together for explanatory purposes everything from bowling leagues and family dinners to the more publicly relevant forms of organizing and joining. We ought to be skeptical that one explanation fits all types of sociopolitical activity, but the vague focus should worry us even more. Publicly relevant voluntary activities are the ones of greatest relevance to the health of American democracy; and to explain transformations in these activities, a focus on changing modes of social interaction cannot be sufficient. The choices masses of citizens make about politics and civic involvement respond, above all, to available avenues of meaningful group participation and publicly relevant clout. Most people need to be directly invited into public engagements, contacted personally by leaders and folks they know. People must also "see themselves" in the shared undertaking. And they must believe an undertaking will really matter— or else they won't bother. All of these considerations direct our attention to the changing roles of leaders, to shifting social identities and modes of organization, and to considerations of power, resources, and institutional leverage. We cannot explain democratically relevant shifts in civil society by focusing on mass attitudes and intimate interactions alone.

As Alexis de Tocqueville recognized long ago, people in a democracy use many of their voluntarily created associations to gain leverage and to express shared identities and widely shared values. That is why civic leaders and organizers are so crucial. They are the ones who take the initiative, who define and jump-start the arts of "combination" Tocqueville rightly considered central to democracy. The kinds of associations leading citizens launch and patronize, the shared values and identities they articulate, and the tactics civic leaders use to gain and exercise public voice and political leverage—all of these matters powerfully influence the menu of possibilities for participation available to most citizens. In a thriving democracy, leaders regularly invite many fellow citizens to join with them in important endeavors. Citizens must respond, of course, or leadership initiatives fail. But it is not foreordained that leaders will emerge to offer the most democratically propitious avenues of shared engagement. Over the sweep of history, elites have often cooperated and contended with one another above the heads of most people living in their societies. Only in special circumstances do elites turn to democratic leadership—above all, to the kinds of democratic leadership that involve mobilizing and organizing others.

Democratic mobilization becomes the norm when would-be leaders can achieve power and influence only by drawing others into movements, associations, and political battles. Elites must have incentives to organize others, if democratic mobilization is to happen regularly. Such incentives were certainly in place in earlier eras of U.S. history—when party politicians could win elected office only in close-fought, high-turnout elections and when association builders could attain national influence only by spreading networks of chapters of dues-paying members all across America. Similar incentives for elites to engage in democratic organizing and mobilization may be lacking today.

Using this frame of reference, this chapter examines roots and results of contemporary shifts in organized American civic life and strategies of civic leadership. A confluence of trends and events sparked a shift from membership mobilization to managerial forms of civic organizing. After 1960 epochal changes in racial ideals and gender relationships delegitimated old-line U.S. membership associations and pushed male and female leaders in new directions. New political opportunities and challenges drew resources and civic activists toward centrally managed lobbying. Innovative technologies and sources of financial support enabled new, memberless models of association building to take hold. And, finally, shifts in America's class structure and elite careers created a broad constituency for professionally managed civic organizing. Many Americans are now relatively

privileged, highly individualistic businesspeople or professionals, with formidable civic resources at their personal disposal. The most privileged
Americans can now organize and contend largely among themselves,
without regularly engaging the majority of citizens. . . .

Determined to take advantage of new opportunities, staff-heavy research and lobbying associations—the proliferating public affairs and social
welfare groups I have already discussed—took much of the action away
from more cumbersome popularly based voluntary federations that had
previously served as important conduits between the federal government
and citizens in the states and districts. Where once it made sense to try
to get things done in Washington by first gauging the opinions of grassroots
association members and influencing officials and representatives in the
localities and states, now it made much more sense for civic activists to
aim their efforts at national media and intervene with staffs or agencies
in Washington. This was especially true where matters of regulation were
at stake—as, increasingly, they were in areas such as environmental protection, civil rights, and consumer or occupational protections. "Since about
the time Martin Luther King, Jr., led a 'march on Washington' by thousands of citizens in the civil rights movement in 1963," Walker concludes,
"there has been a march to Washington by interest groups as well." Activists
have gone where the action is, seeking to harness a more active federal
government to their purposes. . . .

The result was a transformed civic America—still a nation of organizers
but much less a nation of joiners, because civic leaders were no longer
committed to mobilizing vast numbers of fellow citizens into ongoing
membership activities. . . .

Leadership incentives were also very different in classic membership
federations—and this is a key contrast with contemporary civic America.
In huge membership federations, regional or state plus local chapters were
widespread, full of intermediate leaders and members seeking to recruit
others. Hundreds of thousands of local and supralocal leaders had to be
elected and appointed every year. Including the best educated and wealthi-
est, all of the men and women who climbed the ladders of vast membership
associations had to interact in the process with citizens of humble or
middling means and prospects. Classic membership federations built two-
way bridges across classes and places and between local and trans-local
affairs. Now, in a civic America dominated by centralized, staff-driven
advocacy associations, such bridges are eroding. . . .

A Civic Revival After September 11, 2001?

American civic *attitudes*, at least, changed very suddenly in the immediate aftermath of the violent terrorist assaults on U.S. soil on September

11, 2001. As the immediacy of television brought airborne attacks on the World Trade Center and the Pentagon into every living room, the American people responded with an outpouring of patriotism, social solidarity, and renewed hopes for active government. Within a month, more than four out of five Americans were displaying U.S. flags on their homes, clothing, or vehicles. Some 70 percent reported making charitable contributions in response to the events of September 11. Feelings of social solidarity shot up, even across ethnic and racial boundaries where distrust had previously prevailed. . . .

Like the outbreak of earlier wars in U.S. history, September 11 created vast possibilities for civic renewal. Mass outlooks changed, and Americans became eager to cooperate, to reach out, to volunteer. But volunteer for what? Would new attitudes lead to new actions? Would hopes for national solidarity translate into reality, and how sustainable would post-9/11 efforts turn out to be? Worrisome signs soon appeared. . . .

The absence of flourishing membership federations . . . mattered for Americans who wanted to get personally involved, not just give money. After September 11 people had too few opportunities to channel civic urges into ongoing public projects. . . .

. . . America's "new war" after September 11 . . . differed from earlier conflicts in ways that may limit its civic impact. Military actions were conducted by small numbers of highly specialized professional military forces, supported by regular military and National Guard units. No national military draft was deemed necessary. Even after anthrax attacks raised public security concerns at home and underlined the need for much more person power in public health and safety agencies, federal leaders remained uncertain about the value of large numbers of new volunteers. In past wars federal agencies could turn to vast, nationwide voluntary membership federations to orchestrate obviously helpful voluntary contributions in areas such as food conservation or liberty bond drives. But in this new antiterrorist struggle, conducted in a transformed civic universe, professionalism seemed more credible—and it was not clear how to recruit or handle or deploy massive numbers of untrained volunteers. "You just don't put a volunteer out there on the border," explained President Bush's Homeland Security adviser, Tom Ridge. "There are certain levels of law enforcement where you really want professionals involved." . . .

The horrendous events of September 11, 2001, may not, therefore, significantly change the nature of American civic and public life. . . . The potential for heightened popular engagement will continue to exist— because riveting events that reinforce patriotism and a sense of national community are conducive to civic vitality and renewal. Yet as this book has argued, mass willingness is not enough. Institutions and organizations must offer opportunities for people to get involved; and citizens must see ways to have sustained clout. If the promise of civic renewal is to be realized, national leaders, including federal officials, must reach out to organize and involve the American citizenry.

Recurrently throughout U.S. history, wartime crises have triggered eras of civic renewal. But the martial conflicts themselves did not lead to civic revitalization—not in and of themselves, apart from leaders willing to seize the opportunity to engage, or create, popularly rooted organizations to undertake important public tasks. As of the early twenty-first century, the United States has too few associations and leaders able and willing to mobilize citizens for shared national undertakings. September 11, 2001, sparked widespread yearning for expanded public undertakings, but the chance for civic revitalization could all too easily dissipate before America's institutions and leaders catch up with America's people.

5

CORNEL WEST

From *Race Matters*

The opening pages of Professor Cornel West's book tell an unforgettable story of the pervasiveness of racism in the United States. Think about it the next time you wait for a taxi. Think about it when you recall the plight of many of the residents of New Orleans in the aftermath of Hurricane Katrina in 2005. In an America that promises a chance for life, liberty, and the pursuit of happiness to all its citizens, "race matters," West contends. He challenges all Americans to change their thinking about race: the problems of African Americans are not their problems but American problems. West identifies the issues that threaten to disrupt the fabric of the nation—economic, social, political, spiritual—and he suggests a broad outline for solutions.

THIS PAST SEPTEMBER my wife, Elleni, and I made our bi-weekly trek to New York City from Princeton. I was in good spirits. My morning lecture on the first half of Plato's *Republic* in my European Cultural Studies course had gone well. And my afternoon lecture on W. E. B. Du Bois's *The Souls of Black Folk* in my Afro-American Cultural Studies course had left me exhausted yet exhilarated. Plato's powerful symbolism of Socrates' descent to the great port of Piraeus—the multicultural center of Greek trade and commerce and the stronghold of Athenian democracy—still rang in my ears. And Du Bois's prescient pronouncement—"The problem of the twentieth century is the problem of the color line"—haunted me. In a mysterious way, this classic twosome posed the most fundamental challenges to my basic aim in life: to speak the truth to power with love so that the quality of everyday life for ordinary people is enhanced and white supremacy is stripped of its authority and legitimacy. Plato's profound—yet unpersuasive—critique of Athenian democracy as inevitably corrupted by the ignorance and passions of the masses posed one challenge, and Du Bois's deep analysis of the intransigence of white supremacy in the American democratic experiment posed another.

As we approached Manhattan, my temperature rose, as it always does when I'm in a hurry near the Lincoln Tunnel. How rare it is that I miss the grinding gridlock—no matter the day or hour. But this time I drove right through and attributed my good luck to Elleni. As we entered the city, we pondered whether we would have enough time to stop at Sweetwater's (our favorite place to relax) after our appointments. I dropped my wife off for an appointment on 60th Street between Lexington and Park avenues. I left my car—a rather elegant one—in a safe parking lot and stood on the corner of 60th Street and Park Avenue to catch a taxi. I felt quite relaxed since I had an hour until my next engagement. At 5:00 P.M. I had to meet a photographer who would take the picture for the cover of this book on the roof of an apartment building in East Harlem on 115th Street and 1st Avenue. I waited and waited and waited. After the ninth taxi refused me, my blood began to boil. The tenth taxi refused me and stopped for a kind, well-dressed, smiling female fellow citizen of European descent. As she stepped in the cab, she said, "This is really ridiculous, is it not?"

Ugly racial memories of the past flashed through my mind. Years ago, while driving from New York to teach at Williams College, I was stopped on fake charges of trafficking cocaine. When I told the police officer I was a professor of religion, he replied "Yeh, and I'm the Flying Nun. Let's go, nigger!" I was stopped three times in my first ten days in Princeton for driving too slowly on a residential street with a speed limit of twenty-five miles per hour. (And my son, Clifton, already has similar memories at the tender age of fifteen.) Needless to say, these incidents are dwarfed by those like Rodney King's beating* or the abuse of black targets of the

---

*In 1992, four Los Angeles policemen were charged in criminal court with using unnecessary force in the arrest of Rodney King, a black man whom they had stopped while he was driving.—EDS.

FBI's COINTELPRO* efforts in the 1960s and 1970s. Yet the memories cut like a merciless knife at my soul as I waited on that godforsaken corner. Finally I decided to take the subway. I walked three long avenues, arrived late, and had to catch my moral breath as I approached the white male photographer and white female cover designer. I chose not to dwell on this everyday experience of black New Yorkers. And we had a good time talking, posing, and taking pictures.

When I picked up Elleni, I told her of my hour spent on the corner, my tardy arrival, and the expertise and enthusiasm of the photographer and designer. We talked about our fantasy of moving to Addis Ababa, Ethiopia—her home and the site of the most pleasant event of my life. I toyed with the idea of attending the last day of the revival led by the Rev. Jeremiah Wright of Chicago at Rev. Wyatt T. Walker's Canaan Baptist Church of Christ in Harlem. But we settled for Sweetwater's. And the ugly memories faded in the face of soulful music, soulful food, and soulful folk.

As we rode back to Princeton, above the soothing black music of Van Harper's Quiet Storm on WBLS, 107.5 on the radio dial, we talked about what *race* matters have meant to the American past and of how much race *matters* in the American present. And I vowed to be more vigilant and virtuous in my efforts to meet the formidable challenges posed by Plato and Du Bois. For me, it is an urgent question of power and morality; for others, it is an everyday matter of life and death. . . .

What happened in Los Angeles in April of 1992 was neither a race riot nor a class rebellion.† Rather, this monumental upheaval was a multiracial, trans-class, and largely male display of justified social rage. For all its ugly, xenophobic resentment, its air of adolescent carnival, and its downright barbaric behavior, it signified the sense of powerlessness in American society. Glib attempts to reduce its meaning to the pathologies of the black underclass, the criminal actions of hoodlums, or the political revolt of the oppressed urban masses miss the mark. Of those arrested, only 36 percent were black, more than a third had full-time jobs, and most claimed to shun political affiliation. What we witnessed in Los Angeles was the

---

*COINTELPRO was the FBI's "counterintelligence program," conducted over decades but most active in the 1960s. FBI Director J. Edgar Hoover used COINTELPRO to investigate and harass Americans whose activities were considered by the bureau to be subversive: socialist and communist sympathizers; anti-Vietnam War protestors; and especially, black citizens active in the civil rights movement. The press was instrumental in uncovering COINTELPRO's secret machinations in the mid-1970s.—EDS.

†Rioting occurred in Los Angeles after a jury, made up of white citizens, acquitted the policemen who had been accused in the beating of Rodney King.—EDS.

consequence of a lethal linkage of economic decline, cultural decay, and political lethargy in American life. Race was the visible catalyst, not the underlying cause.

The meaning of the earthshaking events in Los Angeles is difficult to grasp because most of us remain trapped in the narrow framework of the dominant liberal and conservative views of race in America, which with its worn-out vocabulary leaves us intellectually debilitated, morally disempowered, and personally depressed. The astonishing disappearance of the event from public dialogue is testimony to just how painful and distressing a serious engagement with race is. Our truncated public discussions of race suppress the best of who and what we are as a people because they fail to confront the complexity of the issue in a candid and critical manner. The predictable pitting of liberals against conservatives, Great Society Democrats against self-help Republicans, reinforces intellectual parochialism and political paralysis.

The liberal notion that more government programs can solve racial problems is simplistic—precisely because it focuses *solely* on the economic dimension. And the conservative idea that what is needed is a change in the moral behavior of poor black urban dwellers (especially poor black men, who, they say, should stay married, support their children, and stop committing so much crime) highlights immoral actions while ignoring public responsibility for the immoral circumstances that haunt our fellow citizens.

The common denominator of these views of race is that each still sees black people as a "problem people," in the words of Dorothy I. Height, president of the National Council of Negro Women, rather than as fellow American citizens with problems. Her words echo the poignant "unasked question" of W. E. B. Du Bois, who, in *The Souls of Black Folk* (1903), wrote:

They approach me in a half-hesitant sort of way, eye me curiously or compassionately, and then instead of saying directly, How does it feel to be a problem? they say, I know an excellent colored man in my town. . . . Do not these Southern outrages make your blood boil? At these I smile, or am interested, or reduce the boiling to a simmer, as the occasion may require. To the real question, How does it feel to be a problem? I answer seldom a word.

Nearly a century later, we confine discussions about race in America to the "problems" black people pose for whites rather than consider what this way of viewing black people reveals about us as a nation.

This paralyzing framework encourages liberals to relieve their guilty consciences by supporting public funds directed at "the problems"; but at the same time, reluctant to exercise principled criticism of black people, liberals deny them the freedom to err. Similarly, conservatives blame the "problems" on black people themselves—and thereby render black social misery invisible or unworthy of public attention.

Hence, for liberals, black people are to be "included" and "integrated" into "our" society and culture, while for conservatives they are to be "well behaved" and "worthy of acceptance" by "our" way of life. Both fail to see that the presence and predicaments of black people are neither additions to nor defections from American life, but rather *constitutive elements of that life*.

To engage in a serious discussion of race in America, we must begin not with the problems of black people but with the flaws of American society—flaws rooted in historic inequalities and longstanding cultural stereotypes. How we set up the terms for discussing racial issues shapes our perception and response to these issues. As long as black people are viewed as a "them," the burden falls on blacks to do all the "cultural" and "moral" work necessary for healthy race relations. The implication is that only certain Americans can define what it means to be American— and the rest must simply "fit in."

The emergence of strong black-nationalist sentiments among blacks, especially among young people, is a revolt against this sense of having to "fit in." The variety of black-nationalist ideologies, from the moderate views of Supreme Court Justice Clarence Thomas in his youth to those of Louis Farrakhan today, rest upon a fundamental truth: white America has been historically weak-willed in ensuring racial justice and has continued to resist fully accepting the humanity of blacks. As long as double standards and differential treatment abound—as long as the rap performer Ice-T is harshly condemned while former Los Angeles Police Chief Daryl F. Gates's antiblack comments are received in polite silence, as long as Dr. Leonard Jeffries's anti-Semitic statements are met with vitriolic outrage while presidential candidate Patrick J. Buchanan's anti-Semitism receives a genteel response—black nationalisms will thrive.

Afrocentrism, a contemporary species of black nationalism, is a gallant yet misguided attempt to define an African identity in a white society perceived to be hostile. It is gallant because it puts black doings and sufferings, not white anxieties and fears, at the center of discussion. It is misguided because—out of fear of cultural hybridization and through silence on the issue of class, retrograde views on black women, gay men, and lesbians, and a reluctance to link race to the common good—it reinforces the narrow discussions about race.

To establish a new framework, we need to begin with a frank acknowledgment of the basic humanness and Americanness of each of us. And we must acknowledge that as a people—*E Pluribus Unum*—we are on a slippery slope toward economic strife, social turmoil, and cultural chaos. If we go down, we go down together. The Los Angeles upheaval forced us to see not only that we are not connected in ways we would like to be but also, in a more profound sense, that this failure to connect binds us even more tightly together. The paradox of race in America is that our common destiny is more pronounced and imperiled precisely when our divisions are deeper. The Civil War and its legacy speak loudly here. And our divisions are growing deeper. Today, eighty-six percent of white suburban Americans live in neighborhoods that are less than 1 percent black, meaning that the prospects for the country depend largely on how its cities fare in the hands of a suburban electorate. There is no escape from our interracial interdependence, yet enforced racial hierarchy dooms us as a nation to collective paranoia and hysteria—the unmaking of any democratic order.

The verdict in the Rodney King case which sparked the incidents in Los Angeles was perceived to be wrong by the vast majority of Americans. But whites have often failed to acknowledge the widespread mistreatment of black people, especially black men, by law enforcement agencies, which helped ignite the spark. The verdict was merely the occasion for deep-seated rage to come to the surface. This rage is fed by the "silent" depression ravaging the country—in which real weekly wages of all American workers since 1973 have declined nearly 20 percent, while at the same time wealth has been upwardly distributed.

The exodus of stable industrial jobs from urban centers to cheaper labor markets here and abroad, housing policies that have created "chocolate cities and vanilla suburbs" (to use the popular musical artist George Clinton's memorable phrase), white fear of black crime, and the urban influx of poor Spanish-speaking and Asian immigrants—all have helped erode the tax base of American cities just as the federal government has cut its supports and programs. The result is unemployment, hunger, homelessness, and sickness for millions.

And a pervasive spiritual impoverishment grows. The collapse of meaning in life—the eclipse of hope and absence of love of self and others, the breakdown of family and neighborhood bonds—leads to the social deracination and cultural denudement of urban dwellers, especially children. We have created rootless, dangling people with little link to the supportive networks—family, friends, school—that sustain some sense of purpose in life. We have witnessed the collapse of the spiritual communities that in the past helped Americans face despair, disease, and death and that transmit through the generations dignity and decency, excellence and elegance.

The result is lives of what we might call "random nows," of fortuitous and feeling moments preoccupied with "getting over"—with acquiring pleasure, property, and power by any means necessary. (This is not what Malcolm X meant by this famous phrase.) Post-modern culture is more and more a market culture dominated by gangster mentalities and self-destructive wantonness. This culture engulfs all of us—yet its impact on the disadvantaged is devastating, resulting in extreme violence in everyday life. Sexual violence against women and homicidal assaults by young black men on one another are only the most obvious signs of this empty quest for pleasure, property, and power.

Last, this rage is fueled by a political atmosphere in which images, not ideas, dominate, where politicians spend more time raising money than debating issues. The functions of parties have been displaced by public polls, and politicians behave less as thermostats that determine the climate of opinion than as thermometers registering the public mood. American politics has been rocked by an unleashing of greed among opportunistic public officials—who have followed the lead of their counterparts in the private sphere, where, as of 1989, 1 percent of the population owned 37 percent of the wealth and 10 percent of the population owned 86 percent of the wealth—leading to a profound cynicism and pessimism among the citizenry.

And given the way in which the Republican Party since 1968 has appealed to popular xenophobic images—playing the black, female, and homophobic cards to realign the electorate along race, sex, and sexual-orientation lines—it is no surprise that the notion that we are all part of one garment of destiny is discredited. Appeals to special interests rather than to public interests reinforce this polarization. The Los Angeles upheaval was an expression of utter fragmentation by a powerless citizenry that includes not just the poor but all of us.

What is to be done? How do we capture a new spirit and vision to meet the challenges of the post-industrial city, post-modern culture, and post-party politics?

First, we must admit that the most valuable sources for help, hope, and power consist of ourselves and our common history. As in the ages of Lincoln, Roosevelt, and King, we must look to new frameworks and languages to understand our multilayered crisis and overcome our deep malaise.

Second, we must focus our attention on the public square—the common good that undergirds our national and global destinies. The vitality of any public square ultimately depends on how much we *care* about the quality of our lives together. The neglect of our public infrastructure, for example—our water and sewage systems, bridges, tunnels, highways, subways, and streets—reflects not only our myopic economic policies, which impede productivity, but also the low priority we place on our common life.

The tragic plight of our children clearly reveals our deep disregard for public well-being. About one out of every five children in this country lives in poverty, including one out of every two black children and two out of every five Hispanic children. Most of our children—neglected by overburdened parents and bombarded by the market values of profit-hungry corporations—are ill-equipped to live lives of spiritual and cultural quality. Faced with these facts, how do we expect ever to constitute a vibrant society?

One essential step is some form of large-scale public intervention to ensure access to basic social goods—housing, food, health care, education, child care, and jobs. We must invigorate the common good with a mixture of government, business, and labor that does not follow any existing blueprint. After a period in which the private sphere has been sacralized and the public square gutted, the temptation is to make a fetish of the public square. We need to resist such dogmatic swings.

Last, the major challenge is to meet the need to generate new leadership. The paucity of courageous leaders—so apparent in the response to the events in Los Angeles—requires that we look beyond the same elites and voices that recycle the older frameworks. We need leaders—neither saints nor sparkling television personalities—who can situate themselves within a larger historical narrative of this country and our world, who can grasp the complex dynamics of our peoplehood and imagine a future grounded in the best of our past, yet who are attuned to the frightening obstacles that now perplex us. Our ideals of freedom, democracy, and equality must be invoked to invigorate all of us, especially the landless, propertyless, and luckless. Only a visionary leadership that can motivate "the better angels of our nature," as Lincoln said, and activate possibilities for a freer, more efficient, and stable America—only that leadership deserves cultivation and support.

This new leadership must be grounded in grass-roots organizing that highlights democratic accountability. Whoever *our* leaders will be as we approach the twenty-first century, their challenge will be to help Americans determine whether a genuine multiracial democracy can be created and sustained in an era of global economy and a moment of xenophobic frenzy.

Let us hope and pray that the vast intelligence, imagination, humor, and courage of Americans will not fail us. Either we learn a new language of empathy and compassion, or the fire this time will consume us all.*

6

MICHAEL KAMMEN

From *People of Paradox*

Thinking about the United States, its history, culture, and politics, as a paradox is one of the most useful ways to tie together all the themes and facts in American government. Historian Michael Kammen offers a sometimes-fanciful, sometimes-profound analysis of the many paradoxes that riddle American life. Citizens expect their leaders to be "Everyman and Superman," he perceptively observes. Kammen takes on the difficult issue of the American melting pot; he substitutes the metaphor of a "super-highway" to explain nicely the country and its people. He points out paradoxes in all aspects of American life, ending with a poetic vision of the super-highway, along the side of the road, at Thanksgiving. Many scholars and thinkers are quoted in Kammen's piece, but his top source opens the selection: "We have met the enemy and he is us," cartoon character Pogo recognizes.

We have met the enemy and he is us.
—POGO

. . . OUR INHERITANCE has indeed been bitter-sweet, and our difficulty in assessing it just now arises from the fact that American institutions have had too many uncritical lovers and too many unloving critics. We have managed to graft pride onto guilt—guilt over social injustice and abuses of power—and find that pride and guilt do not neutralize each other, but make many decisions seem questionable, motives suspect, and consciences troubled.

*In *The Fire Next Time* (1963), African–American writer James Baldwin quotes a black slave's prophecy, found in a song recreated from the Bible, "God gave Noah the rainbow sign, no more water, the fire next time!"—EDS.

Perhaps so many American shibboleths seem to generate their very opposites because they are often half-truths rather than the wholesome verities we believe them to be. Perhaps we ought to recall Alice in Wonderland playing croquet against herself, "for this curious child was very fond of pretending to be two people. 'But it's no use now,' thought poor Alice, 'to pretend to be two people! Why, there's hardly enough of me left to make one respectable person!'" . . .

This dualistic state of mind may be found also in the domestic political values subscribed to by most Americans. We are comfortable believing in both majority rule and minority rights, in both consensus and freedom, federalism and centralization. It may be perfectly reasonable to support majority rule with reservations, or minority rights with certain other reservations. But this has not been our method. Rather, we have tended to hold contradictory ideas in suspension and ignore the intellectual and behavioral consequences of such "doublethink." . . .

Americans have managed to be both puritanical and hedonistic, idealistic and materialistic, peace-loving and war-mongering, isolationist and interventionist, conformist and individualist, consensus-minded and conflict-prone. "We recognize the American," wrote Gunnar Myrdal in 1944, "wherever we meet him, as a practical idealist." . . .

Americans expect their heroes to be Everyman and Superman simultaneously. I once overheard on an airplane the following fragment of conversation: "He has none of the virtues I respect, and none of the vices I admire." We cherish the humanity of our past leaders: George Washington's false teeth and whimsical orthography, Benjamin Franklin's lechery and cunning. The quintessential American hero wears both a halo *and* horns.

Because our society is so pluralistic, the American politician must be all things to all people. Dwight Eisenhower represented the most advanced industrial nation, but his chief appeal rested in a naive simplicity which recalled our pre-industrial past. Robert Frost once advised President Kennedy to be as much an Irishman as a Harvard man: "You have to have both the pragmatism and the idealism." The ambivalent American is ambitious and ambidextrous; but the appearance of ambidexterity—to some, at least—suggests the danger of double-dealing and deceit. The story is told of a U.S. senator meeting the press one Sunday afternoon. "How do you stand on conservation, Senator?" asked one panelist. The senator squirmed. "Well, I'll tell you," he said. "Some of my constituents are for conservation, and some of my constituents are against conservation, and I stand foresquare behind my constituents." . . .

Raymond Aron, the French sociologist, has remarked that a "dialectic of plurality and conformism lies at the core of American life, making for the originality of the social structure, and raising the most contradictory evaluations." Americans have repeatedly reaffirmed the social philosophy of individualism, even making it the basis of their political thought. Yet they have been a nation of joiners and have developed the largest associations and corporations the world has ever known. Nor has American respect for the abstract "individual" always guaranteed respect for particular persons.

There is a persistent tension between authoritarianism and individualism in American history. The genius of American institutions at their best has been to find a place and a use for both innovators and consolidators, rebellious dreamers and realistic adjudicators. "America has been built on a mixture of discipline and rebellion," writes Christopher Jencks, "but the balance between them has constantly shifted over the years." Our individualism, therefore, has been of a particular sort, a collective individualism. Individuality is not synonymous in the United States with singularity. When Americans develop an oddity they make a fad of it so that they may be comfortable among familiar oddities. Their unity, as Emerson wrote in his essay on the New England Reformers, "is only perfect when all the uniters are isolated."

How then can we adequately summarize the buried historical roots of our paradoxes, tensions, and biformities? The incongruities in American life are not merely fortuitous, and their stimuli appear from the very beginning. "America was always promises," as Archibald MacLeish has put it. "From the first voyage and the first ship there were promises." Many of these have gone unfulfilled—an endless source of ambiguity and equivocation. . . .

Above all other factors, however, the greatest source of dualisms in American life has been unstable pluralism in all its manifold forms: cultural, social, sequential, and political. *E pluribus unum* is a misbegotten motto because we have *not* become one out of many. The myth of the melting pot is precisely that: a myth. Moreover, our constitutional system seems to foster fragmentation of power while our economic-technological system seems to encourage consolidation of power. Thus the imperatives of pluralism under conditions of large-scale technology commonly conflict with principles and practices of constitutional democracy. . . .

It has been the impulse of our egalitarianism to make all men American and alike, but the thrust of our social order and intolerance to accentuate differences among groups. We have achieved expertise at both xenophobia and self-hate! At several stages of our history, population growth has outstripped institutional change. The result in many cases has been violence, vigilante movements, or economic unrest, all with the special coloration of unstable pluralism. Because there are significant variations in state laws regulating economic enterprise, taxation, and welfare payments, people and corporations move to tax-sheltered states and to those with the most generous welfare provisions. In this way mobility becomes a function of pluralism.

I do not argue that pluralism is a peculiarly American phenomenon. But I do believe that unstable pluralism on a scale of unprecedented proportion is especially American. . . .

There is a sense in which the super-highway is the most appropriate American metaphor. We have vast and anonymous numbers of people rushing individually (but simultaneously) in opposite directions. In between lies a no-man's-land, usually landscaped with a barrier of shrubs and trees, so that we cannot see the road to Elsewhere, but cannot easily turn back either. Indeed, the American experience in some spheres has moved from unity to diversity (e.g., denominationalism), while in other areas it has flowed in the opposite direction, from diversity to unity (e.g., political institutions). Along both roads we have paused from time to time in order to pay substantially for the privilege of traveling these thoroughfares.

There have always been Americans aware of unresolved contradictions between creed and reality, disturbed by the performance of their system and culture. Told how much liberty they enjoy, they feel less free; told how much equality they enjoy, they feel less equal; told how much progress they enjoy, their environment seems even more out of control. Most of all, told that they should be happy, they sense a steady growth in American unhappiness. Conflicts *between* Americans have been visible for a very long time, but most of us are just beginning to perceive the conflicts *within* us individually.

It is a consequence of some concern that our ambiguities often appear to the wider world as malicious hypocrisies. As when we vacillate, for example, between our missionary impulse and our isolationist instinct. From time to time we recognize that the needs of national security and the furtherance of national ideals may both be served by our vigorous but restrained participation in world affairs. At other times these two desiderata tug in opposite directions. However much we desperately want to be understood, we are too often misunderstood. . . .

Because of our ambivalent ambiance, we are frequently indecisive. "I cannot be a crusader," remarked Ralph McGill, "because I have been cursed all my life with the ability to see both sides." Our experience with polarities provides us with the potential for flexibility and diversity; yet too often it chills us into sheer inaction, or into contradictory appraisals of our own designs and historical development. Often we are willing to split the difference and seek consensus. "It is this intolerable paradox,"

James Reston writes, "of being caught between the unimaginable achievements of men when they cooperate for common goals, and their spectacular failures when they divide on how to achieve the simple decencies of life, that creates the present atmosphere of division and confusion." . . .

We have reached a moment in time when the national condition seems neither lifeless nor deathless. It's like the barren but sensuous serenity of the natural world in late autumn, before Thanksgiving, containing the promise of rebirth and the potential for resurrection. On bare branches whose leaves have fallen, buds bulge visibly in preparation for spring. Along the roadside, goldenrod stands sere and grizzled, and the leafless milkweed with its goosehead pods strews fluff and floss to every breeze, thereby seeding the countryside with frail fertility. The litter of autumn becomes the mulch, and then the humus, for roots and tender seeds. So it was, so it has been, and so it will be with the growth of American Civilization.

7

ROBERT BELLAH/OTHERS

From *Habits of the Heart*

American ideology touches more than just government and politics. It also guides the nation's social, economic, religious, and cultural life. It is fitting, therefore, that an important comment on American ideology comes from the discipline of sociology. Robert Bellah and his colleagues borrow Alexis de Tocqueville's phrase "habits of the heart" to explore the place of individualism in American life. The authors concede that individualism is the single most important ingredient in the nation's values, illustrating it with the symbol of cowboy-heroes Shane and the Lone Ranger. But, they contend, individualism cannot exist without being balanced by a sense of community.

———

INDIVIDUALISM lies at the very core of American culture. Every one of the four traditions we have singled out is in a profound sense individualistic. There is a biblical individualism and a civic individualism as well as a utilitarian and an expressive individualism. Whatever the differences among the traditions and the consequent differences in their understandings of individualism, there are some things they all share, things that are basic to American identity. We believe in the dignity, indeed the sacredness, of the individual. Anything that would violate our right to think for ourselves, judge for ourselves, make our own decisions, live our lives as we see fit, is not only morally wrong, it is sacrilegious. Our highest and noblest aspirations, not only for ourselves, but for those we care about, for our society and for the world, are closely linked to our individualism. Yet, as we have been suggesting repeatedly in this book, some of our deepest problems both as individuals and as a society are also closely linked to our individualism. We do not argue that Americans should abandon individualism—that would mean for us to abandon our deepest identity. But individualism has come to mean so many things and to contain such contradictions and paradoxes that even to defend it requires that we analyze it critically, that we consider especially those tendencies that would destroy it from within. . . .

The question is whether an individualism in which the self has become the main form of reality can really be sustained. What is at issue is not simply whether self-contained individuals might withdraw from the public sphere to pursue purely private ends, but whether such individuals are capable of sustaining either a public *or* a private life. If this is the danger, perhaps only the civic and biblical forms of individualism—forms that see the individual in relation to a larger whole, a community and a tradition—are capable of sustaining genuine individuality and nurturing both public and private life. . . .

America is also the inventor of that most mythic individual hero, the cowboy, who again and again saves a society he can never completely fit into. The cowboy has a special talent—he can shoot straighter and faster than other men—and a special sense of justice. But these characteristics make him so unique that he can never fully belong to society. His destiny is to defend society without ever really joining it. He rides off alone into the sunset like Shane,* or like the Lone Ranger moves on accompanied only by his Indian companion. But the cowboy's importance is not that he is isolated or antisocial. Rather, his significance lies in his unique, individual virtue and special skill and it is because of those qualities that society needs and welcomes him. Shane, after all, starts as a real outsider, but ends up with the gratitude of the community and the love of a woman and a boy. And while the Lone Ranger never settles down and marries the local schoolteacher, he always leaves with the affection and gratitude of the people he has helped. It is as if the myth says you can be a truly good person, worthy of admiration and love, only if you resist fully joining the group. But sometimes the tension leads to an irreparable break. Will Kane, the hero of *High Noon*, abandoned by the cowardly townspeople,

*Shane is the gunfighter-hero of the 1953 western film *Shane.*—EDS.

saves them from an unrestrained killer, but then throws his sheriff's badge in the dust and goes off into the desert with his bride. One is left wondering where they will go, for there is no longer any link with any town. . . .

[T]he cowboy . . . tell[s] us something important about American individualism. The cowboy . . . can be valuable to society only because he is a completely autonomous individual who stands outside it. To serve society, one must be able to stand alone, not needing others, not depending on their judgment, and not submitting to their wishes. Yet this individualism is not selfishness. Indeed, it is a kind of heroic selflessness. One accepts the necessity of remaining alone in order to serve the values of the group. And this obligation to aloneness is an important key to the American moral imagination. Yet it is part of the profound ambiguity of the mythology of American individualism that its moral heroism is always just a step away from despair. . . .

. . . The inner tensions of American individualism add up to a classic case of ambivalence. We strongly assert the value of our self-reliance and autonomy. We deeply feel the emptiness of a life without sustaining social commitments. Yet we are hesitant to articulate our sense that we need one another as much as we need to stand alone, for fear that if we did we would lose our independence altogether. The tensions of our lives would be even greater if we did not, in fact, engage in practices that constantly limit the effects of an isolating individualism, even though we cannot articulate those practices nearly as well as we can the quest for autonomy. . . .

. . . It is now time to consider what a self that is not empty would be like—one that is constituted rather than unencumbered, one that has, let us admit it, encumbrances, but whose encumbrances make connection to others easier and more natural. Just as the empty self makes sense in a particular institutional context—that of the upward mobility of the middle-class individual who must leave home and church in order to succeed in an impersonal world of rationality and competition—so a constituted self makes sense in terms of another institutional context, what we would call, in the full sense of the world, community.

Communities, in the sense in which we are using the term, have a history—in an important sense they are constituted by their past—and for this reason we can speak of a real community as a "community of memory," one that does not forget its past. In order not to forget that past, a community is involved in retelling its story, its constitutive narrative, and in so doing, it offers examples of the men and women who have embodied and exemplified the meaning of the community. These stories of collective history and exemplary individuals are an important part of the tradition that is so central to a community of memory. . . .

Examples of such genuine communities are not hard to find in the United States. There are ethnic and racial communities, each with its own story and its own heroes and heroines. There are religious communities that recall and reenact their stories in the weekly and annual cycles of their ritual year, remembering the scriptural stories that tell them who they are and the saints and martyrs who define their identity. There is the national community, defined by its history and by the character of its representative leaders from [early colonist] John Winthrop to [civil rights leader] Martin Luther King, Jr. Americans identify with their national community partly because there is little else that we all share in common but also partly because America's history exemplifies aspirations widely shared throughout the world: the ideal of a free society, respecting all its citizens, however diverse, and allowing them all to fulfill themselves. Yet some Americans also remember the history of suffering inflicted and the gap between promise and realization, which has always been very great. At some times, neighborhoods, localities, and regions have been communities in America, but that has been hard to sustain in our restless and mobile society. Families can be communities, remembering their past, telling the children the stories of parents' and grandparents' lives, and sustaining hope for the future—though without the context of a larger community that sense of family is hard to maintain. Where history and hope are forgotten and community means only the gathering of the similar, community degenerates into lifestyle enclave. The temptation toward that transformation is endemic in America, though the transition is seldom complete.

People growing up in communities of memory not only hear the stories that tell how the community came to be, what its hopes and fears are, and how its ideals are exemplified in outstanding men and women; they also participate in the practices—ritual, aesthetic, ethical—that define the community as a way of life. We call these "practices of commitment" for they define the patterns of loyalty and obligation that keep the community alive. And if the language of the self-reliant individual is the first language of American moral life, the languages of tradition and commitment in communities of memory are "second languages" that most Americans know as well, and which they use when the language of the radically separate self does not seem adequate. . . . Sometimes Americans make a rather sharp dichotomy between private and public life. Viewing one's primary task as "finding oneself" in autonomous self-reliance, separating oneself not only from one's parents but also from those larger communities and traditions that constitute one's past, leads to the notion that it is in oneself, perhaps in relation to a few intimate others, that fulfillment is to be found. Individualism of this sort often implies a negative view of public life. The impersonal forces of the economic and political worlds are what the individual needs protection against. In this perspective, even occupation, which has been so central to the identity of Americans in the past, becomes instrumental—not a good in itself, but only a means to the attainment of a rich and satisfying private life. But on the basis of what we have seen in our observation of middle-class American life, it would seem that this quest for purely private fulfillment is illusory: it often ends in emptiness instead. On the other hand, we found many people . . . for whom private fulfillment and public involvement are not antithetical. These people evince an individualism that is not empty but is full of content drawn from an active identification with communities and traditions. Perhaps the notion that private life and public life are at odds is incorrect. Perhaps they are so deeply involved with each other that the impoverishment of one entails the impoverishment of the other. Parker Palmer is probably right when he says that "in a healthy society the private and the public are not mutually exclusive, not in competition with each other. They are, instead, two halves of a whole, two poles of a paradox. They work together dialectically, helping to create and nurture one another."

Certainly this dialectical relationship is clear where public life degenerates into violence and fear. One cannot live a rich private life in a state of siege, mistrusting all strangers and turning one's home into an armed camp. A minimum of public decency and civility is a precondition for a fulfilling private life. On the other hand, public involvement is often difficult and demanding. To engage successfully in the public world, one needs personal strength and the support of family and friends. A rewarding private life is one of the preconditions for a healthy public life.

For all their doubts about the public sphere, Americans are more engaged in voluntary associations and civic organizations than the citizens of most other industrial nations. In spite of all the difficulties, many Americans feel they must "get involved." In public life as in private, we can discern the habits of the heart that sustain individualism and commitment, as well as what makes them problematic. . . .

The communities of memory of which we have spoken are concerned in a variety of ways to give a qualitative meaning to the living of life, to time and space, to persons and groups. Religious communities, for example, do not experience time in the way the mass media present it—as a continuous flow of qualitatively meaningless sensations. The day, the week, the season, the year are punctuated by an alternation of the sacred and the profane. Prayer breaks into our daily life at the beginning of a meal, at the end of the day, at common worship, reminding us that our utilitarian pursuits are not the whole of life, that a fulfilled life is one in which God and neighbor are remembered first. Many of our religious traditions recognize the significance of silence as a way of breaking the incessant flow of sensations and opening our hearts to the wholeness of being. And our republican tradition, too, has ways of giving form to time, reminding us on particular dates of the great events of our past or of the heroes who helped to teach us what we are as a free people. Even our private family life takes on a shared rhythm with a Thanksgiving dinner or a Fourth of July picnic.

In short, we have never been, and still are not, a collection of private individuals who, except for a conscious contract to create a minimal government, have nothing in common. Our lives make sense in a thousand ways, most of which we are unaware of, because of traditions that are centuries, if not millennia, old. It is these traditions that help us to know that it does make a difference who we are and how we treat one another.

PART TWO

The Constitution and American Democracy

8

RICHARD HOFSTADTER

From *The American Political Tradition*

Richard Hofstadter, one of the nation's leading historians, explores the real thoughts and motivations behind the men whom all schoolchildren have been taught to revere as Founding Fathers. Hofstadter's classic work points out the ambivalence of those who wrote the Constitution: they viewed human beings as selfish and untrustworthy, yet they strongly believed in the importance of self-government. The founders' ambivalence toward democracy led them to design the political system the United States still lives with today, one in which each interest (or branch or layer of government or economic class or region . . .) would be checked and balanced by competing interests. Hofstadter goes on to interpret what the near-sacred idea of liberty meant to the founders. Liberty was not really related to democracy, he contends, but rather ensured the freedom to attain and enjoy private property. To make this idea clearer, test the author's thesis against the current political debate over health care or social security reform.

———

. . . THE MEN who drew up the Constitution in Philadelphia during the summer of 1787 had a vivid Calvinistic sense of human evil and damnation and believed with Hobbes that men are selfish and contentious. They were men of affairs, merchants, lawyers, planter-businessmen, speculators, investors. Having seen human nature on display in the marketplace, the courtroom, the legislative chamber, and in every secret path and alleyway where wealth and power are courted, they felt they knew it in all its frailty. To them a human being was an atom of self-interest. They did not believe in man, but they did believe in the power of a good political constitution to control him.

This may be an abstract notion to ascribe to practical men, but it follows the language that the Fathers themselves used. General Knox, for example, wrote in disgust to Washington after the Shays Rebellion that Americans were, after all, "men—actual men possessing all the turbulent passions belonging to that animal." Throughout the secret discussions at the Constitutional Convention it was clear that this distrust of man was first and foremost a distrust of the common man and democratic rule. . . .

And yet there was another side to the picture. The Fathers were intellectual heirs of seventeenth-century English republicanism with its opposition to arbitrary rule and faith in popular sovereignty. If they feared the advance of democracy, they also had misgivings about turning to the extreme right. Having recently experienced a bitter revolutionary struggle with an external power beyond their control, they were in no mood to follow Hobbes to his conclusion that any kind of government must be accepted in order to avert the anarchy and terror of a state of nature. . . .

Unwilling to turn their backs on republicanism, the Fathers also wished to avoid violating the prejudices of the people. "Notwithstanding the oppression and injustice experienced among us from democracy," said George Mason, "the genius of the people is in favor of it, and the genius of the people must be consulted." Mason admitted "that we had been too democratic," but feared that "we should incautiously run into the opposite extreme." James Madison, who has quite rightfully been called the philosopher of the Constitution, told the delegates: "It seems indispensable that the mass of citizens should not be without a voice in making the laws which they are to obey, and in choosing the magistrates who are to administer them." James Wilson, the outstanding jurist of the age, later appointed to the Supreme Court by Washington, said again and again that the ultimate power of government must of necessity reside in the people. This the Fathers commonly accepted, for if government did not proceed from the people, from what other source could it legitimately come? To adopt any other premise not only would be inconsistent with everything they had said against British rule in the past but would open the gates to an extreme concentration of power in the future. . . .

If the masses were turbulent and unregenerate, and yet if government must be founded upon their suffrage and consent, what could a Constitution-maker do? One thing that the Fathers did not propose to do, because they thought it impossible, was to change the nature of man to conform with a more ideal system. They were inordinately confident that they knew what man always had been and what he always would be. The eighteenth-century mind had great faith in universals. . . .

. . . It was too much to expect that vice could be checked by virtue; the Fathers relied instead upon checking vice with vice. Madison once objected during the Convention that Gouverneur Morris was "forever inculcating the utter political depravity of men and the necessity of opposing one vice and interest to another vice and interest." And yet Madison himself in the *Federalist* number 51 later set forth an excellent statement of the same thesis:

Ambition must be made to counteract ambition. . . . It may be a reflection on human nature that such devices should be necessary to control the abuses of government. But what is government itself, but the greatest of all reflections on human nature? If men were angels, no government would be necessary. . . . In framing a government which is to be administered by men over men, the great difficulty lies in this: you must first enable the government to control the governed; and in the next place oblige it to control itself.

. . . If, in a state that lacked constitutional balance, one class or one interest gained control, they believed, it would surely plunder all other interests. The Fathers, of course, were especially fearful that the poor would plunder the rich, but most of them would probably have admitted that the rich, unrestrained, would also plunder the poor. . . .

In practical form, therefore, the quest of the Fathers reduced primarily to a search for constitutional devices that would force various interests to check and control one another. Among those who favored the federal Constitution three such devices were distinguished.

The first of these was the advantage of a federated government in maintaining order against popular uprisings or majority rule. In a single state a faction might arise and take complete control by force; but if the states were bound in a federation, the central government could step in and prevent it. . . .

The second advantage of good constitutional government resided in the mechanism of representation itself. In a small direct democracy the unstable passions of the people would dominate lawmaking; but a representative government, as Madison said, would "refine and enlarge the public views by passing them through the medium of a chosen body of citizens." . . .

The third advantage of the government . . . [was that] each element should be given its own house of the legislature, and over both houses there should be set a capable, strong, and impartial executive armed with the veto power. This split assembly would contain within itself an organic check and would be capable of self-control under the governance of the executive. The whole system was to be capped by an independent judiciary. The inevitable tendency of the rich and the poor to plunder each other would be kept in hand. . . .

It is ironical that the Constitution, which Americans venerate so deeply, is based upon a political theory that at one crucial point stands in direct antithesis to the mainstream of American democratic faith. Modern American folklore assumes that democracy and liberty are all but identical, and when democratic writers take the trouble to make the distinction, they usually assume that democracy is necessary to liberty. But the Found-

ing Fathers thought that the liberty with which they were most concerned
was menaced by democracy. In their minds liberty was linked not to
democracy but to property.

What did the Fathers mean by liberty? What did Jay mean when he
spoke of "the charms of liberty"? Or Madison when he declared that to
destroy liberty in order to destroy factions would be a remedy worse than
the disease? Certainly the men who met at Philadelphia were not interested
in extending liberty to those classes in America, the Negro slaves and the
indentured servants, who were most in need of it, for slavery was recognized in the organic structure of the Constitution and indentured servitude
was no concern of the Convention. Nor was the regard of the delegates
for civil liberties any too tender. It was the opponents of the Constitution
who were most active in demanding such vital liberties as freedom of
religion, freedom of speech and press, jury trial, due process, and protection from "unreasonable searches and seizures." These guarantees had to
be incorporated in the first ten amendments because the Convention
neglected to put them in the original document. Turning to economic
issues, it was not freedom of trade in the modern sense that the Fathers
were striving for. Although they did not believe in impeding trade unnecessarily, they felt that failure to regulate it was one of the central weaknesses
of the Articles of Confederation, and they stood closer to the mercantilists
than to Adam Smith. Again, liberty to them did not mean free access to
the nation's unappropriated wealth. At least fourteen of them were land
speculators. They did not believe in the right of the squatter to occupy
unused land, but rather in the right of the absentee owner or speculator
to preempt it.

The liberties that the constitutionalists hoped to gain were chiefly
negative. They wanted freedom from fiscal uncertainty and irregularities
in the currency, from trade wars among the states, from economic discrimination by more powerful foreign governments, from attacks on the creditor
class or on property, from popular insurrection. They aimed to create a
government that would act as an honest broker among a variety of propertied interests, giving them all protection from their common enemies and
preventing any one of them from becoming too powerful. The Convention was a fraternity of types of absentee ownership. All property should
be permitted to have its proportionate voice in government. Individual
property interests might have to be sacrificed at times, but only for the
community of propertied interests. Freedom for property would result in
liberty for men—perhaps not for all men, but at least for all worthy
men. Because men have different faculties and abilities, the Fathers believed, they acquire different amounts of property. To protect property

is only to protect men in the exercise of their natural faculties. Among the many liberties, therefore, freedom to hold and dispose [of] property is paramount. Democracy, unchecked rule by the masses, is sure to bring arbitrary redistribution of property, destroying the very essence of liberty. . . .

A cardinal tenet in the faith of the men who made the Constitution was the belief that democracy can never be more than a transitional stage in government, that it always evolves into either a tyranny (the rule of the rich demagogue who has patronized the mob) or an aristocracy (the original leaders of the democratic elements). . . .

What encouraged the Fathers about their own era, however, was the broad dispersion of landed property. The small land-owning farmers had been troublesome in recent years, but there was a general conviction that under a properly made Constitution a *modus vivendi* could be worked out with them. The possession of moderate plots of property presumably gave them a sufficient stake in society to be safe and responsible citizens under the restraints of balanced government. Influence in government would be proportionate to property: merchants and great landholders would be dominant, but small property-owners would have an independent and far from negligible voice. It was "politic as well as just," said Madison, "that the interests and rights of every class should be duly represented and understood in the public councils," and John Adams declared that there could be "no free government without a democratical branch in the constitution." . . .

. . . At the very beginning contemporary opponents of the Constitution foresaw an apocalyptic destruction of local government and popular institutions, while conservative Europeans of the old regime thought the young American Republic was a dangerous leftist experiment. Modern critical scholarship, which reached a high point in Charles A. Beard's *An Economic Interpretation of the Constitution of the United States*, started a new turn in the debate. The antagonism, long latent, between the philosophy of the Constitution and the philosophy of American democracy again came into the open. Professor Beard's work appeared in 1913 at the peak of the Progressive era, when the muckraking fever was still high; some readers tended to conclude from his findings that the Fathers were selfish reactionaries who do not deserve their high place in American esteem. Still more recently, other writers, inverting this logic, have used Beard's facts to praise the Fathers for their opposition to "democracy" and as an argument for returning again to the idea of a "republic."

In fact, the Fathers' image of themselves as moderate republicans standing between political extremes was quite accurate. They were impelled by class motives more than pietistic writers like to admit, but they were also controlled, as Professor Beard himself has recently emphasized, by a statesmanlike sense of moderation and a scrupulously republican philosophy. Any attempt, however, to tear their ideas out of the eighteenth-century context is sure to make them seem starkly reactionary. Consider, for example, the favorite maxim of John Jay: "The people who own the country ought to govern it." To the Fathers this was simply a swift axiomatic statement of the stake-in-society theory of political rights, a moderate conservative position under eighteenth-century conditions of property distribution in America. Under modern property relations this maxim demands a drastic restriction of the base of political power. A large portion of the modern middle class—and it is the strength of this class upon which balanced government depends—is propertyless; and the urban proletariat, which the Fathers so greatly feared, is almost one half the population. Further, the separation of ownership from control that has come with the corporation deprives Jay's maxim of twentieth-century meaning even for many propertied people. The six hundred thousand stockholders of the American Telephone & Telegraph Company not only do not acquire political power by virtue of their stock-ownership, but they do not even acquire economic power: they cannot control their own company.

From a humanistic standpoint there is a serious dilemma in the philosophy of the Fathers, which derives from their conception of man. They thought man was a creature of rapacious self-interest, and yet they wanted him to be free—free, in essence, to contend, to engage in an umpired strife, to use property to get property. They accepted the mercantile image of life as an eternal battleground, and assumed the Hobbesian war of each against all; they did not propose to put an end to this war, but merely to stabilize it and make it less murderous. They had no hope and they offered none for any ultimate organic change in the way men conduct themselves. The result was that while they thought self-interest the most dangerous and unbrookable quality of man, they necessarily underwrote it in trying to control it. . . .

9

JAMES MADISON

The Federalist 10

This is the most important reading in an American government class. Along with its companion, Federalist 51 (coming in the next section of the book), James Madison's Federalist 10 is the first and last word on U.S. government and politics. In it, he takes up the idea of "faction," by which he means any single group (especially the mob-like majority, but perhaps even a tiny minority) that tries to dominate the political process. Can faction be removed from politics? No, he admits, for a variety of reasons that deeply illuminate his assessment of the American people. But faction can be controlled by a republican (representative) system. Madison favored a large and diverse nation; if there were many groups, no one faction would ever be able to dominate. Signing these papers Publius, Madison, along with Alexander Hamilton and John Jay, wrote eighty-five essays collectively known as The Federalist Papers, *which were published in several New York newspapers on behalf of the ratification of the new Constitution in 1787. James Madison's genius is revealed not only in the workable system of government he helped create for America, but also in his vision of the United States in the future, very much as it is today.*

No. 10: Madison

AMONG the numerous advantages promised by a well-constructed Union, none deserves to be more accurately developed than its tendency to break and control the violence of faction. The friend of popular governments never finds himself so much alarmed for their character and fate as when he contemplates their propensity to this dangerous vice. He will not fail, therefore, to set a due value on any plan which, without violating the principles to which he is attached, provides a proper cure for it. The instability, injustice, and confusion introduced into the public councils have, in truth, been the mortal diseases under which popular governments have everywhere perished, as they continue to be the favorite and fruitful topics from which the adversaries to liberty derive their most specious declamations. The valuable improvements made by the American constitutions on the popular models, both ancient and modern, cannot certainly be too much admired; but it would be an unwarrantable partiality to contend that they have as effectually obviated the danger on this side, as was wished and expected. Complaints are everywhere heard from our most considerate and virtuous citizens, equally the friends of public and private faith and of public and personal liberty, that our governments are too unstable, that the public good is disregarded in the conflicts of rival parties, and that measures are too often decided, not according to the rules of justice and the rights of the minor party, but by the superior force of an interested and overbearing majority. However anxiously we may wish that these complaints had no foundation, the evidence of known facts will not permit us to deny that they are in some degree true. It will be found, indeed, on a candid review of our situation, that some of the distresses under which we labor have been erroneously charged on the operation of our governments; but it will be found, at the same time, that other causes will not alone account for many of our heaviest misfortunes; and, particularly, for that prevailing and increasing distrust of public engagements and alarm for private rights which are echoed from one end of the continent to the other. These must be chiefly, if not wholly, effects of the unsteadiness and injustice with which a factious spirit has tainted our public administration.

By a faction I understand a number of citizens, whether amounting to a majority or minority of the whole, who are united and actuated by some common impulse of passion, or of interest, adverse to the rights of other citizens, or to the permanent and aggregate interests of the community.

There are two methods of curing the mischiefs of faction: the one, by removing its causes; the other, by controlling its effects.

There are again two methods of removing the causes of faction: the one, by destroying the liberty which is essential to its existence; the other, by giving to every citizen the same opinions, the same passions, and the same interests.

It could never be more truly said than of the first remedy that it was worse than the disease. Liberty is to faction what air is to fire, an aliment without which it instantly expires. But it could not be a less folly to abolish liberty, which is essential to political life, because it nourishes faction than it would be to wish the annihilation of air, which is essential to animal life, because it imparts to fire its destructive agency.

The second expedient is as impracticable as the first would be unwise. As long as the reason of man continues fallible, and he is at liberty to exercise it, different opinions will be formed. As long as the connection subsists between his reason and his self-love, his opinions and his passions will have a reciprocal influence on each other; and the former will be objects to which the latter will attach themselves. The diversity in the faculties of men, from which the rights of property originate, is not less an insuperable obstacle to a uniformity of interests. The protection of these faculties is the first object of government. From the protection of different and unequal faculties of acquiring property, the possession of different degrees and kinds of property immediately results; and from the influence of these on the sentiments and views of the respective proprietors ensues a division of the society into different interests and parties.

The latent causes of faction are thus sown in the nature of man; and we see them everywhere brought into different degrees of activity, according to the different circumstances of civil society. A zeal for different opinions concerning religion, concerning government, and many other points, as well of speculation as of practice; an attachment to different leaders ambitiously contending for pre-eminence and power; or to persons of other descriptions whose fortunes have been interesting to the human passions, have, in turn, divided mankind into parties, inflamed them with mutual animosity, and rendered them much more disposed to vex and oppress each other than to co-operate for their common good. So strong is this propensity of mankind to fall into mutual animosities that where no substantial occasion presents itself the most frivolous and fanciful distinctions have been sufficient to kindle their unfriendly passions and excite their most violent conflicts. But the most common and durable source of factions has been the various and unequal distribution of property. Those who hold and those who are without property have ever formed distinct interests in society. Those who are creditors, and those who are debtors, fall under a like discrimination. A landed interest, a manufacturing interest, a mercantile interest, a moneyed interest, with many lesser interests, grow up of necessity in civilized nations, and divide them into different classes, actuated by different sentiments and views. The regulation of these various and interfering interests forms the principal task of modern legislation and involves the spirit of party and faction in the necessary and ordinary operations of government.

No man is allowed to be a judge in his own cause, because his interest would certainly bias his judgment, and, not improbably, corrupt his integrity. With equal, nay with greater reason, a body of men are unfit to be both judges and parties at the same time; yet what are many of the most important acts of legislation but so many judicial determinations, not indeed concerning the rights of single persons, but concerning the rights of large bodies of citizens? And what are the different classes of legislators but advocates and parties to the causes which they determine?

Is a law proposed concerning private debts? It is a question to which the creditors are parties on one side and the debtors on the other. Justice ought to hold the balance between them. Yet the parties are, and must be, themselves the judges; and the most numerous party, or in other words, the most powerful faction must be expected to prevail. Shall domestic manufacturers be encouraged, and in what degree, by restrictions on foreign manufacturers? are questions which would be differently decided by the landed and the manufacturing classes, and probably by neither with a sole regard to justice and the public good. The apportionment of taxes on the various descriptions of property is an act which seems to require the most exact impartiality; yet there is, perhaps, no legislative act in which greater opportunity and temptation are given to a predominant party to trample on the rules of justice. Every shilling with which they overburden the inferior number is a shilling saved to their own pockets.

It is in vain to say that enlightened statesmen will be able to adjust these clashing interests and render them all subservient to the public good. Enlightened statesmen will not always be at the helm. Nor, in many cases, can such an adjustment be made at all without taking into view indirect and remote considerations, which will rarely prevail over the immediate interest which one party may find in disregarding the rights of another or the good of the whole.

The inference to which we are brought is that the *causes* of faction cannot be removed and that relief is only to be sought in the means of controlling its *effects*.

If a faction consists of less than a majority, relief is supplied by the republican principle, which enables the majority to defeat its sinister views by regular vote. It may clog the administration, it may convulse the society; but it will be unable to execute and mask its violence under the forms of the Constitution. When a majority is included in a faction, the form of popular government, on the other hand, enables it to sacrifice to its ruling passion or interest both the public good and the rights of other citizens. To secure the public good and private rights against the danger of such a faction, and at the same time to preserve the spirit and the form of popular government, is then the great object to which our inquiries are directed. Let me add that it is the great desideratum by which alone this form of government can be rescued from the opprobrium under which it has so long labored and be recommended to the esteem and adoption of mankind.

By what means is this object attainable? Evidently by one of two only. Either the existence of the same passion or interest in a majority at the same time must be prevented, or the majority, having such coexistent passion or interest, must be rendered, by their number and local situation, unable to concert and carry into effect schemes of oppression. If the impulse and the opportunity be suffered to coincide, we well know that neither moral nor religious motives can be relied on as an adequate control. They are not found to be such on the injustice and violence of individuals, and lose their efficacy in proportion to the number combined together, that is, in proportion as their efficacy becomes needful.

From this view of the subject it may be concluded that a pure democracy, by which I mean a society consisting of a small number of citizens, who assemble and administer the government in person, can admit of no cure for the mischiefs of faction. A common passion or interest will, in almost every case, be felt by a majority of the whole; a communication and concert results from the form of government itself; and there is nothing to check the inducements to sacrifice the weaker party or an obnoxious individual. Hence it is that such democracies have ever been spectacles of turbulence and contention; have ever been found incompatible with personal security or the rights of property; and have in general been as short in their lives as they have been violent in their deaths. Theoretic politicians, who have patronized this species of government, have erroneously supposed that by reducing mankind to a perfect equality in their political rights, they would at the same time be perfectly equalized and assimilated in their possessions, their opinions, and their passions.

A republic, by which I mean a government in which the scheme of representation takes place, opens a different prospect and promises the cure for which we are seeking. Let us examine the points in which it varies from pure democracy, and we shall comprehend both the nature of the cure and the efficacy which it must derive from the Union.

The two great points of difference between a democracy and a republic are: first, the delegation of the government, in the latter, to a small number of citizens elected by the rest; secondly, the greater number of citizens and greater sphere of country over which the latter may be extended.

The effect of the first difference is, on the one hand, to refine and enlarge the public views by passing them through the medium of a chosen body of citizens, whose wisdom may best discern the true interest of their country and whose patriotism and love of justice will be least likely to sacrifice it to temporary or partial considerations. Under such a regulation it may well happen that the public voice, pronounced by the representatives of the people, will be more consonant to the public good than if pronounced by the people themselves, convened for the purpose. On the other hand, the effect may be inverted. Men of factious tempers, of local prejudices, or of sinister designs, may, by intrigue, by corruption, or by other means, first obtain the suffrages, and then betray the interests of the people. The question resulting is, whether small or extensive republics are most favorable to the election of proper guardians of the public weal; and it is clearly decided in favor of the latter by two obvious considerations.

In the first place it is to be remarked that however small the republic may be the representatives must be raised to a certain number in order to guard against the cabals of a few; and that however large it may be they must be limited to a certain number in order to guard against the confusion of a multitude. Hence, the number of representatives in the two cases not being in proportion to that of the constituents, and being proportionally greatest in the small republic, it follows that if the proportion of fit characters be not less in the large than in the small republic, the former will present a greater option, and consequently a greater probability of a fit choice.

In the next place, as each representative will be chosen by a greater number of citizens in the large than in the small republic, it will be more difficult for unworthy candidates to practise with success the vicious arts by which elections are too often carried; and the suffrages of the people being more free, will be more likely to center on men who possess the most attractive merit and the most diffusive and established characters.

It must be confessed that in this, as in most other cases, there is a mean, on both sides of which inconveniencies will be found to lie. By enlarging too much the number of electors, you render the representative too little acquainted with all their local circumstances and lesser interests; as by reducing it too much, you render him unduly attached to these, and too little fit to comprehend and pursue great and national objects. The federal Constitution forms a happy combination in this respect; the great and aggregate interests being referred to the national, the local and particular to the State legislatures.

The other point of difference is the greater number of citizens and extent of territory which may be brought within the compass of republican than of democratic government; and it is this circumstance principally which renders factious combinations less to be dreaded in the former than in the latter. The smaller the society, the fewer probably will be the distinct parties and interests composing it; the fewer the distinct parties and interests, the more frequently will a majority be found of the same party; and the smaller the number of individuals composing a majority, and the smaller the compass within which they are placed, the more easily will they concert and execute their plans of oppression. Extend the sphere and you take in a greater variety of parties and interests; you make it less probable that a majority of the whole will have a common motive to invade the rights of other citizens; or if such a common motive exists, it will be more difficult for all who feel it to discover their own strength and to act in unison with each other. Besides other impediments, it may be remarked that, where there is a consciousness of unjust or dishonorable purposes, communication is always checked by distrust in proportion to the number whose concurrence is necessary.

Hence, it clearly appears that the same advantage which a republic has over a democracy in controlling the effects of faction is enjoyed by a large over a small republic—is enjoyed by the Union over the States composing it. Does this advantage consist in the substitution of representatives whose enlightened views and virtuous sentiments render them superior to local prejudices and to schemes of injustice? It will not be denied that the representation of the Union will be most likely to possess these requisite endowments. Does it consist in the greater security afforded by a greater variety of parties, against the event of any one party being able to outnumber and oppress the rest? In an equal degree does the increased variety of parties comprised within the Union increase this security? Does it, in fine, consist in the greater obstacles opposed to the concert and accomplishment of the secret wishes of an unjust and interested majority? Here again the extent of the Union gives it the most palpable advantage.

The influence of factious leaders may kindle a flame within their particular States but will be unable to spread a general conflagration through the other States. A religious sect may degenerate into a political faction in a part of the Confederacy; but the variety of sects dispersed over the entire face of it must secure the national councils against any danger from that source. A rage for paper money, for an abolition of debts, for an equal division of property, or for any other improper or wicked project, will be less apt to pervade the whole body of the Union than a particular member of it, in the same proportion as such a malady is more likely to taint a particular county or district than an entire State.

In the extent and proper structure of the Union, therefore, we behold a republican remedy for the diseases most incident to republican government. And according to the degree of pleasure and pride we feel in being republicans ought to be our zeal in cherishing the spirit and supporting the character of federalists. *Publius*

10

MICHAEL KAMMEN

From *A Machine That Would Go of Itself*

Written at the time of the bicentennial of the United States Constitution, historian Michael Kammen's book is of interest to those seeking greater depth on the evolution of the nation's basic document. Kammen traces the shifts in thought about the Constitution's interpretation, from that of a "machine" that once put in motion would function steadily and unchangingly forever, to a more fluid and malleable plan. Particularly memorable is his analogy of a 1966 "Star Trek" episode, "The Omega Glory," in which we see Captain Kirk and the crew of the Enterprise grappling with the same questions that we ask today about the Constitution.

———

THE [metaphor], the notion of a constitution as some sort of machine or engine, had its origins in Newtonian science. Enlightened philosophers, such as David Hume, liked to contemplate the world with all of its components as a great machine. Perhaps it was inevitable, as politics came to be regarded as a science during the 1770s and '80s, that leading revolutionaries in the colonies would utilize the metaphor to suit their purposes. In 1774 Jefferson's *Summary View* mentioned "the great machine of government." . . .

Over the next one hundred years such imagery did not disappear. But neither did it notably increase; and hardly anyone expressed apprehension about the adverse implications of employing mechanistic metaphors. Occasionally an observer or enthusiast might call the Constitution "the best national machine that is now in existence" (1794); or, at the Golden Jubilee in 1839, John Quincy Adams could comment that "fifty years have passed away since the first impulse was given to the wheels of this political machine."

James Fenimore Cooper uttered one of the few expressions of concern couched in this language between 1787 and 1887. "The boldest violations of the Constitution are daily proposed by politicians in this country," he observed in 1848, "but they do not produce the fruits which might be expected, because the nation is so accustomed to work in the harness it has placed on itself, that nothing seems seriously to arrest the movement of the great national car." Although his metaphors are ridiculously muddled, the message is clear enough. Exactly forty years later James Russell Lowell articulated this same apprehension much more cogently in an address to the Reform Club of New York. The pertinent passage marks the apogee of the metaphor, and remains today as profound a warning as it was in 1888.

After our Constitution got fairly into working order it really seemed as if we had invented a machine that would go of itself, and this begot a faith in our luck which even the civil war itself but momentarily disturbed. Circumstances continued favorable, and our prosperity went on increasing. I admire the splendid complacency of my countrymen, and find something exhilarating and inspiring in it. We are a nation which has *struck ile* [sic], but we are also a nation that is sure the well will never run dry. And this confidence in our luck with the absorption in material interests, generated by unparalleled opportunity, has in some respects made us neglectful of our political duties.

That statement epitomizes not merely the main historical theme of this book, but the homily that I hope to convey as well. Machine imagery lingered on for fifty years, casually used by legal scholars, journalists, civics textbooks, even great jurists like Holmes, and by Franklin D. Roosevelt in his first inaugural address. On occasion, during the 1920s and '30s especially, conservatives would declare that the apparatus, being more than adequate, should not be tampered with, whereas reformers insisted that "the machinery of government under which we live is hopelessly antiquated" (a word they loved) and therefore "should be overhauled."

In the quarter century that followed Lowell's 1888 lament, a cultural transition took place that leads us to the last of the major constitutional metaphors. We may exemplify it with brief extracts from three prominent justices: Holmes, who wrote in 1914 that "the provisions of the Constitution are not mathematical formulas . . . they are organic living institutions"; Cardozo, who observed in 1925 that "a Constitution has an organic life"; and Frankfurter, who declared in 1951 that "the Constitution is an organism."

Unlike the other analogies that have been discussed, which were not mutually exclusive, this shift was not merely deliberate but intellectually aggressive at times. The quarter century is punctuated by the declarations of two political scientists deeply involved in public affairs. At the close of the 1880s, A. Lawrence Lowell wrote that "a political system is not a mere machine which can be constructed on any desired plan. . . . It is far more than this. It is an organism . . . whose various parts act and react upon one another." In 1912, when Woodrow Wilson ran for the presidency, a key passage in his campaign statement, *The New Freedom*, elaborated upon

Lowell's assertion. "The makers of our Federal Constitution," in Wilson's words, "constructed a government as they would have constructed an orrery,*—to display the laws of nature. Politics in their thought was a variety of mechanics. The Constitution was founded on the law of gravitation. The government was to exist and move by virtue of the efficacy of 'checks and balances.'"

Lowell and Wilson had obviously responded to the same current of cultural change; but they were not attempting to be intellectually trendy by explaining government in terms of evolutionary theory. The word-concept they both used in condemning a Newtonian notion of constitutionalism was "static." Wilson spelled out the implications: "Society is a living organism and must obey the laws of life, not of mechanics; it must develop. All that progressives ask or desire is permission—in an era when 'development,' 'evolution,' is the scientific word—to interpret the Constitution according to the Darwinian principle; all they ask is recognition of the fact that a nation is a living thing and not a machine." . . .

I would describe the basic pattern of American constitutionalism as one of *conflict within consensus*. At first glance, perhaps, we are more likely to notice the consensus. . . .

The volume of evidence is overwhelming that our constitutional conflicts have been consequential, and considerably more revealing than the consensual framework within which they operate. When Americans have been aware of the dynamic of conflict within consensus, most often they have regarded it as a normative pattern for a pluralistic polity. . . .

There is . . . a . . . closely linked aspect of American constitutionalism about which there has been no consensus: namely, whether our frame of government was meant to be fairly unchanging or flexible. Commentators are quick to quote Justice Holmes's "theory of our Constitution. It is an experiment, as all life is an experiment." Although much less familiar, and less eloquent, more Americans have probably shared this sentiment, written in 1936 by an uncommon common man, the chief clerk in the Vermont Department of Highways: "I regard the Constitution as of too much value to be experimented with."

The assumption that our Constitution is lapidary has a lineage that runs, among the justices, from Marshall and Taney to David J. Brewer and George Sutherland. It has been the dominant assumption for most of our history, and provided the basis for Walter Bagehot, Lord Bryce, and others to regard the U.S. Constitution as "rigid" by comparison with the British. The idea that adaptability was desirable emerged gradually

---

*An apparatus for representing the motions . . . of the planets. . . .

during the mid-nineteenth century, appeared in some manuals aimed at a popular audience by the 1880s, and achieved added respectability in 1906 when Justice Henry Billings Brown spoke at a dinner in his honor. The Constitution, he said, "should be liberally interpreted—interpreted as if it were intended as the foundation of a great nation, and not merely a temporary expedient for the united action of thirteen small States. . . . Like all written Constitutions, there is an underlying danger in its inflexibility." For about a generation that outlook slowly gained adherents, until the two contradictory views were essentially counterpoised in strength by the 1930s.

Meanwhile, a third position appeared during the early decades of the twentieth century—one that might be considered a compromise because it blended facets of the other two. This moderately conservative, evolutionary position was expressed in 1903 by James Ford Rhodes, a nationalistic businessman-turned-historian. The Constitution, in his mind, "is rigid in those matters which should not be submitted to the decision of a legislature or to a popular vote without checks which secure reflection and a chance for the sober second thought, [yet] it has proved flexible in its adaptation to the growth of the country." . . .

Admittedly, our strict constructionists have on occasion stretched the Constitution, as Jefferson did in 1803 to acquire the vast Louisiana Territory. Lincoln, Wilson, and FDR each stood accused of ignoring constitutional restraints; yet each one could honestly respond that, within the framework of a Constitution intended to be flexible in an emergency, his goal had been to preserve the Union, to win a war fought for noble goals, or to overcome the worst and most prolonged economic disaster in American history. In each instance their constitutional critics spoke out clearly, a national debate took place, and clarification of our constitutional values occurred. Sometimes that clarification has come from the Supreme Court; sometimes from a presidential election campaign; sometimes from a combination of the two; and sometimes by means of political compromise. Each mode of resolution is a necessary part of our democratic system. I am led to conclude that Americans have been more likely to read and understand their Constitution when it has been controversial, or when some group contended that it had been misused, than in those calmer moments when it has been widely venerated as an instrument for all time. . . .

During the later 1950s, Robert M. Hutchins and his colleagues at the Center for the Study of Democratic Institutions, located in Santa Barbara, California, began to discuss the desirability of far-reaching constitutional changes. In 1964, following a series of seminars modestly entitled

"Drafting a New Constitution for the United States and the World," Hutchins invited Rexford G. Tugwell, once a member of FDR's "Brain Trust," to direct a reassessment of the Constitution. Tugwell accepted and spent two years conferring with hundreds of jurists, politicians, and scholars. . . .

During the 1970s the Center's primary concerns shifted away from constitutionalism; Tugwell's two major volumes (1974 and 1976) received little attention aside from scholarly journals. When Tugwell died in 1979 at the age of eighty-eight, the *New York Times*'s appreciative editorial did not even mention the revised constitution on which he labored for more than a decade. The *Times* apparently did not regard it as a fitting culmination for a distinguished career in scholarship and public service.

The negligible impact of this seasoned planner's constitutional vision provides a striking contrast with an extremely tradition-oriented interpolation of the U.S. Constitution in science fiction. One popular episode of the television series "Star Trek," written in 1966, received hundreds of reruns during the many years when Tugwell labored over his revision. Millions of Americans watched "The Omega Glory" and recognized its affirmation of the good old Constitution that continued to function even though space, time, and ignorance shrouded its meaning.

Reducing the saga to its ideological essence, Captain Kirk and the starship *Enterprise* land on a planet where the inhabitants are guided by a Prime Directive that must not be violated. Those inhabitants are called Yangs (presumably the descendants of colonizers once known as Yanks), and possess "a worn parchment document" that is "the greatest of holies." Kirk and his crew encounter a bizarre political situation that is not so very different from the one criticized by James Russell Lowell in 1888. The Yangs worship "freedom" but do not understand what it means. Through the ages it has become a ritualized "worship word." The Yangs believe that their ancestors must have been very superior people; they swear an oath to abide by all regulations in the Prime Directive; and they can recite the opening lines of the Prime Directive, but "without meaning."

Following a primitive court scene, complete with jury, it becomes clear that institutions of justice are amazingly resilient—capable of enduring even though their rationale has suffered badly from neglect and amnesia. At the culmination Captain Kirk informs the Yangs that they revere a sacred document without understanding what it is all about. Kirk faces Cloud William, chief of the Yangs, and explains the meaning of the Prime Directive's preamble. Enlightenment then occurs and the great question— is the Prime Directive still operative, and does it apply to this planet?—

achieves a satisfactory resolution. To use the language of yesteryear, "constitutional morality" would surely be restored.

Unlike Rexford Tugwell's new constitution, which kept "emerging" for so long that after a while no one cared, "Star Trek" had a constitutional homily with a happy ending. Americans like happy endings. Hence many younger Americans can still narrate "The Omega Glory" (Old Glory? Ultimate Glory?) flawlessly. How much of the homily got through, however, is another matter. . . .

Ultimately, however, for better and for worse, it is ideological conflict that most meaningfully calls attention to the Constitution. We are then reminded that all Americans do not agree about the most appropriate division of authority: federalism tilting toward states' rights or federalism leaning toward national authority? We are then reminded that we still have broad and strict constructionists, followers of Hamilton and followers of Madison. And we are then reminded that we have had two complementary but divergent modes of constitutional interpretation: a tradition of conflict within consensus. . . .

It is instructive to recall that the founders did not expect their instrument of government to achieve utopia: "merely" national cohesion, political stability, economic growth, and individual liberty. Despite abundant setbacks and imperfections, much of that agenda has been fulfilled for a great many Americans. During the past generation social justice got explicitly added to the agenda as a high priority, and the American Constitution, interpreted by the Supreme Court, was adapted accordingly. For a society to progress toward social justice within a constitutional framework, even by trial and error, is a considerable undertaking. To do so in good faith, more often than not, is equally commendable. If from time to time we require the assistance of gadflies, what flourishing political culture does not? Senator Lowell P. Weicker of Connecticut, for example, has played that role rather well on occasion. As he thundered in 1981, during debate over a legislative amendment to endorse organized prayer in public schools: "To my amazement, any time the word constitutionalism comes up it's looked upon as a threat. A threat! It shouldn't be; it's what holds us all together."

That has been true more often than not. Perhaps those who feel threatened by constitutionalism do not fully understand it. People frequently feel threatened by the unfamiliar. Perhaps it has not been fully understood because it has not been adequately explained. Perhaps it has perplexed us because aspects of its meaning have changed over time. Back in 1786 Benjamin Rush believed it "possible to convert men into republican machines. This must be done if we expect them to perform their parts properly in the great machine of the government of the state." His contemporaries not only took Rush at his word, but regarded the conversion of men into republican machines as a national imperative. . . .

More than a century later, Woodrow Wilson presented a piece of wisdom that tacked the other way. Call it constitutional revisionism if you like. He declared that if the real government of the United States "had, in fact, been a machine governed by mechanically automatic balances, it would have had no history; but it was not, and its history has been rich with the influences and personalities of the men who have conducted it and made it a living reality." Walter Lippmann chose to quote that sentence in 1913 when he wrote *A Preface to Politics*. But he promptly added that "only by violating the very spirit of the constitution have we been able to preserve the letter of it." What Lippmann had in mind was the role played by that palpable reality the Progressives called "invisible government": political parties, interest groups, trade unions, and so on.

Lippmann's remark was not meant to be as cynical as it might sound. It reflects the Progressive desire to be realistic and tough-minded. It also reflects the fact that Americans have been profoundly ambivalent in their feelings about government. Then, too, it reflects the discovery by three overlapping generations of Americans—represented by James Russell Lowell, Wilson, and Lippmann—that the U.S. Constitution is not, and was not meant to be, a machine that would go of itself.

Above all, Lippmann wanted to build upon his excerpt from Wilson and establish the point that there has been more to the story of constitutionalism in American culture than the history of the Constitution itself. The latter is a cherished charter of institutions and a declaration of protections. The former, constitutionalism, embodies a set of values, a range of options, and a means of resolving conflicts within a framework of consensus. It has supplied stability and continuity to a degree the framers could barely have imagined.

II

LANI GUINIER

From *The Tyranny of the Majority*

Law professor Lani Guinier was withdrawn from consideration for the position of assistant attorney general for civil rights in the Justice Department, early in the Clinton administration, because of the storm of controversy over her views on representation in American elections. Critics called her the "quota queen." Professor Guinier explains here that she never advocated quotas, but rather, along with James Madison, she is resisting "the tyranny of the majority." In a diverse society, Guinier believes, winner-take-all elections shut the minority out from having any input at all. Through ideas such as cumulative voting, minorities could elect representatives without damaging the majority's voice. Guinier never received the Senate Judiciary Committee hearing she wished for in order to defend her views, but her ideas remain interesting ones.

———

I HAVE ALWAYS wanted to be a civil rights lawyer. This lifelong ambition is based on a deep-seated commitment to democratic fair play — to playing by the rules as long as the rules are fair. When the rules seem unfair, I have worked to change them, not subvert them. When I was eight years old, I was a Brownie. I was especially proud of my uniform, which represented a commitment to good citizenship and good deeds. But one day, when my Brownie group staged a hatmaking contest, I realized that uniforms are only as honorable as the people who wear them. The contest was rigged. The winner was assisted by her milliner mother, who actually made the winning entry in full view of all the participants. At the time, I was too young to be able to change the rules, but I was old enough to resign, which I promptly did.

To me, fair play means that the rules encourage everyone to play. They should reward those who win, but they must be acceptable to those who lose. The central theme of my academic writing is that not all rules lead to elemental fair play. Some even commonplace rules work against it.

The professional milliner competing with amateur Brownies stands as an example of rules that are patently rigged or patently subverted. Yet, sometimes, even when rules are perfectly fair in form, they serve in practice to exclude particular groups from meaningful participation. When they do not encourage everyone to play, or when, over the long haul, they do not make the losers feel as good about the outcomes as the winners, they can seem as unfair as the milliner who makes the winning hat for her daughter.

Sometimes, too, we construct rules that force us to be divided into winners and losers when we might have otherwise joined together. This idea was cogently expressed by my son, Nikolas, when he was four years old, far exceeding the thoughtfulness of his mother when she was an eight-year-old Brownie. While I was writing one of my law journal articles, Nikolas and I had a conversation about voting prompted by a *Sesame Street Magazine* exercise. The magazine pictured six children: four children had raised their hands because they wanted to play tag; two had their hands down because they wanted to play hide-and-seek. The magazine asked its readers to count the number of children whose hands were raised and then decide what game the children would play.

Nikolas quite realistically replied, "They will play both. First they will play tag. Then they will play hide-and-seek." Despite the magazine's "rules," he was right. To children, it is natural to take turns. The winner may get to play first or more often, but even the "loser" gets something. His was a positive-sum solution that many adult rule-makers ignore.

The traditional answer to the magazine's problem would have been a zero-sum solution: "The children—all the children—will play tag, and only tag." As a zero-sum solution, everything is seen in terms of "I win; you lose." The conventional answer relies on winner-take-all majority rule, in which the tag players, as the majority, win the right to decide for all the children what game to play. The hide-and-seek preference becomes irrelevant. The numerically more powerful majority choice simply subsumes minority preferences.

In the conventional case, the majority that rules gains all the power and the minority that loses gets none. For example, two years ago Brother Rice High School in Chicago held two senior proms. It was not planned that way. The prom committee at Brother Rice, a boys' Catholic high school, expected just one prom when it hired a disc jockey, picked a rock band, and selected music for the prom by consulting student preferences. Each senior was asked to list his three favorite songs, and the band would play the songs that appeared most frequently on the lists.

Seems attractively democratic. But Brother Rice is predominantly white, and the prom committee was all white. That's how they got two proms. The black seniors at Brother Rice felt so shut out by the "democratic process" that they organized their own prom. As one black student put it: "For every vote we had, there were eight votes for what they wanted. . . . [W]ith us being in the minority we're always outvoted. It's as if we don't count."

Some embittered white seniors saw things differently. They complained that the black students should have gone along with the majority: "The majority makes a decision. That's the way it works."

In a way, both groups were right. From the white students' perspective, this was ordinary decisionmaking. To the black students, majority rule sent the message: "we don't count" is the "way it works" for minorities. In a racially divided society, majority rule may be perceived as majority tyranny.

That is a large claim, and I do not rest my case for it solely on the actions of the prom committee in one Chicago high school. To expand the range of the argument, I first consider the ideal of majority rule itself, particularly as reflected in the writings of James Madison and other founding members of our Republic. These early democrats explored the relationship between majority rule and democracy. James Madison warned, "If a majority be united by a common interest, the rights of the minority will be insecure." The tyranny of the majority, according to Madison, requires safeguards to protect "one part of the society against the injustice of the other part."

For Madison, majority tyranny represented the great danger to our early constitutional democracy. Although the American revolution was fought against the tyranny of the British monarch, it soon became clear that there was another tyranny to be avoided. The accumulations of all powers in the same hands, Madison warned, "whether of one, a few, or many, and whether hereditary, self-appointed, or elective, may justly be pronounced the very definition of tyranny."

As another colonist suggested in papers published in Philadelphia, "We have been so long habituated to a jealousy of tyranny from monarchy and aristocracy, that we have yet to learn the dangers of it from democracy." Despotism had to be opposed "whether it came from Kings, Lords or the people."

The debate about majority tyranny reflected Madison's concern that the majority may not represent the whole. In a homogeneous society, the interest of the majority would likely be that of the minority also. But in a heterogeneous community, the majority may not represent all competing interests. The majority is likely to be self-interested and ignorant or indifferent to the concerns of the minority. In such case, Madison observed, the assumption that the majority represents the minority is "altogether fictitious."

Yet even a self-interested majority can govern fairly if it cooperates with the minority. One reason for such cooperation is that the self-interested majority values the principle of reciprocity. The self-interested majority worries that the minority may attract defectors from the majority and become the next governing majority. The Golden Rule principle of reciprocity functions to check the tendency of a self-interested majority to act tyrannically.

So the argument for the majority principle connects it with the value of reciprocity: You cooperate when you lose in part because members of the current majority will cooperate when they lose. The conventional case for the fairness of majority rule is that it is not really the rule of a fixed group—The Majority—on all issues; instead it is the rule of shifting majorities, as the losers at one time or on one issue join with others and become part of the governing coalition at another time or on another issue. The result will be a fair system of mutually beneficial cooperation. I call a majority that rules but does not dominate a Madisonian Majority.

The problem of majority tyranny arises, however, when the self-interested majority does not need to worry about defectors. When the majority is fixed and permanent, there are no checks on its ability to be overbearing. A majority that does not worry about defectors is a majority with total power. . . .

But if a group is unfairly treated, for example, when it forms a racial minority, *and* if the problems of unfairness are not cured by conventional assumptions about majority rule, then what is to be done? The answer is that we may need an *alternative* to winner-take-all majoritarianism. In this book, a collection of my law review articles, I describe the alternative, which, with Nikolas's help, I now call the "principle of taking turns." In a racially divided society, this principle does better than simple majority rule if it accommodates the values of self-government, fairness, deliberation, compromise, and consensus that lie at the heart of the democratic ideal.

In my legal writing, I follow the caveat of James Madison and other early American democrats. I explore decisionmaking rules that might work in a multi-racial society to ensure that majority rule does not become majority tyranny. I pursue voting systems that might disaggregate The Majority so that it does not exercise power unfairly or tyrannically. I aspire to a more cooperative political style of decisionmaking to enable all of the students at Brother Rice to feel comfortable attending the same prom. In looking to create Madisonian Majorities, I pursue a positive-sum, taking-turns solution.

Structuring decisionmaking to allow the minority "a turn" may be necessary to restore the reciprocity ideal when a fixed majority refuses to cooperate with the minority. If the fixed majority loses its incentive to follow the Golden Rule principle of shifting majorities, the minority never gets to take a turn. Giving the minority a turn does not mean the minority gets to rule; what it does mean is that the minority gets to influence decisionmaking and the majority rules more legitimately.

Instead of automatically rewarding the preferences of the monolithic majority, a taking-turns approach anticipates that the majority rules, but is not overbearing. Because those with 51 percent of the votes are not assured 100 percent of the power, the majority cooperates with, or at least does not tyrannize, the minority. . . .

In the end, I do not believe that democracy should encourage rule by the powerful — even a powerful majority. Instead, the ideal of democracy promises a fair discussion among self-defined equals about how to achieve our common aspirations. To redeem that promise, we need to put the idea of taking turns and disaggregating the majority at the center of our conception of representation. Particularly as we move into the twenty-first century as a more highly diversified citizenry, it is essential that we consider the ways in which voting and representational systems succeed or fail at encouraging Madisonian Majorities.

To use Nikolas's terminology, "it is no fair" if a fixed, tyrannical majority excludes or alienates the minority. It is no fair if a fixed, tyrannical majority monopolizes all the power all the time. It is no fair if we engage in the periodic ritual of elections, but only the permanent majority gets to choose who is elected. Where we have tyranny by The Majority, we do not have genuine democracy.

My life's work, with the essential assistance of people like Nikolas, has been to try to find the rules that can best bring us together as a democratic society. Some of my ideas about democratic fair play were grossly mischaracterized in the controversy over my nomination to be Assistant Attorney General for Civil Rights. Trying to find rules to encourage fundamental fairness inevitably raises the question posed by Harvard Professor Randall Kennedy in a summary of this controversy: "What is required to create political institutions that address the needs and aspirations of all Americans, not simply whites, who have long enjoyed racial privilege, but people of color who have long suffered racial exclusion from policy-making forums?" My answer, as Professor Kennedy suggests, varies by situation. But I have a predisposition, reflected in my son's yearning for a positive-sum solution, to seek an integrated body politic in which all perspectives are represented and in which all people work together to find common ground. I advocate empowering voters and their representatives in ways that give even minority voters a chance to influence legislative outcomes. . . .

Concern over majority tyranny has typically focused on the need to monitor and constrain the substantive policy outputs of the decisionmaking process. In my articles, however, I look at the *procedural* rules by which preferences are identified and counted. Procedural rules govern the process by which outcomes are decided. They are the rules by which the game is played.

I have been roundly, and falsely, criticized for focusing on outcomes. Outcomes are indeed relevant, but *not* because I seek to advance particular ends, such as whether the children play tag or hide-and-seek, or whether the band at Brother Rice plays rock music or rap. Rather, I look to outcomes as *evidence* of whether all the children—or all the high school seniors—feel that their choice is represented and considered. The purpose is not to guarantee "equal legislative outcomes"; equal opportunity to *influence* legisative outcomes regardless of race is more like it.

For these reasons, I sometimes explore alternatives to simple, winner-take-all majority rule. I do not advocate any one procedural rule as a universal panacea for unfairness. Nor do I propose these remedies primarily as judicial solutions. They can be adopted only in the context of litigation after the court first finds a legal violation.

Outside of litigation, I propose these approaches as political solutions if, depending on the local context, they better approximate the goals of democratic fair play. One such decisionmaking alternative is called cumulative voting, which could give all the students at Brother Rice multiple votes and allow them to distribute their votes in any combination of their choice. If each student could vote for ten songs, the students could plump or aggregate their votes to reflect the intensity of their preferences. They could put ten votes on one song; they could put five votes on two songs. If a tenth of the students opted to "cumulate" or plump all their votes for one song, they would be able to select one of every ten or so songs played at the prom. The black seniors could have done this if they chose to, but so could any other cohesive group of sufficient size. In this way, the songs preferred by a majority would be played most often, but the songs the minority enjoyed would also show up on the play list.

Under cumulative voting, voters get the same number of votes as there are seats or options to vote for, and they can then distribute their votes in any combination to reflect their preferences. Like-minded voters can vote as a solid bloc or, instead, form strategic, cross-racial coalitions to gain mutual benefits. This system is emphatically not racially based; it allows voters to organize themselves on whatever basis they wish.

Corporations use this system to ensure representation of minority shareholders on corporate boards of directors. Similarly, some local municipal and county governments have adopted cumulative voting to ensure representation of minority voters. Instead of awarding political power to geographic units called districts, cumulative voting allows voters to cast ballots based on what they think rather than where they live.

Cumulative voting is based on the principle of one person—one vote because each voter gets the same total number of votes. Everyone's preferences are counted equally. It is not a particularly radical idea; thirty states either require or permit corporations to use this election system. Cumulative voting is certainly not antidemocratic because it emphasizes the importance of voter choice in selecting public or social policy. And it is neither liberal nor conservative. Both the Reagan and Bush administrations approved cumulative voting schemes pursuant to the Voting Rights Act to protect the rights of racial- and language-minority voters.

But, as in Chilton County, Alabama, which now uses cumulative voting to elect both the school board and the county commission, any politically cohesive group can vote strategically to win representation. Groups of voters win representation depending on the exclusion threshold, meaning the percentage of votes needed to win one seat or have the band play one song. That threshold can be set case by case, jurisdiction by jurisdiction, based on the size of minority groups that make compelling claims for representation.

Normally the exclusion threshold in a head-to-head contest is 50 percent, which means that only groups that can organize a majority can get elected. But if multiple seats (or multiple songs) are considered simultaneously, the exclusion threshold is considerably reduced. For example, in Chilton County, with seven seats elected simultaneously on each governing body, the threshold of exclusion is now one-eighth. Any group with the solid support of one-eighth the voting population cannot be denied representation. This is because any self-identified minority can plump or cumulate all its votes for one candidate. Again, minorities are not defined solely in racial terms.

As it turned out in Chilton County, both blacks and Republicans benefited from this new system. The school board and commission now each have three white Democrats, three white Republicans, and one black Democrat. Previously, when each seat was decided in a head-to-head contest, the majority not only ruled but monopolized. Only white Democrats were elected at every prior election during this century.

Similarly, if the black and white students at Brother Rice have very different musical taste, cumulative voting permits a positive-sum solution to enable both groups to enjoy one prom. The majority's preferences would be respected in that their songs would be played most often, but the black students could express the intensity of their preferences too. If the black students chose to plump all their votes on a few songs, their minority preferences would be recognized and played. Essentially, cumulative voting structures the band's repertoire to enable the students to take turns.

As a solution that permits voters to self-select their identities, cumulative voting also encourages cross-racial coalition building. No one is locked into a minority identity. Nor is anyone necessarily isolated by the identity they choose. Voters can strengthen their influence by forming coalitions to elect more than one representative or to select a range of music more compatible with the entire student body's preferences.

Women too can use cumulative voting to gain greater representation. Indeed, in other countries with similar, alternative voting systems, women are more likely to be represented in the national legislature. For example, in some Western European democracies, the national legislatures have as many as 37 percent female members compared to a little more than 5 percent in our Congress.

There is a final benefit from cumulative voting. It eliminates gerrymandering. By denying protected incumbents safe seats in gerrymandered districts, cumulative voting might encourage more voter participation. With greater interest-based electoral competition, cumulative voting could promote the political turnover sought by advocates of term limits. In this way, cumulative voting serves many of the same ends as periodic elections or rotation in office, a solution that Madison and others advocated as a means of protecting against permanent majority factions. . . .

My nomination became an unfortunate metaphor for the state of race relations in America. My nomination suggested that as a country, we are in a state of denial about issues of race and racism. The censorship imposed against me points to a denial of serious public debate or discussion about racial fairness and justice in a true democracy. For many politicians and policymakers, the remedy for racism is simply to stop talking about race.

Sentences, words, even phrases separated by paragraphs in my law review articles were served up to demonstrate that I was violating the rules. Because I talked openly about existing racial divisions, I was branded "race obsessed." Because I explored innovative ways to remedy racism, I was branded "antidemocratic." It did not matter that I had suggested race-neutral election rules, such as cumulative voting, as an alternative to remedy racial discrimination. It did not matter that I never advocated quotas. I became the Quota Queen.

The vision behind my by-now-notorious law review articles and my less-well-known professional commitments has always been that of a fair and just society, a society in which even adversely affected parties believe in the system because they believe the process is fair and the process is inclusive. My vision of fairness and justice imagines a full and effective voice for all citizens. I may have failed to locate some of my ideas in the specific factual contexts from which they are derived. But always I have tried to show that democracy in a heterogeneous society is incompatible with rule by a racial monopoly of any color.

By publishing these law journal articles as a collection, I hope to spark the debate that was denied in the context of my nomination. We will have lost more than any one individual's opportunity for public service if we fail to pursue the public thirst for information about, and positive-sum solutions to, the issues at the heart of this controversy. The twentieth-century problem—the problem of the color line, according to W. E. B. Du Bois—will soon become a twenty-first-century problem if we allow opposing viewpoints to be silenced on issues of race and racism.

I hope that we can learn three positive lessons from my experience. The first lesson is that those who stand for principles may lose in the short run, but they cannot be suppressed in the long run. The second lesson is that public dialogue is critical to represent all perspectives; no one viewpoint should be permitted to monopolize, distort, caricature, or shape public debate. The tyranny of The Majority is just as much a problem of silencing minority viewpoints as it is of excluding minority representatives or preferences. We cannot all talk at once, but that does not mean only one group should get to speak. We can take turns. Third, we need consensus and positive-sum solutions. We need a broad public conversation about issues of racial justice in which we seek win-win solutions to real-life problems. If we include blacks and whites, and women and men, and Republicans and Democrats, and even people with new ideas, we will all be better off.

12

C. WRIGHT MILLS

From *The Power Elite*

C. Wright Mills's book The Power Elite *stands as a classic in political science. In it he offers one answer to the question "Who rules America?" A three-part elite rules, he believes, composed of corporate, political, and military leaders. These sectors of American life are connected, creating an "interlocking" power structure with highly centralized decision-making. Mills considers a conspiracy theory to account for the power elite's control, but rejects it for something much more frightening. Average Americans are like "trusting children" who rely on the power elite to run things smoothly and well. Today, a half-century after Mills wrote, his ideas seem a bit ultra-dramatic and overstated. Still, Mills offers a warning about power in America that is timeless, one that many people believe is true.*

THE POWERS of ordinary men are circumscribed by the everyday worlds in which they live, yet even in these rounds of job, family, and neighborhood they often seem driven by forces they can neither understand nor govern. "Great changes" are beyond their control, but affect their conduct and outlook none the less. The very framework of modern society confines them to projects not their own, but from every side, such changes now press upon the men and women of the mass society, who accordingly feel that they are without purpose in an epoch in which they are without power.

But not all men are in this sense ordinary. As the means of information and of power are centralized, some men come to occupy positions in American society from which they can look down upon, so to speak, and by their decisions mightily affect, the everyday worlds of ordinary men and women. They are not made by their jobs; they set up and break down jobs for thousands of others; they are not confined by simple family responsibilities; they can escape. They may live in many hotels and houses, but they are bound by no one community. They need not merely "meet the demands of the day and hour"; in some part, they create these demands, and cause others to meet them. Whether or not they profess their power, their technical and political experience of it far transcends that of the underlying population. What Jacob Burckhardt said of "great men," most Americans might well say of their elite: "They are all that we are not."

The power elite is composed of men whose positions enable them to transcend the ordinary environments of ordinary men and women; they are in positions to make decisions having major consequences. Whether they do or do not make such decisions is less important than the fact that they do occupy such pivotal positions: their failure to act, their failure to make decisions, is itself an act that is often of greater consequence than the decisions they do make. For they are in command of the major hierarchies and organizations of modern society. They rule the big corporations. They run the machinery of the state and claim its prerogatives. They direct the military establishment. They occupy the strategic command posts of the social structure, in which are now centered the effective means of the power and the wealth and the celebrity which they enjoy.

The power elite are not solitary rulers. Advisers and consultants, spokesmen and opinion-makers are often the captains of their higher thought and decision. Immediately below the elite are the professional politicians of the middle levels of power, in the Congress and in the pressure groups, as well as among the new and old upper classes of town and city and region. Mingling with them, in curious ways which we shall explore, are those professional celebrities who live by being continually displayed but are never, so long as they remain celebrities, displayed enough. If such celebrities are not at the head of any dominating hierarchy, they do often have the power to distract the attention of the public or afford sensations to the masses, or, more directly, to gain the ear of those who do occupy positions of direct power. More or less unattached, as critics of morality and technicians of power, as spokesmen of God and creators of mass sensibility, such celebrities and consultants are part of the immediate scene in which the drama of the elite is enacted. But that drama itself is centered in the command posts of the major institutional hierarchies.

The truth about the nature and the power of the elite is not some secret which men of affairs know but will not tell. Such men hold quite various theories about their own roles in the sequence of event and decision. Often they are uncertain about their roles, and even more often they allow their fears and their hopes to affect their assessment of their own power. No matter how great their actual power, they tend to be less acutely aware of it than of the resistances of others to its use. Moreover, most American men of affairs have learned well the rhetoric of public relations, in some cases even to the point of using it when they are alone, and thus coming to believe it. The personal awareness of the actors is only one of the several sources one must examine in order to understand the higher circles. Yet many who believe that there is no elite, or at any rate none of any consequence, rest their argument upon what men of affairs believe about themselves, or at least assert in public.

There is, however, another view: those who feel, even if vaguely, that a compact and powerful elite of great importance does now prevail in America often base that feeling upon the historical trend of our time. They have felt, for example, the domination of the military event, and from this they infer that generals and admirals, as well as other men of decision influenced by them, must be enormously powerful. They hear that the Congress has again abdicated to a handful of men decisions clearly related to the issue of war or peace. They know that the bomb was dropped over Japan in the name of the United States of America, although they were at no time consulted about the matter. They feel that they live in a time of big decisions; they know that they are not making any. Accordingly, as they consider the present as history, they infer that at its center, making decisions or failing to make them, there must be an elite of power.

On the one hand, those who share this feeling about big historical events assume that there is an elite and that its power is great. On the other hand, those who listen carefully to the reports of men apparently involved in the great decisions often do not believe that there is an elite whose powers are of decisive consequence.

Both views must be taken into account, but neither is adequate. The way to understand the power of the American elite lies neither solely in recognizing the historic scale of events nor in accepting the personal awareness reported by men of apparent decision. Behind such men and behind the events of history, linking the two, are the major institutions of modern society. These hierarchies of state and corporation and army constitute the means of power; as such they are now of a consequence not before equaled in human history—and at their summits, there are now those command posts of modern society which offer us the sociological key to an understanding of the role of the higher circles in America.

Within American society, major national power now resides in the economic, the political, and the military domains. Other institutions seem off to the side of modern history, and, on occasion, duly subordinated to these. No family is as directly powerful in national affairs as any major corporation; no church is as directly powerful in the external biographies of young men in America today as the military establishment; no college is as powerful in the shaping of momentous events as the National Security Council. Religious, educational, and family institutions are not autonomous centers of national power; on the contrary, these decentralized areas are increasingly shaped by the big three, in which developments of decisive and immediate consequence now occur.

Families and churches and schools adapt to modern life; governments and armies and corporations shape it; and, as they do so, they turn these lesser institutions into means for their ends. Religious institutions provide chaplains to the armed forces where they are used as a means of increasing the effectiveness of its morale to kill. Schools select and train men for their jobs in corporations and their specialized tasks in the armed forces. The extended family has, of course, long been broken up by the industrial revolution, and now the son and the father are removed from the family, by compulsion if need be, whenever the army of the state sends out the call. And the symbols of all these lesser institutions are used to legitimate the power and the decisions of the big three.

The life-fate of the modern individual depends not only upon the family into which he was born or which he enters by marriage, but increasingly upon the corporation in which he spends the most alert hours of his best years; not only upon the school where he is educated as a child and adolescent, but also upon the state which touches him throughout his life; not only upon the church in which on occasion he hears the word of God, but also upon the army in which he is disciplined.

If the centralized state could not rely upon the inculcation of nationalist loyalties in public and private schools, its leaders would promptly seek to modify the decentralized educational system. If the bankruptcy rate among the top five hundred corporations were as high as the general divorce rate among the thirty-seven million married couples, there would be economic catastrophe on an international scale. If members of armies gave to them no more of their lives than do believers to the churches to which they belong, there would be a military crisis.

Within each of the big three, the typical institutional unit has become enlarged, has become administrative, and, in the power of its decisions, has become centralized. Behind these developments there is a fabulous technology, for as institutions, they have incorporated this technology and guide it, even as it shapes and paces their developments.

The economy—once a great scatter of small productive units in autonomous balance—has become dominated by two or three hundred giant corporations, administratively and politically interrelated, which together hold the keys to economic decisions.

The political order, once a decentralized set of several dozen states with a weak spinal cord, has become a centralized, executive establishment which has taken up into itself many powers previously scattered, and now enters into each and every cranny of the social structure.

The military order, once a slim establishment in a context of distrust fed by state militia, has become the largest and most expensive feature of government, and, although well versed in smiling public relations, now has all the grim and clumsy efficiency of a sprawling bureaucratic domain.

In each of these institutional areas, the means of power at the disposal of decision makers have increased enormously; their central executive powers have been enhanced; within each of them modern administrative routines have been elaborated and tightened up.

As each of these domains becomes enlarged and centralized, the consequences of its activities become greater, and its traffic with the others increases. The decisions of a handful of corporations bear upon military and political as well as upon economic developments around the world. The decisions of the military establishment rest upon and grievously affect political life as well as the very level of economic activity. The decisions made within the political domain determine economic activities and military programs. There is no longer, on the one hand, an economy, and, on the other hand, a political order containing a military establishment unimportant to politics and to money-making. There is a political econ-omy linked, in a thousand ways, with military institutions and decisions. On each side of the world-split running through central Europe and around the Asiatic rimlands, there is an ever-increasing interlocking of economic, military, and political structures. If there is government inter-vention in the corporate economy, so is there corporate intervention in the governmental process. In the structural sense, this triangle of power is the source of the interlocking directorate that is most important for the historical structure of the present.

The fact of the interlocking is clearly revealed at each of the points of crisis of modern capitalist society—slump, war, and boom. In each, men of decision are led to an awareness of the interdependence of the major institutional orders. In the nineteenth century, when the scale of all institutions was smaller, their liberal integration was achieved in the automatic economy, by an autonomous play of market forces, and in the automatic political domain, by the bargain and the vote. It was then assumed that out of the imbalance and friction that followed the limited decisions then possible a new equilibrium would in due course emerge. That can no longer be assumed, and it is not assumed by the men at the top of each of the three dominant hierarchies.

For given the scope of their consequences, decisions—and indeci-sions—in any one of these ramify into the others, and hence top decisions tend either to become co-ordinated or to lead to a commanding indeci-sion. It has not always been like this. When numerous small entrepreneurs made up the economy, for example, many of them could fail and the consequences still remain local; political and military authorities did not intervene. But now, given political expectations and military commit-ments, can they afford to allow key units of the private corporate economy to break down in slump? Increasingly, they do intervene in economic affairs, and as they do so, the controlling decisions in each order are inspected by agents of the other two, and economic, military, and political structures are interlocked.

At the pinnacle of each of the three enlarged and centralized domains, there have arisen those higher circles which make up the economic, the political, and the military elites. At the top of the economy, among the corporate rich, there are the chief executives; at the top of the political order, the members of the political directorate; at the top of the military establishment, the elite of soldier-statesmen clustered in and around the Joint Chiefs of Staff and the upper echelon. As each of these domains has coincided with the others, as decisions tend to become total in their consequence, the leading men in each of the three domains of power—

the warlords, the corporation chieftains, the political directorate—tend to come together, to form the power elite of America. . . .

The conception of the power elite and of its unity rests upon the corresponding developments and the coincidence of interests among economic, political, and military organizations. It also rests upon the similarity of origin and outlook, and the social and personal intermingling of the top circles from each of these dominant hierarchies. This conjunction of institutional and psychological forces, in turn, is revealed by the heavy personnel traffic within and between the big three institutional orders, as well as by the rise of go-betweens as in the high-level lobbying. The conception of the power elite, accordingly, does *not* rest upon the assumption that American history since the origins of World War II must be understood as a secret plot, or as a great and co-ordinated conspiracy of the members of this elite. The conception rests upon quite impersonal grounds.

There is, however, little doubt that the American power elite—which contains, we are told, some of "the greatest organizers in the world"— has also planned and has plotted. The rise of the elite, as we have already made clear, was not and could not have been caused by a plot; and the tenability of the conception does not rest upon the existence of any secret or any publicly known organization. But, once the conjunction of structural trend and of the personal will to utilize it gave rise to the power elite, then plans and programs did occur to its members and indeed it is not possible to interpret many events and official policies of the fifth epoch without reference to the power elite. "There is a great difference," Richard Hofstadter has remarked, "between locating conspiracies *in* history and saying that history *is*, in effect, a conspiracy . . . "

The structural trends of institutions become defined as opportunities by those who occupy their command posts. Once such opportunities are recognized, men may avail themselves of them. Certain types of men from each of the dominant institutional areas, more far-sighted than others, have actively promoted the liaison before it took its truly modern shape. They have often done so for reasons not shared by their partners, although not objected to by them either; and often the outcome of their liaison has had consequences which none of them foresaw, much less shaped, and which only later in the course of development came under explicit control. Only after it was well under way did most of its members find themselves part of it and become gladdened, although sometimes also worried, by this fact. But once the co-ordination is a going concern, new men come readily into it and assume its existence without question.

So far as explicit organization—conspiratorial or not—is concerned, the power elite, by its very nature, is more likely to use existing organizations, working within and between them, than to set up explicit organizations whose membership is strictly limited to its own members. But if there is no machinery in existence to ensure, for example, that military and political factors will be balanced in decisions made, they will invent such machinery and use it, as with the National Security Council. Moreover, in a formally democratic polity, the aims and the powers of the various elements of this elite are further supported by an aspect of the permanent war economy: the assumption that the security of the nation supposedly rests upon great secrecy of plan and intent. Many higher events that would reveal the working of the power elite can be withheld from public knowledge under the guise of secrecy. With the wide secrecy covering their operations and decisions, the power elite can mask their intentions, operations, and further consolidation. Any secrecy that is imposed upon those in positions to observe high decision-makers clearly works for and not against the operations of the power elite.

There is accordingly reason to suspect—but by the nature of the case, no proof—that the power elite is not altogether "surfaced." There is nothing hidden about it, although its activities are not publicized. As an elite, it is not organized, although its members often know one another, seem quite naturally to work together, and share many organizations in common. There is nothing conspiratorial about it, although its decisions are often publicly unknown and its mode of operation manipulative rather than explicit.

It is not that the elite "believe in" a compact elite behind the scenes and a mass down below. It is not put in that language. It is just that the people are of necessity confused and must, like trusting children, place all the new world of foreign policy and strategy and executive action in the hands of experts. It is just that everyone knows somebody has got to run the show, and that somebody usually does. Others do not really care anyway, and besides, they do not know how. So the gap between the two types gets wider.

13

RICHARD ZWEIGENHAFT
G. WILLIAM DOMHOFF

From *Diversity in the Power Elite*

In the previous excerpt, C. Wright Mills presented his interpretation of who holds power in America: a small elite. Mills wrote his classic book decades ago. Richard Zweigenhaft and G. William Domhoff revisit Mills's thesis by examining the composition of today's power elite—assuming, of course, that there is such an elite. The authors offer a fascinating account of Jews, women, blacks, Latinos, Asian Americans, and gay men and lesbians in the elite, including many personal stories of powerful individuals. The excerpt here looks at corporate women and African-American men in the military. Yes, the elite looks different today, but no, it is not really so different than when Mills wrote.

INJUSTICES BASED ON race, gender, ethnicity, and sexual orientation have been the most emotional and contested issues in American society since the end of the 1960s, far exceeding concerns with social class, and rivaled only by conflicts about abortion. These issues are now subsumed under the umbrella terms *diversity* and *multiculturalism*, and they have been written about extensively from the perspectives of both the aggrieved and those at the middle and lower levels of the social ladder who resist any changes.

. . . [W]e look at multiculturalism from a new angle: we examine its impact on the small group at the top of American society that we call the power elite—those who own and manage large banks and corporations, finance the political campaigns of conservative Democrats and virtually all Republicans at the state and national levels, and serve in government as appointed officials and military leaders. We ask whether the decades of pressure from civil rights groups, feminists, and gay and lesbian rights activists has resulted in a more culturally diverse power elite. If it has, what effects has this new diversity had on the functioning of the power elite and on its relation to the rest of society? . . .

According to many commentators, the higher circles in the United States had indeed become multicultural by the late 1980s and early 1990s.

Some went even further, saying that the old power elite had been pushed aside entirely. The demise of the "old" power elite was the theme of such books as Nelson Aldrich's *Old Money* and Robert Christopher's *Crashing the Gates*, the latter emphasizing the rise of ethnic minorities. There have also been wide-eyed articles in mainstream magazines, such as one in the late 1980s in *U.S. News and World Report* entitled "The New American Establishment," which celebrated a new diversity at the top, claiming that "new kinds of men and women" have "taken control of institutions that influence important aspects of American life." School and club ties are no longer important, the article announced; the new role of women was highlighted with a picture of some of the "wise women" who had joined the "wise men" who dominated the old establishment.

Then, in July 1995, *Newsweek* ran a cover story on "The Rise of the Overclass," featuring a gallery of one hundred high-tech, media, and Wall Street stars, women as well as men, minorities as well as whites, who supposedly come from all rungs of the social ladder. The term *overclass* was relatively new, but the argument—that the power elite was dead, superseded by a diverse meritocratic elite—was not. . . .

Since the 1870s the refrain about the new diversity of the governing circles has been closely intertwined with a staple of American culture created by Horatio Alger Jr., whose name has become synonymous with upward mobility in America. Born in 1832 to a patrician family—Alger's father was a Harvard graduate, a Unitarian minister, and a Massachusetts state senator—Alger graduated from Harvard at the age of nineteen. There followed a series of unsuccessful efforts to establish himself in various careers. Finally, in 1864 Alger was hired as a Unitarian minister in Brewster, Massachusetts. Fifteen months later, he was dismissed from this position for homosexual acts with boys in the congregation.

Alger returned to New York, where he soon began to spend a great deal of time at the Newsboys' Lodging House, founded in 1853 for footloose youngsters between the ages of twelve and sixteen and home to many youths who had been mustered out of the Union Army after serving as drummer boys. At the Newsboys' Lodging House Alger found his literary niche and his subsequent claim to fame: writing books in which poor boys make good. His books sold by the hundreds of thousands in the last third of the nineteenth century, and by 1910 they were enjoying annual sales of more than one million in paperback.

The deck is not stacked against the poor, according to Horatio Alger. When they simply show a bit of gumption, work hard, and thereby catch a break or two, they can become part of the American elite. The persistence of this theme, reinforced by the annual Horatio Alger Awards to such well-known personalities as Ronald Reagan, Bob Hope, and Billy Graham (who might not have been so eager to accept them if they had known of Alger's shadowed past), suggests that we may be dealing once again with a cultural myth. In its early versions, of course, the story concerned the great opportunities available for poor white boys willing to work their way to the top. More recently, the story has featured black Horatio Algers who started in the ghetto, Latino Horatio Algers who started in the barrio, Asian-American Horatio Algers whose parents were immigrants, and female Horatio Algers who seem to have no class backgrounds—all of whom now sit on the boards of the country's largest corporations.

But is any of this true? Can anecdotes and self-serving autobiographical accounts about diversity, meritocracy, and upward social mobility survive a more systematic analysis? Have very many women and previously excluded minorities made it to the top? Has class lost its importance in shaping life chances?

. . . [W]e address these and related questions within the framework provided by the iconoclastic sociologist C. Wright Mills in his hard-hitting classic *The Power Elite*, published in 1956 when the media were in the midst of what Mills called the Great American Celebration. In spite of the Depression of the 1930s, Americans had pulled together to win World War II, and the country was both prosperous at home and influential abroad. Most of all, according to enthusiasts, the United States had become a relatively classless and pluralistic society, where power belonged to the people through their political parties and public opinion. Some groups certainly had more power than others, but no group or class had too much. The New Deal and World War II had forever transformed the corporate-based power structure of earlier decades.

Mills challenged this celebration of pluralism by studying the social backgrounds and career paths of the people who occupied the highest positions in what he saw as the three major institutional hierarchies in postwar America—the corporations, the executive branch of the federal government, and the military. He found that almost all the members of this leadership group, which he called the power elite, were white Christian males who came from "at most, the upper third of the income and occupational pyramids," despite the many Horatio Algeresque claims to the contrary. . . .

The power elite depicted by C. Wright Mills was, without doubt, an exclusively male preserve. On the opening page of *The Power Elite*—a book with no preface, no introduction, no acknowledgments, just a direct plunge into the opening chapter—Mills stated clearly that "the power elite is composed of men whose positions enable them to transcend the ordinary environments of ordinary men and women." Although there were some women in the corporate, political, and military worlds, very few were in or near the higher circles that constituted the power elite. Are they there now? If so, how substantial and how visible is their presence? When did they arrive, and how did they get there? What are their future prospects? . . .

In 1990, Elizabeth Dole, then secretary of labor, initiated a department-level investigation into the question of whether or not there was a "glass ceiling" blocking women and minorities from the highest ranks of U.S. corporations. When the report was issued by the Federal Glass Ceiling Commission in 1995, comments by the white male managers who had been interviewed and surveyed supported the earlier claims that upper management was willing to accept women and minorities only if they were not too different. As one manager explained, "What's important is comfort, chemistry, relationships, and collaborations. That's what makes a shop work. When we find minorities and women who think like we do, we snatch them up."

Terry Miyamoto, an Asian-American labor relations executive at U.S. West, Inc., a telecommunications company that ranked number 62 on the Fortune 500 list in 1995, uses the term "comfort zone" to make the same point about "chemistry" and reducing "uncertainty": "You need to build relationships," she said, "and you need to be pretty savvy. And for a woman or a person of color at this company, you have to put in more effort to get into this comfort zone."

Much has been made of the fact that men have traditionally been socialized to play competitive team sports and women have not. In *The Managerial Woman*, Margaret Hennig and Anne Jardim argue that the experience of having participated in competitive team sports has provided men with many advantages in the corporate world. Playing on sports teams teaches boys such things as how to develop their individual skills in the context of helping the team to win, how to develop cooperative goal-oriented relationships with teammates, how to focus on winning, and how to deal with losing. "The experience of most little girls," they wrote, "has no parallel." Although the opportunities for young women to participate in competitive sports have increased dramatically in recent years, including team sports like basketball and soccer, few such opportunities were available when most women now in higher management in U.S. corporations were young.

Just as football is often identified as the classic competitive and aggressive team sport that prepares men for the rough and tumble (and hierarchical) world of the corporation, an individual sport—golf—is the more convivial but still competitive game that allows boys to play together, shoot the breeze, and do business. As Marcia Chambers shows in *The Unplayable Lie*, the golf course, and especially the country club, can be as segregated by sex as the football field. Few clubs bar women, but some clubs do not allow women to vote, sit on their governing boards, or play golf on weekend mornings.

Many women managers are convinced that their careers suffer because of discrimination against them by golf clubs. In a study of executives who manage "corporate-government affairs," Denise Benoit Scott found that the women in such positions "share meals with staff members and other government relations officials but never play golf." In contrast, men in such positions "play golf with a broad range of people in business and government, including legislators and top corporate executives." As one of the women she interviewed put it: "I wish I played golf. I think golf is the key. If you want to make it, you have to play golf."

Similarly, when the editors of *Executive Female* magazine surveyed the top fifty women in line-management positions (in sales, marketing, production, and general management with a direct impact on the company's bottom line), they asked them why more women had not made it to the "upper reaches of corporate America." The most frequently identified problem was the "comfort factor"—that the men atop their corporations wanted others around them with whom they were comfortable, and that generally meant other men similar to themselves. One of the other most frequently identified problems, not unrelated to the comfort factor, was the exclusion from "the social networks—the clubs, the golf course—where the informal networking that is so important to moving up the ladder often takes place."

Based on the interviews they conducted for *Members of the Club*, Dawn-Marie Driscoll and Carol Goldberg also conclude that there is an important connection between golf and business. Both Driscoll and Goldberg have held directorships on major corporate boards. They establish their insider status at the beginning of their book: "We are both insiders. We always have been and probably always will be." In a section entitled "The Link That Counts," they explain how they came to realize the importance of golf: "We heard so many stories about golf that we began to pay more attention to the interaction between golf and business. We realized the importance of golf had been right in front of our eyes all the time, but because neither of us played golf, we had missed it as an issue for executive women. But golf is central to many business circles."

A few months before Bill Clinton was elected president, his future secretary of energy had some pertinent comments about the importance of fitting into corporate culture and the relevance of playing golf. "Without losing your own personality," said Hazel O'Leary, then an executive vice president at Northern States Power in Minnesota, "it's important to be part of the prevailing corporate culture. At this company, it's golf. I've resisted learning to play golf all my life, but I finally had to admit I was missing something that way." She took up golf.

There is evidence that the golf anxiety expressed by women executives has its counterpart in the attitudes held by male executives: in its 1995 report, the Federal Glass Ceiling Commission found that many white male executives "fretted" that minorities and women did not know how to play golf.

Whether or not playing golf is necessary to fit in, it is clear that women who make it into the corporate elite must assimilate sufficiently into the predominantly male culture to make it into the comfort zone. . . .

. . . [W]e told of Midshipman Leonard Kaplan's being "sent to Coventry"—which meant that no one spoke to him during his entire four years at the Naval Academy. Benjamin O. Davis Jr., the first black to graduate from the U.S. Military Academy in the twentieth century, had a parallel experience during his four years at that institution. After he had been at West Point for a short time, there was a knock on his door announcing a meeting in the basement in ten minutes. Davis painfully recalls that meeting and its long-term effects in the autobiography he wrote almost sixty years later:

As I approached the assembly where the meeting was in progress, I heard someone ask, "What are we going to do about the nigger?" I realized then that the meeting was about me, and I was not supposed to attend. I turned on my heel and double-timed back to my room.

From that meeting on, the cadets who roomed across the hall, who had been friendly earlier, no longer spoke to me. In fact, no one spoke to me except in the line of duty. Apparently, certain upperclass cadets had determined that I was getting along too well at the Academy to suit them, and they were going to enforce an old West Point tradition—"silencing"—with the object of making my life so unhappy that I would resign. Silencing had been applied in the past to certain cadets who were considered to have violated the honor code and refused to resign. In my case there was no question of such a violation; I was to be silenced solely because cadets did not want blacks at West Point. Their only purpose was to freeze me out.

Except for the recognition ceremony at the end of plebe year, I was silenced for the entire four years of my stay at the Academy.

Davis stuck it out at West Point and graduated near the top of his class. Even after graduation in 1936, his classmates (among them William Westmoreland, from a wealthy textile family in South Carolina) continued their silent treatment of him for years. In fact, for the next fifteen years, as his assignments took him to different locations in the United States and around the world, not only did his classmates continue to give him the silent treatment, but they and their wives also shunned Davis's wife. . . .

Still, a retired black general has become one of the best-known and most admired Americans. It was a major breakthrough in 1989 when Colin Powell was named chairman of the Joint Chiefs of Staff. And, indeed, Powell's ascendance to the top of the military hierarchy has had as much impact for civilians as for soldiers. According to Moskos and Butler, "the elevation of Colin Luther Powell to the chairmanship of the Joint Chiefs of Staff in 1989 was an epic event in American race relations, whose significance has yet to be fully realized."

Powell's parents were both Jamaican immigrants, a fact he makes much of. . . . While a student at the City College of New York, Powell joined ROTC, and when he graduated in 1958, he was commissioned as a second lieutenant. Powell has emphasized that he "found himself" in ROTC: "Suddenly everything clicked. . . . I had found something I was good at. . . . For the first time, in the military I always knew exactly what was expected of me." Equally important, the military had become a place where blacks could do well. "I had an intuitive sense that this was a career which was beginning to open up for blacks," says Powell. "You could not name, in those days, another profession where black men routinely told white men what to do and how to do it."

Powell rose through the ranks. He served as a junior officer in Vietnam, then held a series of command and staff jobs. In 1972 he became a White House Fellow; noting that race worked to his advantage in this appointment, he said to a friend, "I was lucky to be born black." Four years later, Jimmy Carter appointed Clifford Alexander as secretary of the army, and the number of black generals tripled while Alexander held that position. "My method was simple," Alexander revealed. "I just told everyone that I would not sign the goddam promotion list unless it was fair." In 1979, at the age of forty-two, Colin Powell achieved the rank of general. By 1987 he had become national security adviser under Reagan, and in 1989, under Bush, he became the first black—and the youngest man ever—to be chairman of the Joint Chiefs of Staff. After the Gulf War, polls consistently indicated that Powell was among the most admired people in America. . . .

The power elite has been strengthened because diversity has been achieved primarily by the selection of women and minorities who share the prevailing perspectives and values of those already in power. The power elite is not "multicultural" in any full sense of the concept, but only in terms of ethnic or racial origins. This process has been helped along by those who have called for the inclusion of women and minorities without any consideration of criteria other than sex, race, or ethnicity. Because the demand was strictly for a woman on the Supreme Court, President Reagan could comply by choosing a conservative upper-class corporate lawyer, Sandra Day O'Connor. When pressure mounted to have more black justices, President Bush could respond by appointing Clarence Thomas, a conservative black Republican with a law degree from Yale University. It is yet another irony that appointments like these served to undercut the liberal social movements that caused them to happen.

It is not surprising, therefore, that when we look at the business practices of the women and minorities who have risen to the top of the corporate world, we find that their perspectives and values do not differ markedly from those of their white male counterparts. When Linda Wachner, one of the few women to become CEO of a *Fortune*-level company, the Warnaco Group, concluded that one of Warnaco's many holdings, the Hathaway Shirt Company, was unprofitable, she decided to stop making Hathaway shirts and to sell or close down the factory. It did not matter to Wachner that Hathaway, which started making shirts in 1837, was one of the oldest companies in Maine, that almost all of the five hundred employees at the factory were working-class women, or even that the workers had given up a pay raise to hire consultants to teach them to work more effectively and, as a result, had doubled their productivity. The bottom-line issue was that the company was considered unprofitable, and the average wage of the Hathaway workers, $7.50 an hour, was thought to be too high. (In 1995 Wachner was paid $10 million in salary and stock, and Warnaco had a net income of $46.5 million.) "We did need to do the right thing for the company and the stockholders," explained Wachner.

Nor did ethnic background matter to Thomas Fuentes, a senior vice president at a consulting firm in Orange County, California, a director of Fleetwood Enterprises, and chairman of the Orange County Republican Party. Fuentes targeted fellow Latinos who happened to be Democrats when he sent uniformed security guards to twenty polling places in 1988 "carrying signs in Spanish and English warning people not to vote if they were not U.S. citizens." The security firm ended up paying $60,000 in damages when it lost a lawsuit stemming from this intimidation.

We also recall that the Fanjuls, the Cuban-American sugar barons, have had no problem ignoring labor laws in dealing with their migrant labor force, and that the Sakioka family illegally gave short-handled hoes to its migrant farm workers. These people were acting as employers, not as members of ethnic groups. That is, members of the power elite of both genders and all ethnicities have practiced class politics, making it possible for the power structure to weather the challenge created by the social movements that began in the 1960s.

Those who challenged Christian white male homogeneity in the power structure during the 1960s not only sought to create civil rights and new job opportunities for men and women who had previously been mistreated, important though these goals were. They also hoped that new perspectives in the boardrooms and the halls of government would bring greater openness throughout the society. The idea was both to diversify the power elite and to shift some of its power to previously excluded groups and social classes. The social movements of the 1960s were strikingly successful in increasing the individual rights and freedoms available to all Americans, especially African Americans. As we have shown, they also created pressures that led to openings at the top for individuals from groups that had previously been excluded.

But as the concerns of social movements, political leaders, and the courts came to focus more and more on individual rights, the emphasis on social class and "distributive justice" was lost. The age-old American commitment to individualism, reinforced at every turn by members of the power elite, won out over the commitment to greater equality of income and wealth that had been one strand of New Deal liberalism and a major emphasis of left-wing activists in the 1960s.

We therefore have to conclude on the basis of our findings that the diversification of the power elite did not generate any changes in an underlying class system in which the top 1 percent have 45.6 percent of all financial wealth, the next 19 percent have 46.7 percent, and the bottom 80 percent have 7.8 percent. The values of liberal individualism embedded in the Declaration of Independence, the Bill of Rights, and the civic culture were renewed by vigorous and courageous activists, but despite their efforts the class structure remains a major obstacle to individual fulfillment for the overwhelming majority of Americans. This fact is more than an irony. It is a dilemma. It combines with the dilemma of race to create a nation that celebrates equal opportunity but is, in reality, a bastion of class privilege and conservatism.

14

ROBERT DAHL

From *Who Governs?* and from *A Preface to Democratic Theory*

*In any city in the United States—like New Haven, Connecticut—as in
the entire nation, political power is no longer in the hands of a few people
as it once was early in American history. Nor is power spread evenly among
all citizens. Influential political theorist Robert Dahl presents here the classic
statement of pluralism: the dispersion of power among many groups of
people. Dahl differentiates the "political stratum," made up of interested
and involved citizens, from the "apolitical stratum," those who do not take
an active part in government. These two segments of society are vastly
different in their degree of involvement, yet they are closely tied together in
many ways in a pluralist system. At least in theory, anyone can enter the
political stratum where numerous interest groups compete and bargain for
their goals. Public policy is made by "the steady appeasement of relatively
small groups." Because of this "strange hybrid," Dahl contends, pluralism
is the best way to describe how power is distributed in America.*

IN A POLITICAL SYSTEM where nearly every adult may vote
but where knowledge, wealth, social position, access to officials, and other
resources are unequally distributed, who actually governs?

The question has been asked, I imagine, wherever popular government
has developed and intelligent citizens have reached the stage of critical
self-consciousness concerning their society. It must have been put many
times in Athens even before it was posed by Plato and Aristotle.

The question is peculiarly relevant to the United States and to Americans. In the first place, Americans espouse democratic beliefs with a
fervency and a unanimity that have been a regular source of astonishment
to foreign observers . . . [such as] Tocqueville and Bryce. . . .

In the course of the past two centuries, New Haven has gradually
changed from oligarchy to pluralism. Accompanying and probably causing
this change—one might properly call it a revolution—appears to be a
profound alteration in the way political resources are distributed among
the citizens of New Haven. This silent socioeconomic revolution has not
substituted equality for inequality so much as it has involved a shift from
cumulative inequalities in political resources—to use an expression intro-

duced a moment ago—to noncumulative or dispersed inequalities. This point will grow clearer as we proceed. . . .

In the political system of the patrician oligarchy, political resources were marked by a cumulative inequality: when one individual was much better off than another in one resource, such as wealth, he was usually better off in almost every other resource—social standing, legitimacy, control over religious and educational institutions, knowledge, office. In the political system of today, inequalities in political resources remain, but they tend to be *noncumulative*. The political system of New Haven, then, is one of *dispersed inequalities*. . . .

Within a century a political system dominated by one cohesive set of leaders had given way to a system dominated by many different sets of leaders, each having access to a different combination of political resources. It was, in short, a pluralist system. If the pluralist system was very far from being an oligarchy, it was also a long way from achieving the goal of political equality advocated by the philosophers of democracy and incorporated into the creed of democracy and equality practically every American professes to uphold.

An elite no longer rules New Haven. But in the strict democratic sense, the disappearance of elite rule has not led to the emergence of rule by the people. Who, then, rules in a pluralist democracy? . . .

One of the difficulties that confronts anyone who attempts to answer the question, "Who rules in a pluralist democracy?" is the ambiguous relationship of leaders to citizens.

Viewed from one position, leaders are enormously influential— so influential that if they are seen only in this perspective they might well be considered a kind of ruling elite. Viewed from another position, however, many influential leaders seem to be captives of their constituents. Like the blind men with the elephant, different analysts have meticulously examined different aspects of the body politic and arrived at radically different conclusions. To some, a pluralistic democracy with dispersed inequalities is all head and no body; to others it is all body and no head. . . .

Two additional factors help to account for this obscurity. First, among all the persons who influence a decision, some do so more directly than others in the sense that they are closer to the stage where concrete alternatives are initiated or vetoed in an explicit and immediate way. Indirect influence might be very great but comparatively difficult to observe and weigh. Yet to ignore indirect influence in analysis of the distribution of influence would be to exclude what might well prove to be a highly significant process of control in a pluralistic democracy.

Second, the relationship between leaders and citizens in a pluralistic democracy is frequently reciprocal: leaders influence the decisions of constituents, but the decisions of leaders are also determined in part by what they think are, will be, or have been the preferences of their constituents. Ordinarily it is much easier to observe and describe the distribution of influence in a political system where the flow of influence is strongly in one direction (an asymmetrical or unilateral system, as it is sometimes called) than in a system marked by strong reciprocal relations. In a political system with competitive elections, such as New Haven's, it is not unreasonable to expect that relationships between leaders and constituents would normally be reciprocal. . . .

In New Haven, as in other political systems, a small stratum of individuals is much more highly involved in political thought, discussion, and action than the rest of the population. These citizens constitute the political stratum.

Members of this stratum live in a political subculture that is partly but not wholly shared by the great majority of citizens. Just as artists and intellectuals are the principal bearers of the artistic, literary, and scientific skills of a society, so the members of the political stratum are the main bearers of political skills. If intellectuals were to vanish overnight, a society would be reduced to artistic, literary, and scientific poverty. If the political stratum were destroyed, the previous political institutions of the society would temporarily stop functioning. In both cases, the speed with which the loss could be overcome would depend on the extent to which the elementary knowledge and basic attitudes of the elite had been diffused. In an open society with widespread education and training in civic attitudes, many citizens hitherto in the apolitical strata could doubtless step into roles that had been filled by members of the political stratum. However, sharp discontinuities and important changes in the operation of the political system almost certainly would occur.

In New Haven, as in the United States, and indeed perhaps in all pluralistic democracies, differences in the subcultures of the political and the apolitical strata are marked, particularly at the extremes. In the political stratum, politics is highly salient; among the apolitical strata, it is remote. In the political stratum, individuals tend to be rather calculating in their choice of strategies; members of the political stratum are, in a sense, relatively rational political beings. In the apolitical strata, people are notably less calculating; their political choices are more strongly influenced by inertia, habit, unexamined loyalties, personal attachments, emotions, transient impulses. In the political stratum, an individual's political beliefs tend to fall into patterns that have a relatively high degree of coherence and internal consistency; in the apolitical strata, political orientations are disorganized, disconnected, and unideological. In the political stratum, information about politics and the issues of the day is extensive; the apolitical strata are poorly informed. Individuals in the political stratum tend to participate rather actively in politics; in the apolitical strata citizens rarely go beyond voting and many do not even vote. Individuals in the political stratum exert a good deal of steady, direct, and active influence on government policy; in fact some individuals have a quite extraordinary amount of influence. Individuals in the apolitical strata, on the other hand, have much less direct or active influence on policies.

Communication within the political stratum tends to be rapid and extensive. Members of the stratum read many of the same newspapers and magazines; in New Haven, for example, they are likely to read the *New York Times* or the *Herald Tribune*, and *Time* or *Newsweek*. Much information also passes by word of mouth. The political strata of different communities and regions are linked in a national network of communications. Even in small towns, one or two members of the local political stratum usually are in touch with members of a state organization, and certain members of the political stratum of a state or any large city maintain relations with members of organizations in other states and cities, or with national figures. Moreover, many channels of communication not designed specifically for political purposes—trade associations, professional associations, and labor organizations, for example—serve as a part of the network of the political stratum.

In many pluralistic systems, however, the political stratum is far from being a closed or static group. In the United States the political stratum does not constitute a homogeneous class with well-defined class interests. In New Haven, in fact, the political stratum is easily penetrated by anyone whose interests and concerns attract him to the distinctive political culture of the stratum. It is easily penetrated because (among other reasons) elections and competitive parties give politicians a powerful motive for expanding their coalitions and increasing their electoral followings.

In an open pluralistic system, where movement into the political stratum is easy, the stratum embodies many of the most widely shared values and goals in the society. If popular values are strongly pragmatic, then the political stratum is likely to be pragmatic; if popular values prescribe reverence toward the past, then the political stratum probably shares that reverence; if popular values are oriented toward material gain and personal advancement, then the political stratum probably reflects these values; if popular values are particularly favorable to political, social, or economic equality, then the political stratum is likely to emphasize equality. The apolitical strata can be said to "govern" as much through the sharing of common values and goals with members of the political stratum as by other means. However, if it were not for elections and competitive parties, this sharing would—other things remaining the same—rapidly decline.

Not only is the political stratum in New Haven not a closed group, but its "members" are far from united in their orientations and strategies. There are many lines of cleavage. . . .

Because of the ease with which the political stratum can be penetrated, whenever dissatisfaction builds up in some segment of the electorate party politicians will probably learn of the discontent and calculate whether it might be converted into a political issue with an electoral payoff. If a party politician sees no payoff, his interest is likely to be small; if he foresees an adverse effect, he will avoid the issue if he can. As a result, there is usually some conflict in the political stratum between intellectuals, experts, and others who formulate issues, and the party politicians themselves, for the first group often demands attention to issues in which the politicians see no profit and possibly even electoral damage.

The independence, penetrability, and heterogeneity of the various segments of the political stratum all but guarantee that any dissatisfied group will find spokesmen in the political stratum, but to have a spokesman does not insure that the group's problems will be solved by political action. Politicians may not see how they can gain by taking a position on an issue; action by government may seem to be wholly inappropriate; policies intended to cope with dissatisfaction may be blocked; solutions may be improperly designed; indeed, politicians may even find it politically profitable to maintain a shaky coalition by keeping tension and discontent alive and deflecting attention to irrelevant "solutions" or alternative issues. . . .

. . . In devising strategies for building coalitions and allocating rewards, one must take into account a large number of different categories of citizens. It would be dangerous to formulate strategies on the assumption that most or all citizens can be divided into two or three categories, for a successful political coalition necessarily rests upon a multiplicity of groups and categories. . . .*

. . . I defined the "normal" American political process as one in which there is a high probability that an active and legitimate group in the

---

*At this point, the excerpt from *Who Governs?* ends, and *A Preface to Democratic Theory* begins. —EDS.

population can make itself heard effectively at some crucial stage in the process of decision. To be "heard" covers a wide range of activities, and I do not intend to define the word rigorously. Clearly, it does not mean that every group has equal control over the outcome.

In American politics, as in all other societies, control over decisions is unevenly distributed; neither individuals nor groups are political equals. When I say that a group is heard "effectively" I mean more than the simple fact that it makes a noise; I mean that one or more officials are not only ready to listen to the noise, but expect to suffer in some significant way if they do not placate the group, its leaders, or its most vociferous members. To satisfy the group may require one or more of a great variety of actions by the responsive leader: pressure for substantive policies, appointments, graft, respect, expression of the appropriate emotions, or the right combination of reciprocal noises.

Thus the making of governmental decisions is not a majestic march of great majorities united upon certain matters of basic policy. It is the steady appeasement of relatively small groups. . . .

To be sure, reformers with a tidy sense of order dislike it. Foreign observers, even sympathetic ones, are often astonished and confounded by it. Many Americans are frequently dismayed by its paradoxes; indeed, few Americans who look upon our political process attentively can fail, at times, to feel deep frustration and angry resentment with a system that on the surface has so little order and so much chaos.

For it is a markedly decentralized system. Decisions are made by endless bargaining; perhaps in no other national political system in the world is bargaining so basic a component of the political process. In an age when the efficiencies of hierarchy have been re-emphasized on every continent, no doubt the normal American political system is something of an anomaly, if not, indeed, at times an anachronism. For as a means to highly integrated, consistent decisions in some important areas—foreign policy, for example—it often appears to operate in a creaking fashion verging on total collapse.

Yet we should not be too quick in our appraisal, for where its vices stand out, its virtues are concealed to the hasty eye. Luckily the normal system has the virtues of its vices. With all its defects, it does nonetheless provide a high probability that any active and legitimate group will make itself heard effectively at some stage in the process of decision. This is no mean thing in a political system.

It is not a static system. The normal American system has evolved, and by evolving it has survived. It has evolved and survived from aristocracy to mass democracy, through slavery, civil war, the tentative uneasy reconciliation of North and South, the repression of Negroes and their halting liberation; through two great wars of worldwide scope, mobilization, far-flung military enterprise, and return to hazardous peace; through numerous periods of economic instability and one prolonged depression with mass unemployment, farm "holidays," veterans' marches, tear gas, and even bullets; through two periods of postwar cynicism, demagogic excesses, invasions of traditional liberties, and the groping, awkward, often savage, attempt to cope with problems of subversion, fear, and civil tension.

Probably this strange hybrid, the normal American political system, is not for export to others. But so long as the social prerequisites of democracy are substantially intact in this country, it appears to be a relatively efficient system for reinforcing agreement, encouraging moderation, and maintaining social peace in a restless and immoderate people operating a gigantic, powerful, diversified, and incredibly complex society.

This is no negligible contribution, then, that Americans have made to the arts of government—and to that branch, which of all the arts of politics is the most difficult, the art of democratic government.

PART THREE

Separation
of Powers

15

JAMES MADISON

The Federalist 51

In Federalist 10, an earlier selection, one of the Constitution's designers, James Madison, explained his fear of "faction"—any single group that tries to dominate the political process—and why faction cannot be removed from politics. Madison's solution was to accept factions, but control them. Federalist 10 offered a republican (representative) government and a large, diverse nation with many factions as effective controls. In No. 51 he continues, citing the structural features that characterize American government. Power will be separated among different departments, or branches, of government, independent from one another. Then, power will be divided between the national and state levels, a system called federalism. Madison's philosophy for government is here in this essay too: "Ambition must be made to counteract ambition." Don't miss that paragraph, since it contains warnings that resonate across the centuries.

No. 51: Madison

TO WHAT EXPEDIENT, then, shall we finally resort, for maintaining in practice the necessary partition of power among the several departments as laid down in the Constitution? The only answer that can be given is that as all these exterior provisions are found to be inadequate the defect must be supplied, by so contriving the interior structure of the government as that its several constituent parts may, by their mutual relations, be the means of keeping each other in their proper places. Without presuming to undertake a full development of this important idea I will hazard a few general observations which may perhaps place it in a clearer light, and enable us to form a more correct judgment of the principles and structure of the government planned by the convention.

In order to lay a due foundation for that separate and distinct exercise of the different powers of government, which to a certain extent is admitted on all hands to be essential to the preservation of liberty, it is evident that each department should have a will of its own; and consequently should be so constituted that the members of each should have as little agency as possible in the appointment of the members of the others. Were this principle rigorously adhered to, it would require that all the appointments for the supreme executive, legislative, and judiciary magistracies should be drawn from the same fountain of authority, the people, through channels having no communication whatever with one another. Perhaps such a plan of constructing the several departments would be less difficult in practice than it may in contemplation appear. Some difficulties, however, and some additional expense would attend the execution of it. Some deviations, therefore, from the principle must be admitted. In the constitution of the judiciary department in particular, it might be inexpedient to insist rigorously on the principle: first, because peculiar qualifications being essential in the members, the primary consideration ought to be to select that mode of choice which best secures these qualifications; second, because the permanent tenure by which the appointments are held in that department must soon destroy all sense of dependence on the authority conferring them.

It is equally evident that the members of each department should be as little dependent as possible on those of the others for the emoluments annexed to their offices. Were the executive magistrate, or the judges, not independent of the legislature in this particular, their independence in every other would be merely nominal.

But the great security against a gradual concentration of the several powers in the same department consists in giving to those who administer each department the necessary constitutional means and personal motives to resist encroachments of the others. The provision for defense must in this, as in all other cases, be made commensurate to the danger of attack. Ambition must be made to counteract ambition. The interest of the man must be connected with the constitutional rights of the place. It may be a reflection on human nature that such devices should be necessary to control the abuses of government. But what is government itself but the greatest of all reflections on human nature? If men were angels, no government would be necessary. If angels were to govern men, neither external nor internal controls on government would be necessary. In framing a government which is to be administered by men over men, the great difficulty lies in this: you must first enable the government to control the governed; and in the next place oblige it to control itself. A dependence on the people is, no doubt, the primary control on the government; but experience has taught mankind the necessity of auxiliary precautions.

This policy of supplying, by opposite and rival interests, the defect of better motives, might be traced through the whole system of human affairs, private as well as public. We see it particularly displayed in all the subordinate distributions of power, where the constant aim is to divide and arrange the several offices in such a manner as that each may be a check on the other—that the private interest of every individual may be a sentinel over the public rights. These inventions of prudence cannot be less requisite in the distribution of the supreme powers of the State.

But it is not possible to give to each department an equal power of self-defense. In republican government, the legislative authority necessarily predominates. The remedy for this inconveniency is to divide the legislature into different branches; and to render them, by different modes of election and different principles of action, as little connected with each other as the nature of their common functions and their common dependence on the society will admit. It may even be necessary to guard against dangerous encroachments by still further precautions. As the weight of the legislative authority requires that it should be thus divided, the weakness of the executive may require, on the other hand, that it should be fortified. An absolute negative on the legislature appears, at first view, to be the natural defense with which the executive magistrate should be armed. But perhaps it would be neither altogether safe nor alone sufficient. On ordinary occasions it might not be exerted with the requisite firmness, and on extraordinary occasions it might be perfidiously abused. May not this defect of an absolute negative be supplied by some qualified connection between this weaker department and the weaker branch of the stronger department, by which the latter may be led to support the constitutional rights of the former, without being too much detached from the rights of its own department?

If the principles on which these observations are founded be just, as I persuade myself they are, and they be applied as a criterion to the several State constitutions, and to the federal Constitution, it will be found that if the latter does not perfectly correspond with them, the former are infinitely less able to bear such a test.

There are, moreover, two considerations particularly applicable to the federal system of America, which place that system in a very interesting point of view.

First. In a single republic, all the power surrendered by the people is submitted to the administration of a single government; and the usurpations are guarded against by a division of the government into distinct and separate departments. In the compound republic of America, the power surrendered by the people is first divided between two distinct governments, and then the portion allotted to each subdivided among distinct and separate departments. Hence a double security arises to the rights of the people. The different governments will control each other, at the same time that each will be controlled by itself.

Second. It is of great importance in a republic not only to guard the society against the oppression of its rulers, but to guard one part of the society against the injustice of the other part. Different interests necessarily exist in different classes of citizens. If a majority be united by a common interest, the rights of the minority will be insecure. There are but two methods of providing against this evil: the one by creating a will in the community independent of the majority—that is, of the society itself; the other, by comprehending in the society so many separate descriptions of citizens as will render an unjust combination of a majority of the whole very improbable, if not impracticable. The first method prevails in all governments possessing an hereditary or self-appointed authority. This, at best, is but a precarious security; because a power independent of the society may as well espouse the unjust views of the major as the rightful interests of the minor party, and may possibly be turned against both parties. The second method will be exemplified in the federal republic of the United States. Whilst all authority in it will be derived from and dependent on the society, the society itself will be broken into so many parts, interests and classes of citizens, that the rights of individuals, or of the minority, will be in little danger from interested combinations of the majority. In a free government the security for civil rights must be the same as that for religious rights. It consists in the one case in the multiplicity of interests, and in the other in the multiplicity of sects. The degree of security in both cases will depend on the number of interests and sects; and this may be presumed to depend on the extent of country and number of people comprehended under the same government. This view of the subject must particularly recommend a proper federal system to all the sincere and considerate friends of republican government, since it shows that in exact proportion as the territory of the Union may be formed into more circumscribed Confederacies, or States, oppressive combinations of a majority will be facilitated; the best security, under the republican forms, for the rights of every class of citizen, will be diminished; and consequently the stability and independence of some member of the government, the only other security, must be proportionally increased. Justice is the end of government. It is the end of civil society. It ever has been and ever will be pursued until it be obtained, or until liberty be lost in the pursuit. In a society under the forms of which the stronger faction can readily unite and oppress the weaker, anarchy may as truly be said to reign as in a state of nature, where the weaker individual is not secured against the violence of the stronger; and as, in the latter state, even the stronger individuals are prompted, by the uncertainty of their condition, to submit to a government which may protect the weak as well as themselves; so, in the former state, will the more powerful factions or parties be gradually induced, by a like motive, to wish for a government which will protect all parties, the weaker as well as the more powerful. It can be little doubted that if the State of Rhode Island was separated from the Confederacy and left to itself, the insecurity of rights under the popular form of government within such narrow limits would be displayed by such reiterated oppressions of factious majorities that some power altogether independent of the people would soon be called for by the voice of the very factions whose misrule had proved the necessity of it. In the extended republic of the United States, and among the great variety of interests, parties, and sects which it embraces, a coalition of a majority of the whole society could seldom take place on any other principles than those of justice and the general good; whilst there being thus less danger to a minor from the will of a major party, there must be less pretext, also, to provide for the security of the former, by introducing into the government a will not dependent on the latter, or, in other words, a will independent of the society itself. It is no less certain than it is important, notwithstanding the contrary opinions which have been entertained, that the larger the society, provided it lie within a practicable sphere, the more duly capable it will be of self-government. And happily for the *republican cause*, the practicable sphere may be carried to a very great extent by a judicious modification and mixture of the *federal principle*. *Publius*

16

WOODROW WILSON

From *Congressional Government*

Before becoming president of the United States, Woodrow Wilson was governor of New Jersey. Previously, he had been the president of Princeton University and, earlier still, a professor of political science. In his 1885 doctoral writings, Wilson criticizes the fragmentation of power and lack of clear accountability in the American structure of government. The dilution of the national government's authority by state governments excites Wilson's ire, too. He sympathizes with the president's position because of its weakness relative to Congress at the time. Wilson's strongest negative judgment is saved for congressional committees, which he considered major impediments to getting the nation's business accomplished efficiently. Wilson the political scientist makes a good case against the gridlock inherent in the framers' separation of powers design. One wonders whether the beleaguered President

Wilson re-read his own scholarly treatise in 1919, at the end of World War I, when Senator Henry Cabot Lodge led the Foreign Relations Committee in blocking the passage of the Versailles Treaty based on Wilson's Fourteen Points and containing his League of Nations.

———

I KNOW OF few things harder to state clearly and within reasonable compass than just how the nation keeps control of policy in spite of these hide-and-seek vagaries of authority. Indeed, it is doubtful if it does keep control through all the roundabout paths which legislative and executive responsibility are permitted to take. It must follow Congress somewhat blindly; Congress is known to obey without altogether understanding its Committees: and the Committees must consign the execution of their plans to officials who have opportunities not a few to hoodwink them. At the end of these blind processes is it probable that the ultimate authority, the people, is quite clear in its mind as to what has been done or what may be done another time? Take, for example, financial policy,— a very fair example, because, as I have shown, the legislative stages of financial policy are more talked about than any other congressional business, though for that reason an extreme example. If, after appropriations and adjustments of taxation have been tardily and in much tribulation of scheming and argument agreed upon by the House, the imperative suggestions and stubborn insistence of the Senate confuse matters till hardly the Conference Committees themselves know clearly what the outcome of the disagreements has been; and if, when these compromise measures are launched as laws, the method of their execution is beyond the view of the Houses, in the semi-privacy of the departments, how is the comprehension—not to speak of the will—of the people to keep any sort of hold upon the course of affairs? There are no screws of responsibility which they can turn upon the consciences or upon the official thumbs of the congressional Committees principally concerned. Congressional Committees are nothing to the nation; they are only pieces of the interior mechanism of Congress. To Congress they stand or fall. And, since Congress itself can scarcely be sure of having its own way with them, the constituencies are manifestly unlikely to be able to govern them. As for the departments, the people can hardly do more in drilling them to unquestioning obedience and docile efficiency than Congress can. Congress is, and must be, in these matters the nation's eyes and voice. If it cannot see what goes wrong and cannot get itself heeded when it commands, the nation likewise is both blind and dumb.

This, plainly put, is the practical result of the piecing of authority, the cutting of it up into small bits, which is contrived in our constitutional system. Each branch of the government is fitted out with a small section of responsibility, whose limited opportunities afford to the conscience of each many easy escapes. Every suspected culprit may shift the responsibility upon his fellows. Is Congress rated for corrupt or imperfect or foolish legislation? It may urge that it has to follow hastily its Committees or do nothing at all but talk; how can it help it if a stupid Committee leads it unawares into unjust or fatuous enterprises? Does administration blunder and run itself into all sorts of straits? The Secretaries hasten to plead the unreasonable or unwise commands of Congress, and Congress falls to blaming the Secretaries. The Secretaries aver that the whole mischief might have been avoided if they had only been allowed to suggest the proper measures; and the men who framed the existing measures in their turn avow their despair of good government so long as they must intrust all their plans to the bungling incompetence of men who are appointed by and responsible to somebody else. How is the schoolmaster, the nation, to know which boy needs the whipping?

Moreover, it is impossible to deny that this division of authority and concealment of responsibility are calculated to subject the government to a very distressing paralysis in moments of emergency. There are few, if any, important steps that can be taken by any one branch of the government without the consent or cooperation of some other branch. Congress must act through the President and his Cabinet; the President and his Cabinet must wait upon the will of Congress. There is no one supreme, ultimate head—whether magistrate or representative body—which can decide at once and with conclusive authority what shall be done at those times when some decision there must be, and that immediately. Of course this lack is of a sort to be felt at all times, in seasons of tranquil rounds of business as well as at moments of sharp crisis; but in times of sudden exigency it might prove fatal,—fatal either in breaking down the system or in failing to meet the emergency. Policy cannot be either prompt or straightforward when it must serve many masters. It must either equivocate, or hesitate, or fail altogether. It may set out with clear purpose from Congress, but get waylaid or maimed by the Executive.

If there be one principle clearer than another, it is this: that in any business, whether of government or of mere merchandising, *somebody must be trusted*, in order that when things go wrong it may be quite plain who should be punished. In order to drive trade at the speed and with the success you desire, you must confide without suspicion in your chief clerk, giving him the power to ruin you, because you thereby furnish him with a motive for serving you. His reputation, his own honor or disgrace, all his own commercial prospects, hang upon your success. And human nature is much the same in government as in the dry-goods trade. *Power and strict accountability for its use* are the essential constituents of good government. A sense of highest responsibility, a dignifying and elevating sense of being trusted, together with a consciousness of being in an official station so conspicuous that no faithful discharge of duty can go unacknowledged and unrewarded, and no breach of trust undiscovered and unpunished,—these are the influences, the only influences, which foster practical, energetic, and trustworthy statesmanship. The best rulers are always those to whom great power is entrusted in such a manner as to make them feel that they will surely be abundantly honored and recompensed for a just and patriotic use of it, and to make them know that nothing can shield them from full retribution for every abuse of it.

It is, therefore, manifestly a radical defect in our federal system that it parcels out power and confuses responsibility as it does. The main purpose of the Convention of 1787 seems to have been to accomplish this grievous mistake. The "literary theory" of checks and balances is simply a consistent account of what our constitution-makers tried to do; and those checks and balances have proved mischievous just to the extent to which they have succeeded in establishing themselves as realities. It is quite safe to say that were it possible to call together again the members of that wonderful Convention to view the work of their hands in the light of the century that has tested it, they would be the first to admit that the only fruit of dividing power had been to make it irresponsible. . . .

It was something more than natural that the Convention of 1787 should desire to erect a Congress which would not be subservient and an executive which could not be despotic. And it was equally to have been expected that they should regard an absolute separation of these two great branches of the system as the only effectual means for the accomplishment of that much desired end. It was impossible that they could believe that executive and legislature could be brought into close relations of cooperation and mutual confidence without being tempted, nay, even bidden, to collude. How could either maintain its independence of action unless each were to have the guaranty of the Constitution that its own domain should be absolutely safe from invasion, its own prerogatives absolutely free from challenge? "They shrank from placing sovereign power anywhere. They feared that it would generate tyranny; George III had been a tyrant to them, and come what might they would not make a George III." They would conquer, by dividing, the power they so much feared to see in any single hand. . . .

The natural, the inevitable tendency of every system of self-government like our own and the British is to exalt the representative body, the people's parliament, to a position of absolute supremacy. . . . Our Constitution, like every other constitution which puts the authority to make laws and the duty of controlling the public expenditure into the hands of a popular assembly, practically sets that assembly to rule the affairs of the nation as supreme overlord. But, by separating it entirely from its executive agencies, it deprives it of the opportunity and means for making its authority complete and convenient. The constitutional machinery is left of such a pattern that other forces less than that of Congress may cross and compete with Congress, though they are too small to overcome or long offset it; and the result is simply an unpleasant, wearing friction which, with other adjustments, more felicitous and equally safe, might readily be avoided. . . .

The dangers of this serious imperfection in our governmental machinery have not been clearly demonstrated in our experience hitherto; but now their delayed fulfillment seems to be close at hand. The plain tendency is towards a centralization of all the greater powers of government in the hands of the federal authorities, and towards the practical confirmation of those prerogatives of supreme overlordship which Congress has been gradually arrogating to itself. The central government is constantly becoming stronger and more active, and Congress is establishing itself as the one sovereign authority in that government. In constitutional theory and in the broader features of past practice, ours has been what Mr. Bagehot has called a "composite" government.* Besides state and federal authorities to dispute as to sovereignty, there have been within the federal system itself rival and irreconcilable powers. But gradually the strong are overcoming the weak. If the signs of the times are to be credited, we are fast approaching an adjustment of sovereignty quite as "simple" as need be. Congress is not only to retain the authority it already possesses, but is to be brought again and again face to face with still greater demands upon its energy, its wisdom, and its conscience, is to have ever-widening duties and responsibilities thrust upon it, without being granted a moment's opportunity to look back from the plough to which it has set its hands.

The sphere and influence of national administration and national legislation are widening rapidly. Our populations are growing at such a rate that one's reckoning staggers at counting the possible millions that

*Walter Bagehot (1826–1877), British economist, political theorist, and journalist, wrote *The English Constitution*, a book that had great influence on the young Woodrow Wilson. The idealized picture of the virtues of the British polity that informs *Congressional Government* is straight out of Bagehot. — EDS.

may have a home and a work on this continent ere fifty more years shall have filled their short span. The East will not always be the centre of national life. The South is fast accumulating wealth, and will faster recover influence. The West has already achieved a greatness which no man can gainsay, and has in store a power of future growth which no man can estimate. Whether these sections are to be harmonious or dissentient depends almost entirely upon the methods and policy of the federal government. If that government be not careful to keep within its own proper sphere and prudent to square its policy by rules of national welfare, sectional lines must and will be known; citizens of one part of the country may look with jealousy and even with hatred upon their fellow-citizens of another part; and faction must tear and dissension distract a country which Providence would bless, but which man may curse. The government of a country so vast and various must be strong, prompt, wieldy, and efficient. Its strength must consist in the certainty and uniformity of its purposes, in its accord with national sentiment, in its unhesitating action, and in its honest aims. It must be steadied and approved by open administration diligently obedient to the more permanent judgments of public opinion; and its only active agency, its representative chambers, must be equipped with something besides abundant powers of legislation.

As at present constituted, the federal government lacks strength because its powers are divided, lacks promptness because its authorities are multiplied, lacks wieldiness because its processes are roundabout, lacks efficiency because its responsibility is indistinct and its action without competent direction. It is a government in which every officer may talk about every other officer's duty without having to render strict account for not doing his own, and in which the masters are held in check and offered contradiction by the servants. Mr. Lowell has called it "government by declamation." Talk is not sobered by any necessity imposed upon those who utter it to suit their actions to their words. There is no day of reckoning for words spoken. The speakers of a congressional majority may, without risk of incurring ridicule or discredit, condemn what their own Committees are doing; and the spokesmen of a minority may urge what contrary courses they please with a well-grounded assurance that what they say will be forgotten before they can be called upon to put it into practice. Nobody stands sponsor for the policy of the government. A dozen men originate it; a dozen compromises twist and alter it; a dozen offices whose names are scarcely known outside of Washington put it into execution. . . .

An intelligent observer of our politics has declared that there is in the United States "a class, including thousands and tens of thousands of the best men in the country, who think it possible to enjoy the fruits of good government without working for them." Every one who has seen beyond the outside of our American life must recognize the truth of this; to explain it is to state the sum of all the most valid criticisms of congressional government. Public opinion has no easy vehicle for its judgments, no quick channels for its action. Nothing about the system is direct and simple. Authority is perplexingly subdivided and distributed, and responsibility has to be hunted down in out-of-the-way corners. So that the sum of the whole matter is that the means of working for the fruits of good government are not readily to be found. The average citizen may be excused for esteeming government at best but a haphazard affair, upon which his vote and all of his influence can have but little effect. How is his choice of a representative in Congress to affect the policy of the country as regards the questions in which he is most interested, if the man for whom he votes has no chance of getting on the Standing Committee which has virtual charge of those questions? How is it to make any difference who is chosen President? Has the President any very great authority in matters of vital policy? It seems almost a thing of despair to get any assurance that any vote he may cast will even in an infinitesimal degree affect the essential courses of administration. There are so many cooks mixing their ingredients in the national broth that it seems hopeless, this thing of changing one cook at a time.

The charm of our constitutional ideal has now been long enough wound up to enable sober men who do not believe in political witchcraft to judge what it has accomplished, and is likely still to accomplish, without further winding. The Constitution is not honored by blind worship. The more open-eyed we become, as a nation, to its defects, and the prompter we grow in applying with the unhesitating courage of conviction all thoroughly-tested or well-considered expedients necessary to make self-government among us a straightforward thing of simple method, single, unstinted power, and clear responsibility, the nearer will we approach to the sound sense and practical genius of the great and honorable statesmen of 1787. And the first step towards emancipation from the timidity and false pride which have led us to seek to thrive despite the defects of our national system rather than seem to deny its perfection is a fearless criticism of that system. When we shall have examined all its parts without sentiment, and gauged all its functions by the standards of practical common sense, we shall have established anew our right to the claim of political sagacity; and it will remain only to act intelligently upon what our opened eyes have seen in order to prove again the justice of our claim to political genius.

17

JAMES STERLING YOUNG

From *The Washington Community: 1800–1828*

Numerous books and articles have been written about the early years of American government, right after the Constitution was ratified. It seems that scholars have left nothing uncovered in their exploration of that crucial era. But historian James Young succeeds in finding a most unusual angle, one that has great significance for students of American government. He relates the physical living arrangements in early Washington to the separation of powers embodied in the Constitution. Young describes the swamp that delineated parts of the town. He recounts stories about the boardinghouses where legislators lived and sometimes argued vehemently. Young's depiction of House and Senate floor activity can certainly match today's C-SPAN for excitement. Early Washington, D.C., established a clear precedent for the future: many interests were represented, but cooperation was minimal. As Young observes, "Some government!"

DESOLATE IN SURROUNDING, derogatory in self-image, the governmental community was also distinctive for the extraordinary manner in which the personnel chose to situate themselves in Washington—the social formations into which they deployed on the terrain. The settlement pattern of a community is, in a sense, the signature that its social organization inscribes upon the landscape, defining the groups of major importance in the life of the community and suggesting the relationships among them. In the case of the early Washington community that signature is very clear.

The members did not, in their residential arrangements, disperse uniformly or at random over the wide tract of the intended city. Nor did they draw together at any single place. The governmental community rather inscribed itself upon the terrain as a series of distinct subcommunities, separated by a considerable distance, with stretches of empty land between them. Each was clustered around one of the widely separated public buildings; each was a self-contained social and economic entity. The personnel of the governmental community segregated themselves, in short, into distinct groups, and formed a society of "we's" and "they's." . . .

From data gathered in an 1801 survey, listing the location of houses

completed and under construction in the capital, it is possible to recon-
struct the settlement pattern of the early governmental community with
reasonable accuracy. . . .

Members of the different branches of government chose to situate
themselves close by the respective centers of power with which they were
affiliated, seeking their primary associations in extra-official life among
their fellow branch members.

Despite its relative civilization, old Georgetown attracted few members
of government as residents, and most of those who stayed there moved
as soon as they could find quarters in Washington, nearer to their places
of work. . . .

At the opposite end of the city, about five miles from Georgetown,
near the Capitol but separated from it by a dense swamp, was the village
of the armed forces. . . .

. . . Commercialization failing, the environs became the site of the
congressional burying ground, a poorhouse, and a penitentiary with an
arsenal "near, much too near" it, thus associating by coresidence the men
and matériel of war with the dead, the indigent, and the incorrigible.
The settlement was generally shunned by civilian members of the government as a place to live, and high-ranking military and naval officers also
forsook it eventually to take up residence in the executive sector.

The chief centers of activity were the village community of the executives and the village community of the legislators, lying "one mile and a
half and seventeen perches" apart as the crow flies, on the "great heath"
bisected by the River Tiber.

Senators and Representatives lived in the shadow of the Capitol itself,
most of them in knots of dwellings but a moment's walk from their place
of meeting. . . .

The knolltop settlement of legislators was a complete and self-contained village community from beginning to end of the Jeffersonian era.
Neither work nor diversion, nor consumer needs, nor religious needs
required them to set foot outside it. Eight boardinghouses, a tailor, a
shoemaker, a washerwoman, a grocery store, and an oyster house served
the congressional settlement in 1801. Within three years a notary, an
ironmonger, a saddle maker, several more tailors and bootmakers, a liquor
store, bookstores, stables, bakery, and taverns had been added. In twenty
years' time the settlement had increased to more than two thousand people
and the Capitol was nearly surrounded by brick houses "three stories
high, and decent, without being in the least elegant," where the lawmakers
lodged during the session. An itinerant barber served the community,
shuttling between the scattered villages of the capital on horseback, and

a nearby bathhouse catered to congressional clientele. Legislators with
families could send their children to school on the Hill. The members
had their own congressional library and their own post office, dispatching
and receiving mail—which was distributed on the floor of the Senate
and the House daily—without leaving the Hill. Page boys, doorkeepers,
sergeants-at-arms, and other ancillary personnel for Congress were supplied from the permanent population of Capitol Hill—mainly the boardinghouse proprietors and their families. . . . The settlement pattern of
early Washington clearly reveals a community structure paralleling the
constitutional structure of government itself. The "separation of powers"
became a separation of persons, and each of the branches of government
became a self-contained, segregated social system within the larger governmental establishment. Legislators with legislators, executives with executives, judges with judges, the members gathered together in their extra-
official as well as in their official activities, and in their community
associations deepened, rather than bridged, the group cleavages prescribed
by the Constitution.

    Why did the rulers make this highly contrived, unconventional legal
structure into their community structure at Washington? . . . A key factor
contributing to social segregation by branch affiliation is suggested by the
consistency between such behavior and community attitudes about power
and politicians. In the absence of any extrinsic forces compelling the rulers
to segregate in community life, patterned avoidance between executives,
legislators, and judges indicates that they felt a stronger sense of identification with their constitutional roles than with other more partisan roles
they may have had in the community. Social segregation on the basis of
branch affiliation suggests, in other words, that the rulers generally considered themselves executives, legislators, or judges first, and politicians or
party members second. Such a preference for nonpartisan, constitutionally
sanctioned roles fully accords with, and tends to confirm the authenticity
of, the members' disparaging image of politicians. Their decided preference for associating with fellow branch members in extraofficial life is
also precisely the sort of social behavior that was foreshadowed by the
attitudes they held concerning power. Power-holders acculturated to anti-
power values would, it was predicted, be attracted toward behaviors and
associations which were sanctioned by the Constitution. By subdividing
into separate societies of executives, legislators, and judges, the rulers
could not have more literally translated constitutional principles of organization into social realities nor afforded themselves greater security from
reproach in this aspect of their community life at Washington. When one
sees, moreover, the remarkable consistency between the organizational

precepts of the Constitution of 1787 and the community plan of 1791, on the one hand, and, on the other hand, the actual community structure of the governing politicians from 1800 to 1828, one must presume a consistency also in the attitudes from which these principles of organization originally derived, namely, attitudes of mistrust toward political power.

Whatever the underlying causes, here was a community of power-holders who preferred and who sanctioned, in their extraofficial life, a structural configuration that had been designed explicitly to check power. Here was a community of rulers who chose, among all the alternatives of social organization open to them, precisely the one most prejudicial to their capacity to rule. . . . Power made a community of cultural strangers. And power, shared, was hardly a thing to bind strangers together.

To achieve political accord among men of such disparate interests and different acculturation would not have been an easy task even under the most auspicious circumstances. For those gathered to govern on Capitol Hill in the Jeffersonian era, the circumstances were anything but auspicious.

To the political cleavages inherent in any representative assembly were added the deeper social tensions that are generated when men of widely diverging beliefs and behaviors are thrust upon each other in everyday living. Close-quarters living gave rise to personal animus even between "men whose natural interests and stand in society are in many respects similar. . . . The more I know of [two New England Senators] the more I am impressed with the idea how unsuited they are ever to co-operate," commented a fellow lodger; "never were two substances more completely adapted to make each other explode." As social intimacy bared the depth of their behavioral differences, tolerance among men from different regions was strained to the breaking point. Political coexistence with the South and the frontier states was hard enough for New Englanders to accept. Social coexistence was insufferable with slaveholders "accustomed to speak in the tone of masters" and with frontiersmen having "a license of tongue incident to a wild and uncultivated state of society. With men of such states of mind and temperament," a Massachusetts delegate protested, "men educated in . . . New England . . . could have little pleasure in intercourse, less in controversy, and of course no sympathy." Close scrutiny of their New England neighbors in power could convince southerners, in their turn, that there was "not one [who] possesses the slightest tie of common interest or of common feeling with us," planters and gentlemen cast among men "who raised 'beef and pork, and butter and cheese, and potatoes and cabbages'" and carried on "a paltry trade in potash and codfish." Cultural antipathies, crowded barracks, poor rations, and separa-

tion from families left at home combined to make tempers wear thin as
the winters wore on, leading to sporadic eruptions of violence. In a sudden
affray at the table in Miss Shields's boardinghouse, Randolph, "pouring
out a glass of wine, dashed it in Alston's face. Alston sent a decanter at
his head in return, and these and similar missiles continued to fly to and
fro, until there was much destruction of glass ware." The chambers of the
Capitol themselves witnessed more than one scuffle, and, though it was
not yet the custom for legislators to arm themselves when legislating,
pistols at twenty paces cracked more than once in the woods outside the
Capitol.

To those who would seek political agreement in an atmosphere of
social tensions, the rules of proceeding in Congress offered no aid at all.
On the contrary, contentiousness was encouraged by Senate and House
rules which gave higher precedence to raising questions than to deciding
them and which guaranteed almost total freedom from restraint to the
idiosyncratic protagonist. . . . "Political hostilities are waged with great
vigour," commented another observer, "yet both in attack and defence
there is evidently an entire want both of discipline and organization.
There is no concert, no division of duties, no compromise of opinion.
. . . Any general system of effective co-operation is impossible."

The result was a scene of confusion daily on the floor of House and
Senate that bore no resemblance to the deliberative processes of either
the town meeting or the parliamentary assemblies of the Old World.
Congress at work was Hyde Park* set down in the lobby of a busy hotel—
hortatory outcry in milling throngs, all wearing hats as if just arrived or
on the verge of departure, variously attired in the fashions of faraway
places. Comings and goings were continual—to the rostrum to see the
clerk, to the anterooms to meet friends, to the Speaker's chair in a sudden
surge to hear the results of a vote, to the firesides for hasty caucuses and
strategy-planning sessions. Some gave audience to the speaker of the
moment; some sat at their desks reading or catching up on correspondence;
some stood chatting with lady friends, invited on the floor; others dozed,
feet propped high. Page boys weaved through the crowd, "little Mercuries"
bearing messages, pitchers of water for parched throats, bundles of documents, calling out members' names, distributing mail just arrived on the
stagecoach. Quills scratched, bond crackled as knuckles rapped the sand
off wet ink, countless newspapers rustled. Desk drawers banged, feet

---

*Hyde Park, in London, has a corner reserved for those in the public who wish to stand
up in front of the crowd and offer their views on various issues. At any moment of the
day, Hyde Park is filled with raucous, boisterous argument on every subject under the
sun.—EDS.

shuffled in a sea of documents strewn on the floor. Bird dogs fresh from the hunt bounded in with their masters, yapping accompaniment to contenders for attention, contenders for power. Some government! . . .

What emerges from a community study of Capitol Hill is, therefore, a social system which gave probably greater sanction and encouragement to constituency-oriented behavior than any institutional norms or organizational features of the modern Congress. . . . Constituency-oriented behavior, in other words, justified the possession of power in a context of personal and national values which seems to have demanded justification for the possession of power. . . .

As a system for the effective representation of citizen interests the social system of Capitol Hill has probably never been surpassed in the history of republican government. But a fragmented social system of small blocs, more anarchic than cohesive, seems hardly to meet the minimal requirements for a viable system of managing social conflict, for performing "the regulation of . . . various and interfering interests" which the author of *The Federalist*, No. 10 acknowledged to be "the principal task of modern legislation." Far from serving as an institution for the management of conflict, the little democracy on the Hill seems more likely to have acted as a source of conflict in the polity. An ironic and provocative judgment is thus suggested by the community record of Capitol Hill: at a time when citizen interest in national government was at its lowest point in history the power-holders on the Potomac fashioned a system of surpassing excellence for representing the people and grossly deficient in the means for governing the people.

PART FOUR

Federalism

18

JAMES MADISON

From *The Federalist* 39 and 46

Ratification of the Constitution in 1787 required delicate and persuasive diplomacy. The Articles of Confederation, flawed as they were in allowing virtually no centralized governmental power, did give each state the near-total independence valued after their experiences as English colonies. The proponents of the new Constitution had to convince the states to adopt a new structure of government that would strengthen national power. In Nos. 39 and 46, Madison first discusses the importance of representative government. Then he turns to the "bold and radical innovation" that both divided and shared power between the national government and the state governments—what we today call federalism. The approval of the Constitution was to be by the people of the states, and once in operation, the government would be both national and federal. But, Madison explained, the American people would be the ultimate repository of power. State governments would always claim the citizenry's top loyalty, unless the people chose otherwise. Publius argued successfully in the great American tradition of compromise; there was something for everyone in the Constitution.

No. 39: Madison

. . . THE FIRST QUESTION that offers itself is whether the general form and aspect of the government be strictly republican. It is evident that no other form would be reconcilable with the genius of the people of America; with the fundamental principles of the Revolution; or with that honorable determination which animates every votary of freedom to rest all our political experiments on the capacity of mankind for self-government. If the plan of the convention, therefore, be found to depart from the republican character, its advocates must abandon it as no longer defensible.

What, then, are the distinctive characters of the republican form? . . .

If we resort for a criterion to the different principles on which different forms of government are established, we may define a republic to be, or at least may bestow that name on, a government which derives all its powers directly or indirectly from the great body of the people, and is administered by persons holding their offices during pleasure for a limited period, or during good behavior. It is *essential* to such a government that it be derived from the great body of the society, not from an inconsiderable proportion or a favored class of it; otherwise a handful of tyrannical nobles, exercising their oppressions by a delegation of their powers, might aspire to the rank of republicans and claim for their government the honorable title of republic. It is *sufficient* for such a government that the persons administering it be appointed, either directly or indirectly, by the people; and that they hold their appointments by either of the tenures just specified; otherwise every government in the United States, as well as every other popular government that has been or can be well organized or well executed, would be degraded from the republican character. According to the constitution of every State in the Union, some or other of the officers of government are appointed indirectly only by the people. According to most of them, the chief magistrate himself is so appointed. And according to one, this mode of appointment is extended to one of the co-ordinate branches of the legislature. According to all the constitutions, also, the tenure of the highest offices is extended to a definite period, and in many instances, both within the legislative and executive departments, to a period of years. According to the provisions of most of the constitutions, again, as well as according to the most respectable and received opinions on the subject, the members of the judiciary department are to retain their offices by the firm tenure of good behavior. . . .

"But it was not sufficient," say the adversaries of the proposed Constitution, "for the convention to adhere to the republican form. They ought with equal care to have preserved the *federal* form, which regards the Union as a *Confederacy* of sovereign states; instead of which they have framed a *national* government, which regards the Union as a *consolidation* of the States." And it is asked by what authority this bold and radical innovation was undertaken? . . .

First.—In order to ascertain the real character of the government, it may be considered in relation to the foundation on which it is to be established; to the sources from which its ordinary powers are to be drawn; to the operation of those powers; to the extent of them; and to the authority by which future changes in the government are to be introduced.

On examining the first relation, it appears, on one hand, that the Constitution is to be founded on the assent and ratification of the people of America, given by deputies elected for the special purpose; but, on the other, that this assent and ratification is to be given by the people, not as individuals composing one entire nation, but as composing the distinct and independent States to which they respectively belong. It is to be the assent and ratification of the several States, derived from the supreme authority in each State—the authority of the people themselves. The act, therefore, establishing the Constitution will not be a *national* but a *federal* act.

That it will be a federal and not a national act, as these terms are understood by the objectors—the act of the people, as forming so many independent States, not as forming one aggregate nation—is obvious from this single consideration: that it is to result neither from the decision of a *majority* of the people of the Union, nor from that of a *majority* of the States. It must result from the *unanimous* assent of the several States that are parties to it, differing not otherwise from their ordinary dissent than in its being expressed, not by the legislative authority, but by that of the people themselves. . . . Each State, in ratifying the Constitution, is considered as a sovereign body independent of all others, and only to be bound by its own voluntary act. In this relation, then, the new Constitution will, if established, be a *federal* and not a *national* constitution.

The next relation is to the sources from which the ordinary powers of government are to be derived. The House of Representatives will derive its powers from the people of America; and the people will be represented in the same proportion and on the same principle as they are in the legislature of a particular State. So far the government is *national*, not *federal*. The Senate, on the other hand, will derive its powers from the States as political and coequal societies; and these will be represented on the principle of equality in the Senate, as they now are in the existing Congress. So far the government is *federal*, not *national*. The executive power will be derived from a very compound source. The immediate election of the President is to be made by the States in their political characters. The votes allotted to them are in a compound ratio, which considers them partly as distinct and coequal societies, partly as unequal members of the same society. . . . From this aspect of the government it appears to be of a mixed character, presenting at least as many *federal* as *national* features. . . . The idea of a national government involves in it not only an authority over the individual citizens, but an indefinite supremacy over all persons and things, so far as they are objects of lawful government. Among a people consolidated into one nation, this supremacy is completely vested in the national legislature. Among communities united for particular purposes, it is vested partly in the general and partly in the municipal legislatures. In the former case, all local authorities are subordinate to the supreme; and may be controlled, directed, or abolished by it at pleasure. In the latter, the local or municipal authorities form distinct and independent portions of the supremacy, no more subject, within their respective spheres, to the general authority than the general authority is subject to them, within its own sphere. In this relation, then, the proposed government cannot be deemed a *national* one; since its jurisdiction extends to certain enumerated objects only, and leaves to the several States a residuary and inviolable sovereignty over all other objects. . . .

If we try the Constitution by its last relation to the authority by which amendments are to be made, we find it neither wholly *national* nor wholly *federal*. Were it wholly national, the supreme and ultimate authority would reside in the *majority* of the people of the Union; and this authority would be competent at all times, like that of a majority of every national society to alter or abolish its established government. Were it wholly federal, on the other hand, the concurrence of each State in the Union would be essential to every alteration that would be binding on all. The mode provided by the plan of the convention is not founded on either of these principles. In requiring more than a majority, and particularly in computing the proportion by *States*, not by *citizens*, it departs from the national and advances towards the *federal* character; in rendering the concurrence of less than the whole number of States sufficient, it loses again the *federal* and partakes of the *national* character.

The proposed Constitution, therefore, even when tested by the rules laid down by its antagonists, is, in strictness, neither a national nor a federal Constitution, but a composition of both. In its foundation it is federal, not national; in the sources from which the ordinary powers of the government are drawn, it is partly federal and partly national; in the operation of these powers, it is national, not federal; in the extent of them, again, it is federal, not national; and, finally in the authoritative mode of introducing amendments, it is neither wholly federal nor wholly national.   *Publius*

No. 46: Madison

. . . I proceed to inquire whether the federal government or the State governments will have the advantage with regard to the predilection and support of the people. Notwithstanding the different modes in which they are appointed, we must consider both of them as substantially dependent on the great body of the citizens of the United States. I assume this position here as it respects the first, reserving the proofs for another place. The federal and State governments are in fact but different agents and trustees of the people, constituted with different powers and designed for different purposes. The adversaries of the Constitution seem to have lost sight of the people altogether in their reasonings on this subject; and to have viewed these different establishments not only as mutual rivals and enemies, but as uncontrolled by any common superior in their efforts to usurp the authorities of each other. These gentlemen must here be reminded of their error. They must be told that the ultimate authority, wherever the derivative may be found, resides in the people alone, and that it will not depend merely on the comparative ambition or address of the different governments whether either, or which of them, will be able to enlarge its sphere of jurisdiction at the expense of the other. Truth, no less than decency, requires that the event in every case should be supposed to depend on the sentiments and sanction of their common constituents. . . .

Many considerations, besides those suggested on a former occasion, seem to place it beyond doubt that the first and most natural attachment of the people will be to the governments of their respective States. . . .

If . . . the people should in future become more partial to the federal than to the State governments, the change can only result from such manifest and irresistible proofs of a better administration as will overcome all their antecedent propensities. And in that case, the people ought not surely to be precluded from giving most of their confidence where they may discover it to be most due; but even in that case the State governments could have little to apprehend, because it is only within a certain sphere that the federal power can, in the nature of things, be advantageously administered. *Publius*

19

DANIEL ELAZAR

From *American Federalism*

American government has been based on a system of federalism since the Constitution was ratified. Yet, over two centuries, change and flexibility have marked American federalism; the national and state governments have shared power in different ways, to different degrees, with different roles. In the mid-1990s, for example, there is much talk in Washington about moving more governmental programs and policy decisions back to the state level, away from central government edicts. Professor Daniel Elazar offers a classic piece on federalism in which he defends the importance of state governments, even at a time when the national government seemed to dominate. Elazar points to the innovative ideas developed at the state level. He recognizes the states' importance as managers of government programs. Elazar is right on target for today, viewing American federalism as an ever-changing "partnership" between Washington, D.C., and the state capitals.

THE SYSTEM of state-federal relations . . . is not the neat system often pictured in the textbooks. If that neat system of separate governments performing separate functions in something akin to isolation is used as the model of what federalism should be to enable the states to maintain their integrity as political systems, then the states are in great difficulty indeed. If, however, the states have found ways to function as integral political systems—civil societies, if you will—within the somewhat chaotic system of intergovernmental sharing that exists, then they are, as the saying goes, in a different ball game. . . . We have tried to show that the states are indeed in a different ball game and as players in that game are not doing badly at all. Viewed from the perspective of that ball game, the strength and vitality of the states—and the strength and vitality of the American system as a whole—must be assessed by different standards from those commonly used.

In the first place, the states exist. This point is no less significant for its simplicity. The fact that the states survive as going concerns (as distinct from sets of historical boundaries used for the administration of centrally directed programs) after thirty-five years of depression, global war, and then cold war, which have all functioned to reduce the domestic freedom necessary to preserve noncentralized government, is in itself testimony to their vitality as political institutions. . . . Every day, in many ways, the states are actively contributing to the achievement of American goals and to the continuing efforts to define those goals.

Consequently, it is a mistake to think that national adoption of goals shared by an overwhelming majority of the states is simply centralization. To believe that is to deny the operation of the dynamics of history within a federal system. Any assessment of the states' position in the federal union must be made against a background of continuous social change. It is no more reasonable to assume that the states have lost power vis-à-vis the federal government since 1789 because they can no longer maintain established churches than it is to believe that white men are no longer as free as they were in that year because they can no longer own slaves. An apparent loss of freedom in one sphere may be more than made up by gains in another. Massachusetts exercises more power over its economy today than its governors ever hoped to exercise over its churches five generations ago. National values change by popular consensus and *all* governments must adapt themselves to those changes. The success of the states is that they have been able to adapt themselves well.

Part of the states' adaptation has been manifested in their efforts to improve their institutional capabilities to handle the new tasks they have assumed. In the twentieth century, there has been an extensive and continuing reorganization of state governments leading to increased executive responsibility, greater central budgetary control, and growing expertise of state personnel (whose numbers are also increasing). . . .

There has also been a great and continuing increase in the states' supervision of the functions carried out in their local subdivisions. The states' role in this respect has grown as fast as or faster than that of the federal government and is often exercised more stringently, a possibility enhanced by the constitutionally unitary character of the states. The states' supervision has been increased through the provision of technical aid to their localities, through financial grants, and through control of the power to raise (or authorize the raising of) revenue for all subdivisions.

In all this, though, there remains one major unsolved problem, whose importance cannot be overemphasized: that of the metropolitan areas. By and large, the states have been unwilling or unable to do enough to meet metropolitan problems, particularly governmental ones. Here, too, some states have better records than others but none have been able to deal with metropolitan problems comprehensively and thoroughly. It is becoming increasingly clear that—whatever their successes in the past—the future role of the states will be determined by their ability to come to grips with those problems.

A fourth factor that adds to the strength and vitality of the states is the manner in which state revenues and expenditures have been expanding since the end of World War II. . . .

Still a fifth factor is the continuing role of the states as primary managers of great programs and as important innovators in the governmental realm. Both management and innovation in education, for example, continue to be primary state responsibilities in which outside aid is used to support locally initiated ideas.

Even in areas of apparent state deficiencies, many states pursue innovative policies. Much publicity has been generated in recent years that reflects upon police procedures in certain states; yet effective actions to eliminate the death penalty have been confined to the state level. The states have also been active in developing means for releasing persons accused of crimes on their own recognizance when they cannot afford to post bail, thus reducing the imprisonment of people not yet convicted of criminal activity.

Because the states are political systems able to direct the utilization of the resources sent their way, federal grants have served as a stimulus to the development of state capabilities and, hence, have helped enhance their strength and vitality. Federal grants have helped the states in a positive way by broadening the programs they can offer their citizens and strengthening state administration of those programs. Conversely, the grants have prevented centralization of those programs and have given the states the ability to maintain their position despite the centralizing tendencies of the times.

For this reason, and because the concerns of American politics are universal ones, there is relatively little basic conflict between the federal government and the states or even between their respective interests. Most of the conflicts connected with federal-state relations are of two kinds: (1) conflicts between interests that use the federal versus state argument as a means to legitimize their demands or (2) low-level conflicts over the best way to handle specific cooperative activities. There are cases, of course, when interests representing real differences are able to align themselves with different levels of government to create serious federal-state conflict. The civil rights question in its southern manifestation is today's example of that kind of situation.

Finally, the noncentralized character of American politics has served to strengthen the states. Noncentralization makes possible intergovernment cooperation without the concomitant weakening of the smaller partners by giving those partners significant ways in which to preserve their integrity. This is because a noncentralized system functions to a great extent through bargaining and negotiation. Since its components are relatively equal in their freedom to act, it can utilize only a few of the hierarchical powers available in centralized systems. In essence, its general government can only use those powers set forth in the fundamental compact between the partners as necessary to the maintenance of the system as a whole. Stated baldly, congressional authorization of new federal programs is frequently no more than a license allowing federal authorities to begin negotiations with the states and localities. . . .

In the last analysis, the states remain viable entities in a federal system that has every tendency toward centralization present in all strong governments. They remain viable because they exist as civil societies with political systems of their own. They maintain that existence because the American political tradition and the Constitution embodying it give the states an important place in the overall fabric of American civil society. The tradition and the Constitution remain viable because neither Capitol Hill nor the fifty state houses have alone been able to serve all the variegated interests on the American scene that compete equally well without working in partnership.

The states remain vital political systems for larger reasons as well as immediate ones, reasons that are often passed over unnoticed in the public's concern with day-to-day problems of government. These larger reasons are not new; though they have changed in certain details, they remain essentially the same as in the early days of the Union.

The states remain important in a continental nation as reflectors of sectional and regional differences that are enhanced by the growing social and economic complexity of every part of the country, even as the older cultural differences may be diminished by modern communications. They remain important as experimenters and innovators over a wider range of fields than ever before, simply because government at every level in the United States has been expanding. The role of the states as recruiters of political participants and trainers of political leaders has in no way been diminished, particularly since the number of political offices of every kind seems to be increasing at least in proportion to population growth.

In at least two ways, traditional roles of the states have been enhanced by recent trends. They have become even more active promoters and administrators of public services than ever before. In part, this is simply because governments are doing more than they had in the past, but it is also because they provide ways to increase governmental activity while maintaining noncentralized government. By handling important programs at a level that can be reached by many people, the contribute to the maintenance of a traditional interest of democratic politics, namely, the maximization of local control over the political and administrative deci-sion-makers whose actions affect the lives of every citizen in ever-increas-ing ways.

As the population of the nation increases, the states become increasingly able to manage major governmental activities with the competence and expertise demanded by the metropolitan–technological frontier. At the same time, the federal government becomes further removed from popular pres-sures simply by virtue of the increased size of the population it must serve. The states may well be on their way to becoming the most "manageable" civil societies in the nation. Their size and scale remain comprehensible to people even as they are enabled to do more things better.

In sum, the virtue of the federal system lies in its ability to develop and maintain mechanisms vital to the perpetuation of the unique combina-tion of governmental strength, political flexibility, and individual liberty, which has been the central concern of American politics. The American people are known to appreciate their political tradition and the Constitu-tion. Most important, they seem to appreciate the partnership, too, in some unreasoned way, and have learned to use all its elements to reasonably satisfy their claims on government.

20

DAVID OSBORNE

From *Laboratories of Democracy*

Earlier in the twentieth century, Supreme Court Justice Louis Brandeis called state governments "laboratories of democracy." States were where new policy ideas were first developed and tried out. Yet, after President Franklin Roosevelt's New Deal in the 1930s, state governments hardly seemed to be where the action was in government. A strong national government dominated American politics—until recently. Public policy specialist David Osborne looks at the way reinvigorated state governments have taken the lead in developing innovative ideas today. In this excerpt, he focuses on former Arizona governor—later Clinton administration Interior secretary— Bruce Babbitt, who transformed Arizona's old politics-as-usual state government into a modern, forward-looking one. Currently, many states utilize Babbitt's "new paradigm" in their business and educational development.

FRANKLIN ROOSEVELT once said of the New Deal, "Practically all the things we've done in the federal government are like things Al Smith did as governor of New York." There was surprising honesty in Roosevelt's remark, though he might have credited other states as well. Many of FDR's initiatives—including unemployment compensation, massive public works programs, deposit insurance, and social security— were modeled on successful state programs. The groundwork for much of the New Deal social agenda was laid in the states during the Progressive Era.

A similar process is under way today, particularly in the economic arena. The 1980s have been a decade of enormous innovation at the state level. For those unfamiliar with state politics—and given the media's relentless focus on Washington, that includes most Americans—the specifics are often startling. While the Reagan administration was denouncing government intervention in the marketplace, governors of both parties were embracing an unprecedented role as economic activists. Over the past decade, they have created well over 100 public investment funds, to make loans to and investments in businesses. Half the states have set up public venture capital funds; others have invested public money in the creation of private financial institutions. At least 40 states have created programs to stimulate technological innovation, which now number at least 200. Dozens of states have overhauled their public education systems. Tripartite business-labor-government boards have sprung up, often with the purpose of financing local committees dedicated to restructuring labor-management relations. A few states have even launched cooperative efforts with management and labor to revitalize regional industries.

Why this sudden burst of innovation at the state level? Just 25 years ago, state governments were widely regarded as the enemies of change, their resistance symbolized by George Wallace in the schoolhouse door.* The answer has to do with the profound and wrenching economic transition the United States has experienced over the past two decades. In the 1980s, a fundamentally new economy has been born. With it has come a series of new problems, new opportunities, and new challenges. In the states, government has responded.

The notion that America has left the industrial era behind is now commonplace. Some call the new age the "postindustrial era," some the "information age," others the "era of human capital." But most agree that the fundamental organization of the American and international economies that prevailed for three decades after World War II has changed. The United States has evolved from an industrial economy built upon assembly-line manufacturing in large, stable firms to a rapidly changing, knowledge-intensive economy built upon technological innovation.

The most obvious symptoms of this transition are idle factories, dislocated workers, and depressed manufacturing regions. Less obvious are the problems that inhibit our ability to innovate: a poorly educated and trained work force; adversarial relations between labor and management; inadequate supplies of risk capital; and corporate institutions that lag behind their foreign competitors in the speed with which they commercialize the fruits of their research, adopt new production technologies, and exploit foreign markets.

Jimmy Carter was elected just as the public began to sense that something had gone wrong with the American economy. Like other national politicians of his day, he only dimly perceived the emerging realities of the new economy. Ronald Reagan owed his election to the deepening

*George Wallace was the governor of Alabama in 1963, when the federal government forced the state to integrate its schools following the Supreme Court's 1954 *Brown v. Board of Education* decision. President Kennedy mobilized the Alabama National Guard, despite the governor's defiance of the desegregation decree. Governor Wallace gave a speech against desegregation at the schoolhouse door before the guard ushered African–American students into the building. — EDS.

economic crisis, but his solution was to reach back to the free-market myths of the preindustrial era. He had the luxury to do so because he governed an enormously diverse nation, in which rapid growth along both coasts balanced the pain experienced in the industrial and agricultural heartland.

Most governors have not had that luxury. When unemployment approached 13 percent in Massachusetts, or 15 percent in Pennsylvania, or 18 percent in Michigan, governors had to respond. They could not afford to wait for the next recovery, or to evoke the nostrums of free-market theory.

The same dynamic occurred during the last great economic transformation: the birth of our industrial economy. The Progressive movement, which originated at the state and local level, grew up in response to the new problems created by rapid industrialization: the explosion of the cities, the emergence of massive corporate trusts, the growth of urban political machines, the exploitation of industrial labor.* Many Progressive reforms introduced in the cities or states were gradually institutionalized at the federal level—culminating in the New Deal.

This reality led Supreme Court Justice Louis Brandeis to coin his famous phrase, "laboratories of democracy." One of America's leading Progressive activists during the early decades of the twentieth century, Brandeis viewed the states as laboratories in which the Progressives could experiment with new solutions to social and economic problems. Those that worked could be applied nationally; those that failed could be discarded.

Brandeis's phrase captured the peculiar, pragmatic genius of the federal system. As one approach to government—one political paradigm—wears thin, its successor is molded in the states, piece by piece. The process has little to do with ideology and everything to do with trial-and-error, seat-of-the-pants pragmatism. Part of the beauty, as Brandeis pointed out, is that new ideas can be tested on a limited scale—to see if they work, and to see if they sell—before they are imposed on the entire nation.

Today, at both the state and local levels, we are in the midst of a new progressive era. Just as the state and local Progressivism of Brandeis's day

---

*Progressivism was a movement that developed during the first two decades of the twentieth century advocating reform at all levels of government. Well-known as progressives were Governor Robert La Follette of Wisconsin and President Theodore Roosevelt, who ran as a Progressive in the 1912 presidential election. Progressives wanted to clean up urban government, throw out party bosses, and place more power in the hands of ordinary voters through referendum and the direct primary. In journalism, the Muckrakers uncovered political corruption, exploitative working conditions, corporate greed, and consumer abuse as targets for Progressive reform.—EDS.

foreshadowed the New Deal, the state and local experimentation of the 1980s may foreshadow a new national agenda. . . .

Life in Arizona is something few Americans raised east of the Mississippi would recognize. Two-thirds of all state residents were born elsewhere. Half arrived in the last fifteen years. Every fall a third of the students in the typical Phoenix school district are new. In 1986, *61* new shopping centers were completed or under way in the Phoenix metropolitan area.

In the mid-1980s, Phoenix was the nation's fastest growing city; Arizona one of its fastest growing states. At the current pace, the Phoenix area will double its population of 1.9 million—nearly half the state total—within 15 years. Every year this mushrooming metropolis—an endless expanse of one-story, suburban-style homes and shopping centers—gobbles up thousands of acres of desert in a race for the horizon. At 400 square miles, it now covers more ground than New York City.

This explosive growth has transformed a dusty, sparsely populated frontier state into a land of the modern, Sunbelt metropolis. Arizona was the last of the contiguous 48 states to join the union, in 1912. By 1940, it had only 500,000 people, spread out in small, desert towns and over vast Indian reservations. Phoenix had only 65,000 people. But World War II brought military bases and defense plants, and the postwar boom brought air conditioning and air travel. Suddenly Arizona's location and climate were advantages, rather than disadvantages. The defense contractors, aerospace companies, and electronics manufacturers poured in, bringing an army of young engineers and technicians with their wives and their children. This was the Eisenhower generation—raised during the depression, hardened by World War II, anxious for the security of a job, a home, and a future for their children. With their crew cuts and their conservatism, they transformed Arizona from a sleepy, almost southern Democratic state into a bastion of Sunbelt Republicanism.

Before the Republican takeover in the 1950s, the farmers, the mining companies, and the bankers had run the state. Copper, cotton, and cattle were king. "It used to be that there were five or six men who would sit around a luncheon table at the old Arizona Club and pretty much decide on how things were going to be," says Jack Pfister, general manager of the Salt River Project, the state's largest water and power utility. "Some legislators were said to wear a copper collar."

At first, the new suburban middle class did not change this arrangement a great deal. Real estate developers, the new millionaires on the block, joined the club. But even as the Republicans cemented their control in the 1960s, rural legislators held onto the reins of seniority—and thus power. State government was tiny, the governor a figurehead. And the new suburbanites embraced the frontier ethos in which the old Arizona had taken such pride. Ignoring the fact that without major government investments—in military bases, defense plants, and dams—Arizona would still be a rural backwater, they believed their newfound prosperity was the product of untrammeled free enterprise. Beginning in 1952, they voted Republican in every presidential election. They had little truck with Washington. In the 1950s, Arizona declined to participate in the federal Interstate Highway System; in the 1960s, it turned down medicaid. As local people still say with a hint of pride, Arizona is the last preserve of the lone gun slinger.

The combination of explosive growth and a frontier mentality created problems very different from those encountered by the other states profiled in this book. "In the East, you have old cities, old infrastructure, and a fight for economic survival," says Republican Senator Anne Lindemann. "Here, we're trying to control the growth as best we can."

This process was not without its lessons for the rest of the nation, however. Because Arizona is a desert, with a fragile ecosystem, its rapid growth threw into sharp relief the most serious environmental problems of the postindustrial era—particularly those involving water and toxic chemicals. And because the political climate makes public resources so scarce, the struggle to cope with the social problems created by a modern economy stimulated a degree of creativity rarely seen in a conservative state.

The task of dragging Arizona into the modern era fell to Bruce Babbitt, who by the time he left office in 1987 had changed the very nature of the governorship. A lanky, scholarly type whose habitual slouch and thoughtful manner hide an enormous drive, Babbitt looks like a cross between Donald Sutherland and Tom Poston. He has sandy hair, a lined face that has begun to sag with the wear of 14 years in politics, and large, pale eyes that bulge out from behind his eyebrows when he scowls. In a small group, when he is in his natural, analytic mode, Babbitt can be brilliant. On a dais, when he tries to sound like a politician, his body stiffens, his eyes bulge, and he does a good imitation of Don Knotts.

Despite his weakness as a public speaker, Babbitt captivated the Arizona electorate. He was elected in 1978 with 52 percent of the vote, re-elected four years later, during a recession, with 62 percent. Summing up the Babbitt years, the *Arizona Republic*, a conservative newspaper, called him the "take-charge governor." "He is without a doubt the smartest, quickest elected official I have ever met," an environmental activist told me, in a comment echoed by many others. "Babbitt plays it on the precipice," added a state senator. "He is constantly pushing this state forward, and he has an uncanny ability to pull it off." . . .

Traditionally, the governor's office in Arizona had been extremely weak. Arizona was perhaps the only state in the union in which a governor would consider the ambassadorship to Argentina a step up. State government was run by a small group of senior legislators and their staffs, who brought out the governor for ceremonial occasions. The notion that a governor might try to set an agenda for the state, or dare to veto a bill, never crossed most politicians' minds.

Babbitt immediately set out to change that. Six weeks into his term he vetoed two bills on the same day—then timed his veto message for the evening news, knocking the wind out of a planned override. The legislature reacted with shock. "Our idea of an activist governor was one who met with us once a month to seek our advice," said Alfredo Gutierrez. "This guy called us daily to tell us what he wanted to do."

Babbitt vetoed 21 bills in 1979, 30 more over the next two years. His total of 114 vetoes in nine years was more than double the record set by Arizona's first governor, who served for 13 years. "My business friends used to complain that we had a weak governor," says Jack Pfister. "After Babbitt was in there about two or three years, you never heard anybody complain about that again. What he demonstrated was that it was more the individual than the structure of the office itself." . . .

In Arizona, the economic problem has been too much growth, not too little. Ever since Motorola built an R&D center for military electronics in Phoenix in 1948, high-tech manufacturers have flocked to the state. They have been lured—many of them from nearby California—by the cheap land, the cheap labor, and the desert climate, all of which make Arizona perfect for manufacturing precision electronics. As time passed, the only problems they experienced arose from the state's failure to keep up with their growth.

The most pressing problem, aside from water, was the higher education system. Arizona State University, the major school in the Phoenix area, was known for big-time sports and big-time parties. *Playboy* once named it the nation's number one party school. Its engineering and business schools were second rate. As the high-tech industries boomed, they began having trouble recruiting engineers—many of whom wanted to update their education every three to five years to remain on top of their fields— because of the poor reputation of ASU's engineering school. In 1978, industry leaders created an advisory committee to work with the school and took their case to the governor.

Babbitt stole their thunder. His friend Pat Haggerty, the founder and then chairman of Texas Instruments, had convinced him that sustained high-tech growth depended upon top-quality higher education and research institutions. He interrupted the committee presentation, told them about Haggerty, and instructed them to think big. "I'm not interested in being behind short-term or small-time budget increases," he said. "Come back to me with a sweeping multiyear program, and I'll support you."

The advisory committee drew up a five-year plan calling for $32 million in new investments in the engineering school—from industry, from the federal government, and from the state. (As it worked out, industry raised $18.5 million, the federal government contributed about $8 million, and the state provided about $28 million.) With both the governor and the business community pushing the package, the legislature embraced it. Between 1979 and 1984, the College of Engineering and Applied Science built a 120,000-square-foot Engineering Research Center, installed $15 million worth of new equipment, hired 65 new faculty, moved from $1 million a year in research to $9.4 million, and set up a continuing education program that included televised classes beamed right into local plants and offices. In 1984, the National Academy of Sciences ranked ASU's Mechanical Engineering and Electrical Engineering departments second and third in the nation, respectively, in improvement over the previous five years.

In July 1985, the advisory committee and the engineering school adopted a second five-year plan. This one called for $62 million in new money, split among industry, the federal government, and the state. The goal was to move the school into the top ten in the nation.

ASU also launched a university research park. It decided to allow professors to own their own companies, to spend 20 percent of their time working in industry, and to keep a portion of the patent rights on their discoveries. The Babbitt administration played a role in both developments. Babbitt also pushed through a new Disease Control Research Commission, to fund medical research.

Throughout this period, Babbitt worked hard to convince the public that investment in its universities was critical. "In earlier, less complex times, universities were nice to have but not essential to economic growth," he said in a 1983 speech to a high-technology symposium he organized. "When Arizona's first great industry, copper, developed in the late nineteenth century, the main ingredient for success was a strong back and a lot of courage in the face of drought. Then came tourism; its principal ingredients were sunshine and hospitality."

"Now, in 1983, high technology is our growth industry, and the essential resource to sustain high technology cannot be mined from the hills or grown in our soil or derived from hospitality. The main ingredient of the new high-technology evolution is education, in the form of well-educated citizens with strong scientific and technical skills. . . . Universities and colleges are now an economic asset as important to our economic future as copper ore, farms, banks, factories, and airlines." . . .

If traditional liberalism was the thesis and Reagan conservatism was its antithesis, the developments in America's state capitols offer the glimmerings of a new synthesis—a paradigm that may foreshadow the *next* realignment of American politics, as progressivism foreshadowed New Deal liberalism. The thesis, in its purist form, viewed the private sector as the problem and government as the solution. The antithesis, again in its extreme form, viewed government as the problem and the private sector as the solution. The synthesis redefines the nature of both the problem and its solution. It defines the problem as our changing role in the international marketplace. It defines the solution as new roles for and new relationships between our national institutions—public sector and private, labor and management, education and business. The fundamental goal is no longer to create—or eliminate—government programs; it is to use government to change the nature of the marketplace. To boil it down to a slogan, if the thesis was government as solution and the antithesis was government as problem, the synthesis is government as partner.

The new paradigm can be described as a series of interdependent assumptions about political reality, which together form a coherent way of thinking about our problems. The first assumption is that economic growth must be our major priority, but that it can be combined with equity, environmental protection, and other social goals. Whereas interest-group liberals put their social goals first, and Reagan conservatives put growth first, many governors are beginning to understand that in the new economy, growth *requires* equity and environmental protection.

Second, and perhaps most important, the new breed of governor assumes that the real solutions lie in changing the structure of the marketplace. By the late 1960s, many liberals had come to view the market as the problem; often they saw government as a way to overcome or replace the market. If the market would not build low-income housing, government would. If the market would not bring capital into Appalachia, government would. Reagan conservatives, in contrast, wanted government out of the marketplace—a logical contradiction, given that government sets the rules that allow the marketplace to operate. Today both Democratic and Republican governors understand that the market is far more powerful than government—that government cannot "overcome" or "replace" it. But they also understand that government *shapes* the market. To solve problems, they change the rules of the marketplace, or they use government to channel the market in new directions.

A related assumption has to do with attitudes toward government bureaucracies. Today's governors search for nonbureaucratic solutions to problems; if reshaping the marketplace will not suffice, they turn to third-sector organizations. They believe that many of the large, centralized government programs created in the past—medicaid, medicare, welfare, housing programs—have been inefficient and wasteful (often because government had to buy off the private sector, as in the case of medicare and medicaid). . . .

The fourth assumption is that in the newly competitive global economy, our governments have in a sense bumped up against their fiscal limits. Every governor portrayed in this book has taken great pains to make it clear to the electorate that he is not a big spender. . . .

The fifth assumption flows from the fiscal climate: if public resources are relatively scarce, they must be *invested*, not merely spent. Interest-group liberals responded to many problems, as Ronald Reagan likes to say, by "throwing money at them." If people were poor, the solution was higher welfare grants, more food stamps, greater housing subsidies. Reagan and his followers responded to the same problems by taking money away. The failure of both approaches has created a deep ambivalence within the American public, and a desire for a third path. When public opinion polls ask voters if welfare spending should be increased, they overwhelmingly say no. When polls ask if we have a responsibility to improve the plight of the poor, they overwhelmingly say yes. This seeming contradiction actually has a compelling logic: voters want solutions, but not the ones the two parties have traditionally offered.

The governors are gradually working out new ways to address these problems, by investing in the capacities of poor people and poor communities. "I think the American people don't want to simply break with our commitment to improve the lives of the poor; they don't want to throw all that away," says Art Hamilton, the black minority leader of the Arizona House. "But they don't want to have to pay for all the Great Society madness. People don't believe that the welfare system is designed to put itself out of business; that's what bothers a lot of the people I talk to. If the system were designed to lift people from where they are to where their potential can take them, I think people would gladly support that system." . . .

The new paradigm also involves new assumptions about the proper roles of federal, state, and local governments. The New Deal was a time in which America finally accepted bigness: big business, big labor, and big government. An economy dominated by large, stable, mass-production industries required large, centralized institutions in all three areas. Today, however, our economy is decentralizing. Mass production is moving offshore, and smaller, more automated, more flexible manufacturing operations are thriving in the United States. In the service sector small businesses are proliferating, and in both sectors the entrepreneurial process is accelerating. In 1985, seven times as many new businesses were formed as in 1950. . . .

If current state trends do foreshadow national politics, these principles—growth with equity, a focus on market solutions, a search for nonbureaucratic methods, fiscal moderation, investment rather than spending, redistribution of opportunity rather than outcomes, and a new federalism—provide a rough outline of the next political paradigm.

21

LARRY GERSTON
TERRY CHRISTENSEN

From *Recall!*

Few events in state government can compare in drama and publicity with the events in California in 2003. Californians voted Governor Gray Davis out of office in a recall election and replaced him by voting in Arnold Schwarzenegger. Larry Gerston and Terry Christensen examine this exciting moment in recent political history, focusing not only on the winner, a champion bodybuilder and cinema star, but also on the recall process. The authors trace the origin of the Progressive era reforms that created recall, referendum, and initiative, all of which brought direct democracy to the state and local level in some areas of the country. They then turn to the California "earthquake" of 2003: why and how it happened, and the way in which Schwarzenegger ultimately emerged from the recall as the new governor. Students of political science will surely disagree on the wisdom of direct democracy in allowing the people to quickly and directly change policies and even government officials before scheduled elections. Yet the excitement and optimism that "the Governator" engendered cannot be disputed. For Governor Schwarzenegger, the challenge just began with his recall victory. Governing a state with a strong tradition of direct democracy is another matter.

WELCOME TO CALIFORNIA. You'd better have your passport in hand, because this is a different place from just about anywhere else you might go. California is the land of innovation, fads, and extremes. Check out almost any value or concept in the other forty-nine states and you may find it testing the limits and forging new boundaries in California. What you see here today, you will find in the rest of the country tomorrow. The tax revolt, environmental movement, and even anti-spam legislation began in California. And it is in this volatile, changing, strained political environment where the recall—a way for voters to yank elected officials from power at virtually a moment's notice—has taken root and blossomed.

Recall! California's Political Earthquake documents the latest chapter in California's exotic history, explosive present, and unpredictable future. Carried out in a state that is known for make-believe, the events behind *Recall!* are the true story of a polity that almost crashed under the weight of its own problems, a governor unable to manage public expectations, a public that simultaneously demanded answers to expensive questions but wanted them at no financial cost, and a cast of adversaries primed to take advantage of unique political, economic, and social circumstances.

California is not the first state ever to suffer from deficits, power outages, and a decaying infrastructure. But California has a provision in its state constitution that allows the voters, for no particular reason, to remove from office any elected official, thus making it easy to exercise public will on a mere whim. That incredibly low threshold for change was tested in the recall effort against Governor Gray Davis on October 7, 2003. As a result, California's "direct democracy" laboratory exceeded the wildest dreams of the reformers who brought the concept to the state nearly one hundred years ago. . . .

California has long been a source of ideas, policies, and institutions that pop up elsewhere, as trends radiate from the state's constantly changing politics. Direct democracy has been a major source of these trends. While not invented in California, direct democracy reached its apogee there. The concept of direct democracy, especially for amendments to state constitutions, goes back more than one hundred years. South Dakota was the first state to adopt the initiative and referendum—enabling voters to make policy or rescind acts of the legislature—in 1898. A dozen other states followed soon after. Oregon was the first to adopt the recall of elected officials in 1908. California adopted all three tools of direct democracy in one sweeping package in 1911. . . .

No one is more responsible for the introduction of direct democracy to California than Hiram Johnson. The Progressive reformer gained his fame by taking on the much-feared and powerful Southern Pacific Railroad, which had used its economic prowess to dominate state politics. Rejecting what he perceived as an unholy alliance among big business, political parties, and elected officials, Johnson advocated tirelessly for a government where the people could have the final say. His zeal catapulted him to the governor's office where, in his inaugural address, Johnson stated that a successful government "must rest primarily on the rights of men and the absolute sovereignty of the people." Passionately advocating that every citizen be "his own legislature," Johnson called on the legislature and the people to adopt the concepts of direct democracy — the initiative, referendum, and recall. The initiative enables citizens to make policy directly by securing signatures from the voters in order to place issues before them (for laws, 5 percent of those who voted in the previous gubernatorial election is required; for constitutional amendments, 8 percent). The referendum allows voters to overturn acts of the legislature. Referenda qualify for the ballot when petitioners attain a number of signatures equivalent to 5 percent of participants in the most recent gubernatorial election. Finally, if sponsors collect enough signatures to place the issue on the ballot, the recall allows citizens to remove elected officials from their positions.

But while other states have also adopted direct democracy, none have used its mechanisms more frequently than California. Referenda and recalls have been rare, but initiatives have become commonplace in California. Between 1912 and 1977, 159 initiatives qualified for the ballot, although only 43 were approved. Then, in 1978, Californians rediscovered the initiative with Proposition 13, the property tax reform initiative that launched voter revolts around the country and around the world. Angry voters, organized interest groups, candidates on the make, and political consultants latched onto the initiative, placing 132 measures on the ballot between 1978 and 2003; of these, 55 passed.

Among them were many measures restricting the taxing powers of state and local government in California — the progeny of Proposition 13. California became known for "ballot box budgeting," a phenomenon that tied the hands of governors and legislators facing fiscal crises. Noting the success of these efforts in California, other states followed suit. But beyond the use of the initiatives, California had set off a taxpayer revolt that spread to states and nations lacking the option of direct democracy. Antitax sentiment swept the country and the world.

Meanwhile, back at the ballot box, Californians busily set other national and international trends throughout the 1990s. California was among the first states to adopt term limits for state legislators in 1990, cutting their staffs and other resources at the same time; the term limits movement soon spread across the country, almost always by initiative. In 1994, California voters approved Proposition 187, an initiative restricting government services to illegal immigrants. Although the federal courts ruled much of the measure unconstitutional, Californians (not for the first time) expressed their anti-immigrant sentiments and put the immigration issue on the political agenda. That same year, Californians enacted the "three strikes" initiative, imposing strict and lengthy sentences on those who commit three felonies. Other states and the federal government soon adopted the three strikes rule. Two years later, Californians stoked the national debate about affirmative action by approving Proposition 209, an initiative to eliminate affirmative action by California state and local governments. A ban on bilingual education followed in 1998, again a forerunner to a national debate. California is still locked in combat with the federal government over the medical use of marijuana—approved by California voters in 1996 and in other states since then but still banned nationally.

As for the recall, until 2003, this device had been used almost exclusively against local government officials. Depending on the office, anywhere between 10 and 30 percent of the voters are required to sign petitions over periods of time ranging from 40 to 160 days. Historically, recalls have been used against school boards more than any other group of elected officials. The recall has been used successfully on state legislators only four times in its entire history, and no member of the state executive branch had ever been recalled until 2003.

California governors have not been exempt from recall efforts, however. Thirty-one previous attempts have failed to collect the necessary signatures—12 percent of those voting in the previous gubernatorial election. None even came close to qualifying for the ballot. Based on the 12 percent requirement, recall proponents in 2003 needed 897,158 valid signatures. Most experienced political observers doubted that such a number could be reached. But while the requirements for recalling a statewide official in California seem intimidating, it should be noted that the state's 12 percent threshold is the second lowest of the eighteen recall states, perhaps a source of encouragement to proponents in the early days of signature-gathering. Montana has the lowest requirement with 10 percent. Of the seventeen remaining recall states, all but three require 20 percent or more of the voters to sign petitions; most require 25 percent or more, and Kansas requires 40 percent. California also makes recall somewhat easier than some other states by requiring no specific grounds—such as corruption or malfeasance. Californians can recall officials just because they don't like them. But whatever the standard, the recall of statewide officials is extremely rare in American politics. Only one governor, North

Dakota's Lynn Frazier, had been recalled before 2003, and that was in 1921.

The initiative, referendum, and recall have always been powerful potential tools of direct voter involvement in the political process. But whereas the initiative has become a staple of California politics, the recall was more a threat than a reality. That tool was activated in 2003, changing forever the rules of political engagement in California politics. . . .

Governors are the most important of all state officeholders. In more cases than not, they enjoy veto power over legislative decisions, mold the courts by their nominations of judges, and possess superior access to information through management of the bureaucracy. Simply put, governors are at the apex of state power because of the clout associated with their offices—an endowment matched nowhere in American politics other than the U.S. presidency. No wonder that in 2002 alone Frank Murkowski left the U.S. Senate to become Alaska's governor, while Rod Blagojevich and Robert Ehrlich, Jr., gave up seats in the U.S. House of Representatives to become governors of Illinois and Maryland, respectively.

With so much authority at their disposal, governors can initiate, promote, oversee, and control public policies. One well-known book about governors concludes that their ability to manage issues ranging from preschool education to care for the elderly "predicts their chances for advancement" to higher office, perhaps the presidency. This is especially true in California where, with 55 of the nation's 538 electoral votes, the governor is automatically considered presidential timber.

Likewise, failure to manage a state's pressing problems can spell difficult times for a governor. Such a predicament overcame California Governor Gray Davis. Within a period of 2 short years, the state was ravaged by an electrical power crisis, a suddenly depressed economy, and a budget deficit larger than the entire budgets of sixteen states. Regardless of whether these disasters were predictable or avoidable, the responsibility for solving them fell to Governor Gray Davis—at least in the eyes of the public. Whether Davis handled them well became more than a debatable question—it became a theme of the recall election movement. In a state known for bizarre movies with unpredictable endings, it would be hard to imagine more perfect elements for a storm of political revolt. . . .

When California's economy tanked, Gray Davis was in charge because he was governor. Likewise, when the state's power went off, Gray Davis was in charge. And when the deficit spun out of control, Gray Davis was in charge. Whether Davis could have actually fixed these problems by himself is not the question. Simply put, in a state where the public expected its highest elected official to manage the various formal and informal obstacles before him, he did not fulfill expectations. Further, whatever his concerns about these issues, Davis did not seem to relate them to the public in the compassionate, caring way that they expected and needed. For these reasons, Davis's biggest problem may have been in the public's perception of his personality rather than any realistic appraisal of his effort. And in results-oriented, personality-driven California, that lapse in judgment was more than enough to put the governor on the carpet—and send him away. . . .

The entry of Arnold Schwarzenegger into the race to replace Davis was a dream come true for the media. Until the moment of his announcement, Schwarzenegger had told reporters—and even his own campaign consultants—that he would refrain from entering the contest in deference to former Los Angeles Mayor Richard Riordan, once the front runner in the 2002 Republican primary until Davis attack ads tilted the outcome in favor of conservative Bill Simon.

On August 6, [2003,] only 3 days before the filing deadline, Schwarzenegger scheduled an appearance on the *Tonight Show*, ostensibly to explain why he wasn't going to run and why he would defer to long-time friend Riordan. In a vintage Hollywood moment detailing to host Jay Leno his thoughts about the recall, Schwarzenegger declared, "The politicians are fiddling, fumbling and failing, and the man who is failing more than anyone is Gray Davis. He's failing them terribly, and this is why he needs to be recalled. And this is why I'm going to run for governor of California." The crowd burst into cheers and applause as Schwarzenegger orchestrated the first of many well-timed moves to victory. On August 9, the last day of the filing period, Schwarzenegger filed his papers before a national audience of millions of viewers.

Who is Arnold Schwarzenegger? The Davis camp tried to paint him as a one-dimensional action figure who was attempting to leverage his entertainment-generated popularity with the voters. Yet that was only part of the Schwarzenegger persona. Living what he described as the "immigrant's dream," the Austrian-born Schwarzenegger came to the United States as a teenager with $20 in his pocket, put himself through college, and began his now-famous bodybuilding career. From there he became a successful actor. But there were other sides to Schwarzenegger. He became involved in several business ventures and grew more active in politics. As early as 1984, he was active in national Republican campaigns. His 1986 marriage to Maria Shriver, a television journalist and member of the Kennedy clan, drew Schwarzenegger further into the political world. In 2002, he led the way on California's Proposition 49, an initiative that provided surplus state budget money for after-school programs. The initiative passed handily, although no surplus dollars have appeared. Whatever else Schwarzenegger was or was not, he had had exposure to politics in high places.

Indeed, the Schwarzenegger campaign resonated like no other. From his televised appearance on the *Tonight Show* until his election, Schwarzenegger leveraged his movie stardom to political success with masterful, well-planned strokes. Repeatedly, his well-known movie lines became the foundation of his political statements. During the Leno interview, for example, Schwarzenegger warned that elected officials needed to meet the public's expectations, "otherwise you are 'hasta la vista baby,'" referring to a line from his successful role in the *Terminator* movies. As *San Francisco Chronicle* political reporter Carla Marinucci observed, his appearance on Leno's show "had all the elements of another hit movie: suspense, humor and drama, a great script—a surprise Hollywood ending."

But it was more than just drama or the use of clever lines. Schwarzenegger's overall strategy underscored a fundamental point: He used his celebrity as political capital—in place of the traditional building blocks on which seasoned politicians depend. Whereas other major candidates relied on conventional endorsements, phone banking, and historic voting loyalties, Schwarzenegger counted on the personal connection between his movies and his fans. This populist approach gave star-struck voters the feeling that he was talking to them directly.

Despite the informality, there were few ad-libs in Schwarzenegger's campaign. Like a well-scripted movie, every aspect of the effort was carried out with discipline and precision. Early on, he committed to one political debate from the half dozen scheduled among the top-tier candidates, claiming that he would be too busy campaigning and "meeting with the voters." The debate in which he participated was the only one where the candidates knew the questions in advance. Opponents screamed that he was choreographing his campaign and not subjecting himself to the rigors of strict scrutiny; Schwarzenegger stayed on and within his own schedule and campaign design.

Accusations came and went. Nothing stuck, whether it was past statements, past behaviors, or past voting records. And the allegations seemed endless, ranging from illegal entry to being a Nazi sympathizer to having a poor voting record. When he was accused of being a sexist, Schwarzenegger and his wife, NBC correspondent Maria Shriver, appeared on the *Oprah Winfrey Show*, where 86 percent of the viewers are female. With his wife next to him, Schwarzenegger explained his earlier public statements about women as playful, harmless attempts to be friendly. Comedian David Letterman seemed to put the entire issue to rest when, reminding his national audience of former president Bill Clinton's dalliances, said, "I'm telling you, this guy [Schwarzenegger] is presidential material." Quipped fellow comedian Jay Leno, "You've got Arnold, who groped a few women, or Davis, who screwed the whole state." And just like that, the issue was neutralized.

But more than his defense was Schwarzenegger's ability to make his case before a national audience in a controlled environment. Even the groping accusations cited in the *Los Angeles Times* met with more—not less—voter support. Movie stardom had its benefits, about that there was little doubt.

As Schwarzenegger fought off attacks against his character, he defined himself as a political moderate in line with the values of most Californians. He kept his speeches brief and offered few details other than the big picture on major topics. People were less concerned about specifics, he would say, and more interested in leadership and "action, action, action." And with that he straddled the line. On the question of abortion, for example, he identified with a woman's right to choose what to do about an unwanted pregnancy. When asked about gun control, he agreed that the state had the right to control the conditions of gun ownership. And on the question of gay rights, Schwarzenegger stated that he had no opposition to the issue. Each of these positions endeared Schwarzenegger to sizable elements of the moderate electorate. At the same time, he reached out to conservatives when he railed against more taxes, demanded reversal of the automobile license fee increases, and called for California to become business-friendly again. The fact that Schwarzenegger managed to hold onto both conservatives and moderates was a harbinger of the kind of broad support he would develop by the campaign's end. . . .

The voters spoke with amazing clarity on Election Day. On the question of whether Governor Davis should be recalled, the electorate said "yes" by a margin of 55.4 to 44.6 percent. All of the Davis endorsements, appearances by national Democratic heavyweights, and decades of political experience were pushed aside in favor of new leadership. But by whom?

On the question of who would replace Davis, the first choice of the voters was Arnold Schwarzenegger. No, Schwarzenegger did not get a majority, but he came close with 48.6 percent. That percentage was remarkable, given so many other replacement candidates on the ballot. . . .

Schwarzenegger argues that his election was a mandate for change—"the people's veto of politics as usual,"—but he won with 48.6 percent of the vote. Will that be enough or can he build on it? Or will he succumb to politics as usual himself, falling into the fund-raising and deal-making routines of his predecessors? . . .

Whatever happens, the state and nation will witness some interesting moments in the months and years ahead. There is little question that a political earthquake has rocked California. Now we await the aftershocks here and elsewhere.

PART FIVE

Congress

22

DAVID MAYHEW

From *Congress: The Electoral Connection*

Congressional scholar David Mayhew admits from the start that his explanation for the motivation of members of Congress is one-dimensional: they are "single-minded seekers of reelection." While Mayhew's thesis is intentionally narrow and his examples a bit out-of-date (none of the members cited in the excerpt is still in the House), reelection remains a primary motivator for congressional behavior. To attain reelection, representatives use three strategies. They advertise, so that their names are well-known. They claim credit for goodies that flow to their districts. And they take positions on political issues. Mayhew's theme, illustrated with amusing examples, may seem cynical, but it is doubtlessly realistic. Perhaps his analysis should have been fair warning to members of Congress about the public's growing disillusionment with the national legislature.

———

. . . I SHALL CONJURE UP a vision of United States congressmen as single-minded seekers of reelection, see what kinds of activity that goal implies, and then speculate about how congressmen so motivated are likely to go about building and sustaining legislative institutions and making policy. . . .

I find an emphasis on the reelection goal attractive for a number of reasons. First, I think it fits political reality rather well. Second, it puts the spotlight directly on men rather than on parties and pressure groups, which in the past have often entered discussions of American politics as analytic phantoms. Third, I think politics is best studied as a struggle among men to gain and maintain power and the consequences of that struggle. Fourth—and perhaps most important—the reelection quest establishes an accountability relationship with an electorate, and any serious thinking about democratic theory has to give a central place to the question of accountability. . . .

Whether they are safe or marginal, cautious or audacious, congressmen must constantly engage in activities related to reelection. There will be differences in emphasis, but all members share the root need to do things—indeed, to do things day in and day out during their terms. The next step here is to present a typology, a short list of the *kinds* of activities congressmen find it electorally useful to engage in. . . .

One activity is *advertising*, defined here as any effort to disseminate one's name among constituents in such a fashion as to create a favorable image but in messages having little or no issue content. A successful congressman builds what amounts to a brand name, which may have a generalized electoral value for other politicians in the same family. The personal qualities to emphasize are experience, knowledge, responsiveness, concern, sincerity, independence, and the like. Just getting one's name across is difficult enough; only about half the electorate, if asked, can supply their House members' names. It helps a congressman to be known. "In the main, recognition carries a positive valence; to be perceived at all is to be perceived favorably." A vital advantage enjoyed by House incumbents is that they are much better known among voters than their November challengers. They are better known because they spend a great deal of time, energy, and money trying to make themselves better known. There are standard routines—frequent visits to the constituency, nonpolitical speeches to home audiences, the sending out of infant care booklets and letters of condolence and congratulation. . . .

Some routines are less standard. Congressman George E. Shipley (D., Ill.) claims to have met personally about half his constituents (i.e. some 200,000 people). For over twenty years Congressman Charles C. Diggs, Jr. (D., Mich.) has run a radio program featuring himself as a "combination disc jockey–commentator and minister." Congressman Daniel J. Flood (D., Pa.) is "famous for appearing unannounced and often uninvited at wedding anniversaries and other events." Anniversaries and other events aside, congressional advertising is done largely at public expense. Use of the franking privilege has mushroomed in recent years; in early 1973 one estimate predicted that House and Senate members would send out about 476 million pieces of mail in the year 1974, at a public cost of $38.1 million—or about 900,000 pieces per member with a subsidy of $70,000 per member. By far the heaviest mailroom traffic comes in Octobers of even-numbered years. There are some differences between House and Senate members in the ways they go about getting their names across. House members are free to blanket their constituencies with mailings for all boxholders; senators are not. But senators find it easier to appear on national television—for example, in short reaction statements on the nightly news shows. Advertising is a staple congressional activity, and there is no end to it. For each member there are always new voters to be apprised of his worthiness and old voters to be reminded of it.

A second activity may be called *credit claiming*, defined here as acting so as to generate a belief in a relevant political actor (or actors) that one is personally responsible for causing the government, or some unit thereof, to do something that the actor (or actors) considers desirable. The political logic of this, from the congressman's point of view, is that an actor who believes that a member can make pleasing things happen will no doubt wish to keep him in office so that he can make pleasing things happen in the future. The emphasis here is on individual accomplishment (rather than, say, party or governmental accomplishment) and on the congressman as doer (rather than as, say, expounder of constituency views). Credit claiming is highly important to congressmen, with the consequence that much of congressional life is a relentless search for opportunities to engage in it.

Where can credit be found? . . . For the average congressman the staple way of doing this is to traffic in what may be called "particularized benefits." . . .

In sheer volume the bulk of particularized benefits come under the heading of "casework"—the thousands of favors congressional offices perform for supplicants in ways that normally do not require legislative action. High school students ask for essay materials, soldiers for emergency leaves, pensioners for location of missing checks, local governments for grant information, and on and on. Each office has skilled professionals who can play the bureaucracy like an organ—pushing the right pedals to produce the desired effects. But many benefits require new legislation, or at least they require important allocative decisions on matters covered by existent legislation. Here the congressman fills the traditional role of supplier of goods to the home district. It is a believable role; when a member claims credit for a benefit on the order of a dam, he may well receive it. Shiny construction projects seem especially useful. . . .

The third activity congressmen engage in may be called *position taking*, defined here as the public enunciation of a judgmental statement on anything likely to be of interest to political actors. The statement may take the form of a roll call vote. The most important classes of judgmental statements are those prescribing American governmental ends (a vote cast against the war; a statement that "the war should be ended immediately") or governmental means (a statement that "the way to end the war is to take it to the United Nations"). . . .

The ways in which positions can be registered are numerous and often imaginative. There are floor addresses ranging from weighty orations to mass-produced "nationality day statements." There are speeches before home groups, television appearances, letters, newsletters, press releases, ghostwritten books, *Playboy* articles, even interviews with political scientists. . . . Outside the roll call process the congressman is usually able to tailor his positions to suit his audiences. . . .

. . . On a controversial issue a Capitol Hill office normally prepares two form letters to send out to constituent letter writers—one for the pros and one (not directly contradictory) for the antis. Handling discrete audiences in person requires simple agility, a talent well demonstrated in this selection from a Nader profile*:

"You may find this difficult to understand," said Democrat Edward R. Roybal, the Mexican-American representative from California's thirtieth district, "but sometimes I wind up making a patriotic speech one afternoon and later on that same day an anti-war speech. In the patriotic speech I speak of past wars but I also speak of the need to prevent more wars. My positions are not inconsistent; I just approach different people differently." Roybal went on to depict the diversity of crowds he speaks to: one afternoon he is surrounded by balding men wearing Veterans' caps and holding American flags; a few hours later he speaks to a crowd of Chicano youths, angry over American involvement in Vietnam. Such a diverse constituency, Roybal believes, calls for different methods of expressing one's convictions.

Indeed it does.

23

RICHARD FENNO

From *Home Style*

Stated simply, political scientist Richard Fenno had a wonderful idea for a book. Instead of studying members of Congress at work in Washington, D.C., on the House floor, legislating, he researched them in what has always seemed their most obscure, out-of-the-spotlight moments. At home, in their districts, very little was known about legislators until Fenno's work. He opens with the psychological concept of "presentation of self," a technique designed to "win trust" from constituents. Fenno makes mention of the important "delegate" and "trustee" models of representation. Legislators do not explain every detail of their policy positions to the voters, rather, they want voters to trust them enough to allow them "voting leeway" back in Washington.

---

*Ralph Nader is a public-interest activist who has dedicated himself to protecting the American people against both governmental and private industry wrong-doing. One of Nader's best known campaigns came in the 1960s against General Motors, whose Chevrolet Corvair, Nader claimed, was "unsafe at any speed." In the 1996 and 2000 presidential elections, he ran as a third-party candidate.—EDS.

MOST HOUSE MEMBERS spend a substantial proportion of their working lives "at home." Even those in our low frequency category return to their districts more often than we would have guessed. Over half of that group go home more than once a month. What, then, do representatives do there? Much of what they do is captured by Erving Goffman's idea of *the presentation of self*. That is, they place themselves in "the immediate physical presence" of others and then "make a presentation of themselves to others." Goffman writes about the ordinary encounters between people "in everyday life." But, the dramaturgical analogues he uses fit the political world, too. Politicians, like actors, speak to and act before audiences from whom they must draw both support and legitimacy. Without support and legitimacy, there is no political relationship.

In all his encounters, says Goffman, the performer will seek to control the response of others to him by expressing himself in ways that leave the correct impressions of himself with others. His expressions will be of two sorts—"the expressions that he gives and the expression that he gives off." The first are mostly verbal; the second are mostly nonverbal. Goffman is particularly interested in the second kind of expression—"the more theatrical and contextual kind"—because he believes that the performer is more likely to be judged by others according to the nonverbal than the verbal elements of his presentation of self. Those who must do the judging, Goffman says, will think that the verbal expressions are more controllable and manipulable by the performer. And they will, therefore, read his nonverbal "signs" as a check on the reliability of his verbal "signs." Basic to this reasoning is the idea that, of necessity, every presentation has a largely "promissory character" to it. Those who listen to and watch the presentation cannot be sure what the relationship between themselves and the performer really is. So the relationship must be sustained, on the part of those watching, by inference. They "must accept the individual on faith." In this process of acceptance, they will rely heavily on the inferences they draw from his nonverbal expressions—the expressions "given off."

Goffman does not talk about politicians; but politicians know what Goffman is talking about. The response they seek from others is political support. And the impressions they try to foster are those that will engender political support. House member politicians believe that a great deal of their support is won by the kind of individual self they present to others, i.e., to their constituents. More than most other people, they consciously try to manipulate it. Certainly, they believe that what they say, their verbal expression, is an integral part of their "self." But, with Goffman, they place special emphasis on the nonverbal, "contextual" aspects of their presentation. At the least, the nonverbal elements must be consistent with the verbal ones. At the most, the expressions "given off" will become the basis for constituent judgment. Like Goffman, members of Congress are willing to emphasize the latter because, with him, they believe that their constituents will apply a heavier discount to what they say than to how they say it or to how they act in the context in which they say it. In the members' own language, constituents want to judge you "as a person." The comment I have heard most often during my travels is: "he's a good man" or "she's a good woman," unembossed by qualifiers of any sort. Constituents, say House members, want to "size you up" or "get the feel of you" "as a person," or "as a human being." And the largest part of what House members mean when they say "as a person" is what Goffman means by expressions "given off." Largely from expressions given off comes the judgment: "he's a good man," "she's a good woman."

So members of Congress go home to present themselves as a person and to win the accolade: "he's a good man," "she's a good woman." With Goffman, they know there is a "promissory character" to their presentation. And their object is to present themselves as a person in such a way that the inferences drawn by those watching will be supportive. The representatives' word for these supportive inferences is *trust*. It is a word they use a great deal. When a constituent trusts a House member, the constituent is saying something like this: "I am willing to put myself in your hands temporarily; I know you will have opportunities to hurt me, although I may not know when those opportunities occur; I assume— and I will continue to assume until it is proven otherwise—that you will not hurt me; for the time being, then, I'm not going to worry about your behavior." The ultimate response House members seek is political support. But the instrumental response they seek is trust. The presentation of self—that which is given in words and given off as a person—will be calculated to win trust. "If people like you and trust you as individual," members often say, "they will vote for you." So trust becomes central to the representative-constituent relationship. For their part, constituents must rely on trust. They must "accept on faith" that the congressman is what he says he is and will do what he says he will do. House members, for their part, are quite happy to emphasize trust. It helps to allay the uncertainties they feel about their relationship with their supportive constituencies. If members are uncertain as to how to work for support directly, they can always work indirectly to win a degree of personal trust that will increase the likelihood of support or decrease the likelihood of opposition.

Trust is, however, a fragile relationship. It is not an overnight or a one-time thing. It is hard to win; and it must be constantly renewed and rewon. "Trust," said one member, "is a cumulative thing, a totality thing.

. . . You do a little here and a little there." So it takes an enormous amount of time to build and to maintain constituent trust. That is what House members believe. And that is why they spend so much of their working time at home. Much of what I have observed in my travels can be explained as a continuous and continuing effort to win (for new members) and to hold (for old members) the trust of supportive constituencies. Most of the communication I have heard and seen is not overtly political at all. It is, rather, part of a ceaseless effort to reenforce the underpinnings of trust in the congressman or the congresswoman as a person. Viewed from this perspective, the archetypical constituent question is not "What have you done for me lately?" but "How have you looked to me lately?" In sum, House members make a strategic calculation that helps us understand why they go home so much. *Presentation of self enhances trust; enhancing trust takes time; therefore, presentation of self takes time.* . . .

Explaining Washington activity, as said at the outset, includes justifying that activity to one's constituents. The pursuit of power, for example, is sometimes justified with the argument that the representative accumulates power not for himself but for his constituents. In justifying their policy decisions, representatives sometimes claim that their policy decisions follow not what they want but what their constituents want. Recall the member who justified his decision not to support his own highway bill with the comment, "I'm not here to vote my own convictions. I'm here to represent my people." Similarly, the member who decided to yield to his constituent's wishes on gun control said, "I rationalize it by saying that I owe it to my constituents if they feel that strongly about it." But this is not a justification all members use. The independent, issue-oriented Judiciary Committee member mentioned earlier commented (privately) with heavy sarcasm,

All some House members are interested in is "the folks." They think "the folks" are the second coming. They would no longer do anything to displease "the folks" than they would fly. They spend all their time trying to find out what "the folks" want. I imagine if they get five letters on one side and five letters on the other side, they die.

An alternative justification, of course, is that the representative's policy decisions are based on what he thinks is good public policy, regardless of what his constituents want. As the Judiciary Committee member told his constituents often, "If I were sitting where you are, I think what I would want is to elect a man to Congress who will exercise his best judgment on the facts when he has them all." At a large community college gathering in the heart of his district, a member who was supporting President

Nixon's Vietnam policy was asked, "If a majority of your constituents signed a petition asking you to vote for a date to end the war, would you vote for it?" He answered,

It's hard for me to imagine a majority of my constituents agreeing on anything. But if it did happen, then no, I would not vote for it. I would still have to use my own judgment—especially where the security of the country is involved. You can express opinions. I have to make the decision. If you disagree with my decisions, you have the power every two years to vote me out of office. I listen to you, believe me. But, in the end, I have to use my judgment as to what is in your best interests.

He then proceeded to describe his views on the substantive question.

To political scientists, these two kinds of policy justification are very familiar. One is a "delegate" justification, the other a "trustee" justification. The two persist side by side because the set of constituent attitudes on which each depends also exist side by side. Voters, that is, believe that members of Congress should follow constituents' wishes; and voters also believe that members of Congress should use their own best judgment. They want their representatives, it has been said, to be "common people of uncommon judgment." Most probably, though we do not know, voters want delegate behavior on matters most precious to them and trustee behavior on all others. Nonetheless, both kinds of justification are acceptable as a general proposition. Both are legitimate, and in explaining their Washington activity members are seeking to legitimate that activity. They use delegate and trustee justifications because both are legitimating concepts.

If, when they are deciding how to vote, House members think in terms of delegates and trustees, it is because they are thinking about the terms in which they will explain (i.e., justify or legitimate) that vote back home if the need to do so arises. If members never had to legitimate any of their policy decisions back home, they would stop altogether talking in delegate or trustee language. . . .

Members elaborate the linkage between presentation and explanation this way: There are at most only a very few policy issues on which representatives are constrained in their voting by the views of their reelection constituencies. They may not *feel* constrained, if they agree with those views. But that is beside the point; they are constrained nevertheless. On the vast majority of votes, however, representatives can do as they wish—provided only that they can, when they need to, explain their votes to the satisfaction of interested constituents. The ability to get explanations accepted at home is, then, the essential underpinning of a member's voting leeway in Washington.

So the question arises: How can representatives increase the likelihood that their explanations will be accepted at home? And the answer House members give is: They can win and hold constituent trust. The more your various constituencies trust you, members reason, the less likely they are to require an explanation of your votes and the more likely they are to accept your explanation when they do ask for it. The winning of trust, we have said earlier, depends largely on the presentation of self. Presentation of self, then, not only helps win votes at election time. It also makes voting in Washington easier. So members of Congress make a strategic calculation: *Presentation of self enhances trust; trust enhances the acceptability of explanations; the acceptability of explanations enhances voting leeway; therefore, presentation of self-enhances voting leeway.* . . .

The traditional focus of political scientists on the policy aspects of representation is probably related to the traditional focus on activity in the legislature. So long as concentration is on what happens in Washington, it is natural that policymaking will be thought of as the main activity of the legislature and representation will be evaluated in policy terms. To paraphrase Woodrow Wilson, it has been our view that Congress in Washington is Congress at work, while Congress at home is Congress on exhibition. The extrapolicy aspects of representational relationships have tended to be dismissed as symbolic —as somehow less substantial than the relationship embodied in a roll call vote in Washington—because what goes on at home has not been observed. For lack of observation, political scientists have tended to downgrade home activity as mere errand running or fence mending, as activity that takes the representative away from the important things—that is, making public policy in Washington. As one small example, the "Tuesday to Thursday Club" of House members who go home for long weekends—have always been criticized out of hand, on the assumption, presumably, that going home and doing things there was, ipso facto, bad. But no serious inquiry was ever undertaken into what they did there or what consequences—other than their obvious dereliction of duty—their home activity might have had. Home activity has been overlooked and denigrated and so, therefore, have those extra policy aspects of representation which can only be studied at home.

Predictably, the home activities described in this book will be regarded by some readers as further evidence that members of Congress spend too little of their time "on the job"—that is, in Washington, making policy. However, I hope readers will take from the book a different view—a view that values both Washington and home activity. Further, I hope readers will entertain the view that Washington and home activities may even be mutually supportive. Time spent at home can be time spent in developing leeway for activity undertaken in Washington. And that leeway in Washington should be more valued than the sheer number of contact hours spent there. If that should happen, we might then ask House members not to justify their time spent at home, but rather to justify their use of the leeway they have gained therefrom—during the legislative process in Washington. It may well be that a congressman's behavior in Washington is crucially influenced by the pattern of support he has developed at home, and by the allocational, presentational, and explanatory styles he displays there. To put the point most strongly, perhaps we can never understand his Washington activity without also understanding his perception of his various constituencies and the home style he uses to cultivate their support. . . .

24

SARAH BINDER

From *Stalemate*

Writing in 2003, Sarah Binder identifies some reasons for congressional stalemate—gridlock—that became even more pronounced after the 2004 election. First, Binder draws distinctions between lack of legislative action and action based on compromise. She discusses divided government versus control of both houses of Congress and the presidency by the same party. Binder makes the important point that even when the same party controls both branches, stalemate can still happen. As the parties have become more extreme and distant from one another, compromise is less likely. America's bicameral legislature, too, contributes to stalemate. Finally, Binder touches on the Senate filibuster rule that requires a supermajority of 60 votes to end a filibuster as another reason for inaction. Binder's conclusion is that gridlock is a situation not easily remedied and perhaps intrinsic to the "unusual political times" we live in.

——

GRIDLOCK IS NOT a modern legislative condition. Although the term is said to have entered the American political lexicon after the 1980 elections, Alexander Hamilton complained more than two centuries ago about stalemate, at the time rooted in the design of the Continental Congress. In the very first *Federalist*, Hamilton bemoaned the "unequivocal experience of the inefficacy of the subsisting federal government" under the Articles of Confederation.

More than two hundred years later, innumerable critics of American politics still call for more responsive and effective government. The predominance of divided party government in recent decades disheartens many critics. They charge that divided government brings "conflict, delay, and indecision" and frequently leads to "deadlock, inadequate and ineffective policies, or no policies at all." . . .

In many ways, stalemate, a frequent consequence of separated institutions sharing and competing for power, seems endemic to American politics. Periods of lawmaking prowess are the exception, rather than the norm. When they occur, we give them enduring political labels, like the New Deal and the Great Society. Outside of these episodes of significant policy change, the frequency of gridlock varies considerably, variation that has attracted the attention of political observers and political scientists. In this book, I probe these trends in legislative performance, asking questions about the dynamics of lawmaking. How often does gridlock occur? What explains the historical ups and downs in policy stalemate? What are the consequences of Congress's uneven performance over time? How does legislative performance shape the ambitions of members of Congress, their electoral fortunes, and the reputation of the institution in which they serve? . . .

Why study policy gridlock? Normatively, exploring the causes of stalemate is important, regardless of one's party or ideology. Lawmaking is the process by which governments "legitimize substantive and procedural actions to reshape public problems, perhaps to resolve them." If we care about whether and when our political system is able to respond to problems both new and endemic to our common social, economic, and political lives, then explaining the conditions that underscore policy change and stability is a valuable and worthwhile endeavor.

Some might object that interest in gridlock implies a normative preference for legislative activism and liberal policy change. As Jefferson's maxim implies, "that government is best which governs least." If Jefferson was always right, then gridlock might always be a welcome feature of legislative politics. But views about gridlock tend to vary with one's political circumstance. Former Senate majority leader Bob Dole put it best: "If you're against something, you'd better hope there is a little gridlock." Because legislative activism can move the law in either a conservative or liberal direction, calls to end gridlock are not the exclusive province of liberal interests. In some respects, the confusion lies in the choice of words, as we often use the terms *gridlock*, *stalemate*, and *deadlock* to describe legislative inaction. In this book, I too refer to stalemate and gridlock, but more precisely I am exploring Congress's relative ability over time and issues to broach and secure policy compromise on issues high on the national agenda. Framed in this way, a study of legislative performance should interest any keen observer, participant, or student of national performance, regardless of her party or ideology. . . .

Unified party control of government cannot guarantee the compromise necessary for breaking deadlock in American politics. As David Mayhew has argued, looking solely at the *structural* component of the American political system—the separation of powers between Congress and the president—tends to obscure important dynamics in American lawmaking. As the analysis suggests, it is the *pluralist* component that deserves our more focused attention. The distributions of policy views within and across the two major political parties have predictable and important effects on the legislative performance of Congress and the president. The timing of party politics also matters. Long-frustrated congressional minorities often capitalize successfully on electoral mandates when their party gains unified control of Congress. Intrabranch politics, it seems, may be as important as the usual culprit of conflict between the branches. . . .

Two . . . other factors shaping Congress's policy performance command attention: the impact of parties and the consequences of bicameralism. First, consider party effects. My findings suggest that it is premature to reject the idea that political parties influence patterns of legislative outcomes. To be sure, the configuration of party control helps explain just a small portion of deadlock in contemporary politics. But . . . elections do more than divide control of the two major branches. Elections also determine the mix of ideologies within each major party. Such ideological divisions within the parties were decried in the 1950s by the "party government" school whose adherents believed that internal party divisions made it nearly impossible for the major parties to assemble and enact party agendas once they took office.

What is striking about the impact of parties in the latter half of the twentieth century is how strongly that impact differs from the expectations of the party government school. As the American Political Science Association's Committee on Political Parties argued in its often-cited 1950 report, cohesive political parties that offered distinctive choices to the electorate were critical for ensuring responsive and accountable government. The consequences of weak parties were steep: "The very heartbeat of democracy," the committee warned, was threatened by the state of the political parties. Democracy was contingent on organizing and responding to majorities, and cohesive parties were deemed the only viable instrument for doing so.

As the two parties have polarized and the political center has stretched thin over the recent past, little evidence indicates that legislative performance has risen in lockstep. Paradoxically, far from ensuring that voters will be given meaningful choices between competing party programs, the polarization of the parties seems to encourage deadlock. Why should polarization have this effect? One prominent scholar of Congress and electoral politics observes that legislators' desire to be responsive to active constituencies affects the incentive to compromise. "I do not think that one must be overcome by nostalgia," notes Morris P. Fiorina, "to imagine that Everett Dirksen, Mike Mansfield, John McCormack, and Gerald Ford [House and Senate party leaders in the 1960s and 1970s] would have found some common ground and acted. Many of today's leaders, however, would rather have issues to use in the upcoming election than accomplishments to point to." There may be a personal element to these temporal differences in leadership styles, but more likely the differences reflect changes in the makeup and activities of contemporary parties, as party organizations are increasingly defined by issue activists, constituency groups, and large-scale financial contributors with pointed policy and ideological agendas. With limited electoral ties to the mass and moderate middle, legislators have only limited and occasional incentive to craft moderate policy compromises to public problems. The statistical evidence . . . backs up this impression: the larger the political center and the less polarized the Congress, the greater the prospects for measurable policy compromise and change. Parties do affect Congress's capacity to legislate but not strictly according to whether their control is unified or divided.

Bicameralism is perhaps the most critical structural factor shaping the politics of gridlock. Bicameralism—rather than the separation of power between executive and legislative branches—seems most relevant in explaining stalemate in the postwar period. To be sure, both the separation of powers and bicameralism were central to the framers' late-eighteenth-century beliefs about the proper construction of political institutions. Still, with important recent exceptions, the policy consequences of divided government, not bicameralism, feature prominently in theoretical and empirical treatments of legislative gridlock.

Bicameral differences arise of course because structural differences between House and Senate elections ensure that policy views will not be distributed and aggregated identically in the two chambers. Even when both chambers are controlled by the same party, we cannot assume that the two chambers desire the same policy outcomes. The impact of bicameral differences can be seen clearly in the fate of a patients' bill of rights measure in the 106th Congress (1999–2000). Although both chambers passed a version of the bill with the support of Republican majorities, no final agreement emerged from conference negotiations that took place over several months in mid- to late 2000. As one House Republican observed in trying to explain the bicameral impasse, "Just appreciate the fact that Republicans in the House and Senate sometimes have a gulf as large if not larger than some Republicans and Democrats." The looming presence of a Democratic president ready to veto a bill deemed too responsive to the health insurance industry certainly influenced the Republicans' negotiating strategy, as they probably preferred no bill to the more moderate House bill that the president would have signed. But ideological differences between the two chambers also precluded policy compromise, no matter the views of the president. Given median Senate Republican preferences, Senate Republicans had little incentive to compromise with House Republicans in pursuit of a moderate agreement.

Some speculated that the chief Senate Republican negotiator, Don Nickles of Oklahoma, would move closer to the more moderate House bill if vulnerable Republican senators seeking re-election in 2000 could convince Nickles of the electoral imperative to compromise with the House and pass a bill. Despite some senators' efforts to persuade Nickles, no such compromise toward the House bill occurred. As it turned out, this mattered little to the Democrats, as bicameral negotiations were taking place in the run-up to the tightly contested 2000 presidential election. "For us, it's a win-win," explained Senator Minority Leader Tom Daschle (D-S.D.). "We win if we don't get a bill, politically. We win politically and legislatively if we do get a bill." Not only did bicameral differences limit the feasibility of reaching a conference agreement, the polarization of the parties and the electoral rewards of doing nothing limited the incentive to compromise.

The persistence of bicameral effects across the postwar period also sheds some light on the impact of divided and unified government on legislative performance. Spurred by Mayhew's unconventional finding about the limited impact of divided government, recent studies have re-examined "unified gridlock," stalemate that occurs when a single party controls both chambers of Congress and the White House. Most often fingered as potential causes of unified gridlock are supermajority institutions that limit the policymaking capacity of political parties: procedural rules that require three-fifths majorities to limit debate in the Senate in face of a filibuster and constitutional rules that require a two-thirds majority to override a presidential veto. Because presidential vetoes are rare under unified government, I focus on the impact of the Senate filibuster. A recent and compelling argument is that because a supermajority is needed to pass major policy change in the Senate, the majority party's ability to secure policy outcomes favored by its party median is limited. Thus one cannot predict major policy change based on the policy views of the median legislator of the chamber and the majority party. Instead, the views of the sixtieth senator—the senator whose assent is required to invoke cloture and break a filibuster—are pivotal.

However, the severity of the filibuster threat showed little effect on the frequency of deadlock once bicameral differences and party polarization and control were taken into account. Are interchamber differences a more proximate cause of stalemate than supermajority Senate constraints? . . .

Gridlock under unified government may have more to do with differences between the majority party's House and Senate contingents than with supermajority constraints imposed by Senate rules. . . .

. . . If the frequency of deadlock is largely a function of bicameral differences and polarization of the parties, then Congress's legislative performance is a simple function of electoral outcomes and the evolution of constitutional design. There is little that legislators can do to reduce the barriers to legislative stalemate they typically encounter. Legislators can only wait out electoral change that bolsters the presence of moderates and accept the reality of bicameralism. We cannot engineer electoral outcomes, so we should learn to live with gridlock. In a sense, this perspective commits us to accepting the conventional wisdom about the intentions of the framers: legislative inaction was one of their key goals, and thus they designed a political system of checks and balances that would slow down and often thwart efforts to enact major changes in public law.

I think there is some value to interpreting the causes of stalemate in another way. . . .

It is fair to say that legislators today toil in somewhat unusual political times. The decline of the political center has produced a political environment that more often than not gives legislators every incentive not to reach agreement. There are steady partisan and ideological pressures on members not to compromise on firmly held positions. Legislators also work in a remarkably public environment, are followed by an intensely negative media, and face a revolution in communications technology that grants little time or space for methodical deliberation. Legislators also often face an agenda that requires imposing losses rather than distributing benefits, as the promise of budget surpluses has given way to economic

downturns, tax cuts, and politicians' unwillingness to spend from Social
Security reserves. . . .

To be sure, the notion of "fixing gridlock" can be troubling. One
person's stalemate is another's preferred legislative outcome. In the polarized and polarizing era that legislators inhabit today, it is doubtful that
true differences over desirable ends and means can or should always be
negotiated away. But neither can we depend on the emergence of cohesive
political parties to resolve recurring episodes of gridlock, as we see now
that the faith of party government scholars in disciplined parties was
misplaced: gridlock only increases as the political center recedes.

25

BARBARA SINCLAIR

The "60 Vote Senate"

*Professor Barbara Sinclair takes readers deep inside the U.S. Senate. Under-
standing the rules and customs of the chamber is essential to appreciating
the Senate's role in policy-making in the United States, or more accurately,
sometimes the lack of policy-making. Sinclair explains the filibuster and the
cloture rule. She offers some interesting data on the changing use of the
filibuster and cloture over time. Those of you who follow the news about
the nomination of federal judges and other presidential appointees know all
about the filibuster. Sinclair then describes the practice of senators placing
"holds" on matters coming in front of the Senate. Holds, threats of filibusters,
and filibusters all mean that the Senate is the last best hope of the minority.
That was the plan, says Sinclair, but perhaps today's Senate has taken
obstruction beyond the Framers' intent.*

———

WHETHER FROM JIMMY STEWART'S *Mr. Smith Goes to Wash-
ington*, the great civil rights battles of the 1960s, or yesterday evening's
news, Americans, if they know anything about the Senate, know of the
filibuster. Both glorified and reviled, the Senate filibuster has been the
subject of much commentary, written and oral, and some excellent analyses
have recently appeared. Yet there is still much that we do not know
about the impact on the legislative process and on legislative outcomes
of extended debate and related Senate floor rules.

The Senate has always operated under rules that vest enormous power
in each individual senator. In holding the floor and in proposing amend-

ments, senators face fewer constraints than the members of any other legislature in the world. Yet senators have not always exploited the possibilities inherent in the rules to the same extent and in the same way. . . .

The claim that the Senate is a unique legislative chamber rests on the Senate's highly permissive rules concerning floor debate and amending activity. Senators can hold the floor as long as they like so long as cloture is not invoked, a procedure that requires a supermajority. Senators can offer as many amendments as they wish to almost any bill, and usually those amendments need not even be germane.

The Senate has . . . several times altered its debate rules, and the circumstances of its doing so are illuminating. The most important change came in 1917 when the Senate adopted Rule 22, which, for the first time, provided for a way to cut off debate over the objections of some senators. When "a small group of willful men" blocked President Wilson's proposal to arm American merchant ships in 1917, Wilson managed to focus intense public attention on the Senate's debate rules, and public opinion forced the body to agree to a procedure for cutting off debate. Even so, the cloture procedure instituted was cumbersome. Sixteen senators had to file a petition requesting a vote to end debate on the matter at issue; two days after the filing, a vote would be taken, and if two-thirds of those present and voting supported the cloture motion, debate would be limited to one hour per senator.

The rule has been changed several times since. Most importantly, in 1975 the threshold for cutting off debate on legislation was reduced to three-fifths of the total membership (usually sixty), though stopping debate on a proposal to change Senate rules still requires a two-thirds vote. . . .

. . . [A]s the table shows, the use of extended debate and of cloture has increased enormously over the post–World War II period. To be sure, the data must be regarded with some caution. When lengthy debate becomes a filibuster is, in part, a matter of judgment. Furthermore, as I show below, filibusters have changed their form in recent years, and threats to filibuster have become much more frequent than actual talkfests on the floor. As a consequence, cloture is sometimes sought before any overt evidence of a filibuster manifests itself on the floor. Nevertheless, experts and participants agree that the frequency of obstructionism has increased, as the table indicates. In the 1950s, filibusters were rare; they increased during the 1960s and again during the 1970s. By the late 1980s and the 1990s, they had become routine, occurring at a rate of more than one a month—considerably more if only the time the Senate was in session was counted. Cloture votes increased in tandem, and more than one cloture vote per issue is now the norm. Cloture votes are, however,

THE INCREASE IN FILIBUSTERS AND CLOTURE VOTES, 1951–98

Years	Congresses	Filibusters per Congress	Cloture Votes per Congress	Successful Cloture Votes per Congress
1951–60	82–86th	1.0	.4	0
1961–70	87–91st	4.6	5.2	.8
1971–80	92–96th	11.2	22.4	8.6
1981–86	97–99th	16.7	23.0	10.0
1987–92	100–102nd	26.7	39.0	15.3
1993–94	103rd	30	42	14
1995–96	104th	25	50	9
1997–98	105th	29	53	18

Sources: Cloture votes from "A Look at the Senate Filibuster," DSG Special Report, June 13, 1994, No. 103–28, Appendix B (compiled by Congressional Research Service). Successful cloture votes from Ornstein, Mann, and Malbin (1994, 16.2). Data for 103rd Congress from Richard S. Beth, "Cloture in the Senate, 103rd Congress," memorandum, Congressional Research Service, June 23, 1995. Data for the 104th and 105th Congresses from the Congressional Quarterly Almanacs (1995–98).

increasingly less likely to be successful: in the early to mid-1980s, 43 percent of cloture votes got the requisite sixty votes to cut off debate; in the late 1980s and early 1990s, 39 percent did; in the period 1993–1998, only 28 percent did. . . .

From the late 1930s to the late 1960s, when filibustering was strongly associated with civil rights, filibusters were aimed primarily at killing legislation. This was also the era of powerful committee chairmen leading quite autonomous committees; nongermane amendments were most famously used by leaders to circumvent recalcitrant committees. Thus, Majority Leader Lyndon Johnson offered the 1960 civil rights bill as a nongermane amendment on the floor to a bill aiding an impacted school district in Missouri; the Judiciary Committee chaired by Senator James Eastland of Mississippi, an unrelenting foe of civil rights, refused to report such legislation.

With the growth of Senate individualism and senators' increasing exploitation of their prerogatives under Senate rules, the uses to which senators put their powers multiplied. Killing legislation continued to be the aim in many cases, but filibustering also came to be used almost routinely to extract concessions on legislation. Senators as individuals increasingly employed nongermane amendments to pursue their personal agendas, often forcing votes on their issues over and over during a Congress. Also on the rise has been extended–debate–based obstructionism that appears aimed at killing or weakening legislation but actually is a form of position taking—intended to make a statement about a senator's stance and its intensity. Targeting one measure in order to extract concessions on another, sometimes known as hostage taking, has become increasingly frequent. With the growth of partisan polarization, the minorities making use of Senate prerogatives are more often organized partisan ones. In the 1990s especially, exploiting Senate prerogatives to attempt to seize agenda control from the majority party has become a key minority-party strategy.

Certainly since the development of the individualist Senate, senators as individuals have used extended debate, directly and indirectly, to try to kill legislation that they strongly oppose, and they continue to do so today. . . .

Since the 1950s, the Senate has done most of its work through unanimous consent agreements (UCAs). By unanimous consent, senators agree to bring a bill to the floor, perhaps to place some limits on the amendments that may be offered or the length of debate on specific amendments, and then maybe to set a time for the final vote. Some UCAs are highly elaborate and set out agreements on the entire floor consideration of a bill. . . .

The party leaders oversee the negotiation of unanimous-consent agreements and are deeply involved in the more contentious cases. The majority- and the minority-party secretaries of the Senate now are the most important staffers involved and serve as clearinghouses and as a point of continuous contact between the parties. When the majority leader, after consultation with the relevant committee chairman, decides he wants to schedule a bill, he may leave the negotiation of the agreement to the committee chairman, or he may take the lead role himself. The more complex the political situation and the more important to the party the legislation at issue, the more likely the majority leader is to take the lead. In either case, the majority-party secretary will be consulted to ascertain which senators have indicated that they want to be consulted before the bill is scheduled. If a fellow party member has expressed opposition to the bill's being brought to the floor, negotiations may be necessary to take care of his concerns. When the majority has an agreement it can support, the majority party secretary will convey it to the minority party secretary in writing, who will give it to the minority leader and the relevant ranking minority member. The minority secretary will also call any senators on the minority side who have asked to be notified and will find out their concerns. Eventually the minority will respond with a written counteroffer and convey it to the majority through the secretaries. This process may go through several rounds. The leaders will also sometimes negotiate face to face. If and when they reach a tentative agreement, both parties put out a recorded message on their "hot line" to all Senate offices. The message lays out the terms of the agreement and asks senators who have objections to call their leader within a specified period of time. If there are objections, they have to be taken care of. When every senator is prepared to assent to the unanimous-consent agreement, the majority leader takes it to the floor and makes the request.

The two party secretaries maintain the lists of "holds." "A hold," as one knowledgeable participant explained, "is a letter to your leader telling him which of the many powers that you have as a senator you intend to use on a given issue." A typical such letter, addressed to then Majority Leader Trent Lott and copied to the majority secretary, reads, "Dear Trent: I will object to any time agreement or unanimous consent request with respect to consideration of any legislation or amendment that involves_____, as I wish to be accorded my full rights as a Member of the Senate to offer amendments, debate and consider such legislation or amendment. My thanks and kindest personal regards." Each party secretary maintains a list of the "holds" placed by senators of his or her party. The party secretaries confer every morning and tell each other about any new holds on legislation or nominations. They do not, however, reveal the names of their members that have placed the holds.

The hold system is an informal practice, not a matter of Senate rules, and its history is murky. It may well have begun as simply a way of making sure senators were notified before matters of special interest to them were scheduled. Senators might want to be sure that they were not otherwise committed, that they were prepared for floor debate or ready to offer an amendment. Senators still ask to be informed before something of particular interest to them is scheduled; unless they are committee or subcommittee leaders on the issue or otherwise known players, they cannot count on being consulted unless they make such a request. These requests are sometimes called "consults" and are sometimes just lumped under "holds." However, most "holds" are threats to object to a unanimous-consent agreement, and in a body that conducts most of its business through UCAs, that is in effect, as a leadership staffer said, "a threat to filibuster."

Visible filibusters are now just the tip of the iceberg. The Senate's permissive rules have much more effect on the legislative process through filibuster threats than through actual filibusters. "Classic" filibusters, with the Senate in session all night, senators sleeping on cots off the Senate floor, and filibusterers making interminable speeches on the floor, no longer occur. Holds are the "lazy man's filibuster," a staffer complained. Placed sometimes by staff on their own initiative and sometimes at the instigation of lobbyists, "holds" require little effort on the part of senators, the staffer continued, yet they enormously complicate the legislative process and not infrequently kill or severely weaken worthy legislation. Given the secrecy surrounding holds, no data on their frequency exist. However, interview evidence suggests that they are common. One senior aide's claim that "there are holds on virtually everything" may be an exaggeration, but the complaints and frustration expressed by so many senators and aides indicates that holds are an everyday fact of life in the contemporary Senate. . . .

Thus, often simply to get to the floor, a measure must command a substantial supermajority. When time is especially tight — before a recess and at the end of a session — a single objection can kill legislation.

If a majority is willing to pay the price in time and inconvenience, a single senator or a handful cannot stop a majority from bringing a measure to the floor and passing it. Forty-one senators can. With senators as individuals and collectively so willing to use their prerogatives aggressively, anything contentious must command sixty votes in order to pass. "We've developed what I call the 60-vote Senate," a longtime participant said. "We have a lot of cloture votes, but not a lot of successful cloture votes," he continued. "So long as the minority sticks together and has [40-plus] votes, they can prevent that." . . .

The Senate, then, has become a major choke point in the legislative process. . . . During the 1990s not only did much more legislation fail enactment, but that which did was much more likely to be stopped in the Senate than in the House. The combination of senators increasingly exploiting their prerogatives under Senate rules with high partisanship has contributed significantly to the declining rate of enactment.

What evaluative conclusions can be drawn from this? Legislative accomplishment cannot be equated with the number or the percentage of major measures enacted. Whatever one's notions of good public policy, one will find bills killed in the Senate whose fate one bemoans and others for which one applauds the result if not the means by which it came about. Furthermore, the Senate does still function as a legislature; it passes essential legislation such as appropriations bills, though sometimes with difficulty.

Yet the combination of partisanship and individualism does make the legislative process in the Senate fragile and subject to breakdown. Given Senate rules and current expectations about how they may be used, any one senator can cause trouble, and an organized partisan minority can prevent a majority from working its will. In such a body, passing legislation is harder and blocking action easier than in a majoritarian body; minorities command enormous bargaining leverage, especially when time is tight, and intensity counts for more in the legislative process. The "60-vote Senate" poses a significant barrier to the enactment of legislation and to policy change. The existence of a second powerful and independent legislative chamber has always contributed to the status quo bias of the American political system; the ways in which that unique chamber has evolved in recent decades have amplified that effect. . . .

26

MICHELE SWERS

From *The Difference Women Make*

The "difference women make" in the House of Representatives and the Senate, scholar Michele Swers finds, is a big difference. Using many examples of female legislators from the past decade, Swers discusses both the way women candidates campaign and the way women in Congress reflect their gender through the views they hold. Female legislators have become important spokespeople for both Democrats and Republicans on issues ranging from gun control to welfare reform to tax policy. Votes, of course, lie at the core of the parties' goal of attracting women supporters. Swers stresses that beyond just supporters, women legislators bring to congressional issues a distinctive point of view that goes beyond party and politics. In the years after Swers completed her research, the role of women in Congress has continued to grow. Note that Nancy Pelosi (D-CA), cited as a party whip in this selection, became the Democratic leader in the House. Senator Hillary Clinton (D-NY) didn't make it into Swers' discussion, but she certainly could have, as a woman legislator who is making a difference.

———

ON OCTOBER 20, 1999, a group of largely Democratic women took to the floor of the House of Representatives to support an amendment by Congresswoman Patsy Mink (D-HI) that would restore funding for gender equity programs to a Republican bill reauthorizing parts of the 1965 Elementary and Secondary Schools Education Act. As evidence of the continuing need for gender equity programs, Congresswoman Stephanie Tubbs Jones (D-OH) cited women's underrepresentation in Congress. She proclaimed, "Women need to be encouraged to be right here on the floor . . . they need to think about how can we be here on the floor of the U.S. Congress talking about issues that impact the entire country and only fifty-seven of us are women."

Congresswoman Tubbs Jones's comments imply that electing more women to Congress will not just achieve equality but also influence the range of issues considered on the national agenda and the formulation of policy solutions. She is not alone in her belief that electing more women will have a substantive policy impact. Numerous women's Political Action Committees (PACs) raise money to elect liberal or conservative women candidates. For example, the Women in Senate and House (WISH) List raises money for pro-choice Republican women, while the Susan B. Anthony List supports pro-life women. In the 2000 election cycle, Early Money Is Like Yeast's (EMILY's) List raised $21,201,339 to support pro-choice, Democratic women, thus making it one of the leading fundraisers among all PACs. Some women candidates even point to their gender as one of the reasons voters should elect them. Announcing her candidacy for the Senate in 1998, Blanche Lambert Lincoln (D-AR) proclaimed that she was running because "nearly one of every three senators is a millionaire, but there are only five mothers." Similarly, Patty Murray (D-WA) launched her 1992 Senate campaign as "just a mom in tennis shoes." . . .

How important is it to have a Congress that "looks like America"? Do we need more women as mothers in Congress? Do we need more women as women? . . .

. . . [M]any Democratic and moderate Republican women claim that they do feel a special responsibility to represent women in their committee work, and they do lobby male committee leaders to take into account a policy's potential impact on women. For example, Marge Roukema (R-NJ) explained: "But I have to tell you, when I got to Washington, I found that some of the 'women's issues—the family issues'—weren't being addressed by the men in power. Things like child-support enforcement and women's health issues and family safety issues. It wasn't that the men were opposed to these issues—they just didn't get it. They were not sufficiently aware of them. So I realized, in many important areas—if we women in government don't take action, no one else will."

Additionally, in interviews, both Democratic and Republican men and women expressed the belief that women and minorities bring a different perspective to the policy process, and it is important to have these groups at the decision-making table. Many of the Republican and Democratic women who have held party leadership posts also feel a sense of responsibility to represent women. For example, in her congressional memoir, Susan Molinari (R-NY) claimed that she used her position as vice-chair of the Republican conference to act as "the party's champion of women's issues." At the height of the budget-cutting battles of the 104th Congress, she convinced the leadership to increase funding for programs to combat violence against women. When other members rolled their eyes at her suggestions for new women's initiatives, Speaker Gingrich backed her and reminded male members that they could not win the next election without the votes of women. Similarly, in the 103rd Congress, Louise Slaughter (D-NY) used her position on the leadership-controlled Rules Committee to make sure the Freedom of Access to Abortion Clinic Entrances Act was placed on the House calendar before the end of the session and to push a favorable rule through a committee whose members were largely pro-life. Barbara Kennelly (D-CT), who served as a chief deputy whip in the 102nd (1991–92) and 103rd (1993–94) Congresses and conference vice-chair in the 104th (1995–96) Congress, said that "women have a different perspective and you need women to be in the room to make sure it is heard. I worked on women and children's issues over and above committee work, constituent service, and case work."

While both Democratic and Republican women agree that it is important to have women at the table because females bring a different perspective to policy making, Democratic women are more willing to challenge their party leadership explicitly and demand that women be considered for positions because of their gender. According to one Republican staffer, "Republican women do not overtly promote themselves as women" or argue "that we need more women, . . . the Republican Party in general sees a need but it is not overly stated." . . .

On the Democratic side, the more liberal ideological views espoused by the Democratic Party incline members of the caucus to arguments based explicitly on the need for diversity. For example, throughout her campaign to replace David Bonior as whip when he retires in January 2002, Nancy Pelosi maintained that women "deserve a seat at the leadership table." She also argued that her election would allow the party to bring a "fresh face" to the public and would increase the party's advantage with women voters. . . .

Although seniority rules have slowed congresswomen's rise to positions of power in the committees and party leadership, partisan concerns over the potential impact of the gender gap have facilitated women's efforts to raise their profile within their respective party caucuses and to take the lead on gendered issues. Since Republicans seized control of Congress from the Democrats in 1994, they have lost House seats in each succeeding election, and in the 107th Congress their majority control rests on only a six-seat margin. In an era of such tight party competition, party leaders make extra efforts to develop and advertise policy proposals that will attract specific groups of voters and, therefore, both parties are targeting women voters. Although the gender gap is small, women have slightly favored the Democrats since the late 1960s. The gender gap widened in 1996, when 54 percent of women supported Bill Clinton in contrast to only 43 percent of men and when the media focused on the voting behavior of the "soccer mom." Additionally, in 1996, more women voted than men—with 56 percent of women turning out to vote compared to 53 percent of men. The higher turnout among women helped Democrats reclaim House seats in 1996 and 1998. While the Florida recount and the divergence between the popular and Electoral College votes made the 2000 elections a unique historical event, the gender gap continued at the same magnitude, as Al Gore received 12 percent more votes from women than from men. Similarly, across the country, women favored Democratic House candidates, creating a nine-point gender gap, and women helped elect more Democratic women to the Senate.

In response to these trends, Democrats are designing their policy proposals and public appeals with an eye toward maintaining women's support, while Republicans actively work to expand their appeal among women. To achieve these goals, party leaders have increasingly turned to women to act as spokespersons on women's, children's, and family issues and to take a leading role in legislative battles on women's issues. As one Republican congressman complained, "The Democrats will do whatever they can to expand the gender gap." Democratic members and staffers agreed that the party does encourage women to be out in front at press conferences, presidential bill-signing ceremonies, and floor debate on women's issues. As one Democratic staffer explained the dynamic, "The parties are sensitive to the gender gap so they want to appeal to women, children, and family issues. As long as the parties focus on these issues to capture the women's vote, it helps women in office who can be leaders on these issues."

The debates over gun control during the 106th Congress highlight the Democratic strategy. A series of high-profile school shootings brought the issue of gun control back into the public spotlight. Democratic Party polling demonstrated that women care more about gun control legislation than men do and that women are more likely to let their votes be influenced by a candidate's position on gun control. Therefore, Democrats began framing their discussions of gun control in terms of child safety rather than crime, with the presumption that the phrase will resonate especially strongly with women voters. Three Democratic Congresswomen, Carolyn

McCarthy (D-NY), Nita Lowey (D-NY), and Assistant Minority Leader Rosa DeLauro (D-CT), took the lead in organizing press conferences, lobbying colleagues, and counting votes to limit Democratic defectors and to attract Republican support for the McCarthy-Roukema Amendment, which would add gun control provisions to a juvenile justice bill. As the congresswomen explained, they "stepped to the foreground of an issue they had long been passionate about and party leaders almost immediately encouraged them to stay there." Indeed, the murder of her husband and injury of her son in a mass shooting on the Long Island Railroad propelled Congresswoman McCarthy to run for office in the first place. After the House defeated the McCarthy-Roukema Amendment in June 1999, the Democratic women organized a floor protest by lining up to make procedural requests to revise and extend their remarks. In the weeks following the amendment's defeat, Democratic congresswomen used the unconstrained floor time provided by the period for one-minute speeches at the opening of the legislative day to read the names of children who had been killed as a result of gun violence.

As Democrats turn to congresswomen to expand their support among women voters, Republicans, particularly in the 104th Congress, deploy women in a more defensive manner. Discussing her role as conference vice-chair, Susan Molinari described one of her duties as "putting the friendly face on Republican issues," particularly when Republicans feared that Democrats and President Clinton would portray their policies as unfriendly to women in the battle for public opinion. Another Republican staffer close to the leadership explained that "the Republican leaders will ask women to speak when they know the Democrats will have their women out to demagogue an issue. By having women speak at a press conference or in the floor debate, they get women to put a smiley, soft face on issues and prevent Republicans from looking like mean ogres. This happened most often in the 104th and 105th Congresses on welfare reform and other Contract with America items. In the 106th, they [Republicans] have not introduced much extreme legislation. They are not trying to dismantle departments or overhaul social legislation." . . .

Other legislators and staffers explained that, in an effort to narrow the gender gap, Republicans also actively seek out women's issue bills that will improve their standing with women and draw attention away from abortion. As a result, party and committee leaders, often prodded by Republican women, have advanced proposals on such issues as breast cancer, child abuse, violence against women, adoption, and foster care. Since the 104th Congress, Republicans have also made efforts to repackage traditional Republican policies on taxes and other fiscal issues in ways that will attract women. In the 105th and 106th Congresses, Republicans courted women by seeking legislation to eliminate the marriage penalty and protect innocent spouses, often divorced women, who are liable for tax debts resulting from the actions of their former spouses. Jennifer Dunn (R-WA), who leads Republican efforts to bridge the gender gap, utilizes press conferences and public speeches to explain how tax issues affect women. Her congressional Web site includes a special section for women that lists Republican accomplishments on behalf of women and explains how issues like estate taxes disproportionately affect women since, on average, they outlive men. . . .

For the political parties, the crafting of the strategy to sell a policy to the public is as important as the content. Thus, both Democratic and Republican leaders are looking for policies to attract women voters, and they turn to congresswomen to help promote those policies. This concern with the gender gap provides Democratic and Republican women with an opportunity to advance policies related to women's interests, raise their public profiles, and attain power within their party caucuses. Interest groups and individual legislators from both parties seek out women to sponsor or cosponsor gender-related legislation not simply because they have expertise in a particular area but also because they want to connect themselves to the symbolic moral authority these women have as women and/or as mothers.

On the House floor and in press conferences, party leaders rely on women as spokespersons and political symbols in their effort to demonstrate that their party is protecting women's interests. Thus, Democratic leaders turn to their congresswomen to expand the party's traditional advantage with female voters by promoting Democratic initiatives on women's issues and branding Republican policies as antifamily and anti-women. Similarly, Republicans utilize Republican women to combat Democratic efforts to paint their proposals as hurting women. Republican women also craft messages to explain how traditional Republican issues, such as tax cuts, will benefit women. By speaking out on behalf of their party, female legislators raise their own public profile and collect favors that they can use to advance their positions within the party conference, attain support for favored policy initiatives, or gain leeway to defect from their party's position on another issue. . . .

In the final analysis, understanding how politically significant social identities have an impact on the legislative behavior of representatives is not simply a matter of raw numbers in the legislature. The interplay of presence and power is complex. In the case of gender, the unique policy interests of women provide substantive support to those who call for the inclusion of more women in the cabinet choices of presidents and governors and the leadership ranks of Congress and the state legislatures. Electing women has important consequences for the quality of our representational system, thus making the call for more diversity in Congress more than a mere platitude. Presence, however, is only a first step. Power in Congress also depends on access to influential positions within the institution that allow members to exercise strategic influence over the shape of policy outcomes.

27

KATHERINE TATE

From *Black Faces in the Mirror*

The Congressional Black Caucus (CBC) was formed in the early 1970s. Its visibility and influence have grown steadily. Katherine Tate rejects the charge that members of the CBC have delivered only "symbolic" legislation to Black voters. Tate offers a brief history of the caucus and of several key members. She recounts the relationship between the CBC and Jesse Jackson as he twice sought to win the Democratic presidential nomination. The House leadership, especially the Democrats, gradually brought Black legislators into prominent positions on committees and even into the leadership. As more Black representatives are elected today from the South and from other non-urban districts, Tate believes that the CBC will become more internally diverse even as it continues to work toward both symbolic and tangible policy goals.

IN THIS BOOK, I ADDRESS the question of whether or not the racial composition of government is relevant to the political representation of Blacks. Like women, African Americans have made tremendous gains in holding elective office but still fall short of proportional representation. Constituting 12 percent of the population, Blacks hold about two percent of all elected offices in the country. Blacks make up about 7 percent of Congress—the chief lawmaking institution in the U.S. governmental system—with thirty-eight members in the House of Representatives but none currently serving in the Senate.* Today about one-third of Blacks are represented in Washington by Black officeholders. Are these Blacks

*African American Barack Obama was elected to the Senate by Illinois voters in 2004.

better represented in Washington by Blacks than the two-thirds not represented by Blacks? . . .

While the perception of Black legislators is that they are not very successful in winning passage of the bills that they sponsor, I establish . . . that the opposite is true. Black members of Congress are just as successful in bill attainment as White members of Congress are. This stereotype of Black lawmakers in Congress being less successful at bill attainment exists because of their liberal policy agendas. Because public policy-making is a process of coalitions and compromises, Black members are seen as too ideologically extreme to be successful at it. Part of the reputation is based on studies of the Congressional Black Caucus (CBC). Early studies have characterized the CBC as cohesive but ineffectual. As Robert Singh writes in his important work on the CBC, "As an interest group for blacks, the CBC's impact on public policy has been—and remains—marginal." Singh attributes its lack of policy success not only to the institutional features of the American legislative system, but also to the growing diversification of Black members' interests. Other studies challenge the negative depiction of the CBC. Still, the larger question is whether Black representation in the House can deliver anything of substance to Black constituents, or whether at most Black legislators represent symbols that do nothing to improve the lives of African American constituents. The crowning achievement of the CBC in Singh's analysis was the imposition of sanctions against South Africa and the commemoration of Dr. Martin Luther King, Jr.'s birthday as a national holiday, while its "Alternative Budget" legislation faced ignominious defeat after defeat.

To typecast Black legislators as "symbolic" legislators lacks perspective. Much of the legislation initiated in Congress can be labeled symbolic. . . . Black legislators provide Black constituents with the greatest amount of "symbolic" representation, but also initiate and participate in providing their Black constituents with policies of substance, namely those that distribute or redistribute tangible public goods. Legislative success needs to be evaluated on a broader plane than how previous scholars have defined it. Whether one considers symbolic legislation important or not, members of Congress in general spend a great deal of energy providing it to constituents. In the end, if Blacks are to win their fair share of symbolic representation, Black faces need to be a visible part of the U.S. Congress. . . .

The Congressional Black Caucus

As one of its founding members, Representative William Clay (D-MO) offers a richly informative account of the birth of the Congressional

Black Caucus in *Just Permanent Interests* (1992). In 1969, thirteen Blacks were serving in the House during a period of rising Black militancy. President Nixon, writes Clay, perceiving his reelection mandate "to repeal all of the Johnson Great Society programs," had the effect of waving a red flag in front of an impatient and ideologically charged bull. As a means of launching their counteroffensive, the thirteen Black House-members first formed the "Democratic Select Committee," but in 1971 it was renamed Congressional Black Caucus (CBC). The founding members had considered many names, and some others wanted to open the door to other minority legislators, notably Chicanos, Puerto Ricans, and Jewish members. But as Clay writes, these proposals were rejected, as ultimately "it was unanimously agreed that the Caucus be composed of only black members and that the word 'black' remain in the name." Its thirteen founding members were: Representatives Shirley Chisholm, William Clay, George Collins, John Conyers, Ronald Dellums, Charles Diggs, Augustus Hawkins, Ralph Metcalfe, Parren Mitchell, Robert Nix, Charles Rangel, Louis Stokes, and the D.C. delegate, Walter Fauntroy. Organized to maximize their collective influence in Congress, the CBC's mission was to represent the concerns of African Americans.

Early on, the CBC's organizational style was characterized as combative. Rebuffed by President Nixon in their efforts to set up a meeting for over one year, members of the CBC boycotted Nixon's January 1971 State of the Union address. The only African American legislator to attend was Senator Ed Brooke of Massachusetts, then the only Black Republican member of the U.S. Congress. The standoff continued through the second year of President Nixon's second administration. Finally, in March 1971, a meeting was granted, during which the CBC presented the president with sixty policy recommendations. Nixon's response to this list was mixed, but polite.

While the CBC was described as a "concrete manifestation of black political power" within a short period of time, many Black legislators, including some of the CBC's original founders became critical of the organization. By Clay's account, the disagreements and points of disunity were real enough but frequently petty. In a chapter entitled, "The CBC Almost Self-Destructs," he recounts how one member would resign in high drama because the CBC failed to reserve enough tables at a legislative weekend for his campaign contributors, only to rejoin "unceremoniously" four months later. Others would express their grave concerns that a contribution to the organization was accepted from the Coors Company, whose founder was a well-known political conservative. Then there was the presidential bid of one of the CBC's founding members, Shirley

Chisholm (D-NY), which . . . provoked disunity among CBC members.

Beneath all of these issues was obviously a larger conflict between the organization's interests in representing Black interests and members' own political goals. Much feuding took place during President Carter's administration. As members rose in seniority, their loyalty to the organization was stretched and tested by other members who wanted unrelenting and uncompromising resistance to public policies that were perceived as harmful to or dilutive of Black interests—resistance that could jeopardize senior members' own standing in the House. Bill Gray (D-PA)'s service on the Budget Committee and his elevation to Chair in 1985 illustrated this tension well. Chairman Gray clearly became an advocate for the Democratic leadership's budget and a target for CBC's criticism. The conflict was rooted in the organization style that the CBC would adopt. Was the CBC a party within a party, or an organization outside of the Democratic party?

It is instructive that the motto of the CBC is "Black people have no permanent friends, no permanent enemies . . . just permanent interests." Charles Diggs (D-MI), one of its founding members, would claim that the "issues and concerns of this caucus are not partisan ones," implying that the CBC is a party outside of the Democratic organization, willing to align itself with any interest within Congress that will promote the interests of Blacks. Thus, the CBC could conceivably vote across party lines with Republicans in whatever issue was in the interest of African Americans. Political disunity within the Democratic party was injurious to members who wanted to advance within the party ranks. While seniority is a factor in committee assignments, so is party unity. Thus, as Blacks rose in seniority and began to covet positions of power on key committees, the type of strategy exemplified by the CBC's motto was professionally dangerous.

The CBC's political approach, however, was not premised on a "balance of power" equation whereby Black members would position themselves in between the two major parties and vote depending on which group's legislation promised the most by way of benefits for Blacks. This, in fact, is the approach often taken by the Blue Dogs, a group of conservative Democrats. Instead, the CBC's strategy of Black political independence is not unlike that described by Ronald Walters in his analysis of Jesse Jackson's presidential bids. The CBC would organize Black members' votes as a bloc, which could be used to bargain with the larger Democratic party to ensure that its policy agenda moved closer to that of Blacks. Furthermore, the CBC would issue policy statements that could become part of the Democratic party's legislative agenda. By running inside of the Democratic party, Jackson could help mobilize a core segment of Black voters who could be used as bargaining chips with the national Democratic party organization. In addition, Jackson's candidacy could put Black issues on the national political agenda and on the party's policy platform. (The problem is that as a bargaining vehicle for Black Democratic voters, Jackson's two presidential bids were not especially successful.) Like Jackson's bids, the CBC's strategy was entirely intraparty, as they sought to negotiate with the larger Democratic party, and not organize anew from outside of it. . . .

The CBC's legislative strategy is one that was closely followed by Jesse Jackson in his 1984 and 1988 presidential bids. As I note in my analysis of these bids, Jackson "presented himself as both an insider and an outsider. . . . As an insider, he ran as a Democrat and chose not to become a political independent. As an outsider, he challenged party rules and disregarded party norms." After having been its most vocal critic, Jackson in 1996 would fall in line with all the other party leaders, giving his most ringing endorsement ever to Clinton for reelection as president.

As the membership ranks of CBC grew and as members achieved greater seniority, their allegiances transferred increasingly to that of the party. In Singh's analysis of strategic budgetary battles between Democratic leaders and CBC members, those rising fastest in the party's ranks and who were chairs of their own committees and subcommittees were the most likely to vote for the Democratic budget in 1986. Their allegiances were not only divided between their party and the CBC, but also between their positions as chairs of committees and their own re-election and constituency interests. As Singh notes, even Conyers (D-MI), whose positions most consistently corresponded to those of the CBC, voted in 1988 to impeach Alcee Hastings, the first Black federal judge in Florida— even as the CBC refused to adopt a position condemning Hastings, who would later win election in 1992 to the House. The transfer of allegiance to a more solid position within the Democratic party did not come about only because of the growing self-interest of Black members, but as the Democratic party leadership wisely began to appoint Blacks to important committees. Early Black members were put on unimportant committees, deliberately or thoughtlessly, as was the case of Chisholm. But if the function of party leaders is to "keep the peace" by providing members meaningful opportunities to influence the legislative process, party leaders wised up and began to integrate Blacks better. Appointing Gray chair of the Budget Committee in the 99th Congress in 1985, and then as the party's majority whip (the third-ranking party leadership position), was a brilliant way to win votes for the leadership's budget initiatives with, perhaps, less wheeling and dealing on the part of party officials. While Gray attempted to bring fellow CBC members quickly into the party fold, his stronger loyalty to the party was affirmed by voting "present" or abstaining on the CBC alternative budget floor vote. While some may interpret Gray's preference for the party's agenda over that of the CBC as a reflection of an ideological shift, the reason behind his choice, again, probably lay in the incentive and disincentive devices that the party leadership had at its disposal. In their efforts to ensure party discipline, committee chairs were made accountable to the party through a regular secret ballot at the beginning of each Congress. Thus, party chairs could be dumped if the leadership felt they were not sufficiently supportive. Thus, unity is challenged not on the basis of ideology but as individual members rise in the ranks and strive to win greater policy influence over the legislative process on their own.

While some scholars have suggested that the increasing numbers of Blacks in the House would undermine the political solidarity of Blacks as they brought into Congress diverse views and perspectives, the apparent division is less the manifestation of growing ideological disunity than cross-cutting allegiances and a matter of political strategy. The confrontational approach that characterized the early CBC is no longer supported by the majority of Black House members. The additions of Black members from the South add not ideological dissension but different constituency concerns, diluting the overarching urban interests of the previous Caucus members. . . .

Accepting Robert Singh's ultimate conclusion that the CBC, institutionally weak, has amassed at best a "modest record" in delivering public policies of substance to the Black community, I challenge the implications of its increasing irrelevance to the interests of African Americans. Singh's conclusions, after all, are predicated on the assumption that political representation is exclusively substantive, policy representation. Representation as I have defined it, however, is far more encompassing and includes symbolic representation as well. The CBC's primary aim is to give voice and recognition to the interests of Blacks and poor Americans. In the marketplace of ideas and ideologies, this voice and recognition has vital currency. Social groups compete for the positioning of their groups' interests and ultimately of their group's rank with other interests and social groups. Some traces of the old-style protest behavior of the CBC still remain. In the 104th, after Republicans replaced the portrait of the late Democratic chairman of the Rules Committee with the painting of an ardent segregationist, Howard Smith of Virginia, Black members staged a "successful sit-in, demanding the portrait be removed." . . .

While Representative Fattah's (D-PA) bill in the 106th Congress to recognize African American music and its contribution to American society may seem inconsequential, it must be understood as one symbol competing with other symbols in this larger marketplace. It is legislation that is literally in competition with other bills, including those recognizing "classical music." Without Black members taking part in the legislative process, the symbolic interests such as the congressional medals to Rosa Parks, would not be there. Martin Luther King's birthday becoming a national holiday symbolized the role he played in transforming the country into a true democracy. As a national holiday, it becomes difficult to diminish his place in history and the role of African Americans generally in America. Their absence would contribute further to the symbolic marginalization of Blacks' place in American society and in history.

28

PAUL STAROBIN

Pork: A Time-Honored Tradition Lives On

Journalist Paul Starobin's look at congressional "pork" updates a classic subject. Pork, a project that a representative can secure for her or his district, has been a central part of congressional politics from the start. In times past, pork was easier to notice—edifices like canals, highways, bridges—as well as less controversial. The United States needed these infrastructure improvements, and the money was available for a generous pork barrel. Today, pork carries a different connotation. Starobin lists the new forms that pork takes in the "post-industrial" era. Modern pork projects don't look like those of the past. And the pork barrel, while as popular as always, isn't nearly as deep as it once was. Legislators are under pressure to cut, not spend, and pork—often called "earmarks" today—is a perfect target. But what is pork anyway? Some other district's waste-treatment plant.

———

POLITICAL PORK. Since the first Congress convened two centuries ago, lawmakers have ladled it out to home constituencies in the form of cash for roads, bridges and sundry other civic projects. It is a safe bet that the distribution of such largess will continue for at least as long into the future.*

Pork-barrel politics, in fact, is as much a part of the congressional scene as the two parties or the rules of courtesy for floor debate. . . .

And yet pork-barrel politics always has stirred controversy. Critics dislike seeing raw politics guiding decisions on the distribution of federal money for parochial needs. They say disinterested experts, if possible, should guide that money flow.

And fiscal conservatives wonder how Congress will ever get a handle on the federal budget with so many lawmakers grabbing so forcefully for pork-barrel funds. "Let's change the system so we don't have so much porking," says James C. Miller III, director of the White House Office of Management and Budget (OMB). Miller says he gets complaints on the order of one a day from congressional members taking issue with OMB suggestions that particular "pork" items in the budget are wasteful.

But pork has its unabashed defenders. How, these people ask, can lawmakers ignore the legitimate demands of their constituents? When a highway needs to be built or a waterway constructed, the home folks quite naturally look to their congressional representative for help. Failure to respond amounts to political suicide.

"I've really always been a defender of pork-barreling because that's what I think people elect us for," says Rep. Douglas H. Bosco, D-Calif.

Moreover, many accept pork as a staple of the legislative process, lubricating the squeaky wheels of Congress by giving members a personal stake in major bills. . . .

Not only does the flow of pork continue pretty much unabated, it seems to be spreading to areas that traditionally haven't been subject to pork-barrel competition. Pork traditionally was identified with public-works projects such as roads, bridges, dams and harbors. But, as the economy and country have changed, lawmakers have shifted their appetites to what might be called "post-industrial" pork. Some examples:

• *Green Pork.* During the 1960s and 1970s, when dam-builders fought epic struggles with environmentalists, "pork-barrel" projects stereotypically meant bulldozers and concrete. But many of today's projects are more likely to draw praise than blame from environmentalists. The list includes sewer projects, waste-site cleanups, solar energy laboratories,

---

*The interesting, little-known, and ignominious origin of the term "pork barrel" comes from early in American history, when a barrel of salt pork was given to slaves as a reward for their work. The slaves had to compete among themselves to get their piece of the handout. —EDS.

pollution-control research, parks and park improvements and fish hatcheries, to name a few. . . .

• *Academic Pork.* Almost no federal funds for construction of university research facilities are being appropriated these days, except for special projects sponsored by lawmakers for campuses back home. Many of the sponsors sit on the Appropriations committees, from which they are well positioned to channel such funds. . . .

• *Defense Pork.* While the distribution of pork in the form of defense contracts and location of military installations certainly isn't new, there's no question that Reagan's military buildup has expanded opportunities for lawmakers to practice pork-barrel politics. . . .

This spread of the pork-barrel system to new areas raises a question: What exactly is pork? Reaching a definition isn't easy. Many people consider it wasteful spending that flows to a particular state or district and is sought to please the folks back home.

But what is wasteful? One man's boondoggle is another man's civic pride. Perhaps the most sensible definition is that which a member seeks for his own state or district but would not seek for anyone else's constituency.

Thus, pork goes to the heart of the age-old tension between a lawmaker's twin roles as representative of a particular area and member of a national legislative body. In the former capacity, the task is to promote the local interest; in the latter it is to weigh the national interest. . . .

Like other fraternities, the system has a code of behavior and a pecking order. It commands loyalty and serves the purpose of dividing up federal money that presumably has to go somewhere, of helping re-elect incumbents and of keeping the wheels of legislation turning. . . .

When applied with skill, pork can act as a lubricant to smooth passage of complex legislation. At the same time, when local benefits are distributed for merely "strategic" purposes, it can lead to waste. . . .

Just about everyone agrees that the budget crunch has made the competition to get pet projects in spending legislation more intense. Demand for such items has not shrunk nearly as much as the pool of available funds.

29

JOHN ELLWOOD
ERIC PATASHNIK

In Praise of Pork

Pork-barrel spending is high on Americans' list of gripes against Congress. "Asparagus research and mink reproduction" typify the wasteful spending that seems to enrich congressional districts and states while bankrupting the nation. Recently, "earmarks" have been criticized as the newest technique for putting pork into bills. John Ellwood and Eric Patashnik take a different view. Pork is not the real cause of the nation's budget crisis, they feel. In fact, pork projects may be just what members of the House and Senate need to be able to satisfy constituents in order to summon the courage to vote for real, significant, painful budget cuts.

———

IN A WHITE HOUSE address . . . [in] March [1992], President Bush challenged Congress to cut $5.7 billion of pork barrel projects to help reduce the deficit.* Among the projects Bush proposed eliminating were such congressional favorites as funding for asparagus research, mink reproduction, and local parking garages. The examples he cited would be funny, said the President, "if the effect weren't so serious." . . .

Such episodes are a regular occurrence in Washington. Indeed, since the first Congress convened in 1789 and debated whether to build a lighthouse to protect the Chesapeake Bay, legislators of both parties have attempted to deliver federal funds back home for capital improvements and other projects, while presidents have tried to excise pork from the congressional diet. . . .

In recent years, public outrage over government waste has run high. Many observers see pork barrel spending not only as a symbol of an out-of-control Congress but as a leading cause of the nation's worsening

---

*The "pork-barrel" refers to congressional spending on projects that bring money and jobs to particular districts throughout America, thereby aiding legislators in their reelection bids. The interesting, little-known, and ignominious origin of the term "pork barrel" comes from early in American history, when a barrel of salt pork was given to slaves as a reward for their work. The slaves had to compete among themselves to get their piece of the handout. — EDS.

budget deficit. To cite one prominent example, *Washington Post* editor Brian Kelly claims in his recent book, *Adventures in Porkland: Why Washington Can't Stop Spending Your Money*, that the 1992 federal budget alone contains $97 billion of pork projects so entirely without merit that they could be "lopped out" without affecting the "welfare of the nation."

Kelly's claims are surely overblown. For example, he includes the lower prices that consumers would pay if certain price supports were withdrawn, even though these savings (while certainly desirable) would for the most part not show up in the government's ledgers. Yet reductions in pork barrel spending have also been advocated by those who acknowledge that pork, properly measured, comprises only a tiny fraction of total federal outlays. For example, Kansas Democrat Jim Slattery, who led the battle in the House in 1991 against using $500,000 in federal funds to turn Lawrence Welk's birthplace into a shrine, told *Common Cause Magazine*, "it's important from the standpoint of restoring public confidence in Congress to show we are prepared to stop wasteful spending," even if the cuts are only symbolic. In a similar vein, a recent *Newsweek* cover story, while conceding that "cutting out the most extreme forms of pork wouldn't eliminate the federal deficit," emphasizes that doing so "would demonstrate that Washington has the political will to reform its profligate ways."

The premise of these statements is that the first thing anyone—whether an individual consumer or the United States government—trying to save money should cut out is the fluff. As *Time* magazine rhetorically asks: "when Congress is struggling without much success to reduce the federal budget deficit, the question naturally arises: is pork *really* necessary?"

Our answer is yes. We believe in pork not because every new dam or overpass deserves to be funded, nor because we consider pork an appropriate instrument of fiscal policy (there are more efficient ways of stimulating a $5 trillion economy). Rather, we think that pork, doled out strategically, can help to sweeten an otherwise unpalatable piece of legislation.

No bill tastes so bitter to the average member of Congress as one that raises taxes or cuts popular programs. Any credible deficit-reduction package will almost certainly have to do both. In exchange for an increase in pork barrel spending, however, members of Congress just might be willing to bite the bullet and make the politically difficult decisions that will be required if the federal deficit is ever to be brought under control.

In a perfect world it would not be necessary to bribe elected officials to perform their jobs well. But, as James Madison pointed out two centuries ago in *Federalist* 51, men are not angels and we do not live in a perfect world. The object of government is therefore not to suppress the imperfections of human nature, which would be futile, but rather to harness the pursuit of self-interest to public ends.

Unfortunately, in the debate over how to reduce the deficit, Madison's advice has all too often gone ignored. Indeed, if there is anything the major budget-reform proposals of the last decade (Gramm-Rudman, the balanced-budget amendment, an entitlement cap*) have in common, it is that in seeking to impose artificial limits on government spending without offering anything in return, they work against the electoral interests of congressmen instead of with them—which is why these reforms have been so vigorously resisted.

No reasonable observer would argue that pork barrel spending has always been employed as a force for good or that there are no pork projects what would have been better left unbuilt. But singling out pork as the culprit for our fiscal troubles directs attention away from the largest sources of budgetary growth and contributes to the illusion that the budget can be balanced simply by eliminating waste and abuse. While proposals to achieve a pork-free budget are not without superficial appeal, they risk depriving leaders trying to enact real deficit-reduction measures of one of the most effective coalition-building tools at their disposal.

In order to appreciate why congressmen are so enamored of pork it is helpful to understand exactly what pork is. But defining pork is not as easy as it sounds. According to *Congressional Quarterly*, pork is usually considered to be "wasteful" spending that flows to a particular state or district in order to please voters back home. Like beauty, however, waste is in the eye of the beholder. As University of Michigan budget expert Edward M. Gramlich puts it, "one guy's pork is another guy's red meat." To a district plagued by double-digit unemployment, a new highway project is a sound investment, regardless of local transportation needs.

Some scholars simply define pork as any program that is economically inefficient—that is, any program whose total costs exceed its total benefits. But this definition tars with the same brush both real pork and programs that, while inefficient, can be justified on grounds of distributional equity or in which geographic legislative influence is small or nonexistent.

A more promising approach is suggested by political scientist David

---

*Many attempts have been made in past years to lower the deficit. In 1985, the Gramm-Rudman-Hollings law set dollar–limit goals for deficit reduction, to be followed by automatic percentage cuts; however, many programs were exempted. A 1995 balanced-budget amendment passed the House, but failed to get two-thirds of the Senate's approval. Entitlement caps would seek to limit the total amount the federal government could pay out in programs such as Medicare, Medicaid, Social Security, and food stamps.—Eds.

Mayhew in his 1974 book, *Congress: The Electoral Connection*. According to Mayhew, congressional life consists largely of "a relentless search" for ways of claiming credit for making good things happen back home and thereby increasing the likelihood of remaining in office. Because there are 535 congressmen and not one, each individual congressman must try to "peel off pieces of governmental accomplishment for which he can believably generate a sense of responsibility." For most congressmen, the easiest way of doing this is to supply goods to their home districts.

From this perspective, the ideal pork barrel project has three key properties. First, benefits are conferred on a specific geographical constituency small enough to allow a single congressman to be recognized as the benefactor. Second, benefits are given out in such a fashion as to lead constituents to believe that the congressman had a hand in the allocation. Third, costs resulting from the project are widely diffused or otherwise obscured from taxpayer notice.

Political pork, then, offers a congressman's constituents an array of benefits at little apparent cost. Because pork projects are easily distinguished by voters from the ordinary outputs of government, they provide an incumbent with the opportunity to portray himself as a "prime mover" who deserves to be reelected. When a congressman attends a ribbon-cutting ceremony for a shiny new building in his district, every voter can *see* that he is accomplishing something in Washington. . . .

"It's outrageous that you've got to have such political payoffs to get Congress to do the nation's business," says James Miller, OMB director under Ronald Reagan. Miller's outrage is understandable but ultimately unproductive. Human nature and the electoral imperative being what they are, the pork barrel is here to stay.

But if pork is a permanent part of the political landscape, it is incumbent upon leaders to ensure that taxpayers get something for their money. Our most effective presidents have been those who have linked the distribution of pork to the achievement of critical national objectives. When Franklin Roosevelt discovered he could not develop an atomic bomb without the support of Tennessee Senator Kenneth McKellar, chairman of the Appropriations Committee, he readily agreed to locate the bomb facility in Oak Ridge. By contrast, our least effective presidents—Jimmy Carter comes to mind—have either given away plum projects for nothing or waged hopeless battles against pork, squandering scarce political capital and weakening their ability to govern in the process.

The real value of pork projects ultimately lies in their ability to induce rational legislators into taking electorally risky actions for the sake of the public good. Over the last ten years, as the discretionary part of the budget has shrunk, congressmen have had fewer and fewer opportunities to claim credit for directly aiding their constituents. As Brookings scholar R. Kent Weaver has argued, in an era of scarcity and difficult political choices, many legislators gave up on trying to accomplish anything positive, focusing their energies instead on blame avoidance. The result has been the creation of a political climate in which elected officials now believe the only way they can bring the nation back to fiscal health is to injure their own electoral chances. This cannot be good for the future of the republic.

Politics got us into the deficit mess, however, and only politics can get us out. According to both government and private estimates, annual deficits will soar after the mid-1990s, and could exceed $600 billion in 2002 if the economy performs poorly. Virtually every prominent mainstream economist agrees that reducing the deficit significantly will require Congress to do what it has been strenuously trying to avoid for more than a decade—rein in spending for Social Security, Medicare, and other popular, middle-class entitlement programs. Tax increases may also be necessary. From the vantage point of the average legislator, the risk of electoral retribution seems enormous.

If reductions in popular programs and increases in taxes are required to put our national economic house back in order, the strategic use of pork to obtain the support of key legislators for these measures will be crucial. . . .

. . . [T]he president should ignore the advice of fiscal puritans who would completely exorcise pork from the body politic. Favoring legislators with small gifts for their districts in order to achieve great things for the nation is an act not of sin but of statesmanship. To be sure, determining how much pork is needed and to which members it should be distributed is difficult. Rather than asking elected officials to become selfless angels, however, we would ask of them only that they be smart politicians. We suspect Madison would agree that the latter request has a far better chance of being favorably received.

30

DAVID PRICE

From *The Congressional Experience*

From a political science classroom at Duke University in Durham, North Carolina, to the U.S. House of Representatives, David Price describes his background, his decision to run for office, and his concerns for the future of the Congress. Price reveals his typical daily schedule as a representative. He discusses his distaste for "Congress-bashing," the favorite pastime of members of the Congress. Price condemns the "hot-button attack politics" campaigning style that has pushed issues aside and created a negative cynical tone in American politics.

In November 1994, Rep. David Price (D–NC) lost his seat in the House of Representatives to his Republican challenger. Then in November, 1996, Price won back his seat.

———

ON NOVEMBER 4, 1986, I was elected to the U.S. House of Representatives from the Fourth District of North Carolina, a five-county area that includes the cites of Raleigh, Chapel Hill, and Asheboro. Many thoughts crowded in on me on election night, but one of the most vivid was of that spring evening in 1959 when I had first set foot in the part of North Carolina I was now to represent. At the time, I was a student at Mars Hill, a junior college in the North Carolina mountains a few miles from my home in the small town of Erwin, Tennessee. I had taken an eight-hour bus ride from Mars Hill to Chapel Hill to be interviewed for a Morehead Scholarship, a generous award that subsequently made it possible for me to attend the University of North Carolina (UNC). I was awed by the university and nervous about the interview; thinking back on some of the answers I gave the next morning ("Would you say Cecil Rhodes was an imperialist?" "I believe so"), I still marvel that I won the scholarship. But I did, and the next two years were among the most formative and exciting of my life.

I went north in 1961 to divinity school and eventually to graduate school and a faculty appointment in political science at Yale University. But the idea of returning to the Raleigh-Durham-Chapel Hill area of North Carolina exerted a continuing tug on me, particularly as I decided on a teaching career and thought about where I would like to put down personal and academic roots. Fortunately, my wife, Lisa, also found the idea agreeable, despite her budding political career as a member of New Haven's Board of Aldermen. Therefore, when I received an offer to join the political science faculty at Duke University and also to help launch the university's Institute of Policy Sciences and Public Affairs, I jumped at the opportunity. In mid-1973, we moved with our two children— Karen, three, and Michael, one—to Chapel Hill. Though we were delighted with the community and the job and saw the move as a long-term one, I would have been incredulous at the suggestion that within fourteen years I would represent the district in Congress. . . .

Among some voters—and occasionally among congressional colleagues—my academic background has represented a barrier to be overcome. But usually it has not. My district, it is claimed, has the highest number of Ph.D.'s per capita of any comparable area in the country. Certainly, with eleven institutions of higher education and the kind of people who work in the Research Triangle Park, I have some remarkably literate constituents. I sometimes reflect ambivalently on this as I contemplate the piles of well-reasoned letters on every conceivable issue that come into my office. Yet the electoral advantages are considerable. During my first campaign, we polled to test public reactions to my academic affiliation and background, expecting to downplay them in the campaign. Instead, we found highly positive associations and ended up running a television ad that featured me in the classroom! . . .

Becoming a member of the House shakes up not only family life but also the roles and routines associated with one's previous career. I took a special interest, naturally, in [political scientist Richard] Fenno's* interview with a freshman senator who had been a college professor. "Life in the Senate," he said, "is the antithesis of academic life." I would not put it quite that way: Such a view seems both to exaggerate the orderliness and tranquility of modern academic life and to underestimate the extent to which one can impose a modicum of order on life in the Congress. Still, few jobs present as many diverse and competing demands as does service in Congress.

Consider, for example, my schedule for two rather typical days in the spring of 1991, reprinted here without change except for the deletion of

---

*Richard Fenno's most well-known book is his 1978 *Home Style*. It represented a whole new way to study Congress. He followed certain representatives as they returned home, to their districts, to meet with constituents. Fenno found that members of Congress try to build "trust" among the voters so that more "leeway" exists for members in their congressional voting. Much of Fenno's work involved interviewing and observing members of Congress as individuals, to gain insight into their behavior as elected officials.—EDS.

some personal names and the addition of a few explanatory notes. By this time, I had moved to the Appropriations Committee from the three committees on which I sat during my first term, so the hearing schedule was less demanding; nonetheless, the Agriculture Appropriations Subcommittee held hearings on each of these two days. I also testified on a North Carolina environmental matter before a subcommittee of which I was not a member. The Budget Study Group and the Mainstream Forum, two of the informal organizations with which I am affiliated, held meetings, and the Prayer Breakfast, an informal fellowship group, met, as usual, on Thursday morning. I had several scheduled media interviews and probably a number of unscheduled press calls as well. There were a number of party meetings and activities: The Democratic Caucus met to discuss the pending budget resolution; a whip's task force was organized to mobilize Democrats behind the resolution; the caucus held a "party effectiveness" luncheon open to all members to discuss a major pending issue; and I participated in a caucus-organized set of one-minute speeches at the beginning of the House session. The other items are self-explanatory— meetings with North Carolina groups on issues of concern, talks to student groups, and various receptions that substituted for dinner or at least provided enough sustenance to take me through the evening of editing letters and reading in my office. And of course, the schedule does not capture the numerous trips to the House floor for votes, the phone calls, and the staff conferences scattered throughout every day.

These schedules list only events I actually attended; they also reflect the rules of thumb by which my staff and I keep life from getting even more hectic. In general, I talk with groups about pending legislation only when there is a North Carolina connection; most Washington groups are well aware that their delegations need to include at least one representative from the district. I also generally skip receptions at the end of the day unless constituents are to be there or a colleague has asked me to attend.

This sheer busyness in Washington and at home as well surpasses what almost all members have experienced in their previous careers and requires specific survival techniques. Most important, you must set priorities— separate those matters in which you want to invest considerable time and energy from those you wish to handle perfunctorily or not deal with personally at all. Confronted with three simultaneous subcommittee hearings, a member often has a choice: pop in on each of the three for fifteen minutes or choose one and remain long enough to learn and contribute something. It is also essential to delegate a great deal to staff and to develop a good mutual understanding within the office as to when the member's personal direction and attention are required. But there are no manage-

TYPICAL MEMBER'S DAILY SCHEDULE IN WASHINGTON

Wednesday, April 10, 1991

8:00 A.M.	Budget Study Group—Chairman Leon Panetta, Budget Committee, room 340 Cannon Building
8:45 A.M.	Mainstream Forum Meeting, room 2344 Rayburn Building
9:15 A.M.	Meeting with Consulting Engineers Council of N.C. from Raleigh about various issues of concern
9:45 A.M.	Meet with N.C. Soybean Assn. representatives re: agriculture appropriations projects
10:15 A.M.	WCHL radio interview (by phone)
10:30 A.M.	Tape weekly radio show—budget
11:00 A.M.	Meet with former student, now an author, about intellectual property issue
1:00 P.M.	Agriculture Subcommittee Hearing—Budget Overview and General Agriculture Outlook, room 2362 Rayburn Building
2:30 P.M.	Meeting with Chairman Bill Ford and southern Democrats re: HR-5, Striker Replacement Bill, possible amendments
3:15 P.M.	Meet with Close-Up students from district on steps of Capitol for photo and discussions
3:45 P.M.	Meet with Duke professor re: energy research programs
4:30 P.M.	Meet with constituent of Kurdish background re: situation in Iraq
5:30–7:00 P.M.	Reception—Sponsored by National Assn. of Home Builders, honoring new president Mark Tipton from Raleigh, H-328 Capitol
6:00–8:00 P.M.	Reception—Honoring retiring Rep. Bill Gray, Washington Court Hotel
6:00–8:00 P.M.	Reception–Sponsored by Firefighters Assn., room B-339 Rayburn Building
6:00–8:00 P.M.	Reception—American Financial Services Assn., Gold Room

Thursday, April 11, 1991

8:00 A.M.	Prayer Breakfast—Rep. Charles Taylor to speak, room H-130 Capitol
9:00 A.M.	Whip meeting, room H-324 Capitol
10:00 A.M.	Democratic Caucus Meeting, Hall of the House, re: budget
10:25 A.M.	UNISYS reps. in office (staff, DP meets briefly)
10:30 A.M.	Firefighters from Raleigh re: Hatch Act Reform, Manufacturer's Presumptive Liability, etc.

TYPICAL MEMBER'S DAILY SCHEDULE IN WASHINGTON (*continued*)

11:00 A.M.	American Business Council of the Gulf Countries re: rebuilding the Gulf, improving competitiveness in Gulf market
11:15 A.M.	Whip Task Force meeting re: Budget Resolution, room H-114 Capitol
12:00 P.M.	Speech—One Minute on House floor re: budget
12:30 P.M.	Party Effectiveness Lunch—re: banking reform, room H-324 Capitol
1:00 P.M.	Agriculture Subcommittee Hearing—Inspector General Overview and the Office of the General Counsel, room 2362 Rayburn Building
3:00 P.M.	Testify at Oceanography Subcommittee Hearing re: naval vessel waste disposal on N.C. Outer Banks, room 1334 Longworth Building
3:30 P.M.	Speak to Duke public policy students re: operations of Congress, room 188 Russell Building
5:00 P.M.	Interview with Matthew Cross, WUNC stringer re: off-shore drilling
6:45 P.M.	Depart National Airport for Raleigh-Durham

ment techniques on earth that could make a representative's life totally predictable or controllable or that could convert a congressional office into a tidy bureaucracy. A member (or aide) who requires that kind of control—who cannot tolerate, for example, being diverted to talk to a visiting school class or to hear out a visiting delegation of homebuilders or social workers—is simply in the wrong line of work.

. . . Former Congressman Bob Eckhardt (D–Texas) suggested that every member of Congress performs three functions: lawmaker, ombudsman, and educator. This last function, as I have shown, may be closely related to the first: Lawmakers who wish to do more than simply defer to the strongest and best-organized interests on a certain matter must give some attention to explaining their actions and educating their constituents, helping them place the issue in broader perspective or perhaps activating alternative bases of support. And the extent to which a member is willing and able to undertake such explanations is ethically as well as politically significant.

Here, I turn to another facet of the legislators' educative role: their portrayal of Congress itself. On traveling with House members around their districts, Richard Fenno noted that the greatest surprise for him was the extent to which each one "polished his or her individual reputation at the expense of the institutional reputation of Congress":

In explaining what he was doing in Washington, every one of the eighteen House members took the opportunity to picture himself as different from, and better than, most of his fellow members in Congress. No one availed himself of the opportunity to educate his constituents about Congress as an institution—not in any way that would "hurt a little." To the contrary, the members' process of differentiating themselves from the Congress as a whole only served, directly or indirectly, to downgrade the Congress.

This was in the mid-1970s, and every indication is that such tactics have become even more prevalent as Congress-bashing by advocacy groups and in the media has intensified. "We have to differentiate me from the rest of those bandits down there in Congress," Fenno heard a member say to a campaign strategy group. " 'They are awful, but our guy is wonderful'—that's the message we have to get across."

So much for the traditional norm of institutional patriotism! Opinion polls regularly reveal that public officials in general and Congress in particular rank low in public esteem, an evaluation reinforced by the recent spate of ethics charges in both houses but rooted much more deeply in our country's history and political culture. Every indication is that we members reinforce such an assessment by distancing ourselves from any responsibility for the institution's functioning. And we are phenomenally successful at it, matching a 30 percent approval rate for Congress with a 95+ percent reelection rate for ourselves.

My point is not that a member should defend Congress, right or wrong. I understand very well the disadvantages of being put on the defensive about Congress's ethical problems—pointing out that only a small number of members are involved, for example, or that Ethics Committee proceedings are generally bipartisan and fair—although I believe many of these defenses have merit. Rather, I am speaking of a more general tendency to trash the institution. It is often tempting—but I believe, also deceptive and irresponsible—to pose as the quintessential outsider, carping at accommodations that have been reached on a given issue as though problems could simply be ignored, cost-free solutions devised, or the painful necessities of compromise avoided. Responsible legislators will communicate to their constituencies not only the assembly's failings but also what it is fair and reasonable to expect, what accommodations they would be well advised to accept, and so forth. In the past, institutional patriotism has too often taken an uncritical form, assuming that whatever the process produces must be acceptable. But self-righteous, anti-institutional posturing is no better. The moral quixotism to which reelection-minded legislators are increasingly prone too often serves to rationalize their own nonproductive legislative roles and to perpetuate public misperceptions of the criteria one can reasonably apply to legislative performance.

Therefore, although it may be politically profitable to "run *for* Congress by running *against* Congress," the implications for the institution's effectiveness and legitimacy are ominous. As Fenno concluded, "The strategy is ubiquitous, addictive, cost-free, and foolproof. . . . In the short run, everybody plays and nearly everybody wins. Yet the institution bleeds from 435 separate cuts. In the long run, therefore, somebody may lose. . . . Congress may lack public support at the very time when the public needs Congress the most." . . .

My job keeps me very busy and flying, as they say, "close to the ground"—attending to myriad details in dealing with constituents, tracking appropriations, and all the rest. I sometimes feel that I had a better overview of the current state of American politics and even of certain broad policy questions before I was elected than I do now. I have, however, been in a position to observe some alarming trends in our politics and to develop strong convictions about our need to reverse them. I will therefore conclude with a few thoughts on the ominous gap that has opened up between campaigning and governing. . . . It is in the nature of political campaigns to polarize and to oversimplify, but the negative attacks and distortions have increased markedly. And the link between what candidates say in their campaign advertisements and the decisions they make once in office has become more and more tenuous. . . .

This trend has been reinforced by the new technology of campaign advertising and fund-raising; thirty-second television ads and direct mail financial solicitations, for example, put a premium on hard-hitting, oversimplified appeals and the pushing of symbolic hot buttons. The trend has also been both cause and effect of the modern emergence of cultural and value questions, like abortion, race, patriotism, and alternative lifestyles, that lend themselves to symbolic appeals. Republican candidates in particular have found in these issues a promising means of diverting voters' attention from economic and quality-of-life concerns and of driving divisive wedges in the Democratic coalition.

The growing gap between campaigning and governing also bespeaks a certain public alienation and cynicism. Voters complain about the nastiness and irrelevance of campaign advertising, and my campaigns have demonstrated that such tactics can effectively be turned against an opponent. But voters who find little to encourage or inspire them in politics are nonetheless tempted to vote in anger or in protest, inclinations that modern campaign advertising exploits very effectively. As E. J. Dionne suggested, the decline of the "politics of remedy"—that is, politics that attempts "to solve problems and resolve disputes"—seems to have created a vicious cycle:

Campaigns have become negative in large part because of a sharp decline in popular faith in government. To appeal to an increasingly alienated electorate, candidates and their political consultants have adopted a cynical stance which, they believe with good reason, plays into popular cynicism about politics and thus wins them votes. But cynical campaigns do not resolve issues. They do not lead to "remedies." Therefore, problems get worse, the electorate becomes *more* cynical—and so does the advertising.

Responsibility for our descent into attack politics, increasingly divorced from the major problems faced by the American people, is widely shared—by journalists, interest groups, campaign consultants, and the viewing, voting public. Members of Congress are hardly helpless—or blameless—before these trends. For one thing, our defensiveness in the face of tough votes is often exaggerated; members frequently underestimate their ability to deflect attacks or to deal effectively with hostile charges. All of us feel occasionally that "I'd rather vote against this than to have to explain it," but we should worry if we find ourselves taking this way out too often or on matters of genuine consequence. It is our job to interpret and explain difficult decisions, and with sufficient effort, we can usually do so successfully.

We also have some choices about the kind of campaigns we run. By making campaign tactics themselves an issue, we can heighten public awareness of and resistance to distorted and manipulative appeals. Above all, we can tighten the link between what we say in our own campaigns and what we have done and intend to do in office. This is not a plea for dull campaigns; on the contrary, it is our duty to arouse people's concern and anger about areas of neglect, to convince them that we can do better, to inspire them to contribute to the solution. Most people believe that politics and politicians ought to have something constructive to offer in the realms of education, housing, health care, economic development, environmental protection, and other areas of tangible concern. Our task is to get to work on these major challenges in both campaigning *and* governing in a credible way that inspires confidence and enthusiasm. As that happens, hot-button attack politics will increasingly be seen as the sham that it is.

PART SIX

The Presidency

31

RICHARD NEUSTADT

From *Presidential Power and the Modern Presidents*

From this often-read book comes the classic concept of presidential power as "the power to persuade." Richard Neustadt observed the essence of presidential power when working in the executive branch during Franklin Roosevelt's term as president. He stayed to serve under President Truman. It is said that President Kennedy brought Presidential Power *with him to the White House, and Neustadt worked briefly for JFK. The first half of the excerpt, in which he shows how presidents' well-developed personal characteristics permit successful persuasive abilities, comes from the book's first edition. The excerpt's closing pages reflect Neustadt's later musings on the nation, on world affairs, and on the challenges presidents face.*

IN THE EARLY summer of 1952, before the heat of the campaign, President [Harry] Truman used to contemplate the problems of the general-become-President should [Dwight David] Eisenhower win the forthcoming election. "He'll sit here," Truman would remark (tapping his desk for emphasis), "and he'll say, 'Do this! Do that!' *And nothing will happen.* Poor Ike—it won't be a bit like the Army. He'll find it very frustrating."

Eisenhower evidently found it so. "In the face of the continuing dissidence and disunity, the President sometimes simply exploded with exasperation," wrote Robert Donovan in comment on the early months of Eisenhower's first term. "What was the use, he demanded to know, of his trying to lead the Republican Party. . . . " And this reaction was not limited to early months alone, or to his party only. "The President still feels," an Eisenhower aide remarked to me in 1958, "that when he's decided something, that *ought* to be the end of it . . . and when it bounces back undone or done wrong, he tends to react with shocked surprise."

Truman knew whereof he spoke. With "resignation" in the place of "shocked surprise," the aide's description would have fitted Truman. The former senator may have been less shocked than the former general, but he was no less subjected to that painful and repetitive experience: "Do this, do that, and nothing will happen." Long before he came to talk of Eisenhower he had put his own experience in other words: "I sit here all day trying to persuade people to do the things they ought to have sense enough to do without my persuading them. . . . That's all the powers of the President amount to."

In these words of a President, spoken on the job, one finds the essence of the problem now before us: "powers" are no guarantee of power; clerkship is no guarantee of leadership. The President of the United States has an extraordinary range of formal powers, of authority in statute law and in the Constitution. Here is testimony that despite his "powers" he does not obtain results by giving orders—or not, at any rate, merely by giving orders. He also has extraordinary status, ex officio, according to the customs of our government and politics. Here is testimony that despite his status he does not get action without argument. Presidential power is the power to persuade. . . .

The limits on command suggest the structure of our government. The Constitutional Convention of 1787 is supposed to have created a government of "separated powers." It did nothing of the sort. Rather, it created a government of separated institutions *sharing* powers. "I am part of the legislative process," Eisenhower often said in 1959 as a reminder of his veto. Congress, the dispenser of authority and funds, is no less part of the administrative process. Federalism adds another set of separated institutions. The Bill of Rights adds others. Many public purposes can only be achieved by voluntary acts of private institutions; the press, for one, in Douglass Cater's phrase, is a "fourth branch of government." And with the coming of alliances abroad, the separate institutions of a London, or a Bonn, share in the making of American public policy.

What the Constitution separates our political parties do not combine. The parties are themselves composed of separated organizations sharing public authority. The authority consists of nominating powers. Our national parties are confederations of state and local party institutions, with a headquarters that represents the White House, more or less, if the party has a President in office. These confederacies manage presidential nominations. All other public offices depend upon electorates confined within the states. All other nominations are controlled within the states. The President and congressmen who bear one party's label are divided by dependence upon different sets of voters. The differences are sharpest at the stage of nomination. The White House has too small a share in nominating congressmen, and Congress has too little weight in nominating presidents for party to erase their constitutional separation. Party links are stronger than is frequently supposed, but nominating processes assure the separation.

The separateness of institutions and the sharing of authority prescribe the terms on which a President persuades. When one man shares authority with another, but does not gain or lose his job upon the other's whim, his willingness to act upon the urging of the other turns on whether he conceives the action right for him. The essence of a President's persuasive task is to convince such men that what the White House wants of them is what they ought to do for their sake and on their authority. (Sex matters not at all; for *man* read *woman.*)

Persuasive power, thus defined, amounts to more than charm or reasoned argument. These have their uses for a President, but these are not the whole of his resources. For the individuals he would induce to do what he wants done on their own responsibility will need or fear some acts by him on his responsibility. If they share his authority, he has some share in theirs. Presidential "powers" may be inconclusive when a President commands, but always remain relevant as he persuades. The status and authority inherent in his office reinforce his logic and his charm. . . .

A President's authority and status give him great advantages in dealing with the men he would persuade. Each "power" is a vantage point for him in the degree that other men have use for his authority. From the veto to appointments, from publicity to budgeting, and so down a long list, the White House now controls the most encompassing array of vantage points in the American political system. With hardly an exception, those who share in governing this country are aware that at some time, in some degree, the doing of *their* jobs, the furthering of *their* ambitions, may depend upon the President of the United States. Their need for presidential action, or their fear of it, is bound to be recurrent if not actually continuous. Their need or fear is his advantage.

A President's advantages are greater than mere listing of his "powers" might suggest. Those with whom he deals must deal with him until the last day of his term. Because they have continuing relationships with him, his future, while it lasts, supports his present influence. Even though there is no need or fear of him today, what he could do tomorrow may supply today's advantage. Continuing relationships may convert any "power," any aspect of his status, into vantage points in almost any case. When he induces other people to do what he wants done, a President can trade on their dependence now and later.

The President's advantages are checked by the advantages of others. Continuing relationships will pull in both directions. These are relationships of mutual dependence. A President depends upon the persons whom he would persuade; he has to reckon with his need or fear of them. They too will possess status, or authority, or both, else they would be of little use to him. Their vantage points confront his own; their power tempers his. . . .

The power to persuade is the power to bargain. Status and authority yield bargaining advantages. But in a government of "separated institutions sharing powers," they yield them to all sides. With the array of vantage points at his disposal, a President may be far more persuasive than his logic or his charm could make him. But outcomes are not guaranteed by his advantages. There remain the counter pressures those whom he would influence can bring to bear on him from vantage points at their disposal. Command has limited utility; persuasion becomes give-and-take. It is well that the White House holds the vantage points it does. In such a business any President may need them all—and more. . . .

When a President confronts divergent policy advisers, disputing experts, conflicting data, and uncertain outlooks, yet must choose, there plainly *are* some other things he can do for himself besides consulting his own power stakes. But there is a proviso—provided he has done that first and keeps clear in his mind how much his prospects may depend on his authority, how much on reputation, how much on public standing. In the world Reagan inhabited where reputation and prestige are far more intertwined than they had been in Truman's time, or even LBJ's, this proviso is no easy test of presidential expertise. It calls for a good ear and a fine eye. . . .

But when a President turns to others, regardless of the mode, he is dependent on their knowledge, judgment, and good will. If he turns essentially to one, alone, he puts a heavy burden on that other's knowledge. If he chooses not to read or hear details, he puts an even greater burden on the other's judgment. If he consents, besides, to secrecy from everyone whose task in life is to protect his flanks, he courts deep trouble. Good will should not be stretched beyond endurance. In a system characterized by separated institutions sharing powers, where presidential interests will diverge in some degree from those of almost everybody else, that suggests not stretching very far. . . .

Personally, I prefer Presidents . . . more skeptical than trustful, more curious than committed, more nearly Roosevelts than Reagans. I think the former energize our governmental system better and bring out its defects less than do the latter. Reagan's years did not persuade me otherwise, in spite of his appeal on other scores. Every scandal in his wake, for instance, must owe something to the narrow range of his convictions and the breadth of his incuriosity, along with all that trust. A President cannot abolish bad behavior, but he sets a tone, and if he is alert to possibilities he can set traps, and with them limits. Reagan's tone, apparently, was heard by all too many as "enrich yourselves," while those few traps deregulation spared appear to have been sprung and left unbaited for the most part. But this book has not been written to expound my personal preferences. Rather it endeavors to expose the problem for a President of either sort who seeks to buttress prospects for his future influence while making present choices—"looking toward tomorrow from today," as I wrote at the start. For me that remains a crucial enterprise. It is not, of course, the only thing a President should put his mind to, but it is the subject to which I have put my own throughout this book. It remains crucial, in my view, not simply for the purposes of Presidents, but also for the products of the system, whether effective policy, or flawed or none. Thus it becomes crucial for us all.

We now stand on the threshold of a time in which those separated institutions, Congress and the President, share powers fully and uncomfortably across the board of policy, both foreign and domestic. From the 1940s through the 1960s—"midcentury" in this book's terms—Congress, having been embarrassed at Pearl Harbor by the isolationism it displayed beforehand, gave successive Presidents more scope in defense budgeting and in the conduct of diplomacy toward Europe and Japan than was the norm between the two world wars. Once the Cold War had gotten under way, and then been largely militarized after Korea, that scope widened. With the onset of the missile age it deepened. Should nuclear war impend, the President became the system's final arbiter. Thus I characterized JFK against the background of the Cuban missile crisis. But by 1975 the denouement of Watergate and that of Vietnam, eight months apart, had put a period to what remained of congressional reticence left over from Pearl Harbor. And the closing of the Cold War, now in sight though by no means achieved, promises an end to nuclear danger as between the Soviet Union and the United States. Threats of nuclear attack could well remain, from Third World dictators or terrorists, but not destruction of the Northern Hemisphere. So in the realm of military preparations— even, indeed, covert actions—the congressional role waxes as the Cold War wanes, returning toward normality as understood in Franklin Roosevelt's first two terms.

In a multipolar world, crisscrossed by transnational relations, with economic and environmental issues paramount, and issues of security reshaped on regional lines, our Presidents will less and less have reason to seek solace in foreign relations from the piled-up frustrations of home affairs. Their foreign frustrations will be piled high too.

Since FDR in wartime, every President including Bush has found the role of superpower sovereign beguiling: personal responsibility at once direct and high, issues at once gripping and arcane, opposite numbers frequently intriguing and well-mannered, acclaim by foreign audiences echoing well at home, foreign travel relatively glamorous, compared with home, interest groups less clamorous, excepting special cases, authority always stronger, Congress often tamer. But the distinctions lessen—compare Bush's time with Nixon's to say nothing of Eisenhower's—and we should expect that they will lessen further. Telecommunications, trade, aid, banking and stock markets combined with AIDS and birth control and hunger, topped off by toxic waste and global warming—these are not the stuff of which the Congress of Vienna* was made, much less the summits of yore. Moreover, Europeans ten years hence, as well as Japanese, may not resemble much the relatively acquiescent "middle powers" we grew used to in the 1960s and 1970s. Cooperating with them may come to seem to Presidents no easier than cooperating with Congress. Our friends abroad will see it quite the other way around: How are they to cooperate with our peculiar mix of separated institutions sharing powers? Theirs are ordered governments, ours a rat race. Complaints of us by others in these terms are nothing new. They have been rife throughout this century. But by the next, some of the chief complainants may have fewer needs of us, while ours of them grow relatively greater, than at any other time since World War II. In that case foreign policy could cease to be a source of pleasure for a President. By the same token, he or she would have to do abroad as on the Hill and in Peoria: Check carefully the possible effects of present choices on prospective reputation and prestige— thinking of other governments and publics quite as hard as those at home. It is not just our accustomed NATO and Pacific allies who may force the pace here, but the Soviet Union, if it holds together, and potentially great powers—China, India, perhaps Brazil—as well as our neighbors, north and south.

From the multicentered, interdependent world now coming into being, environmentally endangered as it is, Presidents may look back on the Cold War as an era of stability, authority, and glamour. They may yearn for the simplicity they see in retrospect, and also for the solace. Too bad. The job of being President is tougher when incumbents have to struggle for effective influence in foreign and domestic spheres at once, with their command of nuclear forces losing immediate relevance, and the American economy shorn of its former clout. There are, however, compensations,

---

*After the 1814 defeat of the French leader Napoleon by Russia, Prussia, Austria, and Britain, these great powers met in Vienna, Austria, to ensure that the future of Europe would be peaceful. At the Congress of Vienna, they created a "balance of power" system so that no single European nation could dominate the continent.—EDS.

one in particular. If we outlive the Cold War,* the personal responsibility attached to nuclear weapons should become less burdensome for Presidents themselves, while contemplation of their mere humanity becomes less haunting for the rest of us. To me that seems a fair exchange.

32

ARTHUR SCHLESINGER

From *The Imperial Presidency*

Historian Arthur Schlesinger coined one of the most famous and often-quoted political phrases, used not just in academe but in the real world of government too. The demise of Richard Nixon, because of the Watergate scandal, inspired Schlesinger to look back in U.S. history to locate the roots of the tremendous power that the executive had accumulated. His observations led him to develop the idea of an "imperial Presidency," with all the connotations that phrase carries. The author believes that the imperial presidency initially evolved for a clear and identifiable reason; it then grew due to other secondary factors. Certain presidents — Roosevelt and especially Kennedy — garner praise from Schlesinger for their judicious use of imperial powers. Other presidents he condemns. Schlesinger's discussion of Richard Nixon, the ultimate imperial president as well as its destroyer, is a frank and unvarnished critique of the man who turned the imperial presidency homeward, against the American people. After Nixon left office, the phrase was little-used, until President Bush responded to the terrorist attacks of September 11, 2001. To some, President Bush's response to 9/11, especially his "War on Terror" and the invasion of Iraq, signify a rebirth of the "imperial presidency."

IN THE LAST YEARS presidential primacy, so indispensable to the political order, has turned into presidential supremacy. The constitutional Presidency — as events so apparently disparate as the Indochina War and the Watergate affair showed — has become the imperial Presidency and threatens to be the revolutionary Presidency.

*The Cold War refers to the hostility that existed between the United States and the Soviet Union from the end of World War II until recent times. The Cold War involved many forms of hostility: democracy versus communism; America's NATO allies versus the Soviet Union's Warsaw Pact military partners; the threat of nuclear war; economic competition; the dividing of Third World nations into pro-U.S. and pro-Soviet camps. With the demise of communism in Eastern Europe and the disintegration of the Soviet Union, the Cold War era has ended. — EDS.

This book . . . deals essentially with the shift in the *constitutional* balance—with, that is, the appropriation by the Presidency, and particularly by the contemporary Presidency, of powers reserved by the Constitution and by long historical practice to Congress.

This process of appropriation took place in both foreign and domestic affairs. Especially in the twentieth century, the circumstances of an increasingly perilous world as well as of an increasingly interdependent economy and society seemed to compel a larger concentration of authority in the Presidency. It must be said that historians and political scientists, this writer among them, contributed to the rise of the presidential mystique. But the imperial Presidency received its decisive impetus, I believe, from foreign policy; above all, from the capture by the Presidency of the most vital of national decisions, the decision to go to war.

This book consequently devotes special attention to the history of the war-making power. The assumption of that power by the Presidency was gradual and usually under the demand or pretext of emergency. It was as much a matter of congressional abdication as of presidential usurpation. . . .

The imperial Presidency was essentially the creation of foreign policy. A combination of doctrines and emotions—belief in permanent and universal crisis, fear of communism, faith in the duty and the right of the United States to intervene swiftly in every part of the world—had brought about the unprecedented centralization of decisions over war and peace in the Presidency. With this there came an unprecedented exclusion of the rest of the executive branch, of Congress, of the press and of public opinion in general from these decisions. Prolonged war in Vietnam strengthened the tendencies toward both centralization and exclusion. So the imperial Presidency grew at the expense of the constitutional order. Like the cowbird, it hatched its own eggs and pushed the others out of the nest. And, as it overwhelmed the traditional separation of powers in foreign affairs, it began to aspire toward an equivalent centralization of power in the domestic polity.

. . . We saw in the case of Franklin D. Roosevelt and the New Deal that extraordinary power flowing into the Presidency to meet domestic problems by no means enlarged presidential authority in foreign affairs. But we also saw in the case of FDR and the Second World War and Harry S. Truman and the steel seizure that extraordinary power flowing into the Presidency to meet international problems could easily encourage Presidents to extend their unilateral claims at home. . . . Twenty years later, the spillover effect from Vietnam coincided with indigenous developments that were quite separately carrying new power to the Presidency.

For domestic as well as for international reasons, the imperial Presidency was sinking roots deep into the national society itself.

One such development was the decay of the traditional party system. . . . For much of American history the party has been the ultimate vehicle of political expression. Voters inherited their politics as they did their religion. . . . By the 1970s ticket-splitting had become common. Independent voting was spreading everywhere, especially among the young. Never had party loyalties been so weak, party affiliations so fluid, party organizations so irrelevant.

Many factors contributed to the decline of parties. The old political organizations had lost many of their functions. The waning of immigration, for example, had deprived the city machine of its classical clientele. The rise of civil service had cut off the machine's patronage. The New Deal had taken over the machine's social welfare role. Above all, the electronic revolution was drastically modifying the political environment. Two electronic devices had a particularly devastating impact on the traditional structure of politics—television and the computer. . . .

As the parties wasted away, the Presidency stood out in solitary majesty as the central focus of political emotion, the ever more potent symbol of national community. . . .

At the same time, the economic changes of the twentieth century had conferred vast new powers not just on the national government but more particularly on the Presidency. . . .

. . . The managed economy, in short, offered new forms of unilateral power to the President who was bold enough to take action on his own. . . .

. . . The imperial presidency, born in the 1940s and 1950s to save the outer world from perdition, thus began in the 1960s and 1970s to find nurture at home. Foreign policy had given the President the command of peace and war. Now the decay of the parties left him in command of the political scene, and the Keynesian revelation placed him in command of the economy. At this extraordinary historical moment, when foreign and domestic lines of force converged, much depended on whether the occupant of the White House was moved to ride the new tendencies of power or to resist them.

For the American Presidency was a peculiarly personal institution. It remained, of course, an agency of government, subject to unvarying demands and duties no matter who was President. But, more than most agencies of government, it changed shape, intensity and ethos according to the man in charge. . . . The management of the great foreign policy crisis of the Kennedy years—the Soviet attempt to install nuclear missiles

in Cuba—came as if in proof of the proposition that the nuclear age left
no alternative to unilateral presidential decision. . . .

. . . Time was short, because something had to be done before the
bases became operational. Secrecy was imperative. Kennedy took the
decision into his own hands, but it is to be noted that he did not make
it in imperial solitude. The celebrated Executive Committee became a
forum for exceedingly vigorous and intensive debate. Major alternatives
received strong, even vehement, expression. Though there was no legislative consultation, there was most effective executive consultation. . . . But,
even in retrospect, the missile crisis seems an emergency so acute in its
nature and so peculiar in its structure that it did in fact require unilateral
executive decision.

Yet this very acuteness and peculiarity disabled Kennedy's action in
October 1962 as a precedent for future Presidents in situations less acute
and less peculiar. For the missile crisis was unique in the postwar years
in that it *really* combined all those pressures of threat, secrecy and time
that the foreign policy establishment had claimed as characteristic of
decisions in the nuclear age. Where the threat was less grave, the need
for secrecy less urgent, the time for debate less restricted—i.e., in all other
cases—the argument for independent and unilateral presidential action
was notably less compelling.

Alas, Kennedy's action, which should have been celebrated as an
exception, was instead enshrined as a rule. This was in great part because
it so beautifully fulfilled both the romantic ideal of the strong President
and the prophecy of split-second presidential decision in the nuclear age.
The very brilliance of Kennedy's performance appeared to vindicate the
idea that the President must take unto himself the final judgments of war
and peace. The missile crisis, I believe, was superbly handled, and could
not have been handled so well in any other way. But one of its legacies
was the imperial conception of the Presidency that brought the republic
so low in Vietnam. . . .

. . . Johnson talked to, even if he too seldom listened to, an endless
stream of members of Congress and the press. He unquestionably denied
himself reality for a long time, especially when it came to Vietnam. But
in the end reality broke through, forcing him to accept unpleasant truths
he did not wish to hear. Johnson's personality was far closer than Truman's
to imperial specifications. But the fit was by no means perfect. . . .

Every President reconstructs the Presidency to meet his own psychological needs. Nixon displayed more monarchical yearnings than any of
his predecessors. He plainly reveled in the ritual of the office, only regret-
ting that it could not be more elaborate. What previous President, for

example, would have dreamed of ceremonial trumpets or of putting the White House security force in costumes to rival the Guards at Buckingham Palace? Public ridicule stopped this. But Nixon saw no problem about using federal money, under the pretext of national security, to adorn his California and Florida estates with redwood fences, golf carts, heaters and wind screens for the swimming pool, beach cabanas, roof tiling, carpets, furniture, trees and shrubbery. . . . Nixon's fatal error was to institute within the White House itself a centralization even more total than that he contemplated for the executive branch. He rarely saw most of his so-called personal assistants. If an aide telephoned the President on a domestic matter, his call was switched to Haldeman's office.* If he sent the President a memorandum, Haldeman decided whether or not the President would see it. "Rather than the President telling someone to do something," Haldeman explained in 1971, "I'll tell the guy. If he wants to find out something from somebody, I'll do it."

Presidents like Roosevelt and Kennedy understood that, if the man at the top confined himself to a single information system, he became the prisoner of that system. Therefore they pitted sources of their own against the information delivered to them through official channels. They understood that contention was an indispensable means of government. But Nixon, instead of exposing himself to the chastening influence of debate, organized the executive branch and the White House in order to shield himself as far as humanly possible from direct question or challenge—i.e., from reality. . . .

As one examined the impressive range of Nixon's initiatives—from his appropriation of the war-making power to his interpretation of the appointing power, from his unilateral determination of social priorities to his unilateral abolition of statutory programs, from his attack on legislative privilege to his enlargement of executive privilege, from his theory of impoundment to his theory of the pocket veto, from his calculated disparagement of the cabinet and his calculated discrediting of the press to his carefully organized concentration of federal management in the White House—from all this a larger design ineluctably emerged. It was hard to know whether Nixon, whose style was banality, understood consciously where he was heading. He was not a man given to political philosophizing. But he was heading toward a new balance of constitutional powers, an audacious and imaginative reconstruction of the American Constitution.

*Robert Haldeman headed Richard Nixon's White House staff. He was a stern gatekeeper (the president wished it so) before his resignation in the face of the exploding Watergate scandals during the spring of 1973. He was subsequently convicted of criminal charges and imprisoned for his role in Watergate.—EDS.

- FDR relied on cabinet & wife.
- Kennedy relied on cabinet.

- Nixon was paranoid and would confine himself. → cabinet turned on him.

He did indeed contemplate, as he said in 1971 State of the Union message, a New American Revolution. But the essence of this revolution was not, as he said at the time, power to the people. The essence was power to the Presidency. . . . His purpose was probably more unconscious than conscious; and his revolution took direction and color not just from the external circumstances pressing new powers on the Presidency but from the needs and drives of his own agitated psyche. This was the fatal flaw in the revolutionary design. For everywhere he looked he saw around him hideous threats to the national security—threats that, even though he would not describe them to Congress or the people, kept his White House in constant uproar and warranted in his own mind a clandestine presidential response of spectacular and historic illegality. If his public actions led toward a scheme of presidential supremacy under a considerably debilitated Constitution, his private obsessions pushed him toward the view that the Presidency could set itself, at will, *above* the Constitution. It was this theory that led straight to Watergate. . . . .

Secrecy seemed to promise government three inestimable advantages: the power to withhold, the power to leak and the power to lie. . . .

The power to withhold held out the hope of denying the public the knowledge that would make possible an independent judgment on executive policy. The mystique of inside information—"if you only knew what we know"—was a most effective way to defend the national-security monopoly and prevent democratic control of foreign policy. . . .

The power to leak meant the power to tell the people what it served the government's purpose that they should know. . . .

The power to withhold and the power to leak led on inexorably to the power to lie. The secrecy system instilled in the executive branch the idea that foreign policy was no one's business save its own, and uncontrolled secrecy made it easy for lying to become routine. It was in this spirit that the Eisenhower administration concealed the CIA operations it was mounting against governments around the world. It was in this spirit that the Kennedy administration stealthily sent the Cuban brigade to the Bay of Pigs* and stealthily enlarged American involvement in Vietnam. It was in this spirit that the Johnson administration Americanized the Vietnam War, misrepresenting one episode after another to Congress and the peo-

---

*In 1961, President John F. Kennedy accepted responsibility for the disaster at the Bay of Pigs in Cuba. Over a thousand Cuban exiles, trained by the U.S. Central Intelligence Agency (CIA), tried to land in Cuba to overthrow the communist government of Fidel Castro. The invasion was a complete failure, forcing Kennedy to reassess his foreign policy approach, especially toward Latin America.—EDS.

ple—Tonkin Gulf, the first American ground force commitment, the bombing of North Vietnam, My Lai and the rest.*

The longer the secrecy system dominated government, the more government assumed the *right* to lie. . . .

God, it has been well said, looks after drunks, children and the United States of America. However, given the number, the brazen presumption and the clownish ineptitude of the conspirators, if it had not been Watergate, it would surely have been something else. For Watergate was a symptom, not a cause. Nixon's supporters complained that his critics were blowing up a petty incident out of all proportion to its importance. No doubt a burglary at Democratic headquarters was trivial next to a mission to Peking. But Watergate's importance was not simply in itself. Its importance was in the way it brought to the surface, symbolized and made politically accessible the great question posed by the Nixon administration in every sector—the question of presidential power. The unwarranted and unprecedented expansion of presidential power, because it ran through the whole Nixon system, was bound, if repressed at one point, to break out at another. This, not Watergate, was the central issue. . . . Watergate did stop the revolutionary Presidency in its tracks. It blew away the mystique of the mandate and reinvigorated the constitutional separation of powers. If the independent judiciary, the free press, Congress and the executive agencies could not really claim too much credit as institutions for work performed within them by brave individuals, nonetheless they all drew new confidence as institutions from the exercise of power they had forgotten they possessed. The result could only be to brace and strengthen the inner balance of American democracy. . . .

If the Nixon White House escaped the legal consequences of its illegal behavior, why would future Presidents and their associates not suppose themselves entitled to do what the Nixon White House had done? Only condign punishment would restore popular faith in the Presidency and

---

*The Tonkin Gulf incident involved two alleged attacks on American ships in the waters off the coast of Vietnam in 1964. President Lyndon Johnson may have exaggerated the extent of the attacks to gain support for widening the war. In response to the incident, the Senate voted 88 to 2 and the House of Representatives 416 to 0 to allow the president significant latitude in the use of American forces in Vietnam. No formal declaration of war was ever made concerning Vietnam, but the Gulf of Tonkin Resolution became the executive branch's "blank check" to expand the conflict. The 1968 My Lai massacre was a turning point in American public opinion concerning the Vietnam War. U.S. soldiers killed over a hundred Vietnamese villagers. One lieutenant was tried and convicted for the slaughter that had happened because of the inability of American troops to distinguish between enemy soldiers and civilians. Some Americans believed that those higher up in the military, not just Lieutenant William Calley, should have been prosecuted for the massacre. —EDS.

deter future Presidents from illegal conduct—so long, at least, as Watergate remained a vivid memory. We have noted that corruption appears to visit the White House in fifty-year cycles. This suggests that exposure and retribution inoculate the Presidency against its latent criminal impulses for about half a century. Around the year 2023 the American people would be well advised to go on the alert and start nailing down everything in sight.

33

THOMAS CRONIN
MICHAEL GENOVESE

From *The Paradoxes of the American Presidency*

The United States as a nation of paradoxes is a theme frequently used to explain the contradictions found throughout American life. In an earlier selection, Michael Kammen called Americans "people of paradox." Here, political scientists Thomas Cronin and Michael Genovese use the concept of paradox to explore the many images that citizens hold of their president. Each image they describe is accompanied by a contrary image. For example, Cronin and Genovese note, the president is supposed to be an average person just like us, while simultaneously being outstanding and extraordinary. With such paradoxical expectations of a president, is it any wonder that Americans judge the executive so harshly?

THE MIND SEARCHES FOR answers to the complexities of life. We often gravitate toward simple explanations for the world's mysteries. This is a natural way to try and make sense out of a world that seems to defy understanding. We are uncomfortable with contradictions so we reduce reality to understandable simplifications. And yet, contradictions and clashing expectations are part of life. "No aspect of society, no habit, custom, movement, development, is without cross-currents," says historian Barbara Tuchman. "Starving peasants in hovels live alongside prosperous landlords in featherbeds. Children are neglected and children are loved." In life we are confronted with paradoxes for which we seek meaning. The same is true for the American presidency. We admire presidential power, yet fear it. We yearn for the heroic, yet are also inherently suspicious of it. We demand dynamic leadership, yet grant only limited powers to the president. We want presidents to be dispassionate analysts and listeners, yet they must also be decisive. We are impressed with presidents who have great self-confidence, yet we dislike arrogance and respect those who express reasonable self-doubt.

How then are we to make sense of the presidency? This complex, multidimensional, even contradictory institution is vital to the American system of government. The physical and political laws that seem to constrain one president, liberate another. What proves successful in one, leads to failure in another. Rather than seeking one unifying theory of presidential politics that answers all our questions, we believe that the American presidency might be better understood as a series of paradoxes, clashing expectations and contradictions.

Leaders live with contradictions. Presidents, more than most people, learn to take advantage of contrary or divergent forces. Leadership situations commonly require successive displays of contrasting characteristics. Living with, even embracing, contradictions is a sign of political and personal maturity.

The effective leader understands the presence of opposites. The aware leader, much like a first-rate conductor, knows when to bring in various sections, knows when and how to turn the volume up and down, and learns how to balance opposing sections to achieve desired results. Effective presidents learn how to manage these contradictions and give meaning and purpose to confusing and often clashing expectations. The novelist F. Scott Fitzgerald once suggested that, "The test of a first-rate intelligence is the ability to hold two opposed ideas in the mind at the same time." Casey Stengel, long-time New York Yankee manager and occasional (if accidental) Zen philosopher, captured the essence of the paradox when he noted, "Good pitching will always stop good hitting, and vice versa."

Our expectations of, and demands on, the president are frequently so contradictory as to invite two-faced behavior by our presidents. Presidential powers are often not as great as many of us believe, and the president gets unjustly condemned as ineffective. Or a president will overreach or resort to unfair play while trying to live up to our demands.

The Constitution is of little help. The founders purposely left the presidency imprecisely defined. This was due in part to their fears of both the monarchy and the masses, and in part to their hopes that future presidents would create a more powerful office than the framers were able to do at the time. They knew that at times the president would have to move swiftly and effectively, yet they went to considerable lengths to avoid enumerating specific powers and duties in order to calm the then widespread fear of monarchy. After all, the nation had just fought a war against executive tyranny. Thus the paradox of the invention of the presidency: To get the presidency approved in 1787 and 1788, the framers had to leave several silences and ambiguities for fear of portraying the office as an overly centralized leadership institution. Yet when we need central leadership we turn to the president and read into Article II of the Constitution various prerogatives or inherent powers that allow the president to perform as an effective national leader.

Today the informal and symbolic powers of the presidency account for as much as the formal, stated ones. Presidential powers expand and contract in response to varying situational and technological changes. The powers of the presidency are thus interpreted so differently that they sometimes seem to be those of different offices. In some ways the modern presidency has virtually unlimited authority for almost anything its occupant chooses to do with it. In other ways, a president seems hopelessly ensnarled in a web of checks and balances.

Presidents and presidential candidates must constantly balance conflicting demands, cross pressures, and contradictions. It is characteristic of the American mind to hold contradictory ideas without bothering to resolve the conflicts between them. Perhaps some contradictions are best left unresolved, especially as ours is an imperfect world and our political system is a complicated one, held together by countless compromises. We may not be able to resolve many of these clashing expectations. Some of the inconsistencies in our judgments about presidents doubtless stem from the many ironies and paradoxes of the human condition. While difficult, at the least we should develop a better understanding of what it is we ask of our presidents, thereby increasing our sensitivity to the limits and possibilities of what a president can achieve. This might free presidents to lead and administer more effectively in those critical times when the nation has no choice but to turn to them. Whether we like it or not, the vitality of our democracy depends in large measure upon the sensitive interaction of presidential leadership with an understanding public willing to listen and willing to provide support. Carefully planned innovation is nearly impossible without the kind of leadership a competent and fair-minded president can provide.

The following are some of the paradoxes of the presidency. Some are cases of confused expectations. Some are cases of wanting one kind of presidential behavior at one time, and another kind later. Still others stem from the contradiction inherent in the concept of democratic leadership, which on the surface at least, appears to set up "democratic" and "leadership" as warring concepts. Whatever the source, each has implications for presidential performance and for how Americans judge presidential success and failure. . . .

Paradox #1. Americans demand powerful, popular presidential leadership that solves the nation's problems. Yet we are inherently suspicious of strong centralized leadership and especially the abuse of power and therefore we place significant limits on the president's powers.

We admire power but fear it. We love to unload responsibilities on our leaders, yet we intensely dislike being bossed around. We expect impressive leadership from presidents, and we simultaneously impose constitutional, cultural, and political restrictions on them. These restrictions often prevent presidents from living up to our expectations. . . .

Presidents are supposed to follow the laws and respect the constitutional procedures that were designed to restrict their power, yet still they must be powerful and effective when action is needed. For example, we approve of presidential military initiatives and covert operations when they work out well, but we criticize presidents and insist they work more closely with Congress when the initiatives fail. We recognize the need for secrecy in certain government actions, but we resent being deceived and left in the dark—again, especially when things go wrong, as in Reagan's Iranian arms sale diversions to the Contras.

Although we sometimes do not approve of the way a president acts, we often approve of the end results. Thus Lincoln is often criticized for acting outside the limits of the Constitution, but at the same time he is forgiven due to the obvious necessity for him to violate certain constitutional principles in order to preserve the Union. FDR was often flagrantly deceptive and manipulative not only of his political opponents but also of his staff and allies. FDR even relished pushing people around and toying with them. But leadership effectiveness in the end often comes down to whether a person acts in terms of the highest interests of the nation. Most historians conclude Lincoln and Roosevelt were responsible in the use of presidential power, to preserve the Union, to fight the depression and nazism. Historians also conclude that Nixon was wrong for acting beyond the law in pursuit of personal power. . . .

Paradox #2. We yearn for the democratic "common person" and also for the uncommon, charismatic, heroic, visionary performance.

We want our presidents to be like us, but better than us. We like to think America is the land where the common sense of the common person reigns. Nourished on a diet of Frank Capra's "common-man-as-hero" movies, and the literary celebration of the average citizen by authors such as Emerson, Whitman, and Thoreau, we prize the common touch. The plain-speaking Harry Truman, the up-from-the-log-cabin "man or woman of the people," is enticing. Few of us, however, settle for anything but the best; we want presidents to succeed and we hunger for brilliant, uncommon, and semiregal performances from presidents. . . .

It is said the American people crave to be governed by a president who is greater than anyone else yet not better than themselves. We are inconsistent; we want our president to be one of the folks yet also something special. If presidents get too special, however, they get criticized and roasted. If they try to be too folksy, people get bored. We cherish the myth that anyone can grow up to be president, that there are no barriers and no elite qualifications, but we don't want someone who is too ordinary. Would-be presidents have to prove their special qualifications — their excellence, their stamina, and their capacity for uncommon leadership. Fellow commoner, Truman, rose to the demands of the job and became an apparently gifted decision maker, or so his admirers would have us believe.

In 1976 Governor Jimmy Carter seemed to grasp this conflict and he ran as local, down-home, farm-boy-next-door makes good. The image of the peanut farmer turned gifted governor contributed greatly to Carter's success as a national candidate and he used it with consummate skill. Early in his presidential bid, Carter enjoyed introducing himself as peanut farmer *and* nuclear physicist, once again suggesting he was down to earth but cerebral as well.

Ronald Reagan illustrated another aspect of this paradox. He was a representative all-American — small-town, midwestern, and also a rich celebrity of stage, screen, and television. He boasted of having been a Democrat, yet campaigned as a Republican. A veritable Mr. Smith goes to Washington, he also had uncommon star quality. Bill Clinton liked us to view him as both a Rhodes scholar and an ordinary saxophone-playing member of the high school band from Hope, Arkansas; as a John Kennedy and even an Elvis figure; and also as just another jogger who would stop by for a Big Mac on the way home from a run in the neighborhood. . . .

Paradox #3. We want a decent, just, caring, and compassionate president, yet we admire a cunning, guileful, and, on occasions that warrant it, even a ruthless, manipulative president.

There is always a fine line between boldness and recklessness, between strong self-confidence and what the Greeks called "hubris," between dogged determination and pigheaded stubbornness. Opinion polls indicate people want a just, decent, and intellectually honest individual as our chief executive. Almost as strongly, however, the public also demands the quality of toughness.

We may admire modesty, humility, and a sense of proportion, but most of our great leaders have been vain and crafty. After all, you don't get to the White House by being a wallflower. Most have aggressively sought power and were rarely preoccupied with metaphysical inquiry or ethical considerations.

Franklin Roosevelt's biographers, while emphasizing his compassion for the average American, also agree he was vain, devious, and manipulative and had a passion for secrecy. These, they note, are often the standard weaknesses of great leaders. Significant social and political advances are made by those with drive, ambition, and a certain amount of brash, irrational self-confidence. . . .

Perhaps Dwight Eisenhower reconciled these clashing expectations better than recent presidents. Blessed with a wonderfully seductive, benign smile and a reserved, calming disposition, he was also the disciplined, strong, no-nonsense five-star general with all the medals and victories to go along with it. His ultimate resource as president was this reconciliation of decency and proven toughness, likability alongside demonstrated valor. Some of his biographers suggest his success was at least partly due to his uncanny ability to appear guileless to the public yet act with ample cunning in private. . . .

One of the ironies of the American presidency is that those characteristics we condemn in one president, we look for in another. Thus a supporter of Jimmy Carter's once suggested that Sunday school teacher Carter wasn't "rotten enough," "a wheeler-dealer," "an s.o.b."—precisely the virtues (if they can be called that) that Lyndon Johnson was most criticized for a decade earlier. President Clinton was viewed as both a gifted Southern Baptist–style preacher by some of his followers and a man who was character challenged, by opponents. . . .

Paradox #4. We admire the "above politics" nonpartisan or bipartisan approach, yet the presidency is perhaps the most political office in the American system, a system in which we need a creative entrepreneurial master politician.

The public yearns for a statesman in the White House, for a George Washington or a second "era of good feelings"—anything that might prevent partisanship or politics as usual in the White House. Former French President Charles de Gaulle once said, "I'm neither of the left nor of the right nor of the center, but above." In fact, however, the job of president demands that the officeholder be a gifted political broker, ever attentive to changing political moods and coalitions. . . .

Presidents are often expected to be above politics in some respects while being highly political in others. Presidents are never supposed to act with their eyes on the next election, yet their power position demands they must. They are neither supposed to favor any particular group or party nor wheel and deal and twist too many arms. That's politics and that's bad! Instead, a president is supposed to be "president of all the people," above politics. A president is also asked to lead a party, to help fellow party members get elected or reelected, to deal firmly with party barons, interest group chieftains, and congressional political brokers. His ability to gain legislative victories depends on his skills at party leadership and on the size of his party's congressional membership. Jimmy Carter once lamented that "It's very difficult for someone to serve in this office and meet the difficult issues in a proper and courageous way and still maintain a combination of interest-group approval that will provide a clear majority at election time."

To take the president out of politics is to assume, incorrectly, that a president will be generally right and the public generally wrong, that a president must be protected from the push and shove of political pressures. But what president has always been right? Over the years, public opinion has usually been as sober a guide as anything else on the political waterfront. And, lest we forget, having a president constrained and informed by public opinion is what democracy is all about.

The fallacy of antipolitics presidencies is that only one view of the national interest is tenable, and a president may pursue that view only by ignoring political conflict and pressure. Politics, properly conceived, is the art of accommodating the diversity and variety of public opinion to meet public goals. Politics is the task of building durable coalitions and majorities. It isn't always pretty. "The process isn't immaculate and cannot always be kid-gloved. A president and his men must reward loyalty and punish opposition; it is the only way." . . .

Paradox #5. We want a president who can unify us, yet the job requires taking firm stands, making unpopular or controversial decisions that necessarily upset and divide us.

Closely related to paradox #4, paradox #5 holds that we ask the president to be a national unifier and a *harmonizer* while at the same time the job requires priority setting and *advocacy* leadership. The tasks are near opposites. . . .

Our nation is one of the few in the world that calls on its chief executive to serve as its symbolic, ceremonial head of state *and* as its political head of government. Elsewhere, these tasks are spread around. In some nations there is a monarch and a prime minister; in others there are three visible national leaders — a head of state, a premier, and a powerful party chief.

In the absence of an alternative office or institution, we demand that our president act as a unifying force in our lives. Perhaps it all began with George Washington, who so artfully performed this function. At least for a while he truly was above politics, a unique symbol of our new nation. He was a healer, a unifier, and an extraordinary man for several seasons. Today we ask no less of our presidents than that they should do as Washington did, and more.

We have designed a presidential job description, however, that often forces our contemporary presidents to act as national dividers. Presidents must necessarily divide when they act as the leaders of their political parties, when they set priorities to the advantage of certain goals and groups at the expense of others, when they forge and lead political coalitions, when they move out ahead of public opinion and assume the role of national educators, when they choose one set of advisers over another. A president, as a creative executive leader, cannot help but offend certain interests. When Franklin Roosevelt was running for a second term, some garment workers unfolded a great sign that said, "We love him for the enemies he has made." Such is the fate of a president on an everyday basis; if presidents choose to use power they will lose the goodwill of those who preferred inaction. . . .

Paradox #6. We expect our presidents to provide bold, visionary, innovative, *programmatic* leadership and at the same time to *pragmatically* respond to the will of public opinion majorities; that is to say, we expect presidents to lead and to follow, to exercise "democratic leadership."

We want both pragmatic and programmatic leadership. We want principled leadership and flexible, adaptable leaders. *Lead us,* but also *listen to us.*

Most people can be led only where they want to go. "Authentic leadership," wrote James MacGregor Burns, "is a collective process." It emerges from a sensitivity or appreciation of the motives and goals of both followers and leaders. The test of leadership, according to Burns, "is the realization of intended, real change that meets people's enduring needs." Thus a key function of leadership is "to engage followers, not merely to activate them, to commingle needs and aspirations and goals in a common enterprise, and in the process to make better citizens of both leaders and followers."

We want our presidents to offer leadership, to be architects of the future and to offer visions, plans, and goals. At the same time we want them to stay in close touch with the sentiments of the people. We want a certain amount of innovation, but we resist being led too far in any one direction.

We expect vigorous, innovative leadership when crises occur. Once a crisis is past, however, we frequently treat presidents as if we didn't need or want them around. We do expect presidents to provide us with bold, creative, and forceful initiatives "to move us ahead," but we resist radical new ideas and changes and usually embrace "new" initiatives only after they have achieved some consensus.

Most of our presidents have been conservatives or at best "pragmatic liberals." They have seldom ventured much beyond the crowd. They have followed public opinion rather than shaped it. John F. Kennedy, the author of the much-acclaimed *Profiles in Courage*, was often criticized for presenting more profile than courage. He avoided political risks where possible. Kennedy was fond of pointing out that he had barely won election in 1960 and that great innovations should not be forced on the public by a leader with such a slender mandate. President Kennedy is often credited with encouraging widespread public participation in politics, but he repeatedly reminded Americans that caution is needed, that the important issues are complicated, technical, and best left to the administrative and political experts. Seldom did Kennedy attempt to change the political context in which he operated. Instead he resisted, "the new form of politics emerging with the civil rights movement: mass action, argument on social fundamentals, appeals to considerations of justice and morality. Moving the American political system in such a direction would necessarily have been long range, requiring arduous educational work and promising substantial political risk."

Kennedy, the pragmatist, shied away from such an unpragmatic undertaking. . . .

Paradox #7. Americans want powerful, self-confident presidential leadership. Yet we are inherently suspicious of leaders who are arrogant, infallible, and above criticism.

We unquestionably cherish our three branches of government with their checks and balances and theories of dispersed and separated powers. We want our presidents to be successful and to share their power with their cabinets, Congress, and other "responsible" national leaders. In theory, we oppose the concentration of power, we dislike secrecy, and we resent depending on any one person to provide all of our leadership.

But Americans also yearn for dynamic, aggressive presidents—even if they do cut some corners. We celebrate the gutsy presidents who make a practice of manipulating and pushing Congress. We perceive the great presidents to be those who stretched their legal authority and dominated the other branches of government. It is still Jefferson, Jackson, Lincoln, and the Roosevelts who get top billing. Whatever may have been the framers' intentions for the three branches, most experts now agree that most of the time, especially in crises, our system works best when the presidency is strong and when we have a self-confident, assertive president.

There is, of course, a fine line between confidence and arrogance, between firmness and inflexibility. We want presidents who are not afraid to exert their will, but at what point does this become antidemocratic, even authoritarian? . . .

Paradox #8. What it takes to become president may not be what is needed to govern the nation.

To win a presidential election takes ambition, money, luck, and masterful public relations strategies. It requires the formation of an electoral coalition. To govern a democracy requires much more. It requires the formation of a *governing* coalition, and the ability to compromise and bargain.

"People who win primaries may become good presidents—but 'it ain't necessarily so'" wrote columnist David Broder. "Organizing well is important in governing just as it is in winning primaries. But the Nixon years should teach us that good advance men do not necessarily make trustworthy White House aides. Establishing a government is a little more complicated than having the motorcade run on time."

Ambition (in heavy doses) and stiff-necked determination are essential for a presidential candidate, yet too much of either can be dangerous. A candidate must be bold and energetic, but in excess these characteristics can produce a cold, frenetic candidate. To win the presidency obviously requires a single-mindedness, yet our presidents must also have a sense of proportion, be well-rounded, have a sense of humor, be able to take a joke, and have hobbies and interests outside the realm of politics.

To win the presidency many of our candidates (Lincoln, Kennedy, and Clinton come to mind) had to pose as being more progressive or even populist than they actually felt; to be effective in the job they are compelled to appear more cautious and conservative than they often want to be. One of Carter's political strategists said, "Jimmy campaigned liberal but governed conservative." And as Bill Clinton pointed out toward the end of his first year in office, "We've all become Eisenhower Republicans." . . .

We often also want both a "fresh face," an outsider, as a presidential candidate *and* a seasoned, mature, experienced veteran who knows the corridors of power and the back alleyways of Washington. That's why Colin Powell fascinated so many people. Frustration with past presidential performances leads us to turn to a "fresh new face" uncorrupted by Washington's politics and its "buddy system" (Carter, Reagan, Clinton).

But inexperience, especially in foreign affairs, has sometimes led to blunders by the outsiders. . . .

Paradox #9. The presidency is sometimes too strong, yet other times too weak.

Presidents are granted wide latitude in dealing with events abroad. At times, presidents can act unilaterally, without the express consent of Congress. While the constitutional grounds for such action may be dubious, the climate of expectations allows presidents to act decisively abroad. This being the case, the public comes to think the president can do the same at home. But this is usually not the case. A clashing expectation is built into the presidency when strength in some areas is matched with weakness in other areas.

It often seems that our presidency is *always too strong* and *always too weak*. Always too powerful given our worst fears of tyranny and our ideals of a "government by the people." Always too strong, as well, because it now possesses the capacity to wage nuclear war (a capacity that doesn't permit much in the way of checks and balances and deliberative, participatory government). But always too weak when we remember nuclear proliferation, the rising national debt, the budget deficit, lingering discrimination, poverty, and the clutch of other fundamental problems yet to be solved.

The presidency is always too strong when we dislike the incumbent. Its limitations are bemoaned, however, when we believe the incumbent is striving valiantly to serve the public interest as we define it. The Johnson presidency vividly captured this paradox: many who believed he was too strong in Vietnam also believed he was too weak to wage his War on Poverty. Others believed just the opposite. . . .

Ultimately, being paradoxical does not make the presidency incomprehensible. Can we rid the presidency of all paradoxes? We couldn't, even if we wanted to do so. And anyway, what is wrong with some ambiguity? It is in embracing the paradoxical nature of the American presidency that we may be able to arrive at understanding. And with understanding may come enlightened or constructive criticism. This is the basis for citizen democracy.

34

CRAIG RIMMERMAN

From *The Rise of the Plebiscitary Presidency*

Scholars who examine American presidents look not only at individuals who have held the position but also at trends that mark different interpretations of the office. Here, Professor Craig Rimmerman builds on Theodore Lowi's concept of the "plebiscitary presidency," in which the president seeks to govern through the direct support of the American people. Likewise, citizens view the plebiscitary presidency as the focal point of government activity. Rimmerman believes this view to be vastly different from the Constitution's intent. He traces changes in the executive's power through several phases, mentioning the contributions of prominent scholars to an understanding of the presidency. From Presidents Roosevelt to Bush, Rimmerman asks his readers to consider carefully the consequences of such an exalted and unrealistic vision of presidential power.

THE CONSTITUTIONAL framers would undoubtedly be disturbed by the shift to the presidentially centered government that characterizes the modern era. Their fear of monarchy led them to reject the concept of executive popular leadership. Instead, they assumed that the legislative branch would occupy the central policymaking role and would be held more easily accountable through republican government.

Congress has failed, however, to adhere to the framers' intentions and has abdicated its policymaking responsibility. The legislature, with support from the Supreme Court, has been all too willing to promote the illusion of presidential governance by providing the executive with new sources of power, including a highly developed administrative apparatus, and by delegating authority for policy implementation to the executive through vague legislative statutes. . . .

The president-centered government of the modern, plebiscitary era draws much of its power and legitimacy from the popular support of the citizenry, support that is grounded in the development of the rhetorical presidency and the exalted role of the presidency in the American political culture. Theodore Lowi is surely on target when he identifies "the refocusing of mass expectations upon the presidency" as a key problem of presidential governance since Franklin Delano Roosevelt and as a problem associated with the rise of the plebiscitary presidency.

The plebiscitary presidency is characterized by the following: presidential power and legitimacy emanates from citizen support as measured through public opinion polls; in the absence of coherent political parties, presidents forge a direct link to the masses through television; and structural barriers associated with the Madisonian governmental framework make it difficult for presidents to deliver on their policy promises to the citizenry. The framers of the Constitution would hardly have approved of these developments, for they had no intention of establishing a popularly elected monarch. Moreover, the nature of the governmental framework that they created actually prevents occupants of the Oval Office from meeting the heightened citizen expectations associated with the plebiscitary presidency in terms of concrete public policy, especially in the domestic policy arena. This has become particularly clear in the modern era as presidents confront a more fragmented and independent legislature, a decline in the importance of the political party as a governing and coalition-building device, an increase in the power of interest groups and political action committees that foster policy fragmentation, and a bureaucracy that resists centralized coordination. . . .

Throughout much of the nineteenth century, a passive president in domestic policymaking was deemed both acceptable and desirable. Congress took the lead in formulating public policy initiatives and expressed outright hostility toward presidential suggestions that particular legislation should be introduced. In fact, early in the nineteenth century it was commonly believed that the president should not exercise the veto to express policy preferences. The president's primary responsibility was to faithfully execute the laws passed by Congress. For the occupants of the Oval Office in the traditional period, the Constitution imposed "strict limitations on what a President could do." The constitutional separation of powers was taken seriously by all parties, and the prevailing view regarding the proper role of government was "the best government governed least." As opposed to the presidential government of the modern period, the traditional era was characterized by congressional leadership in the policy process.

In the foreign policy arena, however, the president did establish himself through the war-making power. Yet even here the president was restrained when compared to the occupants of the Oval Office in the twentieth century. A prevailing view in the nineteenth century was that the president should avoid involvement with foreign nations, although negotiation with foreign countries was occasionally required. The first president to travel abroad on behalf of the United States was Theodore Roosevelt. Prior to the twentieth century, some members of Congress even argued that the president lacked the necessary legal authority to travel in this manner.

Presidential speechmaking also reflected the largely symbolic chief-of-state roles played by presidents in the traditional era. Jeffrey Tulis's content analysis of presidential speeches reveals that presidents rarely gave the kind of official popular speeches that characterize speech-making in the modern era. When speeches were given, they were considered "unofficial," and they rarely contained policy pronouncements. Tulis concludes that William McKinley's rhetoric was representative of the century as a whole: "Expressions of greeting, inculcations of patriotic sentiment, attempts at building 'harmony' among the regions of the country, and very general, principled statements of policy, usually expressed in terms of the policy's consistency with that president's understanding of republicanism." Virtually all presidents of the time adhered to the same kind of presidential speechmaking. The only exception was Andrew Johnson, who attempted to rally support for his policies in Congress through the use of fiery demagoguery. Johnson's "improper" rhetoric fueled his impeachment charge; yet it is this same kind of rhetoric that today is accepted as "proper" presidential rhetoric.

The reserved role played by the president in the nineteenth century was clearly in keeping with the intention of the constitutional framers. . . .

. . . Yet as the United States headed into its second full century, this situation was to change, as congressional government began to yield to the presidentially centered form of governance that has characterized the modern period.

Students of the presidency have identified a number of factors that have led to the development of the modern, personal, plebiscitary presidency as we know it today. The personal presidency is "an office of tremendous personal power drawn from the people—directly through Congress and the Supreme Court— and based on the new democratic theory that the presidency with all powers is the necessary condition for governing a large, democratic nation. Its development is rooted in changes in presidential rhetoric, the efforts of the progressive reformers of the early twentieth century, the Great Depression and Franklin Delano Roosevelt's New Deal, the role of Congress in granting the executive considerable discretionary power, and Supreme Court decisions throughout the twentieth century that have legitimated the central role that the president should play in the domestic and foreign policy arenas. . . .

Presidential scholars have contributed to the presidentially centered government and the accompanying citizen expectations of presidential performance that characterize the development of presidential power since Franklin Roosevelt. The "cult of the presidency," "textbook presidency," or "savior model" was developed in response to FDR's leadership during the Great Depression, and it prevailed through the presidency of John F. Kennedy. Underlying this "cult" or model approach is a firm commitment to the presidency as a strong office and to the desirability of this condition for the political system as a whole. Political science texts written during this period concluded approvingly that the presidency was growing larger, while gaining more responsibilities and resources. The use of laudatory labels, such as "the Wilson years," "the Roosevelt revolution," "the Eisenhower period," and "the Kennedy Camelot years" also fostered the cult of the presidency and reinforced the notion that the president is the key figure in the American political system. . . .

Perhaps no other work contributed more to the development of this approach that Richard Neustadt's *Presidential Power*, which was first published in 1960. Representing a sharp break with the legalistic and constitutional approach that had dominated presidential scholarship up until that time, *Presidential Power* reinforced the notion that strong presidential leadership should be linked to good government. Neustadt eschewed strict legalistic interpretations of presidential power and instead conceived of power in the following way: "'Power' I defined as personal influence on governmental action. This I distinguished sharply—a novel distinction then—from formal powers vested in the Presidency." For Neustadt, the Franklin Delano Roosevelt activist presidency was the ideal model for presidential leadership and the exercise of power. Future presidents, according to Neustadt, should be evaluated on the basis of how well they achieved the standards set by Roosevelt. Like presidential scholars of his time and many since, Neustadt rejected the framers' view that the Congress should be the chief policymaking branch and that the president should be constrained by numerous checks and balances. Instead, Neustadt spoke of "separated institutions sharing powers."

As Neustadt and other scholars embraced a presidentially centered form of government, they failed to recognize the consequences of imposing a new interpretation of the political order on a governmental framework rooted in Madisonian principles. One such consequence has been that as presidents attempt to meet the heightened expectations associated with the modern presidency, they are sometimes driven to assert presidential prerogative powers in ways that threaten both constitutional and democratic principles. The Johnson and Nixon presidencies, in particular, provided empirical evidence to support this concern. In response, presidential scholars embraced a new model for evaluating presidential power: "the imperial presidency."

Concerns about excessive presidential power were articulated in light of Lyndon Johnson's legislative victories in the 1960s, Johnson's and Nixon's decisionmaking in the Vietnam War, the Nixon/Kissinger Cambodian debacle, and the Nixon presidency's disgrace in the wake of Watergate.* Presidential scholars began to question whether presidential strength would necessarily lead to the promotion of the general welfare. Scholars spoke of the pathological presidency, reinforcing many of the constitutional framers' fears regarding the consequences of concentrating excessive powers in the executive.

Writing in this vein and responding to presidential excesses in the conduct of the Vietnam War and the Watergate scandal, Arthur Schlesinger, Jr., developed the concept of the "imperial presidency." Schlesinger recognized that the system of checks and balances needed vigorous action by one of the three branches if the stalemate built into the system was to be overcome. Schlesinger believed that the presidency was best equipped to fill this role. Rather than rejecting centralized presidential power per se, he spoke of presidential abuses: "In the last years presidential primacy, so indispensable to the political order, has turned into presidential supremacy. The constitutional Presidency—as events so apparently disparate as the Indochina War and the Watergate affair showed—has become the imperial Presidency and threatens to be the revolutionary Presidency." Schlesinger placed much of the blame for the imperial presidency on presidential excesses in foreign policy. . . . Truman, Kennedy, Johnson, and Nixon interpreted the Constitution to permit the president to commit American combat troops unilaterally, and the prolonged Vietnam War encouraged foreign policy centralization and the use of secrecy. The imperial presidency, or "the presidency as satan model," can also be applied to the Nixon administration's domestic activities, including wiretapping, the use of impoundments, executive branch reorganization for political purposes, and expansive interpretations of executive privilege.

Schlesinger's analysis is an important contribution to the study of presidential power because it recognizes the limitations imposed by the framers and the potentially negative consequences of the plebiscitary presidency. . . .

The plebiscitary presidency has been a key source of presidential

---

*Set in motion by strong presidents, these three episodes—the prolonging of the war in Vietnam, the bombing of Vietnam's neutral neighbor, Cambodia, and a presidential administration's heavy involvement in and coverup of the burglary of the Democratic Party's Watergate Hotel–based election headquarters—all greatly divided the nation.—EDS.

power since 1933. For presidents such as Ford and Carter, however, the heightened expectations associated with the personal, plebiscitary presidency have also led to citizen unhappiness and characterizations of presidential failure. The Carter presidency, in particular, reinforced elements of the plebiscitary presidency. As a "trustee" president, Jimmy Carter reinforced the notion that as the elected representative of all the people, "the president must act as the counterforce to special interests" and provide the leadership necessary in setting the policy agenda and introducing "comprehensive policy proposals." Charles Jones makes a persuasive case that Carter's vision of the trustee presidency was anathema to a Congress that had just passed a series of reforms designed to tame the imperial Nixon presidency. When Carter tried to introduce unpopular energy conservation policies and cut back "unnecessary dams and water projects" because they represented the "worst examples of the pork-barrel," he challenged Congress and the American people to reject politics as usual. In this sense, he was displaying a style of presidential leadership unseen in recent years, one that reinforced the plebiscitary presidency while at the same time challenging some of the assumptions on which it is based. Unlike his immediate predecessors and successors, Carter at least tried to heighten the level of dialogue around resource scarcity concerns. He soon learned, however, that his unwillingness to cultivate congressional support for his policies and his call for a shared sacrifice on the part of the American people undermined the plebiscitary foundations of the modern presidency. His 1980 presidential challenger understood Carter's problems quite well and was determined not to repeat them. Ronald Reagan's campaign and governing strategies accepted and extended the plebiscitary presidency. This helps to account for his victories in both 1980 and 1984. . . .

In the American political system, presidents perform two roles that in other countries are often filled by separate individuals. As head of the nation, the president is required to play a unifying role of the kind played by monarchs in Britain, Norway, and the Netherlands or by presidents in France, Germany, and Austria. In addition, presidents serve as political leaders, "a post held in these other nations by a prime minister or chancellor." This dual role virtually guarantees that American presidents will occupy the central political and cultural role as the chief spokesperson for the American way of life. Political scientists, historians, and journalists have all reinforced and popularized the view that the presidency is an office of overwhelming symbolic importance.

Only recently have political scientists begun to challenge this perspective and discuss the negative consequences of such hero worship in a country that purports to adhere to democratic principles. Barbara Hinckley captures these issues well in her recent analysis:

It is the magic of symbolism to create illusion. But illusion has costs that must be considered by journalists, teachers of politics, and future presidents. Is the nation best served by carrying on the symbolism or by challenging it? Should the two contradictory pictures, in a kind of schizophrenic fashion, be carried on together? If so, what line should be drawn and what accommodation made between the two? The questions are compounded by the peculiar openness of the office to changing interpretations. By definition, all institutions are shaped by the expectations of relevant actors. The presidency is particularly susceptible to such influence.

As we have seen in our study of the Reagan and Bush presidencies, presidents attempt to build on their symbolic importance to enhance their public opinion ratings and to extend the plebiscitary presidency. The upshot of this activity over the past sixty years is that the public equates the president with the nation and the values associated with American exceptionalism. A president, such as Jimmy Carter, who attempts to challenge traditional elements of presidential symbolism and demystify the trappings of the White House, is treated with disdain by the public, the press, and to a certain extent by political scientists. . . .

This book suggests that Presidents Reagan and Bush turned to foreign policy when they encountered difficulties in translating their domestic campaign promises into concrete public policy and in meeting the demands of the plebiscitary presidency. Presidents who are caught between citizens' expectations and the constraints of the Madisonian policymaking process* look to the foreign policy arena in an effort to promote the values associated with American exceptionalism.

Any of the examples discussed . . . provide ample opportunity to explore these themes. The Iran-Contra affair,† in particular, raises compelling questions regarding presidential power in the foreign policy arena. In light of the aggrandizement of presidential power that characterized the Vietnam War period and Watergate and the resulting congressional response, it is important to ask students why a president and/or his staff would employ some of the same strategies in dealing with Congress, the media, and the American people. The role of covert activities in a democracy also deserves considerable attention.

---

*James Madison's plan for American government limits each branch by checking and balancing the power of one branch against another.—EDS.

†During President Reagan's administration, members of his National Security Council (NSC) were charged with secretly selling arms to Iran in order to fund anti-communist Nicaraguan Contra activities.—EDS.

If scholars of the presidency are truly concerned with developing a pedagogy and presidential evaluation scheme rooted in critical education for citizenship, then their students must be asked to consider why so little questioning generally occurs regarding the role of the president in committing American troops to war. The Persian Gulf war was a case in point.* It begged for serious discussion, reflection, debate, and questioning about the Bush administration's foreign policy decisionmaking. Some argued that those who dissented from the president's foreign policy strategy were un-American and unpatriotic and were trying to undermine the troops who were already in the Middle East. In fact, if citizens fail to question a president's decisionmaking, then they are giving the president virtually unchecked power to do what he wants with their lives. The failure to question a president abdicates all of the principles of a meaningful and effective democracy and embraces the dictates of an authoritarian and totalitarian regime. This is, of course, the logical consequence of the plebiscitary presidency.

Alexis de Tocqueville spoke of a blind and unreflective patriotism that characterized the American citizenry during the nineteenth century. He would surely see evidence of such patriotism in America today. There is little doubt that such patriotism can be connected to the relationship of the citizenry to the state and the office of the presidency. No modern president can expect to succeed without the support of the public. Yet this support must be grounded in a firm rejection of the unrealistic notion of presidential power. Citizens who respond to the presidency in a highly personalized and reverential manner are likely to be disappointed by presidential performance and are also likely to embrace political passivity and acquiescence in the face of presidential power. In the words of Benjamin Barber, "democratic politics thus becomes a matter of what leaders do, something that citizens watch rather than something they do." As this book has pointed out, Ronald Reagan and George Bush heightened these expectations even further by using techniques that emphasize the plebiscitary, personal character of the modern presidency. Ross Perot's 1992 presidential campaign was firmly rooted in plebiscitary principles.

---

*The Persian Gulf War occurred within a two-month period in early 1991. Backed by House and Senate resolutions of support—not an actual declaration of war—President George H.W. Bush sent U.S. troops to the Persian Gulf as part of a multination coalition to force Iraqi President Saddam Hussein's military out of Kuwait. The United States experienced quick and dramatic success, with CNN's coverage bringing the war directly to Americans daily. Years later, questions remained about the long-term effectiveness of the military strikes in weakening the Iraqi threat. In 2003, President George W. Bush ordered an invasion of Iraq, claiming that Saddam Hussein possessed weapons of mass destruction, an allegation later found to be false.—EDS.

His proposals for nation-wide town meetings and an electronic democracy scheme reflected support for government by plebiscite. To Perot, running as an outsider, anti-establishment candidate, such a plan was desperately needed to challenge the gridlock growing out of the Madisonian policy process and two party system. His proposals also enabled him to emphasize his own leadership abilities and claim that he had the necessary leadership and entrepreneurial abilities to break governmental paralysis. In doing so, Perot reinforced the direct line between the presidency and the American people. Any course on the presidency should examine Perot's government-by-plebiscite proposals and the broader implications of his apparent willingness to bypass the congressional policy process and the two party system. The amount of attention and popularity that Perot's campaign garnered in a short period of time suggests once again that the plebiscitary presidency is an important explanatory construct. It also encourages political scientists to study, with renewed vigor, the relationship between the presidency and the citizenry.

For many students, the presidency is the personification of democratic politics and, as a result, monopolizes "the public space." This view impedes the development of the meaningful and effective participation needed by citizens as they attempt to control decisions that affect the quality and direction of their lives. Presidential scholars have been developing a more realistic understanding of the changing sources of presidential power and how individual presidents have used these powers through the years. We would also do well to consider Murray Edelman's claim that "leadership is an expression of the inadequate power of followers in their everyday lives." This is particularly important as we begin to evaluate the Bush presidency. It is also the first step toward challenging the plebiscitary presidency and achieving a more realistic and successful presidency, one that is grounded in principles of democratic accountability and the development of citizenship.

35

KENNETH MAYER

From *With the Stroke of a Pen*

Students of American government need to understand all the basics of a system of government based on separation of powers: three branches, checks and balances, bicameralism, the veto, war powers, Senate advice and consent, to mention a few key examples. But there are important powers that are less visible and less checked; they do not readily fall into the standard textbook treatment of American government. Kenneth Mayer points out that presidents can have great influence beyond that specifically authorized in the Constitution or gained from a personal ability to persuade. "With the stroke of a pen," a president, without congressional involvement, can issue an executive order that can significantly shape policy. Mayer introduces us to the little-known power of the executive order by citing the often vague contours of the power. He then delineates the policy areas in which executive orders occur, presenting data on the use of the executive order over time. Though perhaps lacking in drama and excitement, executive orders can have great impact.

◆

. . . AMONG POLITICAL SCIENTISTS the conventional wisdom is that the president is weak, hobbled by the separation of powers and the short reach of his formal legal authority. Presidential power, far from being a matter of prerogative or legal rule, "is the power to persuade," wrote Richard Neustadt in the single most influential statement about the office in the past fifty years. Yet throughout U.S. history presidents have relied on their executive authority to make unilateral policy without interference from either Congress or the courts. In this book, I investigate how presidents have used a tool of executive power—the executive order—to wield their inherent legal authority. Executive orders are, loosely speaking, presidential directives that require or authorize some action within the executive branch (though they often extend far beyond the government). They are presidential edicts, legal instruments that create or modify laws, procedures, and policy by fiat.

Working from their position as chief executive and commander in chief, presidents have used executive orders to make momentous policy choices, creating and abolishing executive branch agencies, reorganizing administrative and regulatory processes, determining how legislation is implemented, and taking whatever action is permitted within the boundaries of their constitutional or statutory authority. Even within the confines of their executive powers, presidents have been able to "legislate" in the sense of making policy that goes well beyond simple administrative activity. Yale Law School professor E. Donald Elliot has argued that many of the thousands of executive orders "plainly 'make law' in every sense," and Louis Fisher finds that despite the fact that the Constitution unambiguously vests the legislative function in Congress, "the President's lawmaking role is substantial, persistent, and in many cases disturbing." . . .

A president can declare a national emergency by executive order, a step that authorizes an immense range of unilateral warrants, including—theoretically—the power to restrict travel, impose martial law, and seize property, transportation networks, and communications facilities. And even orders that lack such sweeping effect can still be extraordinarily important to particular interest groups or constituencies, who seek substantive or symbolic redress for their concerns. Congress, in an attempt to protect its own prerogatives, regularly probes the appropriate limits of the executive's independent power through investigations of particular executive orders.

Technically, although the term was not in use at the time, the Louisiana Purchase was carried out by an executive order.

Presidents and their staffs consider executive orders an indispensable policy and political tool. In the wake of the 1994 congressional elections that gave the Republicans control of both chambers for the first time in four decades, Clinton White House officials predicted a renewed emphasis on "regulations, executive orders, and other presidential tools to work around Capitol Hill, much as Ronald Reagan and George Bush did when the House and the Senate were in Democratic hands." In 1998, as Clinton headed for impeachment, his advisors noted that he would resort to executive orders and other unilateral actions to show that he remained capable of governing. In a statement that both summarized the White House position and served to provoke congressional Republicans, advisor Paul Begala outlined the strategy to New York Times reporter James Bennett: "Stroke of the Pen . . . Law of the Land. Kind of cool." . . .

The phrase "stroke of a pen" is now virtually synonymous with executive prerogative, and it is often used specifically to refer to the president's ability to make policy via executive order. *Safire's Political Dictionary* defines the phrase as "by executive order; action that can be taken by a Chief Executive without legislative action." Safire traces the political origins of the phrase to a nineteenth-century poem by Edmund Clarence Stedman, but it was in use long before this, at least as a literary metaphor signifying discretionary power or fiat. The phrase became most widely known during the 1960 presidential election campaign, when Democrats made an issue of Eisenhower's refusal to issue an executive order banning discrimination in housing and federal employment. Kennedy promised to do so, committing himself to ending discrimination by executive order. During the second Kennedy-Nixon debate on October 7, 1960, Kennedy continued his criticism. "What will be the leadership of the President in these areas," he asked, "to provide equality of opportunity for employment? Equality of opportunity in the field of housing, which could be done in all federal-

supported housing by a stroke of the President's pen." After several delays
Kennedy issued the fair housing order in November 1962. . . .

Observers who are even less sympathetic cast executive orders in an
altogether sinister light, seeing in them evidence of a broad conspiracy
to create a presidential dictatorship. The common theme of these complaints is that the executive order is an example of unaccountable power
and a way of evading both public opinion and constitutional constraints.
In the more extreme manifestations, executive orders are portrayed as an
instrument of secret government and totalitarianism. The president says
"Do this! Do that!" and not only is it done, but the government, the
economy, and individual freedom are crushed under the yoke of executive
decree. . . .

In making this argument about the importance of executive power,
I recognize that our "separated system" puts both formal and informal
limits on what presidents can do. Presidents come to office in widely
varying electoral and political contexts that shape their ability to transform
their formal powers into action. Checks and balances were built into
institutional structures of the federal government from the beginning, and
presidents reeling from a prolonged recession, facing united majority party
opposition in Congress, or mired in an unpopular war will find little
solace in the powers specified or implied in Article II of the Constitution.

Nevertheless, in most circumstances presidents retain a broad capacity
to take significant action on their own, action that is meaningful both in
substantive policy terms and in the sense of protecting and furthering
the president's political and strategic interests. Some of this authority,
particularly in regulatory affairs, has been delegated to the president by
Congress, but presidents have also simply assumed many policy-making
powers, especially in national security and foreign policy matters. Although the courts do step in to block presidential action on constitutional
grounds (with *Youngstown* the most notable case), the general pattern has
been more one of judicial deference to executive action than of assertive-
ness. . . .

What, precisely, is an executive order? In the most formal sense, an
executive order is a directive issued by the president, "directing the executive branch in the fulfillment of a particular program," targeted at
executive branch personnel and intended to alter their behavior in some
way, and published in the *Federal Register*. Executive orders are instruments
by which the president carries out the functions of the office, and every
president has issued them (although there was no system for tracking them
until the twentieth century). A 1974 Senate study of executive orders
noted that "from the time of the birth of the Nation, the day-to-day

conduct of Government business has, of necessity, required the issuance of Presidential orders and policy decisions to carry out the provisions of the Constitution that specify that the President 'shall take care that the laws be faithfully executed.' " The lack of any agreed-upon definition means that, in essence, an executive order is whatever the president chooses to call by that name. . . .

It is more useful to think of executive orders as a form of "presidential legislation" or "executive lawmaking," in the sense that they provide the president with the ability to make general policy with broad applicability akin to public law. For over a century the Supreme Court has held that executive orders, when based upon legitimate constitutional or statutory grants of power to the president, are equivalent to laws. In *Youngstown*, the Court concluded with some force that executive orders lacking a constitutional or statutory foundation are not valid, and longstanding judicial doctrine holds that when an executive order conflicts with a statute enacted pursuant to Congress's constitutional authority, the statute takes precedence.

Since executive orders are a tool of the president's executive power, their reach extends as far as executive power itself. The question of when a president can legally rely on an executive order, therefore, is the same as the question of when the president can bring into effect the executive power generally. It is not a coincidence that many of the most important Supreme Court rulings on presidential power have involved executive orders, including *Youngstown*, *Korematsu v. United States*, *Schechter Corp. v. United States*, *Cole v. Young*, and *Ex Parte Merryman*. . . .

The analysis here relies on a random sample of 1,028 executive orders issued between March 1936 and December 1999, drawn from the entire set of all executive orders issued. This sample, which covers 17.6 percent of the approximately 5,800 orders issued since March 1936, can be used to generate inferences about the total population of orders. . . .

The first task is to classify the executive orders in the sample based on subject matter. I created the following exhaustive and mutually exclusive categories. When an order addressed multiple issues or crossed policy boundaries, I assigned it to the category that best described the order's primary focus:

Civil service: Orders dealing with civil service appointments, retirement exemptions, administration of federal personnel, salary, holidays, and so on. I also included personnel loyalty orders and any orders dealing specifically with Foreign Service management or personnel.
Public lands: Orders that withdrew land for public use, restored public

lands, revoked previous land orders, or that established or altered the boundaries of public lands, migratory waterfowl refuges, or airspace reservations.

War and emergency powers: Orders that created or abolished wartime agencies, addressed the exercise of special wartime administrative functions, took possession or control of private economic entities, or established emergency preparedness procedures for federal agencies.

Foreign affairs: Orders dealing with export controls, foreign economic policy, foreign trade, foreign aid, foreign affairs and diplomatic relations generally, establishment of international or treaty-based organizations, management of territories (Philippines, Puerto Rico, the Canal Zone), and immigration.

Defense and military policy: Orders dealing with military personnel, classified information, organization of the intelligence community, administration and reservation of military lands and reservations, and defense policy generally.

Executive branch administration: Orders creating boards, commissions, or interagency councils; orders that delegated presidential power or transferred powers from one agency to another, established civilian awards, administered tax policy (including inspection of tax returns), affected the organization of the Executive Office of the President, administered customs, law enforcement, and commemorative orders; contracting.

Labor policy: Orders creating emergency boards and boards of inquiry to investigate labor disputes, and orders managing federal government labor policy.

Domestic policy: Orders that dealt with domestic policy generally, including energy, the environment, civil rights, the economy, and education.

Tables 1 and 2 show the overall distribution of executive orders in the sample by subject area and across time. Overall, from 1936 to 1999, more than 60 percent of the orders dealt with general executive branch administration, the civil service, or public lands. Most of the remaining orders concerned the president's foreign affairs and war powers, with only a small percentage dealing with domestic and labor policy.

These patters change when orders are broken down by time period. Table 2 shows the distribution of orders across categories for each decade, from the 1930s to the 1990s (the 1930s includes four years, from 1936 to 1939). Several patterns are immediately apparent, especially the sharp drop in the percentage of orders devoted to public land and civil service issues. Over three-fourths of orders in the 1930s dealt with these issues, with nearly half devoted to public lands alone. In the 1990s there were

Table 1 · EXECUTIVE ORDER SUBJECT CATEGORIES,
1936–1999

Type of Order	Percentage of Orders in Sample
Executive branch administration	25.5
Civil service	19.6
Public lands	15.6
Defense and military policy	11.9
Foreign affairs	11.3
War and emergency powers	7.1
Labor policy	5.4
Domestic policy	3.8

Note: Percentages are drawn from a random sample of 1,028 orders.
Margin of error is +/−2.6.

no public land orders, and only one order in eight dealt with the civil service. As I noted above, presidents no longer issue these orders, having delegated these responsibilities to subordinates. The number of orders devoted to war and emergency powers has gone down considerably since the 1940s and 1950s, with the higher figures obviously attributable to the extraordinary impact of World War II and the Korean War.

The percentage of executive orders that deal with foreign affairs, executive branch administration, and domestic policy has grown significantly since the 1930s. Part of this is undoubtedly due to the rise of the presidency as an institution, since as presidents have taken on more and more administrative responsibility they have come to rely on the executive order as an instrument of policy making. . . .

The second area of relative growth in executive orders is in foreign and military affairs. In these areas the absolute number of orders has remained roughly consistent, but they have become a larger percentage of all orders over time. . . .

The tangled history of the executive power points to the conclusion that executive orders matter. Presidents, particularly in the twentieth century (although there are crucial examples from earlier history), have pushed the boundaries of presidential power by taking advantage of gaps in constitutional and statutory language that allow them to fill power vacuums and gain control of emerging capabilities. Because of the inherent ambiguities of the constitutional vestments of executive authority, presidents have expanded their powers outward as a function of precedent, public

Table 2 · EXECUTIVE ORDER SUBJECT CATEGORIES BY DECADE, 1936–1999 (Sample of 1,028 Orders)

	1936–1939	1940s	1950s	1960s	1970s	1980s	1990s
Civil service	30.5%	21.8%	13.8%	11.9%	22.0%	13.1%	12.0%
Public lands	46.1	18.4	10.5	5.0	2.5	1.0	0.0
War and emergency powers	0.0	19.3	3.3	4.0	1.7	1.0	0.0
Foreign affairs	9.6	7.6	9.9	11.9	10.2	20.2	22.7
Defense and military policy	2.4	12.7	27.6	10.9	6.8	6.1	11.9
Executive branch administration	10.8	13.6	28.3	36.6	44.9	41.4	36.6
Labor policy	0.0	4.4	5.9	13.9	3.4	10.1	5.3
Domestic policy	0.6	2.2	0.7	5.9	8.5	7.1	9.3
Number of orders in sample	167	316	152	101	118	99	75
Number of administrations	1	2	2	4	3	3	2
Significant orders	1	50	14	14	26	23	21
Percentage	0.6%	15.8%	9.2%	13.9%	22.0%	23.2%	28.0%

expectations, and deference from the legislative and judicial branches. Executive orders have played a central role in this expansion.

In order to see the importance of constitutional form to the presidency, studies of presidential power must include a broader understanding of the president's formal powers. The notion that studying the president's constitutional authority will not produce useful or interesting findings is shortsighted, and it obscures important elements of the institution. A president's willingness to exercise formal legal authority is conditioned on broader strategic considerations, to be sure, but that does not diminish the powers available. Even within the constitutional constraints of the separation of powers, presidents can use executive orders to alter and adapt government structure, processes, and policies. A president's ability to effect major policy change on his own is in many instances less dependent on personality or powers of persuasion than on the office's formal authority and the inherent characteristics of governing institutions. To understand the nature of the president's legal power, executive orders are a good place to start.

36

BRADLEY PATTERSON

From *The White House Staff: [Chief of Staff]*

Drawing on many examples, Bradley Patterson paints a detailed picture of one of the least public but most important positions in Washington, D.C. The president's chief of staff is in charge of every aspect of the White House office, from the mundane to the weighty. Patterson is a long-time observer of the inside political scene in the nation's capital, and he brings to his prescription for the chief of staff a vast knowledge both of the individuals who have held the job and of the executive branch. The chief of staff must be all things to the president, Patterson feels, but he must be careful in the process not to become isolated and alienated from the numerous people whose requests he has to reject on behalf of his boss.

———

IT SEEMED AS IF two traditions were in the making: Republican presidents, following the Eisenhower model, emplaced chiefs of staff in their White Houses; Democratic presidents, aghast at the Nixon experience, shunned the idea. The second "tradition" came to a halt with

Clinton. As presidential scholar James Pfiffner succinctly put it: "A chief of staff is essential in the modern White House."

. . . Beyond the chief of staff, there is only the president to try to knit his administration into a coherent set of institutions—and the president has vastly graver, and "undelegatable," responsibilities. The chief of staff is *system manager*: boss of none, but overseer of everything.

Does a new president understand this?

One former aide believes that a new chief executive often has a misconception:

[Presidents] always treat chiefs of staff incorrectly. They . . . think of chiefs of staff as nothing more than foremen, hired hands basically. Whereas chiefs of staff and everybody else think of [them] as exalted kinds of rulers with great power. So I think presidents need to think more about staff functions—how the White House operates, how it's going to operate, and the kind of people they choose to be around them. They don't seem to have that sense of history about them. It's like staff history is below them.

Thirty-eight years of experience—nineteen White House chiefs of staff—have, in this author's view, demonstrated a number of principles for effectiveness in fulfilling that central responsibility.

A chief of staff needs to be familiar with the unique pressures and pitfalls of public life in Washington. This means recognizing—and being comfortable with the existence of—the contravening authorities and forces from the vigorously competing centers of power in the nation and in the nation's capital: the cabinet departments, Congress, the courts, the press, the lobbyists, professional societies, interest groups, and the international community. The more successful chiefs of staff have had some thorough experience in one or more of those institutions. Former chief of staff Leon Panetta emphasized: "You really need to have somebody in that position who has some experience in Washington. It's just absolutely essential. The president can have somebody close to him, but it better be somebody who has some experience with what Washington is about, because that person has to make sure that the president isn't making any obvious mistakes."

The chief of staff needs to have firm, four-way support: not only from the president but from the first lady, the vice president, and the vice president's spouse as well. Nagging doubts or lack of confidence on the part of any of these four will eat away at the chief of staff's stature and authority. The wise chief will stay in especially close communication with the vice president and the two spouses. But communication is one thing; responsibility is another. In the end, the chief of staff has only one boss.

The chief of staff should be someone who is not only close to the president but also very familiar with those who operated the campaign. Most of the campaigners will have their hearts set on positions in Washington, hopefully on the White House staff. The incoming chief of staff must be able to distinguish effectiveness in campaigning from effectiveness in the business of governing—and give preference to those who share the president's political ideology rather than to factional advocates who are not necessarily on the same "policy wavelength" as the president.

The chief of staff has comprehensive control over the activities of the White House staff. Comments Panetta:

I had some military background—which was probably of even greater value than any kind of management background you have when you take a position like that. The role of a chief of staff is more like a battlefield commander: you've got a mission to accomplish, and you have to, sometimes, fight your way through a lot of incoming fire to make sure that the mission is done, but you need to have everybody knowing exactly what he or she has to do, in order to accomplish the mission. . . . It was very important to establish that the chief of staff had control.

But what does "control" mean? One Clinton staff chief allegedly tried to keep most of the policy balls bouncing on his own desk: he acted as the budget director, the legislative liaison head, the economic and domestic policy principal—and was the major White House spokesman. He handled all those functions superbly, it was acknowledged, but how long can such concentration be sustained? Another Clinton chief of staff preferred delegation: each senior presidential staffer was given goals, objectives, and guidelines—and then held firmly accountable for achieving them. "You have to empower people!" he said.

Former president George Bush would advise a president: "Get someone [with whom] you are totally comfortable. He/She must be a strong manager. Must be able to inspire confidence and loyalty in the rest of the staff. Must have had enough experience in some phase of life to walk in the White House door with a certain respect level already in place."

None of the policy centers of the White House—including the National Security Council apparat and the offices of the first lady and the vice president—can be allowed to work independently of the rest of the institution. In the Clinton White House, the national security adviser and the vice president's and the first lady's chiefs of staff all attended the chief of staff's senior staff meetings. The chief of staff attended the NSC principals' (cabinet-level) meetings and the intelligence briefings with the president. If even the most sensitive national security issue is being presented to the president, the national security adviser and the chief of staff jointly go into the Oval Office.

Chief of Staff John Podesta described his relationship with national security adviser Samuel (Sandy) Berger: "The one person I do not view, from a policy perspective, as reporting 'through me' is Sandy. I think it works better that way. I am not only comfortable with that; I think that is the better model. As long as we get along. He runs almost every big decision by me; I don't feel left out by him. He can keep a deeper sense of what is going on in his world; I keep a deeper sense of what is going on in my world—and we are pretty well integrated."

All presentations to the president are subject to the chief of staff's review. Issues—particularly those involving differences of opinion—are first vetted around the chief's table. The chief must ask: Is this an open process? Are the right people here? Have we asked the right questions? Are all the key options included? Has the "underbrush" been cleared out and the issues reduced to their core substance? Can consensus be reached on the lesser, "compromisable" differences?

The chief of staff controls the president's schedule. And the look-ahead period is not days but weeks—often, in fact, months. As for the schedule on a given day, the chief of staff's goal is to keep the focus on *the* principal event, ensuring that activities that would compete with news of that principal happening are downplayed or pushed aside. On policy issues awaiting discussion with the president, the chief of staff determines priorities: Which matters require attention and in what order?

The chief of staff controls the president's doorway. Who is invited to meetings and who is not? There may be some hurt feelings, but temporarily bruised egos are a small price to pay for conserving the president's absolutely invaluable time.

Review, by the chief of staff's office, of all papers that come out of the president's office is as important as scrutiny of those that come in. The president's scribbles and marginal comments are likely to be as important as the check marks in the decision box.

The chief will set up a special system for controlling the White House responses to congressional mail that contains important policy questions. Are budgetary issues being raised that require advice from the Office of Management and Budget? Constitutional ones? Is litigation possible? (The counsel must be consulted.) Who will draft the response? Have all the necessary clearances been obtained? Who will sign the outgoing letter?

The chief of staff may wish to have two or three deputy chiefs of staff. One perhaps will specialize in national security issues, another in management and operations matters, a third in domestic or economic questions. The various White House policy units may be divvied up to report on their work to the appropriate deputy *first*—before the chief of staff and the president get involved. Can such sequencing of reporting procedures be put in place without attenuating the relationships between the chief of staff and the principal White House assistants? The three most recent Clinton chiefs of staff all used this system with apparent success.

The chief of staff cannot avoid dealing with Congress. In fact, he may spend a great deal of time negotiating on the Hill on the president's behalf. The chief will likely have to take calls from governors and meet with the leaders of advocacy groups. As the chief does so, however, he always keeps the appropriate White House colleagues—legislative, intergovernmental, public liaison—closely informed and involved. The effective chief sets a firm practice: other staff members are not to be "disempowered." (Such wide-ranging extramural responsibilities are yet another reason that the contemporary White House chief of staff has deputies: to help create time for the chief to handle such external duties and not shirk his own responsibilities to the president.)

Perhaps the chief of staff's most sensitive judgment call is deciding where to draw the line: when to take an issue to the president and when to settle it before it gets that far. Podesta reflects:

I think I have a regulator that says to me, even if the president is likely to be with the consensus of his advisers, I will still have to take it into the Oval Office. There is a level of importance which, even if there is consensus, requires that the decision be signed off by the president. I think Berger would probably agree with that, from the national security viewpoint. He takes care of a lot of issues over in his office. But there is a certain level of decision which you can't just inform the president about; you really have to have his input. He may say, "I don't have a strong view; you decide." Which he will often do, if everybody is on the same page. "We'll just decide it here."

Podesta's predecessor, Erskine Bowles, expressed similar sentiments:

I made a lot of budget decisions that some people would probably have taken, on balance, right in to the president. But the president made it clear to me that he wanted me to do things like that, and the reason is: everyone has individual strengths and weaknesses. I don't have the vision; I can't dream like Bill Clinton. I can't see the things he can see. . . . But I am a doer; I can get things done. I am a negotiator; I can take tough positions and say no. The president would never say, "Erskine, you go out and make this final decision and just bring me the answer." At the same time, I didn't seek permission every time I did something. We would decide in advance what the ground rules were, what he wanted done and what I thought was practical. We would decide together: "This is what we have to have; it's going to be really tough." My job then was to "go to it." If he didn't like what I had negotiated, I expected him to let me know, which he would, quite clearly. At the same time, whether the results were positive or negative, good or bad, the president had to know it all.

Readers will instantly appreciate what a thin line this is—and will recognize how easily an egotistical chief of staff could be tempted to get into the habit of walling off staff or cabinet pleaders with the dictum "Take it from me: the president has decided!" when in fact the chief, rather than the president, was the decisionmaker.

In the decisionmaking process, the chief of staff is always an honest broker. But only an honest broker? By no means. Presidents expect their chiefs of staff to hold, and to express, their own independent judgments about any issue in the Oval Office neighborhood. They must do so, however, without using their stature and their proximity to give their own arguments an "edge" over competing contentions from other staffers or cabinet disputants.

The chief of staff must be possessed of the exceptional sensitivity to recognize a presidential command that is given in unthinking anger, frustration, or exhaustion—and to lay it aside. Scholar Fred Greenstein quotes Eisenhower: "I told my staff . . . once in a while you people have just got to be my safety-valve. So I'll get you in here and I will let go, but this is for you and your knowledge and your knowledge only. Now I've seen these people going out, and I've gotten a little extreme, a little white, but pretty soon one of them comes in and laughs and says, 'Well, you were in good form this morning, Mr. President.'"

Former presidential assistants Bob Haldeman and Joseph Califano both describe similar experiences. When Nixon issued an intemperate instruction on one occasion, Haldeman remembered: "I said nothing more, then stepped out of the office and placed the order immediately on my mental 'no action ever' shelf." President Johnson had the same habit, and Califano used the same response. Califano commented: "After three years of serving on his White House staff, he would have expected me to have some sense of how to measure his true meaning when he spoke in anger." (It is the author's belief that in May of 1993, when faced with what appeared to be a directive from on high to fire the staff of the White House Travel Office, OMA director David Watkins should have emulated the Haldeman practice.)

The chief of staff or one of the deputy chiefs of staff goes on each presidential journey as principal manager of the overall odyssey, since a presidential trip, particularly one overseas, presents a very special challenge for White House preparers and coordinators.

For nearly half a century it has been the chief of staff's responsibility to convene White House staff meetings. Harry S. Truman was the last president to do so personally. Under President Clinton, Chief of Staff Podesta inaugurated what he called strategic management team meetings, a daily morning gathering of the legislative, domestic, economic policy, and national security heads with the deputy chiefs of staff, the director and deputy director of the OMB, the secretary and deputy secretary of Treasury, and a few other senior staff. One could almost have called the group the "White House Executive Committee."

Because of the chief of staff 's stature and proximity to the president, invitations for media appearances—speeches, Sunday television talk shows—pour in. True, the chief is one of those in the White House best positioned to speak for the president—but any chief, even today, remembers Louis Brownlow's long-ago admonition to President Roosevelt: White House staff officers must have a "passion for anonymity." The need to explain or defend a president's actions may be almost overwhelming on some occasions, and a chief may be a spectacularly lucid and persuasive spokesperson. *Each chief of staff and each president will come to their own agreement on how public the chief's persona should be.* The author's personal preference is to give greater weight to Brownlow's advice.

The chief of staff must continually build bridges to the cabinet. While it is the fundamental thesis of this book that policy development and coordination are becoming more and more centralized in the White House staff, there is a risk in this development. Some cabinet secretaries, especially those with narrower and more specialized policy and operational responsibilities—and thus less contact with the White House—may tend to feel isolated, perhaps even alienated. *Locked in the Cabinet,* the memoir of former secretary of labor Robert Reich, evidences this sentiment:

The Secretary of Transportation phones to ask me how I discover what's going on at the White House. I have no clear answer. . . . The decision-making "loop" depends on physical proximity to B—who's whispering into his ear most regularly, whose office is closest to the Oval, who's sitting or standing next to him when a key issue arises. . . . One of the best techniques is to linger in the corridors of the West Wing after a meeting, picking up gossip. Another good place is the executive parking lot between the West Wing and the Old Executive Office Building, where dozens of White House staffers tromp every few minutes. In this administration you're either in the loop or you're out of the loop, but more likely you don't know where the loop is, or you don't even know there *is* a loop.

The chief of staff's antennae must be attuned to pick up such alienation—early.

Concerned that the 1998–99 scandal investigations and impeachment proceedings had led cabinet members to have "gotten kind of distant," Podesta began a series of breakfasts at the White House for small groups of cabinet secretaries. "Seven or eight at a time," he said, "just to kick things around, listen to them, let them tell me what was going on." A former assistant to Chief of Staff Bowles emphasized:

One of the challenges for our office was to act as a nexus, and to remember to keep everyone in the fold, and aware of what was going on in different parts of the White House. It is so big and there are so many different things taking place. There is a certain level of paranoia when you reach certain levels of power in government—in which everybody wants to know what everybody else is doing. The family—the organization—in my mind works better when people understand what's taking place. For the chief of staff to collect information is important, but so is it for the chief of staff to share information.

The chief of staff, finally, runs one more risk: that of becoming insensitive to the perquisites and privileges that necessarily accompany his status. The use of limousines and planes, proximity to the president, the toleration of what may be the chief's personal rudeness, the alacritous attention of subordinates—have gone to the heads of some. Over the years of their incumbency, having had to say no to so many supplicants (including members of Congress) will have added up to a paucity of close friends and a host of enemies. If the chief of staff—a Sherman Adams, a Donald Regan, a John Sununu—makes a stupid, even if unintentional slip, there may be only one friend left: and if he, the president, is embarrassed by the error, there is only the sad and sometimes precipitous exit. Would that the electronics wizards could invent a pocket-size "egometer" that would measure a chief of staff's ego, calculate his insensitivity index—and beep a warning! . . .

PART SEVEN

The Executive Branch

37

HUGH HECLO

From *A Government of Strangers*

To understand Hugh Heclo's intricate analysis of power inside the executive branch, students of American government must first know who the players are. Presidents select a small number (a few thousand) of high-level people to head the executive branch agencies. Among those appointments are cabinet secretaries, undersecretaries, assistant secretaries, and the like. The rest of those who work in the executive branch are civil servants, chosen for government jobs by merit exams, and they remain in government service for many years, even decades. They are the bureaucrats who provide continuity. Appointees come and go—as do presidents—but bureaucrats remain. Heclo identifies the often-unseen tension between a president's appointees and the bureaucrats. Be sure to pay particular attention to his discussion of the "iron triangle," one of the most interesting yet invisible forces in American government.

———

EVERY NEW ADMINISTRATION gives fresh impetus to an age-old struggle between change and continuity, between political leadership and bureaucratic power. Bureaucrats have a legitimate interest in maintaining the integrity of government programs and organizations. Political executives are supposed to have a broader responsibility: to guide rather than merely reflect the sum of special interests at work in the executive branch.

The search for effective political leadership in a bureaucracy of responsible career officials has become extraordinarily difficult in Washington. In every new crop of political appointees, some will have had government experience and a few will have worked together, but when it comes to group commitment to political leadership in the executive branch they constitute a government of strangers. And yet the fact remains that whether the President relies mainly on his White House aides or on his cabinet officials, someone is supposed to be mastering the bureaucracy "out there." For the President, his appointees, and high-ranking bureaucrats, the struggle to control the bureaucracy is usually a leap into the dark.

Despite a host of management and organization studies, Washington exposés and critiques of bureaucracy, very little information is available about the working world and everyday conduct of the top people in government. Even less is known about the operational lessons that could be drawn from their experiences. Congress is widely thought to have lost power to the executive branch, but congressional rather than executive behavior remains a major preoccupation in political research. Observers acknowledge that no president can cope with more than a tiny fraction of the decisionmaking in government, yet we know far more about a president's daily social errands than about the way vital public business is conducted by hundreds of political appointees and several thousand top bureaucrats who take executive actions in the name of the United States government—which is to say, in the name of us all. . . .

If popular impressions are any guide, few job titles are more suspect than "politician" and "bureaucrat." Periodic polls have shown that while most parents might want their offspring to become president, they dislike the notion of their becoming politicians. No pollster has dared to ask Americans what they would think of their children growing up to become Washington bureaucrats.

Yet in many ways the American form of government depends not only on a supply of able politicians and bureaucrats, but even more on a successful interaction between these two unpopular groups. . . .

. . . The administrative machinery in Washington represents a number of fragmented power centers rather than a set of subordinate units under the President. As many observers have noted, the cracks of fragmentation are not random but run along a number of well-established functional specialties and program interests that link particular government bureaus, congressional committees, and interest groups. People in the White House are aware of these subgovernments but have no obvious control over them. They seem to persist regardless of government reorganizations or, perhaps more to the point, they are able to prevent the reorganizations that displease them. In coping with these Washington subgovernments, the real lines of defense and accommodation are out in the departments, with their mundane operations of personnel actions, program approval, budget requests, regulation writing, and all the rest. These are the unglamorous tools with which political leaders in the agencies either help create a broader approach to the conduct of the public's business or acquiesce to the prevailing interest in business as usual. . . .

. . . Political executives who try to exercise leadership within government may encounter intense opposition that they can neither avoid nor reconcile. At such times some agency officials may try to undermine the efforts of political executives. Any number of reasons—some deplorable, some commendable—lie behind such bureaucratic opposition. Executive politics involves people, and certain individuals simply dislike each other and resort to personal vendettas. Many, however, sincerely believe in their bureau's purpose and feel they must protect its jurisdiction, programs, and budget at all costs. Others feel they have an obligation to "blow the whistle" as best they can when confronted with evidence of what they regard as improper conduct. In all these cases the result is likely to strike a political executive as bureaucratic subversion. To the officials, it is a question of higher loyalty, whether to one's self-interests, organization, or conscience.

The structure of most bureaucratic sabotage has been characterized as an "iron triangle" uniting a particular government bureau, its relevant interest group, and congressional supporters. The aims may be as narrow as individual profiteering and empire-building. Or they may be as magnanimous as "public interest" lobbies, reformist bureaucrats, and congressional crusaders all claiming somewhat incongruously to represent the unrepresented. There are alliances with fully developed shapes (e.g., the congressional sponsors of a program, the bureaucrats executing it, and its private clients or suppliers) and those made up of only a few diverse lines (e.g., a civil servant looking forward to post-retirement prospects with a particular lobby association or a congressman unconcerned about a bureaucrat's policy aims but aware that his specific favors can help win reelection). Some bureaucratic entrepreneurs initiate their own outside contacts; others have been pushed into becoming involved in outside alliances by former political appointees.

The common features of these subgovernments are enduring mutual interests across the executive and legislative branches and between the public and private sectors. However high-minded the ultimate purpose, the immediate aim of each alliance is to become "self-sustaining in control of power in its own sphere." The longer an agency's tradition of independence, the greater the political controversy surrounding its subject matter, and the more it is allied with outside groups, the more a new appointee can expect sub rosa opposition to develop to any proposed changes. If political leadership in the executive branch is to be more than the accidental sum of these alliances and if political representation is to be less arbitrary than the demands of any group that claims to speak for the unrepresented, then some conflict seems inevitable between higher political leaders and the subgovernments operating within their sphere.

Often sabotage is unrecognizable because of the virtually invisible ways civil servants can act in bad faith toward political executives. In addition to the bureaucracy's power of withholding needed information and services, there are other means. Like a long-married couple, bureaucrats and those in their networks can often communicate with a minimum of words: "If congressional staffs I trust call up and ask me, I might tell them. But I can also tell them I don't agree with the secretary by offering just technical information and not associating myself with the policy."

An official who does not want to risk direct dealings with Congress can encourage a private interest group to go to the agency's important appropriations and legislative committees, as one political executive discovered: "When we tried to downgrade the . . . bureau, its head was opposed, and he had a friend in a lobby group. After they got together rumblings started from the appropriations committee. I asked [the committee chairman] if he had a problem with this reorganization, and he said, 'No, you have the problem because if you touch that bureau I'll cut your job out of the budget.'" An experienced bureaucrat may not be able to make the decision, but he can try to arrange things to create the reaction he wants. "A colleague of mine," said a supergrade,* "keeps a file on field offices that can be abolished and their political sensitivity. Depending on who's pressing for cuts, he'll pull out those that are politically the worst for that particular configuration." The everyday relationships between people with specialized interests can shade effortlessly into subversion: "You know what it's like," said a bureau chief. "You've known each other and will have a drink complaining about what's happening and work up some little strategy of your own to do something about it." Or bureaucrats can work to get their way simply by not trying to know what is happening. One assistant secretary reported how his career subordinates agreed there might be mismanagement in the regional offices, "but they also said they didn't know what these offices were doing and so there wasn't enough information to justify doing what I wanted." Ignorance may not be bliss, but it can be security.

Political appointees can sometimes encounter much more vigorous forms of sabotage. These range from minor needling to massive retaliation. Since information is a prime strategic resource in Washington, the passing of unauthorized messages outside channels often approaches an art form. There are routine leaks to build credit and keep channels open for when they might be needed, positive leaks to promote something, negative leaks to discredit a person or policy, and counterleaks. There is even the daring reverse leak, an unauthorized release of information apparently for one reason but actually accomplishing the opposite.†

There is no lack of examples in every administration. A political

---

*Though not an official title, a "supergrade" would be a government civil servant in the upper levels of the bureaucracy. — EDS.

†One recent example involved a presidential assistant rather than a bureaucrat. While jockeying with another staff member, the assistant leaked a disclosure of his own impending removal from the West Wing. The opponent, who obviously stood the most to gain from

executive may discover that an agency subordinate "has gone to Congress and actually written the rider to the legislation that nullified the changes we wanted." A saboteur confided that "no one ever found it was [a division chief] who prepared the list showing which lobbyist was to contact which senator with what kind of argument." Still another official reported he had "seen appointees kept waiting in the outer office while their subordinate bureau officials were in private meetings with the congressional staff members." But waiting lines lack finesse. The telephone can be used with more delicacy, particularly after office hours: "The night before the hearings [a bureaucrat] fed the questions to the committee staff and then the agency witnesses spent the next two days having to reveal the information or duck the questions and catch hell." A young staff civil servant described how his superior operated:

I used to sit in [the bureau chief's] office after 6 P.M. when all the important business got done. He'd call up a senator and say, "Tom, you know this program that you and I got through a while back? Well, there's no crisis, but here are some things I'd like to talk to you about." He'd hang up and get on the phone to [a House committee chairman] and say, "I've been talking with Tom about this issue, and I'd like to bring you in on it." Hell, you'd find [the bureau chief] had bills almost drafted before anybody else in the executive branch had ever heard about them.

Encountering such situations, a public executive becomes acutely aware that experience as a private manager provides scant guidance. As one corporate executive with a six-figure salary said, "The end-runs and preselling were incredible. To find an equivalent you'd have to imagine some of your division managers going to the executive board or a major stockholder behind your back." Learning to deal with sabotage is a function of an executive's political leadership, not his private management expertise.

How do political executives try to deal with bureaucratic sabotage? . . . One approach is simply to ignore bureaucratic sabotage. Since the damage that may be done can easily cripple an executive's aims, diminish his reputation, and threaten his circles of confidence, those adopting this strategy can be presumed to have abdicated any attempt at political leadership in the Washington bureaucracy.

A second approach, especially favored by forceful managers, is to try to root out the leakers and prevent any recurrence. But political executives

the story, was naturally asked to confirm or deny the report. Since he was not yet strong enough to accomplish such a removal, the opponent had to deny responsibility for the leak and its accuracy, thereby inadvertently strengthening the position of the presidential assistant who first leaked the story.

usually discover that this straightforward approach has considerable disadvantages. For one thing, it is extremely time-consuming and difficult to actually investigate acts of subversion and pin down blame. For another thing, there are few effective sanctions to prevent recurrences. Moreover, a search for the guilty party can easily displace more positive efforts and leadership initiatives an executive needs to make in dealing with the bureaucracy. Even if it were possible, trying to censor bureaucratic contacts would probably restrict the informal help these outside relationships provide, as well as the harm they do. And in the end any serious sabotage will probably be buttressed by some mandate from Congress; punishing the saboteurs can be seen as an assault on legislative prerogatives and thus invite even sterner retribution. It is circumstances such as these that led an experienced undersecretary to conclude:

Of course you can't be a patsy, but by and large you've got to recognize that leaks and end-runs are going to happen. You can spend all your time at trying to find out who's doing it, and if you do, then what? [One of my colleagues] actually tried to stop some of his bureaucrats from accepting phone calls from the press. They did stop accepting the calls, but they sure as hell returned them quickly. In this town there are going to be people running behind your back, and there's not much you can do to stop it.

However, while academics write about the iron triangle as if it were an immutable force, prudent political executives recognize that although they cannot stop bureaucratic sabotage, neither are they helpless against it. They can use personnel sanctions where misconduct can be clearly proven. But far more important, they can work to counteract sabotage with their own efforts—strengthening their outside contacts, extending their own lines of information and competitive analysis, finding new points of countertension. In general, experienced political executives try to use all their means of self-help and working relations so as to reshape the iron triangles into more plastic polygons.

To deal with sabotage, wise political appointees try to render it more obvious:

I make it clear that all the information and papers are supposed to move through me. It increases your work load tremendously, and maybe you don't understand everything you see, but everyone knows I'm supposed to be in on things and that they are accepting risks by acting otherwise.

They try to counteract unwanted messages with their own accounts to the press and others. The more the agency's boat is leaking, "the more you go out and work the pumps. You can't plug all the leaks, but you can make sure to get your side of the story out."

Political executives also make use of timing to deal with sabotage:

I put in a one-year fudge factor for an important change. That's because I know people are going to be doing end-runs to Congress. This year lets congressmen blow off steam, and for another thing it shows me where the sensitive spots are so I can get busy trying to work out some compromises—you know, things that can serve the congressmen's interest as well as mine.

Substantial results can be achieved by bringing new forces into play, dealing not with just one alliance but creating tests of strengths among the triangles:

It's like when officials were getting together with the unions and state administrators to get at some committee chairman. I hustled out to line up governors and show the congressmen that state administrators weren't speaking for all of state government.

Washington offers more opportunities to search for allies than is suggested by any simple image of political executives on one side and bureaucratic opponents on the other. Political appointees may be "back-doored" by other appointees, higher bureaucrats by lower bureaucrats. Fights may be extended to involve some appointees and bureaucrats versus others. As the leader of one faction put it, "Often a guy preselling things on the Hill is hurting people elsewhere, making it tougher for them to get money and approval and straining their relations. I use this fact to get allies."

A political executive who works hard at outside contacts will discover what subversives may learn too late: that many groups are fickle allies of the bureaucracy. This has seemed especially true as Congress has increased its own bureaucracy of uncoordinated staffs. A veteran bureaucrat described the risks run by would-be saboteurs:

Everybody you might talk to weighs the value of the issue to them against the value of keeping you alive for the next time. I've seen [a congressman] ruin many a good civil servant by getting a relationship going with him and then dropping him to score points off the agency brass. Now, too, there are more Hill staffers running around telling appointees, "Hey, these guys from your department said this and that. How about it?" Then the appointee will go back to the agency and raise hell for the bureaucrat.

Thus the political executives' own positive efforts are the necessary— if not always a sufficient—condition for combating sabotage. Since some bureaucratic subversion is an ever-present possibility and since punishment is difficult, the government executives' real choice is to build and use their political relationships or forfeit most other strategic resources for leadership.

38

JOEL ABERBACH
BERT ROCKMAN

From *In the Web of Politics*

Joel Aberbach and Bert Rockman are leading authorities on the executive branch bureaucracy—the career civil servants who actually run the day-to-day affairs of the cabinet departments and the independent agencies. They are also experts on the "burro pit," as described by one of their interviewees. Aberbach and Rockman describe the push-and-pull between the president's political appointees who head the executive agencies and the bureaucrats who work there. The appointees have the voters' mandate on their side. Bureaucrats have extensive knowledge, years of service, and a grasp of detail on theirs. "Dynamism and ballast" are Aberbach's and Rockman's characterization of this classic political match-up.

MOST PEOPLE THINK of bureaucracy as a downright dull subject. Yet for thirty years the American federal executive has been awash in political controversy. From George Wallace's attacks on "pointy headed bureaucrats," to Richard Nixon's "responsiveness program," to the efforts of Al Gore and Bill Clinton to "reinvent government," the people who administer the American state have stood uncomfortably in the spotlight. . . .

Numerous issues affect the bureaucracy as a whole, including recent emphases on customer satisfaction, downsizing, and employee morale and training. It is, however, at the top levels of the bureaucracy where leadership is demanded and where attention to issues of representativeness, quality, morale, responsiveness, and adaptability is especially crucial. What happens throughout the administrative system is strongly affected by top leadership. Signals and cues are important in organizations. Clarity in them does not ensure that they will be followed, but a lack of clarity or the presence of contradiction ensures that there will be many interpretations about what policy is.

Politics, policy, and expertise meet uneasily at the top of the bureaucracy. A presidential administration's ambitions (and its political appointees) join there with a senior career civil service that is not invested in these ambitions. Presidential administrations demand responsiveness from career officials, but career officials must balance neutrality with helpfulness. The tensions between political direction and skepticism bred from experience are notable at the top levels of any administrative system. Because of the institutional features of the American system of government, these tensions are particularly strong at the top of the federal bureaucracy. Not everything important to the functioning of the federal bureaucracy, of course, occurs at the top levels, but most everything ultimately reverberates from the top. Therefore, we have chosen to focus our attention on the top layers of the bureaucracy—the politically appointed officials of presidential administrations and the senior career executives. . . .

Who answers to whom is at the core of any system of delegation. And administration is inherently such a system. Authorities delegate others to act on their behalf. In any system, including absolute monarchies and dictatorships, bureaucrats respond imperfectly to the authorities' direction. In authoritarian systems, bureaucrats' lack of responsiveness or even just a suspicion about their loyalty has often resulted in suspect administrators losing not merely their jobs, but also their heads. Democracy makes the problem of bureaucratic responsiveness considerably more complex because, among other things, the sanctions for suspect loyalties are far less severe. Also, there is likely to be less continuity of authority in democratic than in authoritarian systems. Democratic politicians do not get elected or anointed for life. Adjustment is difficult. Bureaucrats in a democracy get new bosses with considerable frequency. In a democracy, the chain of command is a bit more convoluted. Louis XIV may have felt relatively little need to answer to others, but democratic politicians cannot afford such self-indulgence. They know they have to answer to others and therefore need to deliver the goods. The flip side of responsiveness is responsibility. In democracies the political leaders are held responsible, so it stands to reason that they are apt to demand responsiveness from the bureaucracy.

Bureaucracy and democracy are thus in inherent tension with one another. First of all, democratic processes are used to select politicians, but not bureaucrats. Despite contemporary pressures for increasing representativeness among civil servants on the basis of characteristics such as gender, race, and ethnicity, bureaucrats still do not have to stand for popular approval at the ballot box. Second, . . . bureaucrats may reflect the preferences of previous regimes and be reluctant to adjust to new policies and leaders. Third, . . . bureaucrats may be especially averse to novelty. Fourth, as policy gets more complex, so does policymaking. The bureaucracy (and in the American case, also the courts) becomes an important venue for policymaking because passing laws is merely the beginning of the policymaking process.

In sum, bureaucrats are involved in policy decisions (even if the fiction remains that they are not), but they are unelected decisionmakers. Moreover, career civil servants, much like federal judges, have lifetime tenure. And this, in turn, brings up yet a further source of tension between bureaucracy and democracy—the expertise of the bureaucrat in contrast to the generalist role of the politician. Most bureaucrats acquire expertise in a particular domain and get to know a great deal about the programs they administer. Politicians, by contrast, can ill afford the luxury of committing so many resources to one of many problems they have to cope with, unless that problem is getting reelected.

Bureaucrats are involved in policymaking mainly because bureaucrats do the details, and, as the saying goes, the devil resides therein. Because political leaders are unlikely to know the details (at least not as well as the bureaucrats do) and because there is inherent slippage in delegation, bureaucrats usually wind up defining the exact terms for implementing what it is that leaders want. In a similar vein, bureaucrats can outline possible paths for their political superiors to follow within the bounds of technical feasibility, legal restriction, and even political reality. These powers are nowhere articulated in formal job descriptions, but to a greater or lesser degree they are real nearly everywhere. The expression "bureaucrats need to be on tap, not on top" is a prescription to counter the reality that the knowledge and experience that career bureaucrats possess make them the professionals of government and give them considerable potential to influence the course of policy. . . .

Responsiveness is a simple concept in theory but a complicated one in practice. In a democracy, it has to do with the straightforward notion that bureaucrats, who are not elected, should be responsible to elected politicians (or their appointed agents). That is the simple part. In practice, it is probably impossible for any set of bureaucratic agents in a truly democratic and constitutional system simply to follow the dictates of their political superiors. In fact, a bureaucracy that consistently did this would likely be regarded as a mere appendage to whichever party happened to be in power. Such a bureaucracy might well become complicit in denying access to the regime's opponents. Indeed, a system of this sort would be regarded as flagrantly violating the democratic rules of the game.

There are four problems with the idea or practice of making bureaucrats completely responsive: signals and directions from political leaders may lack clarity; conflicts sometimes occur between responsiveness to the chain of command and accountability to the law; there is potential conflict between the demand for responsiveness and the need for stability and memory in government; and institutional complications can arise that pit authorities against one another, thus sowing confusion, or fragmenting authority, and thus segmenting responsiveness.

The Problem of Clarity

The problem of directional clarity arises because political leaders sometimes do not know exactly what they want or may even wish to avoid the risk of choosing. Deciphering signals or directions under these circumstances is difficult. This is one reason politicians often resort to *ex post* judgments rather than *ex ante* guidance. The marching orders that President Bush twice articulated to his cabinet are one extreme example of the problem of interpreting political will. Among them were such inspiring messages as "think big" and "challenge the system." The problem was that "the marching orders covered no policy goals for the administration, nor did they provide guidance on policy development." . . .

The Problem of Legality

The second problem arises because not everything political leaders want is consistent with prevailing law. Bureaucrats are supposed to be responsive to the chain of command yet also accountable to the law. Political leaders often want to stretch the boundaries of legal constraints that keep them from doing what they want. In theory, bureaucrats achieve accountability by complying with the chain of command, but this assumes that those up the chain are operating lawfully. To be fully responsive to political authority under such circumstances may well violate the rule of law. A system of divided authority further complicates both accountability and responsiveness. It gives civil servants more potential leeway or cover since they are responsible to more than one set of political authorities and can play one off against the other. It also allows civil servants to delay implementing what they regard as ill-advised directives so as to give other authorities opportunities to act and possibly countermand them. But what gives cover to civil servants fuels the suspicions of political leaders, particularly those in the executive branch.

The Problem of Stability

The third problem arises when political leaders try to budge a recalcitrant bureaucracy. For the most part, politicians tend to think bigger, or perhaps simply more grandiose, thoughts than do bureaucrats. Politicians tend to focus on symbols and desired end states; bureaucrats tend to focus more on the relationship of means to ends and the transaction costs attached to altering existing equilibria. We have noted elsewhere that, untempered by bureaucrats, politicians can be susceptible to a frenzied debate about symbolically laden and ideologically driven proposals with no roots in the past and no assessments of costs, benefits, or feasibilities. But we also observed that, undirected by politicians, bureaucrats would be weighted down by inertia derived from past commitments and thus would be susceptible to "directionless consensus."

There is a sort of yin and yang in government between dynamism and ballast. Politicians tend to provide the dynamics and bureaucrats the ballast. Leadership, drive, and vision are essential to government, but continuity, connections to the past, and an appreciation of policy practicality and political feasibility are equally important. These traits are obviously in tension with one another. Harmonious balance between them is desirable, but it is not self-evident exactly how this can be achieved. To the contrary, as the visions of political leaders widen and the changes they contemplate become more expansive, the tensions are likely to become more pronounced. . . .

The Problem of Institutions

The problems we allude to above are inherent to the responsiveness issue. That is, they are likely to occur anywhere. There is one key exception, however, and that is the institutional problem. The division of authority built into the U.S. Constitution complicates a problem that exists everywhere.

Theorists have noted that U.S. political institutions have different constituencies. This is also true under unified government, when the same political party is in control of the institutions. Even when these relatively favorable circumstances for presidential-congressional comity prevail, informal treaties may be reached so that congressional and executive territory are effectively agreed to, producing what Charles Gilbert referred to as "segmented responsiveness." Under such arrangements, some agencies are more sensitive to key congressional constituencies and interest groups than to the leadership of the executive branch.

In their most extreme form, arrangements of this sort have been characterized as "iron triangles," in which agencies, congressional committees or subcommittees, and interest groups happily coexist. In this setting, at least according to lore, agencies could escape central direction by providing goods to congressional and interest constituencies with a high demand for them. The congressional committees and interest groups would then defend agency interests politically. These arrangements, of course, are merely implicit understandings and do not last forever. They occur when presidential administrations are indifferent to the situation or decide that the costs of dislodging certain agencies from the grip of Congress are too high or the probability of success in such an endeavor too low. However, as divided government has increasingly become the norm, and as policy disagreements across the parties have intensified about such issues as the size and role of government, the stakes for control of the bureaucracy have grown. From this perspective, the political costs of upsetting the prevailing equilibrium, costs that once appeared so formidable, have seemed to decrease in marginal terms precisely because control of the bureaucracy has become so fundamental to an administration's policy success. . . .

Epic struggles have in fact occurred between the branches with regard to the reach of their authority, even when the same party has controlled both the legislative and executive branch. But these struggles are apt to become greater when the branches are divided by party and to become titanic when party cleavages are ideologically sharp. Moreover, when divided government is persistent and the same party remains in control of an institution for a long time, an expectation develops in Washington that the controlling party has a proprietorship over it. From the standpoint of the other party, there is little to be lost and seemingly much to be gained by trying to restrict the prerogatives of the "opposing" branch. As Charles O. Jones puts it, each branch seeks to maximize its share of governmental control. In a system in which each branch is given incomplete resources to govern by itself, each has a tendency to stretch its prerogatives as far as they will go—"to round the O" in the words of Sir Ernest Barker, meaning, to complete the circle of governance by itself.

The bureaucracy frequently becomes the battleground for interbranch conflict because it applies concrete meaning to policy. . . .

Responsiveness has limits, both realistically and normatively. It is necessary for the bureaucracy to put some space between itself and any particular set of governing authorities. In this sense, the bureaucracy represents the continuity of government above and beyond the particular needs of its present incumbents. Of course, this is the heart of the problem. How can the bureaucracy be both independent and democratically controlled? Political authorities may brand such independence, or even a questioning of its proposals, as sheer recalcitrance. Moreover, there is always reason for current authorities to believe that the bureaucracy is more committed to the legacies of the past than the policy agendas of the present.

A bureaucracy wedded to any given political perspective or any particular party inevitably presents problems for the democratic alternation of power. The career civil service may need to be responsive to the present incumbents (a task made difficult by the American system, with its diffused political authority), but it also needs to be regarded as essentially neutral and fair. A senior civil servant from our 1986–87 sample stated in a particularly folksy way the core problem faced by civil servants trying to balance adaptation and neutrality:

> We have to start with the frame of reference of the statute that's passed and to be implemented with a given administration in power. The way that law can be administered can vary within a spectrum, depending upon the lineage of the statute. . . . I think it's our job to try to follow what the administration wants to do in its approach to accomplishing that particular statute's objective, without allowing that statute to be distorted. . . . Let's say I'm a politician; you're the bureaucrat. I'm gonna stand over there and wave at you, and I'm gonna say come on over here in the burro pen and I'm going to get you as far as I can get you, but you better not get there. If you do, you're gonna be in trouble. I try to live by that because I know that the administration is gonna try to pull you to their way of thinking as far as they can, and the next administration is gonna do it the other way. And I think it's our job to keep the objective on the highway without getting into the burro pit. . . .

39

ROBERT REICH

From *Locked in the Cabinet*

University professor Robert Reich was appointed to President Clinton's cabinet in 1993 to be his Secretary of Labor. Writing with all the candor and humor that is Reich's trademark, he gives readers three important criteria he considered in selecting his assistants and then concludes, "I'm flying blind." His daily schedule is packed, and he is motivated to escape from the "bubble" and actually tour the vast buildings of the Labor Department. Finally, Reich offers an instructive anecdote about an idea developed by an obscure civil servant in the department, an idea that turns out to be a real winner and becomes an important new government policy.

February 1, [1993] Washington

I INTERVIEW TWENTY people today. I have to find a deputy secretary and chief of staff with all the management skills I lack. I also have to find a small platoon of assistant secretaries: one to run the Occupational Safety and Health Administration (detested by corporations, revered by unions); another to be in charge of the myriad of employment and job training programs (billions of dollars), plus unemployment insurance (billions more); another to police the nation's pension funds (four trillion dollars' worth); another to patrol the nation's nine million workplaces to make sure that young children aren't being exploited, that workers receive at least a minimum hourly wage plus time and a half for overtime, that sweatshops are relegated to history.

The Department of Labor is vast, its powers seemingly endless. With a history spanning the better part of the twentieth century—involving every major controversy affecting American workers—it issues thousands of regulations, sends vast sums of money to states and cities, and sues countless employers. I can barely comprehend it all. It was created in 1913 with an ambitious mission: *Foster, promote, and develop the welfare of the wage earners of the United States, improve their working conditions, and advance their opportunities for profitable employment.* That about sums it up.

And yet here I am assembling my team before I've even figured it all out. No time to waste. Bill will have to sign off on my choices, then each of them will be nitpicked for months by the White House staff and the FBI, and if they survive those hurdles each must be confirmed by the Senate.

If I'm fast enough out of the starting gate, my team might be fully installed by June. If I dally now and get caught in the traffic jam of subcabinet nominations from every department, I might not see them for a year. And whenever they officially start, add another six months before they have the slightest idea what's going on.

No other democracy does it this way. No private corporation would think of operating like this. Every time a new president is elected, America assembles a new government of 3,000 or so amateurs who only sometimes know the policies they're about to administer, rarely have experience managing large government bureaucracies, and almost never know the particular piece of it they're going to run. These people are appointed quickly by a president-elect who is thoroughly exhausted from a year and a half of campaigning. And they remain in office, on average, under two years—barely enough time to find the nearest bathroom. It's a miracle we don't screw it up worse than we do.

Part of my problem is I don't know exactly what I'm looking for and I certainly don't know how to tell whether I've found it. Some obvious criteria:

1. *They should share the President-elect's values.* But how will I know they do? I can't very well ask, "Do you share the President's values?" and expect an honest answer. Even if they contributed money to the campaign, there's no telling. I've heard of several middle-aged Washington lawyers so desperate to escape the tedium of law practice by becoming an assistant secretary for Anything That Gets Me Out of Here that they've made whopping contributions to both campaigns.

2. *They should be competent and knowledgeable about the policies they'll administer.* Sounds logical, but here again, how can I tell? I don't know enough to know whether someone *else* knows enough. "What do you think about the Employee Retirement Income Security Act?" I might ask, and an ambitious huckster could snow me. "I've thought a lot about this," he might say, "and I've concluded that Section 508(m) should be changed because most retirees have 307 accounts which are treated by the IRS as Subchapter 12 entities." Uttered with enough conviction, bullshit like this could sweep me off my feet.

3. *They should be good managers.* But how to find out? Yesterday I phoned someone about a particular job candidate's management skills, at her suggestion. He told me she worked for him and was a terrific manager. "Terrific?" I repeated. "Wonderful. The best," he said. "You'd recommend her?" I asked. "Absolutely. Can't go wrong," he assured me. I thanked him, hung up the phone, and was enthusiastic for about five minutes, until I realized how little I had learned. How do I know *he* recognizes a good manager? Maybe he's a lousy manager himself and has a bunch of bozos working for him. Why should I trust that he's more interested in my having her on *my* team than in getting her off his?

I'm flying blind. . . .

March 2 Washington

This afternoon, I mount a small revolution at the Labor Department. The result is chaos.

Background: My cavernous office is becoming one of those hermetically sealed, germ-free bubbles they place around children born with immune deficiencies. Whatever gets through to me is carefully sanitized. Telephone calls are prescreened, letters are filtered, memos are reviewed. Those that don't get through are diverted elsewhere. Only [deputy secretary] Tom [Glynn], chief of staff Kitty [Higgins], and my secretary walk into the office whenever they want. All others seeking access must first be scheduled, and have a sufficient reason to take my precious germ-free time.

I'm scheduled to the teeth. Here, for example, is today's timetable:

6:45 A.M.	Leave apartment
7:10 A.M.	Arrive office
7:15 A.M.	Breakfast with MB from the *Post*
8:00 A.M.	Conference call with Rubin
8:30 A.M.	Daily meeting with senior staff
9:15 A.M.	Depart for Washington Hilton
9:40 A.M.	Speech to National Association of Private Industry Councils
10:15 A.M.	Meet with Joe Dear (OSHA enforcement)
11:15 A.M.	Meet with Darla Letourneau (DOL budget)
12:00	Lunch with JG from National League of Cities
1:00 P.M.	CNN interview (taped)
1:30 P.M.	Congressional leadership panel
2:15 P.M.	Congressman Ford
3:00 P.M.	NEC budget meeting at White House
4:00 P.M.	Welfare meeting at White House
5:00 P.M.	National Public Radio interview (taped)
5:45 P.M.	Conference call with mayors
6:15 P.M.	Telephone time
7:00 P.M.	Meet with Maria Echeveste (Wage and Hour)
8:00 P.M.	Kitty and Tom daily briefing
8:30 P.M.	National Alliance of Business reception
9:00 P.M.	Return to apartment.

I remain in the bubble even when I'm outside the building—ushered from place to place by someone who stays in contact with the front office by cellular phone. I stay in the bubble after business hours. If I dine out, I'm driven to the destination and escorted to the front door. After dinner, I'm escorted back to the car, driven to my apartment, and escorted from the car, into the apartment building, into the elevator, and to my apartment door.

No one gives me a bath, tastes my food, or wipes my bottom—at least not yet. But in all other respects I feel like a goddamn two-year-old. Tom and Kitty insist it has to be this way. Otherwise I'd be deluged with calls, letters, meetings, other demands on my time, coming from all directions. People would force themselves on me, harass me, maybe even threaten me. The bubble protects me.

Tom and Kitty have hired three people to handle my daily schedule (respond to invitations, cull the ones that seem most promising, and squeeze all the current obligations into the time available), one person to ready my briefing book each evening so I can prepare for the next day's schedule, and two people to "advance" me by making sure I get where I'm supposed to be and depart on time. All of them now join Tom and Kitty as guardians of the bubble.

"How do you decide what I do and what gets through to me?" I ask Kitty.

"We have you do and see what you'd choose if you had time to examine all the options yourself—sifting through all the phone calls, letters, memos, and meeting invitations," she says simply.

"But how can you possibly *know* what I'd choose for myself?"

"Don't worry," Kitty says patiently. "We know."

They have no way of knowing. We've worked together only a few weeks. Clare and I have lived together for a quarter century and even she wouldn't know.

I trust Tom and Kitty. They share my values. I hired them because I sensed this, and everything they've done since then has confirmed it. But it's not a matter of trust.

The *real* criterion Tom and Kitty use (whether or not they know it or admit it) is their own experienced view of what a secretary of labor with my values and aspirations *should* choose to see and hear. They transmit to me through the bubble only those letters, phone calls, memoranda, people, meetings, and events which they believe *someone like me* ought to have. But if I see and hear only what "someone like me" should see and hear, no original or out-of-the-ordinary thought will ever permeate the bubble. I'll never be surprised or shocked. I'll never be forced to rethink or reevaluate anything. I'll just lumber along, blissfully ignorant of what I *really* need to see and hear—which are things that don't merely confirm my preconceptions about the world.

I make a list of what I want them to transmit through the bubble henceforth:

1. The angriest, meanest ass-kicking letters we get from the public every week.

2. Complaints from department employees about anything.

3. Bad news about fuck-ups, large and small.

4. Ideas, ideas, ideas: from department employees, from outside academics and researchers, from average citizens. Anything that even resem-

bles a good idea about what we should do better or differently. Don't
screen out the wacky ones.

5. Anything from the President or members of Congress.

6. A random sample of calls or letters from real people outside Washington, outside government—people who aren't lawyers, investment
bankers, politicians, or business consultants; people who aren't professionals; people without college degrees.

7. "Town meetings" with department employees here at headquarters
and in the regions. "Town meetings" in working-class and poor areas of
the country. "Town meetings" in community colleges, with adult students.

8. Calls and letters from business executives, including those who
hate my guts. Set up meetings with some of them.

9. Lunch meetings with small groups of department employees, ran-
domly chosen from all ranks.

10. Meetings with conservative Republicans in Congress.

I send the memo to Tom and Kitty. Then, still feeling rebellious and
with nothing on my schedule for the next hour (the NEC meeting
scheduled for 3:00 was canceled) I simply walk out of the bubble. I sneak
out of my big office by the back entrance and start down the corridor.

I take the elevator to floors I've never visited. I wander to places in
the department I've never been. I have spontaneous conversations with
employees I'd never otherwise see. *Free at last.*

Kitty discovers I'm missing. It's as if the warden had discovered an
escape from the state pen. The alarm is sounded: Secretary loose! Secretary
escapes from bubble! Find the Secretary! Security guards are dispatched.

By now I've wandered to the farthest reaches of the building, to
corridors never before walked by anyone ranking higher than GS-12. I
visit the mailroom, the printshop, the basement workshop.

The hour is almost up. Time to head back. But which way? I'm at
the northernmost outpost of the building, in bureaucratic Siberia. I try
to retrace my steps but keep coming back to the same point in the
wilderness.

I'm lost.

In the end, of course, a security guard finds me and takes me back
to the bubble. Kitty isn't pleased. "You shouldn't do that," she says sternly.
"We were worried."

"It was good for me." I'm defiant.

"We need to know where you *are*." She sounds like the mother of a
young juvenile delinquent.

"Next time give me a beeper, and I'll call home to see if you need me."

"You *must* have someone with you. It's not safe."

"This is the Labor Department, not Bosnia."

"You might get lost."

"That's *ridiculous*. How in hell could someone get *lost* in this building?"

She knows she has me. "You'd be surprised." She smiles knowingly and heads back to her office. . . .

March 14 Washington

Tom and Kitty suggest I conduct a "town meeting" of Labor Department employees here at headquarters—give them an opportunity to ask me questions and me a chance to express my views. After all, I've been here almost eight weeks and presumably have a few answers and one or two views.

Some of the other senior staff think it unwise. They point to the risk of gathering thousands of employees together in one place with access to microphones. The cumulative frustrations from years of not being listened to by political appointees could explode when exposed to the open air, like a dangerous gas. Gripes, vendettas, personal slights, hurts, malfeasance, nonfeasance, mistreatments, slurs, lies, deceptions, frauds. Who knows what might be in that incendiary mix?

Secretaries of labor have come and gone, usually within two years. Assistant secretaries, even faster. Only a tiny fraction of Labor Department employees are appointed to their jobs because of who's occupying the White House. The vast majority are career employees, here because they got their jobs through the civil service. Most of them will remain here for decades, some for their entire careers. They have come as lawyers, accountants, economists, investigators, clerks, secretaries, and custodians. Government doesn't pay as well as the private sector, but the jobs are more secure. And some have come because they believe that public service is inherently important.

But for years they've been treated like shit. Republican appointees were often contemptuous of or uninterested in most of what went on here. The Reagan and Bush administrations didn't exactly put workplace issues at the top of their agenda. In fact, Reagan slashed the department's budget and reduced the number of employees by about a quarter. His first appointee as secretary of labor was a building contractor.

The career people don't harbor much more trust for Democrats. It's an article of faith among civil servants that political appointees, of whatever party, care only about the immediate future. They won't be here years from now to implement fully their jazzy ideas, or to pick up the pieces if the ideas fall apart. Career civil servants would prefer not to take short-term risks. They don't want headlines. Even if the headlines are positive, headlines draw extra attention, and in Washington attention can be dangerous.

There is a final reason for their cynicism. Career civil servants feel unappreciated by politicians. Every presidential candidate since Carter has run as a Washington "outsider," against the permanent Washington establishment. Almost every congressional and senatorial candidate decries the "faceless bureaucrats" who are assumed to wield unaccountable power. Career civil servants are easy targets. They can't talk back. This scapegoating parallels the public's mounting contempt for Washington. In opinion polls conducted during the Eisenhower administration, about seventy-five percent of the American public thought that their government "could be trusted to act in the public interest most of the time." In a recent poll, only twenty-five percent expressed similar sentiments. But career civil servants aren't to blame. The disintegration has come on the heels of mistakes and improprieties by political leaders—Vietnam, Watergate, the Iran-*contra* imbroglio, the savings-and-loan scandal. And it accelerated as the nation emerged from five decades of Depression, hot war, and cold war—common experiences that forced us to band together and support a strong government—into a global economy without clear borders or evil empires.

Our "town meeting" is set for noon. A small stage is erected on one side of a huge open hall on the first floor of the department. The hall is about the size of football field. On its walls are paintings of former secretaries of labor.

I walk in exactly at noon. Nervous (Wasn't President James Garfield assassinated by a disgruntled civil servant?)

The hall is jammed with thousands of people. Many are sitting on folding chairs, tightly packed around the makeshift stage. Others are standing. Several hundred are standing on risers around the outer perimeter, near the walls. Is it legal for so many employees to be packed so tightly in one place? Tomorrow's Washington *Post*: Labor Secretary Endangers Workers. Subhead: Violates the Occupational Safety and Health Act.

I make my way up to the small stage and face the crowd. I don't want to speak from behind a lectern, because to see over it I'd have to stand on a stool and would look ridiculous. So I hold the microphone. The crowd quiets.

"Hello."

"Hello!" they roar back in unison. Laughter. A good start, anyway. . . .

"Who's first?" I scan the crowd—left, center, right. No hands. I'm
back in the classroom, first class of the semester. I've asked the question,
but no one wants to break the ice. They have plenty to say, but no one
dares. So I'll do what I always do: I'll just stand here silently, smiling,
until someone gets up the courage. I can bear the silence.

I wait. Thirty seconds. Forty-five seconds. A minute. Thousands of
people here, but no sound. They seem startled. I know they have all sorts
of opinions about what should be done. They share them with each other
every day. But have they ever shared them directly with the Secretary?

Finally, one timid hand in the air. I point to her. "Yes! You! What's
your name?" All eyes on her. The crowd explodes into rumbles, murmurs,
and laughs, like a huge lung exhaling. A cordless mike is passed to her.

"Connie," she answers, nervously.

I move to the front of the stage so I can see Connie better. "Which
agency do you work in, Connie?"

"Employment Standards."

"What's your idea?"

Connie's voice is unsteady, but she's determined. "Well, I don't see
why we need to fill out time cards when we come to work and when
we leave. It's silly and demeaning."

Applause. Connie is buoyed by the response, and her voice grows
stronger. "I mean, if someone is dishonest they'll just fill in the wrong
times anyway. Our supervisors know when we come and go. The work
has to get done. Besides, we're professionals. Why treat us like children?"

I look over at Tom. He shrugs his shoulders: Why not?

"Okay, done. Starting tomorrow, no more time cards."

For a moment, silence. The audience seems stunned. Then a loud
roar of approval that breaks into wild applause. Many who were seated
stand and cheer.

What have I done? I haven't doubled their salaries or sent them on
all-expenses-paid vacations to Hawaii. All I did was accept a suggestion
that seemed reasonable. But for people who have grown accustomed to
being ignored, I think I just delivered an important gift.

The rest of the meeting isn't quite as buoyant. Some suggestions I
reject outright (a thirty-five-hour workweek). Others I write down and
defer for further consideration. But I learn a great deal. I hear ideas I
never would have thought of. One thin and balding man from the Employment and Training Administration has a commonsensical one: When
newly unemployed people register for unemployment insurance, why not

determine whether their layoff is likely to be permanent or temporary—and if permanent, get them retraining and job-placement services right away instead of waiting until their benefits almost run out? He has evidence this will shorten the average length of unemployment and save billions of dollars. I say I'll look into it. . . .

September 20 Washington

Tom tells me that calls are pouring in from members of Congress demanding that unemployment benefits be extended beyond their normal six months. "We've got to find several billion dollars, quick," says Tom. But I don't know where to find the money other than taking it out of job counseling and training—which would be nuts.

"We *won't* extend unemployment benefits if it means less money for finding new jobs!" I'm defiant.

"I don't think you have a choice," says Tom. "People just don't believe there're new jobs out there. All they know is they had a job. They think it's coming back eventually, and they need money to live on in the meantime."

Kitty rushes in. "I've got it!"

"What?"

"The *answer*. Remember the fellow at the department town meeting who had the idea for fixing the unemployment system?"

"Vaguely." I recall a tall, hollow-eyed career employee who spoke toward the end.

"He suggested that when newly unemployed people apply for unemployment insurance they're screened to determine whether their layoff is temporary or permanent—and if *permanent* they immediately get help finding a new job. *Well* . . . " Kitty pauses to catch her breath. "I spoke with him at some length this morning. His name is Steve Wandner. Seems that a few years ago he ran a pilot project for the department, trying his idea out. Get *this*: Where he tried it, the average length of unemployment dropped two to four weeks! The poor guy has been trying to sell the idea since then, but no one has ever listened."

"I don't get it. How does this help us?"

"Think of it! Do what he did all over the country, and cut the average length of unemployment two to four weeks. This saves the government $400 million a year in unemployment benefits. That's $2 billion over the next five years, if you need help with the math."

"I understand the math. I just don't understand the *point*. So what?

That's money saved in the *future*. How does that get us the money we need now?"

Kitty stares at me with her usual what-is-this-man-doing-as-a-cabinet-member expression. "If we can show that we'll save this money over the next five years, we can use it *now* to offset extra unemployment benefits. It's like extra *cash!*" She lunges toward a stack of paper on the corner of my desk and tosses the entire pile into the air. "Manna *from heaven!*"

"I still don't get it. And by the way, you're making a mess."

Kitty is excited, but she talks slowly, as if to a recent graduate of kindergarten. "Try to *understand*. The federal budget law requires that if you want to spend more money, you've got to get the money from somewhere else. Right? One place you can get it is from future savings, but only if the Congressional Budget Office believes you. Follow me?"

"I think so."

"Now comes our brilliant geek from the bowels of the Labor Department with *proof* that we can save around $2 billion during the next five years. And the true *beauty* of it" — Kitty beams — "is that this reform brings us a step closer to what *you've* been talking about. We get a law providing emergency extra unemployment benefits — $2 billion worth — covering the next few months. And *at the same time* we permanently change the whole system so that it's more focused on finding new jobs. It's a twofer! A win-win! Nobody can vote against it! I *love* it!"

I look at Tom. "Is she right?"

"Yup." Tom is impressed.

Kitty begins to dance around the office. She is the only person I have ever met who can fall in love with proposed legislation. . . .

November 24 The White House

B sits at his elaborately carved desk in the Oval Office before the usual gaggle of cameras and spotlights. Clustered tightly around him in order to get into the shot are five smiling senators and ten smiling House members. B utters some sentences about why people who have lost their jobs shouldn't have to worry that their unemployment benefits will run out. He signs the bill into law. The congressmen applaud. He stands and shakes each of their hands. The spotlights go out and the cameras are packed away. The whole thing takes less than five minutes.

Kitty is here, smiling from ear to ear. I congratulate her.

Against a far wall, behind the small crowd, I see Steve Wandner, the hollow-eyed Labor Department employee who first suggested the idea that was just signed into law. I made sure Steve was invited to this signing ceremony. I walk over to where he's standing.

"Good job." I extend my hand.

He hesitates a moment. "I never thought . . . " His voice trails off.

"I want to introduce you to the President."

Steve is reluctant. I pull his elbow and guide him toward where B is chatting energetically with several members of Congress who still encircle him. They're talking football—big men, each over six feet, laughing, telling stories, bonding. It's a veritable huddle. We wait on the periphery.

Several White House aides try to coax the group out of the Oval. It's early in the day, and B is already hopelessly behind schedule. Steve wants to exit, but I motion him to stay put.

The herd begins to move. I see an opening. "Mr. President!" B turns, eyes dancing. He's having fun. It's a good day: signing legislation, talking sports. It's been a good few months: the budget victory, the Middle East peace accord, the NAFTA victory. He's winning, and he can feel it. And when B is happy, the happiness echoes through the White House like a sweet song.

"Come here, pal." B draws me toward him and drapes an arm around my shoulders. I feel like a favorite pet.

"Mr. President, I want you to meet the man who came up with the idea for today's legislation." I motion Steve forward.

With his left arm still around my shoulders, B extends his right hand to Steve, who takes it as if it were an Olympic trophy.

"Good work," is all B says to Steve, but B's tight grip and his fleeting you-are-the-only-person-in-the-world-who-matters gaze into Steve's eyes light the man up, giving him a glow I hadn't thought possible.

It's over in a flash. B turns away to respond to a staffer who has urgently whispered something into his ear. But Steve doesn't move. The hand that had been in the presidential grip falls slowly to his side. He stares in B's direction. The afterglow remains.

I have heard tales of people who are moved by a profound religious experience, whose lives of torment or boredom are suddenly transformed, who actually *look* different because they have found Truth and Meaning. Steve Wandner—the gangly, diffident career bureaucrat who has traipsed to his office at the Labor Department every workday for twenty years, slowly chipping away at the same large rock, answering to the same career executives, coping with silly demands by low-level political appointees to do this or that, seeing the same problems and making the same suggestions and sensing that nothing will ever really change—has now witnessed the impossible. His idea has become the law of the land. . . .

40

JAMES Q. WILSON

From *Bureaucracy*

*It's been twenty years since the "new" ice skating rink was built in New
York's Central Park. Many skaters have enjoyed it since 1986. In that
time, New York City has experienced much change. New mayors have
come and gone. September 11, 2001, happened: The city mourned and
then slowly recovered. But some things in New York City have remained
the same, even if not exactly. Donald Trump still knows how to get
things done. Back in the mid-1980s, before "The Apprentice," Real estate
developer Trump showed that the efficiency of the private sector could accomplish what no public bureaucracy seemed to be able to do: refurbish the
Central Park skating rink, quickly and inexpensively. Today we'd say that
the city fired itself and "privatized" the project by hiring Trump. Renowned
political scientist James Q. Wilson looks at Trump's success with the skating
rink project, but also explains why he had that success. The public sector
has many limitations on its actions that the private sector does not have to
consider. As privatization becomes increasingly popular on the state and
local and even national level of government, it's important to remember
Wilson's caveats: efficiency is not the only worthy goal and not all publicly
run projects are inefficient.*

ON THE MORNING OF MAY 22, 1986, Donald Trump, the
New York real estate developer, called one of his executives, Anthony
Gliedman, into his office. They discussed the inability of the City of New
York, despite six years of effort and the expenditure of nearly $13 million,
to rebuild the ice-skating rink in Central Park. On May 28 Trump offered
to take over the rink reconstruction, promising to do the job in less than
six months. A week later Mayor Edward Koch accepted the offer and
shortly thereafter the city appropriated $3 million on the understanding
that Trump would have to pay for any cost overruns out of his own
pocket. On October 28, the renovation was complete, over a month
ahead of schedule and about $750,000 under budget. Two weeks later,
skaters were using it.

For many readers it is obvious that private enterprise is more efficient
than are public bureaucracies, and so they would file this story away as
simply another illustration of what everyone already knows. But for other

readers it is not so obvious what this story means; to them, business is greedy and unless watched like a hawk will fob off shoddy or overpriced goods on the American public, as when it sells the government $435 hammers and $3,000 coffee-pots. Trump may have done a good job in this instance, but perhaps there is something about skating rinks or New York City government that gave him a comparative advantage; in any event, no larger lessons should be drawn from it.

Some lessons can be drawn, however, if one looks closely at the incentives and constraints facing Trump and the Department of Parks and Recreation. It becomes apparent that there is not one "bureaucracy problem" but several, and the solution to each in some degree is incompatible with the solution to every other. First there is the problem of accountability—getting agencies to serve agreed-upon goals. Second there is the problem of equity—treating all citizens fairly, which usually means treating them alike on the basis of clear rules known in advance. Third there is the problem of responsiveness—reacting reasonably to the special needs and circumstances of particular people. Fourth there is the problem of efficiency—obtaining the greatest output for a given level of resources. Finally there is the problem of fiscal integrity—assuring that public funds are spent prudently for public purposes. Donald Trump and Mayor Koch were situated differently with respect to most of these matters.

Accountability

The Mayor wanted the old skating rink refurbished, but he also wanted to minimize the cost of the fuel needed to operate the rink (the first effort to rebuild it occurred right after the Arab oil embargo and the attendant increase in energy prices). Trying to achieve both goals led city hall to select a new refrigeration system that as it turned out would not work properly. Trump came on the scene when only one goal dominated: get the rink rebuilt. He felt free to select the most reliable refrigeration system without worrying too much about energy costs.

Equity

The Parks and Recreation Department was required by law to give every contractor an equal chance to do the job. This meant it had to put every part of the job out to bid and to accept the lowest without much regard to the reputation or prior performance of the lowest bidder. Moreover, state law forbade city agencies from hiring a general contractor and letting him select the subcontractors; in fact, the law forbade the city from even discussing the project in advance with a general contractor who might later bid on it—that would have been collusion. Trump, by contrast, was free to locate the rink builder with the best reputation and give him the job.

Fiscal Integrity

To reduce the chance of corruption or sweetheart deals the law required Parks and Recreation to furnish complete, detailed plans to every contractor bidding on the job; any changes after that would require renegotiating the contract. No such law constrained Trump; he was free to give incomplete plans to his chosen contractor, hold him accountable for building a satisfactory rink, but allow him to work out the details as he went along.

Efficiency

When the Parks and Recreation Department spent over six years and $13 million and still could not reopen the rink, there was public criticism but no city official lost money. When Trump accepted a contract to do it, any cost overruns or delays would have come out of his pocket and any savings could have gone into his pocket (in this case, Trump agreed not to take a profit on the job).

Gliedman summarized the differences neatly: "The problem with government is that government can't say, 'yes' . . . there is nobody in government that can do that. There are fifteen or twenty people who have to agree. Government has to be slower. It has to safeguard the process." . . .

The government can't say "yes." In other words, the government is constrained. Where do the constraints come from? From us.

Herbert Kaufman has explained red tape as being of our own making: "Every restraint and requirement originates in somebody's demand for it." Applied to the Central Park skating rink Kaufman's insight reminds us that civil-service reformers demanded that no city official benefit personally from building a project; that contractors demanded that all be given an equal chance to bid on every job; and that fiscal watchdogs demanded that all contract specifications be as detailed as possible. For each demand a procedure was established; viewed from the outside, those procedures are called red tape. To enforce each procedure a manager was appointed; those managers are called bureaucrats. No organized group demanded that all skating rinks be rebuilt as quickly as possible, no procedure existed to enforce that demand, and no manager was appointed to enforce it. The political process can more easily enforce compliance with constraints than the attainment of goals.

When we denounce bureaucracy for being inefficient we are saying something that is half true. Efficiency is a ratio of valued resources used to valued outputs produced. The smaller that ratio the more efficient the production. If the valued output is a rebuilt skating rink, then whatever process uses the fewest dollars or the least time to produce a satisfactory rink is the most efficient process. By this test Trump was more efficient than the Parks and Recreation Department.

But that is too narrow a view of the matter. The economic definition of efficiency (efficiency in the small, so to speak) assumes that there is only one valued output, the new rink. But government has many valued outputs, including a reputation for integrity, the confidence of the people, and the support of important interest groups. When we complain about skating rinks not being built on time we speak as if all we cared about were skating rinks. But when we complain that contracts were awarded without competitive bidding or in a way that allowed bureaucrats to line their pockets we acknowledge that we care about many things besides skating rinks; we care about the contextual goals—the constraints—that we want government to observe. A government that is slow to build rinks but is honest and accountable in its actions and properly responsive to worthy constituencies may be a very efficient government, *if* we measure efficiency in the large by taking into account *all* of the valued outputs.

Calling a government agency efficient when it is slow, cumbersome, and costly may seem perverse. But that is only because we lack any objective way for deciding how much money or time should be devoted to maintaining honest behavior, producing a fair allocation of benefits, and generating popular support as well as to achieving the main goal of the project. If we could measure these things, and if we agreed as to their value, then we would be in a position to judge the true efficiency of a government agency and decide when it is taking too much time or spending too much money achieving all that we expect of it. But we cannot measure these things nor do we agree about their relative importance, and so government always will appear to be inefficient compared to organizations that have fewer goals.

Put simply, the only way to decide whether an agency is truly inefficient is to decide which of the constraints affecting its action ought to be ignored or discounted. In fact that is what most debates about agency behavior are all about. In fighting crime are the police handcuffed? In educating children are teachers tied down by rules? In launching a space shuttle are we too concerned with safety? In building a dam do we worry excessively about endangered species? In running the Postal Service is it important to have many post offices close to where people live? In the case of the skating rink, was the requirement of competitive bidding for each contract on the basis of detailed specifications a reasonable one? Probably not. But if it were abandoned, the gain (the swifter completion of the rink) would have to be balanced against the costs (complaints from contractors who might lose business and the chance of collusion and corruption in some future projects).

Even allowing for all of these constraints, government agencies may still be inefficient. Indeed, given the fact that bureaucrats cannot (for the most part) benefit monetarily from their agencies' achievements, it would be surprising if they were not inefficient. Efficiency, in the large or the small, doesn't pay. . . .

Inefficiency is not the only bureaucratic problem nor is it even the most important. A perfectly efficient agency could be a monstrous one, swiftly denying us our liberties, economically inflicting injustices, and competently expropriating our wealth. People complain about bureaucracy as often because it is unfair or unreasonable as because it is slow or cumbersome.

Arbitrary rule refers to officials acting without legal authority, or with that authority in a way that offends our sense of justice. Justice means, first, that we require the government to treat people equally on the basis of clear rules known in advance: If Becky and Bob both are driving sixty miles per hour in a thirty-mile-per-hour zone and the police give a ticket to Bob, we believe they also should give a ticket to Becky. Second, we believe that justice obliges the government to take into account the special needs and circumstances of individuals: If Becky is speeding because she is on her way to the hospital to give birth to a child and Bob is speeding for the fun of it, we may feel that the police should ticket Bob but not Becky. Justice in the first sense means fairness, in the second it means responsiveness. Obviously, fairness and responsiveness often are in conflict.

The checks and balances of the American constitutional system reflect our desire to reduce the arbitrariness of official rule. That desire is based squarely on the premise that inefficiency is a small price to pay for freedom and responsiveness. Congressional oversight, judicial review, interest-group participation, media investigations, and formalized procedures all are intended to check administrative discretion. It is not hyperbole to say that the constitutional order is animated by the desire to make the government "inefficient."

This creates two great tradeoffs. First, adding constraints reduces the efficiency with which the main goal of an agency can be attained but increases the chances that the agency will act in a nonarbitrary manner. Efficient police departments would seek out criminals without reading them their rights, allowing them to call their attorneys, or releasing them in response to a writ of habeas corpus. An efficient building department would issue construction permits on demand without insisting that the applicant first show that the proposed building meets fire, safety, sanitation, geological, and earthquake standards.

The second great tradeoff is between nonarbitrary governance defined as treating people equally and such governance defined as treating each case on its merits. We want the government to be both fair and responsive, but the more rules we impose to insure fairness (that is, to treat all people alike) the harder we make it for the government to be responsive (that is, to take into account the special needs and circumstances of a particular case).

The way our government manages these tradeoffs reflects both our political culture as well as the rivalries of our governing institutions. Both tend toward the same end: We define claims as rights, impose general rules to insure equal treatment, lament (but do nothing about) the resulting inefficiencies, and respond to revelations about unresponsiveness by adopting new rules intended to guarantee that special circumstances will be handled with special care (rarely bothering to reconcile the rules that require responsiveness with those that require equality). And we do all this out of the best of motives: a desire to be both just and benevolent. Justice inclines us to treat people equally, benevolence to treat them differently; both inclinations are expressed in rules, though in fact only justice can be. It is this futile desire to have a rule for every circumstance that led Herbert Kaufman to explain "how compassion spawns red tape." . . .

In the meantime we live in a country that despite its baffling array of rules and regulations and the insatiable desire of some people to use government to rationalize society still makes it possible to get drinkable water instantly, put through a telephone call in seconds, deliver a letter in a day, and obtain a passport in a week. Our Social Security checks arrive on time. Some state prisons, and most of the federal ones, are reasonably decent and humane institutions. The great majority of Americans, cursing all the while, pay their taxes. One can stand on the deck of an aircraft carrier during night flight operations and watch two thousand nineteen-year-old boys faultlessly operate one of the most complex organizational systems ever created. There are not many places where all this happens. It is astonishing it can be made to happen at all.

PART EIGHT

The Judiciary

41

ALEXANDER HAMILTON

From *The Federalist* 78

The 1787 Federalist Papers have been quoted extensively in earlier sections of this book. The most famous selections belong to James Madison, writing about separation of powers and federalism. The Federalist actually had three authors: Madison, Alexander Hamilton, and John Jay. In No. 78, Hamilton expounded on the judicial branch. He makes a strong case for an independent judiciary, separate from the legislative and executive branches. He discusses the lifetime appointment of federal judges. Hamilton was a strong proponent of the courts' power, and as such, he believed that the Supreme Court should have the right to declare an act of Congress unconstitutional. This enormous power, termed judicial review, is explained and justified here by Hamilton, although it was not explicitly stated in the Constitution. In 1803, Chief Justice John Marshall established the precedent for the Supreme Court's use of judicial review in the landmark Marbury v. Madison *case. The year after Marshall's decision, Alexander Hamilton was killed in a duel with Vice-President Aaron Burr.*

No. 78: Hamilton

WE PROCEED now to an examination of the judiciary department of the proposed government. . . .

Whoever attentively considers the different departments of power must perceive that, in a government in which they are separated from each other, the judiciary, from the nature of its functions, will always be the least dangerous to the political rights of the Constitution; because it will be least in a capacity to annoy or injure them. The executive not only dispenses the honors but holds the sword of the community. The legislature not only commands the purse but prescribes the rules by which the duties and rights of every citizen are to be regulated. The judiciary, on the contrary, has no influence over either the sword or the purse; no direction either of the strength or of the wealth of the society, and can take no active resolution whatever. It may truly be said to have neither FORCE nor WILL but merely judgment; and must ultimately depend upon the aid of the executive arm even for the efficacy of its judgments.

This simple view of the matter suggests several important consequences. It proves incontestably that the judiciary is beyond comparison
the weakest of the three departments of power;* that it can never attack
with success either of the other two; and that all possible care is requisite
to enable it to defend itself against their attacks. It equally proves that
though individual oppression may now and then proceed from the courts
of justice, the general liberty of the people can never be endangered from
that quarter; I mean so long as the judiciary remains truly distinct from
both the legislature and the executive. For I agree that "there is no liberty
if the power of judging be not separated from the legislative and executive
powers." And it proves, in the last place, that as liberty can have nothing
to fear from the judiciary alone, but would have everything to fear from
its union with either of the other departments; that as all the effects of
such a union must ensue from a dependence of the former on the latter,
notwithstanding a nominal and apparent separation; that as, from the
natural feebleness of the judiciary, it is in continual jeopardy of being
overpowered, awed, or influenced by its co-ordinate branches; and that
as nothing can contribute so much to its firmness and independence as
permanency in office, this quality may therefore be justly regarded as an
indispensable ingredient in its constitution, and, in a great measure, as
the citadel of the public justice and the public security.

The complete independence of the courts of justice is peculiarly
essential in a limited Constitution. By a limited Constitution, I understand
one which contains certain specified exceptions to the legislative authority;
such, for instance, as that it shall pass no bills of attainder, no *ex post facto*
laws, and the like. Limitations of this kind can be preserved in practice
no other way than through the medium of courts of justice, whose
duty it must be to declare all acts contrary to the manifest tenor of the
Constitution void. Without this, all the reservations of particular rights
or privileges would amount to nothing.

Some perplexity respecting the rights of the courts to pronounce
legislative acts void, because contrary to the Constitution, has arisen from
an imagination that the doctrine would imply a superiority of the judiciary
to the legislative power. It is urged that the authority which can declare
the acts of another void must necessarily be superior to the one whose
acts may be declared void. As this doctrine is of great importance in all
the American constitutions, a brief discussion of the grounds on which
it rests cannot be unacceptable.

---

*The celebrated Montesquieu, speaking of them, says: "Of the three powers above men-
tioned, the JUDICIARY is next to nothing." — *Spirit of Laws*, Vol. I, page 186.

There is no position which depends on clearer principles than that every act of a delegated authority, contrary to the tenor of the commission under which it is exercised, is void. No legislative act, therefore, contrary to the Constitution, can be valid. To deny this would be to affirm that the deputy is greater than his principal; that the servant is above his master; that the representatives of the people are superior to the people themselves; that men acting by virtue of powers may do not only what their powers do not authorize, but what they forbid.

If it be said that the legislative body are themselves the constitutional judges of their own powers and that the construction they put upon them is conclusive upon the other departments it may be answered that this cannot be the natural presumption where it is not to be collected from any particular provisions in the Constitution. It is not otherwise to be supposed that the Constitution could intend to enable the representatives of the people to substitute their *will* to that of their constituents. It is far more rational to suppose that the courts were designed to be an intermediate body between the people and the legislature in order, among other things, to keep the latter within the limits assigned to their authority. The interpretation of the laws is the proper and peculiar province of the courts. A constitution is, in fact, and must be regarded by the judges as, a fundamental law. It therefore belongs to them to ascertain its meaning as well as the meaning of any particular act proceeding from the legislative body. If there should happen to be an irreconcilable variance between the two, that which has the superior obligation and validity ought, of course, to be preferred; or, in other words, the Constitution ought to be preferred to the statute, the intention of the people to the intention of their agents.

Nor does this conclusion by any means suppose a superiority of the judicial to the legislative power. It only supposes that the power of the people is superior to both, and that where the will of the legislature, declared in its statutes, stands in opposition to that of the people, declared in the Constitution, the judges ought to be governed by the latter rather than the former. They ought to regulate their decisions by the fundamental laws rather than by those which are not fundamental. . . .

If, then, the courts of justice are to be considered as the bulwarks of a limited Constitution against legislative encroachments, this consideration will afford a strong argument for the permanent tenure of judicial offices, since nothing will contribute so much as this to that independent spirit in the judges which must be essential to the faithful performance of so arduous a duty.

This independence of the judges is equally requisite to guard the

Constitution and the rights of individuals from the effects of those ill humors which the arts of designing men, or the influence of particular conjunctures, sometimes disseminate among the people themselves, and which, though they speedily give place to better information, and more deliberate reflection, have a tendency, in the meantime, to occasion dangerous innovations in the government, and serious oppressions of the minor party in the community. Though I trust the friends of the proposed Constitution will never concur with its enemies in questioning that fundamental principle of republican government which admits the right of the people to alter or abolish the established Constitution whenever they find it inconsistent with their happiness; yet it is not to be inferred from this principle that the representatives of the people, whenever a momentary inclination happens to lay hold of a majority of their constituents incompatible with the provisions in the existing Constitution would, on that account, be justifiable in a violation of those provisions; or that the courts would be under a greater obligation to connive at infractions in this shape than when they had proceeded wholly from the cabals of the representative body. Until the people have, by some solemn and authoritative act, annulled or changed the established form, it is binding upon themselves collectively, as well as individually; and no presumption, or even knowledge of their sentiments, can warrant their representatives in a departure from it prior to such an act. But it is easy to see that it would require an uncommon portion of fortitude in the judges to do their duty as faithful guardians of the Constitution, where legislative invasions of it had been instigated by the major voice of the community.

But it is not with a view to infractions of the Constitution only that the independence of the judges may be an essential safeguard against the effects of occasional ill humors in the society. These sometimes extend no farther than to the injury of the private rights of particular classes of citizens, by unjust and partial laws. Here also the firmness of the judicial magistracy is of vast importance in mitigating the severity and confining the operation of such laws. It not only serves to moderate the immediate mischiefs of those which may have been passed but it operates as a check upon the legislative body in passing them; who, perceiving that obstacles to the success of an iniquitous intention are to be expected from the scruples of the courts, are in a manner compelled, by the very motives of the injustice they meditate, to qualify their attempts. This is a circumstance calculated to have more influence upon the character of our governments than but few may be aware of. The benefits of the integrity and moderation of the judiciary have already been felt in more States than one; and though they may have displeased those whose sinister expectations they may have disappointed, they must have commanded the esteem and applause of all the virtuous and disinterested. Considerate men of every description ought to prize whatever will tend to beget or fortify that temper in the courts; as no man can be sure that he may not be tomorrow the victim of a spirit of injustice, by which he may be a gainer today. And every man must now feel that the inevitable tendency of such a spirit is to sap the foundations of public and private confidence and to introduce in its stead universal distrust and distress. . . .   *Publius*

42

EUGENE ROSTOW

The Democratic Character of Judicial Review

Written nearly half a century ago, this classic article by legal scholar Eugene Rostow remains the most important analysis written on the theory behind the Supreme Court's power. Judicial review, the ability of the Court to declare an act of Congress or the executive or a state law unconstitutional, may seem on the surface to be "antidemocratic." A handful of lifetime appointees determine the meaning of the Constitution and whether a law passed by Congress and signed by the president is valid. In precise terms and using complex reasoning, Rostow defends the Supreme Court's use of judicial review as being the essence of the American democratic system. In his words, "The political proposition underlying the survival of the power is that there are some phases of American life which should be beyond the reach of any majority, save by constitutional amendment." Rostow's argument is based on what is meant by a democracy. To add a bit to Rostow's explanation, the United States is a "polity" in which the majority rules with protections guaranteed for individuals and minorities. The judiciary ensures that the minority is protected from "tyranny of the majority." Notice the title of this book of readings.

THE IDEA that judicial review is undemocratic is not an academic issue of political philosophy. Like most abstractions, it has far-reaching practical consequences. I suspect that for some judges it is the mainspring of decision, inducing them in many cases to uphold legislative and executive action which would otherwise have been condemned. Particularly in the multiple opinions of recent years, the Supreme Court's self-searching often boils down to a debate within the bosoms of the Justices over the appropriateness of judicial review itself.

The attack on judicial review as undemocratic rests on the premise that the Constitution should be allowed to grow without a judicial check. The proponents of this view would have the Constitution mean what the President, the Congress, and the state legislatures say it means. . . .

It is a grave oversimplification to contend that no society can be democratic unless its legislature has sovereign powers. The social quality of democracy cannot be defined by so rigid a formula. Government and politics are after all the arms, not the end, of social life. The purpose of the Constitution is to assure the people a free and democratic society. The final aim of that society is as much freedom as possible for the individual human being. The Constitution provides society with a mechanism of government fully competent to its task, but by no means universal in its powers. The power to govern is parcelled out between the states and the nation and is further divided among the three main branches of all governmental units. By custom as well as constitutional practice, many vital aspects of community life are beyond the direct reach of government—for example, religion, the press, and, until recently at any rate, many phases of educational and cultural activity. The separation of powers under the Constitution serves the end of democracy in society by limiting the roles of the several branches of government and protecting the citizen, and the various parts of the state itself, against encroachments from any source. The root idea of the Constitution is that man can be free because the state is not.

The power of constitutional review, to be exercised by some part of the government, is implicit in the conception of a written constitution delegating limited powers. A written constitution would promote discord rather than order in society if there were no accepted authority to construe it, at the least in cases of conflicting action by different branches of government or of constitutionally unauthorized governmental action against individuals. The limitation and separation of powers, if they are to survive, require a procedure for independent mediation and construction to reconcile the inevitable disputes over the boundaries of constitutional power which arise in the process of government. . . .

So far as the American Constitution is concerned, there can be little real doubt that the courts were intended from the beginning to have the power they have exercised. The Federalist Papers are unequivocal; the Debates as clear as debates normally are. The power of judicial review was commonly exercised by the courts of the states, and the people were accustomed to judicial construction of the authority derived from colonial charters. Constitutional interpretation by the courts, Hamilton said, does not

by any means suppose a superiority of the judicial to the legislative power. It only supposes that the power of the people is superior to both; and that where the will of the legislature, declared in its statutes, stands in opposition to that of the people, declared in the Constitution, the judges ought to be governed by the latter rather than the former. They ought to regulate their decisions by the fundamental laws, rather than by those which are not fundamental.

Hamilton's statement is sometimes criticized as a verbal legalism. But it has an advantage too. For much of the discussion has complicated the problem without clarifying it. Both judges and their critics have wrapped themselves so successfully in the difficulties of particular cases that they have been able to evade the ultimate issue posed in the Federalist Papers.

Whether another method of enforcing the Constitution could have been devised, the short answer is that no such method has developed. The argument over the constitutionality of judicial review has long since been settled by history. The power and duty of the Supreme Court to declare statutes or executive action unconstitutional in appropriate cases is part of the living Constitution. "The course of constitutional history," Mr. Justice Frankfurter recently remarked, has cast responsibilities upon the Supreme Court which it would be "stultification" for it to evade. The Court's power has been exercised differently at different times: sometimes with reckless and doctrinaire enthusiasm; sometimes with great deference to the status and responsibilities of other branches of the government; sometimes with a degree of weakness and timidity that comes close to the betrayal of trust. But the power exists, as an integral part of the process of American government. The Court has the duty of interpreting the Constitution in many of its most important aspects, and especially in those which concern the relations of the individual and the state. The political proposition underlying the survival of the power is that there are some phases of American life which should be beyond the reach of any majority, save by constitutional amendment. In Mr. Justice Jackson's phrase, "One's right to life, liberty, and property, to free speech, a free press, freedom of worship and assembly, and other fundamental rights may not be submitted to vote; they depend on the outcome of no elections." Whether or not this was the intention of the Founding Fathers, the unwritten Constitution is unmistakable.

If one may use a personal definition of the crucial word, this way of policing the Constitution is not undemocratic. True, it employs appointed officials, to whom large powers are irrevocably delegated. But democracies need not elect all the officers who exercise crucial authority in the name of the voters. Admirals and generals can win or lose wars in the exercise of their discretion. The independence of judges in the administration of justice has been the pride of communities which aspire to be free. Members of the Federal Reserve Board have the lawful power to plunge the country into depression or inflation. The list could readily be extended. Government by referendum or town meeting is not the only possible form of democracy. The task of democracy is not to have the people vote directly on every issue, but to assure their ultimate responsibility for the acts of their representatives, elected or appointed. For judges deciding ordinary litigation, the ultimate responsibility of the electorate has a special meaning. It is a responsibility for the quality of the judges and for the substance of their instructions, never a responsibility for their decisions in particular cases. It is hardly characteristic of law in democratic society to encourage bills of attainder, or to allow appeals from the courts in particular cases to legislatures or to mobs. Where the judges are carrying out the function of constitutional review, the final responsibility of the people is appropriately guaranteed by the provisions for amending the Constitution itself, and by the benign influence of time, which changes the personnel of courts. Given the possibility of constitutional amendment, there is nothing undemocratic in having responsible and independent judges act as important constitutional mediators. Within the narrow limits of their capacity to act, their great task is to help maintain a pluralist equilibrium in society. They can do much to keep it from being dominated by the states or the Federal Government, by Congress or the President, by the purse or the sword.

In the execution of this crucial but delicate function, constitutional review by the judiciary has an advantage thoroughly recognized in both theory and practice. The power of the courts, however final, can only be asserted in the course of litigation. Advisory opinions are forbidden, and reefs of self-limitation have grown up around the doctrine that the courts will determine constitutional questions only in cases of actual controversy, when no lesser ground of decision is available, and when the complaining party would be directly and personally injured by the assertion of the power deemed unconstitutional. Thus the check of judicial review upon the elected branches of government must be a mild one, limited not only by the detachment, integrity, and good sense of the Justices, but by the structural boundaries implicit in the fact that the power is entrusted to the courts. Judicial review is inherently adapted to preserving broad and flexible lines of constitutional growth, not to operating as a continuously active factor in legislative or executive decisions. . . .

Democracy is a slippery term. I shall make no effort at a formal definition here. . . . But it would be scholastic pedantry to define democracy in such a way as to deny the title of "democrat" to Jefferson, Madison, Lincoln, Brandeis, and others who have found the American constitutional system, including its tradition of judicial review, well adapted to the needs of a free society. As Mr. Justice Brandeis said,

the doctrine of the separation of powers was adopted by the Convention of 1787, not to promote efficiency but to preclude the exercise of arbitrary power. The purpose was, not to avoid friction, but, by means of the inevitable friction incident to the distribution of governmental powers among three departments, to save the people from autocracy.

It is error to insist that no society is democratic unless it has a government of unlimited powers, and that no government is democratic unless its legislature had unlimited powers. Constitutional review by an independent judiciary is a tool of proven use in the American quest for an open society of widely dispersed powers. In a vast country, of mixed population, with widely different regional problems, such an organization of society is the surest base for the hopes of democracy.

43

DAVID O'BRIEN

From *Storm Center*

Professor David O'Brien's fine book on the Supreme Court touches on many landmark cases in constitutional law. Few are more important than Brown v. Board of Education of Topeka, Kansas. Today's students of American government often take Brown for granted, since they've lived with the Court's ruling their whole lives; thus they may forget the dramatic events surrounding the 1954 decision. In this excerpt O'Brien revisits the first Brown case, as well as Brown II, exploring the delicate relationship between the Court and public opinion. He then goes back to President Franklin Roosevelt's infamous 1937 "court-packing" scheme to illustrate another aspect of the impact of public opinion on the judiciary. Unlike the citizenry's direct and immediate reaction to Congress and the president, the communication of views between the public and the judiciary is less easy to measure, O'Brien acknowledges. Yet the Supreme Court lies, as it should, at the heart of the process that resolves the nation's monumental political issues.

———

"WHY DOES the Supreme Court pass the school desegregation case?" asked one of Chief Justice Vinson's law clerks in 1952. *Brown v. Board of Education of Topeka, Kansas* had arrived on the Court's docket in 1951, but it was carried over for oral argument the next term and then consolidated with four other cases and reargued in December 1953. The landmark ruling did not come down until May 17, 1954. "Well," Justice Frankfurter explained, "we're holding it for the election"—1952 was a presidential election year. "You're holding it for the election?" The clerk persisted in disbelief. "I thought the Supreme Court was supposed to decide cases without regard to elections." "When you have a major social political issue of this magnitude," timing and public reactions are important considerations, and, Frankfurter continued, "we do not think this is the time to decide it." Similarly, Tom Clark has recalled that the Court awaited, over Douglas's dissent, additional cases from the District of Columbia and other regions, so as "to get a national coverage, rather than a sectional one." Such political considerations are by no means unique. "We often delay adjudication. It's not a question of evading at all," Clark concluded. "It's just the practicalities of life—common sense."

Denied the power of the sword or the purse, the Court must cultivate its institutional prestige. The power of the Court lies in the pervasiveness of its rulings and ultimately rests with other political institutions and public opinion. As an independent force, the Court has no chance to resolve great issues of public policy. *Dred Scott v. Sandford* (1857) and *Brown v. Board of Education* (1954) illustrate the limitations of Supreme Court policy-making. The "great folly," as Senator Henry Cabot Lodge characterized *Dred Scott*, was not the Court's interpretation of the Constitution or the unpersuasive moral position that blacks were not persons under the Constitution. Rather, "the attempt of the Court to settle the slavery question by judicial decision was simple madness." . . . A hundred years later, political struggles within the country and, notably, presidential and congressional leadership in enforcing the Court's school desegregation ruling saved the moral appeal of *Brown* from becoming another "great folly."

Because the Court's decisions are not self-executing, public reactions inevitably weigh on the minds of the justices. . . .

. . . Opposition to the school desegregation ruling in *Brown* led to bitter, sometimes violent confrontations. In Little Rock, Arkansas, Governor Orval Faubus encouraged disobedience by southern segregationists. The federal National Guard had to be called out to maintain order. The school board in Little Rock unsuccessfully pleaded, in *Cooper v. Aaron* (1958), for the Court's postponement of the implementation of *Brown's* mandate. In the midst of the controversy, Frankfurter worried that Chief Justice Warren's attitude had become "more like that of a fighting politician than that of a judicial statesman." In such confrontations between the Court and the country, "the transcending issue," Frankfurter reminded the brethren, remains that of preserving "the Supreme Court as the authoritative organ of what the Constitution requires." When the justices move too far or too fast in their interpretation of the Constitution, they threaten public acceptance of the Court's legitimacy.

The political struggles of the Court (and among the justices) continue after the writing of opinions and final votes. Announcements of decisions trigger diverse reactions from the media, interest groups, lower courts, Congress, the President, and the general public. Their reactions may enhance or thwart compliance and reinforce or undermine the Court's prestige. Opinion days thus may reveal something of the political struggles that might otherwise remain hidden within the marble temple. They may also mark the beginning of larger political struggles for influence in the country. . . .

When deciding major issues of public law and policy, justices must consider strategies for getting public acceptance of their rulings. When striking down the doctrine of "separate but equal" facilities in 1954 in *Brown v. Board of Education (Brown I)*, for instance, the Warren Court waited a year before issuing, in *Brown II*, its mandate for "all deliberate speed" in ending racial segregation in public education.

Resistance to the social policy announced in *Brown I* was expected. A rigid timetable for desegregation would only intensify opposition. During oral arguments on *Brown II*, devoted to the question of what kind of decree the Court should issue to enforce *Brown*, Warren confronted the hard fact of southern resistance. The attorney for South Carolina, S. Emory Rogers, pressed for an open-ended decree—one that would not specify when and how desegregation should take place. He boldly proclaimed

Mr. Chief Justice, to say we will conform depends on the decree handed down. I am frank to tell you, right now [in] our district I do not think that we will send—[that] the white people of the district will send their children to the Negro schools. It would be unfair to tell the Court that we are going to do that. I do not think it is. But I do think that something can be worked out. We hope so.

"It is not a question of attitude," Warren shot back, "it is a question of conforming to the decree." Their heated exchange continued as follows:

CHIEF JUSTICE WARREN: But you are not willing to say here that there
  would be an honest attempt to conform to this decree, if we did leave
  it to the district court [to implement]?
MR. ROGERS: No, I am not. Let us get the word "honest" out of there.
CHIEF JUSTICE WARREN: No, leave it in.
MR. ROGERS: No, because I would have to tell you that right now we
  would not conform—we would not send our white children to the
  negro schools. . . .

Agreement emerged that the Court should issue a short opinion-
decree. In a memorandum, Warren summarized the main points of
agreement. The opinion should simply state that *Brown I* held radically
segregated public schools to be unconstitutional. *Brown II* should acknowledge that the ruling creates various administrative problems, but emphasize
that "local school authorities have the primary responsibility for assessing
and solving these problems; [and] the courts will have to consider these
problems in determining whether the efforts of local school authorities"
are in good-faith compliance. . . .

Enforcement and implementation required the cooperation and coordination of all three branches. Little progress could be made, as Assistant
Attorney General Pollack has explained, "where historically there had
been slavery and a long tradition of discrimination [until] all three branches
of the federal government [could] be lined up in support of a movement
forward or a requirement for change." The election of Nixon in 1968
then brought changes both in the policies of the executive branch and
in the composition of the Court. The simplicity and flexibility of *Brown*,
moreover, invited evasion. It produced a continuing struggle over measures, such as gerrymandering school district lines and busing in the 1970s
and 1980s, because the mandate itself had evolved from one of ending
segregation to one of securing integration in public schools. . . .

"By itself," the political scientist Robert Dahl observed, "the Court is
almost powerless to affect the course of national policy." *Brown* dramatically
altered the course of American life, but it also reflected the justices'
awareness that their decisions are not self-executing. The rulings [in] *Brown*
. . . were unanimous but ambiguous. The ambiguity in the desegregation
rulings . . . was the price of achieving unanimity. Unanimity appeared
necessary if the Court was to preserve its institutional prestige while
pursuing revolutionary change in social policy. Justices sacrificed their
own policy preferences for more precise guidelines, while the Court
tolerated lengthy delays in recognition of the costs of open defiance and
the pressures of public opinion. . . .

Public opinion serves to curb the Court when it threatens to go too far or too fast in its rulings. The Court has usually been in step with major political movements, except during transitional periods or critical elections. It would nevertheless be wrong to conclude, along with Peter Finley Dunne's fictional Mr. Dooley, that "th' supreme court follows th' iliction returns." To be sure, the battle over FDR's "Court-packing" plan and the Court's "switch-in-time-that-saved-nine" in 1937 gives that impression. Public opinion supported the New Deal, but turned against FDR after his landslide reelection in 1936 when he proposed to "pack the Court" by increasing its size from nine to fifteen. In a series of five-to-four and six-to-three decisions in 1935–1936, the Court had struck down virtually every important measure of FDR's New Deal program. But in the spring of 1937, while the Senate Judiciary Committee considered FDR's proposal, the Court abruptly handed down three five-to-four rulings upholding major pieces of New Deal legislation. Shortly afterward, FDR's close personal friend and soon-to-be nominee for the Court, Felix Frankfurter, wrote Justice Stone confessing that he was "not wholly happy in thinking that Mr. Dooley should, in the course of history turn out to have been one of the most distinguished legal philosophers." Frankfurter, of course, knew that justices do not simply follow the election returns. The influence of public opinion is more subtle and complex.

Life in the marble temple is not immune from shifts in public opinion. . . . The justices, however, deny being directly influenced by public opinion. The Court's prestige rests on preserving the public's view that justices base their decisions on interpretations of the law, rather than on their personal policy preferences. Yet, complete indifference to public opinion would be the height of judicial arrogance. . . .

"The powers exercised by this Court are inherently oligarchic," Frankfurter once observed when pointing out that "[t]he Court is not saved from being oligarchic because it professes to act in the service of humane ends." Judicial review is antidemocratic. But the Court's power stems from its duty to give authoritative meaning to the Constitution, and rests with the persuasive forces of reason, institutional prestige, the cooperation of other political institutions, and, ultimately, public opinion. The country, in a sense, saves the justices from being an oligarchy by curbing the Court when it goes too far or too fast with its policy-making. Violent opposition and resistance, however, threaten not merely the Court's prestige but the very idea of a government under law.

Some Court watchers, and occasionally even the justices, warn of "an imperial judiciary" and a "government by the judiciary." For much of the Court's history, though, the work of the justices has not involved

major issues of public policy. In most areas of public law and policy, the
fact that the Court decides an issue is more important than what it decides.
Relatively few of the many issues of domestic and foreign policy that
arise in government reach the Court. When the Court does decide major
questions of public policy, it does so by bringing political controversies
within the language, structure, and spirit of the Constitution. By deciding
only immediate cases, the Court infuses constitutional meaning into the
resolution of the larger surrounding political controversies. But by itself
the Court cannot lay those controversies to rest.

The Court can profoundly influence American life. As a guardian of
the Constitution, the Court sometimes invites controversy by challenging
majoritarian sentiments to respect the rights of minorities and the principles of a representative democracy. The Court's influence is usually more
subtle and indirect, varying over time and from one policy issue to another.
In the end, the Court's influence on American life cannot be measured
precisely, because its policy-making is inextricably bound up with that of
other political institutions. Major confrontations in constitutional politics,
like those over school desegregation, school prayer, and abortion, are
determined as much by what is possible in a system of free government
and in a pluralistic society as by what the Court says about the meaning
of the Constitution. At its best, the Court appeals to the country to
respect the substantive value choices of human dignity and self-governance
embedded in our written Constitution.

44

PETER IRONS

From *Brennan vs. Rehnquist*

*The U.S. Supreme Court today is different than it was when President
Franklin Roosevelt called the justices "Nine Old Men." The Court's
membership now includes justices who are black, female, and young, and
they come from different regions, religions, and socioeconomic backgrounds.
Yet the fundamental issues faced by the Court have not changed. Legal
scholar Peter Irons examines a primary philosophical battle on the Supreme
Court: individual and minority rights protected by an active judicial branch
versus majority power, expressed by strong legislative and executive branches,
with the Court exercising judicial restraint. The battle was never better
illustrated than in the contrast between Justice William J. Brennan (d.
1990) and Chief Justice William H. Rehnquist (d. 2005).*

WILLIAM J. BRENNAN, JR., and William H. Rehnquist served together on the United States Supreme Court between 1972 and 1990. During these eighteen years, they headed the Court's liberal and conservative wings, and lobbied for the votes of moderate justices. They provided intellectual and political leadership to contending sides in a battle over the Constitution that affected the lives of every American. The two justices brought divergent judicial philosophies to the Court, rooted in different values and views about the relations of individuals and the state. Each won major victories, but neither won a final triumph. . . . Setting aside unanimous decisions, Brennan and Rehnquist agreed in only 273 of 1,815 case in which one or more justices dissented, just 15 percent of the Court's divided decisions over a span of almost two decades. This was the lowest rate of agreement of any pair of justices over those years. And they disagreed in virtually every case that raised important constitutional issues.

Brennan and Rehnquist are almost totally opposite in background, philosophy, and judicial voting. During their years together, they battled over the Constitution, each trying to rally the Court's moderates to his side. The stakes were high—questions of abortion, affirmative action, capital punishment, and other controversial issues hung in the balance. . . .

This book perceives the Supreme Court as a political institution, and constitutional litigation as a form of politics. These are hardly radical—or recent—notions. "Scarcely any political question arises in the United States," Alexis de Tocqueville observed in 1835, "that is not resolved, sooner or later, into a judicial question." The Court's first major decision, *Marbury v. Madison* in 1803, drew the justices into an intensely political conflict among all three branches of the federal government. Chief Justice John Marshall did not shrink from this dispute. "It is emphatically the province and duty of the judicial department," he wrote, "to say what the law is." His opinion established the Court as the ultimate arbiter of political disputes the other branches could not resolve.

The Supreme Court remains embroiled in political disputes. . . .

There is little question that William Brennan brought with him to the Supreme Court bench a well-formed constitutional philosophy. Shaped in childhood and sharpened by law practice and judicial experience, it can be capsulized in one word: dignity. . . .

The Due Process clauses of the Constitution, added by the Fifth and Fourteenth amendments, were designed to limit governmental authority by protecting the "life, liberty, or property" of Americans from arbitrary official action. As Brennan put it, "Due process required fidelity to a more basic and more subtle principle: the essential dignity and worth of each individual." The Constitution required officials "to treat citizens not as subjects but as fellow human beings." Brennan added that "due process asks whether government has treated someone fairly, whether individual dignity has been honored, whether the worth of an individual has been acknowledged." Officials cannot answer these questions "solely by pointing to rational action taken according to standard rules. They must plumb their conduct more deeply, seeking answers in the more complex equations of human nature and experience." . . .

Another central theme of Brennan's judicial philosophy is that "due process" is a concept whose meaning is not static, frozen by the Framers in 1787, but one that changes over time, as society changes. The Framers did not intend, he argued, to impose on judges an inflexible definition of "a clause that reflects a principle as elusive as human dignity." . . .

The notion that the meaning of "due process" shifts over time imposes a burden on judges who share this approach to the Constitution. Placed by history within a "given age," Brennan said, judges "must draw on our own experience as inhabitants of that age, and our own sense of the uneven fabric of social life. We cannot delude ourselves that the Constitution takes the form of a theorem whose axioms need mere logical deduction." . . .

. . . [There is] another important theme of Brennan's jurisprudence. "The view that all matters of substantive policy should be resolved through the majoritarian process," he says, "has appeal under some circumstances, but I think ultimately it will not do." What the principle of majority rule cannot do, Brennan argues, is "to rectify claims of minority right that arise as a response to the outcomes of that very majoritarian process." When those outcomes—in voting booths and legislative chambers—display prejudice against the "outsiders" in American society, the Constitution requires judicial intervention. In Brennan's view, judges have the power and, in appropriate cases, the duty to displace majority rule when it violates the rights of minorities. "Faith in democracy is one thing," he says, "blind faith quite another." The Constitution was designed to place fundamental rights "beyond the reach of temporary political majorities."

This defense of minority rights does not lead Justice Brennan to advocate replacing what he calls legislative "imperialism" with an equivalent judicial imperialism. The Constitution does not empower judges to impose their own personal values on its provisions. But it does require them to speak, individually and collectively, for American society as a whole. "When Justices interpret the Constitution," Brennan says, "they speak for their community, not for themselves alone." This statement, of course, begs the question of how any justice can determine which "community" is relevant to the decision of a case. Some communities are delimited by geography as local, state, or national; others are defined as ethnic, religious, or racial. And the nation can be considered a "community" as a whole. Beyond these questions are those of public opinion and personal sentiment. No justice has ever proposed that the Court rely on public opinion polls in deciding controversial cases. And no justice has suggested that personal views are superior to the Constitution's demand for impersonal judging.

Justice Brennan does not evade these hard questions. He acknowledges that judges must make "substantive value choices" when they interpret constitutional provisions and that they "must accept the ambiguity inherent in the effort to apply them to modern circumstances." Justices, he says, "read the Constitution in the only way that we can: as twentieth-century Americans." He adds these words: "We look to the history of the time of framing and to the intervening history of interpretation. But the ultimate question must be: What do the words of the text mean in our time? For the genius of the Constitution rests not in any static meaning it might have had in a world that is dead and gone, but in the adaptability of its great principles to cope with current problems and current needs."

Brennan agrees that allowing unelected judges to reverse the decisions of elected lawmakers goes against the grain of democratic government. "These are important, recurrent worries," he admits. But he does not shrink from advocating "an active judiciary" as a counterweight to "legislative irresponsibility." He cites as examples of "panic" by majorities the prosecution of those who criticized American involvement in both world wars. Judges failed in each case to protect the victims of wartime hysteria, and the results "are among the least proud moments in the Court's history."

In summary, Justice Brennan's judicial philosophy begins with his deep religious faith in the "dignity" of every person, moves to the principle that government exists to serve the needs of individuals and to protect their dignity, and ends with the notion that the meaning of the Constitution must change as society changes. Judges speak for a community that is diverse and disputatious, and they must step in to prevent majorities, permanent or temporary, from trampling on the rights of minorities. The foundation of Brennan's jurisprudence is his view of the Constitution as "a living, evolving document that must be read anew" by each generation. . . .

William Rehnquist came to the bench with a clear, consistent political and legal philosophy, but without a judicial record that would show his philosophy in action. It took only a few years of votes and opinions to provide evidence that his judicial philosophy followed the path of his earlier positions. Speaking at the University of Texas Law School in 1976, he outlined his views in a speech entitled "The Notion of a Living Constitution." Of all his speeches, articles, and opinions, this address presents Rehnquist's jurisprudence in its most developed form.

In many ways, his Texas speech was simply an expanded version of the views expressed in Rehnquist's 1948 letter to the *Stanford Daily*, in which he argued that "one personal conviction is no better than another" and rejected "the implication that humanitarianism is desirable" as a moral value. His speech explicitly adopted the position of legal positivism, the notion that the legislative will is supreme and that the content of laws is not a proper concern of judges. If legislators follow the rules, they are constrained only by the explicit commands of the Constitution. The most extreme form of legal positivism—approached in the civil law system of continental Europe—does not allow for judicial review of legislation. The American form of positivism—articulated most forcefully by Robert Bork—gives judges an independent but limited role in reviewing laws, constrained by precedent and the constitutional text. In both systems, judges are expected to show deference to the legislative will. . . .

Rehnquist admitted that "in exercising the very delicate responsibility of judicial review," judges had authority to strike down laws they "find to violate some provision of the Constitution." But he took a narrow view of this authority. The concept of judicial review, he said, "has basically antidemocratic and antimajoritarian facets that require some justification" in a system based on majority rule. The idea of a "living Constitution" struck Rehnquist as a negation of "the nature of political value judgments in a democratic society." He agreed that constitutional safeguards for individual liberty "take on a generalized moral rightness or goodness." But this goodness has no source outside the premise of majority rule, no basis in any "morality" that relies on personal conscience. Constitutional protections "assume a general social acceptance," Rehnquist asserted, "neither because of any intrinsic worth nor because of any unique origins in someone's idea of natural justice but instead simply because they have been incorporated in a constitution by the people."

The major theme of Rehnquist's speech was that political majorities are entitled to enact "positive law" and to impose their moral views on minorities. Laws "take on a form of moral goodness because they have been enacted into positive law," he argued. One complement of legal positivism is moral relativism, the notion that no moral value is inherently superior to another. Rehnquist took this position as a college student and stuck by it as a justice. "There is no conceivable way," he told his Texas audience, "in which I can logically demonstrate to you that the judgments of my conscience are superior to the judgments of your conscience, and vice versa." The "goodness" of any value is decided in the voting booth. . . .

This record shows that Rehnquist is a principled political conservative. But is he also, as he describes himself, a judicial conservative? His philosophy of deference to legislative acts is not, by itself, either liberal or conservative. Laws can be "liberal" by granting rights to minorities, or "conservative" by placing burdens on them. For example, a legislature can pass laws that protect homosexuals from discrimination, or laws that make homosexual behavior a crime. However, in consistently voting to uphold criminal convictions, to deny First Amendment claims, and to reject the claims of racial minorities and women, Rehnquist has taken a "conservative" position on the political issues raised in these cases. He is equally *not* a conservative in the sense of displaying the respect for precedent shown by those who profess "judicial restraint" as a principle. . . .

The jurisprudence of Justice Rehnquist does, in fact, distinguish him from *all* of his colleagues since he joined the Court. None has voted more consistently to uphold governmental actions, legislative and executive. And none has voted more consistently against the claims of dissenters and minorities. His "deference" principle stands in stark contrast to the "dignity" value of Justice Brennan. Their competing visions of the Constitution are rooted in historic struggles over American law and politics. . . .

Supreme Court justices are placed on the bench by elected officials who owe their positions to the electorate. How we vote in elections for senators and presidents will affect the outcome of the Court's decisions in years and decades to come. This is an awesome power, one that every American should ponder before entering the voting booth. Justices Brennan and Rehnquist have offered persuasive arguments on either side of a continuing constitutional debate. But in the end, the decision is ours.

45

DAVID YALOF

From *Pursuit of Justices*

In selecting nominees to the Supreme Court, the president faces a daunting task. Legal scholar David Yalof takes readers inside the process, pointing out the many factions in the nation, in the branches of government, and even within the president's own circle that must be considered when making a nomination. The president today has access to large amounts of information about a potential justice, but so does everyone else in the political process. After all, remember that a Supreme Court justice is often the most significant and long lasting legacy that a president leaves behind.

———

ON JUNE 27, 1992, the Supreme Court inserted itself once again into the national debate over abortion with its surprising decision in *Planned Parenthood v. Casey*. Specifically, five of the nine justices refused to cast aside *Roe v. Wade*, the Court's controversial 1973 opinion establishing a constitutional right to abortion. Included among *Roe*'s saviors that day were Sandra Day O'Connor and Anthony Kennedy, both appointees of former President Ronald Reagan. As a candidate for the presidency in 1980 and 1984, Reagan had supported a constitutional amendment to overturn *Roe*, a ruling considered to be among the most vilified of public targets for social conservatives in his party. As president, Reagan had publicly promised to appoint justices to the Supreme Court willing to reverse *Roe v. Wade*. Yet just the opposite occurred in *Casey*: a majority of the Court reaffirmed the core right to privacy first discovered in *Roe*. And in a touch of irony, two of President Reagan's own nominees had played significant roles in safeguarding the decision from the Court's conservatives.

Obviously the selection of Supreme Court nominees is among the president's most significant duties. Yet as the outcome in *Casey* demonstrates, it is a task beset with difficulties and potential frustrations. On one hand, a president ordinarily tries to choose a nominee whose influence will reach beyond the current political environment. As a beneficiary of life tenure, a justice may well extend that president's legacy on judicial matters long into the future. Yet in selecting a nominee the president must also successfully maneuver through that immediate environment, lest he suffer politically or (as in some cases) see his nominee rejected by the Senate outright. In recent years internal strife and factionalism within the executive branch have only further complicated what was already a delicate undertaking. . . .

A central question remains: why were these particular candidates chosen over others possessing similar—and in some cases superior—qualifications? The classic "textbook" portrayal of the Supreme Court nomination process depicts presidents as choosing Supreme Court justices more for their judicial politics than for their judicial talents. By this version of events, presidents, by nominating justices whose political views appear compatible with their own, try to gain increased influence over the Supreme Court. Once on the Court, a justice may then satisfy or disappoint the appointing president by his decisions. Such an oversimplified view of nomination politics usually ignores the more complex political environment in which modern presidents must act, including the various intricacies and nuances of executive branch politics.

. . . I contend that modern presidents are often forced to arbitrate among factions within their own administrations, each pursuing its own interests and agendas in the selection process. At first glance, presidential reliance on numerous high-level officials equipped with a variety of perspectives might seem a logical response to the often hostile and unpredictable political environment that surrounds modern appointments to the Court. Yet conflicts within the administration itself may have a debilitating effect on that president's overall interests. High-level advisors may be sincerely pursuing their own conceptions of what makes up the administration's best interests; but to achieve their own maximum preferred outcomes, they may feel compelled to skew the presentation of critical information, if not leave it out altogether. In recent administrations the final choice of a nominee has usually reflected one advisor's hard-won victory over his rivals, without necessarily accounting for the president's other political interests. . . .

The New Deal marked the beginning of a fundamental transformation in American politics. A national economic crisis demanded national solutions, and the government in Washington grew exponentially to meet these new demands. Beginning in the 1930s, the federal government entered one policy area after another that had previously been the exclusive province of state governments. Emergency conditions required quick institutional responses, and the executive branch in particular was drawn into critical aspects of national policymaking. Just as the character of national politics changed dramatically, the Supreme Court was undergoing a transformation of its own. Fundamental changes in the political landscape affecting Supreme Court appointments were a by-product of these changes. At least ten critical developments in American politics substantially altered the character of the modern selection process for justices:

1. The *growth and bureaucratization of the Justice Department* facilitated the investment of considerable manpower and other resources towards the consideration of prospective Supreme Court candidates. As the size of the national government grew dramatically during the early twentieth century, the government's overall legal responsibilities quickly expanded. Congress reacted by increasing the size of the Justice Department and transferring to it most litigating functions from other federal agencies. Armed with a full staff of attorneys and more extensive bureaucratic support, attorneys general in modern times have enjoyed more regular input into the selection of Supreme Court nominees, often consulting with the president well before a vacancy on the Court even arises. . . .

2. The *growth and bureaucratization of the White House* has also had an impact on the nomination process. The White House staff, once limited to a handful of personal assistants, was barely a factor in political decision-making for most of the nineteenth and early twentieth centuries. Starting with Franklin Roosevelt's administration, however, the White House staff experienced prodigious growth, expanding from just thirty-seven employees in the early 1930s to more than nine hundred by the late 1980s. As the modern presidency has brought more policymaking activities within the White House, the White House staff has increasingly figured in matters of high presidential priority.

Modern presidents often rely on the White House Counsel's Office to assist them in screening and selecting prospective Supreme Court nominees. Thus, increasingly, the attorney general's most constant and genuine competitor for influence has been the White House Counsel. Theodore Sorenson, John Kennedy's special counsel, asserted that his duties did not overlap with the attorney general's; rather he was involved "as a policy advisor to the president with respect to legislation, with respect to his programs and messages, with respect to executive orders, and with respect to those few formally legal problems, which come to the White House." But those supposed lines of demarcation have blurred considerably during the past thirty years. Today, a president has at his disposal two distinct organizations, each with its own bureaucratic resources; the president may rely on either or both offices for counsel concerning the selection of Supreme Court nominees.

3. Paralleling the increased role for national political institutions in American life has been the *growth in size and influence of federal courts.* Congress's willingness in the past to meet increased caseloads with new

judgeships has steadily multiplied the president's opportunities to place his imprint on lower court policymaking. The total number of district and circuit judgeships rose from under two hundred in 1930 to well over seven hundred by the late 1980s. Thus between thirty and forty vacancies may occur annually on the federal bench. These federal judges must be counted on to interpret, enforce, and in some cases limit the expansion of federal governmental authority. At times federal courts have even fashioned national law and policy, serving as key facilitators of social, economic, and political growth.

Senatorial courtesy, to be sure, remains the dominant factor in lower court selections, but the steady increase in the number of judgeships has provided presidents with more than an occasional opportunity to nominate candidates of their own choosing after the preferences of individual senators have been satisfied. The growing size and prestige of the D.C. Circuit have given presidents additional opportunities to hand out plum assignments: because senatorial courtesy does not apply to those seats, presidents may freely nominate ideologically compatible law professors, former administration officials, and others to positions of considerable prestige in the federal judicial system. Thus more than ever before, the federal courts today provide an especially useful "proving ground" for candidates who might one day be considered for a seat on the high court.

4. *Divided party government* has become a recurring theme in American government since World War II. Between 1896 and 1946, opposing parties controlled the White House and the Senate during just two sessions of Congress. By contrast, split party conditions now seem almost routine. . . .

5. The *confirmation process has become increasingly public*. For much of our nation's history the confirmation process unfolded largely behind closed doors. Though the Senate Judiciary Committee often met and offered recommendations on nominees during the nineteenth century, closed investigative hearings were not conducted until 1873 when President Ulysses Grant unsuccessfully nominated George Williams to be chief justice. Open hearings were held for the first time only in 1916, when the Senate considered Louis Brandeis's candidacy. Nine years later Harlan Fiske Stone became the first nominee in history to appear before the committee personally. Full-fledged public hearings were finally instituted on a regular basis beginning in 1930 with President Hoover's nomination of John J. Parker.

Since 1955, virtually all Supreme Court nominees have formally testified before the Senate Judiciary Committee. Hearings have been televised live since 1981, insuring heightened public access to the process. The increasingly public nature of confirmation-stage politics has placed added strain on senators, many of whom may be reluctant to spend their time and political capital on an arduous process that will only create enemies back home. Meanwhile, the president must now find nominees who, aside from meeting ideological or professional criteria, will fare well in front of television cameras when facing a barrage of senators' questions.

6. The *rise in power of the organized bar* has figured significantly in recent Supreme Court selections. The American Bar Association's Special Committee on the (federal) Judiciary (later renamed the "Standing Committee on Federal Judiciary") was founded in 1947 to "promote the nomination of competent persons and to oppose the nomination of unfit persons" to the federal courts. During the past half-century that committee has played a significant if uneven role in the appointment of lower federal court judges. Not surprisingly, the ABA has taken an especially strong interest in the nomination of Supreme Court justices as well. Beginning with Eisenhower's nomination of Harlan in 1954, the ABA has formally reviewed all Supreme Court nominees for the Senate Judiciary Committee. Thus in selecting nominees, presidents must incorporate into their calculations the possibility that a less-than-exceptional rating from the ABA could serve as a rallying point for opposition during the subsequent confirmation process. Still, the bar's actual influence over the choice of nominees has varied largely depending upon the administration in power. In 1956, the Eisenhower administration began to submit names of potential Supreme Court nominees to the ABA at the same time that the FBI began its background check. During this period the ABA exerted little direct influence during initial deliberations over prospective candidates. By contrast, subsequent administrations have often enlisted the committee's services during much earlier stages of the process. High-ranking officials in the Justice Department have consulted with committee members to gauge potential support for and opposition to a prospective candidate. . . .

7. *Increased participation by interest groups* has also altered the character of the Supreme Court nomination process. This is not an entirely new phenomenon. Organized interests (including the National Grange and the Anti-Monopoly League) figured significantly in defeating Stanley Matthews's nomination to the Court in 1881. Almost fifty years later, an unlikely coalition of labor interests and civil rights groups joined together to defeat the nomination of John Parker. Since World War II, interest groups have extended their influence into the early stages of nominee selection by virtue of their increased numbers and political power. Groups such as the Alliance for Justice, People for the American Way, and the Leadership Conference on Civil Rights have made Supreme Court ap-

pointments a high priority in their respective organizations. Many interest groups now conduct their own research into the backgrounds of prospective nominees and inundate the administration with information and analysis about various individual candidates.

8. *Increased media attention* has further transformed nominee selection politics. Presidents in the nineteenth and early twentieth centuries, working outside the media's glare, could often delay the selection of a nominee for many months while suffering few political repercussions. By contrast, contemporary presidents must contend with daily coverage of their aides' ruminations concerning a Supreme Court vacancy. Reporters assigned to the "Supreme Court beat" often provide their readership with the most recent "shortlists" of candidates under consideration by the president. A long delay in naming a replacement may be viewed by the press as a sign of indecision and uncertainty on the part of the president. Delay may also work to an administration's benefit, especially if media outlets expend their own resources investigating prospective candidates and airing potential political liabilities prior to any formal commitment by the administration.

9. *Advances in legal research technology* have had a pronounced effect on the selection process. All modern participants in the appointment process, including officials within the White House and the Justice Department, enjoy access to sophisticated tools for researching the backgrounds of prospective Supreme Court candidates. Legal software programs such as LEXIS/NEXIS and WESTLAW allow officials to quickly gather all of a prospective candidate's past judicial opinions, scholarship, and other public commentary as part of an increasingly elaborate screening process. Computer searches may be either tailored around narrow subject issues or they may be comprehensive in scope. The prevalence of C-SPAN and other cable and video outlets has made it possible to analyze prospective candidates' speeches and activities that would have otherwise gone unnoticed. Of course, advanced research technology is a double-edged sword: media outlets and interest groups may just as effectively publicize negative information about prospective candidates, undermining the president's carefully laid plans for a particular vacancy.

10. Finally, the *more visible role the Supreme Court has assumed in American political life* has increased the perceived stakes of the nomination process for everyone involved. Several of the critical developments listed above, including increased media attention and interest group influence in the nominee selection process, stem from a larger political development involving the Court itself: during this century the Supreme Court has entrenched itself at the forefront of American politics. Prior to the New

Deal, the Court only occasionally tried to compete with other governmental institutions for national influence. For example, the Taney Court
inserted itself into the debate over slavery with its decision in *Dred Scott
v. Sanford* (1857). The Court's aggressive protection of property rights in
the late nineteenth century pitted it first against state governments, and
then later against Congress and the president during the early part of the
twentieth century. In each instance the judiciary usually represented a
political ideology in decline; after a period of time the Court eventually
returned to its role as an essentially reaffirming institution.

Since the early 1940s, however, the Supreme Court has positioned
itself at the center of major political controversies on a nearly continuous
basis. Driven by a primarily rights-based agenda, the Court has found itself
wrestling with matters embedded in the American psyche: desegregation,
privacy rights, affirmative action, and law enforcement. With the Court's
continuously high visibility in the American political system, each appointment of a new justice now draws the attention of nearly all segments of
society. The stakes of Supreme Court appointments may only seem higher
than before, but that perception alone has caused a veritable sea change
in the way presidents . . . must treat the selection of Supreme Court nominees.

46

Kelo v. City of New London

*In 2005, the Supreme Court ruled that New London, Connecticut, could
legally force the last holdouts living in the Fort Trumbull area to leave their
homes under the Constitution's Fifth Amendment doctrine of eminent
domain. The case immediately became the center of much national controversy, since the city's hopes for economic rejuvenation involved a private
developer's plan to bring Pfizer Inc. and other businesses to Fort Trumbull
at the expense of tearing down homes. Unlike other eminent domain
situations where property is seized for public use—a road or a school—
New London officials invoked eminent domain for private development that
the city construed as "in the public's interest." The 5-4 decision was based
on Justice John Paul Stevens' view that the Connecticut state law used by
New London officials did allow for the principle of eminent domain to be
applied in this case. Yet the dissent by Justice Sandra Day O'Connor, who
retired from the Court soon after this case, raises important issues. Because
of the majority's decision, she wrote, "all private property is now vulnerable
to being taken and transferred to another private owner, so long as it might
be upgraded. . . . " Those are not the words in the Constitution, O'Connor*

added, and it is a special danger to the property of those who are few in
number or weak in political power. After the Kelo *decision, which united*
liberal and conservative critics, many state legislatures responded to the
public's disapproval by quickly considering new state laws to limit eminent
domain.

Kelo v. City of New London
545 U.S. _____ 125 S.Ct. 2655 (2005)

JUSTICE STEVENS DELIVERED the opinion of the Court.

In 2000, the city of New London approved a development plan that, in the words of the Supreme Court of Connecticut, was "projected to create in excess of 1,000 jobs, to increase tax and other revenues, and to revitalize an economically distressed city, including its downtown and waterfront areas." 268 Conn. 1, 5, 843 A. 2d 500, 507 (2004). In assembling the land needed for this project, the city's development agent has purchased property from willing sellers and proposes to use the power of eminent domain to acquire the remainder of the property from unwilling owners in exchange for just compensation. The question presented is whether the city's proposed disposition of this property qualifies as a "public use" within the meaning of the Takings Clause of the Fifth Amendment to the Constitution.* . . .

The city of New London (hereinafter City) sits at the junction of the Thames River and the Long Island Sound in southeastern Connecticut. Decades of economic decline led a state agency in 1990 to designate the City a "distressed municipality." In 1996, the Federal Government closed the Naval Undersea Warfare Center, which had been located in the Fort Trumbull area of the City and had employed over 1,500 people. In 1998, the City's unemployment rate was nearly double that of the State, and its population of just under 24,000 residents was at its lowest since 1920.

These conditions prompted state and local officials to target New London, and particularly its Fort Trumbull area, for economic revitalization. To this end, respondent New London Development Corporation (NLDC), a private nonprofit entity established some years earlier to assist the City in planning economic development, was reactivated. In January 1998, the State authorized a $5.35 million bond issue to support the

---

*The Fifth Amendment deals mostly with citizens' protections in criminal due process, as in "taking the Fifth," but its last clause states: "nor shall private property be taken for public use, without just compensation."—EDS.

NLDC's planning activities and a $10 million bond issue toward the creation of a Fort Trumbull State Park. In February, the pharmaceutical company Pfizer Inc. announced that it would build a $300 million research facility on a site immediately adjacent to Fort Trumbull; local planners hoped that Pfizer would draw new business to the area, thereby serving as a catalyst to the area's rejuvenation. After receiving initial approval from the city council, the NLDC continued its planning activities and held a series of neighborhood meetings to educate the public about the process. . . .

The NLDC intended the development plan to capitalize on the arrival of the Pfizer facility and the new commerce it was expected to attract. In addition to creating jobs, generating tax revenue, and helping to "build momentum for the revitalization of downtown New London," *id.*, at 92, the plan was also designed to make the City more attractive and to create leisure and recreational opportunities on the waterfront and in the park.

The city council approved the plan in January 2000, and designated the NLDC as its development agent in charge of implementation. See Conn. Gen. Stat. §8-188 (2005). The city council also authorized the NLDC to purchase property or to acquire property by exercising eminent domain in the City's name. §8-193. The NLDC successfully negotiated the purchase of most of the real estate in the 90-acre area, but its negotiations with petitioners failed. As a consequence, in November 2000, the NLDC initiated the condemnation proceedings that gave rise to this case. . . .

Petitioner Susette Kelo has lived in the Fort Trumbull area since 1997. She has made extensive improvements to her house, which she prizes for its water view. Petitioner Wilhelmina Dery was born in her Fort Trumbull house in 1918 and has lived there her entire life. Her husband Charles (also a petitioner) has lived in the house since they married some 60 years ago. In all, the nine petitioners own 15 properties in Fort Trumbull—4 in parcel 3 of the development plan and 11 in parcel 4A. Ten of the parcels are occupied by the owner or a family member; the other five are held as investment properties. There is no allegation that any of these properties is blighted or otherwise in poor condition; rather, they were condemned only because they happen to be located in the development area.

In December 2000, petitioners brought this action in the New London Superior Court. They claimed, among other things, that the taking of their properties would violate the "public use" restriction in the Fifth Amendment. . . .

We granted certiorari to determine whether a city's decision to take property for the purpose of economic development satisfies the "public use" requirement of the Fifth Amendment. 542 U. S. _____ (2004). . . .

Two polar propositions are perfectly clear. On the one hand, it has long been accepted that the sovereign may not take the property of *A* for the sole purpose of transferring it to another private party *B*, even though *A* is paid just compensation. On the other hand, it is equally clear that a State may transfer property from one private party to another if future "use by the public" is the purpose of the taking; the condemnation of land for a railroad with common-carrier duties is a familiar example. Neither of these propositions, however, determines the disposition of this case. . . .

The disposition of this case therefore turns on the question whether the City's development plan serves a "public purpose." Without exception, our cases have defined that concept broadly, reflecting our longstanding policy of deference to legislative judgments in this field. . . .

Viewed as a whole, our jurisprudence has recognized that the needs of society have varied between different parts of the Nation, just as they have evolved over time in response to changed circumstances. Our earliest cases in particular embodied a strong theme of federalism, emphasizing the "great respect" that we owe to state legislatures and state courts in discerning local public needs. See *Hairston v. Danville & Western R. Co.*, 208 U. S. 598, 606–607 (1908) (noting that these needs were likely to vary depending on a State's "resources, the capacity of the soil, the relative importance of industries to the general public welfare, and the long-established methods and habits of the people"). For more than a century, our public use jurisprudence has wisely eschewed rigid formulas and intrusive scrutiny in favor of affording legislatures broad latitude in determining what public needs justify the use of the takings power. . . .

Those who govern the City were not confronted with the need to remove blight in the Fort Trumbull area, but their determination that the area was sufficiently distressed to justify a program of economic rejuvenation is entitled to our deference. The City has carefully formulated an economic development plan that it believes will provide appreciable benefits to the community, including—but by no means limited to—new jobs and increased tax revenue. As with other exercises in urban planning and development, the City is endeavoring to coordinate a variety of commercial, residential, and recreational uses of land, with the hope that they will form a whole greater than the sum of its parts. To effectuate this plan, the City has invoked a state statute that specifically authorizes the use of eminent domain to promote economic development. Given the comprehensive character of the plan, the thorough deliberation that preceded its adoption, and the limited scope of our review, it is appropriate for us, as it was in *Berman*, to resolve the challenges of the individual owners, not on a piecemeal basis, but rather in light of the entire plan. Because that plan unquestionably serves a public purpose, the takings challenged here satisfy the public use requirement of the Fifth Amendment. . . .

Petitioners contend that using eminent domain for economic development impermissibly blurs the boundary between public and private takings. Again, our cases foreclose this objection. Quite simply, the government's pursuit of a public purpose will often benefit individual private parties. . . .

Just as we decline to second-guess the City's considered judgments about the efficacy of its development plan, we also decline to second-guess the City's determinations as to what lands it needs to acquire in order to effectuate the project. "It is not for the courts to oversee the choice of the boundary line nor to sit in review on the size of a particular project area. Once the question of the public purpose has been decided, the amount and character of land to be taken for the project and the need for a particular tract to complete the integrated plan rests in the discretion of the legislative branch." *Berman*, 348 U. S., at 35-36.

In affirming the City's authority to take petitioners' properties, we do not minimize the hardship that condemnations may entail, notwithstanding the payment of just compensation. We emphasize that nothing in our opinion precludes any State from placing further restrictions on its exercise of the takings power. Indeed, many States already impose "public use" requirements that are stricter than the federal baseline. Some of these requirements have been established as a matter of state constitutional law, while others are expressed in state eminent domain statutes that carefully limit the grounds upon which takings may be exercised. As the submissions of the parties and their *amici* make clear, the necessity and wisdom of using eminent domain to promote economic development are certainly matters of legitimate public debate. This Court's authority, however, extends only to determining whether the City's proposed condemnations are for a "public use" within the meaning of the Fifth Amendment to the Federal Constitution. Because over a century of our case law interpreting that provision dictates an affirmative answer to that question, we may not grant petitioners the relief that they seek.

The judgment of the Supreme Court of Connecticut is affirmed.

JUSTICE O'CONNOR, with whom THE CHIEF JUSTICE [REHN-QUIST], JUSTICE SCALIA, and JUSTICE THOMAS join, dissenting.

Over two centuries ago, just after the Bill of Rights was ratified, Justice Chase wrote:

"An *act* of the Legislature (for I cannot call it a law) contrary to the great first principles of the social compact, cannot be considered a rightful exercise of legislative authority. . . . A few instances will suffice to explain what I mean. . . . [A] law that takes property from A. and gives it to B: It is against all reason and justice, for a people to entrust a Legislature with *such* powers; and, therefore, it cannot be presumed that they have done it." *Calder v. Bull*, 3 Dall. 386, 388 (1798) (emphasis deleted).

Today the Court abandons this long-held, basic limitation on government power. Under the banner of economic development, all private property is now vulnerable to being taken and transferred to another private owner, so long as it might be upgraded—*i.e.*, given to an owner who will use it in a way that the legislature deems more beneficial to the public—in the process. To reason, as the Court does, that the incidental public benefits resulting from the subsequent ordinary use of private property render economic development takings "for public use" is to wash out any distinction between private and public use of property—and thereby effectively to delete the words "for public use" from the Takings Clause of the Fifth Amendment. Accordingly I respectfully dissent. . . .

The Fifth Amendment to the Constitution, made applicable to the States by the Fourteenth Amendment, provides that "private property [shall not] be taken for public use, without just compensation." When interpreting the Constitution, we begin with the unremarkable presumption that every word in the document has independent meaning, "that no word was unnecessarily used, or needlessly added." *Wright v. United States*, 302 U. S. 583, 588 (1938). In keeping with that presumption, we have read the Fifth Amendment's language to impose two distinct conditions on the exercise of eminent domain: "the taking must be for a 'public use' and 'just compensation' must be paid to the owner." *Brown v. Legal Foundation of Wash.* 538 U. S. 216, 231-232 (2003).

These two limitations serve to protect "the security of Property," which Alexander Hamilton described to the Philadelphia Convention as one of the "great obj[ects] of Gov[ernment]." 1 Records of the Federal Convention of 1787, p. 302 (M. Farrand ed. 1934). Together they ensure stable property ownership by providing safeguards against excessive, unpredictable, or unfair use of the government's eminent domain power—

particularly against those owners who, for whatever reasons, may be unable to protect themselves in the political process against the majority's will. . . .

This case returns us for the first time in over 20 years to the hard question of when a purportedly "public purpose" taking meets the public use requirement. It presents an issue of first impression: Are economic development takings constitutional? I would hold that they are not. . . .

In moving away from our decisions sanctioning the condemnation of harmful property use, the Court today significantly expands the meaning of public use. It holds that the sovereign may take private property currently put to ordinary private use, and give it over for new, ordinary private use, so long as the new use is predicted to generate some secondary benefit for the public—such as increased tax revenue, more jobs, maybe even aesthetic pleasure. But nearly any lawful use of real private property can be said to generate some incidental benefit to the public. Thus, if predicted (or even guaranteed) positive side-effects are enough to render transfer from one private party to another constitutional, then the words "for public use" do not realistically exclude *any* takings, and thus do not exert any constraint on the eminent domain power. . . .

Any property may now be taken for the benefit of another private party, but the fallout from this decision will not be random. The beneficiaries are likely to be those citizens with disproportionate influence and power in the political process, including large corporations and development firms. As for the victims, the government now has license to transfer property from those with fewer resources to those with more. The Founders cannot have intended this perverse result. "[T]hat alone is a *just* government," wrote James Madison, "which *impartially* secures to every man, whatever is his *own*." For the National Gazette, Property, (Mar. 29, 1792), reprinted in 14 Papers of James Madison 266 (R. Rutland et al. eds. 1983). . . .

PART NINE

Civil Liberties and Civil Rights

47

ANTHONY LEWIS

From *Gideon's Trumpet*

Written in 1964, Gideon's Trumpet *is one of the most-assigned books in American government courses. The excerpt presented here touches on all the major points in the legal and personal story of Clarence Earl Gideon, the Florida prisoner whose case,* Gideon v. Wainwright *(1963), transformed American justice. As Gideon's story unfolds, notice the following elements in journalist Anthony Lewis's account of the landmark case that ensured all defendants legal counsel in state criminal cases:* in forma pauperis; *writ of certiorari;* Betts v. Brady; *stare decisis; Attorney Abe Fortas; Fourteenth Amendment; selective incorporation of the Bill of Rights; "a great marble temple"; "Oyez, oyez, oyez"; Justice Black; 9–0; court-appointed attorney Fred Turner; public defenders; not guilty; the Bay Harbor Poolroom.*

IN THE MORNING MAIL of January 8, 1962, the Supreme Court of the United States received a large envelope from Clarence Earl Gideon, prisoner No. 003826, Florida State Prison, P.O. Box 221, Raiford, Florida. Like all correspondence addressed to the Court generally rather than to any particular justice or Court employee, it went to a room at the top of the great marble steps so familiar to Washington tourists. There a secretary opened the envelope. As the return address had indicated, it was another petition by a prisoner without funds asking the Supreme Court to get him out of jail—another, in the secretary's eyes, because pleas from prisoners were so familiar a part of her work. . . .

. . . A federal statute permits persons to proceed in any federal court *in forma pauperis,* in the manner of a pauper, without following the usual forms or paying the regular costs. The only requirement in the statute is that the litigant "make affidavit that he is unable to pay such costs or give security therefor."

The Supreme Court's own rules show special concern for *in forma pauperis* cases. Rule 53 allows an impoverished person to file just one copy of a petition, instead of the forty ordinarily required, and states that the Court will make "due allowance" for technical errors so long as there is substantial compliance. In practice, the men in the Clerk's Office—a half dozen career employees, who effectively handle the Court's relations with the outside world—stretch even the rule of substantial compliance. Rule 53 also waives the general requirement that documents submitted to the Supreme Court be printed. It says that *in forma pauperis* applications should be typewritten "whenever possible," but in fact handwritten papers are accepted.

Gideon's were written in pencil. They were done in carefully formed printing, like a schoolboy's, on lined sheets evidently provided by the Florida prison. Printed at the top of each sheet, under the heading Correspondence Regulations, was a set of rules ("Only 2 letters each week . . . written on one side only . . . letters must be written in English . . . ") and the warning: MAIL WILL NOT BE DELIVERED WHICH DOES NOT CONFORM TO THESE RULES. Gideon's punctuation and spelling were full of surprises, but there was also a good deal of practiced, if archaic, legal jargon, such as "Comes now the petitioner . . . ".

Gideon was a fifty-one-year-old white man who had been in and out of prisons much of his life. He had served time for four previous felonies, and he bore the physical marks of a destitute life: a wrinkled, prematurely aged face, a voice and hands that trembled, a frail body, white hair. He had never been a professional criminal or a man of violence; he just could not seem to settle down to work, and so he had made his way by gambling and occasional thefts. Those who had known him, even the men who had arrested him and those who were now his jailers, considered Gideon a perfectly harmless human being, rather likeable, but one tossed aside by life. Anyone meeting him for the first time would be likely to regard him as the most wretched of men.

And yet a flame still burned in Clarence Earl Gideon. He had not given up caring about life or freedom; he had not lost his sense of injustice. Right now he had a passionate—some thought almost irrational—feeling of having been wronged by the State of Florida, and he had the determination to try to do something about it. Although the Clerk's Office could not be expected to remember him, this was in fact his second petition to the Supreme Court. The first had been returned for failure to include a pauper's affidavit, and the Clerk's Office had enclosed a copy of the rules and a sample affidavit to help him do better next time. Gideon persevered. . . .

Gideon's main submission was a five-page document entitled "Petition for a Writ of Certiorari Directed to the Supreme Court State of Florida." A writ of certiorari is a formal device to bring a case up to the Supreme Court from a lower court. In plain terms Gideon was asking the Supreme Court to hear his case.

What was his case? Gideon said he was serving a five-year term for "the crime of breaking and entering with the intent to commit a misdemeanor, to wit, petty larceny." He had been convicted of breaking into the Bay Harbor Poolroom in Panama City, Florida. Gideon said his conviction violated the due-process clause of the Fourteenth Amendment to the Constitution, which provides that "No state shall . . . deprive any person of life, liberty, or property, without due process of law." In what way had Gideon's trial or conviction assertedly lacked "due process of law"? For two of the petition's five pages it was impossible to tell. Then came this pregnant statement:

"When at the time of the petitioners trial he ask the lower court for the aid of counsel, the court refused this aid. Petitioner told the court that this Court made decision to the effect that all citizens tried for a felony crime should have aid of counsel. The lower court ignored this plea."

Five more times in the succeeding pages of his penciled petition Gideon spoke of the right to counsel. To try a poor man for a felony without giving him a lawyer, he said, was to deprive him of due process of law. There was only one trouble with the argument, and it was a problem Gideon did not mention. Just twenty years before, in the case of *Betts v. Brady*, the Supreme Court had rejected the contention that the due-process clause of the Fourteenth Amendment provided a flat guarantee of counsel in state criminal trials.

Betts v. Brady was a decision that surprised many persons when made and that had been a subject of dispute ever since. For a majority of six to three, Justice Owen J. Roberts said the Fourteenth Amendment provided no universal assurance of a lawyer's help in a state criminal trial. A lawyer was constitutionally required only if to be tried without one amounted to "a denial of fundamental fairness." . . .

Later cases had refined the rule of *Betts v. Brady*. To prove that he was denied "fundamental fairness" because he had no counsel, the poor man had to show that he was the victim of what the Court called "special circumstances." Those might be his own illiteracy, ignorance, youth, or mental illness, the complexity of the charge against him or the conduct of the prosecutor or judge at the trial. . . .

But Gideon did not claim any "special circumstances." His petition made not the slightest attempt to come within the sophisticated rule of *Betts v. Brady*. Indeed, there was nothing to indicate he had ever heard of the case or its principle. From the day he was tried Gideon had had one idea: That under the Constitution of the United States he, a poor man, was flatly entitled to have a lawyer provided to help in his defense. . . .

Gideon was wrong, of course. The United States Supreme Court had not said he was entitled to counsel; in *Betts v. Brady* and succeeding cases it had said quite the opposite. But that did not necessarily make Gideon's petition futile, for the Supreme Court never speaks with absolute finality when it interprets the Constitution. From time to time—with due solemnity, and after much searching of conscience—the Court has overruled its own decisions. Although he did not know it, Clarence Earl Gideon was calling for one of those great occasions in legal history. He was asking the Supreme Court to change its mind. . . .

Clarence Earl Gideon's petition for certiorari inevitably involved, for all the members of the Court, the most delicate factors of timing and strategy. The issue he presented—the right to counsel—was undeniably of first-rank importance, and it was an issue with which all of the justices were thoroughly familiar. . . .

. . . Professional comment on the Betts case, in the law reviews, had always been critical and was growing stronger, and within the Supreme Court several justices had urged its overruling. On the other hand, a majority might well draw back from so large a step. . . . At the conference of June 1, 1962, the Court had before it two jurisdictional statements asking the Court to hear appeals, twenty-six petitions for certiorari on the Appellate Docket, ten paupers' applications on the Miscellaneous Docket and three petitions for rehearing. . . .

The results of the deliberations at this conference were made known to the world shortly after ten A.M. the following Monday, June 4th, when a clerk posted on a bulletin board the mimeographed list of the Supreme Court's orders for that day. One order read:

Gideon v. Cochran 890 Misc.

The motion for leave to proceed *in forma pauperis* and the petition for writ of certiorari are granted. The case is transferred to the appellate docket. In addition to other questions presented by this case, counsel are requested to discuss the following in their briefs and oral argument:

"Should this Court's holding in *Betts v. Brady*, 316 U.S. 455, be reconsidered?" . . .

In the Circuit Court of Bay County, Florida, Clarence Earl Gideon had been unable to obtain counsel, but there was no doubt that he could have a lawyer in the Supreme Court of the United States now that it had agreed to hear his case. It is the unvarying practice of the Court to appoint a lawyer for any impoverished prisoner whose petition for review has been granted and who requests counsel.

Appointment by the Supreme Court to represent a poor man is a great honor. For the eminent practitioner who would never, otherwise, dip his fingers into the criminal law it can be an enriching experience, making him think again of the human dimensions of liberty. It may provide the first, sometimes the only, opportunity for a lawyer in some distant corner of the country to appear before the Supreme Court. It may also require great personal sacrifice. There is no monetary compensation of any kind—only the satisfaction of service. The Court pays the cost of the lawyer's transportation to Washington and home, and it prints the briefs, but there is no other provision for expenses, not even secretarial help or a hotel room. The lawyer donates that most valuable commodity, his own time. . . .

The next Monday the Court entered this order in the case of *Gideon v. Cochran:*

"The motion for appointment of counsel is granted and it is ordered that Abe Fortas, Esquire, of Washington, D.C., a member of the Bar of this Court be, and he is hereby, appointed to serve as counsel for petitioner in this case.

Abe Fortas is a high-powered example of that high-powered species, the Washington lawyer. He is the driving force in the firm of Arnold, Fortas and Porter. . . . A lawyer who has worked with him says: "Of all the men I have met he most knows why he is doing what he does. I don't like the s.o.b., but if I were in trouble I'd want him on my side. He's the most resourceful, the boldest, the most thorough lawyer I know." . . .

. . . "The real question," Fortas said, "was whether I should urge upon the Court the special-circumstances doctrine. As the record then stood, there was nothing to show that he had suffered from any special circumstances. . . .

When that transcript was read at Arnold, Fortas and Porter, there was no longer any question about the appropriateness of this case as the vehicle to challenge *Betts v. Brady*. Plainly Gideon was not mentally defective. The charge against him, and the proof, were not particularly complicated. The judge had tried to be fair; at least there was no overt bias in the courtroom. In short, Gideon had not suffered from any of the special circumstances that would have entitled him to a lawyer under the limited rule of *Betts v. Brady*. And yet it was altogether clear that a lawyer would have helped. The trial had been a rudimentary one, with a prosecution case that was fragmentary at best. Gideon had not made a single objection or pressed any of the favorable lines of defense. An Arnold, Fortas and Porter associate said later: "We knew as soon as we read that transcript that here was a perfect case to challenge the assumption of *Betts* that a man could have a fair trial without a lawyer. He did very well for a

ANTHONY LEWIS

layman, he acted like a lawyer. But it was a pitiful effort really. He may
have committed this crime, but it was never proved by the prosecution.
A lawyer—not a great lawyer, just an ordinary, competent lawyer—could
have made ashes of the case." . . .

As Abe Fortas began to think about the case in the summer of 1962,
before Justice Frankfurter's retirement, it was clear to him that overruling
Betts v. Brady would not come easily to Justice Frankfurter or others of
his view. This was true not only because of their judicial philosophy in
general, but because of the way they had applied it on specific matters.
One of these was the question of precedent.

"In most matters it is more important that the applicable rule of law
be settled than that it be settled right." Justice Brandeis thus succinctly
stated the basic reason for *stare decisis*, the judicial doctrine of following
precedents. . . .

Another issue . . . cut even deeper than *stare decisis*, and closer to
Gideon's case. This was their attitude toward federalism—the independence of the states in our federal system of government. . . .

The Bill of Rights is the name collectively given to the first ten
amendments to the Constitution, all proposed by the First Congress of
the United States in 1789 and ratified in 1791. The first eight contain
the guarantees of individual liberty with which we are so familiar: freedom
of speech, press, religion and assembly; protection for the privacy of the
home; assurance against double jeopardy and compulsory self-incrimination; the right to counsel and to trial by jury; freedom from cruel and
unusual punishments. At the time of their adoption it was universally
agreed that these eight amendments limited only the Federal Government
and its processes. . . .

There matters stood until the Fourteenth Amendment became part
of the Constitution in 1868. A product of the Civil War, it was specifically
designed to prevent abuse of individuals by state governments. Section 1
provided: "No State shall make or enforce any law which shall abridge
the privileges or immunities of citizens of the United States; nor shall
any State deprive any person of life, liberty, or property, without due
process of law; nor deny to any person within its jurisdiction the equal
protection of the laws." Soon the claim was advanced that this section
had been designed by its framers to *incorporate*, and apply to the states, all
the provisions of the first eight amendments.

This theory of wholesale incorporation of the Bill of Rights has been
adopted by one or more Supreme Court justices from time to time, but
never a majority. . . .

But if wholesale incorporation has been rejected, the Supreme Court has used the Fourteenth Amendment to apply provisions of the Bill of Rights to the states *selectively.* The vehicle has been the clause assuring individuals due process of law. The Court has said that state denial of any right deemed "fundamental" by society amounts to a denial of due process and hence violates the Fourteenth Amendment. . . .

The difficult question has been which provisions of the first eight amendments to absorb. . . .

Grandiose is the word for the physical setting. The W.P.A. Guide to Washington* called the Supreme Court building a "great marble temple" which "by its august scale and mighty splendor seems to bear little relation to the functional purposes of government." Shortly before the justices moved into the building in 1935 from their old chamber across the street in the Capitol, Justice Stone wrote his sons "The place is almost bombastically pretentious, and thus it seems to me wholly inappropriate for a quiet group of old boys such as the Supreme Court." He told his friends that the justices would be "nine black beetles in the Temple of Karnak."

The visitor who climbs the marble steps and passes through the marble columns of the huge pseudo-classical facade finds himself in a cold, lofty hall, again all marble. Great bronze gates exclude him from the area of the building where the justices work in private—their offices, library and conference room. In the courtroom, which is always open to the public, the atmosphere of austere pomp is continued: there are more columns, an enormously high ceiling, red velvet hangings, friezes carved high on the walls. The ritual opening of each day's session adds to the feeling of awe. The Court Crier to the right of the bench smashes his gavel down sharply on a wooden block, everyone rises and the justices file in through the red draperies behind the bench and stand at their places as the Crier intones the traditional opening: "The honorable, the Chief Justice and the Associate Justices of the Supreme Court of the United States. Oyez, oyez, oyez. All persons having business before the honorable, the Supreme Court of the United States, are admonished to draw near and give their attention, for the Court is now sitting. God save the United States and this honorable Court."

But then, when an argument begins, all the trappings and ceremony seem to fade, and the scene takes on an extraordinary intimacy. In the most informal way, altogether without pomp, Court and counsel converse.

*The WPA, the Works Progress Administration, was started by President Franklin Roosevelt as part of the New Deal in 1935. WPA projects, designed to put people back to work during the Depression, included school and park building, theater and music performances, and map and guidebook writing.—EDS.

It is conversation—as direct, unpretentious and focused discussion as can be found anywhere in Washington. . . .

Chief Justice Warren, as is the custom, called the next case by reading aloud its full title: Number 155, Clarence Earl Gideon, petitioner, versus H. G. Cochran, Jr., director, Division of Corrections, State of Florida. . . .

The lawyer arguing a case stands at a small rostrum between the two counsel tables, facing the Chief Justice. The party that lost in the lower court goes first, and so the argument in *Gideon v. Cochran* was begun by Abe Fortas. As he stood, the Chief Justice gave him the customary greeting, "Mr. Fortas," and he made the customary opening: "Mr. Chief Justice, may it please the Court. . . . "

This case presents "a narrow question," Fortas said—the right to counsel—unencumbered by extraneous issues. . . .

"This record does not indicate that Clarence Earl Gideon was a person of low intelligence," Fortas said, "or that the judge was unfair to him. But to me this case shows the basic difficulty with Betts versus Brady. It shows that no man, however intelligent, can conduct his own defense adequately." . . .

"I believe we can confidently say that overruling Betts versus Brady at this time would be in accord with the opinion of those entitled to an opinion. That is not always true of great constitutional questions. . . . We may be comforted in this constitutional moment by the fact that what we are doing is a deliberate change after twenty years of experience—a change that has the overwhelming support of the bench, the bar and even of the states." . . .

It was only a few days later, as it happened, that *Gideon v. Wainwright* was decided. There was no prior notice; there never is. The Court gives out no advance press releases and tells no one what cases will be decided on a particular Monday, much less how they will be decided. Opinion days have a special quality. The Supreme Court is one of the last American appellate courts where decisions are announced orally. The justices, who divide on so many issues, disagree about this practice, too. Some regard it as a waste of time; others value it as an occasion for descending from the ivory tower, however briefly, and communicating with the live audience in the courtroom. . . .

Then, in the ascending order of seniority, it was Justice Black's turn. He looked at his wife, who was sitting in the box reserved for the justices' friends and families, and said: "I have for announcement the opinion and judgment of the Court in Number One fifty-five, Gideon against Wainwright."

Justice Black leaned forward and gave his words the emphasis and the drama of a great occasion. Speaking very directly to the audience in the courtroom, in an almost folksy way, he told about Clarence Earl Gideon's case and how it had reached the Supreme Court of the United States.

"It raised a fundamental question," Justice Black said, "the rightness of a case we decided twenty-one years ago, Betts against Brady. When we granted certiorari in this case, we asked the lawyers on both sides to argue to us whether we should reconsider that case. We do reconsider Betts and Brady, and we reach an opposite conclusion."

By now the page boys were passing out the opinions. There were four—by Justices Douglas, Clark and Harlan, in addition to the opinion of the Court. But none of the other three was a dissent. A quick look at the end of each showed that it concurred in the overruling of *Betts v. Brady*. On that central result, then, the Court was unanimous. . . .

That was the end of Clarence Earl Gideon's case in the Supreme Court of the United States. The opinions delivered that Monday were quickly circulated around the country by special legal services, then issued in pamphlets by the Government Printing Office. Eventually they appeared in the bound volumes of Supreme Court decisions, the United States Reports, to be cited as *Gideon v. Wainwright*, 372 U.S. 335—meaning that the case could be found beginning on page 335 of the 372nd volume of the reports.

Justice Black, talking to a friend a few weeks after the decision, said quietly: "When *Betts v. Brady* was decided, I never thought I'd live to see it overruled." . . .

The reaction of the states to *Gideon v. Wainwright* was swift and constructive. The most dramatic response came from Florida, whose rural-dominated legislature had so long refused to relieve the problem of the unrepresented indigent such as Gideon. Shortly after the decision Governor Farris Bryant called on the legislature to enact a public-defender law. . . .

Resolution of the great constitutional question in *Gideon v. Wainwright* did not decide the fate of Clarence Earl Gideon. He was now entitled to a new trial, with a lawyer. Was he guilty of breaking into the Bay Harbor Poolroom? The verdict would not set any legal precedents, but there is significance in the human beings who make constitutional-law cases as well as in the law. And in this case there was the interesting question whether the legal assistance for which Gideon had fought so hard would make any difference to him. . . .

. . . After ascertaining that Gideon had no money to hire a lawyer of his own choice, Judge McCrary asked whether there was a local law-

yer whom Gideon would like to represent him. There was: W. Fred
Turner.

"For the record," Judge McCrary said quickly, "I am going to appoint
Mr. Fred Turner to represent this defendant, Clarence Earl Gideon." . . .

The jury went out at four-twenty P.M., after a colorless charge by the
judge including the instruction—requested by Turner—that the jury must
believe Gideon guilty "beyond a reasonable doubt" in order to convict
him. When a half-hour had passed with no verdict, the prosecutors were
less confident. At five twenty-five there was a knock on the door between
the courtroom and the jury room. The jurors filed in, and the court clerk
read their verdict, written on a form. It was *Not Guilty.*

"So say you all?" asked Judge McCrary, without a flicker of emotion.
The jurors nodded. . . .

After nearly two years in the state penitentiary Gideon was a free
man. . . . That night he would pay a last, triumphant visit to the Bay
Harbor Poolroom. Could someone let him have a few dollars? Someone
did.

"Do you feel like you accomplished something?" a newspaper reporter
asked.

"Well I did."

48

Miranda v. Arizona

*Chief Justice Earl Warren, the great liberal judge whose Court had already
handed down a number of landmark rulings—among them,* Brown v.
Board of Education *(1954) on desegregation in public schools,* Mapp v.
Ohio *(1961) on search and seizure by police, and* Gideon v. Wainwright
*(1963) on the right to counsel in criminal trials in state courts—wrote the
opinion in another major case,* Miranda v. Arizona *(1966). The case
involved Ernesto Miranda, who had been arrested for kidnapping and rape,
and who had been identified by the victim in a police lineup. Police officers
then interrogated Miranda, who subsequently signed a confession at the top
of which read that he had done so "with full knowledge of my legal rights,
understanding that any statement I make may be used against me." During
the trial, Miranda's confession was entered as evidence, and despite the
officer's testimony that Miranda had not been told of his right to have an
attorney present during interrogation, Miranda was found guilty. The Supreme Court of Arizona upheld the conviction on the grounds that Miranda*

had not specifically requested an attorney. The case went to the U.S. Supreme Court whose ruling resulted in what we now know as the "Miranda rights," a statement read to any suspect by law enforcement officers during an arrest.

Miranda v. Arizona
384 U.S. 436, 86 S.Ct. 1602 (1966)

CHIEF JUSTICE WARREN DELIVERED the opinion of the Court.

The cases before us raise questions which go to the roots of our concepts of American criminal jurisprudence: the restraints society must observe consistent with the Federal Constitution in prosecuting individuals for crime. More specifically, we deal with the admissibility of statements obtained from an individual who is subjected to custodial police interrogation and the necessity for procedures which assure that the individual is accorded his privilege under the Fifth Amendment to the Constitution not to be compelled to incriminate himself.

We dealt with certain phases of this problem recently in *Escobedo v. Illinois*, 378 U.S. 478 (1964). There, as in the four cases before us, law enforcement officials took the defendant into custody and interrogated him in a police station for the purpose of obtaining a confession. The police did not effectively advise him of his right to remain silent or of his right to consult with his attorney. Rather, they confronted him with an alleged accomplice who accused him of having perpetrated a murder. When the defendant denied the accusation and said "I didn't shoot Manuel, you did it," they handcuffed him and took him to an interrogation room. There, while handcuffed and standing, he was questioned for four hours until he confessed. During this interrogation, the police denied his request to speak to his attorney, and they prevented his retained attorney, who had come to the police station, from consulting with him. At his trial, the State, over his objection, introduced the confession against him. We held that the statements thus made were constitutionally inadmissible. . . . We adhere to the principles of *Escobedo* today.

Our holding will be spelled out with some specificity in the pages which follow but briefly stated it is this: the prosecution may not use statements, whether exculpatory or inculpatory, stemming from custodial interrogation of the defendant unless it demonstrates the use of procedural safeguards effective to secure the privilege against self-incrimination. By custodial interrogation, we mean questioning initiated by law enforcement officers after a person has been taken into custody or otherwise deprived of his freedom of action in any significant way. As for the procedural safeguards to be employed, unless other fully effective means are devised to inform accused persons of their right of silence and to assure a continuous opportunity to exercise it, the following measures are required. Prior to any questioning, the person must be warned that he has a right to remain silent, that any statement he does make may be used as evidence against him, and that he has a right to the presence of an attorney, either retained or appointed. The defendant may waive effectuation of these rights, provided the waiver is made voluntarily, knowingly and intelligently. If, however, he indicates in any manner and at any stage of the process that he wishes to consult with an attorney before speaking there can be no questioning. Likewise, if the individual is alone and indicates in any manner that he does not wish to be interrogated, the police may not question him. The mere fact that he may have answered some questions or volunteered some statements on his own does not deprive him of the right to refrain from answering any further inquiries until he has consulted with an attorney and thereafter consents to be questioned. . . .

The constitutional issue we decide in each of these cases [being decided today] is the admissibility of statements obtained from a defendant questioned while in custody or otherwise deprived of his freedom of action in any significant way. In each, the defendant was questioned by police officers, detectives, or a prosecuting attorney in a room in which he was cut off from the outside world. In none of these cases was the defendant given a full and effective warning of his rights at the outset of the interrogation process. In all the cases, the questioning elicited oral admissions, and in three of them, signed statements as well which were admitted at their trials. They all thus share salient features—incommunicado interrogation of individuals in a police-dominated atmosphere, resulting in self-incriminating statements without full warnings of constitutional rights. . . . We stress that the modern practice of in-custody interrogation is psychologically rather than physically oriented. . . . Interrogation still takes place in privacy. Privacy results in secrecy and this in turn results in a gap in our knowledge as to what in fact goes on in the interrogation rooms. A valuable source of information about present police practices, however, may be found in various police manuals and texts which document procedures employed with success in the past, and which recommend various other effective tactics. . . .

The officers are told by the manuals that the "principal psychological factor contributing to a successful interrogation is *privacy*—being alone with the person under interrogation." The efficacy of this tactic has been explained as follows:

"If at all practicable, the interrogation should take place in the investigator's office or at least in a room of his own choice. The subject should be deprived of every psychological advantage." . . .

After this psychological conditioning, however, the officer is told to point out the incriminating significance of the suspect's refusal to talk:

"Joe, you have a right to remain silent. That's your privilege and I'm the last person in the world who'll try to take it away from you. If that's the way you want to leave this, O.K. But let me ask you this. Suppose you were in my shoes and I were in yours and you called me in to ask me about this and I told you, 'I don't want to answer any of your questions.' You'd think I had something to hide, and you'd probably be right in thinking that. That's exactly what I'll have to think about you, and so will everybody else. So let's sit here and talk this whole thing over."

Few will persist in their initial refusal to talk, it is said, if this monologue is employed correctly.

In the event that the subject wishes to speak to a relative or an attorney, the following advice is tendered:

"[T]he interrogator should respond by suggesting that the subject first tell the truth to the interrogator himself rather than get anyone else involved in the matter. If the request is for an attorney, the interrogator may suggest that the subject save himself or his family the expense of any such professional service, particularly if he is innocent of the offense under investigation. The interrogator may also add, 'Joe, I'm only looking for the truth, and if you're telling the truth, that's it. You can handle this by yourself.'" . . .

Even without employing brutality, the "third degree" or the specific stratagems described above, the very fact of custodial interrogation exacts a heavy toll on individual liberty and trades on the weakness of individuals. . . .

. . . In each of the cases [heard by the court], the defendant was thrust into an unfamiliar atmosphere and run through menacing police interrogation procedures. The potentiality for compulsion is forcefully apparent, for example, in *Miranda*, where the indigent Mexican defendant was a seriously disturbed individual with pronounced sexual fantasies, and in *Stewart*, in which the defendant was an indigent Los Angeles Negro who had dropped out of school in the sixth grade. To be sure, the records do not evince overt physical coercion or patent psychological ploys. The fact remains that in none of these cases did the officers undertake to afford appropriate safeguards at the outset of the interrogation to insure that the statements were truly the product of free choice.

It is obvious that such an interrogation environment is created for no purpose other than to subjugate the individual to the will of his examiner. This atmosphere carries its own badge of intimidation. To be sure, this is not physical intimidation, but it is equally destructive of human dignity. The current practice of incommunicado interrogation is at odds with one of our Nation's most cherished principles—that the individual may not be compelled to incriminate himself. Unless adequate protective devices are employed to dispel the compulsion inherent in custodial surroundings, no statement obtained from the defendant can truly be the product of his free choice. . . .

To summarize, we hold that when an individual is taken into custody or otherwise deprived of his freedom by the authorities in any significant way and is subjected to questioning, the privilege against self-incrimination is jeopardized. Procedural safeguards must be employed to protect the privilege, and unless other fully effective means are adopted to notify the person of his right of silence and to assure that the exercise of the right will be scrupulously honored, the following measures are required. He must be warned prior to any questioning that he has the right to remain silent, that anything he says can be used against him in a court of law, that he has the right to the presence of an attorney, and that if he cannot afford an attorney one will be appointed for him prior to any questioning if he so desires. Opportunity to exercise these rights must be afforded to him throughout the interrogation. After such warnings have been given, and such opportunity afforded him, the individual may knowingly and intelligently waive these rights and agree to answer questions or make a statement. But unless and until such warnings and waiver are demonstrated by the prosecution at trial, no evidence obtained as a result of interroga- tion can be used against him. . . . We turn now to these facts to consider the application to these cases of the constitutional principles discussed above. . . .

On March 13, 1963, petitioner, Ernesto Miranda, was arrested at his home and taken in custody to a Phoenix police station. He was there identified by the complaining witness. The police then took him to "Interrogation Room No. 2" of the detective bureau. There he was questioned by two police officers. The officers admitted at trial that Miranda was not advised that he had a right to have an attorney present. Two hours later, the officers emerged from the interrogation room with a written confession signed by Miranda. At the top of the statement was a typed paragraph stating that the confession was made voluntarily, without threats or promises of immunity and "with full knowledge of my legal rights, understanding any statement I make may be used against me."

At his trial before a jury, the written confession was admitted into evidence over the objection of defense counsel, and the officers testified to the prior oral confession made by Miranda during the interrogation. Miranda was found guilty of kidnapping and rape. He was sentenced to 20 to 30 years' imprisonment on each count, the sentences to run concurrently. On appeal, the Supreme Court of Arizona held that Miranda's constitutional rights were not violated in obtaining the confession and affirmed the conviction. 98 Ariz. 18, 401 P. 2d 721. In reaching its decision, the court emphasized heavily the fact that Miranda did not specifically request counsel.

We reverse. From the testimony of the officers and by the admission of respondent, it is clear that Miranda was not in any way apprised of his right to consult with an attorney and to have one present during the interrogation, nor was his right not to be compelled to incriminate himself effectively protected in any other manner. Without these warnings the statements were inadmissible.

49

DONALD KETTL

From *System under Stress*

The USA PATRIOT Act was one of the American government's first responses to the September 11, 2001, terrorist attacks. It is also one of the most controversial responses. Professor Donald Kettl first recounts some of the bureaucratic failures that led up to the attacks. He then discusses the legislation proposed immediately after September 11. The debate over the USA PATRIOT Act exposed the tension between officials who favored a broad expansion of government's power to ensure security and those who feared a drastic loss of civil liberties. The Act, itself, is long and complicated; learn here a little about the key provisions. Finally, Kettl takes up the question of whether the PATRIOT Act was passed too quickly, without sufficient consideration of the civil liberties that Americans were sacrificing. This excerpt raises important questions about the balance between protecting the nation and guarding people's freedoms. The real question is: Can we find the right balance?

OF ALL THE SURPRISES IN THE AFTERMATH of the September 11 terrorist attacks, one of the biggest was the discovery that the four teams of hijackers had been living undetected in the United States for many months. Two had settled in San Diego in January 2000. Several had spent time in the United States in the early 1990s, taking language instruction and, later, flight lessons. The "muscle" hijackers, whose job it was to overcome the pilots and control the passengers, began arriving in April 2001. The four pilot hijackers flew dry runs across the country early in the year and, for reasons investigators could never determine, spent layovers in Las Vegas.

All of the hijackers had entered the country with what appeared to be valid passports. By the day of the attacks, the visas of two of them had expired, and a third hijacker had failed to register for classes and thus violated the terms of his student visa. But federal authorities did not discover any of this until after the attacks. Just as importantly, sixteen of the hijackers were in the country legally. All managed to live comfortable lives, blending into the fabric of American society.

Americans have always treasured their ability to go where they want when they want. They have long valued the freedom to choose their jobs and chart their careers, to live their lives without government scrutiny, and to associate with people of their own choosing. So important are these values, in fact, that many states refused to ratify the U.S. Constitution until, in 1789, Congress proposed a bill of rights. But at the same time, Americans have always expected their government to protect them from threats. That the country was attacked by people who had so easily integrated themselves into the nation's daily life raised a dilemma: How much should government intrude into the lives of citizens in its quest to provide protection?

That question raised a second point. Americans have always accepted any expansion of government power grudgingly. When government has expanded, people have tended to trust state and local governments, to which they are closer, more than the federal government. But to the degree that homeland security strengthens government power, it tends to strengthen the power of the federal government. Therefore, it not only shifts the balance from individual freedom to government control, but it also shifts the balance from state and local authority to federal power. In the long run, the most lasting and important effects of the September 11 attacks could prove to be these changes in individual liberty and governance.

The discovery that the attackers had so easily entered the country and managed to plot the attacks without detection (except by a handful of suspicious FBI agents, whose memos had not gained attention at headquarters) stunned federal officials. A congressional investigation, completed in 2002 but whose report was not released until six months later in early 2003, offered a scathing assessment. "At home, the counterterrorism effort suffered from the lack of an effective domestic intelligence capability. The FBI was unable to identify and monitor effectively the extent of activity by al Qaeda and other international terrorist groups operating in the United States." Coupled with the CIA's problems in tracking foreign threats, "these problems greatly exacerbated the nation's vulnerability to an increasingly dangerous and immediate international terrorist threat inside the United States." Sixteen of the nineteen hijackers had come from Saudi Arabia, and an American who had worked for the Saudi foreign ministry said, "The visa operation is a joke over there." Nationals from other countries handled the initial processing of the applications, and that made it easy for even questionable individuals to slip through the process. "The State Department does not do a quality control check," the former employee charged. As a result, *Boston Globe* reporters concluded, "With its borders so porous and its recordkeeping so unreliable, the United States has little ability to keep all criminals—or terrorists— out of the country and has no system to track them once they're in."

According to the *Washington Post*, the whole star-crossed system was "a portrait of terrorists who took advantage of America's open society as they planned their murderous assault on the Pentagon and the World Trade Center." The story was dismaying: a student visa process that one terrorist had exploited; easy issuance of new passports to foreign travelers; a lack of careful screening at American immigration facilities; failure to create effective watch lists and match them to those trying to enter the country; and weak information systems to track foreign travelers once they entered the country. Americans and their officials wondered if the nation's tradition of openness and minimal intrusion of government had allowed the hijackers an advantage that they had exploited to horrendous result.

Americans were rocked not only by the enormity of the attacks but also by the fact that the terrorists had walked among them for months or years. Even worse, intelligence analysts warned that more al Qaeda operatives might be waiting in "sleeper cells" to stage more attacks. Investigators found evidence that some of the September 11 hijackers had studied crop dusters. Was al Qaeda planning to distribute anthrax or some other biotoxin from the air? Was another round of airline hijackings in the offing? How could the nation protect itself without turning into a police state? The *Boston Globe* said that the terrorists "exploited one of the most

enduring tenets of American freedom: its open society." A week after the
attacks, columnist Martin Wolf sharply summarized the budding dilemma in London's *Financial Times*. "The biggest long-term challenge to any
open society vulnerable to assaults on so vast a scale is striking the balance
between safety and freedom. The attack of September 11 took advantage
of the ease of movement and low security levels of air transport inside
the U.S." He concluded, "We must balance the needs of security with
the demands of freedom."

Even the staunchest advocates of civil liberties knew that the horror
of the September 11 attacks and the fact that the terrorists had exploited
American freedom in an effort to weaken the nation would inevitably
mean some sacrifice of civil rights and civil liberties to provide greater
security. Intelligence analysts discovered that the terrorists were using
satellite phones and coded e-mail. By contrast, American officials charged
with guarding the borders and ferreting out terrorist cells had to sift
through reams of paper and deal with databases that did not connect and
computer systems that could not network. Sen. Edward M. Kennedy of
Massachusetts, long an advocate of an open immigration policy, nonetheless recognized that things had to change. "We're dealing with horse-and-
buggy technology," he said. "We're dealing with handwritten notes. It's
a shocking indictment." U.S. intelligence had to enter the twenty-first
century. . . .

Attorney General John Ashcroft, along with other senior administration officials, was at a secure location, a carefully guarded and undisclosed
site away from Washington, for the first days after the attacks. But Ashcroft
sent word to his staff that he wanted tough, new authority to help the
FBI and the Justice Department find and break up terrorist cells. One of
his aides later remembered that Ashcroft's charge was clear: "all that is
necessary for law enforcement, within the bounds of the Constitution,
to discharge the obligation to fight this war against terror." Not only did
department officials feel the need to act, but the heat of press scrutiny
created an inescapable need to be *seen* to be acting as well.

That imperative created a flurry of proposals on the floor of Congress.
Some members proposed an aggressive new authority that would allow
the federal government to intercept e-mail and telephone calls. Proposals
surfaced to allow the government to increase monitoring of foreign agents
and to infiltrate religious services even if there was no prior evidence of
criminal activity. Investigators, in fact, had complained that the law made
it easier to infiltrate the Mafia than al Qaeda cells and this had to be
corrected. For their part, civil libertarians worried that Congress would
rush to enact sweeping new legislation without stopping to consider what

impact it might have on civil rights and civil liberties. Security experts struggled to find a way to balance concerns for liberty with the need for stronger homeland defense.

A plan began to take shape. Members of Congress agreed on new legislation to make it easier to track the origin and destination of telephone calls and to increase the authority of government to track e-mail. They agreed on broader wiretap authority and new measures to track the flow of money to terrorist groups. The Bush administration, however, wanted to go much further. Ashcroft, for example, wanted the authority to indefinitely detain noncitizens who the Justice Department believed might be planning acts of terrorism. He wanted greater flexibility in sharing grand jury and eavesdropping data throughout the federal government and in tapping into e-mail chats. And he wanted the new authority to be made permanent, so that the federal government could create new and aggressive long-term strategies to go after potential terrorists. Just a week after the attacks, Ashcroft announced at a press conference that he expected the administration's proposal to be ready very shortly—and that he wanted Congress to act on it within a few days. "We need these tools to fight the terrorism threat which exists in the United States," Ashcroft said.

Most members of Congress agreed that the nation needed tougher penalties for terrorists and that the federal government needed broader investigative powers. But Sen. Patrick J. Leahy, D-Vt., chair of the Judiciary Committee, warned that "the biggest mistake we could make" was to conclude that the terrorist threat was so great "that we don't need the Constitution." He added, "The first thing we have to realize is this is not either/or—this is not the Constitution versus capturing the terrorists. We can have both." The American Civil Liberties Union echoed Leahy's concern in a set of ten principles endorsed by scores of civil rights and civil liberties groups. "We need to consider proposals calmly and deliberately with a determination not to erode the liberties and freedoms that are at the core of the American way of life," the ACLU said on September 20.

Fundamental issues were at stake. Citizens expect a right of privacy in their homes and workplaces, but government intelligence analysts believed that they needed broader powers to wiretap phones and track e-mail. They sought new powers to search the homes and belongings of individuals suspected to have terrorist links, without informing the individuals in advance. The rationale behind all of this was that the government suspected that terrorists worked in secret cells. Conducting a search of one cell member's home might alert the others that the government was on to them and frustrate the government's ability to arrest all of the cell's members.

Civil libertarians worried that in its zeal to capture and interrogate potential terrorists, the government might violate the long-standing principle of habeas corpus. Literally translated as "you have the body," the principle traces its lineage back to the Magna Carta. A writ of habeas corpus, issued by a court, requires the government to bring a prisoner to court to show that it has reasonable cause for holding the person or the prisoner must be released. Federal officials said they believed that some potential terrorists should be held as "enemy combatants," which would allow them to be imprisoned indefinitely, without trial, to permit prolonged investigation and questioning. That, civil libertarians worried, would open the door to broad abuse of government power.

Congress did not come close to meeting Ashcroft's deadline, but it did complete its work in near-record time. The legislation's authors formally labeled it the "Uniting and Strengthening America by Providing Appropriate Tools Required to Intercept and Obstruct Terrorism Act"—or the "USA Patriot Act," surely one of the most clever and symbolically powerful Washington acronyms of all time. It not only found the right words to spell out the title for the act, but it wrapped the legislation in the cloak of patriotism, which the drafters hoped no one could resist in the frightening days after September 11. The bill won House approval on October 24. The Senate agreed the next day by a vote of 98–1, with Sen. Russ Feingold, D-Wis., casting the only "nay" vote. President Bush signed the bill promptly on October 26, just six weeks after the attacks. "Today, we take an essential step in defeating terrorism, while protecting the constitutional rights of all Americans," Bush said that morning. "With my signature, this law will give intelligence and law enforcement officials important new tools to fight a present danger."

The USA Patriot Act gives the federal government broad new powers to investigate and detain potential terrorists:

• It facilitates the tracking and gathering of information with new technologies. The law allows federal officials greater authority to use a kind of "secret caller ID," which can identify the source and destination of calls made to and from a particular telephone. Existing laws allowed such "trap and trace" orders for phone calls. The new law permits them for other electronic communications, including e-mail.

• The law permits "roving surveillance," which means that surveillance can occur without being limited to a particular place or instrument. In the past, court orders allowed surveillance only on telephones or places identified in advance. Since terrorists often change locations and sometimes discard cellular telephones after a single use, court orders could not keep up with their activities. The new law permits investigators to obtain authority to track targets as they move or switch phones and e-mails. It also allows investigators to obtain a court order to examine any "tangible item," rather than just business records. For example, investigators can probe voice mails and library records showing who borrowed which books.

• It increases federal authority to investigate money laundering. The new law requires financial institutions to keep more complete records of the financial activities of suspicious individuals and to allow federal investigators broader access to them. In the aftermath of September 11, federal officials had discovered that hundreds of thousands of dollars had flowed through the financial system to terrorist cells undetected, and they wanted stronger authority to trace this flow of money.

• The law strengthens the authority of border agents to prevent possible terrorists from entering the United States. It gives authorities greater power to detain and deport suspicious individuals and those suspected of supporting them. To signal that these provisions were not aimed at punishing foreigners, the law also provides humanitarian assistance for foreign victims of the September 11 attacks.

• The law defines a broad array of activities—terrorist attacks on mass transportation facilities, biological attacks, harboring of terrorists, money laundering to support terrorism, and fraudulent solicitation of money to support terrorism—as federal crimes. Federal officials were concerned that the ingenuity of terrorists had grown faster than criminal law, and they were intent on capturing the full range of terrorist activities as crimes.

• It allows so called sneak-and-peek searches in which investigators can enter homes and facilities and conduct searches without informing those searched until sometime later. Under previous law, those searched had to be informed before the search began. Federal officials said that giving even a few minutes' notice might disrupt their investigations and tip off members of a terrorist cell. Sneak-and-peek searches, they said, permit more effective investigations.

• It expands the government's authority to prosecute computer hackers. Government officials increasingly worried that terrorists, or even ordinary hackers, would exploit vulnerabilities in the Internet to flood the system with e-mail or to damage computer records. With the growing dependence of the world economy on electronic commerce and communication, officials wanted to increase the system's protection against cyberterror attacks and to provide stronger remedies to those hurt by hackers.

Such attacks had not occurred on a broad scale at that point, but security analysts warned that the system was vulnerable and that they could occur in the future. Over the next few years, hackers proved them right.

Administration officials maintained that the USA Patriot Act gave the government valuable new powers that only terrorists needed to fear. The line, often repeated, was that the government needed the same power to investigate potential terrorists that it had long used to stop organized crime. Civil rights experts acknowledged the need for new government powers but worried that there were few checks on the new powers and that the government would push them too far. The government could conduct searches without informing those searched. It could hold prisoners without informing them of the charges or bringing them to trial. And the issue not only was *what* the government could do. It was also the uncertainty about how the new powers would be used and what protections citizens would have to ensure that government officials did not abuse those powers.

For the new wiretap and surveillance powers, the law created a "sunset" (an automatic expiration of the authority) at the end of 2005, unless Congress extended them. Within an hour of Bush's signing the act, Ashcroft put ninety-four federal attorneys and fifty-six FBI field offices to work implementing its provisions. In September 2003, he hailed the Patriot Act as one of the Justice Department's best tools to "connect the dots" in fighting terrorist activity. Congress passed the law with overwhelming, bipartisan support. But almost immediately, critics began worrying about just how the government would use the act's new powers. . . .

In the months after the passage of the USA Patriot Act, worries about the ramifications of post–September 11 policies on civil rights and civil liberties steadily grew. Constant criticism from international human rights organizations of U.S. treatment of Taliban and al Qaeda prisoners failed to attract much attention within the United States. At least initially, many Americans were simply in no mood to worry about the possible mistreatment of those allied with the September 11 terrorists. For the USA Patriot Act, however, domestic criticism was broad based and sharp. The legislatures of Alaska and Hawaii passed resolutions condemning it. So did the councils of more than 160 local governments, including Baltimore, Denver, Detroit, Minneapolis, Oakland, San Francisco, and Seattle. Alaska Rep. Don Young, a Republican, said, "I think the Patriot Act was not really thought out." He added, "I'm very concerned that, in our desire for security and our enthusiasm for pursuing supposed terrorists, sometimes we might be on the verge of giving up the freedoms which we're trying to protect." Attorney General Ashcroft decided to meet the critics head-on by going on an eighteen-city speaking tour in August 2003 to sell the act and its accomplishments. It was an unusual tactic by such a senior official for a program that had been in place so long.

Critics on both the right and the left complained that Congress had rushed to judgment. They charged that, under heavy pressure to act, Congress had given too little attention to the measure's effects on civil rights and civil liberties. At the conservative Cato Institute, Robert A. Levy said that "Congress's rush job" had produced a bill that was "unconstitutionally vague" and dangerous. In fact, he charged, the bill gutted "much of the Fourth Amendment [the protection against unreasonable searches and seizures] in far less time than Congress typically expends on routine bills that raise no constitutional concerns." The Patriot Act, Levy said, did not provide sufficient judicial oversight to prevent possible abuses. He contended that the law was too broad and that it aggressively threatened the rights of individual citizens under the guise of protecting against terrorism. He worried that the sunset was too narrow and too long—that the law did not provide a sufficient opportunity to revisit the broad questions to see how well it was working. "Any attempt by government to chip away at constitutionally guaranteed rights must be subjected to the most painstaking scrutiny to determine whether less invasive means could accomplish the same ends. The USA-Patriot anti-terrorism bill does not survive that demanding test. In a free society, we deserve better," he concluded.

From the left came equally harsh criticism. "In its rush to pass the Patriot Act just six weeks after the September 11 attacks, Congress overlooked one of our most fundamental rights—the right to express our political beliefs, especially those that are controversial," said senior attorney Nancy Chang of the Center for Constitutional Rights, which filed suit to block the act. Chang added, "Now it is up to the judiciary to correct Congress's excesses." The ACLU filed its own suit against the Patriot Act, claiming that the provision allowing broader searches of "tangible things" was unconstitutional. Even librarians found themselves in the battle. They feared that the extensive powers the act gave the government to probe "tangible things" would enable federal investigators to examine the reading habits of their patrons without their knowledge or consent. These actions, the American Library Association (ALA) warned in a 2003 resolution, could "threaten civil rights and liberties guaranteed under the United States Constitution and Bill of Rights." That drew a retaliatory charge from Ashcroft, in the midst of his multicity campaign, that the ALA was fueling a "baseless hysteria."

The charges and countercharges finally led the Justice Department to release a count of how many times the "tangible thing" provision had been used in the act's first two years: zero. Department officials argued that this was evidence that the critics did not need to worry. The critics countered that if the provision had not been used at all, it could not have been important in the antiterror war. Rep. John Conyers Jr., D-Mich., said that "if this authority was not needed to investigate September 11," he wondered if "it should stay on the books any longer." . . .

Nevertheless, the USA Patriot Act was a highly unusual piece of federal legislation. Rarely had any public policy issue united critics from both conservative and liberal ends of the political spectrum. On the right, condemnation came from those who had long worried that a strong government might hinder the exercise of individual freedom. On the left, opponents were concerned that innocent individuals would be swept up in the administration's zeal to fight terrorists. Critics from both sides quietly suggested that the administration was using the war against terrorism to promote new governmental powers that Congress had rejected in years past. No one argued for being soft on terrorists, and no one wanted to risk another big attack, but many involved felt that some kind of line had to be drawn in the shifting sand of homeland security legislation. . . .

While the debate raged, there was widespread disagreement on just where to draw this line between the stronger powers the government said it needed and the protections of civil rights and civil liberties that had, for many decades, been fundamental to American democracy. Having stood atop the pile of debris that once had been the World Trade Center, inhaling the pungent smoke and surrounded by determined rescue workers, President Bush had developed an unshakable commitment to making the country as safe as possible. Civil libertarians, conservatives and liberals alike, worried that the post–September 11 changes could transform American society. The USA Patriot Act and the president's proposals for a second, stronger version, they feared, could have as lasting an impact on the country as the American Revolution. This time, however, the legacy would be one of enduring restrictions on liberty, the opposite of the legacy of freedom established by the nation's founders. Both sides knew that the struggle was titanic. Rarely does a nation face such fundamental choices about its future.

The debate gained steam as the issue developed. Unlike most public policy controversies, in which debate peaks during the congressional battle over proposed legislation and then wanes with time, concern about the Patriot Act only grew following its passage. The number of state and local governments passing resolutions against it swelled. The confidence of critics—and the concern of Bush administration officials—increased, in part because of what now appeared to be legitimate worry that in the weeks after September 11 high emotions had led Congress to pass the measure too quickly, without careful examination. As the act's details became clearer, they stirred up more worry. Moreover, as the immediate effects of September 11 faded slightly, so did concern about another imminent attack, and concerns about the threat to traditional liberties grew. Reports such as the one about the imprisonment of children at Guantanamo and the complaints of the librarians motivated critics to ask what the administration truly had in mind. The second wave of Bush administration proposals led both members of Congress and civil liberties activists to dig in for what they expected would be a protracted battle. . . .

"When dangers increase, liberties shrink. That has been our history, especially in wartime," explains Stuart Taylor Jr. Unquestionably, the nation must recalibrate the balance between liberty and security, but in determining how best to do so, Taylor argues, "We are also stuck in habits of mind that have not yet fully processed how dangerous our world has become or how ill-prepared our legal regime is to meet the new dangers." This predicament proved especially devilish because the only way to know how low to set the security bar was to take a chance on an attack and risk the devastating consequences that could occur from miscalculation. After September 11, administration officials did not want to be in a position of having to defend themselves against charges that they failed to protect the nation ever again. They realized that there were risks to civil liberties in their approach, but they believed that they had to take those risks to secure the nation.

How could officials know whether they had gone too far? The absence of a terrorist attack might mean that the administration had calibrated its strategy just right, or simply that terrorists had changed their strategies and were planning something different. On the other hand, an attack could occur in the future because it is fundamentally impossible to protect everyone against everything all of the time. Even seemingly absurd and paranoid government restrictions on civil rights and civil liberties might not necessarily defend against all terrorist threats. It is impossible ever to know where best to set the balance—safety is no guarantee that the government did not go too far, and attack is not necessarily a sign that the government did not go far enough. As cases challenging the USA Patriot Act and the Bush administration's strategy of detaining prisoners in Guantanamo began wending their way through the federal courts, even some early proponents began worrying that the policies had gone too far.

Thus, homeland security is about setting a balance. Where that balance is set must ultimately be a political judgment, made by political officials through the rough-and-tumble debates of the political process. The tough and sometimes nasty battles over the USA Patriot Act in many ways represent the process at its best. With the nation tiptoeing into new problems it had never faced before, it needed to devise untested policies to solve uncertain issues. To make the problem even more devilish, it was one in which citizens, quite rightly, expected their public officials to provide them protection and safety in their homes and workplaces—as well as freedom and liberty in their daily lives.

50

RICHARD KLUGER

From *Simple Justice*

No Supreme Court case has so changed the United States as did Brown v. Board of Education of Topeka, Kansas *(1954). Volumes have been written on* Brown *and the aftermath of* Brown, *but the best place to start is with Richard Kluger's classic work. The selection here focuses on Earl Warren, the chief justice who wrote the landmark decision. The case that would reverse* Plessy v. Ferguson *(1896) and the "separate but equal" doctrine that the Court had upheld for half a century, was waiting to be heard when the death of Chief Justice Fred Vinson put Warren on the Court. Kluger quotes Justice Frankfurter as saying on hearing of Vinson's death, "This is the first indication I have ever had that there is a God." Kluger explores the intricate process Warren faced in forging a majority, and eventually unanimity, for overturning "separate but equal." While those Americans who were born after* Brown *cannot remember a time when it was not the law of the land, Kluger takes us back to that thrilling moment of change.*

IN THE TWO AND A HALF YEARS since they had last sat down to decide a major racial case, the Justices of the Supreme Court had not grown closer. Indeed, the philosophical and personal fissures in their ranks had widened since they had agreed—unanimously—to side with the Negro appellants in *Sweatt, McLaurin,* and *Henderson* in the spring of 1950. That had been a rare show of unanimity. By the 1952 Term, the Court was failing to reach a unanimous decision 81 percent of the time, nearly twice as high a percentage of disagreement as it had recorded a decade earlier. . . .

It was perhaps the most severely fractured Court in history—testament, on the face of it, to Vinson's failure as Chief Justice. Selected to lead the Court because of his skills as a conciliator, the low-key, mournful-visaged Kentuckian found that the issues before him were far different from, and far less readily negotiable than, the hard-edged problems he had faced as Franklin Roosevelt's ace economic troubleshooter and Harry Truman's Secretary of the Treasury and back-room confederate.

Fred Vinson's lot as Chief Justice . . . had not proven a happy one. . . .

What, then, could be expected of the deeply divided Vinson Court as it convened on the morning of December 13, 1952, to deliberate on the transcendent case of *Brown v. Board of Education*? The earlier racial cases—*Sweatt* and *McLaurin*—they had managed to cope with by chipping away at the edges of Jim Crow but avoiding the real question of *Plessy*'s continued validity.* The Court could no longer dodge that question, though it might continue to stall in resolving it. Hovering over the Justices were all the repressive bugaboos of the Cold War era. The civil rights of Negroes and the civil liberties of political dissenters and criminal defendants were prone to be scrambled together in the public mind, and every malcontent was a sitting target for the red tar of anti-Americanism. No sector of the nation was less hospitable to both civil-liberties and civil-rights claimants than the segregating states of the South, and it was the South with which the Justices had primarily to deal in confronting *Brown.* . . .

And so they were divided. But given the gravity of the issue, they were willing to take their time to try to reconcile their differences. They clamped a precautionary lid on all their discussions of *Brown* as the year turned and Fred Vinson swore in Dwight David Eisenhower as the thirty-fourth President of the United States. The Justices seemed to make little headway toward resolving the problem, but they all knew that a close vote would likely be a disaster for Court and country alike. The problem of welding the disparate views into a single one was obviously complicated

---

*The Supreme Court in *Plessy v. Ferguson* (1896) interpreted the equal protection clause of the Fourteenth Amendment to mean that the states could require separation of the races in public institutions if these institutions were equal (the "separate but equal doctrine"). From 1937 until 1954 the Court subjected "separate but equal" to increasingly rigorous scrutiny. In *Sweatt v. Painter* (1950) and *McLaurin v. Oklahoma State Regents* (1950), for example, the Court invalidated specific state racial segregationist practices in higher education on grounds that they did not permit truly equal access to black students. Yet, the Court had not overturned *Plessy*.—EDS.

by the ambivalence afflicting the Court's presiding Justice. As spring came and the end of the Court's 1952 Term neared, Fred Vinson seemed to be in increasingly disagreeable and edgy spirits. Says one of the people at the Court closest to him then: "I got the distinct impression that he was distressed over the Court's inability to find a strong, unified position on such an important case."

What evidence there is suggests that those on or close to the Court thought it was about as severely divided as it could be at this stage of its deliberations. . . .

During the last week of the term in June, the law clerks of all the Justices met in an informal luncheon session and took a two-part poll. Each clerk was asked how he would vote in the school-segregation cases and how he thought his Justice would vote. According to one of their number, a man who later became a professor of law: "The clerks were almost unanimous for overruling *Plessy* and ordering desegregation, but, according to their impressions, the Court would have been closely divided if it had announced its decision at that time. Many of the clerks were only guessing at the positions of their respective Justices, but it appeared that a majority of the Justices would not have overruled *Plessy* but would have given some relief in some of the cases on the ground that the separate facilities were not in fact equal." . . .

All such bets on the alignment of the Court ended abruptly a few days later when the single most fateful judicial event of that long summer occurred. In his Washington hotel apartment, Fred M. Vinson died of a heart attack at 3:15 in the morning of September 8 [1953]. He was sixty-three.

All the members of the Court attended Vinson's burial in Louisa, Kentucky, his ancestral home. But not all the members of the Court grieved equally at his passing. And one at least did not grieve at all. Felix Frankfurter had not much admired Fred Vinson as judge or man. And he was certain that the Chief Justice had been the chief obstacle to the Court's prospects of reaching a humanitarian and judicially defensible settlement of the monumental segregation cases. In view of Vinson's passing just before the *Brown* reargument, Frankfurter remarked to a former clerk, "This is the first indication I have ever had that there is a God." . . . Fred Vinson was not yet cold in his grave when speculation rose well above a whisper as to whom President Eisenhower would pick to heal and lead the Supreme Court as it faced one of its most momentous decisions in the segregation cases. . . .

Dwight Eisenhower's principal contribution to the civil rights of Americans would prove to be his selection of Earl Warren as Chief

Justice—a decision Eisenhower would later say had been a mistake. The President was on hand, at any rate, on Monday, October 5, when just after noon the clerk of the Supreme Court read aloud the commission of the President that began, "Know ye: That reposing special trust and confidence in the wisdom, uprightness and learning of Earl Warren of California, I do appoint him Chief Justice of the United States. . . . " Warren stood up at the clerk's desk to the side of the bench and read aloud his oath of office. At the end, Clerk Harold Willey said to him, "So help you God." Warren said, "So help me God." Then he stepped quickly behind the velour curtains and re-emerged a moment later through the opening in the center to take the presiding seat. His entire worthy career to that moment would be dwarfed by what followed. . . . At the reargument, Earl Warren had said very little. The Chief Justice had put no substantive questions to any of the attorneys. Nor is it likely that he had given any indication of his views to the other Justices before they convened at the Saturday-morning conference on December 12. But then, speaking first, he made his views unmistakable.

Nearly twenty years later, he would recall, "I don't remember having any great doubts about which way it should go. It seemed to me a comparatively simple case. Just look at the various decisions that had been eroding *Plessy* for so many years. They kept chipping away at it rather than ever really facing it head-on. If you looked back—to *Gaines*, to *Sweatt*, to some of the interstate-commerce cases—you saw that the doctrine of separate-but-equal had been so eroded that only the *fact* of segregation itself remained unconsidered. On the merits, the natural, the logical, and practically the only way the case could be decided was clear. The question was *how* the decision was to be reached."

At least two sets of notes survive from the Justices' 1953 conference discussion of the segregation cases—extensive ones by Justice Burton and exceedingly scratchy and cryptic ones by Justice Frankfurter. They agree on the Chief Justice's remarks. The cases had been well argued, in his judgment, Earl Warren told the conference, and the government had been very frank in both its written and its oral presentations. He said he had of course been giving much thought to the entire question since coming to the Court, and after studying the briefs and relevant history and hearing the arguments, he could not escape the feeling that the Court had "finally arrived" at the moment when it now had to determine whether segregation was allowable in the public schools. Without saying it in so many words, the new Chief Justice was declaring that the Court's policy of delay, favored by his predecessor, could no longer be permitted.

The more he had pondered the question, Warren said, the more he had come to the conclusion that the doctrine of separate-but-equal rested upon the concept of the inferiority of the colored race. He did not see how *Plessy* and its progeny could be sustained on any other theory—and if the Court were to choose to sustain them, "we must do it on that basis," he was recorded by Burton as saying. He was concerned, to be sure, about the necessity of overruling earlier decisions and lines of reasoning, but he had concluded that segregation of Negro schoolchildren had to be ended. The law, he said in words noted by Frankfurter, "cannot in 'this day and age' set them apart." The law could not say, Burton recorded the Chief as asserting, that Negroes were "not entitled to *exactly same* treatment of all others." To do so would go against the intentions of the three Civil War amendments.

Unless any of the other four Justices who had indicated a year earlier their readiness to overturn segregation—Black, Douglas, Burton, and Minton—had since changed his mind, Warren's opening remarks meant that a majority of the Court now stood ready to strike down the practice.

But to gain a narrow majority was no cause for exultation. A sharply divided Court, no matter which way it leaned, was an indecisive one, and for Warren to force a split decision out of it would have amounted to hardly more constructive leadership on this transcendent question than Fred Vinson had managed. The new Chief Justice wanted to unite the Court in *Brown*. . . .

He recognized that a number of Court precedents of long standing would be shattered in the process of overturning *Plessy*, and he regretted that necessity. It was the sort of reassuring medicine most welcomed by Burton and Minton, the least judicially and intellectually adventurous members of the Court.

He recognized that the Court's decision would have wide repercussions, varying in intensity from state to state, and that they would all therefore have to approach the matter in as tolerant and understanding a way as possible. Implicit in this was a call for flexibility in how the Court might frame its decree.

But overarching all these cushioning comments and a tribute to both his compassion as a man and his persuasive skills as a politician was the moral stance Earl Warren took at the outset of his remarks. Segregation, he had told his new colleagues, could be justified only by belief in the inferiority of the Negro; any of them who wished to perpetuate the practice, he implied, ought in candor to be willing to acknowledge as much. These were plain words, and they did not have to be hollered. They cut across all the legal theories that had been so endlessly aired and went straight to the human tissue at the core of the controversy. . . .

The Warren opinion was "finally approved" at the May 15 conference, Burton noted in his diary. The man from California had won the support of every member of the Court.

. . . Not long before the Court's decision in *Brown* was announced, Warren told *Ebony* magazine twenty years later, he had decided to spend a few days visiting Civil War monuments in Virginia. He went by automobile with a black chauffeur.

At the end of the first day, the Chief Justice's car pulled up at a hotel, where he had made arrangements to spend the night. Warren simply assumed that his chauffeur would stay somewhere else, presumably at a less expensive place. When the Chief Justice came out of his hotel the next morning to resume his tour, he soon figured out that the chauffeur had spent the night in the car. He asked the black man why.

"Well, Mr. Chief Justice," the chauffeur began, "I just couldn't find a place—couldn't find a place to . . . "

Warren was stricken by his own thoughtlessness in bringing an employee of his to a town where lodgings were not available to the man solely because of his color. "I was embarrassed, I was ashamed," Warren recalled. "We turned back immediately. . . . "

. . . In the press room on the ground floor, reporters filing in at the tail end of the morning were advised that May 17, 1954, looked like a quiet day at the Supreme Court of the United States.

All of the opinions of the Court were announced on Mondays in that era. The ritual was simple and unvarying. The Justices convened at noon. Lawyers seeking admission to the Supreme Court bar were presented to the Court by their sponsors, greeted briefly by the Chief Justice, and sworn in by the clerk of the Court. Then, in ascending order of seniority, the Justices with opinions to deliver read them aloud, every word usually, without much effort at dramaturgy. Concurrences and dissents were read after the majority opinion. And then the next case, and then the next. There was no applause; there were no catcalls. There were no television or newsreel cameras. There were no questions from the newsmen in the audience. There was no briefing session in the press room or the Justices' chambers after Court adjourned. There were no weekly press conferences. There were no appearances on *Meet the Press* the following Sunday. There were no press releases elaborating on what the Court had said or meant or done. The opinions themselves were all there was. . . .

Down in the press room, as the first three routine opinions were distributed, it looked, as predicted, like a very quiet day at the Court. But then, as Douglas finished up, Clerk of the Court Harold Willey dispatched a pneumatic message to Banning E. Whittington, the Court's dour press officer. Whittington slipped on his suit jacket, advised the press-room contingent, "Reading of the segregation decisions is about to begin in the courtroom," added as he headed out the door that the text of the opinion would be distributed in the press room afterward, and then led the scrambling reporters in a dash up the marble stairs.

"I have for announcement," said Earl Warren, "the judgment and opinion of the Court in No. 1 — *Oliver Brown et al. v. Board of Education of Topeka.*" It was 12:52 P.M. In the press room, the Associated Press wire carried the first word to the country: "Chief Justice Warren today began reading the Supreme Court's decision in the public school segregation cases. The court's ruling could not be determined immediately." The bells went off in every news room in America. The nation was listening.

It was Warren's first major opinion as Chief Justice. He read it, by all accounts, in a firm, clear, unemotional voice. If he had delivered no other opinion but this one, he would have won his place in American history.

Considering its magnitude, it was a short opinion. During its first part, no one hearing it could tell where it would come out. . . .

Without in any way becoming technical and rhetorical, Warren then proceeded to demonstrate the dynamic nature and adaptive genius of American constitutional law. . . . Having declared its essential value to the nation's civic health and vitality, he then argued for the central importance of education in the private life and aspirations of every individual. . . . That led finally to the critical question: "Does segregation of children in public schools solely on the basis of race . . . deprive the children of the minority group of equal educational opportunities?"

To this point, nearly two-thirds through the opinion, Warren had not tipped his hand. Now, in the next sentence, he showed it by answering that critical question: "We believe that it does." . . .

This finding flew directly in the face of *Plessy.* And here, finally, Warren collided with the 1896 decision. . . .

The balance of the Chief Justice's opinion consisted of just two paragraphs. The first began: "We conclude" — and here Warren departed from the printed text before him to insert the word "unanimously," which sent a sound of muffled astonishment eddying around the courtroom — "that in the field of public education the doctrine of 'separate but equal' has no place. Separate educational facilities are inherently unequal." The plaintiffs and others similarly situated — technically meaning Negro children within the segregated school districts under challenge — were therefore being deprived of the equal protection of the laws guaranteed by the Fourteenth Amendment.

The concluding paragraph of the opinion revealed Earl Warren's political adroitness both at compromise and at the ready use of the power of his office for ends he thought worthy. "Because these are class actions, because of the wide applicability of this decision, and because of the great variety of local conditions," he declared, "these cases present problems of considerable complexity. . . . In order that we may have the full assistance of the parties in formulating decrees," the Court was scheduling further argument for the term beginning the following fall. The attorneys general of the United States and all the states requiring or permitting segregation in public education were invited to participate. In a few strokes, Warren thus managed to (1) proclaim "the wide applicability" of the decision and make it plain that the Court had no intention of limiting its benefits to a handful of plaintiffs in a few outlying districts; (2) reassure the South that the Court understood the emotional wrench desegregation would cause and was therefore granting the region some time to get accustomed to the idea; and (3) invite the South to participate in the entombing of Jim Crow by joining the Court's efforts to fashion a temperate implementation decree — or to forfeit that chance by petulantly abstaining from the Court's further deliberations and thereby run the risk of having a harsh decree imposed upon it. It was such dexterous use of the power available to him and of the circumstances in which to exploit it that had established John Marshall as a judicial statesman and political tactician of the most formidable sort. The Court had not seen his like since. Earl Warren, in his first major opinion, moved now with that same sure purposefulness. . . .

It was 1:20 P.M. The wire services proclaimed the news to the nation. Within the hour, the Voice of America would begin beaming word to the world in thirty-four languages: In the United States, schoolchildren could no longer be segregated by race. The law of the land no longer recognized a separate equality. No Americans were more equal than any other Americans.

51

CHARLES OGLETREE

From *All Deliberate Speed*

The impact of the Supreme Court case, Brown v. Board of Education,
*certainly did not end in 1954 when the decision was handed down. Legal
scholar Charles Ogletree picks up the story of Brown with the events after
the landmark decision. Ogletree looks at Brown II, the subsequent decision
that required school desegregation "with all deliberate speed." Contrary to
common belief, the real meaning of this phrase, Ogletree asserts, is that
change could come slowly, not right away. Ogletree then takes readers decades
ahead to three classic civil rights cases based on affirmative action. He
explores the 1978 Bakke decision and the recent Gratz and Grutter cases
from the University of Michigan: the issues in all three involve the value
of diversity and the means to achieve it. To close the excerpt, Ogletree looks
ahead to the way in which all these cases may affect education in the United
States in the coming decades. The meaning of "all deliberate speed" has
proven crucial to the lives of millions of American young people.*

───

ON MAY 17, 1954, AN OTHERWISE UNEVENTFUL Monday
afternoon, fifteen months into Dwight D. Eisenhower's presidency, Chief
Justice Earl Warren, speaking on behalf of a unanimous Supreme Court,
issued a historic ruling that he and his colleagues hoped would irrevocably
change the social fabric of the United States. "We conclude that in the
field of public education the doctrine of 'separate-but-equal' has no place.
Separate educational facilities are inherently unequal." Thurgood Marshall,
who had passionately argued the case before the Court, joined a jubilant
throng of other civil rights leaders in hailing this decision as the Court's
most significant opinion of the twentieth century. The *New York Times*
extolled the *Brown* decision as having "reaffirmed its faith and the underlying American faith in the equality of all men and all children before the
law." . . .

At the time, no one doubted the far-reaching implications of the
Court's ruling. The *Brown* lawyers had apparently accomplished what
politicians, scholars, and others could not—an unparalleled victory that
would create a nation of equal justice under the law. The Court's decision
seemed to call for a new era in which black children and white children

would have equal opportunities to achieve the proverbial American Dream. It did not come too soon for the families whose children were victims of segregation. . . .

Having broadly proclaimed its support of desegregating public schools, the Supreme Court shortly thereafter issued [a second] opinion [*Brown II*]—the opinion that legitimized much of the social upheaval that forms the central theme of this book. Fearful that southern segregationists, as well as the executive and legislative branches of state and federal governments, would both resist and impede this courageous decision, the Court offered a palliative to those opposed to *Brown's* directive. Speaking again with one voice, the Court concluded that, to achieve the goal of desegregation, the lower federal courts were to "enter such orders and decrees consistent with this opinion as are necessary and proper to admit to public schools on a racially nondiscriminatory basis *with all deliberate speed* the parties to these cases."

As Thurgood Marshall and other civil rights lawyers pondered the second decision, they tried to ascertain what the Court meant in adding the crucial phrase "all deliberate speed" to its opinion. It is reported that, after the lawyers read the decision, a staff member consulted a dictionary to confirm their worst fears—that the "all deliberate speed" language meant "slow" and that the apparent victory was compromised because resisters were allowed to end segregation on their own timetable. These three critical words would indeed turn out to be of great consequence, in that they ignore the urgency on which the *Brown* lawyers insisted. When asked to explain his view of "all deliberate speed," Thurgood Marshall frequently told anyone who would listen that the term meant S-L-O-W. . . .

Nearly twenty-five years after the landmark *Brown* decision, a major challenge to its underlying principles of equality in education was emerging. The timing was significant for me in that I was among the large wave of first-generation African-Americans going to college and graduate school. Even though *Brown* paved the way by removing the barrier of segregated educational systems, it remained to be seen who would now have the opportunity to attend the prestigious institutions that had been substantially, if not completely, closed to African-Americans. While the battle for integration continued in the courtrooms around America, the shocking assassination of Martin Luther King, Jr., in April 1968, triggered a chain reaction of nationwide black protest; it also forced many institutions to open their doors much faster than they had contemplated. Harvard Law School was no different. A private institution, it claimed that its doors had always been open to people regardless of color (although women were not admitted until 1953), and it could point out that George Lewis Ruffin, an African-American, had graduated from the law school in 1869 (which, coincidentally, was the year that Howard Law School was founded), but there was still no real effort to seek out and admit African-Americans. . . .

When I arrived in the fall of 1975, Harvard Law School was admitting fifty to sixty African-American students each year, nearly 10 percent of its entering class. Harvard was, in fact, admitting more African-American students than any of its peer institutions and, with the exception of Howard Law School, was at the top of all law schools in the number of minority students enrolled. Some twenty-five years after *Brown*, diversity appeared to be a permanent part of Harvard's educational mission. Our sense of comfort was nearly shattered, however, when Allan Bakke, a white student who had applied to the University of California at Davis Medical School and been rejected, filed a suit challenging an admissions program that affirmatively recruited and admitted African-American and Chicano applicants. The lawsuit called the *Brown* case into question, and squarely raised the issue of what public institutions could do, or not do, to increase the deplorably low representation of minorities in their universities and graduate schools. . . .

In *Bakke*, Justice Powell asserted that Title VI of the Civil Rights Act of 1964 proscribed only racial classifications that would be unconstitutional if used by a state. He applied strict scrutiny and concluded that, although achieving a diverse student body constituted a compelling state interest, the California program was not narrowly tailored to meet that end. He upheld the aspect of the UC Davis plan as that allowed the consideration of diversity, as articulated in the Harvard plan, as one factor, in selecting a class of students to pursue higher education. . . .

What differentiates *Brown* from *Bakke* is the forced abandonment of a legal and intellectual justification of integration based on remedying past discrimination. *Bakke* placed the legitimacy of affirmative action in universities squarely on educational diversity rather than on remedial aims. . . .

I routinely discuss legal, personal, and social issues with my friend John Payton, and in 1997, John called with some exciting news. His law firm had been approached by the University of Michigan to represent it in a lawsuit filed by some white applicants who had unsuccessfully applied to Michigan's law school and undergraduate program. The white applicants were represented by the Center for Individual Rights (CIR), a conservative Washington, D.C.-based organization. . . .

The Michigan lawsuits demanded, among other things, the end to any program that considered an applicant's race, the immediate admission of those whites who were allegedly qualified and denied admission, and money damages. . . .

The civil rights community and those private and public universities committed to maintaining a diverse pool of applicants for their institutions learned some painful lessons from the *Bakke* case, and they decided to develop a more focused effort this time around. More than 150 groups filed briefs in support of the Michigan diversity plan; they included law schools, universities, members of Congress, and corporations. Retired members of the armed forces, reporting that the military could not have credibility without an affirmative action plan that recruited minority officers into its ranks, filed a highly influential brief. Their brief caused a stir, in that it went against the public position of President George W. Bush, who filed a brief opposing the Michigan plan and labeled it a quota. There were further splits within the Republican ranks, as the highest-ranked and best-known African-Americans in the Bush administration, Colin Powell and Condoleezza Rice, also supported diversity and, in Powell's case, supported Michigan explicitly. Despite all of this external agitation, only nine votes counted, and I was carefully counting to see whether we could muster five votes. . . .

In *Gratz v. Bollinger* and *Grutter v. Bollinger*, the Supreme Court answered the central question, debated since *Bakke*, of the propriety of university or college affirmative action programs. The results were, at best, a moderate success for affirmative action. They remain, in the context of the Court's jurisprudence on race- and economic-based educational programs, an important setback to the mission established in *Brown*. By a vote of 5 to 4, the Court upheld the Michigan Law School's affirmative action plan. By a vote of 6 to 3, it held that the undergraduate program was tantamount to a quota system, and unconstitutional. It was a day to celebrate, largely because a contrary decision in the law school case would have been unfathomable.

In *Grutter*, O'Connor presented a robust endorsement of the principle of diversity as a factor in university admissions. Justice O'Connor not only endorsed Justice Powell's broad mandate in *Bakke* but went even further in embracing the significance of diversity in the *Grutter* decision:

Justice Powell emphasized that *nothing less* than the "nation's future depends upon leaders trained through wide exposure to the ideas and mores of students as diverse as this Nation of many peoples."

So long as the admissions program does not constitute the type of quota system of "racial balancing" outlawed by *Bakke*, it may admit a "critical mass" of minority students in an effort to obtain a racially diverse student body. Educational institutions are permitted to use race as a factor (in the words of *Bakke*, quoted in *Grutter*, as a "plus") in minority admissions, so long as the decision to admit the student is "flexible enough to ensure that each applicant is evaluated as an individual and not in a way that makes an applicant's race or ethnicity the defining feature of his or her application."

In the *Gratz* opinion, Chief Justice Rehnquist, writing for a 6-to-3 majority, found the undergraduate admissions program unconstitutional. He was joined by the conservative justices Scalia, Kennedy, O'Connor, and Thomas. The centrist justice Breyer concurred in the judgment of the Court while not joining the chief justice's opinion. The chief justice found that awarding a blanket score—in this case, 20 points, or just over 13 percent of the maximum 150 points used to rank applicants—ensured that the university would admit all qualified minority applicants. He held that the scoring system, "by setting up automatic, predetermined point allocations for the soft variables [including race], ensures that the diversity contributions of applicants cannot be individually assessed." The university's failure to consider individualized features of the diversity of each applicant rendered its affirmative action plan unconstitutional and required the Court to strike it down.

Grutter held that attainment of the educational benefits flowing from diversity (such as promoting cross-racial understanding that breaks down racial stereotypes) constitutes a compelling interest, and deferred to the university's determination that diversity is essential to its educational mission. The law school's position was further bolstered by numerous expert studies and reports, as well as the experience of major American businesses, retired military officers, and civilian military officials. Finally, universities and, more especially, law schools are training grounds for future leaders, and "the path to leadership must be visibly open to talented and qualified individuals of every race and ethnicity."

Moreover, the individualized consideration, the absence of quotas, and the recognition of diversity stemming from sources other than race (all of which resemble the Harvard approach that Justice Powell praised in *Bakke*) render the plan narrowly tailored. However, affirmative action must be limited in time, and the Court expects it will no longer be necessary twenty-five years from now. . . .

Collectively, *Grutter* and *Gratz* preserved the institution of affirmative action in American higher education and, to that extent, are important. Nonetheless, both cases—*Grutter* by what it did *not* say and *Gratz* by what it *did* say—are troubling in that they will likely fail to be the catalysts for dispensing with the "all deliberate speed" mentality adopted in *Brown*.

With the decisions, the Court did not erect a further barrier in the path of the struggle to true integration and equality; it also did little to promote that struggle. . . .

. . . My fear that *Brown's* vision is being accomplished only with "all deliberate speed" is now supplanted by my greater fear that resegregation of public education is occurring at a faster pace. While we celebrate the Michigan decision as a vindication of the principles articulated in *Brown*, we must also be vigilant to make sure that the progress of fifty years is not compromised any further. . . .

Racial segregation today is the result of a complicated mix of social, political, legal, and economic factors, rather than the result of direct state commands ordering racial separation. Yet, whatever the causes, it remains overwhelmingly true that black and Latino children in central cities are educated in virtually all-minority schools with decidedly inferior facilities and educational opportunities. Even when students in suburban and rural schools are included, a majority of black and Latino students around the country still attend predominantly minority schools.

The effective compromise reached in the United States at the close of the twentieth century is that schools may be segregated by race as long as it is not due to direct government fiat. Furthermore, although *Brown I* emphasized that equal educational opportunity was a crucial component of citizenship, there is no federal constitutional requirement that pupils in predominantly minority school districts receive the same quality of education as students in wealthier, largely all-white suburban districts. Although these suburban districts appear as healthy as ever, the public school system in many urban areas is on the brink of collapse. Increasing numbers of parents who live in these urban areas are pushing for charter schools, home schooling, or vouchers for private schools in order to avoid traditional public school education. At the start of the twenty-first century, the principle of *Brown* seems as hallowed as ever, but its practical effect seems increasingly irrelevant to contemporary public schooling.

Indeed, the United States has been in a period of resegregation for some time now. Resegregation is strongly correlated with class and with poverty. Today, white children attend schools where 80 percent of the student body is also white, resulting in the highest level of segregation of any group. Only 15 percent of segregated white schools are in areas of concentrated poverty; over 85 percent of segregated black and Latino schools are. Schools in high-poverty areas routinely show lower levels of educational performance; even well-prepared students with stable family backgrounds are hurt academically by attending such schools.

U.S. public schools as a whole are becoming more nonwhite as minority enrollment approaches 40 percent of all students, nearly twice the percentage in the 1960s. In the western and southern regions of the country, almost half of all students are minorities. In today's schools, blacks make up only 8.6 percent of the average white student's school, and just over 10 percent of white students attend schools that have a predominantly minority population. Even more striking is the fact that over 37 percent of black and Latino students attend 90–100 percent minority schools.

This trend has led to the emergence of a substantial number of public schools where the student body is almost entirely nonwhite. The 2000 United States Department of Calculation data showed that there has been a very rapid increase in the number of multiracial schools where three different racial groups comprise at least one-tenth of the total enrollment. However, these schools are attended by only 14 percent of white children. Most of the shrinking white enrollment occurs in the nation's largest city school systems.

Minority segregated schools have much higher concentrations of poverty and much lower average test scores, lower levels of student and teacher qualifications, and fewer advanced courses. They are often plagued by limited resources and social and health problems. High-poverty schools have been shown to increase educational inequality for the students who attend them because of such problems as a lack of resources, shortage of qualified teachers, lower parent involvement, and higher teacher turnover. Almost half of the students in schools attended by the average black or Latino student are poor or nearly poor. By contrast, less than one student in five in schools attended by the average white student is classified as poor. As Gary Orfield, co-director of the Civil Rights Project (CRP) at Harvard University, and Susan E. Eaton, researcher at CRP, note, "Nine times in ten, an extremely segregated black and Latino school will also be a high-poverty school. And studies have shown that high-poverty schools are overburdened, have high rates of turnover, less qualified and experienced teachers, and operate a world away from mainstream society." . . .

Certainly, there must be some form of social change on the education front. Whether this occurs through separation or in an integrated environment is a matter of great consequence for American society. Our experiment with integration started with a pronouncement, half a century ago in *Brown*, that integration was an important value with positive social consequences that should be embraced by all Americans. Twenty years later, real action to integrate our schools had only just started. We are but one generation into an integrated society, and the signs are that the majority of the population is tired with the process. Those at the top want to stay there, and those in the middle would rather hold on to what they have than give a little to get a lot. We have to decide whether this is a country that is comfortable with discrimination. Are we satisfied with the fact that many whites find minorities so repellent that they will move and change their children's schooling to avoid us? For, make no mistake, that is what underpins the supposedly "rational" decisions based on racial stereotyping: an inability on the part of the majority of Americans to acknowledge that minority citizens are "just like us."

There is little surprise in acknowledging that there was substantial resistance by the white community to integration and later to affirmative action. But the theory of interest convergence suggests that most Americans cannot be bothered to engage that problem unless it directly affects them. They would rather turn away, uninterested, and perpetuate racial disadvantage than acknowledge it, let alone confront it. We have witnessed the *Brown* decision, followed by *Bakke* and, more recently, *Grutter v. Bollinger.* We have witnessed Dr. King's historic "I Have a Dream" speech and his subsequent assassination. We have heard the powerful words of President Johnson in his commitment to affirmative action, and President Bush's criticism of the Michigan plan as a program promoting racial preferences. We have seen diversity plans approved by the Supreme Court and, in the same year, some HBCUs [historically black colleges and universities] lose their accreditation and close. We continue to make progress, and suffer setbacks, in grappling with the persistent problem of race in America. But we must remain vigilant in our commitment to confront racial inequalities, even when we face persistent, even increasing resistance. . . .

The decision in *Brown I*, ending segregation in our public schools — and by implication de jure segregation everywhere is justly celebrated as one of the great events in our legal and political history. Precedent did not compel the result, nor was the composition of the Court indicative of a favorable outcome. There is no doubt that the circumstances of many African-Americans are better now than they were before the *Brown* decision. But the speed with which we have embraced the society made possible by *Brown I* has indeed been all too deliberate. It has been deliberate meaning "slow," "cautious," "wary," as if Americans remained to be convinced of the integration ideal. It has been deliberate in the sense of "ponderous" or "awkward," as if each step had been taken painfully and at great cost. Yet the speed with which we have embraced integration has not been deliberate in the sense of "thoughtful" or "reflective" — on the contrary, our response has been emotional and instinctive, perhaps on both sides of the debate. These reactions, anticipated and epitomized in *Brown II*, I suggest, are the real legacy of *Brown I*.

It would be foolhardy to deny that progress has been made, or to dismiss the reality that *Brown I* is a momentous decision both for what it says and for what it has achieved. But there is more yet to do. *Brown I* should be celebrated for ending de jure segregation in this country—a blight that lasted almost four hundred years and harmed millions of Americans of all races. Far too many African-Americans, however, have been left behind, while only a relative few have truly prospered. For some, the promise of integration has proved ephemeral. For others, short-term gains have been replaced by setbacks engendered by new forms of racism. School districts, briefly integrated, have become resegregated. Some distinctively African-American institutions have been permanently destroyed and others crippled. As we stand near the end or the transformation of affirmative action, things look set to get worse, not better.

For all their clear vision of the need to end segregation, *Brown I* and *II* stand as decisions that see integration as a solution that is embraced only grudgingly. Subsequent courts do not even seem to recognize integration as an imperative. And that, perhaps, is the worst indictment of the *Brown* decisions: their faith in progress and their failure to see how quickly people of a different mind could not only resist but, once the tide had turned, even reverse the halting progress toward a fully integrated society. . . .

52

CRAIG RIMMERMAN

From *From Identity to Politics*

The current decade has brought much attention to issues involving the gay and lesbian community. Divides in American society that have been termed the "culture wars" have centered around gay rights as one of several key areas of disagreement. In this excerpt, Professor Craig Rimmerman points out that the gay and lesbian movement is itself not one monolithic movement. He describes the "assimilationist" and the "liberationist" approaches, as well as some of the strategies used by both groups to achieve their goals. To illustrate the movement's strategies and goals, Rimmerman focuses on the multifaceted and changing ways that gays and lesbians have brought national attention to the AIDS epidemic. In discussing the several marches on Washington to fight AIDS, Rimmerman gives readers an interesting lesson in the politics of effective community organizing.

———

We forget that all significant political change,
and this is going to be the case for gays more than anyone,
doesn't just need a wide spectrum of styles and strategies
— it depends on a wide range of styles and strategies.

—FRANKLIN KAMENY
veteran Washington, D.C., activist

FRANKLIN KAMENY'S OBSERVATION CAPTURES both the limitations and the possibilities of the contemporary lesbian and gay movements. He reminds us that, like most other contemporary social movements, they have made progress by embracing an array of approaches to political, social, and economic change. Indeed, to talk about "the movement" essentializes the rich number of communities, approaches, and debates that have contributed to the lengthy struggle for lesbian, gay, transgendered, and bisexual rights in this country.

Yet regardless of how we conceptualize "the movement," lesbians and gay men can celebrate progress. Over the past twenty-five years, the lesbian and gay movements have achieved greater visibility and more legal protections. How has this progress been manifested? There are open communities of lesbians and gay men in urban areas throughout the United States. In addition, openly gay men and lesbians have been successful in the electoral arena, as they have been elected to city councils, state legislatures, and the United States Congress. Community organizations and businesses exist that appeal directly to the needs of the lesbian and gay population. Lesbians and gay men have infiltrated mainstream culture in television, film, and music. The 1998 Pulitzer Prize for fiction was awarded to Michael Cunningham, an openly gay man, for his powerful novel, *The Hours*.

But for all of the so-called "progress," lesbians and gay men remain second-class citizens in vital ways. Fewer than one-tenth of one percent of all elected officials in the United States are openly lesbian, gay, or bisexual. Lesbians and gay men are forbidden to marry, to teach in many public schools, to adopt children, to provide foster care, to serve in the armed forces, National Guard, reserves, or the ROTC. If evicted from their homes, expelled from their schools, fired from their jobs, or refused public lodging, they usually are not able to seek legal redress. The topic of homosexuality is often deemed inappropriate for discussion in public schools, including in sex education courses. Many public school libraries refuse to own some of the many books that address the issue in important ways. Lesbians and gays are often reviled by the church and barred from membership in the clergy. They are the victims of hate crimes and targets of verbal abuse. Their parents reject them, and many gay youth have either attempted or contemplated suicide. Indeed, one political scientist concludes that "no other group of persons in American society today, having been convicted of no crime, is subject to the number and severity of legally imposed disabilities as are persons of same-sex orientation."

Like all other social movements, the lesbian and gay rights movements have often been divided over approaches to political, social, and cultural change. In one major approach, the assimilationists typically embrace a rights-based perspective and work within the broader framework of liberal, pluralist democracy, fighting for a seat at the table. Theirs is a "work within the system" approach to political and social change. Typically, they espouse a "let us in" approach to political activism, rather than the "let us show you a new way of conceiving the world" style associated with lesbian and gay liberation. Assimilationists are more likely to accept that progress will have to be incremental, and that slow, gradual change is built into the very framework of our government. A second approach, the liberationist perspective, favors more radical, cultural change, change that is transformational in nature and that often arises from outside the political mainstream. Much of the conflict within the lesbian and gay movements concerning political and social strategy has reflected disagreements over assimilation and liberation. It is far too facile to reduce this conflict to a simple dualism. However, the assimilation and liberation categories are useful for understanding the dominant strains within the lesbian and gay movements in the United States over the past fifty years. Liberationists argue that there is a considerable gap between access and power, and that it is not enough simply to have a seat at the table. For many liberationists, what is required is a strategy that embraces both structural political and cultural change, often through "outsider" political tactics. . . .

Why have the lesbian and gay movements turned to unconventional politics over the years? Are unconventional politics a viable political and social strategy? What is the connection between unconventional outsider politics and the insider-based electoral and legal strategies? If we accept that there are fundamental flaws with the electoral-politics and legal-rights strategies, should the lesbian and gay movements reject a mainstream assimilationist strategy and embrace progressive change that is transformative in nature? These are the questions at the core of this chapter, and they will be explored in both historical and contemporary context.

Unconventional politics require participants to go outside the formal channels of the American political system (voting and interest-group politics) to embrace the politics of protest, direct action, and mass involvement. This form of politics was employed with great success by the African-American civil rights movement and has been used in contemporary American politics by groups across the ideological spectrum, including Earth First!, ACT UP, Operation Rescue, and the militias.

This chapter explores the use of unconventional politics within the contemporary lesbian and gay movements. It devotes considerable attention to AIDS policy and to the way AIDS altered the landscape of lesbian and gay politics in the 1980s and 1990s, as large numbers of newly politicized activists mobilized in the midst of a hideous epidemic. ACT UP, Queer Nation, and the Lesbian Avengers all developed at the height of the AIDS crisis. As we will see, the movements associated with AIDS "pioneered new and sophisticated forms of cultural politics." The "sex-panic" debates and the debates over the de-gaying and re-gaying of AIDS in the 1990s provide a window for assessing the contemporary landscape of lesbian and gay politics in light of the epidemic. The chapter also considers marches and demonstrations and the debate over whether valuable movement resources should be used to promote such unconventional politics, with specific attention to the 1993 March on Washington and the 2000 Millennium March. Finally, several activists and scholars identified a decline in political activism and unconventional politics in the 1990s. If such a decline is real, what accounts for it? . . .

The core argument of this chapter is one that underlies this entire book. It is difficult to foster and maintain a relationship between the mainstream, assimilationist lesbian and gay movements and outsider, lesbian and gay activists organizing at the grass roots, as we have seen in the discussion of conflicts over various organizing strategies. Yet this relationship is an important one and it needs to be developed and encouraged, as the case study of AIDS policy in this chapter suggests. AIDS first appeared on the scene in the summer of 1981, when the *New York Times* reported on July 3 that forty-one gay men were dying from a rare cancer as well as infectious complications that stemmed "from an unexplainable depression of the immune system." By 1982 and 1983, the seriousness of the AIDS epidemic "was widely experienced by gay men, not only as a threat to new-found sexual freedoms, but to the broad social and political gains of the community as a whole." How the lesbian and gay movements responded to these challenges is a central focus of our inquiry. . . .

. . . In the end, what was missing was unconventional, outsider politics as a political strategy for capturing the attention of public policy decision makers. Such a strategy emerged with the birth of ACT UP in 1987. . . .

ACT UP, the commonly used acronym for the AIDS Coalition to Unleash Power, is a grassroots organization associated with nonviolent civil disobedience. In the late 1980s and early 1990s, ACT UP became the standard-bearer for protest against governmental and societal indifference to the AIDS epidemic. As we have seen, the group is part of a long tradition of grassroots initiatives in American politics, especially in the African American civil rights movement, which used unconventional politics to promote political and social change. ACT UP has been influenced by the civil rights movement to the extent that it, too, has used boycotts, marches, demonstrations, and nonviolent civil disobedience to attract media coverage of its direct action. With the birth of ACT UP, we witnessed a return to a style of political organizing that had connections to the lesbian and gay liberation movements of the early 1970s, although ACT UP was more successful in garnering national and international attention.

The organization was founded in March 1987 by playwright and AIDS activist Larry Kramer. Kramer had become increasingly unhappy with the GMHC [Gay Men's Health Crisis] focus on providing social services and its "bearing witness" approach to those services. Finally, he publicly disengaged himself from what he labeled "GMHC's Red Cross role." In a speech at the Lesbian and Gay Community Services Center of New York, Kramer challenged the lesbian and gay movements to organize, mobilize, and demand an effective AIDS policy response. He informed the audience of gay men that two-thirds of them might be dead within five years. In Kramer's view, the mass media ought to be the central vehicle for conveying the message that the government had hardly begun to address the AIDS crisis. In his speech, he asked, "Do we want to start a new organization devoted solely to political action?"

Kramer's speech inspired another meeting at the Community Services Center several days later, which more than three hundred people attended. This event essentially signaled the birth of ACT UP. Thereafter, ACT UP/New York routinely drew more than eight hundred people to its weekly meetings. As the organization grew, it remained the largest and most influential of all the chapters. By early 1988, active chapters had appeared throughout the country, including in Los Angeles, Boston, Chicago, and San Francisco. At the beginning of 1990, ACT UP had spread around the globe, with more than a hundred chapters worldwide. . . .

Throughout its existence, ACT UP has made an effort to recruit women and minorities into the organization. This made considerable sense given that AIDS has clearly broadened the lesbian and gay rights movements' agenda. Women in ACT UP organized a series of national actions aimed at forcing the U.S. Centers for Disease Control and Prevention to change its definition of AIDS to include those illnesses contracted by HIV-positive women. But despite its efforts at inclusion, many ACT UP chapters were riddled with gender conflicts. Arlene Stein attributes these to "real, persistent structural differences in style, ideology, and access to resources among men and women." Lesbians and gay men often experienced the same kinds of divisions that arose between heterosexual men and women. . . .

Like other social movements in the United States, the lesbian and gay movements have used marches and demonstrations as vehicles for voicing anger, communicating ideas for political and social change, and attracting media attention. The largest of these marches have logically taken place in Washington, D.C. The first March on Washington occurred on October 14, 1979; march organizers estimated that around a hundred thousand people participated. Lucia Valeska, co-director of the National Gay Task Force, claimed that it symbolized "the birth of a national gay movement." Reflecting on the major differences between it and the first march against the Vietnam war, held ten years earlier [on October 15, 1969], another march participant, James M. Saslow, said, "Then the order of the day was Quaker solemnity, panicky outrage, and some rather naive notions about the ingredients of social change. The men made speeches, and the women made coffee. I am a decade older now, and so is Stonewall; today the women lead off the march, and there is a mood of celebration, a sense that this time we're all marching not merely against something, but *for* something."

By the second March on Washington in October 1987, the political and social landscape had radically changed. Ronald Reagan had been President for six years, and the lesbian and gay movements were experiencing the holocaust called AIDS. The news media dutifully reported the police estimate that some two hundred thousand marched, but others on the scene believed that number was too low. Regardless of the actual figure, many more marchers participated in 1987 than in 1979. This is no surprise, given the changed historical circumstances of the time, most notably the urgency of the AIDS crisis, made visible by the Names Project's AIDS Memorial Quilt. More than six hundred people were arrested during a protest on the steps of the U.S. Supreme Court, the largest number of people who participated in any act of civil disobedience since the antiwar demonstrations. The mainstream news media offered considerably more coverage of this march than it had in 1979, although inexplicably the three national newsmagazines, *Newsweek*, *Time*, and *U.S. News and World Report*, provided no coverage at all. Urvashi Vaid, then media director of the National Gay and Lesbian Task Force, devised a smart strategy for attracting the attention of those journalists who did cover the march. She advised protesters that they should carry signs identifying the city and state they represented. Vaid recognized that reporters needed a local angle in order to satisfy their hometown editors, and if the organizers provided that, they would receive important coverage in their local press. She explained, "I told the press they would see protesters from every corner of the nation, and when they held up their signs, the media swarmed all over them. It was the best. We gave the media what they wanted, and the people who got the coverage went on to be major spokespersons in their media at home." . . .

[The] . . . 1993 march attempted to define itself by its name: the March on Washington for Lesbian, Gay and Bi Equal Rights and Liberation. The march liberally invoked the memory of Dr. Martin Luther King and championed a strategy modeled on the African American civil rights movement and its 1963 March on Washington. As the march platform suggests, this civil rights strategy now completely dominated the broader movements' approach to political and social change. Indeed, despite the reference to "liberation" in its title, very little in the platform suggested a broadly political, cultural, and liberationist strategy. The amount of media coverage for this march was "unprecedented." Gregory Adams, the communications director for the march, said that "the media really seemed to get it this time. Consistent and distinct messages of justice, fair treatment, and equality ran through nearly every article or broadcast we saw." Ohio University professors Joseph Bernt and Marilyn Greenwald supported Adams's assessment with their empirical analysis of march coverage in thirty newspapers. Bernt said, "It extended over a long period of time, including the week after the march. This [march] generated much more sophisticated stories; it got into local gay and lesbian communities." Despite the fact that more people participated in this march than in either 1979 or 1987, there was controversy within the larger lesbian and gay movements over whether such marches have any meaningful, tangible impact.

Rep. Barney Frank (D-Mass.) was among the strongest critics. Over the years, Frank had maintained a fairly close and favorable relationship to the direct-action wing of the lesbian and gay movements, "despite publicly voicing criticism of some tactics, and a distaste for the all-or-nothing purism he sees as widespread in them." One ACT UP member offered this endorsement of Frank in 1992: "He maintains a certain distance from direct-action groups, but there aren't many people in the halls of Congress who call ACT UP and Queer Nation on a regular basis and ask what they're up to." But Frank broke with many direct-action group members when he publicly voiced his disapproval of the 1993 March on Washington:

> It's not that the people in the gay and lesbian community are not energetic. They are very energetic; they just wasted all their energy. When they came to Washington they surrounded the Capitol and turned their backs and held hands. That had zero impact on public policy zero. But it took a lot of energy, and they thought it would have an impact. The debate about whether or not we are 300,000 people or a million people [at the March on Washington] is irrelevant. The point is that nobody in Congress cares. Literally, nobody cares. What they care about is how many of those people they heard from. And if there were a million people but nobody heard from them, that is not as good as 10,000 people everybody heard from. . . . The March was an important cultural event; it was an important self-actualizing event; but it had no short-term political impact for us. . . . So by May I was very discouraged about our inability to make the transition from a marginal to a mainstream political group. And that is the problem when people have the preference for the tactics of the margins—sit-ins, demonstrations. When is the last time the NRA had a sit-in, or a demonstration, or a shoot-in? They don't do that. Who is more influential?

Frank's frustration erupted during the debate on the military ban. He joined other "insider" politicians in lamenting the failure of the lesbian and gay movements to do the tough day-to-day organizing and lobbying of Congress that were clearly needed if the ban had any chance at all of being overturned.

Frank's critique is also relevant as we consider the planning for the 2000 Millennium March, which took place on April 30, 2000. In February 1998, two organizations—the Human Rights Campaign (HRC) and the Universal Fellowship of Metropolitan Community Churches (UFMCC)—publicly announced that they were starting to organize another march on Washington. With the encouragement of organizer Robin Tyler, the two organizations made preliminary decisions about the march itself and agreed to provide funding for the planning efforts. A number of critics quickly pointed out that no other organizations had been consulted in advance, nor had the broader lesbian and gay communities. And decisions had already been made: The march would be held in the year 2000, it would be called the "Millennium March," and the central organizing theme would be issues of "faith and family."

This was hardly the kind of open and democratic process that organizational and community members had a right to expect. Should such a march even be held? Might the resources of the movements better be used in other ways? If the march did occur, what should its message be? And who should be involved in planning the march? These questions were never satisfactorily addressed early in the planning process, a failure that caused considerable consternation within the broader lesbian and gay movements. Elizabeth Birch, executive director of HRC, eventually came to believe that the original call for the march was "a colossal error in judgment," but the damage had already been done (Gamson 2000, 18). To some critics, "the Millennium March [came] to symbolize . . . a movement increasingly run by what is essentially a national, corporate, business-as-usual political lobby [HRC], which collects funds while local and state groups struggle against attack" (ibid., 16). The so-called planning for this march also reflected the top-down, hierarchical proclivities of the mainstream lesbian and gay movements. Worse yet, the march organizers did not seem to have seriously engaged the thoughtful criticisms that Barney Frank offered regarding the 1993 March on Washington. The controversy over the march is an important reminder that many movement members resist this model of political organizing, and believe it is crucial to have open, participatory, and democratic conversations about strategy, message, and use of resources. . . .

53

ELLEN ALDERMAN
CAROLINE KENNEDY

From *In Our Defense*

Two noted attorneys have chosen to examine the Bill of Rights not from the perspective of landmark Supreme Court cases, but from a grassroots perspective. Ellen Alderman and Caroline Kennedy present the story behind an obscure federal case involving the First Amendment and freedom of religion. The U.S. Forest Service had decided to build a logging road through public lands in northern California. The land is sacred to the Yurok tribe, and the tribe hoped that the Constitution's First Amendment would protect them in their free exercise of religion. However, in 1987 the Supreme Court, in a close vote, decided otherwise. Alderman and Kennedy note, however, that Congress intervened, and the land was named protected wilderness in 1990. For now, the Yurok's sacred land is undisturbed, but without the Supreme Court's help.

———

"Congress shall make no law respecting an establishment of religion,
or prohibiting the free exercise thereof . . . "

WHEN THE DOGWOOD TREE blossomed twice and a whale
swam into the mouth of the Klamath River, the Yurok medicine man
knew it was time for the tribe to perform the White Deer Skin Dance.
He knew that these natural signs were messengers sent by the Great Spirit
to tell the people things were out of balance in the world. The White Deer
Skin Dance and Jump Dance are part of the World Renewal Ceremonies of
the Yurok, Karok, Tolowa, and Hoopa Indian tribes of northern California. The World Renewal Ceremonies are performed to protect the earth
from catastrophe and humanity from disease and to bring the physical
and spiritual world back in balance. Preparations for the ceremonies begin
far up in the mountains, in the wilderness known to the Indians as the
sacred "high country."

According to Indian mythology, the World Renewal Ceremonies were
initiated by the *woge*, spirits that inhabited the earth before the coming
of man. The *woge* gave culture and all living things to humanity, and the
ceremonies are held at sites along the river where these gifts were given.
The *woge* then became afraid of human contamination and retreated to
the mountains before ascending into a hole in the sky. Because the mountains were the *woge*'s last refuge on earth, they are the source of great
spiritual power.

In recent years, there has been a quiet resurgence of traditional Indian
religion in the high country. Young Indians who left to find jobs on the
"other side of the mountain" are returning to their ancestral grounds.
Lawrence "Tiger" O'Rourke, a thirty-two-year-old member of the Yurok
tribe, worked for eight years around the state as a building contractor
before returning to raise fish in the traditional Indian way.

"In the white man's world . . . you just spend all of your lifetime
making money and gathering up things around you and it doesn't really
have any value," Tiger says. "Here, the Spirit is still in everything—the
trees, the rocks, the river . . . the different kinds of people. It's got a life
spirit, so we're all connected. . . . The concrete world, it's kind of dead.
It feels like something's missing and the people are afraid. . . . So this place
is just right for me, I guess."

There are about five thousand others who, like Tiger, are happy to
live in isolation from the "white man's world"; indeed the spiritual life

of the high country depends on it. But when the U.S. Forest Service announced plans to build a logging road through the heart of the high country, many of the Yurok tribe decided they could not remain quiet any longer.

They went to court, claiming that the logging road would violate their First Amendment right to freely exercise their religion. They said it was like building a "highway through the Vatican." What the Indians wanted the courts to understand was that the salmon-filled creeks, singing pines, and mountain trails of the high country were their Vatican.

To prepare for the World Renewal Ceremony, the medicine man first notifies the dance givers that it is time. According to Indian law, only certain families are allowed to give dances and to own dance regalia. The privilege and the responsibility are passed down from generation to generation.

"In the beginning," says Tiger, a member of such a family, "the Spirit came up the river and he stayed at different people's houses. He only knocked and went in where he knew the people would take care of him. They would have a responsibility to the people, and the world, and the universe to make the ceremony, and they would always do it. It's a lot of work. You have to live a good life, you have to live with truth. Not everybody could do it."

The dance giver is also responsible for paying up all debts before the dance. Indian law puts a price on everything, and by paying the price the social balance is restored. If you insult someone, you owe that person a certain amount; if you kill a person, you must pay that person's family. Payment prevents hatred and anger from spreading to infect the community and brings the world back into harmony. . . .

The most sacred area of the high country is known as Medicine Mountain, a ridge dominated by the peaks of Doctor Rock, Peak 8, and Chimney Rock. Chimney Rock, a majestic outcropping of pinkish basalt, rises sixty-seven hundred feet above sea level. From its summit, views of receding blue waves of mountain ridges fade into the horizon in all directions. On a clear day, the shimmer of the Pacific Ocean gleams at the end of the winding silver ribbon of the Smith River below. . . .

Although only a few medicine men and Indian doctors actively use the sacred sites of the high country, the spiritual well-being of the entire tribe depends on performance of the ancient rituals. Despite more than a half century during which the government removed Indians from their villages and prohibited them from speaking their own language or practicing their religion, a few elderly Indians never left or gave up the old ways. Some young Indians, like Tiger, are returning to their homeland. And others, like Walter "Black Snake" Lara, are trying to balance the old world with the new.

Black Snake works felling trees. He says it is an honorable job in many parts of the lush California forests, but not in the high country. Of the sacred grounds he says, "The Creator fixed it that way for us. We're responsible for it."

Tiger, Black Snake, and others are struggling to maintain their fragile way of life. They are succeeding in part because the steep mountains, dense forests, and nonnavigable streams have protected their cemeteries, villages, and high country from encroachment by the "concrete" world. To them, the proposed highway was more than just a symbol of that concrete world. By the Forest Service's own estimates, each day it would bring about seventy-two diesel logging trucks and ninety other vehicles within a half mile of Chimney Rock.

Actually, the Forest Service started constructing a logging road through the Six Rivers National Forest in the 1930s. It began at either end, in the lumber-mill towns of Gasquet to the north and Orleans to the south, thus becoming known as the G-O Road. Under the Forest Service's management plan, once the road was completed, the towns would be connected and timber could be hauled to mills at either end of the forest. In the meantime, as construction inched toward Chimney Rock, new areas of timber were opened up to logging. "They snuck that road in from both sides," says Black Snake.

By the 1970s, the two segments of the seventy-five-mile road dead-ended in the forest. Black pavement simply gave way to gravel and dirt, and then the side of a mountain. The final six-mile section needed to complete the road was known as the Chimney Rock section of the G-O Road.

The Indians feared that if the road was built it would destroy the sanctity of the high country forever. As Sam Jones, a full-blooded Yurok dance giver put it. "When the medicine lady goes out there to pray, she stands on these rocks and meditates. The forest is there looking out. [She] talks to the trees and rocks, whatever is out there. After they get through praying, their answer comes from the mountain. Our people talk in their language to them and if it's all logged off and all bald there, they can't meditate at all. They have nothing to talk to."

An influx of tree fellers, logging trucks, tourists, and campers would also destroy the ability to make medicine in the high country. The consequences were grave; if the medicine man could not bring back the power for the World Renewal Ceremonies, the people's religious existence would be threatened. And because the land itself is considered holy by the Indians, they could not move their "church" to another location. "People don't understand about our place," Black Snake says, "because they can build a church and worship wherever they want."

The Indians filed a lawsuit in federal district court in San Francisco: *Northwest Indian Cemetery Protective Association v. Peterson.* (R. Max Peterson was named as defendant in his capacity as chief of the U.S. Forest Service.) They claimed that construction of the G-O Road would destroy the solitude, privacy, and undisturbed natural setting necessary to Indian religious practices, thereby violating their First Amendment right to freely exercise their religion.

By invoking the First Amendment, the Indians joined those before them who had sought religious freedom in America. After all, many colonists came to the New World to escape religious persecution in the Old, establishing colonies that reflected the varied beliefs of their inhabitants. The Puritans of Massachusetts sought to build their "City on a Hill," Lord Baltimore founded Maryland as a colony where Catholics and Protestants would live together and prosper, William Penn led the Quakers to Philadelphia, and the Virginia planters were strong supporters of the Church of England. . . .

[Thomas] Jefferson's [1785 Virginia] statute served as one of [James] Madison's models for the First Amendment, which, as adopted and ratified, has two components: the establishment clause and the free exercise clause. In general terms, according to the Supreme Court, the "establishment of religion clause of the First Amendment means at least this: Neither a state nor the Federal Government can set up a church. Neither can pass laws which aid one religion, aid all religions, or prefer one religion over another. . . . In the words of Jefferson, the clause against establishment of religion by law was intended to erect 'a wall of separation between church and State.'" Courts have relied on the establishment clause to strike down state support for parochial schools, statutes mandating school prayer, and the erection of religious displays (for example, nativity scenes or menorahs) on public property.

In contrast, the free exercise clause forbids the government from outlawing religious belief. It also forbids the government from unduly burdening the exercise of a religious belief. However, some regulation of conduct expressing belief is permitted. If a person claims that a government action violates his right to freely exercise his religion, courts must first determine if the asserted religious belief is "sincerely held." If so, then the burden on individual worship must be balanced against the state's interest in proceeding with the challenged action. Only if the state's interest is "compelling" will it outweigh the individual's right to the free exercise of religion.

In the two hundred years since the First Amendment was ratified, the free exercise clause has protected many whose religious beliefs have differed from those of the majority. For example, the Supreme Court has held that unemployment benefits could not be denied to a Seventh-Day Adventist fired for refusing to work on Saturday, her sabbath; nor to a Jehovah's Witness who quit his job in a weapons production factory for religious reasons. Forcing these individuals to choose between receiving benefits and following their respective religious practices violated their right to the free exercise of religion.

In 1983, the Federal District Court for the Northern District of California held that completion of the G-O Road would violate the Northwest Indians' right to freely exercise their religion. The court concluded that the G-O Road would unconstitutionally burden their exercise of sincerely held religious beliefs, and the government's interest in building the road was not compelling enough to override the Indians' interest. Therefore, the court enjoined, or blocked, the Forest Service from completing the road. When the decision was announced, the group of fifty to a hundred Indians who had traveled south to attend the trial were convinced that their medicine had been successful.

The government appealed the decision to the Ninth Circuit Court of Appeals. While the case was pending, Congress passed the California Wilderness Act, which designated much of the sacred high country as a wilderness area. Thus all commercial activity, including mining or timber harvesting, was forever banned. But as part of a compromise worked out to secure passage of the act, Congress exempted a twelve-hundred foot wide corridor from the wilderness, just enough to complete the G-O Road. So although the surrounding area could not be destroyed, the road could still be built. That decision was left to the Forest Service. The medicine was still working, however; in July 1986, the Ninth Circuit affirmed the district court's decision and barred completion of the road.

The government then appealed the case to the U.S. Supreme Court. It filed a "petition for certiorari," a request that the Court hear the case. The Supreme Court receives thousands of these "cert" petitions each year, but accepts only about 150 for argument and decision. In order to take the case, four justices must vote to grant "cert." If they do not, the lower-court ruling stands. Because freedom of religion is so important in the constitutional scheme, and because the case involved principles affecting the management of vast tracts of federal land, *Northwest Indian Cemetery Protective Association* was one of the 150 cases accepted.

The Indians based their Supreme Court arguments on their victories in the lower courts and on a landmark 1972 Supreme Court case, *Wisconsin v. Yoder.* In *Yoder,* three Amish parents claimed that sending their children to public high school, as required by law, violated their right to free exercise of religion. They explained that the Old Order Amish religion was devoted to a simple life in harmony with nature and the soil, untainted by influence from the contemporary world. The Amish said that public schools emphasized intellectual accomplishment, individual distinction, competition, and social life. In contrast, "Amish society emphasize[d] informal learning-through-doing; a life of 'goodness,' rather than a life of intellect; wisdom, rather than technical knowledge; community welfare, rather than competition; and separation from, rather than integration with, contemporary worldly society." The Amish said that forcing their children out of the Amish community into a world undeniably at odds with their fundamental beliefs threatened their eternal salvation. Therefore, they claimed, state compulsory education laws violated their right to freely exercise their religion. The Supreme Court agreed.

If the Supreme Court could find that freedom of religion outweighed the state's interest in compulsory education, the Indians believed that the Constitution would make room for them too. After all, Chief Justice Warren Burger had written in *Yoder,* "A way of life that is odd or even erratic but interferes with no rights or interests of others is not to be condemned because it is different." The Indians argued that, like the Amish, they wanted only to be left alone to worship, as they had for thousands of years.

But the Forest Service argued that the Indians were seeking something fundamentally different from what the Amish had won. Whereas the exemption from a government program in *Yoder* affected only the Amish, and "interfere[d] with no rights or interests of others," the Indians were trying to stop the government from managing its own resources. From the government's point of view, if the courts allowed these Indians to block the G-O Road, it would open the door for other religious groups to interfere with government action on government lands everywhere. (It did not matter to the government that the Indians considered the high country to be *their* land.) The Forest Service produced a map marked to indicate sacred religious sites in California; the red markers nearly covered the state. Giving the Indians veto power over federal land management decisions was not, in the government's view, what the free exercise clause was intended to protect. As Justice William O. Douglas once wrote, "The

Free Exercise Clause is written in terms of what the government cannot do to the individual, not in terms of what the individual can exact from the government."

The singing pines, soaring eagles, and endless mountain vistas of northern California are about as far from the white marble Supreme Court on Capitol Hill as it is possible to get in the United States. Yet like thousands of Americans before them, a small group of Indians came in November 1987 to watch their case argued before the highest court in the land. Though the Indians had never put much faith in any branch of the government, they had come to believe that if the justices could see the case through "brown eyes," they would finally make room in the Bill of Rights for the "first Americans."

Some did not realize that by the time a case reaches the Supreme Court, it no longer involves only those individuals whose struggle initiated it, but has enduring repercussions throughout the country. Unlike a legal code or statute that is written with specificity, "a constitution," wrote Chief Justice John Marshall, "is framed for ages to come, and is designed to approach immortality, as nearly as human institutions can approach it." When the Supreme Court decides a case based on the Bill of Rights, it enunciates principles that become the Supreme Law of the Land, and are used by lower courts across the United States to guide their decisions.

The Indians lost by one vote. "The Constitution simply does not provide a principle that could justify upholding [the Indians'] legal claims," Justice Sandra Day O'Connor wrote for the majority. "However much we wish that it were otherwise, government simply could not operate if it were required to satisfy every citizen's religious needs and desires."

The Court accepted that the G-O Road could have "devastating effects on traditional Indian religious practices." Nonetheless, it held that the G-O Road case differed from *Yoder* because here, the government was not *coercing* the Indians to act contrary to their religious beliefs. In what may prove to be an important development in the law, the Court concluded that unless the government *coerces* individuals to act in a manner that violates their religious beliefs, the free exercise clause is not implicated, and the government does not have to provide a compelling reason for its actions.

The Court also noted the broad ramifications of upholding the Indians' free exercise claim. While the Indians did not "at present" object to others using the high country, their claim was based on a need for privacy in the area. According to the Court, under the Indians' reasoning there was nothing to prevent them, or others like them, from seeking to exclude all human activity but their own from land they held sacred. "No disrespect for the [Indian] practices is implied when one notes that such beliefs could easily require *de facto* beneficial ownership of some rather spacious tracts of public property," the Court wrote.

Justice William Brennan's emotional dissent rejected the Court's reasoning and result. The religious freedom remaining to the Indians after the Supreme Court's decision, according to Justice Brennan, "amounts to nothing more than the right to believe that their religion will be destroyed . . . the safeguarding of such a hollow freedom . . . fails utterly to accord with the dictates of the First Amendment." Justice Brennan and the two justices who joined him, Thurgood Marshall and Harry Blackmun, rejected the Court's new "coercion test."

"The Court . . . concludes that even where the government uses federal land in a manner that threatens the very existence of a Native American religion, the Government is simply not 'doing' anything to the practitioners of that faith," Justice Brennan wrote. "Ultimately the Court's coercion test turns on a distinction between government actions that compel affirmative conduct inconsistent with religious belief, and those governmental actions that prevent conduct consistent with religious belief. In my view, such a distinction is without constitutional significance." The dissenters believed instead that the Indians' religion would be severely burdened, indeed made "impossible," by the government's actions, and that the government had not shown a compelling interest in completing the road.

"They might as well rewrite the Constitution. They teach us we have freedom of religion and freedom of speech, but it's not true," says Tiger O'Rourke. "This was our place first time, our home. It's still our home, but we don't have the same rights as other Americans."

Currently, the G-O Road is stalled. The Indians are challenging the Forest Service on environmental grounds and attempting to get Congress to add the G-O Road corridor to the existing, protected wilderness area.

Like many Americans, Tiger and Black Snake say they never thought much about the Constitution until it touched their lives directly. Among the tribes of northern California, defeat has fired a new fight for their way of life, spurred intertribal outreach and educational efforts, and brought a new awareness of the legal system. "We *have* to understand the Constitution now," says Tiger O'Rourke. "We still need our line of warriors, but now they've got to be legal warriors. That's the war now, and it's the only way we're going to survive."

N.B. On October 28, 1990, the last day of its session, the 101st Congress passed legislation adding the G-O Road corridor to the Siskiyou Wilderness. This legislation ensures that the logging road will not be completed; its two spurs will remain dead-ended in the forest beneath Chimney Rock. Because the area was protected to preserve the environment rather than the Indians' religion, the Indians found their victory bittersweet. "It's all right for us. We'll use the area as we always have," says Black Snake. "But we didn't accomplish what we set out to accomplish for other tribes. [We] can't win one on beliefs." But, he adds, "maybe it's the Creator's way of seeing just how sincere we are."

54

MARY ANN GLENDON

From *Rights Talk*

Individual rights lie at the heart of America's political system. Unfortunately, in the view of legal scholar Mary Ann Glendon, today's "rights talk" makes a mockery of the real meaning of rights. Legitimate, deeply-rooted rights have given way to what are nothing more than demands. Little thought is given to whether a right is basic or merely a convenience; to the effect of one person's claim of a right on others; to the weighing of rights versus responsibilities. Glendon, as a strong supporter of individual rights, asks people to return to a more common-sense, less artificial, definition of rights. Daily, in their private lives, Americans embrace a genuine and true concept of rights, not the "rights talk" of the public arena.

IN THE SPRING of 1990, men and women in East Germany and Hungary participated in the first fully free elections that had taken place in any of the East European countries since they came under Soviet control in 1945. Excitement ran high. The last people to have voted in that part of the world were now in their seventies. Some young parents, casting a ballot for the first time, brought their children with them to see the sight. Many, no doubt, will long remember the day as one marked with both festivity and solemnity. Meanwhile, in the United States, public interest in politics appears to be at an all-time low. Two months before the 1988 presidential election, polls revealed that half the voting-age public did not know the identity of the Democratic vice-presidential candidate and could not say which party had a majority in Congress. In that election, only half the eligible voters cast ballots, thirteen percent less than in 1960. Americans not only vote less than citizens of other liberal democracies, they display a remarkable degree of apathy concerning public affairs. Over a period of twenty years, daily newspaper readership has fallen from seventy-three percent of adults to a mere fifty-one percent. Nor have the readers simply become viewers, for ratings of network evening news programs have dropped by about twenty-five percent in the past ten years, and the slack has not been taken up by cable television news. Cynicism, indifference, and ignorance concerning government appear to be pervasive. By all outward indicators, the right and obligation to vote—a subject of wonder to East Europeans, and the central concern of many of us who worked in the civil rights movement in the 1960s—is now held here in rather low esteem.

Poor voter turnouts in the United States are, of course, mere symptoms of deeper problems, not least of which are the decline of broadly representative political parties, and the effect of the "sound-bite" on serious and sustained political discussion. On this deeper level lies the phenomenon with which this book is concerned: the impoverishment of our political discourse. Across the political spectrum there is a growing realization that it has become increasingly difficult even to define critical questions, let alone debate and resolve them.

Though sound-bites do not permit much airing of issues, they seem tailor-made for our strident language of rights. Rights talk itself is relatively impervious to the other more complex languages we still speak in less public contexts, but it seeps into them, carrying the rights mentality into spheres of American society where a sense of personal responsibility and of civic obligation traditionally have been nourished. An intemperate rhetoric of personal liberty in this way corrodes the social foundations on which individual freedom and security ultimately rest. While the nations of Eastern Europe are taking their first risk-laden and faltering steps toward democracy, the historic American experiment in ordered liberty is thus undergoing a less dramatic, but equally fateful, crisis of its own. It is a crisis at the very heart of the American experiment in self-government, for it concerns the state of public deliberation about the right ordering of our lives together. In the home of free speech, genuine exchange of ideas about matters of high public importance has come to a virtual standstill.

This book argues that the prominence of a certain kind of rights talk in our political discussions is both a symptom of, and a contributing factor to, this disorder in the body politic. Discourse about rights has become the principal language that we use in public settings to discuss weighty questions of right and wrong, but time and again it proves inadequate, or leads to a standoff of one right against another. The problem is not, however, as some contend, with the very notion of rights, or with our strong rights tradition. It is with a new version of rights discourse that has achieved dominance over the past thirty years.

Our current American rights talk is but one dialect in a universal language that has developed during the extraordinary era of attention to civil and human rights in the wake of World War II. It is set apart from rights discourse in other liberal democracies by its starkness and simplicity, its prodigality in bestowing the rights label, its legalistic character, its exaggerated absoluteness, its hyper-individualism, its insularity, and its silence with respect to personal, civic, and collective responsibilities.

This unique brand of rights talk often operates at cross-purposes with our venerable rights tradition. It fits perfectly within the ten-second formats currently preferred by the news media, but severely constricts opportunities for the sort of ongoing dialogue upon which a regime of ordered liberty ultimately depends. A rapidly expanding catalog of rights— extending to trees, animals, smokers, nonsmokers, consumers, and so on—not only multiplies the occasions for collisions, but it risks trivializing core democratic values. A tendency to frame nearly every social controversy in terms of a clash of rights (a woman's right to her own body vs. a fetus's right to life) impedes compromise, mutual understanding, and the discovery of common ground. A penchant for absolute formulations ("I have the right to do whatever I want with my property") promotes unrealistic expectations and ignores both social costs and the rights of others. A near-aphasia concerning responsibilities makes it seem legitimate to accept the benefits of living in a democratic social welfare republic without assuming the corresponding personal and civic obligations.

As various new rights are proclaimed or proposed, the catalog of individual liberties expands without much consideration of the ends to which they are oriented, their relationship to one another, to corresponding responsibilities, or to the general welfare. Converging with the language of psychotherapy, rights talk encourages our all-too-human tendency to place the self at the center of our moral universe. In tandem with consumerism and a normal dislike of inconvenience, it regularly promotes the short-run over the long-term, crisis intervention over preventive measures, and particular interests over the common good. Saturated with rights, political language can no longer perform the important function of facilitating public discussion of the right ordering of our lives together. Just as rights exist for us only through being articulated, other goods are not even available to be considered if they can be brought to expression only with great difficulty, or not at all.

My principal aim . . . has been to trace the evolution of our distinctive current rights dialect, and to show how it frequently works against the conditions required for the pursuit of dignified living by free women and men. With stories and examples drawn from disputes over flag-burning, Indian lands, plant closings, criminal penalties for homosexual acts, eminent domain, social welfare, child support, and other areas, I have endeavored to demonstrate how our simplistic rights talk simultaneously reflects and distorts American culture. It captures our devotion to individualism and liberty, but omits our traditions of hospitality and care for the community. In the images of America and Americans that it projects, as well as in the ideals to which it implicitly pays homage, our current rights talk is a verbal caricature of our culture — recognizably ours, but with certain traits wildly out of proportion and with some of our best features omitted.

Our rights-laden political discourse does provide a solution of sorts to the communications problems that beset a heterogeneous nation whose citizens decreasingly share a common history, literature, religion, or customs. But the "solution" has become part of the problem. The legal components of political discourse, like sorcerers' apprentices, have taken on new and mischief-making connotations when liberated from their contexts in the speech community of lawyers. (A person has no duty to come to the aid of a "stranger.") With its nonlegal tributaries rapidly dwindling, political rhetoric has grown increasingly out of touch with the more complex ways of speaking that Americans employ around the kitchen table, in their schools, workplaces, and in their various communities of memory and mutual aid.

Under these circumstances, what is needed is not the abandonment, but the renewal, of our strong rights tradition. But it is not easy to see how we might develop a public language that would be better suited in complexity and moral seriousness to the bewildering array of difficulties that presently face us as a mature democracy in an increasingly interdependent world. Nor is it readily apparent how the public forum, dominated as it is by images rather than ideas, could be reclaimed for genuine political discourse.

We cannot, nor would most of us wish to, import some other country's language of rights. Nor can we invent a new rhetoric of rights out of whole cloth. A political Esperanto* without roots in a living cultural

---

*Esperanto was a language created in the late 1880s using simplified grammar and vocabulary borrowed from many languages in an attempt to create a common, universal method of communication. Esperanto was not accepted by people, however, and never achieved wide popularity. — EDS.

tradition would die on the vine. . . . In many settings, employing a grammar of cooperative living, American women and men sound better and smarter than our current political discourse makes them out to be. The best resource for renewing our political discourse, therefore, may be the very heterogeneity that drives us to seek a simple, abstract, common language. The ongoing dialogue between freedom and responsibility, individualism and community, present needs and future plans, that takes place daily in a wide variety of American speech communities could help to revitalize our rights tradition as well as our political life.

PART TEN

Public Opinion

55

WALTER LIPPMANN

From *The Phantom Public*

Walter Lippmann was a prominent American journalist who wrote during the first half of the twentieth century. In his much-read book on public opinion, The Phantom Public, *Lippmann took a hard and realistic look at the role played by the American people in government decision-making. His conclusions were startlingly critical. He portrayed citizens as relatively uninformed, often disinterested, and usually haphazard in their views. Opinions emerge only in time of crisis, and then fade quickly. Many people do not participate at all. Lippmann extended his harsh judgment to political leaders who skillfully manipulate public opinion. To soften his criticisms, Lippmann pointed to what he believed to be the fallacy behind public opinion: "It is bad for a fat man to try to be a ballet dancer." To expect more of the public, Lippmann felt, was an unrealistic and self-defeating illusion.*

———

THE PRIVATE CITIZEN today has come to feel rather like a deaf spectator in the back row, who ought to keep his mind on the mystery off there, but cannot quite manage to keep awake. He knows he is somehow affected by what is going on. Rules and regulations continually, taxes annually and wars occasionally remind him that he is being swept along by great drifts of circumstance.

Yet these public affairs are in no convincing way his affairs. They are for the most part invisible. They are managed, if they are managed at all, at distant centers, from behind the scenes, by unnamed powers. As a private person he does not know for certain what is going on, or who is doing it, or where he is being carried. No newspaper reports his environment so that he can grasp it; no school has taught him how to imagine it; his ideals, often, do not fit with it; listening to speeches, uttering opinions and voting do not, he finds, enable him to govern it. He lives in a world which he cannot see, does not understand and is unable to direct.

In the cold light of experience he knows that his sovereignty is a fiction. He reigns in theory, but in fact he does not govern. . . .

There is then nothing particularly new in the disenchantment which the private citizen expresses by not voting at all, by voting only for the head of the ticket, by staying away from the primaries, by not reading speeches and documents, by the whole list of sins of omission for which he is denounced. I shall not denounce him further. My sympathies are with him, for I believe that he has been saddled with an impossible task and that he is asked to practice an unattainable ideal. I find it so myself for, although public business is my main interest and I give most of my time to watching it, I cannot find time to do what is expected of me in the theory of democracy; that is, to know what is going on and to have an opinion worth expressing on every question which confronts a self-governing community. And I have not happened to meet anybody, from a President of the United States to a professor of political science, who came anywhere near to embodying the accepted ideal of the sovereign and omnicompetent citizen. . . .

[Today's theories] assume that either the voters are inherently competent to direct the course of affairs or that they are making progress toward such an ideal. I think it is a false ideal. I do not mean an undesirable ideal. I mean an unattainable ideal, bad only in the sense that it is bad for a fat man to try to be a ballet dancer. An ideal should express the true possibilities of its subject. When it does not it perverts the true possibilities. The ideal of the omnicompetent, sovereign citizen is, in my opinion, such a false ideal. It is unattainable. The pursuit of it is misleading. The failure to achieve it has produced the current disenchantment.

The individual man does not have opinions on all public affairs. He does not know how to direct public affairs. He does not know what is happening, why it is happening, what ought to happen. I cannot imagine how he could know, and there is not the least reason for thinking, as mystical democrats have thought, that the compounding of individual ignorances in masses of people can produce a continuous directing force in public affairs. . . .

The need in the Great Society not only for publicity but for uninterrupted publicity is indisputable. But we shall misunderstand the need seriously if we imagine that the purpose of the publication can possibly be the informing of every voter. We live at the mere beginnings of public accounting. Yet the facts far exceed our curiosity. . . . A few executives here and there . . . read them. The rest of us ignore them for the good and sufficient reason that we have other things to do. . . .

Specific opinions give rise to immediate executive acts; to take a job, to do a particular piece of work, to hire or fire, to buy or sell, to stay here or go there, to accept or refuse, to command or obey. General opinions give rise to delegated, indirect, symbolic, intangible results: to a vote, to a resolution, to applause, to criticism, to praise or dispraise, to audiences, circulations, followings, contentment or discontent. The specific opinion may lead to a decision to act within the area where a man has personal jurisdiction, that is, within the limits set by law and custom, his personal power and his personal desire. But general opinions lead only to some sort of expression, such as voting, and do not result in executive acts except in coöperation with the general opinions of large numbers of other persons.

Since the general opinions of large numbers of persons are almost certain to be a vague and confusing medley, action cannot be taken until these opinions have been factored down, canalized, compressed and made uniform. . . . The making of one general will out of a multitude of general wishes . . . consists essentially in the use of symbols which assemble emotions after they have been detached from their ideas. Because feelings are much less specific than ideas, and yet more poignant, the leader is able to make a homogeneous will out of a heterogeneous mass of desires. The process, therefore, by which general opinions are brought to cooperation consists of an intensification of feeling and a degradation of significance. Before a mass of general opinions can eventuate in executive action, the choice is narrowed down to a few alternatives. The victorious alternative is executed not by the mass but by individuals in control of its energy. . . .

. . . We must assume, then, that the members of a public will not possess an insider's knowledge of events or share his point of view. They cannot, therefore, construe intent, or appraise the exact circumstances, enter intimately into the minds of the actors or into the details of the argument. They can watch only for coarse signs indicating where their sympathies ought to turn.

We must assume that the members of a public will not anticipate a problem much before its crisis has become obvious, nor stay with the problem long after its crisis is past. They will not know the antecedent events, will not have seen the issue as it developed, will not have thought out or willed a program, and will not be able to predict the consequences of acting on that program. We must assume as a theoretically fixed premise of popular government that normally men as members of a public will not be well informed, continuously interested, nonpartisan, creative or executive. We must assume that a public is inexpert in its curiosity, intermittent, that it discerns only gross distinctions, is slow to be aroused and quickly diverted; that, since it acts by aligning itself, it personalizes whatever it considers, and is interested only when events have been melodramatized as a conflict.

The public will arrive in the middle of the third act and will leave before the last curtain, having stayed just long enough perhaps to decide who is the hero and who the villain of the piece. Yet usually that judgment will necessarily be made apart from the intrinsic merits, on the basis of a sample of behavior, an aspect of a situation, by very rough external evidence. . . .

. . . The ideal of public opinion is to align men during the crisis of a problem in such a way as to favor the action of those individuals who may be able to compose the crisis. The power to discern those individuals is the end of the effort to educate public opinion. . . .

Public opinion, in this theory, is a reserve of force brought into action during a crisis in public affairs. Though it is itself an irrational force, under favorable institutions, sound leadership and decent training the power of public opinion might be placed at the disposal of those who stood for workable law as against brute assertion. In this theory, public opinion does not make the law. But by canceling lawless power it may establish the condition under which law can be made. It does not reason, investigate, invent, persuade, bargain or settle. But, by holding the aggressive party in check, it may liberate intelligence. Public opinion in its highest ideal will defend those who are prepared to act on their reason against the interrupting force of those who merely assert their will.

That, I think, is the utmost that public opinion can effectively do. With the substance of the problem it can do nothing usually but meddle ignorantly or tyrannically. . . .

For when public opinion attempts to govern directly it is either a failure or a tyranny. It is not able to master the problem intellectually, nor to deal with it except by wholesale impact. The theory of democracy has not recognized this truth because it has identified the functioning of government with the will of the people. This is a fiction. The intricate business of framing laws and of administering them through several hundred thousand public officials is in no sense the act of the voters nor a translation of their will. . . .

Therefore, instead of describing government as an expression of the people's will, it would seem better to say that government consists of a body of officials, some elected, some appointed, who handle professionally, and in the first instance, problems which come to public opinion spasmodically and on appeal. Where the parties directly responsible do not work out an adjustment, public officials intervene. When the officials fail, public opinion is brought to bear on the issue. . . .

This, then, is the ideal of public action which our inquiry suggests. Those who happen in any question to constitute the public should attempt only to create an equilibrium in which settlements can be reached directly and by consent. The burden of carrying on the work of the world, of inventing, creating, executing, of attempting justice, formulating laws and moral codes, of dealing with the technic and the substance, lies not upon public opinion and not upon government but on those who are responsibly concerned as agents in the affair. Where problems arise, the ideal is a settlement by the particular interests involved. They alone know what the trouble really is. No decision by public officials or by commuters reading headlines in the train can usually and in the long run be so good as settlement by consent among the parties at interest. No moral code, no political theory can usually and in the long run be imposed from the heights of public opinion, which will fit a case so well as direct agreement reached where arbitrary power has been disarmed.

It is the function of public opinion to check the use of force in a crisis, so that men, driven to make terms, may live and let live.

56

V. O. KEY

From *Public Opinion and American Democracy*

Professor V. O. Key was a pioneer in the study of many facets of modern American politics, including elections, political parties, and public opinion. His detailed study of public opinion attempted to explain the relationship between the people's opinions and the political leadership's opinions. Key's analysis is complicated but clear in its recognition of both elite and mass influence. A particularly useful concept is Key's "opinion dike." He believed that the public's opinion keeps leaders from straying too far outside the parameters acceptable to the people in the making of policy. Most important, Key lifted the blame for "indecision, decay, and disaster" from the shoulders of the public onto the leadership stratum where, he alleged, it really belongs.

————

THE EXPLORATION of public attitudes is a pursuit of endless fascination—and frustration. Depiction of the distribution of opinions within the public, identification of the qualities of opinion, isolation of the odd and of the obvious correlates of opinion, and ascertainment of the modes of opinion formation are pursuits that excite human curiosity. Yet these endeavors are bootless unless the findings about the preferences, aspirations, and prejudices of the public can be connected with the work-ings of the governmental system. The nature of that connection has been suggested by the examination of the channels by which governments become aware of public sentiment and the institutions through which opinion finds more or less formal expression.

When all these linkages are treated, the place of public opinion in government has still not been adequately portrayed. The problem of opinion and government needs to be viewed in an even broader context. Consideration of the role of public opinion drives the observer to the more fundamental question of how it is that democratic governments manage to operate at all. Despite endless speculation on that problem, perplexities still exist about what critical circumstances, beliefs, outlooks, faiths, and conditions are conducive to the maintenance of regimes under which public opinion is controlling, at least in principle, and is, in fact, highly influential. . . . Though the preceding analyses did not uncover the secret of the conditions precedent to the practice of democratic politics, they pointed to a major piece of the puzzle that was missing as we sought to assemble the elements that go into the construction of a democratic regime. The significance of that missing piece may be made apparent in an indirect manner. In an earlier day public opinion seemed to be pictured as a mysterious vapor that emanated from the undifferentiated citizenry and in some way or another enveloped the apparatus of government to bring it into conformity with the public will. These weird conceptions, some of which were mentioned in our introductory chapter, passed out of style as the technique of the sample survey permitted the determination, with some accuracy, of the distribution of opinions within the population. Vast areas of ignorance remain in our information about people's opinions and aspirations; nevertheless, a far more revealing map of the gross topography of public opinion can now be drawn than could have been a quarter of a century ago.

Despite their power as instruments for the observation of mass opinion, sampling procedures do not bring within their range elements of the political system basic for the understanding of the role of mass opinion within the system. Repeatedly, as we have sought to explain particular distributions, movements, and qualities of mass opinion, we have had to go beyond the survey data and make assumptions and estimates about the role and behavior of that thin stratum of persons referred to variously as the political elite, the political activists, the leadership echelons, or the influentials. In the normal operation of surveys designed to obtain tests of mass sentiment, so few persons from this activist stratum fall into the sample that they cannot well be differentiated, even in a static description, from those persons less involved politically. The data tell us almost nothing about the dynamic relations between the upper layer of activists and mass opinion. The missing piece of our puzzle is this elite element of the opinion system. . . .

While the ruling classes of a democratic order are in a way invisible because of the vagueness of the lines defining the influentials and the relative ease of entry to their ranks, it is plain that the modal norms and standards of a democratic elite have their peculiarities. Not all persons in leadership echelons have precisely the same basic beliefs; some may even regard the people as a beast. Yet a fairly high concentration prevails around the modal beliefs, even though the definition of those beliefs must be imprecise. Fundamental is a regard for public opinion, a belief that in some way or another it should prevail. Even those who cynically humbug the people make a great show of deference to the populace. The basic doctrine goes further to include a sense of trusteeship for the people generally and an adherence to the basic doctrine that collective efforts should be dedicated to the promotion of mass gains rather than of narrow class advantage; elite elements tethered to narrow group interest have no slack for maneuver to accommodate themselves to mass aspirations. Ultimate expression of these faiths comes in the willingness to abide by the outcome of popular elections. The growth of leadership structures with beliefs including these broad articles of faith is probably accomplished only over a considerable period of time, and then only under auspicious circumstances.

If an elite is not to monopolize power and thereby to bring an end to democratic practices, its rules of the game must include restraints in the exploitation of public opinion. Dimly perceptible are rules of etiquette that limit the kinds of appeals to public opinion that may be properly made. If it is assumed that the public is manipulable at the hands of unscrupulous leadership (as it is under some conditions), the maintenance of a democratic order requires the inculcation in leadership elements of a taboo against appeals that would endanger the existence of democratic practices. Inflammation of the sentiments of a sector of the public disposed to exert the tyranny of an intolerant majority (or minority) would be a means of destruction of a democratic order. Or by the exploitation of latent differences and conflicts within the citizenry it may at times be possible to paralyze a regime as intense hatreds among classes of people come to dominate public affairs. Or by encouraging unrealistic expectations among the people a clique of politicians may rise to power, a position to be kept by repression as disillusionment sets in. In an experienced democracy such tactics may be "unfair" competition among members of the politically active class. In short, certain restraints on political competition help keep competition within tolerable limits. The observation of a few American political campaigns might lead one to the conclusion that there are no restraints on politicians as they attempt to humbug the people. Even so, admonitions ever recur against arousing class against class, against stirring the animosities of religious groups, and against demagoguery in its more extreme forms. American politicians manifest considerable restraint in this regard when they are tested against the standards of behavior of politicians of most of those regimes that have failed in the attempt to establish or maintain democratic practices. . . .

. . . Certain broad structural or organizational characteristics may need to be maintained among the activists of a democratic order if they are to perform their functions in the system. Fundamental is the absence of sufficient cohesion among the activists to unite them into a single group dedicated to the management of public affairs and public opinion. Solidification of the elite by definition forecloses opportunity for public choice among alternative governing groups and also destroys the mechanism for the unfettered expression of public opinion or of the opinions of the many subpublics. . . .

. . . Competitive segments of the leadership echelons normally have their roots in interests or opinion blocs within society. A degree of social diversity thus may be, if not a prerequisite, at least helpful in the construction of a leadership appropriate for a democratic regime. A series of independent social bases provide the foundations for a political elite difficult to bring to the state of unification that either prevents the rise of democratic processes or converts them into sham rituals. . . .

Another characteristic may be mentioned as one that, if not a prerequisite to government by public opinion, may profoundly affect the nature of a democratic order. This is the distribution through the social structure of those persons highly active in politics. By various analyses, none founded on completely satisfactory data, we have shown that in the United States the political activists—if we define the term broadly—are scattered through the socio-economic hierarchy. The upper-income and occupational groups, to be sure, contribute disproportionately; nevertheless, individuals of high political participation are sprinkled throughout the lesser occupational strata. Contrast the circumstances when the highly active political stratum coincides with the high socioeconomic stratum. Conceivably the winning of consent and the creation of a sense of political participation and of sharing in public affairs may be far simpler when political activists of some degree are spread through all social strata. . . .

Allied with these questions is the matter of access to the wider circles of political leadership and of the recruitment and indoctrination of these political activists. Relative ease of access to the arena of active politics may be a preventive of the rise of intransigent blocs of opinion managed by those denied participation in the regularized processes of politics. In a sense, ease of access is a necessary consequence of the existence of a somewhat fragmented stratum of political activists. . . .

This discussion in terms of leadership echelons, political activists, or elites falls painfully on the ears of democratic romantics. The mystique of democracy has in it no place for ruling classes. As perhaps with all powerful systems of faith, it is vague on the operating details. Yet by their nature governing systems, be they democratic or not, involve a division of social labor. Once that axiom is accepted, the comprehension of democratic practices requires a search for the peculiar characteristics of the political influentials in such an order, for the special conditions under which they work, and for the means by which the people keep them in check. The vagueness of the mystique of democracy is matched by the intricacy of its operating practices. If it is true that those who rule tend sooner or later to prove themselves enemies of the rights of man—and there is something to be said for the validity of this proposition—then any system that restrains that tendency however slightly can excite only awe. . . .

Analytically it is useful to conceive of the structure of a democratic order as consisting of the political activists and the mass of people. Yet this differentiation becomes deceptive unless it is kept in mind that the democratic activists consist of people arranged along a spectrum of political participation and involvement, ranging from those in the highest posts of official leadership to the amateurs who become sufficiently interested to try to round up a few votes for their favorite in the presidential campaign. . . . It is in the dynamics of the system, the interactions between these strata, that the import of public opinion in democratic orders becomes manifest. Between the activists and the mass there exists a system of communication and interplay so complex as to defy simple description; yet identification of a few major features of that system may aid in our construction of a general conception of democratic processes.

Opinion Dikes

In the interactions between democratic leadership echelons and the mass of people some insight comes from the conception of public opinion as a system of dikes which channel public action or which fix a range of discretion within which government may act or within which debate at official levels may proceed. This conception avoids the error of personifying "public opinion" as an entity that exercises initiative and in some way functions as an operating organism to translate its purposes into governmental action.

In one of their aspects the dikes of opinion have a substantive nature in that they define areas within which day-to-day debate about the course of specific action may occur. Some types of legislative proposals, given the content of general opinion, can scarcely expect to attract serious attention. They depart too far from the general understandings of what is proper. A scheme for public ownership of the automobile industry, for example, would probably be regarded as so far outside the area of legitimate public action that not even the industry would become greatly concerned. On the other hand, other types of questions arise within areas of what we have called permissive consensus. A widespread, if not a unanimous, sentiment prevails that supports action toward some general objective, such as the care of the ill or the mitigation of the economic hazards of the individual. Probably quite commonly mass opinion of a permissive character tends to develop in advance of governmental action in many areas of domestic policy. That opinion grows out of public discussion against the background of the modal aspirations and values of people generally. As it takes shape, the time becomes ripe for action that will be generally acceptable or may even arouse popular acclaim for its authors. . . .

The idea of public opinion as forming a system of dikes which channel action yields a different conception of the place of public opinion than does the notion of a government by public opinion as one in which by some mysterious means a referendum occurs on very major issue. In the former conception the articulation between government and opinion is relatively loose. Parallelism between action and opinion tends not to be precise in matters of detail; it prevails rather with respect to broad purpose. And in the correlation of purpose and action time lags may occur between the crystallization of a sense of mass purpose and its fulfillment in public action. Yet in the long run majority purpose and public action tend to be brought into harmony. . . .

The argument amounts essentially to the position that the masses do not corrupt themselves; if they are corrupt, they have been corrupted. If this hypothesis has a substantial strain of validity, the critical element for the health of a democratic order consists in the beliefs, standards, and competence of those who constitute the influentials, the opinion-leaders, the political activists in the order. That group, as has been made plain, refuses to define itself with great clarity in the American system; yet analysis after analysis points to its existence. If a democracy tends toward indecision, decay, and disaster, the responsibility rests here, not in the mass of the people.

57

THOMAS CRONIN

From *Direct Democracy*

Although the United States is a representative—republican—system of government, elements of direct democracy have been introduced on the state and local levels over time, especially in the early twentieth century during the Progressive era. Initiative, referendum, and recall give citizens an immediate and direct voice in their government, beyond just electing officials. Professor Thomas Cronin explains these instruments of direct democracy and cites California's 1978 tax-cutting Proposition 13 as a leading example of an important statewide ballot question. Controversy swirls over the wisdom of such exercises in direct democracy. Cronin weighs the advantages against the potential problems of allowing voters to have a direct say in policy-making. His conclusion is that initiative, referendum, and recall will neither destroy American government nor save it. Yet in the twenty-first century, with voters' openly-expressed distrust of public officials, direct democracy will surely become more and more a part of the state and local political scene.

———

FOR ABOUT A hundred years Americans have been saying that voting occasionally for public officials is not enough. Political reformers contend that more democracy is needed and that the American people are mature enough and deserve the right to vote on critical issues facing their states and the nation. During the twentieth century, American voters in many parts of the country have indeed won the right to write new laws and repeal old ones through the initiative and referendum. They have also thrown hundreds of state and local officials out of office in recall elections.

Although the framers of the Constitution deliberately designed a republic, or indirect democracy, the practice of direct democracy and the debate over its desirability are as old as English settlements in America. Public debate and popular voting on issues go back to early seventeenth-century town assemblies and persist today in New England town meetings.

Populist democracy in America has produced conspicuous assets and conspicuous liabilities. It has won the support and admiration of many enthusiasts, yet it is also fraught with disturbing implications. Its most important contributions came early in this century in the form of the initiative, referendum, and recall, as a reaction to corrupt and unresponsive state legislatures throughout the country. Most of us would not recognize what then passed for representative government. "Bills that the machine and its backers do not desire are smothered in committee; measures which they do desire are brought out and hurried through their passage," said Governor Woodrow Wilson at the time. "It happens again and again that great groups of such bills are rushed through in the hurried hours that mark the close of the legislative sessions, when everyone is withheld from vigilance by fatigue and when it is possible to do secret things." The threat, if not the reality, of the initiative, referendum, and recall helped to encourage a more responsible, civic-minded breed of state legislator. These measures were not intended to subvert or alter the basic character of American government. "Their intention," as Wilson saw it, was "to restore, not to destroy, representative government."

The *initiative* allows voters to propose a legislative measure (statutory initiative) or a constitutional amendment (constitutional initiative) by filing a petition bearing a required number of valid citizen signatures.

The *referendum* refers a proposed or existing law or statute to voters for their approval or rejection. Some state constitutions require referenda; in other states, the legislature may decide to refer a measure to the voters. Measures referred by legislatures (statutes, constitutional amendments, bonds, or advisory questions) are the most common ballot propositions. A *popular* or *petition referendum* (a less frequently used device) refers an already enacted measure to the voters before it can go into effect. States allowing the petition referendum require a minimum number of valid citizen signatures within a specified time. There is confusion about the difference between the initiative and referendum because *referendum* is frequently used in a casual or generic way to describe all ballot measures.

The *recall* allows voters to remove or discharge a public official from office by filing a petition bearing a specified number of valid signatures demanding a vote on the official's continued tenure in office. Recall procedures typically require that the petition be signed by 25 percent of those who voted in the last election, after which a special election is almost always required. The recall differs from impeachment in that the people, not the legislature, initiate the election and determine the outcome with their votes. It is a purely political and not even a semijudicial process.

American voters today admire and respect the virtues of representative government, yet most of them also yearn for an even greater voice in how their laws are made. They understand the defects of both representative and direct democracy and prefer, on balance, to have a mixture of the two. Sensible or sound democracy is their aspiration.

Although Americans cannot cast votes on critical national issues, voters in twenty-six states, the District of Columbia, and hundreds of localities do have the right to put measures on their ballots. Legislatures can also refer measures to the public for a general vote. And constitutional changes in every state except Delaware must be approved by voters before becoming law. Voters in fifteen states and the District of Columbia can also recall elected state officials, and thirty-six states permit the recall of various local officials.

When Americans think of their right to vote, they think primarily of their right to nominate and elect legislators, members of school boards and of city councils, and the American president. Yet California's famous Proposition 13 in June 1978 focused nationwide attention on the public's right to participate in controversial tax decision making, as Californians voted to cut their property taxes by at least half. More voters participated in this issue contest than in the same day's gubernatorial primaries.

California's Proposition 13 had two additional effects. It triggered similar tax-slashing measures (both as bills and as direct legislation by the people) in numerous other states, and it encouraged conservative interest groups to use the initiative and referendum processes to achieve some of their goals. In the past decade conservative interests have placed on state and local ballots scores of measures favoring the death penalty, victims' rights, English-only regulations, and prayer in schools, and opposing taxation or spending, pornography, abortion, and homosexuality. Several states have regularly conducted referenda on issues ranging from a nuclear freeze to seat-belt laws. Citizens are now voting on hundreds of initiatives and referenda at state and local levels. . . .

Skeptics, however, worry about tyranny by the majority and fear voters are seldom well enough informed to cast votes on complicated, technical national laws. People also worry, and justifiably, about the way well-financed special interest groups might use these procedures. Corruption at the state level is much less common today than it was early in the century, but special interests are surely just as involved as ever. The power of campaign contributions is clear. The advantages to those who can afford campaign and political consultants, direct mail firms, and widespread television and media appeals are very real. Although in theory Americans are politically equal, in practice there remain enormous disparities in individuals' and groups' capacities to influence the direction of government. And although the direct democracy devices of the initiative, referendum, and recall type are widely available, the evidence suggests it is generally the organized interests that can afford to put them to use. The idealistic notion that populist democracy devices can make every citizen a citizen-legislator and move us closer to political and egalitarian democracy is plainly an unrealized aspiration.

The initiative, referendum, and recall were born in an era of real grievances. They made for a different kind of democracy in those areas that permitted them. At the very least, they signaled the unacceptability of some of the most corrupt and irresponsible political practices of that earlier era. It is fashionable among political analysts today to say that although they have rarely lived up to their promises, neither have they resulted in the dire outcomes feared by critics. Yet they have had both good and questionable consequences. . . .

By examining direct democracy practices we can learn about the strengths and weaknesses of a neglected aspect of American politics, as well as the workings of representative democracy. We seek to understand it so we can improve it, and to improve it so it can better supplement rather than replace our institutions of representative government. . . .

A populist impulse, incorporating notions of "power to the people" and skepticism about the system has always existed in America. Americans seldom abide quietly the failings and deficiencies of capitalism, the welfare state, or the political decision rules by which we live. We are, as historian Richard Hofstadter wrote, "forever restlessly pitting ourselves against them, demanding changes, improvements, remedies." Demand for more democracy occurs when there is growing distrust of legislative bodies and when there is a growing suspicion that privileged interests exert far greater influences on the typical politician than does the common voter.

Direct democracy, especially as embodied in the referendum, initiative, and recall, is sometimes viewed as a typically American political response to perceived abuses of the public trust. Voters periodically become frustrated with taxes, regulations, inefficiency in government programs, the inequalities or injustices of the system, the arms race, environmental hazards, and countless other irritations. This frustration arises in part because more public policy decisions are now made in distant capitals, by remote agencies or private yet unaccountable entities—such as regulatory bodies, the Federal Reserve Board, foreign governments, multinational alliances, or foreign trading combines—instead of at the local or county level as once was the case, or as perhaps we like to remember.

Champions of populist democracy claim many benefits will accrue from their reforms. Here are some:

• Citizen initiatives will promote government responsiveness and accountability. If officials ignore the voice of the people, the people will have an available means to make needed law.

• Initiatives are freer from special interest domination than the legislative branches of most states, and so provide a desirable safeguard that can be called into use when legislators are corrupt, irresponsible, or dominated by privileged special interests.

• The initiative and referendum will produce open, educational debate on critical issues that otherwise might be inadequately discussed.

• Referendum, initiative, and recall are nonviolent means of political participation that fulfill a citizen's right to petition the government for redress of grievances.

• Direct democracy increases voter interest and election-day turnout. Perhaps, too, giving the citizen more of a role in governmental processes might lessen alienation and apathy.

• Finally (although this hardly exhausts the claims), citizen initiatives are needed because legislators often evade the tough issues. Fearing to be ahead of their time, they frequently adopt a zero-risk mentality. Concern with staying in office often makes them timid and perhaps too wedded to the status quo. One result is that controversial social issues frequently have to be resolved in the judicial branch. But who elected the judges?

For every claim put forward on behalf of direct democracy, however, there is an almost equally compelling criticism. Many opponents believe the ordinary citizen usually is not well enough informed about complicated matters to arrive at sound public policy judgments. They also fear the influence of slick television advertisements or bumper sticker messages.

Some critics of direct democracy contend the best way to restore faith in representative institutions is to find better people to run for office. They prefer the deliberations and the collective judgment of elected representatives who have the time to study complicated public policy matters, matters that should be decided within the give-and-take process of politics. That process, they say, takes better account of civil liberties.

Critics also contend that in normal times initiative and referendum voter turnout is often a small proportion of the general population and so the results are unduly influenced by special interests: big money will win eight out of ten times.

A paradox runs throughout this debate. As the United States has aged, we have extended the suffrage in an impressive way. The older the country, the more we have preached the gospel of civic participation. Yet we also have experienced centralization of power in the national government and the development of the professional politician. The citizen-politician has become an endangered species.

Representative government is always in the process of development and decay. Its fortunes rise and fall depending upon various factors, not least the quality of people involved and the resources devoted to making it work effectively. When the slumps come, proposals that would reform and change the character of representative government soon follow. Direct democracy notions have never been entirely foreign to our country— countless proponents from Benjamin Franklin to Jesse Jackson, Jack Kemp, and Richard Gephardt have urged us to listen more to the common citizen. . . .

The American experience with direct democracy has fulfilled neither the dreams and expectations of its proponents nor the fears of its opponents.

The initiative and referendum have not undermined or weakened representative government. The initiative, referendum, and recall have been no more of a threat to the representative principle than has judicial review or the executive veto. Tools of neither the "lunatic fringe" nor the rich, direct democracy devices have become a permanent feature of American politics, especially in the West.

The initiative, referendum, and recall have not been used as often as their advocates would have wished, in part because state legislatures have steadily improved. Better-educated members, more-professional staff, better media coverage of legislative proceedings, and longer sessions have transformed the legislative process at the state level, mostly for the better. Interest groups once denied access to secret sessions now regularly attend, testify, and participate in a variety of ways in the legislative process. Although individuals and some groups remain frustrated, the level and intensity of that frustration appear to be lower than the discontent that prompted the popular democracy movements around the turn of the century.

Still, hundreds of measures have found their way onto ballots in states across the country, and 35 to 40 percent of the more than 1,500 citizen-initiated ballot measures considered since 1904 have won voter approval. About half of these have been on our ballots since World War II. A few thousand legislatively referred measures have also been placed on the ballot, and at least 60 percent of these regularly win voter approval. Popular, or petition, referenda, placed on the ballot by citizens seeking a voter veto of laws already passed by state legislatures, have been used infrequently. . . . Recall, used mainly at the local and county level, is seldom used against state officials. The marvel is that all these devices of popular democracy, so vulnerable to apathy, ignorance, and prejudice, not only have worked but also have generally been used in a reasonable and constructive manner. Voters have been cautious and have almost always rejected extreme proposals. Most studies suggest that voters, despite the complexity of measures and the deceptions of some campaigns, exercise shrewd judgment, and most students of direct democracy believe most American voters take this responsibility seriously. Just as in candidate campaigns, when they give the benefit of the doubt to the incumbent and the burden of proof is on the challenger to give reasons why he or she should be voted into office, so in issue elections the voter needs to be persuaded that change is needed. In the absence of a convincing case that change is better, the electorate traditionally sticks with the status quo.

Few radical measures pass. Few measures that are discriminatory or would have diminished the rights of minorities win voter approval, and most of the exceptions are ruled unconstitutional by the courts. On balance, the voters at large are no more prone to be small-minded, racist, or sexist than are legislators or courts.

A case can be made that elected officials are more tolerant, more educated, and more sophisticated than the average voter. "Learning the arguments for freedom and tolerance formulated by notables such as Jefferson, Madison, Mill, or the more libertarian justices of the Supreme Court is no simple task," one study concludes. "Many of those arguments are subtle, esoteric, and difficult to grasp. Intelligence, awareness, and education are required to appreciate them fully." Yet on the occasional issues affecting civil liberties and civil rights that have come to the ballot, voters have generally acted in an enlightened way. This is in part the case because enlightened elites help shape public opinion on such occasions through endorsements, news editorials, talk-show discussions, public debates, and legislative and executive commentary. Further, those voting on state and local ballot measures are usually among the top 30 or 40 percent in educational and information levels.

The civic and educational value of direct democracy upon the electorate has been significant, but this aspect of the promise of direct democracy was plainly overstated from the start. Most voters make up their minds on ballot issues or recall elections in the last few days, or even hours, before they vote. The technical and ambiguous language of many of these measures is still an invitation to confusion, and about a quarter of those voting in these elections tell pollsters they could have used more information in making their decisions on these types of election choices.

Like any other democratic institution, the initiative, referendum, and recall have their shortcomings. Voters are sometimes confused. On occasion an ill-considered or undesirable measure wins approval. Large, organized groups and those who can raise vast sums of money are in a better position either to win, or especially to block, approval of ballot measures. Sometimes a recall campaign is mounted for unfair reasons, and recall campaigns can stir up unnecessary and undesirable conflict in a community. Most of these criticisms can also be leveled at our more traditional institutions. Courts sometimes err, as in the *Dred Scott* decision and in *Plessy v. Ferguson* or *Korematsu*. Presidents surely make mistakes (FDR's attempt to pack the Supreme Court, 1937; Kennedy's Bay of Pigs fiasco, 1961; Nixon's involvement in the Watergate break-in and subsequent coverup, 1972–1974; Reagan's involvement in the Iran-contra arms deal, 1986). And legislatures not only make mistakes about policy from time to time but wind up spending nearly a third of their time amending, changing, and correcting past legislation that proved inadequate or wrong. In short, we pay a price for believing in and practicing democracy—whatever the form.

Whatever the shortcomings of direct democracy, and there are several, they do not justify the elimination of the populist devices from those state constitutions permitting them. Moreover, any suggestion to repeal the initiative, referendum, and recall would be defeated by the voters. Public opinion strongly supports retaining these devices where they are allowed. . . .

In sum, direct democracy devices have not been a cure-all for most political, social, or economic ills, yet they have been an occasional remedy, and generally a moderate remedy, for legislative lethargy and the misuse and nonuse of legislative power. It was long feared that these devices would dull legislators' sense of responsibility without in fact quickening the people to the exercise of any real control in public affairs. Little evidence exists for those fears today. When popular demands for reasonable change are repeatedly ignored by elected officials and when legislators or other officials ignore valid interests and criticism, the initiative, referendum, and recall can be a means by which the people may protect themselves in the grand tradition of self-government.

58

LAWRENCE JACOBS
ROBERT SHAPIRO

From *Politicians Don't Pander*

Lawrence Jacobs and Robert Shapiro challenge the premise popular in the 1990s that politicians cater to what the public wants: a finger in the wind of public opinion makes policy. No, they find, politicians don't pander. In fact, the authors suggest that the opposite is true. More often, politicians ignore what the mainstream of the public wants, attempting instead to create a version of public opinion that accords with the politicians' views. Media coverage aids in this upside down relationship between the people and their representatives. The end result is that the American people do not believe that the government reflects their views; they do not trust their leaders. To Jacobs and Shapiro, the question of how much public opinion truly shapes policy lies at the heart of American democracy.

———

THE WAY CONGRESS HANDLED the impeachment of President Bill Clinton revealed a lot about American politics. Commentators and the American public were visibly struck by the unyielding drive of congressional Republicans to remove Clinton from office in the face of clear public opposition. The Republicans' disregard for the preferences of the great majority of Americans contradicted perhaps the most widely accepted presumption about politics—that politicians slavishly follow public opinion.

There was little ambiguity about where Americans stood on Clinton's personal behavior and impeachment. The avalanche of opinion polls during 1998 and early 1999 showed that super-majorities of nearly two-thirds of Americans condemned the president's personal misdeeds, but about the same number approved his job performance, opposed his impeachment and removal from office, and favored a legislative censure as an appropriate alternative punishment.

Despite Americans' strong and unchanging opinions, congressional Republicans defied the public at almost every turn. Beginning in the fall of 1998, the Republican-led House of Representatives initiated impeachment proceedings; its Judiciary Committee reported impeachment articles; and it passed two articles of impeachment on the House floor. Neither the House nor the Senate allowed a vote on the option supported by the public—censure. For all the civility in the Senate trial of the president on the House-passed articles of impeachment, the Republicans' pursuit of Clinton was checked not by a sudden attentiveness to public opinion but rather by the constitutional requirement of a two-thirds vote and the bipartisan support that this demanded.

The impeachment spectacle reveals one of the most important developments in contemporary American politics—the widening gulf between politicians' policy decisions and the preferences of the American people toward specific issues. The impeachment of Clinton can be added to the long list of policies that failed to mirror public opinion: campaign finance reform, tobacco legislation, Clinton's proposals in his first budget for an energy levy and a high tax on Social Security benefits (despite his campaign promises to cut middle-class taxes), the North American Free Trade Agreement (at its outset), U.S. intervention in Bosnia, as well as House Republican proposals after the 1994 elections for a "revolution" in policies toward the environment, education, Medicare, and other issues.

Recent research . . . provides evidence that this list is not a quirk of recent political developments but part of a trend of declining responsiveness to the public's policy preferences. The conventional wisdom that politicians habitually respond to public opinion when making major policy decisions is wrong. . . .

The Republicans' handling of impeachment fits into a larger pattern in contemporary American politics. . . .

. . . First, Republicans disregarded public opinion on impeachment because their political goals of attracting a majority of voters was offset by their policy goals of enacting legislation that politicians and their supporters favored. The ideological polarization of congressional Republicans and Democrats since the mid-1970s, the greater institutional independence of individual lawmakers, and other factors have raised the political benefits of pursuing policy goals that they and their party's activists desire. Responding to public opinion at the expense of policy goals entailed compromising their own philosophical convictions and risked alienating ideologically extreme party activists and other supporters who volunteer and contribute money to their primary and general election campaigns. Only the heat of an imminent presidential election and the elevated attention that average voters devote to it motivate contemporary politicians to respond to public opinion and absorb the costs of compromising their policy goals.

Indeed, the Republicans' relentless pursuit of impeachment was largely driven by the priority that the domineering conservative wing of the party attached to their policy goal (removing Clinton) over their political goals (appealing to a majority of Americans). Moderate Republicans could not ignore the risk of opposing impeachment—it could lead to a challenge in the next primary election and diminished campaign contributions.

Our second point is that politicians pursue a strategy of *crafted talk* to change public opinion in order to offset the potential political costs of not following the preferences of average voters. Politicians track public opinion not to make policy but rather to determine how to craft their public presentations and win public support for the policies they and their supporters favor. Politicians want the best of both worlds: to enact their preferred policies and to be reelected.

While politicians devote their resources to changing public opinion, their actual influence is a more complex story. Politicians themselves attempt to change public opinion not by directly persuading the public on the merits of their policy choices but by "priming" public opinion: they "stay on message" to highlight standards or considerations for the public to use in evaluating policy proposals. Republicans, for example, emphasized "big government" to prompt the public to think about its uneasiness about government. Politicians' efforts to sway the public are most likely to influence the perceptions, understandings, and evaluations of specific policy proposals such as Republican proposals in 1995 to significantly reduce spending on Medicare to fund a tax cut. But even here, politicians' messages promoting their policy proposals often provoke new or competing messages from their political opponents and the press that complicate or stymie their efforts to move public opinion. In addition, efforts to influence the public's evaluations of specific proposals are unlikely to affect people's values and fundamental preferences (such as those underlying support for Medicare, Social Security, and other well-established programs). We distinguish, then, between political leaders' attempts to alter the public's perceptions, evaluations, and choices concerning very specific proposals (which are susceptible but not certain to change) and Americans' values and long-term preferences (which tend to be stable and particularly resistant to short-term manipulation). In short, politicians' confidence in their ability to move public opinion by crafting their statements and actions boosts their willingness to discount majority opinion; but the reality is that efforts to change public opinion are difficult and are often most successful when deployed against major new policy proposals by the opposition, which has the more modest task of increasing the public's uncertainty and anxiety to avoid risk.

Politicians respond to public opinion, then, but in two quite different ways. In one, politicians assemble information on public opinion to design government policy. This is usually equated with "pandering," and this is most evident during the relatively short period when presidential elections are imminent. The use of public opinion research here, however, raises a troubling question: why has the derogatory term "pander" been pinned on politicians who respond to public opinion? The answer is revealing: the term is deliberately deployed by politicians, pundits, and other elites to belittle government responsiveness to public opinion and reflects a long-standing fear, uneasiness, and hostility among elites toward popular consent and influence over the affairs of government. It is surely odd in a democracy to consider responsiveness to public opinion as disreputable. We challenge the stigmatizing use of the term "pandering" and adopt the neutral concept of "political responsiveness." We suggest that the public's preferences offer both broad directions to policymakers (e.g., establish universal health insurance) and some specific instructions (e.g., rely on an employer mandate for financing reform). In general, policymakers should follow these preferences.

Politicians respond to public opinion in a second manner—they use research on public opinion to pinpoint the most alluring words, symbols, and arguments in an attempt to move public opinion to support their desired policies. Public opinion research is used by politicians to manipulate public opinion, that is, to move Americans to "hold opinions that they would not hold if aware of the best available information and analysis. . . . " Their objective is to *simulate responsiveness*. Their words and presentations are crafted to change public opinion and create the *appearance* of responsiveness as they pursue their desired policy goals. Intent on lowering the potential electoral costs of subordinating voters' preferences to their policy goals, politicians use polls and focus groups not to move their positions closer to the public's but just the opposite: to find the most effective means *to move public opinion closer to their own desired policies.*

Political consultants as diverse as Republican pollster Frank Luntz and Clinton pollster Dick Morris readily confess that legislators and the White House "don't use a poll to reshape a program, but to reshape your argumentation for the program so that the public supports it." Indeed, Republicans' dogged pursuit of impeachment was premised on the assumption that poll-honed presentations would ultimately win public support for their actions. We suggest that this kind of overconfidence in the power of crafted talk to move public opinion explains the political overreaching and failure that was vividly displayed by Clinton's health reform effort during the 1993–94 period and the Republicans' campaign for their policy objectives beginning with their "Contract with America" during 1995–96. Crafted talk has been more effective in opposing rather than promoting policy initiatives partly because the news media represent and magnify disagreement but also because politicians' overconfidence in crafted talk has prompted them to promote policy goals that do not enjoy the support of most Americans or moderate legislators.

Our argument flips the widespread image of politicians as "pandering" to public opinion on its head. Public opinion is not propelling policy decisions as it did in the past. Instead, politicians' own policy goals are increasingly driving major policy decisions and public opinion research, which is used to identify the language, symbols, and arguments to "win" public support for their policy objectives. Responsiveness to public opinion and manipulation of public opinion are not mutually exclusive: politicians manipulate public opinion by tracking public thinking to select the actions and words that resonate with the public.

Our third point is that politicians' muted responsiveness to public opinion and crafting of their words and actions has a profound impact on the mass media and on public opinion itself. In contrast to others who emphasize the nearly unlimited independence and power of the mass media, we argue that press coverage of national politics has been driven by the polarization of politicians and their reliance on crafting their words and deeds. The press focuses on political conflict and strategy because these are visible and genuine features of contemporary American politics. The combination of politicians' staged displays and the media's scrutiny of the motives behind them produced public distrust and fear of major government reform efforts. We do not treat policymaking, media coverage, and public opinion as parts that can be studied one at a time; rather, we study their dynamic configurations and processes of interdependence. Democratic governance and the process of public communications are inseparably linked. . . .

We argue that politicians' pursuits of policy goals have created a reinforcing spiral or cycle that encompasses media coverage and public opinion. It is characterized by three features. First, the polarization of Washington political elites and their strategies to manipulate the media and gain public support have prompted the press to increasingly emphasize or frame its coverage in terms of political conflict and strategy at the expense of the substance of policy issues and problems. Although news reports largely represent the genuine contours of American politics, the media's organizational, financial, and professional incentives prompt them to exaggerate the degree of conflict in order to produce simple, captivating stories for their audiences.

Second, the increased political polarization and politicians' strategy of crafting what they say and do (as conveyed through press coverage) raise the probability of both changes in public understandings and evaluations of specific policy proposals, and public perceptions that proposals for policy change make uncertain or threaten the personal well-being of individual Americans. The presence of a vocal political opposition, combined with the media's attentiveness to the ensuing conflict and the public's skittishness about change, often prevents reformers from changing public opinion as they intended.

Third, the cycle closes as the media's coverage and the public's reaction that was initially sparked by politicians' actions feed back into the political arena. How politicians appraise the media's coverage of their initial actions affects their future strategy and behavior. Politicians latch on to any evidence of changes in public opinion that are favorable to their positions in order to justify their policies and to increase the electoral risk of their rivals for opposing them. . . .

The public's perception that government officials do not listen to or care much about their views accelerated in the 1970s and peaked in the 1990s. Paralleling this trend, polls by Gallup, the Pew Center, and the Center on Policy Attitudes during the second half of the 1990s consistently found that large majorities doubted the founding premise of American government—popular sovereignty and consent of the governed. Over 60 percent of the public (according to responses to a diverse set of survey questions) believed that elected officials in Washington and members of Congress "lose touch" or are "out of touch with average Americans" and do not understand what "most Americans" or "people like you" think. . . .

Increasing political responsiveness to centrist opinion would not produce neutral changes in government policy but ones that can have profound political implications. Politicians who respond to public opinion would enact policies that defied today's calcified political categories of liberal and conservative. The public, on balance, is more conservative on social issues than Democrats; it is less liberal, for instance, toward homosexuality and criminal behavior. On the other hand, the public is supportive of proposals for political reforms and progressive economic, health, and environmental programs, which Republicans reject. More responsive government might well pursue more conservative social policies and more progressive economic and political ones.

The most important implication of raising responsiveness is to reaffirm the spirit and content of democracy in America. The continued slippage in government responsiveness threatens the foundation of our democratic order and the meaning of rule by and for the people. Whether *democratic* government survives is not foreordained or guaranteed; it is the challenge of each generation to be vigilant and reassert its importance. Insisting that politicians follow the popular will and allow citizens to engage in unfettered public debate is central to that struggle.

PART ELEVEN

Interest Groups

59

ALEXIS DE TOCQUEVILLE

From *Democracy in America*

Interest-group politics remains a big part of U.S. government today—for good and bad. But it is not as new a part as it may seem. Young French aristocrat Alexis de Tocqueville, visiting in 1831, observed how naturally Americans formed "associations." Just like today, groups were formed "to promote the public safety, commerce, industry, morality, and religion." In a country that emphasized individuality, Tocqueville felt, group allegiances gave people the power to work together to reach shared goals. American interest groups were out in the open, meeting freely to advance their viewpoints. Tocqueville, whose earlier selection from Democracy in America *opened this book, placed great faith in interest groups as a way that minorities could protect themselves from "tyranny of the majority." Today, one wonders how he would suggest that the nation protect itself from the tyranny of interest groups.*

———

IN NO COUNTRY IN the world has the principle of association been more successfully used, or more unsparingly applied to a multitude of different objects, than in America. Besides the permanent associations, which are established by law under the names of townships, cities, and counties, a vast number of others are formed and maintained by the agency of private individuals.

The citizen of the United States is taught from his earliest infancy to rely upon his own exertions, in order to resist the evils and the difficulties of life; he looks upon the social authority with an eye of mistrust and anxiety, and he only claims its assistance when he is quite unable to shift without it. This habit may even be traced in the schools of the rising generation, where the children in their games are wont to submit to rules which they have themselves established, and to punish misdemeanors which they have themselves defined. The same spirit pervades every act of social life. If a stoppage occurs in a thoroughfare, and the circulation of the public is hindered, the neighbors immediately constitute a deliberative body; and this extemporaneous assembly gives rise to an executive power, which remedies the inconvenience, before anybody has thought of recurring to an authority superior to that of the persons immediately concerned. If the public pleasures are concerned, an association is formed to provide for the splendor and the regularity of the entertainment. Societies are formed to resist enemies which are exclusively of a moral nature, and to diminish the vice of intemperance: in the United States associations are established to promote public order, commerce, industry, morality, and religion, for there is no end which the human will seconded by the collective exertions of individuals, despairs of attaining. . . .

An association consists simply in the public assent which a number of individuals give to certain doctrines; and in the engagement which they contract to promote the spread of those doctrines by their exertions. The right of associating with such views is very analogous to the liberty of unlicensed writing; but societies thus formed possess more authority than the press. When an opinion is represented by a society, it necessarily assumes a more exact and explicit form. It numbers its partisans, and compromises their welfare in its cause: they, on the other hand, become acquainted with each other, and their zeal is increased by their number. An association unites the efforts of minds which have a tendency to diverge in one single channel, and urges them vigorously towards the one single end which it points out.

The second degree in the right of association is the power of meeting. When an association is allowed to establish centres of action at certain important points in the country, its activity is increased, and its influence extended. Men have the opportunity of seeing each other; means of execution are more readily combined; and opinions are maintained with a warmth and energy which written language cannot approach.

Lastly, in the exercise of the right of political association, there is a third degree: the partisans of an opinion may unite in electoral bodies, and choose delegates to represent them in a central assembly. This is, properly speaking, the application of the representative system to a party.

Thus, in the first instance, a society is formed between individuals professing the same opinion, and the tie which keeps it together is of a purely intellectual nature: in the second case, small assemblies are formed which only represent a faction of the party. Lastly, in the third case, they constitute a separate nation in the midst of the nation, a government within the Government. . . .

It cannot be denied that the unrestrained liberty of association for political purposes is the privilege which a people is longest in learning how to exercise. If it does not throw the nation into anarchy, it perpetually augments the chances of that calamity. On one point, however, this perilous liberty offers a security against dangers of another kind; in countries where associations are free, secret societies are unknown. In America, there are numerous factions, but no conspiracies. . . .

The most natural privilege of man, next to the right of acting for himself, is that of combining his exertions with those of his fellow-creatures, and of acting in common with them. I am therefore led to conclude that the right of association is almost as inalienable as the right of personal liberty. . . .

60

E. E. SCHATTSCHNEIDER

From *The Semisovereign People*

The late 1950s and early 1960s was a time when political scientists placed their focus on the interest group theory of American politics. Although hardly a new idea, interest group politics was studied intensely, sometimes to be idealized as the perfect model of government and other times critiqued as the downfall of democracy. Scholar E. E. Schattschneider's much-cited book explored the "pressure system" in American politics, dominated by "organized" (as opposed to informal), "special-interest" (not public-interest) groups. Schattschneider's conclusion was that "the pressure system has an upper-class bias." Decades later, political scientists might not use the exact same language as Schattschneider, who relied on the concept of class in his analysis. Today, vastly different degrees of organization, financial resources, and intensity separate interest group claimants in the competition for getting their issues heard by the government.

MORE THAN any other system American politics provides the raw materials for testing the organizational assumptions of two contrasting kinds of politics, *pressure politics* and *party politics*. The concepts that underlie these forms of politics constitute the raw stuff of a general theory of political action. The basic issue between the two patterns of organization is one of size and scope of conflict; pressure groups are small-scale organizations while political parties are very large-scale organizations. One need not be surprised, therefore, that the partisans of large-scale and small-scale organizations differ passionately, because the outcome of the political game depends on the scale on which it is played.

To understand the controversy about the scale of political organization it is necessary first to take a look at some theories about interest-group politics. Pressure groups have played a remarkable role in American politics, but they have played an even more remarkable role in American political theory. Considering the political condition of the country in the first third of the twentieth century, it was probably inevitable that the discussion of special interest pressure groups should lead to development of "group" theories of politics in which an attempt is made to explain everything in terms of group activity, i.e., an attempt to formulate a universal group theory. Since one of the best ways to test an idea is to ride it into the ground, political theory has unquestionably been improved by the heroic attempt to create a political universe revolving about the group. Now that we have a number of drastic statements of the group theory of politics pushed to a great extreme, we ought to be able to see what the limitations of the idea are. . . .

One difficulty running through the literature of the subject results from the attempt to explain *everything* in terms of the group theory. On general grounds it would be remarkable indeed if a single hypothesis explained everything about so complex a subject as American politics. Other difficulties have grown out of the fact that group concepts have been stated in terms so universal that the subject seems to have no shape or form.

The question is: Are pressure groups the universal basic ingredient of all political situations, and do they explain everything? To answer this question it is necessary to review a bit of rudimentary political theory.

Two modest reservations might be made merely to test the group dogma. We might clarify our ideas if (1) we explore more fully the possibility of making a distinction between public interest groups and special-interest groups and (2) if we distinguished between organized and unorganized groups. . . .

As a matter of fact, the distinction between *public* and *private* interests is a thoroughly respectable one; it is one of the oldest known to political theory. In the literature of the subject the public interest refers to general or common interests shared by all or by substantially all members of the community. Presumably no community exists unless there is some kind of community of interests, just as there is no nation without some notion of national interests. If it is really impossible to distinguish between private and public interests the group theorists have produced a revolution in political thought so great that it is impossible to foresee its consequences. For this reason the distinction ought to be explored with great care.

At a time when nationalism is described as one of the most dynamic forces in the world, it should not be difficult to understand that national interests actually do exist. It is necessary only to consider the proportion of the American budget devoted to national defense to realize that the common interest in national survival is a great one. Measured in dollars this interest is one of the biggest things in the world. Moreover, it is difficult to describe this interest as special. The diet on which the American leviathan feeds is something more than a jungle of disparate special interests. In the literature of democratic theory the body of common agreement found in the community is known as the "consensus" without which it is believed that no democratic system can survive.

The reality of the common interest is suggested by demonstrated capacity of the community to survive. There must be something that holds people together.

In contrast with the common interests are the special interests. The implication of this term is that these are interests shared by only a few people or a fraction of the community; they *exclude* others and may be *adverse* to them. A special interest is exclusive in about the same way as private property is exclusive. In a complex society it is not surprising that there are some interests that are shared by all or substantially all members of the community and some interests that are not shared so widely. The distinction is useful precisely because conflicting claims are made by people about the nature of their interests in controversial matters. . . .

Is it possible to distinguish between the "interests" of the members of the National Association of Manufacturers and the members of the American League to Abolish Capital Punishment? The facts in the two cases are not identical. First, *the members of the A.L.A.C.P. obviously do not expect to be hanged.* The membership of the A.L.A.C.P. is not restricted to persons under indictment for murder or in jeopardy of the extreme penalty. *Anybody* can join A.L.A.C.P. Its members oppose capital punishment although they are not personally likely to benefit by the policy they advocate. The inference is therefore that the interest of the A.L.A.C.P. is not adverse, exclusive or special. It is not like the interest of the Petroleum Institute in depletion allowances. . . .

We can now examine the second distinction, the distinction between organized and unorganized groups. The question here is not whether the distinction can be made but whether or not it is worth making. Organization has been described as "merely a stage or degree of interaction" in the development of a group.

The proposition is a good one, but what conclusions do we draw from it? We do not dispose of the matter by calling the distinction between organized and unorganized groups a "mere" difference of degree because some of the greatest differences in the world are differences of degree. As far as special-interest politics is concerned the implication to be avoided is that a few workmen who habitually stop at a corner saloon for a glass

E. E. SCHATTSCHNEIDER

of beer are essentially the same as the United States Army because the difference between them is merely one of degree. At this point we have a distinction that makes a difference. . . .

If we are able, therefore, to distinguish between public and private interests and between organized and unorganized groups we have marked out the major boundaries of the subject; *we have given the subject shape and scope*. We are now in a position to attempt to define the area we want to explore. Having cut the pie into four pieces, we can now appropriate the piece we want and leave the rest to someone else. For a multitude of reasons *the most likely field of study is that of the organized, special-interest groups*. The advantage of concentrating on organized groups is that they are known, identifiable and recognizable. The advantage of concentrating on special-interest groups is that they have one important characteristic in common: they are all exclusive. This piece of the pie (the organized special-interest groups) we shall call the *pressure system*. The pressure system has boundaries we can define; we can fix its scope and make an attempt to estimate its bias. . . .

The organized groups listed in the various directories (such as *National Associations of the United States*, published at intervals by the United States Department of Commerce) and specialty yearbooks, registers, etc., and the *Lobby Index*, published by the United States House of Representatives, probably include the bulk of the organizations in the pressure system. All compilations are incomplete, but these are extensive enough to provide us with some basis for estimating the scope of the system. . . .

When lists of these organizations are examined, the fact that strikes the student most forcibly is that *the system is very small*. The range of organized, identifiable, known groups is amazingly narrow; there is nothing remotely universal about it. There is a tendency on the part of the publishers of directories of associations to place an undue emphasis on business organizations, an emphasis that is almost inevitable because the business community is by a wide margin the most highly organized segment of society. Publishers doubtless tend also to reflect public demand for information. Nevertheless, the dominance of business groups in the pressure system is so marked that it probably cannot be explained away as an accident of the publishing industry. . . .

The business or upper-class bias of the pressure system shows up everywhere. Businessmen are four or five times as likely to write to their congressmen as manual laborers are. College graduates are far more apt to write to their congressmen than people in the lowest educational category are. . . .

Broadly, the pressure system has an upper-class bias. There is overwhelming evidence that participation in voluntary organizations is related to upper social and economic status; the rate of participation is much higher in the upper strata than it is elsewhere. . . .

The bias of the system is shown by the fact that *even nonbusiness organizations reflect an upper-class tendency.* . . .

The class bias of associational activity gives meaning to the limited scope of the pressure system, because *scope and bias are aspects of the same tendency.* The data raise a serious question about the validity of the proposition that special-interest groups are a universal form of political organization reflecting *all* interests. As a matter of fact, to suppose that everyone participates in pressure-group activity and that all interests get themselves organized in the pressure system is to destroy the meaning of this form of politics. The pressure system makes sense only as the political instrument of a segment of the community. It gets results by being selective and biased; *if everybody got into the act the unique advantages of this form of organization would be destroyed, for it is possible that if all interests could be mobilized the result would be a stalemate.*

Special-interest organizations are most easily formed when they deal with small numbers of individuals who are acutely aware of their exclusive interests. To describe the conditions of pressure-group organization in this way is, however, to say that it is primarily a business phenomenon. Aside from a few very large organizations (the churches, organized labor, farm organizations, and veterans' organizations) the residue is a small segment of the population. *Pressure politics is essentially the politics of small groups.*

The vice of the groupist theory is that it conceals the most significant aspects of the system. The flaw in the pluralist heaven is that the heavenly chorus sings with a strong upper-class accent. Probably about 90 percent of the people cannot get into the pressure system.

The notion that the pressure system is automatically representative of the whole community is a myth fostered by the universalizing tendency of modern group theories. *Pressure politics is a selective process* ill designed to serve diffuse interests. The system is skewed, loaded and unbalanced in favor of a fraction of a minority. . . .

The competing claims of pressure groups and political parties for the loyalty of the American public revolve about the difference between the results likely to be achieved by small-scale and large-scale political organization. Inevitably, the outcome of pressure politics and party politics will be vastly different.

61

THEODORE LOWI

From *The End of Liberalism*

No assessment of the importance of interest groups in American politics would be complete without this classic work by Theodore Lowi. Lowi presents a ground-breaking criticism of interest-group politics, which he calls "interest-group liberalism" and "pluralism." Look for his arguments about the supposed-balance among groups. Note Lowi's view about government's role in perpetuating interest-group politics. His questioning of the actual definition of an interest group is important. Lowi then considers how interest-group politics treats the American people as a whole: "The public is shut out." His final argument is stunning: interest groups resist change; they become institutionalized, with government approval, and in the end are really conservative.

———

THE MOST clinically accurate term to capture the American variant . . . is *interest-group liberalism*. It is liberalism because it is optimistic about government, expects to use government in a positive and expansive role, is motivated by the highest sentiments, and possesses a strong faith that what is good for government is good for the society. It is interest-group liberalism because it sees as both necessary and good a policy agenda that is accessible to all organized interests and makes no independent judgment of their claims. It is interest-group liberalism because it defines the public interest as a result of the amalgamation of various claims. A brief sketch of the working model of interest-group liberalism turns out to be a vulgarized version of the pluralist model of modern political science: (1) Organized interests are homogeneous and easy to define. Any duly elected representative of any interest is taken as an accurate representative of each and every member. (2) Organized interests emerge in every sector of our lives and adequately represent most of those sectors, so that one organized group can be found effectively answering and checking some other organized group as it seeks to prosecute its claims against society. And (3) the role of government is one of insuring access to the most effectively organized, and of ratifying the agreements and adjustments worked out among the competing leaders.

This last assumption is supposed to be a statement of how a democracy works and how it ought to work. Taken together, these assumptions amount to little more than the appropriation of the Adam Smith "hidden hand" model for politics, where the group is the entrepreneur and the equilibrium is not lowest price but the public interest. . . .

. . . Interest-group liberalism . . . had the approval of political scientists because it could deal with so many of the realities of power. It was further appealing because large interest groups and large memberships could be taken virtually as popular rule in modern dress. . . . And it fit the needs of corporate leaders, union leaders, and government officials desperately searching for support as they were losing communal attachments to their constituencies. . . .

A[n] . . . increasingly important positive appeal of interest-group liberalism is that it helps create the sense that power need not be power at all, control need not be control, and government need not be coercive. If sovereignty is parceled out among groups, then who is out anything? As a major *Fortune* editor enthusiastically put it, government power, group power, and individual power may go up simultaneously. If the groups to be controlled control the controls, then "to administer does not always mean to rule." The inequality of power and the awesome coerciveness of government are always gnawing problems in a democratic culture. . . .

In sum, leaders in modern, consensual democracies are ambivalent about government. Government is obviously the most efficacious way of achieving good purposes, but alas, it is efficacious because it is coercive. To live with that ambivalence, modern policy-makers have fallen prey to the belief that public policy involves merely the identification of the problems toward which government ought to be aimed. It pretends that through "pluralism," "countervailing power," "creative federalism," "partnership," and "participatory democracy" the unsentimental business of coercion need not be involved and that unsentimental decisions about how to employ coercion need not really be made at all. Stated in the extreme, the policies of interest-group liberalism are end-oriented but ultimately self-defeating. Few standards of implementation, if any, accompany delegations of power. The requirement of standards has been replaced by the requirement of participation. The requirement of law has been replaced by the requirement of contingency. As a result, the ends of interest-group liberalism are nothing more than sentiments and therefore not really ends at all. . . .

. . . Interest-group liberals have the pluralist paradigm in common and its influence on the policies of the modern state has been very large and very consistent. Practices of government are likely to change only if there is a serious reexamination of the theoretical components of the public philosophy and if that reexamination reveals basic flaws in the theory. Because they guide so much of the analysis of succeeding chapters, contentions about the fundamental flaws in the theory underlying interest-group liberals ought to be made explicit here at the outset. Among the many charges to be made against pluralism, the following three probably best anticipate the analysis to come.

1. The pluralist component has badly served liberalism by propagating the faith that a system built primarily upon groups and bargaining is self-corrective. Some parts of this faith are false, some have never been tested one way or the other, and others can be confirmed only under very special conditions. For example, there is the faulty assumption that groups have other groups to confront in some kind of competition. Another very weak assumption is that people have more than one salient group, that their multiple or overlapping memberships will insure competition, and at the same time will keep competition from becoming too intense. This concept of overlapping membership is also supposed to prove the voluntary character of groups, since it reassures us that even though one group may be highly undemocratic, people can vote with their feet by moving over to some other group to represent their interests. Another assumption that has become an important liberal myth is that when competition between or among groups takes place the results yield a public interest or some other ideal result. As has already been observed, this assumption was borrowed from laissez-faire economists and has even less probability of being borne out in the political system. One of the major Keynesian* criticisms of market theory is that even if pure competition among factors of supply and demand did yield an equilibrium, the equilibrium could be at something far less than the ideal of full employment at reasonable prices. Pure pluralist competition, similarly, might produce political equilibrium, but the experience of recent years shows that it occurs at something far below an acceptable level of legitimacy, or access, or equality, or innovation, or any other valued political commodity.

2. Pluralist theory is also comparable to laissez-faire economics in the extent to which it is unable to come to terms with the problem of imperfect competition. When a program is set up in a specialized agency,

---

*Keynesians are economists who subscribe to the ideas of Englishman John Maynard Keynes. Keynes provided the economic basis for President Franklin Roosevelt's New Deal in the 1930s by advocating government intervention in the economy to "prime the pump" during the Depression. Keynesians opposed pure market theory in which the economy would balance itself by competition. Instead, they believed that government must create jobs by spending money it borrowed, in order to stimulate employment and consumption, thereby eventually building the economy back to prosperity.—EDS.

the number of organized interest groups surrounding it tends to be reduced, reduced precisely to those groups and factions to whom the specialization is most salient. That almost immediately transforms the situation from one of potential competition to one of potential oligopoly. As in the economic marketplace, political groups surrounding an agency ultimately learn that direct confrontation leads to net loss for all the competitors. Rather than countervailing power there is more likely to be accommodating power. Most observers and practitioners continue to hold on to the notion of group competition despite their own recognition that it is far from a natural state. [Economist John Kenneth] Galbraith was early to recognize this but is by no means alone is his position that "the support of countervailing power has become in modern times perhaps the major peace-time function of the Federal government." Group competition in Congress and around agencies is not much of a theory if it requires constant central government support.

3. The pluralist paradigm depends upon an idealized conception of the group. Laissez-faire economics may have idealized the enterprise and the entrepreneur but never more than the degree to which the pluralist sentimentalizes the group, the group member, and the interests. We have already noted the contrast between the traditional American or Madisonian definition of the group as adverse to the aggregate interests of the community with the modern view that groups are basically good things unless they break the law or the rules of the game. To the Madisonian, groups were a necessary evil much in need of regulation. To the modern pluralist, groups are good, requiring only accommodation. Madison went beyond his definition of the group to a position that "the regulation of these various interfering interests forms the principal task of modern legislation." This is a far cry from the sentimentality behind such notions as "supportive countervailing power," "group representation in the interior processes of . . . ," and "maximum feasible participation." . . .

The problems of pluralist theory are of more than academic interest. They are directly and indirectly responsible for some of the most costly attributes of modern government: (1) the atrophy of institutions of popular control; (2) the maintenance of old and the creation of new structures of privilege; and (3) conservatism in several senses of the word. These three hypotheses do not exhaust the possibilities but are best suited to introduce the analysis of policies and programs in the next six chapters.

1. In *The Public Philosophy*, Walter Lippmann was rightfully concerned over the "derangement of power" whereby modern democracies tend first toward unchecked elective leadership and then toward drainage of public authority from elective leaders down into the constituencies. How-

ever, Lippmann erred if he thought of constituents as only voting constituencies. Drainage has tended toward "support-group constituencies," and
with special consequences. Parceling out policy-making power to the
most interested parties tends strongly to destroy political responsibility. A
program split off with a special imperium to govern itself is not merely
an administrative unit. It is a structure of power with impressive capacities
to resist central political control.

When conflict of interest is made a principle of government rather
than a criminal act, programs based upon such a principle cut out all of
that part of the mass of people who are not specifically organized around
values salient to the goals of that program. The people are shut out at
the most creative phase of policy-making—where the problem is first
defined. The public is shut out also at the phase of accountability because
in theory there is enough accountability to the immediate surrounding
interests. In fact, presidents and congressional committees are most likely
to investigate an agency when a complaint is brought to them by one of
the most interested organizations. As a further consequence, the accountability we do get is functional rather than substantive; and this involves
questions of equity, balance, and equilibrium, to the exclusion of questions
of the overall social policy and whether or not the program should be
maintained at all. It also means accountability to experts first and amateurs
last; and an expert is a person trained and skilled in the mysteries and
technologies of that particular program.

Finally, in addition to the natural tendencies, there tends also to be a
self-conscious conspiracy to shut out the public. One meaningful illustration, precisely because it is such an absurd extreme, is found in the
French system of interest representation in the Fourth Republic. As the
Communist-controlled union, the Confédération Générale du Travail
(CGT), intensified its participation in postwar French government, it was
able to influence representatives of interests other than employees. In a
desperate effort to insure that the interests represented on the various
boards were separated and competitive, the government issued a decree
that "each member of the board must be *independent of the interests he is
not representing.*"

2. Programs following the principles of interest-group liberalism tend
to create and maintain privilege; and it is a type of privilege particularly
hard to bear or combat because it is touched with a symbolism of the
state. Interest-group liberalism is not merely pluralism but is *sponsored*
pluralism. Pluralists ease our consciences about the privileges of organized
groups by characterizing them as representative and by responding to their
"iron law of oligarchy" by arguing that oligarchy is simply a negative
name for organization. Our consciences were already supposed to be

partly reassured by the notion of "overlapping memberships." But however true it may be that overlapping memberships exist and that oligarchy is simply a way of leading people efficiently toward their interests, the value of these characteristics changes entirely when they are taken from the context of politics and put into the context of pluralistic government. The American Farm Bureau Federation is no "voluntary association" if it is a legitimate functionary within the extension system. Such tightly knit corporate groups as the National Association of Home Builders (NAHB), the National Association of Real Estate Boards (NAREB), the National Association for the Advancement of Colored People (NAACP), or the National Association of Manufacturers (NAM) or American Federation of Labor-Congress of Industrial Organizations (AFL-CIO) are no ordinary lobbies after they become part of the "interior processes" of policy formation. Even in the War on Poverty, one can only appreciate the effort to organize the poor by going back and pondering the story and characters in *The Three Penny Opera*. The "Peachum factor" in public affairs may be best personified in Sargent Shriver and his strenuous efforts to get the poor housed in some kind of group before their representation was to begin. . . .

The more clear and legitimized the representation of a group or its leaders in policy formation, the less voluntary its membership in that group and the more necessary is loyalty to its leadership for people who share the interests in question. And, the more widespread the policies of recognizing and sponsoring organized interest, the more hierarchy is introduced into our society. It is a well-recognized and widely appreciated function of formal groups in modern society to provide much of the necessary everyday social control. However, when the very thought processes behind public policy are geared toward these groups they are bound to take on the involuntary character of *public* control.

3. The conservative tendencies of interest-group liberalism can already be seen in the two foregoing objections: weakening of popular control and support of privilege. A third dimension of conservatism, stressed here separately, is the simple conservatism of resistance to change. David Truman, who has certainly not been a strong critic of self-government by interest groups, has, all the the same, provided about the best statement of the general tendency of established agency-group relationships to be "highly resistant to disturbance":

New and expanded functions are easily accommodated, provided they develop and operate through existing channels of influence and do not tend to alter the relative importance of those influences. Disturbing changes are those that modify either the content or the relative strength of the component forces operating through an administrative agency. In the face of such changes, or the threat of them, the "old line" agency is highly inflexible.

If this already is a tendency in a pluralistic system, then agency-group relationships must be all the more inflexible to the extent that the relationship is official and legitimate.

Innumerable illustrations will crop up throughout the book. They will be found in new areas of so-called social policy, such as the practice early in the War on Poverty to co-opt neighborhood leaders, thereby creating more privilege than alleviating poverty. . . . Old and established groups doing good works naturally look fearfully upon the emergence of competing, perhaps hostile, new groups. That is an acceptable and healthy part of the political game—until the competition between them is a question of "who shall be the government?" At that point conservatism becomes a matter of survival for each group, and a direct threat to the public interest. Ultimately this threat will be recognized.

62

JEFFREY BIRNBAUM

From *The Lobbyists*

Journalist Jeffrey Birnbaum takes readers back to 1990, when Republican President Bush and the Democratic Congress took on the budget bill. From the start, the complex negotiations were fertile territory for Washington's corporate lobbyists. Lobbying is not a much-loved or well-respected activity. It epitomizes life "inside the Beltway." This excerpt from Birnbaum's fascinating account focuses on Wayne Thevenot, one of the many lobbyists who got involved in 1990's behind-the-scenes budget maneuverings. Thevenot, of Concord Associates (whose most important client was the National Realty Committee) was a Washington veteran who began as a congressional aide decades ago. Interest groups and lobbying, as James Madison anticipated, are inevitable in a large, diverse nation. Still, K Street, where many lobbying firms have their offices, might not have been exactly what Madison had in mind. Events in the early 21st century confirm the questionable tactics used by some, not all, lobbyists.

"Okay," the President says. "Let's talk."

IT IS THE BRIGHT, clear morning of Tuesday, June 26, 1990, and President George Bush is meeting in the White House with

his economic advisers and the congressional leaders of both parties. Together, over steaming coffee in the private quarters, they face a crisis.
The federal budget deficit is careening out of control, and efforts to
negotiate a solution are getting nowhere. At around 8:30 A.M., after an
hour of fruitless talk, the Democrats finally assert that the President has
run out of choices. He must renounce his "no new taxes" pledge—the
oath that was instrumental in getting him elected. He must make a public
statement, they say, about the need to raise taxes.

The room grows silent.

Then the President utters those fateful words.

Not long thereafter, a short statement is quietly tacked on to a bulletin
in the White House press room. "It is clear to me that both the size of
the deficit problem and the need for a package that can be enacted require
all of the following," it reads, including the real shocker: "tax revenue
increases."

The announcement hits Washington like an explosion. . .

Later that morning in another part of town, the phones start ringing
at Concord Associates, a small lobbyists-for-hire company that overlooks
the Treasury Department in the Willard Office Building. Wayne Thevenot, a balding former staffer in the Senate, gets a call from his wife, Laura,
who is also a lobbyist. And James Rock, a bearded former aide in the
House, hears from his wife, Sue, who works inside the government on
the staff of the Senate's budget committee. Both women bring the same
news about the President's announcement, and both men confess embarrassment. "How could I not have known?" they each wonder. As lobbyists,
they are no longer part of the government, but they know enough high
officials in Washington to hear about most significant things before they
are announced.

This time, as usual, they had plenty of opportunity to know in advance.
Four days earlier, Rock had attended a lobbyists' breakfast where Robert
C. Byrd, the powerful chairman of the Senate Appropriations Committee,
was the featured speaker. And just the day before, Thevenot had been
among a small group of lobbyists who paid Senate Minority Leader Robert
Dole to have lunch with them at the 116 Club, an exclusive haunt for
lobbyists on Capitol Hill. If anyone in Washington had known what the
President was going to do, these two would have. But apparently they
knew nothing; neither had breathed a word about the momentous change.

Thevenot and Rock are surprised about the turn of events, but they
are not disappointed. Far from it. This is just the kind of news lobbyists
love; it gives them something to act on. As a result, their expensively
decorated offices now hum with excitement. Unlike [American Trucking
Association lobbyist Thomas] Donohue and [his aide, Kenneth] Simonson,

who work only for the truckers, Thevenot and Rock are freelance lobby-ists. They sell their services to almost anyone who is willing to pay their fees. That means that bad news for corporate America is good news for them. Crisis is their stock-in-trade, and that is precisely what the President's statement has created. His words have greatly enhanced the prospect for a big tax increase and that probably will mean more clients for Thevenot and Rock—if they are able to act quickly. So Rock parks himself in a chair across from Thevenot, who sits behind his oversized partner's desk, and they begin to plot and plan. They decide to contact the liquor distributors with whom they had once met; surely they will fear a tax increase now and will want to hire more lobbyists. Maybe there is reason to talk to securities firms too, they speculate; and some extra retainers from the real estate industry ought to be easy to find. "It's time to go to work," Rock concludes. "Now!" . . .

Washington has become a club in which the line between those inside and those outside the government is not clearly drawn. Corporate lobbyists have so suffused the culture of the city that at times they seem to be part of the government itself. One result is that corporate America, once a perennial sacrificial lamb when it came to government crackdowns, has become something of a sacred cow. Not only are lawmakers and policy-makers reluctant to make changes that would hurt businesses, they even have a tendency to try to help them, as long as budgetary pressures do not interfere. In 1990, Congress passed, and President Bush signed, the biggest deficit-reduction bill ever. But of its approximately $140 billion in tax increases over five years, only 11 percent came from corporations. The rest came from individual, taxpaying families.

Most people outside of Washington see the world of corporate lobby-ists in caricature: fat, cigar-smoking men who wine and dine the nation's lawmakers while shoving dollar bills into their pockets. If lobbyists were always so crass, surely they would be easier to understand. If they were so blatant, they would not be nearly as effective as they often are. And they are effective, at least on the margins. But it is there, in relatively small changes to larger pieces of legislation, that big money is made and lost. Careful investment in a Washington lobbyist can yield enormous returns in the form of taxes avoided or regulations curbed—an odd, negative sort of calculation, but one that forms the basis of the economics of lobbying.

The lobbyists' trade bears close similarity to the ancient board game Go, the object of which is to surround the enemy completely, cut him off from any avenue of escape, and thus defeat him. Blocking the decision-maker at every turn is the object of any successful lobbying campaign.

Equally important is not to allow the decision-maker to know that he or she is being entrapped. That makes lobbying both high-powered and discreet, a dangerous combination.

Over time, the sheer pervasiveness of corporate lobbyists has had a major impact on government policy, beyond just the lucrative margin of legislation. The fact that lobbyists are everywhere, all the time, has led official Washington to become increasingly sympathetic to the corporate cause. This is true among Democrats as well as among Republicans.

Lawmakers' workdays are filled with meetings with lobbyists, many of whom represent giant corporations. And their weekends are stocked with similar encounters. When lawmakers travel to give speeches, they rarely address groups of poor people. The big-money lobbies often pick up the tab, and their representative fill the audiences, ask the questions, and occupy the luncheon tables and throng the cocktail parties that accompany such events. "That's the bigger issue," contends one congressional aide. "Who do these guys hang out with? Rich people. If you spend your time with millionaires, you begin to think like them." Lobbyists provide the prism through which government officials often make their decisions. . . .

Every lawmaker's chief interest is getting reelected. So lobbyists see it as their job to persuade lawmakers that voters are on the lobbyists' side. To that end, Washington has become a major marketing center, in which issues are created by interest groups and then sold like toothpaste to voters from Portland, Maine, to Portland, Oregon. Thanks to Washington-based direct-mail and telemarketing wizardry, corporations can solicit letters and phone calls from voters in any district in the nation. And clever Washington-based lobbyists know that the best way to guarantee that their point of view will be heard is to take constituents with them when they go to speak to members of Congress.

Lobbyists also function as unpaid staff to the decision-makers, who often don't have enough people on their own payrolls. Lobbyists contribute the money that lawmakers need to get reelected. And, more important, lobbyists provide information about both policy and process that government officials often cannot get from their own, often underfunded government agencies. Lobbyists are the foot soldiers and the friends of the people who run the government.

Sometimes corporate lobbyists are adversaries of the men and women who wield the federal government's enormous power. In every battle, there are winners and losers. And, sometimes, the lobbyists are the losers. Lobbyists also fight among themselves, because the corporate world is far from monolithic. As in any industry, there are also plenty of bad lobbyists.

Money is wasted; campaigns can be sloppy and ham-handed. Sometimes corporate lobbyists seem to succeed despite themselves. They are the gang that couldn't shoot straight, but they manage to hit their target often enough to make a difference.

Despite their key role in the world of government, lobbyists are almost always the junior players, because, ultimately, they do not make the decisions. Taken as a group, they are a kind of underclass in the nation's capital, a lower caste that is highly compensated, in part, to make up for their relatively low stature in the city's severely stratified culture. At the top of the hierarchy are members of Congress and Cabinet secretaries. Next come congressional and Cabinet staffs. And then, at the bottom, come lobbyists. Lobbyists chafe at this. But their status is readily apparent. Frequently they suffer the indignity of standing in hallways or reception areas for hours at a time. Theirs are the first appointments canceled or postponed when other business calls. They do not even like to be called "lobbyists." They prefer "consultants" or "lawyers." They also use euphemisms like "When I left the Hill . . . " to describe the moment they left the congressional payroll to take a lobbying job.

One lobbyist put his predicament succinctly: "My mother has never introduced me to her friends as 'my son, the lobbyist.' My son, the Washington representative, maybe. Or the legislative consultant. Or the government-relations counsel. But never as the lobbyist. I can't say I blame her. Being a lobbyist has long been synonymous in the minds of many Americans with being a glorified pimp." . . .

The Main Street of lobbying is K Street, a short stretch through the heart of the sleek downtown. Spanking-new office buildings, filled with law firms, lobbying firms, and the allied services of the influence industry, sprang up everywhere in the city, eventually forming an almost unbroken corridor that stretched from Georgetown at one end of the city to Capitol Hill at the other. When even more office space was needed, metal and stone edifices were built on the Virginia side of the Potomac River. By the 1990s, Washington was home to about eighty thousand lobbyists of one kind or another, and the number was still growing. . . .

Thevenot could ingratiate himself with the best of them, and often did. He once declared at a lobbyists' Christmas party that he wished one day to be the "kissee rather than the kisser." But he was not cloying in his demeanor. He could be full of country charm and bawdy wit, with a hail-fellow manner to match. Yet he carried himself with the broad-shouldered confidence of the weight lifter he once was. He drove big cars and worked for big money. But more than that, he was a big man in Washington, a member in good standing of the political fraternity there. He might have been just a lobbyist, but in some circles he was a near equal of the lawmakers whose votes he worked to influence. He had been around for so long, he said, that to many lawmakers he was "as familiar as an old shoe." And he liked it that way.

At age fifty-four, Thevenot was sometimes bored by the repetitiveness of the legislative process. Other times he was frustrated by his inability to get things done. And having come of age in the Washington of the 1960s and early 1970s, he was forever bemoaning the "bullshitters and hurrah merchants" who were calling themselves politicians in the 1980s. But he still had not lost his touch or enthusiasm. He said he was "barnacle-encrusted," and deep down, still found fun—and, more important, profit—in playing the insider's game.

Thevenot was an access man. He survived on his ability to be accepted and trusted by the people with clout in Congress; his reputation rose and fell on having his telephone calls returned. He was not a technician. When he lobbied for changes in the tax code, for instance, he usually was versed only in the basic facts of the matter. For answers to deeper questions, he brought along an expert. But almost no one considered his need for backup a deficiency. Thevenot's job was more about strategy than details. He had to know whom to ask, when to ask, and how to ask for help, none of which was a simple question in the Byzantine world of Washington.

The secret of Thevenot's entrée was buried deep in the bayous and cotton fields of rural Louisiana. The third-oldest of eight children, Thevenot was the son of a failed farmer. "We built a house, started a farm, and proceeded to get poor," Thevenot recalled. "We also were the only ones who spoke clear English" in a region where Cajun patois was more the norm. His skill with language and his interest in government had brought him to where he was.

In the early 1960s, Thevenot worked as a television reporter for the NBC affiliate in Baton Rouge, and was part of the gang that covered the antics of the colorful governor, Earl Long. In 1963, Thevenot went over to the other side and became campaign manager for Gillis Long, a cousin of Russell's, who was waging an uphill fight for the U.S. House of Representatives against a two-term incumbent. Thevenot did a tremendous volume of work: everything from hiring hillbilly bands to trying to keep the candidate's driver out of jail. And when Gillis Long won, Thevenot's ticket to Washington had been punched.

The only problem was that the headstrong Thevenot was not interested in working for the even more headstrong Gillis Long. Thevenot told Long that he would be his friend forever, but never again his employee.

So Gillis Long telephoned Russell Long, then a U.S. senator, and asked him to find Thevenot a job. The one he found turned out to be as an elevator operator, but, in the hands of the resourceful Thevenot, it became a job with possibilities.

Between trips, Thevenot wrote speeches for his Senate patron. Soon, he moved out of the elevator and into more responsible positions on the staffs of committees that were run by Russell Long. These included panels with jurisdiction over small-business and post-office legislation. No matter what his title was officially, Thevenot always functioned as a top aide to Russell Long, who went on to become one of the most powerful men in Washington as chairman of the Senate Finance Committee.

When Russell Long had been drinking and was bruising for a brawl, Thevenot was there to spirit him away. He was also confidant to the mighty and friend to those who would become that way. He knew "Johnny" Breaux when he was a fellow staffer on Capitol Hill; Breaux went on to become a U.S. senator—in the seat vacated by Russell Long. Thevenot knew "Tommy" Boggs when he was the chubby teenage son of House Majority Leader Hale Boggs of Louisiana; in 1989 Boggs was running one of the biggest lobbying law firms in Washington. In short, Thevenot belonged to Washington's tight-knit Louisiana mafia, which like the Tabasco sauce from back home, wielded a fiery punch even in small quantities. "Thevenot's a piece of work," Senator Breaux explained. "He adds color to an otherwise bland city."

When Thevenot first left the Hill in 1975, he worked briefly for an investment-banking firm. But he soon realized that his life was too closely tied to Congress to abandon the Hill completely. Besides, he thought, becoming a lobbyist would get him faster to what was then his goal: making lots of money. "I decided that there was a point of diminished returns to being a staffer. I got to a point where I just sort of ran out of good ideas," he said. "I also had a family and financial obligations. I was making thirty-five thousand dollars a year, with four kids who had to go to college eventually. It was just not enough. So after nearly thirteen years it was just time to get out and cash in.

"I gave up the idea of changing the world. I set about to get rich."

With two friends, Thevenot set up the lobbying firm of Thevenot, Murray and Scheer. They represented a variety of business interests, but Thevenot was most drawn to real estate. After a few years, he left the partnership to become president and chief lobbyist for the National Realty Committee, one of the burgeoning new trade associations that represented specialized industry factions. The business world had grown too complex and too fragmented for huge umbrella organizations, such as the U.S.

Chamber of Commerce and the National Association of Manufacturers, to represent adequately. So in 1969 the biggest real estate developers banded together to form an elite group. In the early 1980s, Thevenot became its most successful and best-known mouthpiece, and helped lead it to many victories on Capitol Hill.

The National Realty Committee's most sweeping win came in 1981, when real estate was lavished with new tax breaks at the prodding of President Reagan. That caused a spurt in development around the country, which redefined the skylines of the nation's cities and filled the pockets of Thevenot's clients with gold. Projects were planned not so much for the rent that they would bring in as for the tax benefits. The boom, however, was so excessive that it was not long before the tax goodies were taken away. "See-through skyscrapers" with no occupants to speak of were becoming a national embarrassment, and there was nothing that Thevenot could do about it. The Tax Reform Act of 1986 made real estate one of its biggest victims. Not only were the 1981 benefits excised, but some tax breaks of older vintage were trimmed away as well. It was a bloodbath for the industry. But, in typical form, Thevenot expressed his chagrin with a smile. "At least our people have nice big buildings of their own to jump from," he said.

Thevenot was not blamed for the disaster. Lobbyists rarely are when the industries they represent lose a legislative fight. He could have stayed with the National Realty Committee forever; indeed, he was on retainer to the group through 1989, at $7,500 a month plus expenses, and continued to function as its top lobbyist. But he wanted a change, and a chance to make more money. So he decided to leave the full-time employ of the real estate industry and go out on his own. He affiliated with William Boardman, a tax lawyer and lobbyist for the engineering and construction industries, who had rented some fancy new office space (at about $45 a square foot) in the Willard Office Building, which had been renovated with the help of Thevenot's early 1980s tax breaks. The two men called themselves Concord Associates, a reference to Boardman's Boston-area roots; on the elegantly papered walls they hung drawings of Revolutionary War scenes from battles around Concord.

In appearance, Thevenot was an odd mixture that mirrored the competing demands of his vocation—one part soft, another part hard as nails. He had the cherubic face of a Kewpie doll, and only slightly more hair. But he also had the beefy hands and swagger of the roughneck he was during the hardworking summers of his youth in sweltering Morgan City, Louisiana. Thevenot had come a long way since then. When Congress reconvened in January 1989, he had been an invited guest at some of the

fanciest gatherings in the nation's capital, and he spent most of his time
hopping from one private party to another. Senator Charles Robb of
Virginia had held a bash for three thousand people at Union Station to
celebrate his election. But thanks to the National Realty Committee
checks that Thevenot had delivered to Robb's campaigns in the past,
Thevenot had been invited to a far smaller, more intimate party in the
new senator's office.

What Thevenot did there was collect information, which for him was
no insignificant task. He explained, "We're talking to everybody we can
about what the general mood of the Congress is. What issues are they
going to deem important? How are the members lining up? How strongly
they feel, for example, about new taxes to deal with the deficit problem.
That is what we do, it's a network, it's a game. All the people that we
know, and we've done favors for, gotten jobs for, sent them business, are
part of it. What you know and your ability to interpret it—your ability
to understand what's important and what's not—is what it's all about."

63

WILLIAM GREIDER

From *Who Will Tell the People*

*Almost every excerpt in this section is a criticism of interest groups. Students
of American government need to know the problems inherent in group-
based politics. Journalist William Greider, whose approach to writing about
government is undeniably counter-culture, provides a story both tragic and
uplifting. He details the politicization of Washington, D.C. janitors from
powerless working-poor laborers, into the "Justice for Janitors" organization.
Greider's account of the janitors' "rude and crude" tactics is both sad and
shocking. The lesson to be drawn from the janitors' strategy, however, is
depressing. Think about Greider's janitors as you sit in college classrooms
or the professional offices college graduates occupy. How do they get cleaned
and neatened for us each morning?*

THE QUALITY OF democracy is not measured in the contentment of the affluent, but in how the political system regards those who
lack personal advantages. Such people have never stood in the front ranks
of politics, of course, but a generation ago, they had a real presence, at

least more than they have now. The challenging conditions they face in their daily lives were once part of the general equation that the political system took into account when it decided the largest economic questions. Now these citizens are absent from politics—both as participants and as the subjects of consideration.

These citizens are not the idle poor, though many hover on the edge of official poverty and virtually all exist in a perpetual condition of economic insecurity. These are working people—the many millions of Americans who fill the society's least glamorous yet essential jobs and rank at the bottom of the ladder in terms of compensation. A large segment of working-class Americans has effectively become invisible to the political debate among governing elites. They are neither seen nor heard nor talked about.

Their absence is a crucial element in the general democratic failure of modern politics. . . .

Like other citizens who have lost power, the humblest working folk have figured out how politics works in the modern age. They know that their only hope is "rude and crude" confrontation. To illustrate this reality, we turn to a group of citizens in Washington, D.C., who are utterly remote from power—the janitors who clean the handsome office buildings in the nation's capital. In a sense, they clean up each night after the very people and organizations that have displaced people like themselves from the political debate. While they work for wages that keep them on the edge of poverty, their political grievances are not heard through the regular channels of politics.

Like other frustrated citizens, the janitors have taken their politics, quite literally, into the streets of the nation's capital.

In late afternoon on a warm June day, while the people in suits and ties were streaming out of downtown office buildings and heading home, a group of fourteen black and Hispanic citizens gathered on the sidewalk in front of 1150 Seventeenth Street Northwest and formed a loose picket line. They were the janitors who cleaned this building every night and, though hardly anyone noticed or cared, they were declaring themselves "on strike" against poverty wages.

"Fire me? Don't bother me one bit. Can't do worse than this," Lucille Morris, a middle-aged black woman with two daughters, said. She was passing out picket signs to hesitant coworkers, most of them women. "Hold 'em up!" she exhorted the others. "Let 'em know you're tired of this mess."

Others grinned nervously at her bravado. An older Hispanic woman dressed in work clothes started into the building and was intercepted by one of the strikers. "She says she's just going in to use the bathroom," Leila Williams reported, "but she's coming back out." Williams, a sweet-faced grandmother who lives with her sixteen-year-old grandson in one of the poorest wards of southeast Washington, was wearing a bright red union tee-shirt that proclaimed: "Squeeze Me Real Hard—I'm Good Under Pressure."

"No one is working—this building isn't going to get cleaned tonight," the organizer from the Services Employees International Union announced with satisfaction. "And nobody's going to get fired," Jay Hessey reassured. "The company can't find enough people to do these jobs at this pay."

"I've been here eleven years and I still get the same pay the newcomers get—$4.75 an hour," Lucille Morris said. "We be doing like two people's work for four hours a night. We don't get nothing in the way of benefits. You get sick, you sick. You stay out too long, they fire you."

"One lady been here for fourteen years and she still get five dollars an hour for doing the bathrooms," Leila Williams added. "They give you another quarter an hour for doing the toilets. When we pass inspections, you know, they always treat us. They give us pizza or doughnuts, like that. We don't want no treats. We want the money."

The SEIU, a union that mainly represents people who do society's elementary chores, launched its "Justice for Janitors" strategy nationwide in 1987 and has staged scores of similar strikes in downtown Washington as well as other major cities. Because of the way federal government now regulates the workers' right to organize for collective action, regular union-organizing tactics have been rendered impotent. So the workers mostly stage symbolic one-night walkouts to grab attention.

The real organizing tactic is public shame—theatrical confrontations intended to harass and embarrass the owners and tenants of the buildings. The janitors will crash the owner's dinner parties and leaflet his neighborhood with accusatory handbills. They will confront the building's tenants at social events and demand help in pressuring the owners.

They, for instance, targeted Mortimer Zuckerman, the real-estate developer who owns *The Atlantic* magazine and *U.S. News & World Report*, with a nasty flier that declared: "Mort Zuckerman might like to be seen as a public citizen, responsible editor, intellectual and all-around good guy. To the janitors who clean his buildings, he is just another greedy real-estate operator." They hounded Zuckerman at important banquets and even in the Long Island Hamptons at celebrity softball games, in which he is a pitcher.

The owners and managers of some five hundred office buildings in Washington have developed an efficient system that insulates them from both unions and higher wages. Each owner hires an independent contractor to service the building and the competitive bidding for contracts is naturally won by the firm that pays the least to the janitors. About six thousand workers—most of them black or Hispanic—are left without any practical leverage over the arrangement. When the union signs up workers and demands its legal right to bargain for a contract in their behalf, the building owner promptly fires the unionized cleaning contractor and hires a new one who is nonunion. Old janitors are fired, new ones are recruited and the treadmill continues.

This management device keeps janitors like Lucille Morris stuck permanently at the same wage level year after year, hovering just above the legal minimum required by law, a wage level that provides less than $10,000 a year at full-time hours.

But these janitors do not even get full-time work from their employers. By doubling the size of the crews, the contractors can hold the workers to a four-hour shift each night and, thus, legally exclude the janitors from all of the employee benefits the firms provide to full-time employees—health insurance, pensions, paid vacations, paid sick leave. The law protects this practice too.

In order to survive, these women and men typically shuttle each day between two or three similar low-wage jobs, all of which lack basic benefits and other protections. Some of the janitors, those who are supporting families, qualify as officially poor and are eligible for food stamps, public housing or other forms of government aid. In effect, the general taxpayers are subsidizing these low-wage employers—the gleaming office buildings of Washington and their tenants—by providing welfare benefits to people who do work that is necessary to the daily functioning of the capital's commerce.

In another era, this arrangement might have been called by its right name—exploitation of the weak by the strong—but in the contemporary political landscape that sort of language is considered passé. Exploitative labor practices are subsumed under the general principle of economic efficiency and the consequences are never mentioned in the political debates on the great social problems afflicting American cities. The government may authorize welfare for the indigent, but it will not address the wages and working conditions that impoverish these people. . . .

For the city of Washington, the political neglect constitutes a social irony, for many of these janitors live in the same troubled neighborhoods where the vicious street combat over drugs occurs. The community is naturally horrified by the violence among the young drug merchants and, without much success, has deployed both police and National Guard to suppress it. Yet the city is oblivious to the plight of the janitors—the people who are working for a living, trying to be self-supporting citizens and must live in the midst of the dangerous social deterioration.

Economists might not see any connection between these two social problems, but any teenager who lives in one of the blighted neighborhoods can grasp it. One group of poor people, mostly young and daring, chooses a life of risk and enterprise with the promise of quick and luxurious returns. Another group of poor people, mostly older men and women, patiently rides the bus downtown each night, and in exchange for poverty wages, they clean the handsome office buildings where the lawyers and lobbyists work. When the janitors stage their occasional strikes, they are harassing the very people who have helped block them out of governing issues—the policy thinkers, the lawyers and lobbyists and other high-priced talent who have surrounded the government in order to influence its decisions.

By coincidence, one of the tenants at 1150 Seventeenth Street, where they were picketing, was the American Enterprise Institute, the conservative think tank that produces policy prescriptions for the political debates of Washington. When the service-employees union organizers approached AEI for support, their request was brushed off, but AEI has had quite a lot to say about minimum-wage laws and their supposedly deleterious effects. In recent years, AEI has published at least nine different scholarly reports arguing against the minimum wage. This position faithfully represents the interests of AEI's sponsoring patrons—the largest banks and corporations in America.

But the SEIU organizers insisted they were not trying to make an ideological point by picking on AEI. The real target was the building owner, which operated a dozen downtown buildings in a similar manner. Besides, they explained, most of the ostensibly liberal policy groups in Washington are no different, from the janitors' point of view.

Indeed, the next strike was planned against another building, also owned by the Charles E. Smith Management Company, which served as the home of the Urban Institute, a liberal think tank that specializes in studying the afflictions of the urban poor. The Urban Institute, though presumably more sympathetic to the working poor, has also published scholarly pamphlets questioning the wisdom of laws to improve their wages.

The Urban Institute scholars are regarded as a liberal counterpoise to such conservative institutions as AEI but, in fact, the liberals are financed, albeit less generously, by the same business and financial interests that pay for the conservative thinkers—Aetna Insurance, $75,000; Chase Manhattan Bank, $15,000; Exxon, $75,000; General Electric, $35,000; Southwestern Bell, $50,000 and so on. The commonly held illusion in Washington politics is that supposedly disinterested experts contend with each other over defining the "public good" from different viewpoints. Yet many of them get their money from the same sources—business and financial interests.

Like other tenants, officials at the Urban Institute insisted the janitors' pay was not their problem. It was a dispute for the cleaning contractor or the building owner to resolve. The SEIU organizers were twice turned down in their efforts to meet with the Urban Institute's officers, so they went out to picket their private homes and tried to crash the institute's banquet for its board of directors.

"Isn't it the same kind of issue any time you pass someone on the street who's homeless?" asked Isabel V. Sawhill, a senior fellow at the institute who is an authority on the "underclass" and related social questions. "It's hard to get involved as an individual in all these microdecisions to change the system. It can't be done at that level. Laws and policies have to be changed."

But these weren't exactly distant strangers one passed on the street. They were the very people who cleaned the office each night, carried out the trash, vacuumed the carpet and scrubbed the sinks and toilets.

"Actually, we never see them," Sawhill allowed. "I do sometimes see them, I admit, because I hang around late, but most people don't."

The janitors, it is true, were mostly invisible. Despite several years of flamboyant efforts, the janitors' campaign had gained very little presence in the civic consciousness of Washington. Public shame is not a terribly reliable lever of political power. For one thing, it only works if widely communicated, and the major media, including *The Washington Post*, had largely ignored the fractious little dramas staged by the janitors.

"People are yawning at them," said Richard Thompson, president of General Maintenance Service, Inc., the largest employer of low-wage janitors. "If there were really a justice question, people in this city would react. There are a lot of government and city government folks who wouldn't stand for it."

The janitors thought they would embarrass both local politicians and congressional Democrats when they targeted a strike at the new shopping complex in Union Station, which is owned by the federal government. Instead, the janitors were fired and commerce continued without interference from the government. Though the Democratic party is ostensibly sympathetic to people like the janitors, Democrats also rely on the real-estate industry as a major source of campaign money.

After an hour or so of picketing on Seventeenth Street, the janitors got into vans and drove over to a museum at New York Avenue and Thirteenth Street where a local charity was holding its annual fund-raising gala. The strikers had no quarrel with the charity, but they did wish to embarrass David Bruce Smith, a young man who is an officer in his grandfather's real-estate company and was serving as chairman of the benefit dinner.

The women in red tee-shirts and the union organizers spread out along the sidewalk and began giving handbills to any who would take them. "Talk with David Bruce Smith," the leaflet asked. "The Janitors Deserve Some Benefits Too!"

The encounter resembled a sidewalk parody of class conflict. As people began arriving for the event, an awkward game of dodging and ducking ensued between the black janitors and the white dinner guests in evening dress. Women from the charity dinner stationed themselves at curbside and, as cars pulled up for the valet parking, they warned the arriving guests about what awaited them. The black women came forward offering their leaflets, but were mostly spurned, as people proceeded swiftly to the door.

"Look, we are a charitable organization and this is political," a man complained bitterly to the union organizers. "People are going to see this and say, what? Are you trying to embarrass me? They're coming here to enjoy themselves."

Jay Hessey reminded him of the constitutional right to petition for redress of grievances. Three D.C. police cars were on hand in the event the janitors violated the law by blocking the doorway or waving placards. It's unfair, the official sputtered, to target an organization that is devoted to charitable activities. It was unfair, the janitors agreed, but then so is life itself. Some people get valet parking. Some people get an extra quarter for cleaning the toilets.

As tempers rose, Hessey stood toe-to-toe with the angry officials and rebuffed them with an expression of utter indifference to their distress. Hessey's colloquial term for the janitor's rude theater—"In your face"— was the essence of their politics. Cut off from the legitimate avenues of political remedy, the janitors had settled on what was left. Like it or not, fair or unfair, people were going to consider, at least for a few uncomfortable moments, the reality known to these janitors.

Most of the guests followed instructions and darted past the demonstrators to the door, but this greatly amused Lucille Morris and Leila Williams and their companions. It had taken considerable courage for these black and Hispanic cleaning women to stand on a sidewalk in downtown Washington and confront well-to-do white people from the other side of town. Once they were there, the women found themselves enjoying the encounter.

It was the white people who turned grim and anxious. Without much success, the black women followed couples to the doorway, urging them to read the handbills. An elegantly dressed woman in silk turned on them and snapped: "You know what? For three hundred dollars, you should be able to enjoy your evening!"

When a mother and daughter streaked past Leila Williams, refusing her handbill, she called after them: "All right, ladies. But you might be standing out here yourself sometime."

"That's right," another janitor exclaimed. "The Lord gave it all, the Lord can take it away."

Their exercise in public shame was perhaps not entirely futile. The elegant woman in silk evidently thought better of her harsh words to the black women because, a few minutes later, she returned outside and discreetly asked them for a copy of their leaflet. She mumbled an expression of sympathy and promised to help, then returned to the banquet.

The janitors may lack formal educations and sophisticated experience with finance but they understand the economic situation well enough.

They know, for instance, that unionized janitors in New York City or Philadelphia will earn two or three times more for doing the very same work. They know that in Washington the federal government and some major private employers, like *The Washington Post* and George Washington University, pay nearly twice as much to janitors and also provide full employee benefits. They know, because the union has explained it for them, that janitorial services represent a very small fraction of a building's overall costs and that even dramatic pay increases would not wreck the balance sheets of either the owners or the tenants.

The problem, as they see it, is not economics. Their problem is power and no one has to tell the janitors that they don't have any. Collective action is the only plausible means by which they can hope to change things. But even the opportunity for collective action has been gravely weakened for people such as these.

The janitors' predicament provides a melodramatic metaphor for a much larger group of Americans—perhaps 20 million or more—who have also lost whatever meager political presence they once had. These are not idlers on welfare or drug addicts, though they often live among them. These are working people, doing necessary jobs and trying to live on inadequate incomes.

These Americans have been orphaned by the political system. They work in the less exalted occupations, especially in the service sector, making more than the minimum wage but less than a comfortable middle-class income. Most have better jobs and higher wages than the Washington janitors—office clerks, hospital attendants, retail salespeople—but are trapped by similar circumstances. Among health-care workers, for instance, one third earn less than $13,000 a year. Some occupations that used to be much higher on the wage scale—airline stewardesses or supermarket clerks—have been pushed closer to the low end by the brutal giveback contracts that labor unions were compelled to accept during the 1980s.

The incomes of the group I'm describing range roughly upward from the poverty line (around $10,000 for a family of three) to somewhere just short of the median household income of around $35,000. "Working poor" does not accurately describe most of them but then neither does "middle class." The poor still suffer more in their daily lives, of course, but even the poor are represented in politics by an elaborate network of civic organizations.

If one asks—Who are the biggest losers in the contemporary alignment of governing power?—it is these people who are economically insecure but not officially poor. During the last generation and especially the last decade, they have been effectively stripped of political protections against exploitation in the workplace. Neither party talks about them or has a serious plan to address their grievances. In the power coordinates that govern large national questions, these people literally do not exist. . . .

After many weeks of pressure and rude confrontations, the D.C. janitors found that some people do respond to the tactics of public embarrassment. After twice rebuffing them, officials at the Urban Institute agreed to support the janitors' plea for better wages. Mortimer Zuckerman also evidently had a change of heart, for his real-estate company abruptly agreed to bargain with the union for contracts at three buildings. The Charles E. Smith Company retreated too after the expressions of community concern generated by the janitors' appearance at the charity dinner.

These breakthroughs for "Justice for Janitors" might be taken as heart-warming evidence that "the system works," as Washington political columnists like to say. But the real meaning was the contrary. The janitors' union, like others, has figured out that the way politics gets done nowadays is not by electing people to office or passing bills in Congress. Politics gets done by confronting power directly, as persistently and rudely as seems necessary.

For all its weaknesses, the irregular methodology exemplified by "Justice for Janitors" has become the "new politics" of the democratic breakdown. Other labor unions, large and small, have adopted similar strategies designed to "shame" corporations into accepting decent labor relations. They confront prominent shareholders at public gatherings or testify against the companies at zoning hearings and before government agencies. They assemble critical dossiers on a corporation's environmental record that will shock the public and drive off consumers. These and other corporate-campaign strategies are sometimes effective in forcing a company to respond to its workers. Like the "Justice for Janitors" campaign, however, the tactics are driven by the worker's essential weakness, not the potential power that lies in their collective strength. In the present circumstances, what else works?

64

ROBERTO SURO

From *Strangers Among Us*

This selection offers insights on how one Hispanic activist group developed. Author Roberto Suro first takes readers into the Los Angeles Flats to watch las madres, *the unofficial protectors of this Hispanic immigrant neighborhood. From their role in stopping street gang violence, las madres has grown into a grassroots political organization with broader goals. This group represents an important part of a large and growing new political constituency. Among its concerns are immigration, citizenship, and California's Proposition 187 that removed many benefits from illegal immigrants. The process of absorbing new citizens remains a real challenge for America, Suro notes, but one that cannot and should not be ignored.*

———————

DOWN IN THE FLATS [east of the Los Angeles River] in the evenings, a third group roams the street, moving through the shadows between the day people and the night people. They are *las madres* (the mothers). Dressed in blue jeans or simple cotton dresses, they make sandwiches for the laborers, and then many nights, especially on weekends, they set out to street corners where there might be trouble among the thirteen street gangs that inhabit the Flats. The mothers are immigrants and natives, Spanish speakers, English speakers, and bilinguals. Most have big families in poor households, and most of them work—sewing in sweatshops, cleaning other people's homes and offices. "*Caminadas de amor*" (strolls for love) are what they call their forays. Carrying snacks and soft drinks, they go to the corners, sometimes as many as twenty of them at a time, and encircle their heavily armed progeny.

"They wait for us. They know we are coming and they wait for us because they like it," said Paula Hernández, one of the stalwarts of the group. "All we ever ask of them is to show respect for others. That, and we pray for them and listen to them. They are always having problems with other gangs and the police, and if we listen to them and treat them in a serious way, we can tell them they cannot solve their problems without showing respect for others."

The mothers deal with the police through a neighborhood watch organization, run clothing drives, operate a day-care center, and help support an alternative school for dropouts. With the Jesuits at the Dolores Mission, they also help run a shelter for battered women and a bakery to provide jobs for neighborhood boys. Considering how bad things are, *las madres* are not going to redeem the Flats anytime soon. But, amid the bougainvillea and the bungalows, beneath the freeway overpasses, they try to maintain order. At the heart of a sophisticated metropolis and within sight of office towers housing international banks, the mothers are the most coherent civilizing force in their community, more potent than the police, more consistent than any government agency, more respected than the schools. They represent yet another form of identity that is growing in the barrios. The mothers are a voice of resistance against life at the bottom of a stratified society. They echo the protests of the civil rights era, but in immigrant tones. They use Spanish words to master the downtown bureaucracies of public housing and Medicaid. *Las madres* represent a form of Latino identity that is as pragmatic as it is cultural and that remains proudly ethnic even as it seeks to engage America.

"Of course we are scared, and we get tired because we work all day and then come back to this," said Mrs. Hernández, gesturing down a dark alley where young male voices could be heard cackling.

Sheltered in the orange glare of a streetlight, the mothers formed a tight circle. They are bound together by more than civic spirit. Like most Latinos, *las madres* emerge from a culture that places little stock in institutions. They are at most a generation or two removed from countries where governments are more feared than trusted.

They've grown up believing that *compadrazgo* is the strongest bond outside the family. When the parents of a newborn child ask another couple to serve as the baby's godparents, the four become *compadres*, and it is understood that thenceforth their friendship is a bond for life that can be relied on for practical and emotional support even when relatives fail to heed the call. The baptism ceremony celebrates the ties among the adults as much as the arrival of an infant. And *compadrazgo* is just a formal expression of the kind of networking that begins with kinship and that usually goes much further in Latino cultures, especially in small towns and rural areas.

So there is something very Mexican about six women standing under a streetlight, looking out for their families and for one another, just as there was something very Mayan about how Juan Chanax and his *compadres* helped one another find work. But in places like the Flats, those linkages are finding new expressions and are being put to new purposes as these communities contend with the twin challenges of urban decay and steady immigration.

The mothers of the Dolores Mission are allied with an umbrella group called Las Madres de East L.A. It became one of the best-known community organizations in the city after it won a long battle to keep a prison out of the barrio, and then it won national fame by enlisting middle-class Anglo environmental groups to help it defeat plans to build a toxic-waste incinerator nearby. These battles in the 1980s helped promote a new civil rights cause, environmental racism, which alleges that environmental hazards have been inordinately, even intentionally, concentrated in poor and minority communities.

With little coordination or hierarchy, the mothers in the Flats and all across East L.A. also form a powerful grassroots political force. They helped elect Gloria Molina as the first Hispanic on the Los Angeles County Commission, and they have given important backing to several other insurgent political campaigns. When Proposition 187, the anti–illegal immigration initiative, held a huge lead in the polls, they went door-to-door to make sure that at least barrio voters would reject it.*

And this is not just a Los Angeles phenomenon. In the late 1980s and during the 1990s, barrio community organizations helped elect candidates, most of them women, to top offices in El Paso, Houston, Miami, and New York. In defiance of well-established Latino political bosses, many of these *madres* became the fresh faces and surprise winners when the ballots were counted.

---

*Proposition 187 would prohibit illegal immigrants from receiving social or welfare services, ban them from public schools and universities, and prevent them from receiving publicly funded health care except in emergencies. —EDS.

"Sometimes someone says they wish things could be like they are in
Mexico," Paula Hernández said. "They think women don't have to worry
about their families so much there. Well, it is true women have to do
more here. We are away from the children more because we work more,
and that makes problems. But it is here that we have learned to get over
our fear of saying what we think. It is here we have learned to work
together as mothers. That happened because we were here."

Whether they are in Congress or out in the streets pacifying gang
bangers, all this activism by Hispanic women reflects two political developments that are fundamentally American: the increasing prominence of
women in electoral politics and the growing dynamism of community-
action groups that coalesce on specific issues at the neighborhood level.
These are national trends that cut across regions, economic classes, and
racial or ethnic groups, and there is nothing distinctly Latino or immigrant
about them. Indeed, outside the United States, Latino political culture
remains male-dominated despite significant changes in the status of women
over the past thirty years.

Using minority-group status to get leverage on institutions, electing
female politicians, creating community-based organizations to funnel government funds into their neighborhoods—on all these many fronts Latino
immigrants are adapting to the United States and learning to use American
tools to fix their problems. But at the end of the day as they walk in the
dark, traveling between the day people and the night people, making a
community out of both, they are *comadres*, creating a sisterhood just as
their mothers and grandmothers and generations of Latinas did before
them in places far away. The *madres* are neither American nor Mexican.
They are creating something new in the barrios out of the old ways they
brought from the south and the tools they discovered on American terrain.

Down in the Flats when it started getting late, the mothers had gone
home, and the night people dispersed to make their rounds. Cars screeched
away. As one big black-and-red sedan pulled out, four or five firecrackers
flew from the windows in a kind of mock drive-by. Some of the remaining
lads flinched, their hands reaching to their pockets.

At the mission door, the day people started filing in, giving their
number to a man with a clipboard. They rolled themselves in olive drab
blankets, propped bundled clothes under their heads, and read *fotonovelas*,
which are comic books with photos of actors instead of drawings and
with soap-opera plots instead of superhero fantasies.

"*Los Angeles ya es Latino,*" Los Angeles is already Latino. The sentence
was spoken by a man in white painter pants and a faded work shirt as he

smoked a last cigarette before going in to stretch out on his pew. Earlier, he had entertained me and several other of the laborers with stories of how he had crossed the border so many times that he no longer used a *coyote*, a guide. He told tales of escaping from police who pursued him unjustly in Mexico and of eluding immigration agents in the United States. It was a migrant's *corrido* sung by a nicotine campfire. The mission door was about to close, and now the man was talking about California's [then] governor, Pete Wilson, who had been much in the news those days with his plans to balance the state government's budget by shutting down the border.

"Los Angeles is already Latino. It is too late for Wilson. What is he going to do? Deport us and all the Chicanos, too? If he wants to send two million people to Mexico, okay, let him do it; Mexico will send six million back. Then all of California will be Latino."

Two young laborers, teenagers by their looks, were terribly amused by this and so the older man indulged them. He was a natural-born ham, and before he had finished his cigarette, he had them in stitches.

"If he tries to send all the Latinos out of Los Angeles, all the *blancos* will go crazy in their dirty houses and all the *koreanos* with no one to work for them will go crazy, too. And so they will invite us—yes, *invite* us—to build a subway from Tijuana to Los Angeles that goes right under the border and under the noses of *la migra* [the immigration authorities]."

One of the boys tried to put icing on the joke as they walked into the church. "Yeah, we will get on the subway in Tijuana and they will serve us steaks at tables with napkins, and by the time we are finished eating, we will be here at Union Station."

"*Los Angeles ya es Latino.*" . . .

In old downtown Los Angeles on land not far from where the Spanish monks built their mission, an odd sight developed during the winter of 1994–1995. Crowds of Latinos began forming on the sidewalks in the chilly predawn hours. They lined up and waited for the offices of the Immigration and Naturalization Services to open so that they could apply for citizenship. In Los Angeles and then in every major city across the country, immigrants suddenly rushed to seek naturalized status in such numbers that they quickly overwhelmed the bureaucracy. It started shortly after the election that produced Proposition 187 and the Republican majority in Congress, and it occurred spontaneously, with little direction or encouragement from political leaders or advocacy groups. As months and then years passed and the number of Latinos seeking citizenship remained at flood stage, it became apparent that something fundamental had changed in the mentality of the barrio.

Prior to this boom in naturalization, conventional wisdom held that immigrants in the United States acquired citizenship in proportion to the distance they had traveled to get here. So, Asians and Europeans routinely naturalized almost as soon as they became eligible, usually after five years as permanent legal immigrants. By contrast, Canadians and Mexicans rarely would become citizens even after living in the United States for decades. Along with immigrants from the Caribbean and Central America, they retained intense ties to their homelands and often lived with the dream of returning.

As a result, every barrio had a huge supply of potential citizens. That reservoir had swelled when the immigrants who came in the surge of the 1980s reached eligibility, and then it grew even larger as the nearly 3 million beneficiaries of the 1986 amnesty became eligible. In 1995, applications for citizenship topped a million nationwide, nearly twice as many as the year before. By 1997, the INS was expecting close to 2 million citizenship applications.

The long lines of Latinos seeking U.S. citizenship marked a turning point. Like the Dominicans in Washington Heights after the 1992 riots, Latino newcomers all around the country were shocked out of their sojourner mentality by the anti-immigrant backlash. Legal immigrants realized that even though they paid taxes like everyone else, they could still lose access to a social safety net that citizens took for granted. The backlash, however, did not generate the kind of counterreaction typical of minority-group politics. Latinos did not protest or march to demand recognition of their rights. They did not mobilize as a group, nor did they generate a telegenic leader who spoke for their interests. The rush to naturalization was a simple act of self-defense, in part because citizenship offered some protection from the loss of benefits. More important, however, it was a declaration by people who had long lived between two lands that they had begun to consider the United States their permanent home.

Latino immigrants will become citizens with the same quiet relentlessness they showed in entering the country, creating communities, and getting jobs. They are also becoming voters. Together with native-born Latinos, they already make up a significant slice of the electorate in New York, Chicago, Los Angeles, and a number of smaller cities. As with the Irish and the Jews early in this century, the Latinos' political importance will be magnified because they are concentrated in a few highly visible places and because they may be able to swing key states in very close races. Southern California has the potential to become a Latino political bastion in the next twenty years even with no further immigration. More than half of all the youths in Los Angeles County are Latinos, and by the year 2010 Latinos will considerably outnumber Anglos in the entire L.A. metropolitan area. All those kids who carried Mexican flags to protest Proposition 187 have only to grow up and the politics of California and the nation will change for a generation or more. Despite the mathematical inexorability of this change, its direction is not clear. There is always the chance Latinos might fail to translate their numbers into real clout. With the exception of the Miami Cubans, Latino voters have gone Democratic so predictably and by such large margins in the past that the new citizens might suffer the fate of African-Americans, who are often taken for granted because Democrats know they have nowhere else to go. Or if the new Latinos fail to articulate a distinct political identity for themselves, they might eventually resemble the Puerto Ricans and become secondary players who are constantly struggling to make themselves heard.

Initially the leaders and candidates will emerge from the ranks of Mexican-American and Puerto Rican activists who are steeped in minority-group politics, but over time, as immigrants and the children of immigrants enter the arena, it seems likely that Latinos will develop a broader political identity. Their attitudes and agendas will necessarily evolve as a reaction to their experiences with American public institutions, everything from the neighborhood school to Congress. This is perhaps the greatest source of uncertainty about the future, because Latinos are becoming American citizens at a time when America is at best ambivalent about their presence. After the backlash embodied in Proposition 187 and the restrictionist proposals in Washington, many politicians reversed field. The 1996 election produced intimations of how fast the Latino vote was growing, and leaders of both parties grew apprehensive about seeming blatantly anti-immigrant. So, elderly immigrants were not kicked out of nursing homes, and in 1997 a few provisions of immigration law were modified to soften punitive actions against Central Americans who had overstayed temporary permits and illegals in the process of fixing their status. But all that amounted to mollification at a time when a continued economic expansion generated demand for new workers and temporarily relieved some of the nation's anti-immigrant anxiety. Even with sinking welfare rolls and a shrinking budget deficit, new immigrants are still denied access to America's social safety net. Immigration is widely regarded as convenient, even desirable in good economic times, but that is not a commitment to ensuring the successful integration of a large number of newcomers, especially those who most need help from their hosts. The potential for a renewed backlash remains very real, and so it is likely that today's Latino immigrants will establish their political identity in a nation that oscillates between uneasy acceptance and fearful rejection of them.

For the first time since the Voting Rights Act of 1965 opened polling places in the Deep South to blacks, the United States is enfranchising a large new group of people who have been marked as outsiders. This is not primarily a political process or a matter that can be settled with legislation and policy directives. Latino immigrants are on the brink of taking important steps that will define their place in American society for generations to come. Latino newcomers are well along in this process, but much of what they have accomplished thus far has been done quietly. Most Americans hardly noticed the barrios until they grew large. Now the key tasks ahead can only be accomplished loudly and in the public arena. Immigrants must establish links with the United States as vibrant as those they have maintained with their home countries. The barrios must be converted from self-enclosed enclaves into organic American communities intimately connected with the cities around them. Businesses and neighborhood organizations created primarily to facilitate migration and settlement must now turn to long-term goals. And the United States must stop looking at recently arrived immigrants as appendages that can be disposed of when they are unwanted. That means reaching a new understanding of how American society cares for and absorbs people who come from abroad, work hard, remain poor, and fill their homes with children. In the early part of the next century, the new Latino immigrants will become part of the American nation. They are here already. They are not going to leave. It will happen, but the process of integration is never easy or peaceful. There is conflict on the horizon, but beyond the conflict, there may be signs of hope.

65

DAN BALZ
RONALD BROWNSTEIN

From *Storming the Gates*

Dan Balz and Ronald Brownstein bring readers into a National Rifle Association leadership meeting. The NRA is one of the most powerful interest groups in the United States. While gun ownership is the group's main focus, its broader mission is to resist what members see as the ever-increasing power of the national government. Other groups, based on their own particular issues, share the NRA's basic distrust of Washington.

WHAT BOTHERS JOHN COLLINS is not so much the new gun-control laws—he expected as much from Bill Clinton and the Democrats in Congress—as the video cameras on the highways in his hometown of Las Vegas. The progression worries him, the small steps, the imperceptible advances. Remember, at first, they were supposed to keep an eye on traffic? Now the cameras are being used to give out traffic tickets. What's next? Monitoring where people drive? Cataloguing license plates? "Little by little," he said ominously, letting the thought trail off in a haze of cigarette smoke.

Tanned and leathery, Collins delivered this warning while standing outside a ballroom in a downtown Phoenix hotel one sizzling afternoon in May 1995. Inside, leaders of the National Rifle Association (NRA), at once perhaps the most powerful and embattled lobby in the country, were handing out awards at a gala luncheon. Collins was one of some twenty thousand gun enthusiasts who had gathered for the NRA's annual convention. A few blocks away, in the Phoenix Convention Center, dozens of manufacturers had set up booths, displaying the latest in shotguns and handguns and telescopic sights. There were hunting bows, crafted as carefully as sculptures, and camouflage outfits and leather jackets with the names of gun manufacturers emblazoned across the back like baseball teams.

Browsing through the stacks of merchandise (down to infant-sized NRA T-shirts that read "Protecting your right to keep and bear arms, for now and for the future") was one of the two principal activities at the convention. The other was talking politics. Stephen Donnell, an NRA board member who has been with the organization for fifty years, waited until Collins had finished his disquisition on highway cameras before offering his own opinion on the state of the nation. "The real issue isn't gun control," he said. "The question is whether we are going to be subjects of the government or whether we are going to be citizens and the government is going to be subject to us." Donnell suggested digging up old newsreels of Hitler and Mussolini to gain an understanding of where Clinton was trying to take the country. What was the connection? "The similarity," John Collins jumped in, "is in the direction they are going."

Not far from Collins and Donnell, David Dutton, a slim, bearded psychologist from the small town of Coarsegold, California, was sitting on a bench, wearing a T-shirt with pictures of Bill and Hillary Clinton above the inscription "Dual Airbags." Friendly but passionate, Dutton picked up where Collins and Donnell left off. "The federal government has become a hydra-headed monster," Dutton said. "Almost any federal agency they want to cut, I would be in favor of. It's grown out of hand. It's a malignant cancer." People used to be free in America, he said almost wistfully. "Now if you pump leaded gas in your car, it's a federal offense."

Not everyone who gathered at the NRA convention was so angry at government. But most were. Like Collins, they had grievances that extended well beyond guns and gun control. Indeed, few of them said they had suffered any personal inconvenience from either the ban on semi-automatic assault weapons or the waiting period for handgun purchases Congress had approved over the previous two years. To most of them, gun control had ascended from the practical to the symbolic. Gun control was just the means to the end of enlarging government and giving Washington more power to control the lives of its citizens. Washington was taking away guns to clear the path for taking away other rights: This was the article of faith. One man from Colorado raged at being required to give his fingerprints to obtain a driver's license. Another complained about federal environmental regulations that favored turtles over farmers and snails over ranchers. Another said government welfare programs were undermining traditional moral values. Speed limits, restraints on the use of public lands, all the infringements on liberty that society demands to uphold order seemed to them an intolerable web of rules and regulations too thick to evade or even comprehend.

What made these sentiments all the more remarkable was their source. The NRA convention had a small-town, blue-collar flavor, and the men who pored over shotguns and swapped hunting stories seemed like the sort who might have broken up antiwar demonstrations with their fists twenty-five years ago. Now they sounded like the Weathermen themselves, branding the government as corrupt, voracious, malevolent. "We're going into a situation where there is a police state mentality," one man said. Another man added: "I'm not saying there is any definite, immediate conspiracy to turn America into a tyranny. But as a matter of principle, people should be afraid of their government."

At their most extreme, these beliefs bordered on the antigovernment paranoia expressed by the two men accused of blowing up a federal office building in Oklahoma City just a month before the NRA meeting. Yet they usually stopped short. Everyone in Phoenix condemned the violence, and if there was any sympathy for the bombers it was kept well hidden. Still, the intensity of the alienation from government was palpable. When these men talked about Washington, many of them conjured up images of revolution—peaceful or political, but revolution nonetheless. In the same way they once might have spoken of Moscow as a threat to their freedom, now they pointed at their own capital. "I consider the federal government to be the greatest threat to our liberty today," Dutton said. "We've defeated communism. We've defeated Nazism. The last threat is inside the Beltway."

These angry white men are one legion in a grassroots movement that has rewritten the political equation of the 1990s, and in the process helped to transform the Republican Party. With social movements on the left like labor unions and civil rights organizations diminished in power, an army of conservative grassroots groups has mobilized middle-class discontent with government into a militant political force, reaching for an idealized past with the tools of the onrushing future: fax machines, computer bulletin boards, and the shrill buzz of talk radio. They have forged alliances with the Gingrich generation of conservatives and strengthened their hand as the dominant voice within the GOP family. Like a boulder in a highway, the conservative populist movement has become an enormous, often impassable obstacle in the path of President Clinton. No single factor in the Republican revival after Bush's defeat has been more important than the party's success at reconnecting with and invigorating the profusion of anti-Washington and antigovernment movements sprouting in every state.

These movements exist in concentric circles of alienation from government. At the farthest edge are extremist tax protesters, survivalists, and elements of the militia movement so alienated from society that they can imagine taking up arms against it. But most of the energy has been contained within the boundaries of mainstream politics. Probably not in this century have so many distinct groups, with such a broad range of grievances, simultaneously targeted the government in Washington as their enemy. The conservative, or antigovernment, populist coalition operates on at least half a dozen fronts: gun owners led by the 3.5-million-member NRA; Christian conservatives organized primarily through televangelist Marion G. (Pat) Robertson's Christian Coalition, which now counts 1.7 million members in seventeen hundred local chapters; the movement to impose term limits on members of Congress; the network of more than eight hundred state and local antitax organizations; small-business owners spearheaded by the six-hundred-thousand-member National Federation of Independent Business (NFIB), which has surpassed more conciliatory big business organizations as a legislative force in Washington; the Perot movement; and the "wise use" and property rights movements that have amalgamated ranchers, farmers, off-road enthusiasts, loggers, and miners—as well as multinational mining and timber companies—into a coalition demanding the rollback of environmental regulations, increased access to public lands, and government compensation for environmental rules that prevent landowners from developing their property.

Even this list doesn't encompass the entire range of populist right-of-center uprisings through the early 1990s, from the movements that opposed the North American Free Trade Agreement (NAFTA) and the world trade treaty known as GATT to the anti-immigration and anti-affirmative action movements that began in California and have spread elsewhere over time. "There is a synergy," said conservative political consultant Craig Shirley. "It is feeding on itself. It is keeping itself in motion."

These movements sort largely into two camps. In one are the Christian Coalition and other groups drawn to politics primarily by fears of cultural decline and the breakdown of the family. In the other are the secular organizations—like the National Federation of Independent Business, the followers of Ross Perot, the term limits and property rights movements, and the NRA—motivated mostly by opposition to the expansion of government spending and regulation. There are significant differences between and even within these camps, but the conservative populist coalition is more demographically and ideologically coherent than many on the left assume. To a striking degree, Americans in these groups express common attitudes and exhibit similar lifestyles. Gun ownership is considerably more common among groups within the antigovernment coalition than among the population as a whole. Nearly half of small-business owners consider themselves born-again Christians. Gun owners, Christian conservatives, and small-business owners are all heavy listeners to talk radio. In many states, small-business owners, antitax advocates, and Perot activists provided the foundation of support for the term limits movement. The 1995 term limits ballot initiative in Mississippi, for example, was directed by Mike Crook, a field organizer for the Christian Coalition who was also a member of the NRA. "The links are all there," Crook says. "They are all interrelated. All of these grassroots organizations . . . amount to taking back our country for the people."

PART TWELVE

Voting and Elections

66

DANTE SCALA

From *Stormy Weather*

It's the fall of 2007. You're in school. Congress and the president are at work in Washington, D.C. A presidential election is a year away, far into the future. But for the candidates, the future is now and the place is New Hampshire. How can a tiny northern non-demographically representative locale be the critical focus of American politics? The New Hampshire primary, held early in the winter of a presidential election year, can become the source of "momentum," explains Dante Scala: that precious and unmeasurable quality that can make or break a campaign. Scala points to the realities of momentum and the media attention it garners; with media attention come donations. Scala takes readers through the Exhibition Season, a bizarre combination of grassroots politics based on winning over local activists and simultaneously catering to the national press corps. Then comes the Media Fishbowl, the New Hampshire primary that occurs right after the Iowa caucuses. New Hampshire has had its moment in the spotlight. It has given and taken away candidates' momentum. Soon, the fall of 2011 will be here.

———◆———

THE FACT THAT CANDIDATES for the highest office in the land must pass muster with the residents of New Hampshire, a small New England state, is one of the greatest eccentricities of the American electoral calendar. This eccentricity is embraced by those who consider New Hampshire the last bastion of grassroots politics in the presidential selection process, a place where a politician seeking the highest office in the land must look a voter in the eye, shake hands, and answer questions on a one-to-one basis. Critics dismiss the New Hampshire primary as an annoying appendix to the presidential nomination process, a model of grassroots democracy now much more myth than reality. They charge that the primary gives vastly disproportionate influence to a relatively small group of voters who are unrepresentative of the national electorate, pointing to the Granite State's peculiarly libertarian brand of conservatism, its aversion to taxes, and its homogeneous, white population.

That such a small state came to play such a large role in choosing major-party nominees for president—and thus a significant role in choosing the next occupant of the White House—is a uniquely American story of the idiosyncrasies of local politics mixing with national trends to produce an unforeseen development. When the state's political elites scheduled the presidential primary to coincide with Town Meeting Day in March, they did so in order to save the money and trouble of holding two separate events. Not in their wildest dreams did the frugal Yankees realize that they were gaining squatter's rights to the most valuable real estate in presidential nomination politics. . . .

The fuel New Hampshire has provided, in a word, is "momentum." Momentum sometimes takes on a mystical, ill-defined quality for observers and participants in a campaign, something akin to "team chemistry" in sports. A losing team is often said to suffer from bad chemistry among its members, but that chemistry magically transforms when the same team has a winning streak. Candidates often claim to have momentum until results at the polls prove otherwise. . . .

. . . In the presidential primaries, a candidate's momentum is judged on a weekly, even daily, basis by the answer to a single question: What is the likelihood that the candidate will go on to win the support of a majority of the delegates to the party's national convention and the nomination? A candidate is said to have momentum if that likelihood is on the rise. In the course of the campaign, that likelihood will rise and fall as political handicappers compare a candidate's progress in relation to his competitors and consider what opportunities are left for the candidate to pick up more delegates. . . .

. . . Media attention along with financial contributions and standings in the polls are the three main measurements of momentum. Often these measures all affect one another in a cyclical manner. A flurry of stories on a candidate boosts name recognition; increased name recognition leads to better standings in the polls; and better showings in the polls prompt more contributors to send funds to the campaign. . . . At a certain point, the momentum may be seen as ineluctable as the candidate takes on, or is given, an "aura of success."

A candidate gains that aura by exceeding expectations or a series of markers that observers such as the national media lay down as criteria for successful results. The media's expectations are often criticized as arbitrary, especially by those candidates who fail to meet them or feel that the media have been too lenient on their opponents. Expectations, however, do have their roots in a comparison of assumptions about how a candidate will do—based on evidence such as historical precedents, poll standings, results from neighboring states, and the efforts of campaigns—with how a candidate actually does. Expectations and momentum are a zero-sum game: a *better than expected performance* fuels momentum, increasing the candidate's likelihood of winning the nomination while reducing that of the opponent; *performing no better than expectations but no worse* means the candidate remains moving at the same pace toward the nomination, with little advantage for either the candidate or the opponent; *performing worse than expectations* puts the brakes on a candidate's momentum, harming his chances of winning the nomination and advancing those of the opponent.

Momentum can thus be fleeting, an important consideration given that the presidential nomination "process" is really more a series of loosely connected electoral contests held at irregular intervals over a prolonged period of time. Each state has its own peculiarities, its own set of factions and differing proportions of factions, so that momentum created in one primary can be dashed as the successful message employed there backfires in subsequent states.

Momentum can be a valuable addition to the other types of resources that a candidate carries with him into the presidential nomination process. Some of these, such as a candidate's ideological reputation or his inherent abilities as a campaigner, are established prior to the beginning of the campaign. A candidate's liberalism, for example, will aid him in a liberal state but harm him in a conservative one. The availability of vital re- sources—money, attention from the media, and overall popularity—may depend on the success of the candidate's campaign, such as a strong performance in a competitive primary that attracts media coverage. With all other factors equal, candidates with more resources will do better than candidates with fewer resources, and early success can generate increased resources, such as the backing of donors who prefer to send their donations to perceived winners. . . .

First Stage: The Exhibition Season

Also referred to as the invisible primary, this is the period that extends from the morning after a general presidential election, until the first contests in Iowa and New Hampshire more than three years later. "The exhibition season is a building and testing period," Cook wrote, "in which candidates are free to fashion campaign themes and to discover which constituencies are receptive to their appeals." Key tasks include fund- raising; the early stages of organization building in various primary states; and seeking the support of key interest groups such as labor unions. Although no votes are cast in the exhibition season, the games played at this time clearly count on the candidate's record.

The ability to raise money is one of the chief benchmarks for a successful campaign during the exhibition season. Conventional political wisdom places the prerequisite amount for a viable primary campaign at roughly $20 million. Candidates with lots of cash on hand have obvious advantages in a nomination campaign, including the capability to pay for staffers, to put advertising on the airwaves, and to garner valuable data from polling. Money alone may not necessarily decide a nomination, but money does make it possible for a candidate to employ certain means that help to secure a victory, such as advance polling.

The task of raising campaign funds, however, has been greatly complicated by the campaign finance reforms of the 1970s. Prior to these reforms, a presidential candidate was able to rely on a small group of wealthy donors to provide invaluable seed money for the initial stages of a campaign. After the reforms, which placed a ceiling of $1,000 on individual donations (now raised to $2,000 for the 2004 election cycle, after the passage of the McCain-Feingold campaign finance reform legislation), reliance on a few fat-cat donors was no longer possible. In order to run a viable campaign, presidential candidates instead have to collect thousands upon thousands of donations, in addition to obtaining matching public funding. Campaigns employ a variety of strategies to accomplish this daunting task. While insurgent ideological candidates can patch together a viable campaign by using direct mail or even 1-800 numbers, candidates who can raise money in thousand-dollar increments, as opposed to hundred-dollar increments, undoubtedly are able to raise large amounts of money more efficiently while still being eligible for matching public financing as well. The ability to raise funds is, in many ways, the first real contest of the nomination season. . . .

Much media speculation inevitably focuses on how candidates are doing in the first-in-the-nation primary in New Hampshire. Thus, in addition to fundraising trips to money centers such as New York and California, New Hampshire's Manchester International Airport is a frequent stop for candidates playing in the exhibition season. One weekend in fall 2002, for instance, Senator John Edwards of North Carolina did no fewer than a dozen events in a three-day tour of the state, beginning with a speech at the state Democratic Party's annual Jefferson-Jackson dinner Friday night in Manchester. The events ranged widely in size and were held all over the state, from the smallest, a coffee with four or five people, to house parties with dozens of people, including one at the home of Peter Burling, leader of the Democratic delegation in the New Hampshire House of Representatives. At one point during Edwards's whirlwind weekend, the van taking the candidate from Claremont to Cornish in western New Hampshire got lost. Edwards's political consultant, Nick Baldick, himself a New Hampshire primary veteran, chalked this up as par for the course: "This is New Hampshire," he said. "There are no signs. People are going to get lost."

For many aspiring presidential candidates, a trip to New Hampshire is indeed similar to an educated business traveler's first voyage to a far-off land. The traveler needs to accomplish a number of things on his first visit. He needs to make acquaintances and discover friends. He needs a base of operations that will run and expand while he is away on business elsewhere. Most of all, though, the traveler needs a guide from among the natives. But how should he choose? Dayton Duncan, veteran New Hampshire activist and author of *Grass Roots*, a book on activists in the 1988 presidential campaign, described the dilemma of finding good advice this way:

You're a wealthy Englishman going big-game hunting in a foreign country. . . . [You] might be very good at firing your big gun. But you're in a foreign country, and [depending on] which guides you hire when you arrive, they might lead you to where you get a good shot off, or they might lead you to where all you get is malaria. And part of it is, before you made your choice of guides, had you done some previous work on that, of trying to determine who the guides ought to be? Or, do you also just have innate, common sense or innate political ability to figure it out?

Answering these questions, Duncan said, is key to this first stage of the New Hampshire primary: the competition among the candidates to lure activists and build an organization. This contest ends by the close of September or early October, months before the primary; by this time, the courtship of activists is mostly complete, and organizations are well along in their setup. Courting activists is more an art than a science, in part because there are as many motivations that draw activists to candidates as there are activists, said Manchester Democratic party chair Ray Buckley:

Some people just like personal attention. If you're running for president, and you call this person once a week for six months, you've got him. Other people, they want you to be the . . . craziest liberal. Another person, it's because you're on a particular committee in the Senate, and so you did something on an issue, they're attracted on the issue. . . . They happened to have been at an event, and you gave an amazing speech, and you showed charisma, so the person was excited by that. You get this one person in, because they know forty other activists, you happen to get that whole clique.

Unlike the early days of the New Hampshire primary, candidates must now undertake this competition in the media spotlight, knowing that their every move is scrutinized by the political cognoscenti. When the New Hampshire Democratic Party held a fund-raising dinner in February

2003, for instance, the list of presidential candidate attendees made not just the *Manchester Union Leader* but also ABCNews.com's "The Note," a daily must-read for the national political elite. American politics today, including media coverage of politics, "lends itself to endless speculation, and gum-chewing, and thumb-sucking about what's going to happen, versus real reporting on what actually is happening," Duncan said. In that type of environment, grassroots campaigning in New Hampshire is important in part because of the image such action conveys to the watching media. "Having that as your backdrop to how you're campaigning is a good backdrop to have. It also saves you from getting a rap going, particularly early on, that you're doing it wrong." . . .

Second Stage: The Media Fishbowl

The seemingly interminable exhibition season finally ends in January of the year of the presidential election, when Iowa holds its caucuses and, soon after, New Hampshire its primary.

The Iowa caucuses are both inconclusive and definitive for candidates' fortunes. On one hand, the January caucuses held in precincts across the state do not actually award convention delegates to candidates; this occurs months later at state party conventions. On the other hand, and more important, the Iowa caucuses are "the gateway to a long and complex nomination process, and all players and all observers very much want whatever information they can glean" from the results, however transitory they may be. The media turn their attention from speculation on a candidate's prospects to analysis of the verdict from actual voters: "Iowa results, plus media spin" set the story line for New Hampshire and establish the roles of front runner, lead challenger (or challengers), and the remaining bit players who have the unenviable parts of long shots or also-rans.

For the week between the Iowa caucuses and New Hampshire's first-in-the-nation primary, the attention of the national political media descends on New Hampshire in a deluge. "That week is full of electricity," said Pat Griffin, executive vice president for the advertising firm O'Neil Griffin Bodi and a veteran of several political campaigns. In jest, he compared the last week before the primary to being on the set of *Doctor Zhivago*:

All these Washington types buy their mukluks . . . to come up once every four years. . . . They come up and say, "My God, where can I get my hair done? Where can I find arugula salad?" . . . Go to [Manchester restaurant] Richard's Bistro at night, they're all at the same places, [saying] "My goodness, can you believe this tundra where these people live?"

The national political media venture into the tundra—at least as far as Manchester and its environs, if not the seacoast or the Connecticut River valley or the North Country—because the people who live there possess something they want dearly: information on how actual voters feel about the presidential candidates. The Iowa caucuses, in which participants have to devote hours of time on a single evening, are usually low-turnout events attended by party faithful, in which strong organizations are often vital to a good showing. The New Hampshire primary, in contrast, turns out a much higher percentage of voters, and candidates must therefore be able to appeal to a variety of constituencies. Iowa and New Hampshire together, plus the media's interpretations of those two contests, winnow the field to a front runner and one or, at most, two or three challengers. . . .

Perhaps one of the reasons New Hampshire has been and remains an indicator is that it is an early testing ground of candidates' organizational skills, charisma, and appeal to the broad range of the relevant electorate. For, notwithstanding its idiosyncrasies—and what state is not idiosyncratic?—New Hampshire's populace is composed of various factions that have their analogues in the rest of the nation. How a candidate crafts a message to appeal to those factions or constituencies in New Hampshire does affect how he or she will be perceived thereafter. New Hampshire's ability to determine the nomination may be in question; that it is an early indicator of how a candidate plans on running a campaign and the likely chances of the success of that message, however, is not.

67

DENNIS JOHNSON

From *No Place for Amateurs*

Behind the scenes of every political campaign today is a political consultant. Political consulting is a thriving business whose skills are employed not just by candidates for national office, but those running for state and local positions too. Referendum questions placed on state ballots are managed by consultants. No race is too small or too obscure to be aided by consulting firms, whether big time ones led by the famous (James Carville, Dick Morris) or the anonymous one or two person basement operation. Dennis Johnson reveals the multitude of tasks that consultants perform for a campaign. He also gives some good tips on movies to rent on the topic: The War Room *and* Wag the Dog *are particularly good choices for those who enjoy the blend of fact and fiction.*

———

I don't want to read about you in the press.
I'm sick and tired of consultants getting famous at my expense.
Any story that comes out during the campaign undermines my candidacy.
—BILL CLINTON to his new 1996 reelection consultants
Dick Morris and Doug Schoen

JUST DAYS BEFORE THE 1996 Democratic National Convention, a smiling, confident Bill Clinton was featured on the cover of *Time* magazine. Pasted on Clinton's right shoulder was a cut-out photo of political consultant Dick Morris, "the most influential private citizen in America," according to *Time*. On the eve of Clinton's renomination, *Time* was sending its readers a backhanded pictorial message: here is the most powerful man in the world, who fought his way back from political oblivion, and perched on his shoulder is the reason why. Suddenly the once-secretive, behind-the-scenes consultant was a household name. In the early months of the reelection campaign, Morris worked hard at being the unseen political mastermind and strategist. "Being a man of mystery helps me work better," he confided to George Stephanopoulos. While Bill Clinton's 1992 consultants were talk-show regulars, wrote best-sellers, and traveled the big-dollars lecture circuit, Morris was the backroom schemer. Many media outlets had trouble even finding a file photo of the elusive Dick Morris, adding to the mystery and illusion of power.

Morris had been Clinton's earliest political adviser back in Arkansas during the first run for governor. They had a rocky relationship over the years, but following the Republican takeover of Congress in November 1994, Bill Clinton began meeting secretly with Morris. Working out of the Jefferson Hotel in Washington, using the code name "Charlie," Morris plotted the president's comeback. He was the anonymous, behind-the-scenes consultant who would retool Clinton's image, reposition his policies, and help revive his faltering presidency.

Throughout his career, Bill Clinton had a reputation for discarding political consultants. Those who helped him capture the White House in 1992—Mandy Grunwald, Stanley Greenberg, Paul Begala, and James Carville—were nowhere to be seen following the 1994 election upheaval. By the spring of 1995, Morris had assembled his own team, including veteran media consultants Bob Squier, Bill Knapp, and Hank Sheinkopf, and pollsters Mark Penn and Doug Schoen. They met regularly with several White House insiders to plan the remarkable political comeback of Bill Clinton.

Morris's anonymity was shattered when he was caught with his long-time prostitute companion by the supermarket tabloid the *Star*. The tabloid deliberately timed its bombshell story for maximum effect on the Democratic convention, with the scandal erupting on the day that Bill Clinton accepted his party's renomination for the presidency. Morris and his wife immediately left the Chicago convention and the Clinton campaign, retreating to their Connecticut home, besieged by reporters and photographers. Morris, the political consultant turned nefarious celebrity, had become a late-night dirty joke, damaged goods, and certainly a political liability. There were rumors that he was sharing sensitive White House information with his prostitute girlfriend, and Morris shocked many by announcing that months earlier he had signed a secret book deal to write the inside story of Clinton's reelection comeback. Morris now had plenty of free time to write his version of the 1996 campaign, work the talk-show circuit, join a twelve-step sex addiction program, retool his tarnished image, and pocket his $2.5 million book advance. Though the Morris scandal scarcely damaged the Clinton campaign, it ended up being everything President Clinton objected to: Dick Morris was getting famous—and rich—at his expense. For the moment, Morris joined a short list of celebrity political consultants who became as famous and often far more handsomely paid than their clients.

For years Americans had been unwittingly exposed to campaign posturing and manipulation engineered by political consultants. In the 1990s they grew curious about the manipulators. Suddenly, political consultants were hot properties. Movies, documentaries, and books gave us a glimpse of consultants at work. A film documentary, *The War Room*, made media stars of James Carville and George Stephanopoulos in Bill Clinton's 1992 presidential campaign headquarters. Reporter Joe Klein's best-selling roman à clef, *Primary Colors*, detailed with unnerving accuracy the seamy side of the presidential quest by an ambitious young Southern governor and his avaricious campaign team. Later John Travolta starred as the silver-haired young presidential candidate in the inevitable movie version. *Vote for Me*, a PBS documentary, showed hard-charging New York media consultant Hank Sheinkopf patiently coaching his candidate, an Alabama Supreme Court judge, on the fine points of camera angles and voice projection. Another film documentary, *The Perfect Candidate*, chronicled the highly charged campaign of conservative lightning rod Oliver North and his consultant Mark Goodin as they battled and lost to the uninspiring, wooden Charles Robb in the 1994 Virginia Senate race.

In the movie *Wag the Dog*, the president's spin doctor (Robert De Niro) and a high-powered Hollywood myth-maker (Dustin Hoffman) conjure up a wartime incident in Albania to cover up the president's sexual indiscretions with a twelve-year-old girl. Michael J. Fox portrayed the energetic, earnest young White House aide, a George Stephanopoulos clone, in the film *An American President* (1995), and later reprised the role in a television series, *Spin City*, with Fox serving as an aide to an unprincipled, vacuous mayor of New York City.

The bookshelf was suddenly filling up with insider accounts by political consultants. Well-traveled, controversial Republican consultant Ed Rollins skewered many of his campaign rivals and former clients in a book entitled *Bare Knuckles and Back Rooms*. On the dust jacket was the middle-aged, balding Rollins, poised with his boxing gloves, ready to take on the rough and tumble of politics. Carville and his Republican-operative wife, Mary Matalin, teamed up on the lecture circuit, hawked credit cards and aspirin in television commercials, and wrote a best-selling memoir, *All's Fair: Love, War, and Running for President*.

Carville, Stephanopoulos, and Paul Begala reappeared during the Lewinsky scandal* and the impeachment hearings. Begala returned as the loyal defender inside the White House bunker, while Carville attacked special prosecutor Kenneth Starr on television talk shows and through an angry book. . . . *And the Horse He Rode in On: The People v. Kenneth Starr*. Stephanopoulos, meanwhile, singed by the president's betrayal, distanced himself from the White House and publicly criticized Clinton's behavior in his 1999 book, *All Too Human*. Morris, too, resurfaced on talk shows, wrote political columns, advised Clinton on how to deflect criticism during the Lewinsky scandal, and penned another book, immodestly titled *The New Prince: Machiavelli Updated for the Twenty-first Century*.

Despite the notoriety and self-promotion of Morris, Carville, and others, the celebrity consultant is the exception, not the rule. Most political consultants toil in the background, content to ply their craft in anonymity. Even at the presidential campaign level, consultants generally labor in obscurity. Few Americans had ever heard of Don Sipple or Bill McInturff, consultants in Bob Dole's dysfunctional 1996 presidential race, or Bill Clinton's 1996 consultants Bill Knapp, Doug Schoen, and Marius Penczner. Very few have ever heard of George W. Bush's chief strategist Karl Rove, Al Gore's media consultant Carter Eskew, or John McCain's consultant Mike Murphy.

Political consultants, both controversial and anonymous, have become

---

*The Lewinsky scandal led to President Bill Clinton's 1998–99 impeachment by the House of Representatives and subsequent acquittal in a Senate trial. Clinton was charged with being untruthful, in legal proceedings, about revealing his sexual relationship with Monica Lewinsky, a White House intern. —EDS.

essential players in the increasingly technological, fast-paced, often brutal world of modern elections. Through it all, they have changed the face of modern American politics.

Political Consultants at Work

In earlier decades, campaigns were financed and run by local or state political parties. They were fueled by local party activists and volunteers, by family, friends, and close political supporters. By the early 1960s presidential campaigns and statewide campaigns for governor and senator began seeking out media and polling firms to help deliver their messages to voters. During the next two decades, there emerged both a new industry, political management, and a new professional, the campaign consultant. By the 1980s every serious presidential candidate, nearly every statewide candidate, and a large number of congressional candidates were using the services of professional political consultants.

The 1990s witnessed yet another transformation. Candidates for office below the statewide level were beginning to seek the advice of professional political consultants. For many candidates, the dividing line was the $50,000 campaign: those who could not raise that kind of money had to rely solely on volunteer services, and those above this threshold usually sought professional assistance. In some local political jurisdictions, record amounts of campaign funds were being raised to pay for campaign services, and races for medium-city mayor, county sheriff, or local judge took on the techniques and tactics once seen only in statewide, professionally managed contests. Professional consulting services, such as phone banks, telemarketing, and direct mail, were supplanting the efforts once provided by volunteers and party loyalists. This multibillion-dollar industry is now directed by professional consultants who make the key decisions, determine strategy, develop campaign communications, and carry out campaign tactics for their clients.

The influence of political consultants goes well beyond getting candidates elected to office. They play an increased role in ballot measures by helping clients determine ballot strategy, framing issues, and even providing the campaign foot soldiers who gather signatures for ballot petitions. Consultants use marketing and mobilization skills to orchestrate pressure on legislators. Political telemarketers link angered constituents directly with the telephones of members of Congress. Overnight, they can guarantee five thousand constituent telephone calls patched directly to a legislator's office. Political consultants are also finding lucrative markets internationally, serving presidential and other candidates throughout the world.

In the commercial world, a business that generates less than $50 million is considered a small enterprise. By that measure, every political consulting firm, except for some of the vendors, is a small business. Most of the estimated three thousand firms that specialize in campaigns and elections have ten or fewer staffers and generate just several hundred thousand dollars in revenue annually. Only a few firms, such as media consultant Squier, Knapp, and Dunn, generate millions of dollars in revenue; most of this money, however, passes through the consultants' hands to pay television advertising costs.

Leading polling firms, such as the Tarrance Group or Public Opinion Strategies, may have forty to eighty employees; most are support staff working the telephones and part of the back office operations. Quite a few firms are cottage enterprises—one- or two-person boutiques, often in speciality markets such as event planning, opposition research, fund-raising, or media buying. Many political consulting firms operate out of the basement of the principal's home with no more than telephone lines, computers, fax machines, and online access. For example, even after he became famous as Clinton's principal political adviser, James Carville and his assistants worked out of the "bat cave," a basement studio apartment on Capitol Hill that served as Carville's home and nerve center for his far-flung political operations.

Firms that rely solely on campaign cycles are exposed to the roller-coaster of cash flow: many lean months, with very little money coming in from clients, countered by a few fat months, when the bulk of the revenue pours in. In addition to the on-off flow of cash, the firms must deal with the logistical difficulties of juggling many candidates during the crucial last weeks of the campaign cycle and the enormous time pressures of a busy campaign season. Some consulting firms have around-the-clock operations during critical weeks of the campaign. These political emergency rooms are geared to handle any last-minute crisis. During long stretches when there are few campaign opportunities, professionals and support staff may have to be let go until the cycle picks up again.

One of the most difficult but necessary tasks is to even out the steep curves in the election cycle so that money and resources flow more regularly. Consultants have developed several strategies for this: convincing candidates to hire consultants earlier in the cycle, stretching out the amount of time they stay with campaigns, and seeking out off-year races, especially down the electoral ladder, such as mayoral races, general assembly, and other local contests, many of which in past years would not have sought professional assistance. Consultants are becoming more involved in the growing business of initiatives, referenda, and issues management. Many of these campaigns are tied to the same election cycle as candidate campaigns, but others are tied to local, state, or congressional issue cycles. Political consulting firms also pursue clients from the corporate and trade association world and international clients. By spreading out business, consulting firms are able to stay competitive, smooth out the peaks and valleys of the election cycle, and keep their heads above water.

In the 1980s firms began to shift away from heavy reliance on candidate campaigns. For example, the late Matt Reese, one of the founders of the political consulting business, who had worked for more than four hundred Democratic candidates, changed direction after the 1982 elections to concentrate on corporate and trade association clients. Republican consultant Eddie Mahe shifted his business from 100 percent candidate-based in 1980 to about fifteen percent candidate-based in the early 1990s, picking up corporate and other clients. In the mid-1970s Wally Clinton's pioneering political telemarketing firm, the Clinton Group, gained 90 percent of its work from candidates, but has since moved away from reliance on candidates to issues and corporate work. Many successful consulting firms have followed this pattern and now have much of their business coming from noncandidate campaigns.

As corporations have discovered the value of grassroots lobbying and issues management, consultants who specialize in direct mail and political telemarketing have shifted focus to legislative and issues work. Corporate and trade association organizations took special notice of the successful political consultant-orchestrated grassroots campaign run against President Clinton's 1993–94 health care proposal. For political consultants, such work is often far more lucrative, more reliable, and less stress-inducing than working for candidates in competitive election cycles. Some of the most successful political consulting firms have less than half of their revenue coming from candidate campaigns. . . .

What Consultants Bring to Campaigns

Candidates, not consultants, win or lose elections. In 1996 voters chose Bill Clinton, not media consultant Bob Squier; they rejected Bob Dole, not pollster Bill McInturff. Candidates alone face the voters and ultimately bear the responsibility for the tone and expression of their campaign. Sometimes reputations are diminished and images tarnished by the campaign itself. For example, George Bush will be remembered for permitting a down-and-dirty campaign that included the infamous

"Revolving Door" and Willie Horton* commercials in his 1988 presidential campaign. In that same year, Michael Dukakis will be remembered for his ride in a military vehicle, hunkered down in an oversized battle helmet, looking goofy. Alphonse D'Amato and Charles Schumer will be remembered for the abusive, in-your-face campaigns they waged in the 1998 New York Senate race.

While candidates are ultimately responsible for their campaigns, there is no way they can compete, let alone win, without professional help. Professional consultants bring direction and discipline to the campaign. Few enterprises are as unpredictable, vulnerable, and chaotic as a modern campaign. So much can go wrong: the candidate might go "off message," in which case the campaign loses focus; internal party feuds might threaten the success of the entire campaign; fund-raising might fall short of expectations, choking the life out of the entire enterprise. All the while, the opponent's campaign is raising more money, attacking with a sharp, clear message, redefining the race in its own terms, grabbing media attention, and efficiently mobilizing its resources. Campaign professionals are needed to bring order out of chaos, maintain message and strategy discipline, and keep the campaign focused.

The best consultants are able to define the race on their own terms—not the terms set by the opposition, the media, or outside third parties. In the end, the campaign boils down to letting voters know the answers to some very simple questions: who the candidate is, what the issues are, and why this race is important. Following are some examples of defining issues and messages.

From the 1996 Clinton-Gore reelection campaign:

DEFINING ISSUE: Who is better prepared to lead this country into the next century?
MESSAGE: "Building a bridge to the twenty-first century."

From the 1980 Reagan-Bush campaign:

DEFINING ISSUE: The shortcomings of the Carter administration's policies.
MESSAGE: "Are you better off today than you were four years ago?"

---

*The Willie Horton ad is a famous—or infamous—negative ad from the 1988 Bush-Dukakis presidential campaign. An independent PAC created the initial ad that accused Democratic candidate, Gov. Michael Dukakis of Massachusetts, of allowing convicted murderer William Horton out of prison on a weekend furlough; Horton committed several violent crimes while on furlough. Because Horton was black and his victims were white, the ad stirred up racial tensions that lurked not too far beneath the surface of the 1988 Bush-Dukakis campaign. —EDS.

Republican consultant Lee Atwater was fond of saying that he knew that the message of his campaign was hitting home when he would go to a local Kmart and ask shoppers what they thought of the contest, and they'd simply parrot the message he had developed.

Professionals also take campaign burdens off the candidate. Campaigns are exhausting, placing extraordinary physical and emotional demands upon the candidate. The campaign staff, and especially the campaign manager, absorb as much of the stress of the campaign as possible. A campaign manager may serve as official campaign optimist, psychologist, and hand-holder for the candidate or, often, the candidate's spouse. The manager will make the tough personnel and tactical choices when the campaign starts going bad, and be the unofficial heavy (or whipping boy) when needed.

Consultants, particularly those in niche or vendor industries, provide legal, tax, and accounting services for the increasingly complex financial disclosure reporting requirements. They provide expertise in buying television time and placing radio and television commercials. Consulting firms capture and analyze television commercials aired by opponents and other races, and offer both quantitative and qualitative analysis from survey research, focus-group, and dial-group findings. Increasingly campaigns depend on specialists who also can provide a technological edge. Consultants provide online retrieval systems and websites, computer-assisted telephone technology, voter and demographic databases, and geo-mapping and sophisticated targeting techniques so that a campaign can know, block by block and house by house, who is likely to vote and for whom they would cast a ballot. Strategists are able to use predictive technologies, traditional statistical techniques such as regression analysis, and new artificial intelligence technologies such as neural nets and genetic algorithms to target potential voters.

Above all, consultants bring experience from other campaigns. Every campaign has its unique circumstances, events, and dynamics. But campaigns are also great recycling bins. When a consultant has worked for fifteen or twenty-five races, campaigns begin to fall into predictable patterns: messages and themes, issues, and tactics reappear, taking on slight variations—new twists to old challenges. Veteran consultants can save a candidate from making mistakes, spot opportunities quickly, and take advantage of changing circumstances. As veteran consultant Joseph R. Cerrell put it, tongue in cheek, we need consultants—"to have someone handy who has forgotten more about media, mail, fund-raising and strategy than most candidates will ever know."

Growing reliance on professional consultants is costly: the price of admission to elections has risen substantially. The campaign, for many candidates, becomes a perverse full-time game of chasing dollars. Consultants have seen business grow because of the superheated fund-raising activities of the national Democratic and Republican parties, the explosion of soft money, and issues advocacy.

The best consultants aren't afraid of a fight. They know that in many cases an election can be won only if they drop the pretense of reasoned, civilized campaigning and take the gloves off. Campaigns engage in rough tactics because they work. Opposition researchers dig deep into personal lives, seeking out misdeeds and character flaws. Pollsters test-market negative material before focus and electronic dial meter groups. Then the media team cuts slash-and-burn thirty-second clips, using all the tricks of the trade: unflattering black-and-white photos of the opponent, ominous music and sound effects, and distorted features, salted with authentic-sounding textual material, often taken out of context. The direct mail pieces may get even uglier. The goal is to drive up the opponent's negatives, to paint the opponent in such unflattering ways that enough voters have only a negative view of that candidate.

Certainly not all campaigns use negative tactics. Candidates are often very reluctant to engage in mudslinging or demagoguery. Voters are turned off by negative campaigns and feel alienated from the democratic process. But campaign consultants see negative campaigning as a tool, not so much a question of political ethics or morality. If the only way to win is to go negative, then negative it is.

Professional consultants bring many weapons to a campaign. The campaign's theme and message are communicated through television and radio commercials, through direct mail pieces, and increasingly through campaign websites. Those communications are developed and honed through the use of sophisticated research analyses, especially survey research, focus groups, and dial meter sessions. Even more fundamental is the campaign's deadliest weapon, candidate and opposition research. . . .

Professional campaigns and the political consulting industry will flourish in the decades to come. Candidates for public office—both incumbents and challengers—will not hesitate to raise increasingly larger sums of campaign funds to pay for professional consultants and their services. Despite the occasional outburst from elected officials or the public, candidates need, want, and for the most part appreciate the assistance they receive from professional consultants. We may see profound changes in campaign financing, communications, and technology. Through it all, professional consulting will endure, adapt, and prosper. Professionals have become indispensable players in modern campaigns.

68

WILLIAM EGGERS

From *Government 2.0*

The Internet has arrived on the American political scene. Former Minnesota governor Jesse Ventura used the Internet in his upset independent party victory in 1998. Senator John McCain raised money and communicated views on the Net in his 2000 run for the Republican presidential nomination. Howard Dean relied on the Internet to take him from former Vermont governor to serious presidential candidate in 2004. William Eggers traces the rise of online campaigning, detailing the Dean campaign's clever and innovative use of the Internet for everything from fundraising to volunteer organizing. Using the Internet, Dean's campaign manager Joe Trippi, "helped bring Dean to the dance," Eggers writes, "but when it came time to dance with the homecoming queen, the underdog turned frontrunner just couldn't get his feet right." Ventura, McCain, and Dean are only the early pioneers of Internet campaigning, to be sure.

WHEN FORMER WRESTLING STAR Jesse Ventura toppled both Republican and Democratic opponents to win the 1998 Minnesota governor's race, the Internet got almost as much credit as the governor's "maverick celebrity" persona. Ventura began his campaign with no major party (and no major-party war chest), no endorsements, and no public recognition of his ideas. For several months, he didn't even have an office.

But Ventura did have a webmaster: Phil Madsen, a former auto mechanic, wilderness camp guide, sales manager, and church youth director who, when the campaign began, had never even built a website. No problem. Madsen bought a copy of Microsoft FrontPage 98 and turned www.jesseventura.org into a miniature campaign headquarters, where supporters could do everything from join the JesseNet email list to purchase a Jesse action figure. The Jesse dolls made a mint for the Ventura campaign, over a third of whose contributions were collected online. Ventura even added a second line of dolls with outsized nodding heads to finance his reelection campaign. These dolls, the "bobbleheads," sold out.

Ventura's website helped his campaign in strictly political terms as well. The campaign published scads of policy positions on the site, and the media responded by moving off the wrestling theme and taking the candidate more seriously. One newspaper even called him "Jesse 'The Wonk' Ventura." When he made controversial remarks (which he did quite often) or was misquoted (such as when it was widely reported that he favored legalizing prostitution), JesseNet subscribers instantly received emailed clarifications, unfiltered by reporters. JesseNet, says Madsen, effectively replaced the major political parties that his boss disdained, creating "a statewide force of truth-telling missionaries" bent on spreading the gospel of Jesse.

The Ventura campaign also used the Internet to recruit, coordinate, and motivate volunteers. "In the old days, we used to call people on the telephone one at a time to raise volunteers," says Madsen. "Now we can raise them by the dozens with a single email message." JesseNet also replaced more traditional advance teams, mobilizing volunteers whenever Ventura thundered into town. With few computers in the campaign office, the campaign even used JesseNet to let volunteers do online data entry from the comfort of their homes.

The Ventura campaign marked a milestone for e-campaigning. Until his election, the Internet had never been used in a sophisticated way by a major political campaign. Candidates would put up the obligatory website and use email to connect with staff and key volunteers, but most communications were still done by traditional media like phone, mail, and television. Ventura changed that by demonstrating just how valuable the Net could be to a political campaign. He showed how a candidate who catches fire can make up for a lack of traditional party infrastructure by using the Internet to market himself directly to voters, raise money, organize volunteers, and get voters to the polls—four of every campaign's most important tasks. There were too many other factors—notably, the candidate's beefy persona—to give the Internet all the credit for his startling victory. But without the Net, says Madsen, "we couldn't have won the election." . . .

Online campaigning has made huge strides since Ventura's shocking netfueled election. In fact, by today's standards, Ventura's then trailblazing foray into Internet campaigning might now even seem a bit primitive, that is until you stop to consider two important facts: Ventura was the first major candidate to do this; and, unlike Howard Dean and John McCain—two more recent Internet campaigning pioneers—Jesse actually won his race.

Thanks at least in part to Ventura's success, candidates for offices at all levels of government have begun to exploit the potential of a medium which can, according to PoliticsOnline.com president Phil Noble, deliver "everything a campaign is already doing, but faster, smarter and cheaper." "Everything except kissing babies," he amends. "There are no cyber-lips yet." Instead of simply posting their brochures online, tech-savvy candidates are making the Net the hub of their campaign. . . .

As more and more candidates embrace email, the Internet, and other information technologies, many changes coming to government in general are guiding political campaigns as well. Just as citizen expectations are rising with regard to the ease and speed of government services, so are voter expectations. "Netizens" expect to not only scan candidate websites but to have a variety of options while there. Voter contact is becoming more personalized and more targeted. The ability to turn scads of voter information into useful knowledge about which voters to target and how to win them over can mean the difference between winning and losing a campaign. Campaign spending is more transparent than ever before thanks to the Net. Want to know the names of the well-heeled Bush Rangers, each one of whom raised a whopping $200,000 for President Bush in 2004? They're listed right there on www.georgewbush.com. Even volunteering is going high-tech. Many campaigns are outfitting volunteers with PDAs to share voter information when they hit the precincts. . . .

> Jesse Ventura was the hop.
> John McCain was the skip.
> And Howard Dean is the quantum leap.
>
> —MICHAEL CORNFIELD
> George Washington University's
> Institute for Politics, Democracy and the Internet

Ventura's breakthrough campaign helped to inspire a presidential bid that, although it did not ultimately win the White House, nonetheless marked Internet campaigning's big-time debut. After all, Ventura was several different kinds of anomaly—how many politicians can get away with posing as Rodin's "Thinker" in an ad during the last days of the campaign? Sen. John McCain's massive Internet fund-raising push during the 2000 presidential primary proved that "normal" (or at least seminormal) candidates could use the new medium as well.

Max Fose, McCain's webmaster, likes to joke that his B.A. in Criminal Justice made him a natural for work in politics. Fose fits the role of Weird-Web-Guy perfectly, with his spiky hair and sweaters, sitting in the back of McCain headquarters in a cramped little room lit by a flickering neon

bulb and a green scented candle. Fose knew McCain was fighting an
uphill battle against both public expectations and presidential son George
W. Bush's vast network of party support. His own online role, he felt,
would be crucial to overcoming the obstacles in McCain's path. "If this
is David vs. Goliath," he said, "then the Internet is our slingshot."

He began by placing McCain banner ads on popular sites like the
New York Times, the *Wall Street Journal*, *Los Angeles Times*, and *Slate*
magazine, and it worked; about 3 percent of viewers who saw the ads
"clicked through" to McCain's campaign site—a much higher percentage
than is garnered by most direct-mail campaigns. Like Ventura, McCain
used the Internet to gather volunteers and cash, to exercise damage control,
and to present the candidate's views. On just one Saturday during the
California primary campaign, the site sent out twenty-two emails to
different groups of supporters. In New York, the campaign had forty-
nine different people across the state, each representing a different geographical area, updating their part of the campaign site daily.

But it was McCain's upset victory in the New Hampshire primary
that most strikingly illustrated the Internet's potential political power.
McCain showed future dark-horse candidates how to capitalize on early
wins by converting his political momentum almost immediately into
dollars, which in turn, he used to build more momentum. Previously,
candidates would have to wait weeks for donations in the wake of a New
Hampshire win, by which time their comet may have already burnt out.
McCain, by contrast, raked in $20,000 via his website in the first hour
after he won the primary; $300,000 by the next morning; and $2 million
by the end of the week. "The Internet transforms the action-reaction
dynamic of defining events," write Michael Cornfield and Jonah Sieger
of George Washington University. "If an organization is prepared for a
surge of traffic to arrive at some point during the campaign, it can put
it to work, not only to redefine public perceptions, but to raise money,
recruit volunteers, and otherwise multiply the impact of an event." All
in all, the Arizona Senator raised nearly one-third of all his campaign
funds, $6.4 million, online—something that had never been done be-
fore. . . .

It was audacious. It was inspired. It was vintage Howard Dean. In
four days, Vice President Cheney was slated to raise $300,000 for the
Bush-Cheney reelection committee at an event for 150 well-to-do GOP
donors in South Carolina. Alongside a picture of him biting into a turkey
sandwich on his website, Dean issued a challenge to his supporters: over
the next four days help me raise more money than the vice president will

receive in South Carolina. There was one catch. Instead of throwing $2,000-a-plate fund-raisers, Dean wanted to beat Cheney without spending a dime—by raising all the money online.

It was no contest.

Dean raised $508,640 over the Internet in four days—almost 70 percent more than Cheney's haul. Fully 9,621 supporters answered the Vermont governor's call. The average donation: about $50 a piece. The best part of the story is that the idea didn't come from Dean or his campaign manager, or some highly paid campaign consultant. In fact it didn't come from anyone on the campaign at all. It came from a blogger on his website.

The Cheney Challenge was but one example of Dean's Internet fundraising prowess. By the summer of 2003, he had shocked the political world. In just six months Dean had gone from long-shot candidate with no money in his campaign kitty to the Dem with the most money, the most supporters and the best polling numbers. His silver bullet? The Internet. Dean garnered tens of millions of dollars worth of donations and hundreds of thousands of supporters from the Net. Most of the money came from small donors that Dean could go back to several times without hitting up against the $2,000 federal spending limit. His Internet fundraising was so strong that this governor from one of the least populated states in the nation decided to opt out of public financing altogether.

In the second quarter of 2003, more than 73,000 people contributed to Dean's campaign, a full 50,000 more than to John Kerry. In the fourth quarter, Dean broke the record for campaign fund-raising in a single quarter, bringing in $15.9 million, far outdistancing Bill Clinton, who had taken in $10.5 million as a sitting president. By the time he withdrew from the race, 670,000 donors had given the Vermont governor more than $45 million. . . .

Dean and McCain both benefited greatly from the "clean" image of Internet money: no chicken-or-fish dinners with wealthy donors, no photos of the candidate in compromising proximity to honey-tongued lobbyists. The Internet, it turns out, is highly conducive to new, small-dollar donors. Thirty-one percent of McCain's Internet contributions came from people who'd never given to a political campaign before, and 71 percent came from people who had either not given money before or had given only once before. Not to be outdone, Dean raised more money from $25 and $75 donations than any Democratic campaign in history. As Internet fundraising becomes more common, the percentage of small-dollar, first-time donors is likely to rise even more.

Ironically, McCain, and to some extent Dean, were both known for an issue—campaign finance reform—which many observers believe will be rendered less pressing by online fund-raising (and maybe even made obsolete), as increased contributions by small online donors balance out the lobbyists' moneybags. According to Fose, when these small donors give online, they give significantly more than they do by mail or by phone because it is more of an impulse buy. Internet contributions can be rapidly tallied and published online, thus enhancing campaign transparency.

E-campaigners also may need less money to run. After all, email is free, and as former Louisiana legislator Ron Faucheux says, "The biggest cost item in political campaigns is *postage*." . . .

> We didn't know what we were doing half the time.
> We were doing things that were being tried for the first time in this
> country's political history.
>
> —JOE TRIPPI
> Howard Dean's former campaign manager

Fund-raising, of course, was only one facet of online campaigning that the Dean campaign mastered like no campaign had before. By running the first presidential campaign organized primarily through the web, Dean demonstrated how an underdog candidate with a compelling message can exploit the speed and decentralized nature of the Internet to go from relative obscurity to a front-runner for the presidency in a very short period of time. Dean was the first presidential campaign to have a blog, the first (at least in America) to experiment with wireless and text messaging, and the first to use a popular gathering spot called Meetup.com, which coordinates local gatherings for people with similar interests, to bring volunteers together from all over the country to coordinate events and discuss campaign issues.

The Meetup meetings started off as unsanctioned events spontaneously put together by supporters and morphed into monthly meetings with Dean and his senior campaign staff attending. Each month, tens of thousands of volunteers got together at restaurants, cafes, and student unions in more than one thousand cities and towns across the country to discuss the Dean campaign and listen to the candidate. By the time he dropped out of the race, more than 200,000 people had registered at Meetup.com for Howard Dean, making it the most popular Meetup group on the web—right ahead of witches, pagans, and Elvis enthusiasts. Dean used Meetup and other web-based tools such as DeanLink, a Friendstar-like program that helped supporters recruit their friends and family to join the campaign, to create hundreds of networks of loosely organized volunteers who in turn were linked to each other and to the national campaign. "When you don't have money for mailings and fund-raisers and you're outside the power structure, the Net is just a wonderful tool to get things rolling," said Mark Naccarato, cochairman of the Dean campaign in Nashville, Tennessee, "The Internet is just a very efficient way to connect people . . . what it changes is the ability to organize quickly and efficiently."

By the beginning of 2004, Dean had signed up nearly 900,000 people online to assist his campaign in one way or another. These supporters, who the campaign team called the "Net roots," were the heart and the soul of the Dean campaign. They helped him walk away with MoveOn.org's highly publicized Internet-based Democratic presidential primary, winning 44 percent of the vote—not to mention millions of dollars worth of free publicity and $3 million in campaign donations that came in the week following the vote.

The really novel part about the Dean campaign was not that it managed to recruit a lot of supporters—other campaigns had done that before—but that it moved beyond the one-way conversation national campaigns traditionally had with their supporters to a genuine dialogue. The Dean campaign vested a tremendous amount of trust and authority in the Net roots. A handful of the most innovative ideas from the campaign, such as the Cheney Challenge, came from bloggers on Dean's website. When Dean was deciding whether or not to opt out of public financing—and thereby the campaign spending limits—he spelled out the pros and cons on his weblog and then left the decision up to his supporters via a national online vote. "We're actually trying to get people to participate in democracy again," explained Dean's tech-savvy campaign manager Joe Trippi at the time. "And we're using the Internet to get the message out faster and earlier and asking supporters to help spread the word."

Dean, of course, ultimately lost the Democratic primary in what surely will go down as one of the fastest and steepest crashes in recent presidential history. Countless political wags likened the Dean flameout to the dot-com crash. The meltdown, we were told, demonstrated that the Internet model of political organization was a failure—or at least that it failed Dean. "Dean offered the Democratic Party a different model of organizing, a distinctive approach to political mobilization," wrote David Broder, the Beltway's dean of political journalism. "Its conspicuous failure in its first road tests . . . brings into question the whole notion that Internet-based populism is the wave of the future."

The Internet didn't fail Dean. Dean failed Dean. Once subjected to the "front-runner's glare," he made a bevy of mistakes: a gaffe a day for

weeks on end (from Osama to Saddam to Confederate flags), the refusal
to talk at all about his family (thereby making it hard for voters to get to
know him as a person), spending millions of dollars on television commercials outside of Iowa months before a single primary was held (who could
forget the $100,000 in Texas), and, of course, "the scream" (enough said).
Smelling blood, his primary opponents, as well as the media, were happy
to pile on and the rest was history. "This [wasn't] a dot-com crash," argues
Trippi. "It's a dot-com miracle being shot down is what it is . . . the dot-
com was supposed to make money, and the Howard Dean campaign put
more money together than any Democrat in history so where did it mess
up there? It's the broadcast politics of the party, it's the scream speech run
over and over again, and yes to be honest about it, the governor admits
it's himself."

To be sure Trippi has a vested interest in this account, but he is
nonetheless correct. The Internet-based model Trippi pioneered helped
bring Dean to the dance, but when it came time to dance with the
homecoming queen, the underdog turned frontrunner just couldn't get
his feet right.

69

KATHLEEN HALL JAMIESON

From *Dirty Politics*

*One of the most memorable campaign ads from a presidential election is
the famous—or infamous—1988 Willie Horton ad. The original ad came
from a political action committee (PAC) independent of President Bush's
campaign. Political scientist Kathleen Hall Jamieson describes the content
of the anti-Dukakis message. It showed William Horton, whom the ad
referred to as "Willie," a convicted murderer, who had been given a weekend
furlough while Michael Dukakis was governor of Massachusetts. The ad
tells viewers that during this furlough, Horton kidnapped a couple and
stabbed the man and raped the woman. Jamieson examines the Bush
campaign's follow-up spot and reveals how the Willie Horton story became
like a drama, filled with dangerous misinterpretations and untrue implications about the crime. William Horton was black. The couple was white.*

The Republicans had successfully played the "race card," with fear being a winning issue in the 1988 presidential election.

ALMOST THREE YEARS after George Bush decisively defeated Democrat Michael Dukakis to become the president of the United States, a group of voters in Pineville, Louisiana, was asked, "Can you tell me what you remember as being important in the 1988 presidential campaign?" The individuals in the group responded.

Hmm.

I'm trying to think.

1988?

LEADER: '88.

That's the last one.

Dukakis.

That was Dukakis.

It's about time for another one isn't it?

That time again. It was Dukakis wasn't it?

I just knew I couldn't vote for him.

Seems like the Democratic man that ran, he had a lot of problems. His wife and so forth.

A lot of that didn't come out 'til after the election, though.

That's right.

A lot of us didn't know of her personal problems. They hid . . . that was pretty well hid. She admitted that was . . . I don't know that was a . . .

I think the big thing against him was that, wasn't his criminal . . . I mean not his criminal record, but his . . . the handling of, um . . .

The handling of his state programs.

His state programs. I think that influenced a lot of people, how they voted.

And again, it was still a social aspect of dealing with social issues. And, uh, Bush was more international and people developing things for themselves. Giving them an opportunity to do their own thing and that will support our country. By that I mean build up business and the taxes then, and the income from growth and everything will take care of our country. I saw those as two distinct things.

FOCUS GROUP LEADER: You had just mentioned how he handled state issues. Can you think of any specific issues?

Well, I think right off the . . . the one I'm thinking about was his . . . his handling of a criminal, um, and I can't right now . . .

What do you mean, a pardon of someone who has . . .

Willie Horton.

Yeah. A pardon.

Pardon.

Yeah. He pardoned that guy that went out and killed someone.

Afterwards. You know, he released this known . . . I guess he was a murderer wasn't he? Originally. And they released him anyway and he went out and killed . . .

Immediately and killed people again.

Right after getting out.

And this was brought out that he was releasing people really without seemingly too much thought. I think that had a lot to do with it.

William Horton and Michael Dukakis are now twinned in our memory. The fact that the memories are factually inaccurate does not diminish their power. Dukakis did not pardon Horton nor did the furloughed convict kill.

Although it does recount the facts of the Horton case, this chapter is not one more rehash of who did what to whom in the 1988 campaign. Instead, it sets a context for the book by examining how voters and reporters came to know what they know of politics. It argues that, in politics as in life, what is known is not necessarily what is believed, what is shown is not necessarily what is seen, and what is said is not necessarily what is heard. It then examines how in the Horton case consultants exploited the psychological quirks that characterize humans.

These quirks include a pack-ratlike tendency to gather up and interrelate information from various places, a disposition to weigh accessible, dramatic data more heavily than abstract statistical information, and a predilection for letting fears shape perception of what constitutes "fact."

At the same time, we have conventionalized journalistic norms that reward messages that are dramatic, personal, concise, visual, and take the form of narrative. In 1988, the psychological dispositions of the public coupled with the news norms to produce an environment in which an atypical but dramatic personification of deep-seated fears would displace other issues and dominate the discourse of the campaign. That dramatic, visual, personalized narrative told the "story" of William Horton.

The role that ads, Bush rhetoric, news, and audience psychology played in transforming William Horton's name for some into a symbol of the terrors of crime and for others of the exploitation of racist fears shows the powerful ways in which messages interact and the varying responses they evoke in individuals. Like pack rats, voters gather bits and pieces of political information and store them in a single place. Lost in the storage is a clear recall of where this or that "fact" came from. Information obtained from news mixes with that from ads, for example.

Although Bush had been telling the tale on the stump since June, in the second week in September 1988, the Horton story broke into prime time in the form of a National Security Political Action Committee (NSPAC) ad. The ad tied Michael Dukakis to a convicted murderer who had jumped furlough and gone on to rape a Maryland woman and assault her fiancé. The convict was black, the couple white.*

The ad opens with side-by-side pictures of Dukakis and Bush. Dukakis's hair is unkempt, the photo dark. Bush, by contrast, is smiling and bathed in light. As the pictures appear, an announcer says "Bush and Dukakis on crime." A picture of Bush flashes on the screen. "Bush supports the death penalty for first-degree murderers." A picture of Dukakis. "Dukakis not only opposes the death penalty, he allowed first degree murderers to have weekend passes from prison." A close-up mug shot of Horton flashes onto the screen. "One was Willie Horton, who murdered a boy in a robbery, stabbing him nineteen times." A blurry black-and-white photo of Horton apparently being arrested appears. "Despite a life sentence, Horton received ten weekend passes from prison." The words "kidnapping," "stabbing," and "raping" appear on the screen with Horton's picture as the announcer adds, "Horton fled, kidnapping a young couple, stabbing the man and repeatedly raping his girlfriend." The final photo again shows Michael Dukakis. The announcer notes "Weekend prison passes. Dukakis on crime."

When the Bush campaign's "revolving door" ad began to air on October 5, viewers read Horton from the PAC ad into the furlough ad. This stark black-and-white Bush ad opened with bleak prison scenes. It then cut to a procession of convicts circling through a revolving gate and marching toward the nation's living rooms. By carefully juxtaposing words and pictures, the ad invited the false inference that 268 first-degree murderers were furloughed by Dukakis to rape and kidnap. As the bleak visuals appeared, the announcer said that Dukakis had vetoed the death penalty and given furloughs to "first-degree murderers not eligible for parole. While out, many committed other crimes like kidnapping and rape."

The furlough ad contains three false statements and invites one illegitimate inference. The structure of the ad prompts listeners to hear "first-degree murderers not eligible for parole" as the antecedent referent for "many." Many of whom committed crimes? First-degree murderers not

*In his article "The Road to Here," included in Larry Sabato's *Toward the Millennium: The Elections of 1996*, journalist Tom Rosenstiel points out that much negative campaigning ironically originates in the primaries among fellow party members. It was fellow Democrat Al Gore who first unearthed the Willie Horton incident regarding Democrat Michael Dukakis during the presidential primaries in 1988. — EDS.

eligible for parole. Many of whom went on to commit crimes like kidnapping and rape? First-degree murderers not eligible for parole.

But many unparoleable first-degree murderers did not escape. Of the 268 furloughed convicts who jumped furlough during Dukakis's first two terms, only four had ever been convicted first-degree murderers not eligible for parole. Of those four not "many" but one went on to kidnap and rape. That one was William Horton. By flashing "268 escaped" on the screen as the announcer speaks of "many first-degree murderers," the ad invites the false inference that 268 murderers jumped furlough to rape and kidnap. Again, the single individual who fits this description is Horton. Finally, the actual number who were more than four hours late in returning from furlough during Dukakis's two and a half terms was not 268 but 275. In Dukakis's first two terms, 268 escapes were made by the 11,497 individuals who were given a total of 67,378 furloughs. In the ten-year period encompassing his two completed terms and the first two years of his third term (1987–88), 275 of 76,455 furloughs resulted in escape.

This figure of 275 in ten years compares with 269 who escaped in the three years in which the program was run by Dukakis's Republican predecessor, who created the furlough program.

Still the battle of drama against data continued. After the Bush campaign's furlough ad had been on the air for two and a half weeks, in the third week of October, PAC ads featuring the victims of Horton began airing. One showed the man whose fiancée had been raped by the furloughed Horton. "Mike Dukakis and Willie Horton changed our lives forever," said Cliff Barnes, speaking in tight close-up. "He was serving a life term, without the possibility of a parole, when Governor Dukakis gave him a few days off. Horton broke into our home. For twelve hours, I was beaten, slashed, and terrorized. My wife, Angie, was brutally raped. When his liberal experiment failed, Dukakis simply looked away. He also vetoed the death penalty bill. Regardless of the election, we are worried people don't know enough about Mike Dukakis."

The second ad was narrated by the sister of the teenager killed by Horton. "Governor Dukakis's liberal furlough experiments failed. We are all victims. First, Dukakis let killers out of prison. He also vetoed the death penalty. Willie Horton stabbed my teenage brother nineteen times. Joey died. Horton was sentenced to life without parole, but Dukakis gave him a furlough. He never returned. Horton went on to rape and torture others. I worry that people here don't know enough about Dukakis's record." The words that recur in the two ads are: "liberal," "experiment," "rape," worry that "people don't know enough about Dukakis," "vetoed the death penalty."

Taken together the ads created a coherent narrative. Dukakis furloughed Horton (PAC ads), just as he had furloughed 267 other escapees (Bush revolving door ad). Horton raped a woman and stabbed her fiancé (crime-quiz and victim PAC ads). Viewers could infer what must have happened to the victims of the other 267 escapees. . . .

The Horton narrative fit the requirements of news. Unlike the "soft" news found in feature stories of the sort pioneered by Charles Kuralt on television, hard news is about an event that treats an issue of ongoing concern. Because violent crime is dramatic, conflict ridden, evokes intense emotions, disrupts the social order, threatens the community, and can be verified by such official sources as police, it is "newsworthy." If one believed Bush's version of the facts, a convicted murderer who should have been executed had been furloughed to rape, torture, and murder again. In newscasts, the villain Horton appeared incarnated in a menacing mug shot. To personalize and dramatize, the news camera showed him in close-up; the less inflammatory visuals in the controversial PAC ad were shot mid-screen. Appearing in tight close-ups both in news and in the ads, the sister of the teenager Horton allegedly killed and the fiancé and now husband of the woman he raped told of their torment and urged a vote against the second villain in the story, Michael Dukakis. . . .

Helping propel the false generalizations from the isolated case of Horton to hordes of others who presumably did what he had done were complex and unspoken references to race. "'Crime' became a shorthand signal," note Thomas and Mary Edsall, "to a crucial group of white voters, for broader issues of social disorder, evoking powerful ideas about authority, status, morality, self-control, and race." "Any reference to capital punishment," argues political scientist Murray Edelman, "is also a reference to the need to restrain blacks and the poor from violence. The liberal argument that poor people and blacks are disproportionately targeted by capital punishment laws doubtless fuels this fear in a part of the public. That the association is subtle makes it all the more potent, for 'capital punishment,' like all condensation symbols, draws its intensity from the associations it represses." Without actually voicing the repressed associations, the image of Horton on the screen as the announcer notes that Dukakis opposes the death penalty serves to raise them. "'Weekend Passes' [which I have called the Horton ad] is not about Willie Horton," says NSPAC's Floyd Brown. "It's about the death penalty. George Bush stood on the side of the majority. Michael Dukakis stood on the side of the minority. The death penalty is where we win our audience."

The 1990 General Social Survey of Racial Stereotyping among White Americans demonstrates that racial prejudice correlates with support for capital punishment. According to Kinder and Mendelberg, "white Americans who regard blacks as inferior are quite a bit more likely to favor the death penalty for convicted murderers."

In the last week of October 1988, ninety-three members of ten focus groups demonstrated the power of the Horton narrative to elicit racially based fear. "If you saw an ad on prison furloughs with scenes in a prison," these voters were asked, "remember as best you can" the "race or ethnic identity" of the "people you saw in the ad. . . . " Of those who did recall the ad, nearly 60 percent (59.9 percent, 43 individuals) reported that most of the men were black. In fact, only two of the "prisoners" are identifiably black. One of them is the only one in the ad to ever look directly into the camera.

When asked to write out everything "you know about William Horton," all but five of the focus group respondents included the fact that Horton is black in their description. All but twelve wrote that the woman raped was white. One-third of the respondents indicated Horton's race twice in their descriptions. And one focus group respondent referred to Horton throughout his description as "this Black Man." Twenty-eight percent of those in the focus groups indicated that he had committed murder while on furlough. . . .

All narrative capitalizes on the human capacity and disposition to construct stories. A compelling narrative such as the Horton saga controls our interpretation of data by offering a plausible, internally coherent story that resonates with the audience while accounting causally for otherwise discordant or fragmentary information.

When news and ads trace the trauma and drama of a kidnapping and rape by a convicted murderer on furlough, the repetition and the story structure give it added power in memory. Visceral, visual identifications and appositions are better able to be retrieved than statistical abstractions.

Repeatedly aired oppositional material carries an additional power. Material aired again and again is more likely to stay fresh in our minds. The same is true for attacks.

Cognitive accessibility is upped by those message traits that characterize the Republicans' use of Horton: the dramatic, the personally relevant, the frequently repeated topic or claim—the menacing mug shot, circling convicts, empathic victims—and seemingly uncaring perpetrator—the Massachusetts governor.

When it came to William Horton, our quirks as consumers of political information worked for the Republicans and against the Democrats. In our psychic equations, something nasty has greater power and influence than something nice. When evaluating "social stimuli," negative information carries more weight than positive information. Additionally, negative information seems better able than positive to alter existing impressions and is easier to recall. Televised images that elicit negative emotion result in better recall than those that evoke positive ones. As a result, attacks are better remembered than positive reasons for voting for a candidate. And dissatisfied, disapproving voters are more likely to appear at their polling place than their more satisfied neighbors.

Messages that induce fear dampen our disposition to scrutinize them for gaps in logic. When the message is fear arousing, personal involvement and interest in it minimize systematic evaluation. In the language of cognitive psychology, "[L]arge levels of negative affect such as fear may override cognitive processing."

The Horton story magnifies fear of crime, identifies that fear with Dukakis, and offers a surefire way of alleviating the anxiety—vote for Bush. . . .

The power of the Horton mini-series was magnified as it unfolded soap-opera-like in news and ads; broadcasts that focused on the tale's strategic intent and effect couldn't effectively challenge its typicality. And since statistics don't displace stories nor data, drama, the native language of Dukakis didn't summon persuasive visions of the cops he had put on the street or the murders and rapes that hadn't been committed in a state whose crime rate was down. Abetted by news reports, amplified by Republican ads, assimilated through the cognitive quirks of audiences, William Horton came to incarnate liberalism's failures and voters' fears.

70

STEPHEN ANSOLABEHERE
SHANTO IYENGAR

From *Going Negative*

The weakening of political parties, growing voter cynicism, and negative campaign advertising: Political scientists Stephen Ansolabehere and Shanto Iyengar interrelate these complex developments in American politics. Illustrating their thesis with some memorable election campaign attack ads, the authors contend that a vicious cycle has developed. Middle-of-the-road, independent-minded voters are increasingly alienated by negative campaigns, with the result that politics becomes more and more the province of those on the ideological extremes.

ONCE UPON A TIME, this country divided itself neatly along party lines. Most people voted; those who did not tended to be poorer, less well-educated, and more apathetic, but still party loyal. The line between participants and nonparticipants was a fault line of sorts, but it was not terribly worrisome. Civic duty ideally would involve everyone, but, even falling short of the ideal, we were at least expressing our national will in our elections. Television has changed all that. Now, we are split by a new division: between loyalists and apathetics. On the one hand, media propaganda can often shore up loyalists to vote for their traditional party; on the other hand, that same propaganda is increasingly peeling off a band of citizens who turn from independence to apathy, even antipathy, toward our political institutions.

Pollsters and political scientists first noticed this new fault line in 1964. The number of people who proclaimed themselves independent of traditional party labels rose sharply in the mid-1960s. At the same time, candidates embraced television as a new means of independent communication with the voters. Politicians no longer needed the legions of party workers to get their messages across; they could effectively establish personal connections with their constituents using television advertising. In addition, there arose a new class of campaign manager—the media consultant, who typically had worked on Madison Avenue and viewed selling politics much like selling any other product. By the end of the 1960s, media consultants had filled the shoes left vacant by the then-extinct ward healers and precinct captains. Within the political parties, chaos reigned. The old-style politicos in both the Democratic and Republican parties battled and lost to a new regime of populists and progressives, who opened up the parties' nominating process to all comers. By most accounts, these reforms did even greater harm to the parties, shamelessly opening schisms that in earlier years were smoothed over behind closed doors.

At the time many observers mistakenly saw in the combination of televised political advertising and the nonpartisan voter the advent of a new age in America. Television advertising was to have produced a new kind of independent politician, not beholden to special interests and not part of the problems that voters increasingly associated with Washington.

That day has not dawned. To be sure, the ranks of Independent voters have swollen since 1964, and television advertising is now the mainstay of contemporary political campaigns. The political parties, however, remain ascendent in elections and in government. Despite an occasional Independent candidacy and the rise of the personal electoral followings of many candidates, electoral competition is still between Republicans and Democrats. What is more, government, especially Congress, has become even more polarized and partisan than ever. The parties in Congress represent two increasingly cohesive and extreme positions.

The electorate has reacted with frustration and anger. In recent years, the political pulsetakers have registered record lows in political participation, record highs in public cynicism and alienation, and record rates of disapproval of the House of Representatives, the institution designed to represent the public will.

The single biggest cause of the new, ugly regime is the proliferation of negative political advertising on TV. Our argument is that a new synthesis in American politics has failed to emerge precisely because of the ways that partisans and nonpartisans react to televised political messages. Like product advertising, successful political advertising reflects people's beliefs, experiences, and preferences. One consequence of this simple axiom is that political campaigns reinforce the loyalties of partisans. Nonpartisans, by contrast, usually tune out political advertising. They find politicians, politics, and government distasteful; political advertising simply sounds like more of the same. Only negative messages resonate with such attitudes. As political campaigns have become more hostile over the last two decades, nonpartisans have heard plenty to reinforce their low opinions of politics. Unfortunately, negative campaigning only reinforces the nonpartisans' disillusionment and convinces them not to participate in a tainted process. As a result, nonpartisans have not become the electoral force that they might have. Instead, political advertising has produced a party renaissance, even though partisans are an increasingly unrepresentative segment of the public. . . .

The electorate has grown weary of the nastiness and negativity of campaigns. They are mad at the candidates, mad at the parties, mad at the media, and mad at anyone else who steps into the electoral arena. Many people now choose to stay home on election day; others openly express their dissatisfaction with the candidates and the parties among which they must choose. People no longer feel that they vote *for*, only against. If venom isn't really what the public is after, why do candidates insist on going negative?

Politicians and campaign consultants are, by and large, not mean-spirited people who conspire to scare voters away from the polls. The reality is more complex. The negative tenor of campaigns can be traced to the competitive nature of political advertising, to the activities of organized interests, and, last but not least, to the ways in which reporters cover the campaign. Politicians, interest groups, and journalists all act in ways that serve their own best interests. Few of these players really want to produce highly negative campaigns, but the interplay among them produces the kind of campaigns that voters have come to loathe.

"Politics," Lloyd Bentsen reflected after the 1988 election, "is a contact sport." The main event is the head-to-head competition between the candidates. This, above all else, drives candidates to assail one another with thirty-second spot ads. Put bluntly, candidates attack out of fear: fear that the opposition will throw the first punch, fear that they will appear weak if they don't respond in kind. In politics, the best defense is a strong offense, and negative advertising is the most expedient way to fend off the opposition's attacks.

In addition, candidates attack to expand the scope of the political conflict, to drag organized interests and the media into the fray. Political campaigns have about them the same excitement as a prize fight. The more intense the conflict, the more people are drawn to it. Political campaigns, however, are not nearly as orderly as professional boxing matches. No ropes keep the audience from joining in. The more a candidate attacks, the more she makes news; the more conflict there is, and stories about the conflict, the more likely the candidate's proponents are to join the fray. Corporations, professional associations, unions, and other organizations have large stakes in the outcomes of elections, and they don't remain on the sidelines long. These organizations put up millions of dollars to underwrite the candidate's campaign activities; they also aggressively publicize their support of and opposition to politicians independent of the candidate's own campaigning. Through unrestrained independent advertising, interest groups can and do influence the tone, the issues, and even the outcome of elections.

The media are less partisan, but have an equally important effect on the tenor of campaigns. Journalists report the campaign with the verve of sportswriters covering a title fight. Their job, after all, is to sell papers and attract viewers, and elections are full of great material—the mistakes and weaknesses of the candidates, the twists and turns of public opinion, and the jabs and hooks of political debate. Campaign commercials, especially the negative ones, are ideally suited to the dictates of a good news story. They pack a sensational story with good visuals and good sound into thirty brief seconds. Nothing grabs the public's attention like the smell of a scandal or the prospect of a political upset. Such stories make for entertaining reading, but they don't instill confidence in the political system. . . .

. . . [M]ost consultants subscribe to Roger Ailes's first dictum of politics: "If you get punched, punch back." The best way to defuse an attack is typically to counterattack. Here are examples of three common tactics.

---

1. DEFEND AGAINST THE CHARGES

Attack by Representative Wayne Dowdy against Senator Trent Lott, Mississippi U.S. Senate race, 1988.

SCENE: A stretch limousine barrels through a small town.

ANNOUNCER: Trent Lott says he needs to keep his taxpayer-paid, $50,000-a-year chauffeur in Washington. You can vote for a party politician who looks at life through tinted windows. Or you can vote for a Senator who sees Mississippi through the eyes of its people.

Response by Trent Lott.

GEORGE AWKWARD [Lott's African-American bodyguard, speaking directly into the camera, with the American flag in the background]: I've been a detective in a security police force in Washington, D.C., for 27 years. Wayne Dowdy calls me a chauffeur. He offends every law enforcement officer who puts his life on the line every day. Mr. Dowdy, I'm nobody's chauffeur. [pause] Got it?

---

2. COUNTERATTACK ON THE SAME QUESTION OR ON ISSUES THAT ARE OF GREATER CONCERN TO VOTERS

Attack by Bruce Herschensohn on Barbara Boxer, California Senate race, 1992.

HERSCHENSOHN [speaking directly into the camera]: Ya know. A hundred and forty-three bounced checks. Wow, that's . . . that's . . . a lot. That's really a lot. That's what my opponent did. It added up to more than what most Californians make in well over a year. Forty-one thousand dollars in bounced checks. Boy. I Mean, do you want her trying to balance your budget? Our government's budget? Gee.

ANNOUNCER: Fight back with Herschensohn.

Boxer's response.

HERSCHENSOHN [newsclips]: "What I want is the repeal of *Roe v. Wade*" . . . "We need more offshore oil drilling and nuclear power plants" . . . "Demolish the Department of Energy and Education" . . . "I oppose any cuts in defense."

ANNOUNCER: That's what Bruce Herschensohn wants. Is that what you want?

---

3. ASSAIL THE OPPOSITION'S CREDIBILITY

Attack by Russell Feingold on Senator Robert Kasten, Wisconsin U.S. Senate race, 1992.

FEINGOLD [holding newspaper with headline about Senator Robert Kasten's negative campaign tactics]: If things are going to change around here, this man must be defeated in November. Not much has been written about Russ Feingold to attack. So the only option is to make something up.

FEINGOLD [holding up mock tabloid endorsement by Elvis Presley]: You voters know better than to believe everything you read.

Senator Robert Kasten's counterattack.

ELVIS IMPERSONATOR [sitting in pink Cadillac with 1950s music blaring, looking at cardboard cutout of Feingold holding mock tabloid]: I don't make many appearances. But when I heard that he was telling tales how I endorsed him, I had to come forward. You know that Russ has been in politics for more than a decade. Feingold plans to raise our taxes over $300 billion. Well, the King would never support that. Take it from the King, this Russ Feingold record has got me all shook up.

Feingold's parting shot.

FEINGOLD [close up]: A while ago, I warned you about my opponent's history of making things up. I figured when he started distorting the truth about me, you'd take it with a grain of salt.

[Feingold picks up a jar of salt and starts pouring it on the ground. The camera zooms in on the growing pile.]

FEINGOLD: Well, get ready, because now he's telling you I have a plan to raise thousands of dollars of taxes on the middle class. Not true. Senator Kasten knows I haven't proposed any such tax increases. Period. The truth is the Senator has made up something so big that a few grains of salt won't be enough. A shovelful would be more like it.

[Camera pulls back to show Feingold holding a shovel.]

Tit-for-tat. And so it goes with many campaigns today. A negative advertisement triggers a negative response and, in turn, a negative reply. Increasingly, even positive commercials provoke attacks. Candidates who promote a particular ideology or program seem especially susceptible to criticism. Stick your neck out and get your head chopped off. . . .

Whatever its causes, negative politics generates disillusionment and distrust among the public. Attack advertisements resonate with the popular beliefs that government fails, that elected officials are out of touch and quite corrupt, and that voting is a hollow act. The end result: lower turnout and lower trust in government, regardless of which party rules.

The marginal voter—the Independent—feels the pinch of negative advertisements most sharply. Attack ads produce the highest drop in political efficacy and in intentions to participate among nonpartisans. Most of these people have shed their traditional party attachments not because they feel ambivalent about which of the two parties they should support, but because they dislike politics in general. The hostile tenor of campaign advertising further reinforces their contempt for candidates, parties, and government. As a result, negative campaigning divides the American electorate into a voting public of party loyalists and a nonvoting public of apathetics.

With each election this schism widens. Though their growth has been glacial, Independents are now the single largest of the "partisan" groups in the electorate—36 percent, according to the Gallup poll. They tend not to vote, and regardless of which party is in the majority, they do not feel that the government represents their ideas and interests. Each succeeding election raises their frustration higher yet. Our evidence is that the political campaigns deserve much of the blame for the Independents' retreat from the polls. Positive campaign advertising generally fails to reach Independents. Nonpartisans do not find the typical political commercial compelling or persuasive, and they are only further angered, frustrated, and alienated by negative campaigning. The current climate of attack politics strengthens their resolve to remain Independents, but weakens their electoral voice.

As a consequence, electoral politics [is] becoming less representative. Elected officials respond mainly to the opinions of those who vote, which is increasingly a partisan and ideologically extreme crowd. Contemporary campaigning discourages nonpartisans from expressing their interests and frustrations at the polls; it thus obstructs politicians from hearing their anger.

71

JAMES CEASER
ANDREW BUSCH

From *Red Over Blue*

In their look back at the 2004 presidential election James Ceaser and Andrew Busch open with an account of Senator John Kerry's nomination at the Democratic convention. "I'm John Kerry, and I'm reporting for duty," announced the candidate, a decorated Vietnam War veteran. But right after receiving his party's nomination, a group who called themselves Swift Boat Veterans for Truth began an anti-Kerry campaign that had a significant impact during the months leading up to the November election. The swift boat vets were a 527 organization, a new type of political group that arose as a response to the McCain-Feingold campaign finance reforms. While many factors led to the incumbent president's reelection, the Swift Boat Veterans for Truth were instrumental in John Kerry's defeat at the hands of National Guardsman George W. Bush.

————

THE DEMOCRATS ENTERED THEIR CONVENTION week buoyant at their prospects for the election in November. Party strategists were eager to tell any and all members of the media—including "bloggers," who for the first time ever had space reserved for them on press row—that the party was more united than ever behind a presidential candidate. The race, Kerry's advisers offered, was coming to resemble that of 1980, with President Bush in the role of Jimmy Carter and John Kerry playing "The Gipper." In 1980, polls consistently showed Carter with low job approval and high wrong track numbers. According to the mythology of the 1980 campaign, voters had decided to fire Carter, and all Reagan needed to do was present himself as a credible alternative. The Kerry strategists argued that the 2004 polls displayed a similar desire to fire Bush.

The primary goal of the convention accordingly became to convince voters of Senator Kerry's fitness to become Commander in Chief Kerry. Once that threshold was crossed, Kerry could then turn to domestic issues where he held an advantage in the polls over Bush. But how to cross it? Here Kerry faced several difficulties, some of his own making, others reflecting divisions within his political base. Kerry's last twenty years had been spent as a legislator, not an executive, and within the Senate he had not held a major leadership post or been directly responsible for any pieces of landmark legislation. He had built one of the more dovish records on foreign policy and defense in the Senate from his election in 1984 until 1997, when he began to echo President Clinton's tough rhetoric against Saddam Hussein. His record of votes on domestic issues was also highly liberal. There was much, in short, to gloss over. Kerry also had to deal with trying to unify Democrats on national security issues. A majority of Democrats were antiwar, but a significant minority supported the Iraq War while being critical of Bush's plan of execution. The same was true of many swing voters. Kerry sought to handle these dilemmas by a political balancing that emphasized his Vietnam service. He would resume the cloak of the reluctant warrior who fought for his country when called, but who could also offer a levelheaded assessment of the prospects for success in a difficult situation. Both elements—pro and antiwar Democrats—could find reason to support Kerry.

Conventions were once seething cauldrons of political infighting and intrigue over party platforms and nominees, but the modern convention is a scripted and organized show designed to sell the party and its candidate to the American public. In a display of disdain for what many journalists called party infomercials, the major networks reduced their coverage of the conventions to only three prime-time hours of the four-day event, forcing both parties to schedule their most prominent speakers to appear at those times. Viewers were treated, among others, to former President Carter, who lamented Bush's policy failures with regard to the Middle East, Iran, and North Korea; former President Clinton, who mused about a return to the better days of the Clinton economy; Senator Ted Kennedy, who tried to stir the echoes of his family's past; and Howard Dean, who issued a (for him) mild declamation on the future of the party. All of them, including ex-Senator Max Cleland, who introduced Kerry, played up Kerry's service in Vietnam. The result was a convention that seemed to focus more on the past than on the future. The most positive and prospective message of the convention was the keynote address delivered by an Illinois state senator, Barack Obama, who was all but assured of election to the U.S. Senate. Unfortunately for Democrats, Obama's speech was delivered on the night on which the network coverage went dark.

On the final night of the convention John Kerry strode through the crowd to the podium, smartly saluted the audience, and announced, "I'm John Kerry, and I'm reporting for duty." The speech that followed brimmed with homespun history. Kerry offered loving details of his childhood and suggested that his time served in Vietnam would put him in good stead to act as commander in chief. He spent a scant ninety seconds explaining his twenty years in the Senate, before mentioning his plans for the future, which could be found in more detail at JohnFKerry.com. Minimizing both record and issues, Kerry staked his claim for the presidency on biography to a greater extent than any presidential candidate since Dwight D. Eisenhower in 1952, except that Eisenhower never had to call attention to his own biography. It was a well-delivered oration, but longer on style than content.

One remarkable aspect of the convention was the degree to which the social and cultural liberalism of the delegates was kept under wraps. At previous Democratic conventions full-throated affirmations of a woman's "right to choose" and calls for gun control were de rigueur rhetoric from the podium, but not at the 2004 convention. With the exception of a single speech by Representative Barney Frank, which was not delivered during prime time, no pronouncements were made in favor of same-sex marriage. The only social policy that the Democrats dared to support was increased funding for embryonic stem cell research. Beyond this one paean to liberal social policy, however, the silence suggested a tacit recognition that the Democratic Party was not eager to play up the cultural divide. Outright denunciations of the war in Iraq were likewise strictly limited, although Michael Moore was granted a privileged and highly visible seat in the presidential box next to Jimmy Carter.

As the convention closed, most analysts applauded the Democratic Party for having run such a successful convention. The party had kept anti-Bush vitriol to a minimum, rekindled fond memories of Democrat presidents past, and established its nominee as a man of character who, in his own words, could "make America stronger at home and respected in the world." All that was left was to see how large a margin Kerry had opened over his rival in the postconvention polls. Those polls suggested that Kerry had indeed improved his standing with voters: he was seen as more likable and as a stronger leader. But he received little if any of the anticipated "bump" or "bounce" in the head-to-head polls against Bush.

(By past standards, most candidates can expect a six-point bump, with the nominee of the out-party receiving closer to nine points.) Most postconvention polls showed Kerry and Edwards ticking up two or three points, but others—including a Gallup survey—actually showed Kerry losing ground to Bush. These perplexing poll results puzzled pundits, forcing many to reevaluate the success of the convention. Many now wondered whether the convention had underplayed a discussion of issues in favor of personal biography. But there was another and more hopeful view for Democrats. It was that the American public was now so firmly divided that there were fewer swing voters or persuadables in the electorate. If Kerry had received no postconvention bump, the silver lining was that Bush would be unable to receive one either. The electorate was "unbumpable." As long as Kerry could maintain his lead through August, he would be in the driver's seat heading into the debates and the final weeks of the campaign. . . .

Instead, throughout the month of August, Bush whittled away at John Kerry's five- or six-point lead. Bush may have profited a bit from the national glow surrounding American success in the Olympics and from the participation of athletes, including women athletes, from Iraq and Afghanistan. The Bush campaign also scored a coup when it badgered Kerry into conceding on August 9 that, knowing everything that he then knew, he would still have voted to authorize the Iraq War (though Kerry went on to explain that he would have exercised the authority differently). This admission, often repeated without the qualification, not only deflated many of Kerry's supporters, but it also contributed to a growing impression that Kerry's position on Iraq was more than nuanced; it was opaque. Bush's efforts to claim that Kerry now agreed with him almost certainly prompted Kerry's turn, a month later, to a clear anti-war stance. But this matter, important as it was, was put on hold when the ad of an anti-Kerry organization threw the entire race into a spin, effectively eliminating a key prop of Kerry's campaign strategy.

On August 5, Kerry's campaign-by-biography came under challenge from the Swift Boat Veterans for Truth, a new 527 organization consisting of men who had served in John Kerry's swift boat unit in Vietnam. This group came out with its first attack ad questioning Kerry's heroism in Vietnam and by extension his fitness to serve as commander in chief. The ad featured fellow swift boat vets addressing the camera and stating that Kerry did not deserve the medals he received. Accompanying the criticism were pictures of the men as young soldiers standing near Kerry in Vietnam. Although the group's initial ad buy was small—about $500,000 and limited to three states—it created a firestorm of enormous proportions.

Much of the interest was generated by the new media, where the allegations were aired and analyzed. The attention quickly led to a spike in online donations for the group that paid for a second attack ad that contained another, and potentially more damning, set of charges against Kerry. It featured snippets of John Kerry's testimony before a U.S. Senate committee in 1971, speaking in opposition to the Vietnam War. Interspersed were clips of former prisoners of war commenting on how Kerry's statements adversely affected their treatment at the hands of their North Vietnamese captors. In his Senate testimony Kerry cited reports accusing soldiers of having raped and pillaged the countryside in a fashion reminiscent of Genghis Khan. One former POW stated that "John Kerry gave the enemy for free what we endured torture not to admit." These two ads, although miniscule in what they cost, turned out to be far more influential than all of the other ads of the campaign, on which millions were spent. At the end of August, the Kerry campaign finally broke down and bought advertising time in the markets where the swift boat vet ads had aired, but by then the Internet and media coverage had enhanced the reach of the ads to the extent that almost 80 percent of the population was familiar with their content.

The ads and the subsequent release of a book, *Unfit for Command*, written by one of the founders of the 527 group, John O'Neill, and making specific allegations about Kerry's combat and postwar actions, sparked a debate within the Kerry campaign about how best to respond. The initial decision was to ignore the message and to attack the messenger as being a pawn of the GOP. The seed money for the group had come from a deep-pocketed Republican from Texas who had previous associations with Karl Rove, and two individuals ultimately had to quit the Bush campaign because of their association with the swift boat ads. Kerry called on President Bush to denounce the swift boat veterans directly. Bush responded by calling on Kerry to join him in condemning all 527 groups in their efforts to influence the election. The back-and-forth over the arcane legal provisions governing the actions of 527 groups continued for a couple of weeks, while the charges made by the swift boat vets were allowed to fester nearly unchallenged.

As it became clearer that Kerry could not eliminate the swift boat vets' challenge through indirect means, his campaign team (aided by the mainstream media) adopted a new tactic: discredit the most attenuated charges. The *Boston Globe*, the *New York Times*, and the *Chicago Tribune*—among others—ran accounts calling into question some of the swift boat veterans claims that challenged Kerry's heroism in Vietnam. Few papers, however, tackled Kerry's persistent and problematic claims to have ventured into Cambodia during his four-month stint as a swift boat captain. Nor did many wish to examine the POWs' charges that Kerry's congressional testimony had caused them distress.

Besides creating disarray in the Kerry campaign over how to respond, the initial swift boat ad effectively took away Kerry's Vietnam security blanket. Kerry could no longer freely invoke Vietnam without the risk of having to personally engage the questions about his war record and his postwar activities. Many Democrats, including former President Clinton, now advised him to drop the subject, and the campaign began to downplay the issue, with some going even so far as to deny that Kerry had ever made very much of his service in the first place. One way or another, the question of military service in Vietnam faded from the campaign as an issue. Bush certainly did not want to talk about it, and now Kerry dared not to. In fact, Kerry by and large ceased taking questions of any kind from the press. With his biography now a matter of contention, a pivotal part of Kerry's candidacy was diminished. By the end of the month of August, when the Republicans began their convention, John Kerry had lost his lead and the two candidates were in a statistical dead heat in the polls. . . .

George Bush was selected in a close race in which more people, 118 million, voted than in any previous election. The president won a total of 51 percent of the vote to John Kerry's 48 percent. Compared to the 2000 election, Bush improved his share of the total vote in forty-eight out of fifty states, with some of his biggest gains coming in the blue states. For the aficionados of the now famous red-blue maps, the nation as a whole appeared redder after 2004, with New Mexico and Iowa added to the Republican column and New Hampshire alone switching to the Democrats. The county version of the red-blue map showed expanding swaths of red, with blue areas receding and being largely confined to urban zones and university-town enclaves. . . .

72

FRANCES FOX PIVEN
RICHARD CLOWARD

From *Why Americans Still Don't Vote*

This is not the first book that Frances Fox Piven and Richard Cloward have written on voting—or more precisely, nonvoting—among the American public. More than a decade after writing Why Americans Don't Vote, *the authors observe that many Americans still don't vote, despite reforms such as the 1993 National Voter Registration Act— "motor voter." The reasons behind nonvoting go deeper than ease of registration, Piven and Cloward believe. Many potential voters, especially people with low incomes and from minority groups, don't participate because they are alienated from the entire political process. As activists in the Human Service Employees Registration and Voter Education program, Piven and Cloward place blame on politicians who have failed to capture the attention and allegiance of America's unrepresented millions.*

THIS BOOK IS ABOUT AN electoral reform project called Human SERVE (Human Service Employees Registration and Voter Education), which we initiated in 1983. Our purpose was to make voter registration available in welfare and unemployment offices, and in private sector agencies such as day care and family planning. The book discusses the ideas that informed the project, the complex dynamics of the reform effort itself, and the outcome.

We undertook the project because it was clear by 1980 that a Republican/business/Christian Right coalition was coming to power and that the New Deal and Great Society programs—which have always been of central interest to us—were seriously threatened. At the same time, registration and voting levels among the recipient constituencies of these programs were low and falling. We thought it might be possible to raise voting levels through registration reform and thus strengthen resistance to the attack on entitlements.

In the late 1980s, a national voting rights coalition of civil rights, good government, labor, and religious groups took up this strategy of registration reform, and persuaded Democrats in Congress (joined by several Republicans) to pass the National Voter Registration Act of 1993, which a Democratic president signed in May of that year. The Act required that, beginning in 1995, voter registration be made available in AFDC, Food Stamps, Medicaid, and WIC agencies and in agencies serving disabled Americans. It also required that people be allowed to register when they get or renew driver's licenses. It was this last provision that gave the Act its tag name "motor voter." The states were also required to permit people to register by mail, and the Federal Election Commission was ordered to design a mail form that the states were required to use if they failed to design their own. With this reform, historic barriers to voter registration that had kept voting down among blacks and many poor whites in the South and among many in the northern industrial working class were largely abolished. . . .

The right to vote is the core symbol of democratic politics. Of course, the vote itself is meaningless unless citizens have other rights, such as the right to speak, write, and assemble; unless opposition parties can compete for power by offering alternative programs, cultural appeals, and leaders; and unless diverse popular groupings can gain some recognition by the parties. And democratic arrangements that guarantee formal equality through the universal franchise are inevitably compromised by sharp social and economic inequalities. Nevertheless, the right to vote is the feature of the democratic polity that makes all other political rights significant. "The electorate occupies, at least in the mystique of [democratic] orders, the position of the principal organ of governance."

Americans generally take for granted that ours is the very model of a democracy. Our leaders regularly proclaim the United States to be the world's leading democracy and assert that other nations should measure their progress by the extent to which they develop electoral arrangements that match our own. At the core of this self congratulation is the belief that the right to vote is firmly established here. But in fact the United States is the only major democratic nation in which the less-well-off, as well as the young and minorities, are substantially underrepresented in the electorate. Only about half of the eligible population votes in presidential elections, and far fewer vote in off-year elections. As a result, the United States ranks at the bottom in turnout compared with other major democracies. Moreover, those who vote are different in politically important respects from those who do not. Voters are better off and better educated, and nonvoters are poorer and less well educated. Modest shifts from time to time notwithstanding, this has been true for most of the twentieth century and has actually worsened in the last three decades. In sum, the active American electorate overrepresents those who have more and underrepresents those who have less. . . .

Three conditions made the National Voter Registration Act of 1993 possible. One was the growth of an influential national voting rights coalition committed to making government agency registration the law of the land.

A second condition was the rapid spread of motor voter programs in the states. When the NVRA was enacted in 1993, twenty-nine states had motor voter programs. Most were just starting up and had registered few people. Still, it mattered in the congressional debates that more than half the states had opted for this reform. John L. Sousa, chief counsel of the Senate committee that had jurisdiction over voter registration, would later say, "We wanted this voter registration reform bill to reflect what's already happening in the states." When the National Voter Registration Act came up for consideration in the early 1990s, *Washington Post* political columnist David Broder remarked that "by building on the State experience, its sponsors have done something that is all too rare in Washington: They allowed the design to be field-tested before taking it national."

The third condition explaining why reform succeeded is ironic. Neither party thought that voter registration reform would change electoral outcomes. One report after another appeared in the 1980s concluding that nonvoters were "carbon copies" of voters. It was not self-evident that the Democrats would benefit more; greater voting for the Democrats by the poor and minorities could potentially be offset by higher voting for the Republicans by young people.

This political situation was altogether different from the circumstances preceding the enactment of the Voting Rights Act of 1965. Then, the endangered southern Democratic political leadership fought tooth and nail to prevent the enfranchising of blacks, since new black voters would undermine the apartheid basis of the "Southern Democracy." It took massive turbulence—civil disobedience campaigns in the South and civil disorder in the northern cities—to force national Democratic leaders to override southern opposition. But nothing like that was necessary to win voter registration reform three decades later. . . .

The NVRA reforms produced an unprecedented increase in voter registration. Turnout, however, did not rise. . . .

. . . Four years into the NVRA system, turnout had fallen another 2.8 percentage points, from 38.8 percent in 1994 to 36 percent in 1998. Moreover, "Southern turnout dropped 3.6 points to 30.5 percent, a larger drop than the rest of the nation." Florida and Kentucky reported that as few as 20 percent of those registered in public assistance agencies went to the polls. In sum, more accessible registration procedures did not increase voting rates.

Why? A formidable body of evidence and opinion predicted that what Arend Lijphart calls "voter-friendly" registration rules lead to higher turnout levels. In fact, we think the procedures of the National Voter Registration Act (NVRA) should over time bring us close to the automatic voter registration procedures that characterize European polities, which Powell concluded could boost turnout by 14 percentage points. More recently, in 1992, Ruy Teixiera conducted an exhaustive review of the American data and reported that, while voter registration barriers could not explain the recent declines in turnout, they nevertheless remained the most costly feature of the voting act in the United States. He concluded that the reduction of these costs was the single most credible reform that would increase turnout, by 8 to 15 percentage points. Comparisons of turnout in states with the least restrictive registration arrangements and in other states yield similar estimates of a potential increase of from 9 to 15 percentage points. So why have the expectations implicit in these arguments so far been disappointed? Why the continuing fall in turnout, rising registration rates notwithstanding?

Most studies of voter turnout attempt to disaggregate the effects of registration barriers and an array of other influences. If registration barriers are less significant in depressing turnout, then other factors must be more significant. Consistent with the traditional emphasis on social-psychological explanations, the usual approach has been to scrutinize changes in the capacities and attitudes of individual voters in the search for the factors contributing to the demobilization of the electorate. All else being equal, some changes in the characteristics of voters are expected to raise turnout while other factors depress turnout. Thus the growing numbers of young people in the electorate, who have traditionally voted less, at least in the United States, should depress turnout. But rising educational levels should increase turnout, at least in the United States. All this is familiar. The new variable proposed by recent analyses is that lower turnout seems to be associated with the fact that Americans are less embedded in social networks that encourage participation. Teixiera, for example, emphasizes "a substantial decline in social connectedness" through family and church.

The perspective on the causes of low turnout . . . reveals the limits of attempts to disaggregate the impact of particular variables on voter turnout. The effects of legal and procedural barriers are closely intertwined with the political factors that draw people to the ballot box, and especially with the strategies the political parties employ to attract or pull voters to the polls. Moreover, the barriers and political appeals and strategies together go far to determine which individual-level variables are related to turnout. When issue and cultural appeals resonate with the electorate, contests are tight, and the parties work to get the vote out, then legal and procedural barriers matter much less—as in the big cities in the years immediately after the introduction of voter registration barriers at the beginning of the century. And under these conditions, the relationship between turnout and education and income evaporates. To put the matter clearly, hotly contested elections about intensely felt issues still draw voters, and when they do, the impact of barriers dwindles, and so do differentials in turnout that can be ascribed to individual-level social and psychological traits. Rosenstone and Hansen point to the mayoral election in Chicago in 1983 when the nomination of Harold Washington raised black turnout by 17 percentage points, despite a restrictive voter registration system, because the keenly felt issue in the election was racial ascendance in the city's political regime.

But when political appeals lose their salience and party efforts to bring people to the polls slacken, as they did in the wake of progressive-era party reforms, voter registration barriers loom much larger, class-related disparities in voting widen, and so should the impact of such individual traits as education, income, or social connectedness. Moreover, the pattern of nonparticipation that is initially constructed by the interplay of barriers and party indifference tends to reproduce itself over time. Party operatives assume, even naturalize, low participation rates, and hence tend to take the absence of the marginalized for granted in fashioning appeals and mobilizing strategies. In time the attitudes of the marginalized come to reflect their disaffection with a party system that pays them little heed.

Thus, the most provocative data reported in recent studies purporting to account for declining turnout describe dramatic changes in attitudes toward politics over the past three decades. "Americans," say Rosenstone and Hansen, "have lost their confidence in the effectiveness of their actions." They have also lost their attachment to electoral politics: Americans are less satisfied with the electoral choices offered them and, indeed, had less good to say even about the parties and candidates they favored than they had in the 1960s. Abramson, Aldrich, and Rohde also emphasize the erosion of party loyalties and a declining belief in the responsiveness of politicians to voter influence. And Teixiera reports consistent findings.

Changes in political attitudes are of course changes in individual-level traits, but since the traits at issue are attitudes toward politics, and since they have changed so rapidly, it seems reasonable to suspect that the broader political system is implicated. If turnout is falling because of declining party loyalties or lowered feelings of political efficacy, something is probably going on in the larger environment of American politics.

. . . [W]e argued that the correlation of such individual-level attributes as education with turnout was misleading, that it did not reflect the direct impact of education on participation but the tilt of party appeals and strategies away from the less educated and worse-off, and toward the more educated and better-off. The decline in political efficacy and increase in political alienation, and the impact of these attitudes on turnout, suggests a further elaboration of the relationship between individual-level attributes and politics. The political system not only selectively mobilizes people according to their class-related attributes, but it also creates the attributes that depress turnout. On both these counts, the statistical evidence on the bearing of individual attributes on turnout points the finger of blame at the performance of the American political parties.

This . . . is not the place to begin an examination of the features of recent American electoral politics that are increasing various measures of political alienation. The much discussed and debated decline of party organization (at least in the Democratic party), the flood of special interest money pouring into the campaigns, the growing presence of the K Street lobbyists, the gap between the issues Americans say are important and the national legislative agenda, the increasing complexity of policy initiatives riddled with pork barrel giveaways—all of these probably contribute to growing public cynicism. Perhaps the rise of neoliberalism as the current ideological orthodoxy also turns people away from electoral politics, if only because it argues the futility of government intervention in a world dominated by markets, especially international markets. In short, the political parties and their interest-group allies are constructing a political environment that is demobilizing the American electorate, lowered barriers notwithstanding.

The very success of this development may even help to explain why the business opposition to government agency registration we initially anticipated never materialized. In the late nineteenth century, at least some business interests treated the shape and scale of electoral participation as a potential threat to their influence and worked to reduce participation by the lower strata. But on the eve of the twenty-first century, the big automobile companies readily conceded Election Day as a paid holiday to unionized auto workers. Predictably, Republican party leaders railed at the contract concession, as they had railed at the NVRA. But General Motors, Ford, and Daimler Chrysler, the world's three largest auto compa-

nies, were unfazed. Perhaps electoral politics has evolved to the stage
where money, advertising, and special-interest lobbies, together with the
dampening effect on democratic aspirations of neoliberal ideology, have
combined to neutralize the age-old class threat posed by an enfranchised
population.

It followed from our perspective on the closely interbraided causes of
low turnout that we did not think voter registration would have its most
important effects on turnout directly. True, accessible voter registration
procedures would lower the costs, in rational-choice terms, of the voting
act, and Human SERVE's public relations material emphasized that if
registration barriers were eliminated, millions of new voters could flock
to the polls. But we personally did not believe that the mere fact of lower
costs was likely to draw people to the polls in large numbers. Rather,
. . . our hope was that once rates of registration rose among low income
and minority citizens, this pool of newly available voters would attract at
least some entrepreneurial politicians who would then begin to raise the
issues and organize the get-out-the-vote efforts that would bring new
voters to the polls.

That has yet to happen. In fact, however logical such recruitment
efforts might seem from a narrow focus on electoral incentives, the cen-
tury-long reliance of the American parties on electoral demobilization
. . . suggests that it may never happen. So does our own very limited
success in trying to make allies, even of politicians who were likely to
benefit at the polls. Some Democratic governors issued executive orders to
be sure, but then declined to implement them. Even when state legislatures
controlled by Democrats mandated motor voter, they refused to include
social agencies as registration sites. Our successes at initiating registration
in some municipal agencies were typically short-lived; when we stopped
prodding, registration flagged or ceased. . . .

The moral seems to us clear. The scale and shape of the active electorate
can determine electoral outcomes. But left to themselves, the parties are
unlikely to work to expand participation. Perhaps part of the reason is
simply that politicians have come to absorb the conventional wisdom that
ascribes nonparticipation to the individual traits of voters. More likely,
they mouth such explanations for comfort. Indeed, party competition is
more likely to take the form of strategies to demobilize sectors of the
electorate, than of strategies to expand it. . . .

In sum, we think it possible that the NVRA and the pool of potential
voters it is creating might yet matter in American politics. If it does, it
is not likely to be because the dynamic of electoral competition itself
prods the major parties to reach out to new voters. It is more likely to

be because a new surge of protest, perhaps accompanied by the rise of minor parties and the electoral cleavages that both movements and minor parties threaten, forces political leaders to make the programmatic and cultural appeals, and undertake the voter recruitment, that will reach out to the tens of millions of Americans who now remain beyond the pale of electoral politics.

PART THIRTEEN

Political Parties

73

WALTER DEAN BURNHAM

From *Critical Elections and the Mainsprings of American Politics*

Political science can offer few clear-cut theories of how politics works. Because of the variable of human nature as well as the impossibility of measuring and predicting political events with exactness, political science is often less a "science" and more an "art." A few attempts at developing major theories to explain and predict politics have been made, however. One is the theory of "critical realignments." Professor Walter Dean Burnham was one of the first to try to explain why certain presidential elections throughout American history mark significant long-term changes in the social and economic direction of the nation. Citing 1800, 1828, 1860, 1896, and 1932, Burnham describes the characteristics of a critical or realigning election, the most dramatic being its supposed "uniform periodicity." They occur at roughly equal intervals apart in time.

FOR MANY DECADES it has been generally recognized that American electoral politics is not quite "all of a piece" despite its apparent diverse uniformity. Some elections have more important long-range consequences for the political system as a whole than others, and seem to "decide" substantive issues in a more clear-cut way. There has long been agreement among historians that the elections of those of 1800, 1828, 1860, 1896, and 1932, for example, were fundamental turning points in the course of American electoral politics.

Since the appearance in 1955 of V. O. Key's seminal article, "A Theory of Critical Elections," political scientists have moved to give this concept quantitative depth and meaning. . . .

It now seems time to attempt at least an interim assessment of the structure, function, and implications of critical realignments for the American political process. Such an effort is motivated in particular by the author's view that critical realignments are of fundamental importance not only to the system of political action called "the American political process" but also to the clarifications of some aspects of its operation. It seems particularly important in a period of obvious political upheaval not only to identify these phenomena and place them in time, but to integrate them into a larger (if still very modest) theory of movement in American politics.

Such a theory must inevitably emphasize the elements of stress and abrupt transformation in our political life at the expense of the consensual, gradualist perspectives which have until recently dominated the scholar's vision of American political processes and behavior. For the realignment phenomenon focuses our attention on "the dark side of the moon." It reminds us that politics as usual in the United States is not politics as always; that there are discrete types of voting behavior and quite different levels of voter response to political stimuli, depending on what those stimuli are and at what point in time they occur; and that American political institutions and leadership, once defined (or redefined) in a "normal phase" of our politics, seem to become part of the very conditions that threaten to overthrow them. . . .

In its "ideal-typical" form, the critical realignment differs from stable alignments eras, secular [gradual] realignments, and deviating elections in the following basic ways.

1. The critical realignment is characteristically associated with short-lived but very intense disruptions of traditional patterns of voting behavior. Majority parties become minorities; politics which was once competitive becomes noncompetitive or, alternatively, hitherto one-party areas now become arenas of intense partisan competition; and large blocks of the active electorate—minorities, to be sure, but perhaps involving as much as a fifth to a third of the voters—shift their partisan allegiance.

2. Critical elections are characterized by abnormally high intensity as well.

a. This intensity typically spills over into the party nominating and platform-writing machinery during the upheaval and results in major shifts in convention behavior from the integrative "norm" as well as in transformations in the internal loci of power in the major party most heavily affected by the pressures of realignment. Ordinarily accepted "rules of the game" are flouted; the party's processes, instead of performing their usual integrative functions, themselves contribute to polarization.

b. The rise in intensity is associated with a considerable increase in ideological polarizations, at first within one or more of the major parties and then between them. Issue distances between the parties are markedly increased, and elections tend to involve highly salient issue-clusters, often with strongly emotional and symbolic overtones, far more than is customary in American electoral politics. One curious property of established leadership as it drifts into the stress of realignment seems to be a tendency to become more rigid and dogmatic, which itself contributes greatly to the explosive "bursting stress" of realignment. . . .

c. The rise in intensity is also normally to be found in abnormally heavy voter participation for the time. . . .

3. Historically speaking, at least, national critical realignments have not occurred at random. Instead, there has been a remarkably uniform periodicity in their appearance. . . .

4. It has been argued, with much truth, that American political parties are essentially constituent parties. That is to say, the political-party subsystem is sited in a socioeconomic system of very great heterogeneity and diversity. . . .

Critical realignments emerge directly from the dynamics of this constituent-function supremacy in American politics. . . . In other words, realignments are themselves constituent acts: they arise from emergent tensions in society which, not adequately controlled by the organization or outputs of party politics as usual, escalate to a flash point; they are issue-oriented phenomena, centrally associated with these tensions and more or less leading to resolution adjustments; they result in significant transformations in the general shape of policy; and they have relatively profound aftereffects on the roles played by institutional elites. They are involved with redefinitions of the universe of voters, political parties, and the broad boundaries of the politically possible.

To recapitulate, then, eras of critical realignment are marked by short, sharp reorganizations of the mass coalitional bases of the major parties which occur at periodic intervals on the national level; are often preceded by major third-party revolts which reveal the incapacity of "politics as usual" to integrate, much less aggregate, emergent political demand; are closely associated with abnormal stress in the socioeconomic system; are marked by ideological polarizations and issue-distances between the major parties which are exceptionally large by normal standards; and have durable consequences as constituent acts which determine the outer boundaries of policy in general, though not necessarily of policies in detail. . . . There is much evidence . . . that realignments do recur with rather remarkable regularity approximately once a generation, or every thirty to thirty-eight years.

The precise timing of the conditions which conduce to realignment is conditioned heavily by circumstance, of course: the intrusion of major crises in society and economy with which "politics as usual" in the United States cannot adequately cope, and the precise quality and bias of leadership decisions in a period of high political tension, cannot be predicted in specific time with any accuracy. Yet a broadly repetitive pattern of oscillation between the normal inertia of mass electoral politics and the ruptures of the normal which realignments bring about is clearly evident from the data. So evident is this pattern that one is led to suspect that the truly "normal" structure of American electoral politics at the mass base is precisely this dynamic, even dialectic polarization between long-term inertia and concentrated bursts of change in this open system of action. It may well be that American political institutions, including the major political parties, are so organized that they have a chronic, cumulative tendency toward underproduction of other than currently "normal" policy outputs. They may tend persistently to ignore, and hence not to aggregate, emergent political demand of a mass character until a boiling point of some kind is reached.

In this context, the rise of third-party protests as what might be called protorealignment phenomena would be associated with the repeated emergence of a rising gap between perceived expectations of the political process and its perceived realities over time, diffused among a constantly increasing portion of the active electorate and perhaps mobilizing many hitherto inactive voters. . . .

The periodic rhythm of American electoral politics, the cycle of oscillation between the normal and the disruptive, corresponds precisely to the existence of largely unfettered developmental change in the socioeconomic system and its absence in the country's political institutions. Indeed, it is a prime quantitative measure of the interaction between the two. The socioeconomic system develops but the institutions of electoral politics and policy formation remain essentially unchanged. Moreover, they do not have much capacity to adjust incrementally to demand arising from socioeconomic dislocations. Dysfunctions centrally related to this process become more and more visible, until finally entire classes, regions, or other major sectors of the population are directly injured or come to see themselves as threatened by imminent danger. Then the triggering event occurs, critical realignments follow, and the universe of policy and of electoral coalitions is broadly redefined. It is at such moments that the constitution-making role of the American voter becomes most visible, and his behavior, one suspects, least resembles the normal pattern. . . .

In this context, then, critical realignment emerges as decisively important in the study of the dynamics of American politics. It is as symptomatic of political nonevolution in this country as are the archaic and increasingly rudimentary structures of the political parties themselves. But even more importantly, critical realignment may well be defined as the chief tension-management device available to so peculiar a political system. Historically it has been the chief means through which an underdeveloped political

system can be recurrently brought once again into some balanced relationship with the changing socioeconomic system, permitting a restabilization
of our politics. . . . Granted the relative inability of our political institutions
to make gradual adjustments along vectors of *emergent* political demand,
critical realignments have been as inevitable as they have been necessary
to the normal workings of American politics. Thus once again there is a
paradox: the conditions which decree that coalitional negotiation, bargaining, and incremental, unplanned, and gradual policy change become the
dominant characteristic of American politics in its normal state also decree
that it give way to abrupt, disruptive change with considerable potential
for violence. . . .

Such a dynamically oriented frame of reference presupposes a holistic
view of American politics which is radically different from that which
until very recently has tended to dominate the professional literature. The
models of American political life and political processes with which we are
most familiar emphasize the well-known attributes of pluralist democracy.
There are not stable policy majorities. Intense and focused minorities with
well-defined interests exert influence on legislation and administrative rule
making out of all proportion to their size. The process involves gradual,
incremental change secured after bargaining has been completed among
a wide array of interested groups who are prepared to accept the conditions
of bargaining. It is true that such descriptions apply to a "politics as usual"
which is an important fragment of political reality in the United States,
but to describe this fragment as the whole of that reality is to assume
an essentially ideological posture whose credibility can be maintained
only by ignoring the complementary dynamics of American politics as a
whole. . . .

The reality of this process taken as a whole seems quite different from
the pluralist vision. It is one shot through with escalating tensions, periodic
electoral upheavals, and repeated redefinitions of the rules and outcomes-
in-general of the political game, as well as redefinitions—by no means
always broadening ones—of those who are in fact permitted to play it.
One very basic characteristic of American party politics which emerges
from a contemplation of critical realignments is a profound incapacity
of established political leadership to adapt itself sequentially—or even
incrementally?—to emergent political demand generated by the losers in
our stormy socioeconomic transformations. American political parties are
not action instrumentalities of definable and broad social collectivities; as
organizations they are, consequently, interested in control of offices but
not of government in the broader sense of which we have been speaking.

It follows from this that once successful routines are established or reestablished for winning office, there is no motivation among party leaders to disturb the routines of the game. These routines are disturbed not by adaptive change within the party-policy system, but by the application of overwhelming external force.

74

JAMES CEASER
ANDREW BUSCH

From *Red Over Blue*

James Ceaser and Andrew Busch begin their discussion of the red state-blue state divide with an explanation of what the terms "red" and "blue" have come to mean in American politics: the parts of the country that vote Republican and those with strong Democratic leanings. Attitudes on moral issues are an important part of the partisan divide, Ceaser and Busch acknowledge, but there are other reasons for the division also. Nor is the red-blue divide a totally accurate characterization; the authors point to purple and fuchsia areas. Especially interesting is the authors' contention that the commonly accepted view of the United States as a polarized nation is incorrect. The country is actually less polarized today than in the past in terms of demographic measures. Ceaser and Busch take up the question of whether a major party realignment has occurred. They discuss recent political trends, in light of Walter Dean Burnham's classic theory as well as David Mayhew's criticism of the realignment concept. The conclusion? The 2004 election does mark a significant change in party politics but maybe not one that will last over time.

USING COLORS TO DESCRIBE political divisions is a practice that was employed at least as early as the sixth century, when Byzantine politics was riven by a division between the "blues" and the "greens," rival political factions that based their names on the colors worn by their favorite chariot teams. The political theorist and historian Niccolò Machiavelli records that in his native city of Florence, after a brief period of domestic peace that ended in 1300, "the whole city became divided, the people as well as the nobility, and the parties took the names of the Bianchi (Whites) and the Neri (Blacks)." The labels appear to have originated in an earlier blood feud between two families in the neighboring city of Pistoia, where one of the families descended from a woman named Bianca (White), prompting the other to call itself Blacks. But these origins were quickly forgotten as the factional names of Whites and Blacks spread across Northern Italy.

America's experience with the palette did not begin until just after the 2000 election, when an electoral map appeared in the *New York Times* showing the states that gave a plurality to George W. Bush in red and those going for Al Gore in blue. Other renditions followed illustrating the national vote by counties. The visual impression created by these maps was striking. Given the geographical distribution of the vote, in which most areas favored George Bush, what the viewer saw was a vast sea of red surrounding a few beleaguered islands of blue. In the bitter dispute that followed Election Day in 2000, Republicans seized on this image and circulated these maps on the Internet with great enthusiasm. Democrats dismissed these pictures as wholly misleading, reminding everyone that what counts is the number of inhabitants in a district, not the expanse of its territory; it is people who vote, not rocks or stones or trees.

The battle of the colors in America had begun. . . .

Americans in the 2004 election chose red over blue. They made this choice not crushingly or overwhelmingly, but clearly and decisively. No one could call the 2004 election a landslide, but Republicans emerged from the election ascendant as the nation's majority party. Republicans defeated Democrats across the board and improved their position inside each national institution. President Bush defeated Senator John Kerry in the popular vote 51 percent to 48 percent, increasing the Republican share from the 2000 election by nearly three points. The Republicans won a majority in the House of Representatives, 232 to 201, upping their total by eleven seats from 2000 (and three seats from 2002). Finally, Republicans were victors in 19 of the 34 Senate races, giving them a solid 55-44 majority in that body and increasing their number by five seats from 2000 (and four from 2002). America was not just more red than blue in 2004, but it was considerably redder than it had been in 2000. George W. Bush's personal victory may have been narrow, but the victory he brought his party was substantial indeed. . . .

When the policy reasons given for the voters' decision are analyzed, a rough picture emerges of what moved them. "Rough" is the word to stress because there is much less science to interpreting voter choice than many pollsters like to pretend. Not only are the poll questions often vague and confusing, but the actual line of causality can run in a different direction than many suppose: people often make a general overall decision about which individual they prefer, after which they embrace some policy explanations to justify that choice. Still, there is some utility to this line of analysis, as students of elections seek to interpret the "meaning" of the popular voice. Over the years, electoral analysts have identified four major policy dimensions: the economy, welfare issues (health, education, etc.), national security, and what has variously been called "social" or "moral" concerns. . . .

The return of the national security issue in 2004 did help George Bush, although not unambiguously. Looking at the indicator of what voters selected as "the most important issue," Bush "won" with voters who framed the national security issue in the first instance in terms of the general war on terrorism, while he "lost" with voters who saw it in the first instance as the Iraq War. Since there were more of the former than the latter (and since Bush's margin of approval was greater within that group than was Kerry's on the Iraq War), it can be concluded that Bush in the end held the edge on the national security dimension. It was widely speculated that Bush's large gains among women voters from 2000 had much to do with this factor. A segment of the women voters, popularly dubbed "security moms," put terrorism first and apparently saw George Bush as the one best-suited to protecting their families. George Bush was perceived as the steadier or firmer candidate in keeping the nation safe from the threat of terror. It may even be that the negative character trait that the Kerry campaign identified to counter the Bush charge of Kerry as a flip-flopper—namely that Bush was "stubborn"—helped the president on the issue of fighting terrorism.

From the way questions are posed in the polls, it is difficult to establish a clear ranking of the relative importance of the four different dimensions of policy. But using the figures available, and sorting them by the different categories, national security concerns come out on top (and favored Bush), followed by economic issues (which helped Kerry), moral issues (strongly Bush), and finally welfare concerns (strongly Kerry). (See table.)

Given this ranking, how did it happen in the immediate aftermath of the election that a widespread view emerged, especially on the Left, that the moral dimension was the most important factor in the 2004 election? The explanation had something to do with a purely technical issue of how the poll questions were formulated, but even more with the psychological state of those seeking a justification for defeat. The technical issue was this: in asking the question about the most important issue, the national election poll supplied a list that broke the foreign policy dimension and economic dimension into subissues (e.g., terrorism and the Iraq War), so that the issue of "moral values" appeared as the single highest response. In addition, in looking back to this same question in the 2000 polls, the

MOST IMPORTANT ISSUES FOR VOTERS IN THE 2004 ELECTION

Issues	Selected By	% for Bush	% for Kerry
National Security Issues	34%	58	42
Iraq	15%	26	73
Terrorism	19%	80	14
Economic Issues	25%	26	74
Economy/Jobs	20%	18	80
Taxes	5%	57	43
Moral Issues	22%	80	18
Welfare Issues	12%	24	76
Health Care	8%	23	77
Education	4%	26	73

Source: CNN.com exit poll, available at www.CNN.com/ELECTION/2004/pages/results/
states/US/P/00/epolls.0.html.

choice of "moral values" had not been offered, so that a superficial analysis might have concluded that it jumped from nowhere to the top. (In fact, other poll evidence from 2000 clearly shows that with the Clinton scandals so prominent, the dimension of "moral values" was of enormous importance in that election.) These technical issues, however, were only the backdrop to the psychological wish many had to believe that the election was determined by millions upon millions of evangelical voters who had turned out in a fit of primitive prejudice to express their fear of homosexual marriage. According to Garry Wills, writing in the *New York Times*, Bush mobilized those who believe "more fervently in the Virgin birth than in evolution" and was able to be reelected "precisely by being a divider, pitting the reddest aspects of the red states against the blue nearly half of the nation." This view of the electorate was frightening to those who espoused it, but it was also consoling: it proved that defeat was at the hands of those whose votes had no moral, ethical, or intellectual worth.

In response to this highly polemical interpretation, a number of Republicans and conservatives understandably rushed to downplay the significance of the moral issue—perhaps too much so. They were correct to deny its primary importance, but the truth of the matter lies in an appreciation of degree. The "moral issue," although not the most important dimension in 2004, was nevertheless quite important, just as it had been in 2000. Nor was it synonymous with the issue of single-sex marriage. It spread across a whole range of ethical issues, including abortion, stem cell research, the character of schooling, and the tone of mass entertainment. These issues also turn out to be highly important not just to religious-minded voters (who are more apt to respond to the specific cue of "moral issues") but also to many strongly secular voters (who tend to hold opposite views and who apparently prefer to refer to these matters as "policy questions" rather than "moral issues"). Democrats no less than Republicans brought some of these questions into the campaign debate. The division on this set of questions shows up repeatedly in the connections between more religious Americans, who vote more strongly (but by no means exclusively) Republican, and more secular-minded Americans, who vote more strongly (but by no means exclusively) Democratic. There is clearly nothing new in this division. . . .

The terms "red" and "blue" have come to be used not just politically, to designate partisan leanings, but anthropologically, to describe cultural proclivities. This expansion of the metaphor, though it is suggestive in some ways, has had the unfortunate effect of conflating these two realms and of equating political divisions entirely with "cultural" divisions. The "cultural" component, which is only one part of the political equation (albeit, an important one), is wrongly taken to characterize the whole. In some presentations, the red-blue divide is evoked to express the idea of a radically polarized society split between two conflicting ways of life: a red America that is small-town, religious, and dominated by the church steeple, and a blue America that is secular, urban, and dominated by Thai restaurants. And in the most facile characterizations, everyone living in the first kind of area is imagined to vote Republican, while everyone in the second votes Democratic. It is as if Republicans and Democrats never meet, except perhaps in a chance encounter at an airport or a Division of Motor Vehicles. No one, of course, who has studied voting patterns would ever subscribe to such a view, although one ill effect of the color scheme is that it can contribute to this kind of dichotomous thinking. It was accordingly very helpful when a number of electoral analysts took up their pens to remind people that many of the geographic areas colored in red in 2000 (and now in 2004) only barely sided with President Bush (and other Republicans), and that the same was the case for the blue areas. Some clever cartographers followed, introducing different shades between the colors—purple or even fuchsia—reflecting their relative degree of support for Republicans and Democrats.

Geography, especially when it relies on units as large as states, is a fairly crude way to try to discuss the scope of cultural divisions in America. But since this theme was pursued so widely in these terms in 2000, it needs to be considered briefly for 2004. The results on this score may surprise many who have imbibed the notion that this election led to greater geographic "polarization." The opposite in fact was the case. George Bush's percentage share of the vote, as one might have expected, increased almost everywhere in the United States, the only exceptions being Vermont (a blue state, where he dropped by almost two points) and South Dakota (a red state, which Bush won by a landslide both times, dropping this time by a tiny fraction). But of the eight states in which Bush gained the most from 2000 (over five percentage points), five of them were blue states: Hawaii (7.8 percent), Rhode Island (6.8 percent), Connecticut (5.5 percent), New Jersey (5.9 percent), and New York (5.0 percent). Overall, the blue states moved in the direction of red by more than the national average as a whole. Geographically, the nation in 2004 was less, not more, polarized.

Looking ahead, Democrats have cast their eyes on states like Colorado and Virginia, where Kerry ran surprisingly well. The Democratic hope in these states rests on the demographic expansion of certain suburban areas that are filled with the kind of upper-middle-class professionals who tend increasingly to vote Democratic—areas like Fairfax and Albemarle counties in Virginia and Jefferson County in Colorado. Republicans rely on the demographic fact that Republican families, and now many of the red-state areas, are the fastest growing parts of the population. The long-term national outcome, in this view, boils down to a race between Republicans' efforts to produce more babies and Democrats' efforts to produce more lawyers and professors. Which group of partisans will derive the greater pleasure in this contest remains unknown.

Whether the nation became more polarized in 2004 depends on exactly what are the criteria of polarization. Only recently, race and minority divisions from the rest of the populace were singled out as the most worrisome source of polarization. By this standard, there was much less polarization in 2004. Race was largely absent from the 2004 campaign as an electoral theme, in contrast to 2000 when ads castigating Bush for opposing hate crimes legislation in Texas were a part of the campaign. While African Americans continued to vote overwhelmingly Democratic (88 percent), Bush gained some ground from 2000. Among Latino voters, the degree of polarization decreased dramatically. In what was one of the keys of Bush's victory, his share of the Latino vote rose from just a third in 2000 to 44 percent in 2004. If gender is taken as the source of division, here again there was less polarization: the eleven-percentage-point difference between men and women in 2000, with women favoring Al Gore over George Bush, shrunk to just three points this time. Men and women are getting back together, a development likely to make members of both sexes more content. It may be, as some contend, that the reduction in the gaps between these demographic groups is being replaced by a common division on the basis of "cultural" beliefs that is cutting through all groups in the same way. The evidence here is not conclusive, but even if this were true, would the nation really be more polarized, or less? . . .

The 2004 election marks a decisive point . . . , less because of the magnitude of the Republican gains in this election than because of the significance of crossing a critical political threshold. For the first time since 1952, Republicans won a recognizable majority in all three of the elected institutions of the national government, which after all is the main political prize associated with being a majority party. In 2000 Republicans managed to attain unified control of the federal government, but without really winning that election. They backed into the position, electing a president who trailed in the plurality vote, dropping two seats in the House (while retaining a razor-thin majority of 221-212), and losing four seats in the Senate (leaving that chamber in a 50-50 tie, broken only by Vice President Dick Cheney's vote). Another such "victory" and the Republicans would have been undone. By contrast, the Republican victories in 2004 were real, even if not huge, allowing Republicans to be able to claim the status of being, for the moment at least, the majority party.

This change in the relative strength of the two parties over the last generation is the most notable fact in the electoral history of our time. By what name should it be called? The simplest and most descriptive term, it would seem, is "realignment," and a few analysts, including a handful of Democrats, have not hesitated to employ this word. But most political scientists have resisted doing so, not necessarily because of a partisan aversion to placing this crown on the head of the Republican Party, but because they have concluded the term itself should be retired. The reason is that it has been tied in the literature of political science to a grand theory of electoral and political change that most have come to believe is false. According to the "classic" theory, realignment is a great event that respects the dramatic unities of time, place, and action; it is the electoral version of an exploding nova star, generating in a single moment (one national election or at most two) a massive amount of energy that reshapes all political matter for the next era. The introduction of this energy into the political system, which generally follows in the wake of a national crisis, produces three effects: (1) a decisive shift in the relative electoral strength of the parties, accompanied by internal changes in the character of the parties' internal coalition, in which the previous minority party (or a new party) sometimes takes over as the majority party; (2) a change in the agenda of national politics and in the dominant ideas governing public life, corresponding to the program or the public philosophy of the majority party; and (3) a change in the way politics is conducted and in how political information is transferred and received in society. To top it all off, realignments come with a predictable regularity, occurring roughly every thirty-two to thirty-six years.

This remarkable, not to say fantastic, theory was developed largely by Walter Dean Burnham, a professor of political science who began his career at Kenyon College before going on to teach at MIT and the University of Texas, from which he recently retired. Part statistician, part seer, Burnham not only claimed to have discovered this pattern historically, but he has also never been shy about insisting, beginning as early as 1968, that the phenomenon still applies to our own era. Mesmerized by the richness of this analysis, many scholars spent much of their careers awaiting the next realignment, only to grow impatient with its tardiness in arriving before finally beginning to entertain doubts about the validity of the concept itself. The misgivings were recently cataloged and given systematic expression by David Mayhew, one of the nation's leading political scientists. Mayhew put the theory under a clinical microscope and judged it to be inaccurate or wanting in almost every particular. He recommended abandoning the term, concluding that the "realignment perspective" is "too slippery, too binary, too apocalyptic, and it has come to be too much of a dead end." There Mayhew ends his little book, having demolished an edifice but without having put anything else in its place.

For those left with the task of trying to situate the 2004 election in some historical perspective, there seems to be no alternative for the time being other than to try to combine the best of Burnham and the best of Mayhew. This act of forced union can be accomplished, first, by setting forth a minimal definition of a realignment that, in the spirit of Mayhew's critique, divorces the concept from the grand theoretical claims made on its behalf; but second, by drawing on Burnham, by treating the imaginative claims linked to realignment theory as questions or hypotheses, which can be analyzed to see what light, if any, they shed on the current situation. This approach is not offered as a new theory of electoral change, but simply as a way to consider the larger implications of this particular election.

Relaxing, then, Burnham's dramatic assumptions about the great unities of time, place, and action, a realignment can be conceived simply as a major change in the underlying strength of the two parties during a specified period of time. By this definition, a realignment has already taken place in the time period between the 1960s or 1979, when the Democratic Party was in the clear majority, and today, when the Republican Party holds an edge. (How long the Republican advantage will hold, no one can know for certain.) Distinguishing this change from the change posited in a "pure" realignment in the classic theory, it is clear that in the current case not all of the energy for the transformation has flowed from a single explosion. It has taken twenty-four years to achieve the "equivalent" of what was supposedly achieved in a single election, such as 1800, 1860, or 1932. This rolling realignment nevertheless possesses a kind of unity, as the three most important Republican victories during this period—1980, 1994, and 2004—are all slightly different versions of the new conservatism inaugurated in 1980. It took one initial explosion and two secondary ones to generate the energy sufficient for Republicans to reach the critical threshold of majority status.

Where does this account leave the 2004 election? It is not, clearly, the election that launched the process. Burnham, who has always been more eclectic in the application of "theory" than some make out, has aptly characterized 2004 as the election that "consolidates" the realignment. For those still wedded to the classic theory, Burnham has divined a likely future of Republican dominance: "If Republicans keep playing the religious card along with the terrorism card, this could last a long time." He has referred to 2004 as perhaps "the most important election of [his] lifetime." At seventy-five, he could presumably be including 1932 in the comparison, although even the precocious Burnham may not have been charting electoral patterns when he was three. If this realignment has been consolidated, it should now be possible to look back on this period as one event and to ask what are some of its distinctive properties. The time may have arrived to begin speaking of a "system of 2004" that is different in important respects from the system of 1932. The new system, which emerged with a gradual but clear shift in party strength and a reorientation in the internal party coalitions, is characterized by an increase in partisan consistency, the ascendance of a new set of political ideas supported by a new kind of intellectual infrastructure, and the advent of a new mode of political communication. America is living in a new political universe.

A realignment in the classic theory is said to provoke a major change in the internal coalition of the parties. This hypothesis clearly holds true of the two parties in the current period, although it is a much more difficult task to describe internal coalitional changes over a long period than in a single moment. In a pure realignment, when everything happens suddenly, the changes take place in the same electorate; what one side loses, the other side gains (or picks up from existing nonvoters). Over a longer period, many changes that occur are unrelated to the energy released by the realignment—for example, in the current realignment, the emergence of Latino voters, who hardly existed a generation ago, or the shrinking proportion of blue-collar workers, who were previously a much larger contingent in the Democratic Party. Nevertheless, many of the recent changes have been realignment-driven. The Republican Party a generation ago was chiefly a coalition of small business owners and entrepreneurs, mainline Protestants of the middle and upper classes, plus a large set of partially disgruntled Democrats, among labor and throughout the South, who often supported Republican presidential candidates but not Republicans for other offices. The geographical base of the party was in the Midwest and, for a time, the Northeast. By 2004, the party still holds its business and entrepreneurial part, but it has added an important new element: the religious voters, found either in the new Protestant evangelical sects or among the more orthodox of Catholics, Jews, and older Protestant sects.

As the foundation of American politics is still geographical, the most important changes are tied to geography. Here the most notable feature of American politics in this realigning period has been a massive regional shift. The South has become the major geographical base of the Republican Party, while New England—a much smaller region—has become a bastion of the Democratic Party. The change in the South, which was already well under way in voting behavior at the presidential level before 1980, has since steadily worked its way down to other offices, with the final level, not yet reached in all of the southern states, being the state legislatures. Today, in the eleven states of the Old South, 85 percent of the senators from the region and 63 percent of the members of the House are Republican. Meanwhile, an opposite, although less complete, change has been taking place in New England. . . .

. . . [Another] effect of realignment posited in the classic theory is a change in the dominant set of ideas that governs the nation and sets the national agenda. This part of the theory also has application to the current realignment, but again with similar difficulties in applying the idea neatly to a change that has taken place over so long a period of time. The main lines are nevertheless clear. A nation that once was best described as being guided by liberalism (under Lyndon Johnson) or at least progressivism (under Jimmy Carter) is now better described as being strongly influenced by conservatism. Of course the meaning of both liberalism and conservatism has shifted and altered somewhat, in part as each has responded to the other. The liberalism of Bill Clinton, if it was that, became much more centrist or "third way" in the aftermath of the Reagan years and the Republican victory in 1994, while the conservatism of George Bush became more centrist (or compassionate) in response to Bill Clinton's reelection in 1996 and Republican reversals in Congress in 1998. But in the end, after all of the swings of the pendulum, it is conservatism in one form or another that has gained enormous ground. . . .

One of David Mayhew's most trenchant critiques of classic realignment theory is that it posited an inevitability to affairs that is simply not appropriate in a world defined by contingency. Who, after all, would have predicted September 11? That something resembling a realignment system can be observed is no prediction that it will endure and no guarantee that the process that brought it about is closer to its beginning than to its end. The future, if it can be seen at all, is best left to prophets. . . .

Politically, 2004 illustrated the outlines of a new electoral system, long in the making but now fully revealed. That system consists of a (slight) Republican majority, built on a reshuffling and rationalizing of party coalitions over several decades that has, on balance, favored Republicans; the ascendancy of a conservative public philosophy, which occurred hand-in-hand with the development of an infrastructure of conservative intellectual institutions; and the gradual rise of the new media, which fundamentally transformed the delivery of news and commentary in America, aiding Republicans in the process.

Any account of the rise of the Republicans must admit the importance of contingency. The GOP might still be the minority party, it could be argued, if not for vexing events in 1968 (Vietnam, race riots, and the rise of the counterculture), 1980 (stagflation, Iran, and Afghanistan), and 2002 and 2004 (September 11). But almost every majority party has owed much to events, many of them traumatic and unforeseen, which the public perceived that it handled better than its opponents. Where would the New Deal coalition have been without the Great Depression and Pearl Harbor, or McKinley without the Depression of 1893, or the first Republicans without Fort Sumter and Appomattox? In any event, if Republicans owed their political success after 2001 to September 11, it was largely because they had spent more than a generation establishing their bona fides as the national security party.

The 2004 election has a number of implications for the future. Republicans in Congress seem to possess a number of structural advantages that present a steep hill for Democrats to climb in their quest for a takeover. In presidential politics, the tide in 2004 ran in the Republicans' favor, making red states redder and blue states purpler. Bush's win was broad, as he gained ground in almost every demographic group. And, to a greater degree than at any time in recent American history, a president and Congress of the same party successfully pursued a comprehensive and unified strategy that wove together the political, the electoral, and the legislative. . . .

A new system—the system of 2004—is in place, culminating a long process of partisan change. Yet even if Republicans gained ascendancy through a "rolling realignment" that resulted in an undisputed national majority in 2004, there can be no telling how long it will last. When Democrats looked out from the summit of their landslide of 1964—a victory much more impressive than the Republican win forty years later—they perceived an endless horizon of electoral success stretching before them. In retrospect, though, 1964 was the apogee of their power. They were undone not by the mechanistic workings of an inevitable cycle, but by events, their own mistakes, and a Republican Party agile enough to take advantage of those errors.

Someday, the reds and the blues of America in the twenty-first century will seem as quaint and curious as the blues and the greens of Byzantium or the whites and blacks of Florence. For the moment, red stands atop blue in the "51 percent nation," like Hercules standing astride the world itself. Only Hercules has a narrow toehold indeed. Like a mythic Greek, Republicans may find that hubris and fate are their most threatening enemies.

75

EARL BLACK
MERLE BLACK

From *The Rise of Southern Republicans*

What was once the Solid Democratic South is no longer solid nor Democratic. Sibling political scientists Earl and Merle Black, experts on southern politics, dissect an important change that has been occurring since the 1980s. First with support for Republican President Ronald Reagan in 1980 and 1984 and then for Republican congressional candidates in subsequent elections, southern white voters now back Republican candidates more than Democratic ones. Professors Black find that the source of this "Great White Switch" was due initially to the issue of race and civil rights. Nowadays, the appeal of the Republican party for white southerners lies in its conservative party positions on issues like the scope of the federal government's power, taxes, and family values. African American Democrats and moderate independent southerners still count, of course, and that's why the South today is a competitive, up-for-grabs region at election time—just like the rest of the nation.

———

REPUBLICANS FROM THE SOUTH have transformed American politics. The collapse of the solid Democratic South and the emergence of southern Republicanism, first in presidential politics and later in elections for Congress, have established a new reality for America: two permanently competitive national political parties. Not since Democrats battled Whigs before the Civil War has there been such a thoroughly nationalized two-party system. The Democratic party has always been a national enterprise, commanding durable strength in both the South and the North. Traditionally, the Republican party's geographic reach was quite different. A broadly based *northern* party, Republicans maintained active wings in the Northeast, Midwest, West, and Border states but secured only a nominal presence in the South. Apart from the short-lived Reconstruction era, for many generations southern Republicanism "scarcely deserve[d] the name of party. It waver[ed] somewhat between an esoteric cult on the order of a lodge and a conspiracy for plunder in accord with the accepted customs of our politics."

When the Republicans recaptured both houses of Congress in 1994 for the first time since 1952, they did not construct their Senate and House majorities in the old-fashioned way. Republican control of Congress traditionally involved a purely sectional strategy in which enormous Republican surpluses in the North trumped huge Republican deficits in the South. The novel feature of the Republicans' 1994 breakthrough was its national character. Republicans won majorities of House and Senate seats in both the North *and* the South, a feat they had not achieved since 1872, and their new southern majorities were vital to the Republicans' national victories. Across the nation Republicans as well as Democrats now realistically believe they have fighting chances to win both the White House and Congress in any particular election. Focusing on elections to both the Senate and the House of Representatives, this book examines the regional causes and national consequences of rising southern Republicanism.

It is easy to forget just how thoroughly the Democratic party once dominated southern congressional elections. In 1950 there were no Republican senators from the South and only 2 Republican representatives out of 105 in the southern House delegation. Nowhere else in the United States had a major political party been so feeble for so many decades. A half-century later Republicans constituted *majorities* of the South's congressional delegations—13 of 22 southern senators and 71 of 125 representatives. This immense partisan conversion is our subject. Just as the emergence of southern Republicanism restored competition to America's presidential politics, so has the rise of Republican senators and representatives from the South revitalized congressional politics.

The old southern politics was transparently undemocratic and thoroughly racist. "Southern political institutions," as V. O. Key Jr. demonstrated, were deliberately constructed to subordinate "the Negro population and, externally, to block threatened interferences from the outside with these local arrangements." By protecting white supremacy, southern Democrats in Congress institutionalized massive racial injustice for generations. Eventually the civil rights movement challenged the South's racial status quo and inspired a national political climate in which southern Democratic senators could no longer kill civil rights legislation. Led by President Lyndon B. Johnson of Texas, overwhelming majorities of northern Democrats and northern Republicans united to enact the Civil Rights Act of 1964 and the Voting Rights Act of 1965. Landmark federal intervention reformed southern race relations and helped destabilize the traditional one-party system. In the fullness of time the Democratic party's supremacy gave way to genuinely competitive two-party politics.

But if the old solid Democratic South has vanished, a comparably solid Republican South has not developed. Nor is one likely to emerge. Republican politicians hold majorities of the region's House and Senate seats, but their majorities are much smaller than those traditionally maintained by southern Democrats. Even more important, neither Republicans nor Democrats enjoy majority status among the southern electorate. In the old southern politics, whites overwhelmingly considered themselves Democrats and voted accordingly. Political battles in the contemporary South feature two competitive minority parties rather than the unmistakable domination of a single party. . . .

Modern competitive two-party politics is grounded in the region's rapidly growing and immensely diverse population. The central political cleavage, as ancient as the South itself, involves race. When the Republican party nominated Arizona Senator Barry Goldwater—one of the few northern senators who had opposed the Civil Rights Act—as their presidential candidate in 1964, the party attracted many racist southern whites but permanently alienated African-American voters. Beginning with the Goldwater-versus-Johnson campaign more southern whites voted Republican than Democratic, a pattern that has recurred in every subsequent presidential election. Two decades later, in the middle of Ronald Reagan's presidency, more southern whites began to call themselves Republicans than Democrats, a development that has also persisted. These two Great White Switches, first in presidential voting and then almost a generation later in partisan identification, laid the foundations for highly competitive two-party politics in the South. Gradually a new southern politics emerged in which blacks and liberal to moderate whites anchored the Democratic party while many conservative and some moderate whites formed a grow-ing Republican party that owed little to Abraham Lincoln but much to Goldwater and even more to Reagan. Elections in the contemporary South ordinarily separate extraordinarily large Democratic majorities of blacks from smaller Republican majorities of whites.

Yet modern southern politics involves more than its obvious racial divisions. The South, an increasingly complex society, is the largest region in the United States. More than 84 million people, three of every ten Americans according to the 2000 Census, now reside in the eleven states of the old Confederacy. During the 1990s the region's population grew by 19 percent, much faster than the increase (11 percent) that occurred in the rest of the nation, and its congressional delegation expanded from 125 to 131 seats in the 2002 apportionment. The South's population growth was rooted in the liberating effects of civil rights legislation and the tremendous expansion of the economy. As Dan Balz and Ronald Brownstein have concluded, "The decline of the agrarian South and the rise of a modern economy grounded in manufacturing, defense, tourism, services, and tech-nology has been, by anyone's measure, one of the great success stories of the late twentieth century—but in creating a more diversified society, the South's transformation made it difficult for Democrats to speak for the interests of all, as they once claimed to do." Whites and blacks born and raised in the region no longer had to leave in search of better opportunities in the North. Many individuals reared elsewhere in the nation and world— whites, blacks, Hispanics, Asians, and others—now found the South an acceptable, even desirable, place in which to work and retire.

The rise of a middle and upper-middle class has produced millions of voters with substantial incomes subject to substantial federal and state taxation. Many of these upwardly mobile individuals, wanting to keep the lion's share of their earnings, view the Republicans as far more sympa-thetic than the Democrats to their economic interests and aspirations. Another major fault line divides white southerners who are part of the religious right political movement (strongly pro-Republican) from the much larger group who are not (slightly pro-Republican). And among whites who are not attracted to conservative religious groups, men are strongly pro-Republican while women are more evenly divided in their partisanship. Thus economic class, religion, and gender also structure the social foundations of southern two-party politics. . . .

The unique characteristics of the South's modern House delegation can best be appreciated when set against historical patterns of representation. . . .

White supremacy was the undisguised political theory and standard practice of the racist white Democrats who ended Reconstruction. Violence, intimidation, and extensive ballot-box fraud converted a congressional delegation that was nine-tenths white Republican in 1866 into one that was almost four-fifths white Democratic by 1874. An artificially Democratic electorate replaced an artificially Republican electorate. There was nothing remotely "normal" or "constitutional" about the relentlessly undemocratic and morally corrosive mechanisms that restored white Democrats to their preeminence in the southern House delegation.

Although white Republicans (unlike black Republicans) could never be stamped out completely, the term "Solid South" accurately described the white Democrats' prominence in Congress. As the protracted agrarian upheavals of the late nineteenth century subsided and the remaining black voters were driven out of the political system, the southern delegation settled down to almost perfect white Democratic domination. Having eliminated their racial and partisan opponents from the electorate, racially conservative white Democrats chosen by racially conservative white voters easily monopolized the region's congressional delegation.

The Great Depression and New Deal maintained the lopsided partisan division of the southern House delegation. Outside the South the greatest economic catastrophe of the twentieth century revived the Democratic party and discredited the Republican party in many congressional districts. Because southern Republicans already hovered close to zero, in the South the Great Depression simply gave most whites additional reasons to hate Republicans and powerfully reinforced Democratic supremacy. Before federal intervention into southern race relations, congressional representation in the region amounted to a simple story of sustained white Democratic power.

Most of the white Democrats who served through the mid-1960s defended racial segregation and worked hard to prevent civil rights legislation. Gradually, however, as the older Democratic segregationists departed, they were replaced by younger white Democratic politicians who understood that cultivating biracial coalitions was essential to their survival. Many of the white Republicans who began to win congressional elections positioned themselves as far more conservative on racial issues than their Democratic opponents. Yet with widespread acceptance of the finality of

racial change, little remains of the overt racial rhetoric that often characterized the first generation of southern Republican congressmen. By and
large, Republican House members from the South emphasize their economic and social conservatism. After federal intervention the gap between
white Democrats and white Republicans began to narrow, but as late as
1990 white Democrats still outnumbered white Republicans by better
than three to two.

Striking partisan changes in southern representation occurred during
the 1990s. In 1991, following the last election based on districts established
after the 1980 Census, the South's delegation consisted of 72 white Democrats, 39 white Republicans, and 5 black Democrats. Ten years later, after
the creation of many new majority black districts, it included 71 white
Republicans, 1 white independent . . . who caucused with the Republicans, 37 white Democrats, and 16 black Democrats. . . .

In the South the Reagan realignment of the 1980s was a momentous
achievement. By transforming the region's white electorate, Ronald
Reagan's presidency made possible the Republicans' congressional breakthrough in the 1990s. The secular realignment of southern white voters,
chiefly involving conservative men and women, occurred in two distinct
stages. Greater white support for Republican *presidential candidates* com-
menced in 1964, but the more fundamental Republican advantage in
partisan identification emerged two decades later. The extended lag between
the presidential and partisan realignments allowed Democrats to dominate
southern elections to Congress long after federal intervention had ended
racial segregation and started to destabilize the one-party system.

The Great White Switch in presidential voting appeared immediately
after Congress passed and Democratic president Lyndon Johnson signed
the 1964 Civil Rights Act. Republican Barry Goldwater easily defeated
Johnson among white southerners. Since 1964 more whites have voted
Republican than Democratic in every single presidential election. Similar
changes in southern party affiliation, however, did not immediately accompany the white switch in presidential voting. Partisan realignments
require political leaders whose performance in office expands the party's
base of reliable supporters. Not until Reagan's presidency did more southern whites begin to think of themselves as Republicans than as Democrats.
Reagan was the first Republican presidential candidate to poll back-to-
back landslide majorities from white southerners; and his vice president,
George Bush, captured the presidency in 1988 by running on the strategy
that Reagan had mastered: attracting substantial majorities from conservative and moderate whites, while implicitly conceding the votes of blacks
and liberal whites.

Important as his electoral victories were, Reagan's presidency had a far more crucial impact upon many southern whites. His optimistic conservatism and successful performance in office made the Republican party respectable and useful for millions of southern whites. Many of them, for the first time in their lives, began to think of themselves as Republicans. The Great White Switch in partisan identification created a much more competitive playing field for two-party politics, one that ultimately encouraged, expanded, and intensified Republican campaign activity for Senate and House seats.

The Republican approach to top-down party building in the South was modeled upon its successful strategy in presidential elections: realign white conservatives as a reliable source of Republican support and neutralize white moderates as a consistent foundation of Democratic strength. Reagan attracted a majority of white conservatives into the Republican party and persuaded many other conservatives to think of themselves as "independents" rather than as Democrats. The Republican president had a different impact on southern white moderates. He eroded their traditional attachment to the Democratic party and increased their Republican ties, thereby neutralizing a huge, longstanding Democratic advantage among this critically important segment of the southern electorate.

By *realigning* white conservatives and *dealigning* white moderates, Reagan produced a *partial* realignment of the southern white electorate. . . .

"The situation was ripe for the culmination of the Republican southern strategy," emphasized [Numan] Bartley. The California Republican turned out to be the most popular president among southern whites since Franklin Roosevelt. Utilizing "anecdote over analysis," acting from "ideological principles when possible" but willing to "compromise when necessary," as Charles W. Dunn and J. David Woodward characterized his style, Reagan appealed to the emotions, aspirations, and interests of the region's conservative and moderate white voters. According to journalist Lou Cannon, who had covered Reagan's entire political career, "the ideological core of Reaganism" encompassed three priorities: "lower tax rates, a stronger military force and reduced government spending." These objectives resonated powerfully among conservative and moderate whites in the South. Deliberately avoiding any explanation of how his priorities might be simultaneously achieved, Reagan instead promoted "values that have a base in the collective subconscious of every American," according to Dunn and Woodward. Reagan "promised a new era of national renewal emphasizing traditional values—the dignity of work, love for family and neighborhood, faith in God, belief in peace through strength and a commitment to protect freedom as a legacy unique to America."

In 1980 the Democratic and Republican parties also differed in many important respects over the proper role of the federal government. "The Democratic party platform favored affirmative action, federally funded abortions, and busing, and it endorsed the Equal Rights Amendment to the point of denying party support to candidates who opposed the amendment and encouraging boycotts of states that refused to ratify it," Bartley noted, whereas "Reagan's Republican platform disavowed busing and abortion, ignored the Equal Rights Amendment, demanded prayer be allowed in the schools, and advocated family values." Throughout the campaign he emphasized "a visceral hatred of burgeoning federalism," of the ever-growing presence of federal laws, rules, and regulations in domestic affairs. "I would take the lead in getting the government off the *backs* of the people of the United States and turning you loose," promised Reagan. As a former Democrat who had switched to the Republican party late in his life, Reagan knew how to appeal to a southern white electorate that contained many born-and-bred Democrats. "Now I know what it's like to pull that Republican lever for the first time because I used to be a Democrat myself," Reagan would say. "But I can tell you— it only hurts for a minute." . . .

Rising congressional Republicanism in the oldest regional stronghold of the Democratic party has reshaped the Republicans into a truly national party for the first time since Reconstruction. Not since Whigs fought Democrats in the 1830s and 1840s has American politics been based on a thoroughly nationalized two-party system. Because leaders in both parties can easily see ways to win or lose their House and Senate majorities, the national stakes of each election cycle are permanently high. A retirement here, an unexpected death there, to say nothing about short-term political trends helping one party or the other—all these factors contribute to the seesaw nature of the modern party battle. In its unmitigated ferocity contemporary congressional partisanship reflects the new reality that the results of national elections are no longer foregone Democratic victories or assured Republican triumphs.

Thus the South's political transformation holds extraordinary consequences for America. Old-fashioned sectional conflict has dissipated, but sectional considerations continue to pervade national politics through the conservative agenda pursued by Republican congressional leaders from the South. As it has been in presidential politics for some time, the South is now at the epicenter of Republican and Democratic strategies to control Congress. In order to comprehend national political dynamics, it is therefore more important than ever to understand the changing South.

76

JOHN GARCÍA

From *Latino Politics in America*

In his study of Latino gains in the political arena, John García bases his research on the 2000 election — and his findings are even more valid as the decade continues. His list of Hispanics in the House of Representatives and in the Senate ends with 2001 data, but it could easily be brought up to date, adding several more Latinos to both lists. As the Latino population in the United States has grown, so has Latino participation in politics. Both political parties know this, and both are trying hard to win Hispanic votes. García discusses the movement of Latinos into new areas of the country where their presence is significant in schools, in the workplace, and in politics. Surely, this is only the first edition of what will be many editions of Latino Politics in America.

———

THE CLOSENESS OF THE [2000] presidential election, growth of the Latino electorate, notable partisan attention directed to the Latino communities, and more Latinos seeking elected office all provide evidence for the political gains that Latinos take into the new millennium. Amid another round of elections . . . , at all levels there are important developments that Latinos can impact, as well as be impacted by. Both parties are vigorously contesting for control of both chambers of Congress; the latest round of redistricting opens more opportunities for Latino office competition; gains in naturalization and voter registration afford another chance to exercise political clout; and both political parties are continuing their targeted efforts to expand their respective Latino support. . . .

As already noted, gains in political representation, increased participation, and impact on the public policy-making process have been continuous objectives for the Latino community. Following the 2000 elections, there were high expectations among Latinos for gains in presidential appointments at the cabinet and White House staff levels. At this time, only one Latino (HUD Secretary Mel Martínez) serves in the cabinet, and Antonio González serves as special counsel to the president; there have been other Latinos appointed to various sub-cabinet positions, commissions, and some judgeships.* President George W. Bush initiated the first presidential radio broadcast in Spanish in 2002 as part of his (and the Republican Party's) efforts to establish closer links with the Latino community. In addition, the Republican Party initiated a weekly "news-oriented" broadcast on Spanish-language television. To some extent, the Democratic Party has sought to strengthen its support within the Latino community through policy proposals focusing on immigration reform, greater access by permanent legal residents to social welfare programs, minority small business support, health care coverage, and racial profiling. Thus the carryover from the 2000 elections of directed attention by the major political parties continues.

In May 2002, poll results from eight hundred Latinos were presented at a gathering of the New Democratic Network: support for President George W. Bush would draw even against Al Gore if the two were to meet in the 2004 presidential elections. In the 2000 election, Al Gore outdistanced George W. Bush by 20 percentage points, but the current poll results indicate a near toss-up (46 percent versus 44 percent) if the election were held today. Explanations for closing this gap are attributed to a rising Latino middle class, policy responsiveness by the Bush administration (i.e., Bush reiterated continued support of U.S. economic embargo of Cuba), and a "softening of the GOP's image." Part of the White House strategy is based on the 7–8 percent of the electorate that Latinos now assume and building on the 35 percent Latino vote received in 2000. The other finding was that the same Latinos indicated support for the Democratic congressional candidate (49 percent to 23 percent) over Republican candidates. . . .

. . . The first "fact" lies with the projected population growth of Latinos. While much has been made of the rapid and continuous growth of the "largest minority," this pattern will be reinforced in the future. Census Bureau population decennial counts and future projections into mid-century continue to show the Latino growth rate exceeding that of all other populations. It is estimated that by 2050, Latinos will make up one-fourth of the U.S. population (currently they constitute one-eighth). The other major development in this continued population growth is their geographic dispersion throughout all regions of the United States. In 1990 approximately 90 percent of all Latinos lived in ten states.

The influx of Latinos into less "traditional" areas is becoming more evident. For example, during a Christmas season Protestant service in

---

*Alberto Gonzáles became the Attorney General in George W. Bush's Administration in 2005. —EDS.

HISPANICS IN THE U.S. CONGRESS

Hispanic Representative	Years Served	State	Partisan Affiliation	Congressional District
House of Representatives				
Romualdo Pacheco	1877–1878	California	Republican	4th
Ladislas Lazaro	1913–1927	Louisiana	Democrat	7th
Benigno C. Hernandez	1915–1917, 1919–1921	New Mexico	Republican	at-large
Dennis Chavez	1931–1935	New Mexico	Democrat	1st
Joachim O. Fernandez	1931–1941	Louisiana	Democrat	1st
Antonio M. Fernandez	1943–1956	New Mexico	Democrat	1st
Joseph Montoya	1957–1964	New Mexico	Democrat	1st
Henry B. González	1961–1998	Texas	Democrat	20th
Edward Roybal	1963–1993	California	Democrat	33rd
Eligio de la Garza	1965–1997	Texas	Democrat	15th
Manuel Lujan Jr.	1969–1989	New Mexico	Republican	1st
Herman Baldillo	1971–1977	New York	Democrat	21st
Robert García	1978–1990	New York	Democrat	21st
Anthony L. Coehlo	1979–1989	California	Democrat	15th
Matthew Martínez	1982–2001	California	Democrat	31st
William B. Richardson	1983–1997	New Mexico	Democrat	3rd
Solomon Ortiz	1983–	Texas	Democrat	27th
Esteban Torres	1983–1999	California	Democrat	34th
Albert G. Bustamante	1985–1993	Texas	Democrat	23rd
Ileana Ros-Lehtinen	1989–	Florida	Republican	18th
Jose E. Serrano	1990–	New York	Democrat	16th
Ed L. Pastor	1991–	Arizona	Democrat	2nd
Frank M. Tejada	1993–1997	Texas	Democrat	28th
Xavier Becerra	1993–	California	Democrat	30th
Henry Bonilla	1993–	Texas	Republican	23rd
Lincoln Díaz-Balart	1993–	Florida	Republican	21st
Robert Menendez	1993–	New Jersey	Democrat	13th
Lucille Allard-Roybal	1993–	California	Democrat	37th
Nydia M. Velasquez	1993–	New York	Democrat	12th
Luis Gutierrez	1993–	Illinois	Democrat	4th
Silvestre Reyes	1996–	Texas	Democrat	16th
Ruben Hinojosa	1997–	Texas	Democrat	15th
Ciro D. Ródriguez	1997–	Texas	Democrat	28th
Loretta Sanchez	1997–	California	Democrat	46th
Joe Baca	1999–	California	Democrat	42nd
Charles A. González	1999–	Texas	Democrat	20th
Grace Napolitano	1999–	California	Democrat	34th
Hilda Solís	2001–	California	Democrat	31st
United States Senate				
Octaviano Larrazolo	1928–1929	New Mexico	Republican	
Dennis Chavez	1935–1962	New Mexico	Democrat	
Joseph M. Montoya	1964–1977	New Mexico	Democrat	

HISPANICS WHO HAVE SERVED AS CABINET SECRETARIES

Hispanic Cabinet Officer	Years Served	President in Office When Nominated	Cabinet Office Held
Mel Martínez	2001–	George W. Bush	Dept. of Housing and Urban Development
William Richardson	1998–2000	William Clinton	Dept. of Energy
Federico Peña	1997–2000	William Clinton	Dept. of Energy
	1993–1997	William Clinton	Dept. of Transportation
Henry Cisneros	1992–1997	William Clinton	Dept. of Housing and Urban Development
Martin Lujan	1989–1992	George H. W. Bush	Dept. of Interior
Lauro Cavazos	1988–1992	Ronald Reagan	Dept. of Education

suburban Portland, Oregon, a call went out to congregational members to give clothing, books, and other practical gifts to needy individuals. The organizer said that the first twenty-eight of the seventy-five households on the list were Spanish speakers. There was another call for persons who could speak Spanish to help deliver the gifts. Similar indicators are present in Portland, Oregon, as signs in Spanish are posted throughout the Oregon Museum of Science and Industry, as well as signs and voice recordings on the MAX (the light rail system).

A Latino transformation is occurring in Dalton, Georgia (northwestern part of the state), where Latinos have been migrating, mostly from Mexico, to the "carpet capital of the world." In fall 2000, Latinos constituted a majority (51.4 percent) of the students in the public schools in this town of 23,000. Across northern Georgia, an influx of mostly Latino immigrants is arriving to work in the poultry processing plants and carpet mills. This scenario can be recounted in many other communities throughout the South, the Rocky Mountain States, America's heartland, New England, and the suburban Northeast.

Finally, there is the burgeoning growth of Central and South Americans within the Latino community. While persons of Mexican origin continue to maintain high growth rates (both birth rates and immigration), it is Latinos from the Dominican Republic, Colombia, El Salvador, Guatemala, and the like, who are growing faster and becoming more geographically important. Latinos from Central and South America have settled for the most part in areas where Mexican-origin, Cubans, and Puerto Ricans are located. While contributing to the overall Latino growth, this pattern also represents a broader mix of Latino interests and potential resource building. . . .

The expansion of Latinos into metropolitan areas and regions of the country where they have been less evident serves a couple of political and social purposes. First, the continuing growth (but more geographically varied settlement patterns) provides Latinos with an even greater national presence. Even though the public and political-economic institutions are aware of the Latino communities, there are regions, especially the South, Northwest, and upper Midwest, in which public awareness of and experience with Latinos had been virtually nonexistent. At the same time, the expansion of Latinos into more locales can produce positive and negative consequences. The above-mentioned Latino movement to Dalton, Georgia, has helped meet the demand for jobs and workers. The other side of this rapid transformation is inter-group tensions and anti-immigrant sentiments among "native" Georgians.

For example, in 1989 there were 3,131 non–Latino white students enrolled in Dalton schools, or almost 80 percent of the student enrollment. In the fall of 2000, there were only 1,893 white students, many having transferred to private schools. Some parents complained that their English-speaking children were ignored as teachers paid more attention to children learning the English language. One store's plywood sign condemns "uncontrollable immigration" and declares, "Congress sold us for cheap labor." On the other hand, Dalton's carpet industry clearly supports the Latino immigrants. Dalton produces 40 percent of the world's carpet, and in a community where the unemployment rate is less than 3 percent, carpet mills are worried about maintaining reliable workers.

Obviously, part of the future of Latino politics is the process of community building within the Latino community, as well as bridging within existing community interests and institutions in more recently settled areas. Continued growth exceeding the national average and movement into lower and/or fewer Latino populated areas are some of the basic facts about the future profile of Latinos in the United States. They represent both challenges and opportunities for Latinos to establish their roots in the community and develop the resource base and interest to influence local policy makers and employers. . . .

The second basic "fact" that bears relevance to the future of Latino politics is the existence of a pan-ethnic community. I have questioned the existence and form of community that may exist among the various Latino subgroups in the United States. Our examination of this question demonstrates that some level of pan-ethnic community exists among Latinos. Organizations continue to represent and advocate on behalf of Latinos, and numerous newer organizations have been formed. They have organized around issues of civil and political rights and salient policy areas (immigration, language policies, etc.), as well as work-related groups and culture- and neighborhood-based interests. Political and economic elites have established networks and, at times, cooperative activities that cut across specific Latino subgroups (Cubans, Dominicans, Salvadorans, etc.).

The dispersion of Latinos across different regions of the country has brought more Latinos into contact where only one group previously predominated. For example, the Latino mix in the Miami metropolitan area has changed, and a majority of Latinos are now non-Cubans. While inter-Latino group interactions may vary by group and they may be more competitive than cooperative in nature (competition for scarce public and private resources, political resources, etc.), the changed Latino landscape has created pressures and incentives to come together as a broader community. These developments in conjunction with the media's attention have continued to reinforce the expansion and activities of Latinos throughout the country. These developments serve to influence Latino community building. . . .

The mid-1990s firmly established the real "political capital" of Latinos in American politics. Metaphors of "invisibility," "a sleeping giant," and "soon to have your place in the sun" have been used for decades, especially in references to the Mexican-origin population. More recently, similar themes of potentiality and conversion of a significant, growing population into a major political, economic, and cultural force were evident in the mass media, espoused by political and economic leaders, and by activists and organizational leaders from the different Latino communities. Since the mid-1990s, there is greater evidence that Latinos have moved to more concrete indicators that the "Latino vessel has arrived" on the American political and social shores.

77

JOHN WHITE

From *The Values Divide*

Quite a while before the significance of morality and values as a dividing line within the American polity became a standard line of analysis by political scientists and commentators, John White had already spotted it. The "values divide" began decades ago, based on issues that had not yet entered the political arena directly. White discusses clashing views on the family, on marriage, on church attendance, on lifestyles. The way that public officials from both political parties have reacted to the struggle over values is significant for political discourse in America. Instead of looking for middle ground, White observes, most politicians have fled to the extremes where the Democrats and Republicans find themselves most at odds with one another.

THIS BOOK DESCRIBES the values divide that began in the 1960s and accelerated during the Clinton years. This is not my first look at the subject. In 1988, I completed *The New Politics of Old Values*, which studied how Ronald Reagan transformed the presidency by emphasizing the values of "family, work, neighborhood, peace and freedom." Reagan's values politics worked well in his day. But we are now as far removed from Reagan's inauguration as Reagan himself was from John F. Kennedy's swearing-in. In the intervening decades, it is undoubtedly clear that something far more politically significant than the victories of Bill Clinton or George W. Bush has occurred. One incident illustrates the change; back in 1988 when I was completing *The New Politics of Old Values*, Democrat Gary Hart removed himself from the presidential contest when rumors of his purported adultery became the focus of constant media attention. Hart complained that excessive media attention to his personal life had driven the issues he wanted to raise off the front pages: "That link with the voters that lets you listen to their concerns and often your ideas and proposals had been broken." That link broke when a reporter asked if Hart had ever committed adultery. After an awkward silence, the former Colorado senator replied that rumors of his infidelity had nothing to do with his qualifications to be president. By not answering, Hart explicitly refused to endorse the 1960s emblem adopted by civil rights and women's groups that "the personal is political." Hart subsequently exited the race, and Michael Dukakis, whose moral rectitude was never in doubt, was nominated instead.

In contrast, the Clinton presidency was all about the politics of persona. By making the personal so political, Bill Clinton confronted a public that since 1988 had either "matured" in its thinking about its leaders and was more realistic in its expectations, or an electorate whose tolerance of indecency in the Oval Office was the single best indicator that the country's values had gone awry. Clinton's actions—and, indeed, his entire personal history—made clear that the 1960s aphorism that "the personal is political" has come to dominate all aspects of public life. Clinton's own story, first as an Oxford student who avoided the draft and experimented with drugs and later as the married man who conducted numerous extramarital affairs, became a symbol for the loose morality many saw embodied in the 1960s generation that has contributed so mightily to the present values divide. Today, Clinton's wife, Hillary, embodies several of the contradictions many citizens have regarding their own values standards. Supporters see the former Barry Goldwater girl as a role model for independent-minded women who enjoy separate careers apart from their husbands, and they rejoiced when she won a Senate seat from New York. But these same defenders were dismayed when she adopted a Tammy Wynette-like stance (something she once vowed she would never do) and stood by her man during the Monica Lewinsky affair.

Even as powerful and untold a tale as the complicated marriage of Bill and Hillary Clinton, pales in contrast to the values shift that has occurred in everyday family lives of ordinary Americans. How we live, work, and interact with each other, and who we have sex with (and how often), has altered the way we think about each other and ourselves. Not surprisingly, these alterations have animated and transformed present-day politics. For the moment, Americans have been given a respite from the values controversy. George W. Bush is no Bill Clinton, and he is unlikely to challenge the public much when it comes to reconstructing old values to fit present circumstances. Instead of pointing the way to the future, George and Laura Bush are emblematic of the sedate 1950s, a far cry from Bill and Hillary Clinton who seemed to enjoy challenging conventional mores. Yet, even with George and Laura Bush as the present-day incarnation of Dwight and Mamie Eisenhower, a new values politics continues to echo in the nation's civic life. By making the personal entirely political, it is clear that the values divide, which intensified during Bill Clinton's presidency and marked George W. Bush's election in 2000, is *the* demarcation line for an intensely personal politics as it is practiced at the beginning of the twenty-first century. . . .

Defining what it means to be an American is subject to considerable and varied interpretation. . . . Each side in the culture wars is fighting a battle that gives very different answers to the question, "What does it mean to be an American?" One faction emphasizes duty and morality; another stresses individual rights and self-fulfillment. The result is a values divide. As one activist put it, "This is a war of ideology, it's a war of ideas, it's a war about our way of life. And it has to be fought with the same intensity, I think, and dedication as you would fight a shooting war."

The values divide has created its own political lexicon. Liberals routinely label their orthodox counterparts "right-wing zealots," "religious nuts," "fanatics," "extremists," "moral zealots," "fear brokers," "militants," "demagogues," "homophobes," "latter-day Cotton Mathers," or "patriots of paranoia." They maintain that their opponents are "anti-intellectual and simplistic," with a message that is "vicious," "cynical," "narrow," "divisive," and "irrational." While serving as president of Yale University, the late A. Bartlett Giamatti once told the freshman class that the religious right is "angry at change, rigid in the application of chauvinistic slogans, absolutist in morality, [and threatens] through political pressure or public denunciation whoever dares to disagree with their authoritarian positions." Giamatti felt certain that his Yale freshmen would find a more enlightened answer to the question, "What does it mean to be an American?"

Newly formed liberal organizations have sought to promote their interpretation of freedom, individualism, and equality of opportunity. The National Organization for Women (NOW) advocates greater economic and cultural freedoms for women: "We believe that a true partnership between the sexes *demands a different concept of marriage,* an equitable sharing of the responsibilities of home and children and of the economic burdens of their support." The People for the American Way likewise sees itself as promoting an authentic Americanism: "In Congress and state capitals, in classrooms and in libraries, in courthouses and houses of worship, on the airwaves and on the printed page, on sidewalks and in cyberspace, we work to promote full citizen participation in our democracy and safeguard the principles of our Constitution from those who threaten the American dream. Join us in defending the values our country was founded on: pluralism, individuality, and freedom of thought, expression, and religion."

Those who belong to the NOW and People for the American Way, like many others who espouse liberal causes, extol the new freedoms individuals have to make choices in their personal lives. When asked by pollster John Zogby whether there are "absolute moral truths that govern our lives," those who classified themselves as "progressives" or "very liberal" were evenly divided: 48 percent agreed, 46 percent disagreed. Those who were "very conservative" were much more emphatic: 74 percent said there are absolute truths; only 25 percent disagreed.

As these poll numbers indicate, the values divide between liberals and conservatives over lifestyle issues has become a chasm. Jen Morgan, a conservative Christian from San Diego, worried that the messages conveyed by the popular culture represent a wholesale attack on the biblical truism that two-parent families work best: "Society wants us to think that two women are just as qualified to raise children, or two men are just as qualified to raise children. All of the . . . wrong morals that go along with that sort of a lifestyle and . . . because of that, the whole definition of the family is changing. . . . It all is breaking the family down, because God wanted it to be man and woman raising a family. He must have had a reason for that." . . .

Nowhere are the cultural differences greater than they are between those who attend church frequently (whatever their denomination) and those who go less regularly or not at all. This gap between the "churched" and the "less churched" has contributed to the passions behind the debate about the country's values. Without a doubt, the United States is a very religious country. More than 90 percent believe in God; 85 percent view the Bible as the actual or inspired word of God; and 52 percent have an unfavorable view of atheists. Back in 1958, 83 percent told the Gallup Organization that the "ideal president of the United States" would be someone who attended church regularly. And most Americans continue to pay homage to religion: 72 percent believe that religious groups should be permitted to use public school grounds to hold their after-school meetings; 66 percent favor daily prayer in public classrooms; and 80 percent want prayers said at high school commencements. Running for the U.S. Senate in 1998, Arkansas Democrat Blanche Lincoln touted her "personal relationship with Jesus Christ," which began in college when she became a member of Billy Graham's Campus Crusade for Christ. At a church gathering, Lincoln addressed her "brothers and sisters in Christ," saying, "When I talk to Him, it's pretty informal. I just lay it all out there, say it like it is." Lincoln won easily, with 55 percent of the vote. Two years later, George W. Bush roused audiences by proposing a greater government role in assisting faith-based social programs, and 72 percent said that the discussion of religion and God in the presidential campaign had been good for the country.

But since the 1960s there has been a substantial increase in those who do not attend church. In 1963, 49 percent told the Gallup Organization they attended church regularly; 27 percent were occasional churchgoers; 4 percent seldom attended; and 19 percent did not go to a church at all. According to the latest Gallup data, 42 percent claim to attend church "at least once a week" or "almost every week," while 57 percent say they go to religious services "about once a month," "seldom," or "never." The result has been a diminution of the moral authority religious institutions once wielded. In 1988, three-quarters believed that a person can be a good Christian or Jew *without* attending a church or synagogue. Twelve years later an astonishing 58 percent agreed with the statement: "It is *not* necessary to believe in God in order to be moral and have good values." Finally, 53 percent believe it is possible to improve the nation's moral values without placing more emphasis on religion.

As the number of churchgoers decreases, those who remain in their pews are even more devoted to their religious beliefs. Jen Morgan, the fundamentalist San Diego Christian, is angry that those who are less religious have such influence in educational and cultural institutions. Speaking of atheists, Morgan says, "They are winning. We don't say 'Merry Christmas' anymore in the public school. We say 'Happy Holiday' because Christmas denotes God, denotes Jesus. There are a lot of Roman Catholics in the schools. There are a lot of Protestants. They still believe in God. . . . But here comes along people who are atheists and who are only a certain portion of the population, and they are the ones being heard." Across the other side of the values divide, Patricia Bates of DeKalb County, Georgia, counters: "The Scripture says 'Only my Father can judge which is heaven.' All of you are playing God here. Get a mirror. Are you that great? If everybody would step back and look at themselves, take a mirrored look at themselves and then ask, 'What is my purpose? Where do I fit [in] this puzzle?,' then we'd be much better off."

Unlike the early twentieth century, when many Americans battled against an influx of members of other religious groups (especially newly arrived Catholic and Jewish immigrants), today's religious controversies are with the religious institutions themselves. Those who belong to an organized religion often find answers to today's problems in God's revealed truth. The less-churched question God and seek answers from within themselves. Today there are more Americans than ever before who do *not* find answers to life's difficulties in the practice of any religious faith. The Gallup Organization has compiled an index of leading religious indicators, which measures the importance Americans place on religion, weekly church or synagogue attendance, confidence in religious institutions, and belief in God. In 1941, the index stood at 730; today it reads 673. The result is a growing values gap between those who are "churched" and the increasing number of "less-churched" Americans. According to a survey conducted by the *Washington Post* and the Henry J. Kaiser Family Foundation, of those who agreed that the federal government should take steps to protect the nation's religious heritage, 64 percent said religion was very important in their life. Likewise, of those who agreed with the proposition that there should be a high degree of separation between church and state, 84 percent said religion was not important at all to them. . . .

In a country that is increasingly diverse and tolerant, there is also a greater sense of discomfiture as different lifestyles, and the individual outlooks that prompt them, gain greater acceptance. The question that plagues virtually all contemporary political debate, "Whose country is it anyway?" divides Americans by their religious beliefs, age, race, ethnicity, and region. It is a debate destined to transform American politics. . . .

This cultural divide created its own moral federalism [in the 2000 presidential election]. Simply put, if you were gay, you were more likely to live in Vermont; if you wanted the Ten Commandments posted in the courts, you liked living in Alabama; if you were antigun, you had lots of company in Massachusetts; but if you were pro-gun, you were not alone in Wyoming. The result was an increased partisanship thanks to the cultural divide separating Democrats and Republicans on most moral issues: 91 percent of all Republicans supported Bush; 86 percent of Democrats backed Gore. But the party gap was only one of many. The gender gap returned with a vengeance: 54 percent of women supported Gore, and 53 percent of men voted for Bush. Other gaps included married versus single; churched versus less churched; the religious right versus those who were not "born again"; whites versus blacks versus Latinos; working women versus stay-at-home moms; union members versus non-union members; working class versus the prosperous middle versus the brie-and-chablis set; liberals versus conservatives; gays versus straights; gun owners versus those who didn't have guns in their homes; rural versus urban America; and in Vermont, those who were enthusiastic about civil unions versus those angry at the idea.

The gaps created by this new moral federalism were especially present in how voters viewed the country's moral direction. Overall, 39 percent said that the moral climate was headed in the right direction, whereas 57 percent said things were on the wrong track. Not surprisingly, Bush voters saw the nation's morals askew, with 62 percent answering "wrong track." Gore voters were considerably happier with the status quo: 70 percent of them thought that the country's morals were going in the right direction. The state of the country's moral values became a prism through which voters saw politics. Blacks, liberals, and Democrats, for example, thought the country's morals were just fine. Whites, conservatives, and Republicans disagreed. How one viewed the country's moral condition also colored perceptions of the presidency, of life for the next generation, of Bill Clinton's legacy, whether the country needed a fresh start or should stay on course, whether the military had become too weak, and whether they could trust the candidates. . . .

Prior to the 2000 election, Congressman David Price, a respected North Carolina Democrat, called for a "subdued partisanship." But the passions that rule today's congressional parties make subdued partisanship an almost impossible goal. It is not only the issues separating the two congressional parties that makes bipartisanship more difficult to achieve, but it is also the demeanor of both parties. In March 2001, only one-third of House members showed up at a resort in Greenbrier, West Virginia, for the annual bipartisan retreat. [Former] Democratic minority leader Dick Gephardt stated the obvious, "Bipartisanship is over—not that it ever began." Gephardt should know. His relationships with Speakers Newt Gingrich and Dennis Hastert have been almost nonexistent. Moreover, George W. Bush has done very little negotiating with congressional Democratic leaders. But, says Gephardt, the lack of civility at the top extends to those of a lesser rank: "Democrats and Republicans don't even make eye contact when they pass one another in the halls of Congress, unless it's to exchange furious glares."

Rather than engaging in the hard task of governing, many congressional partisans find it more enticing to be sought-after guests on cable television programs such as *Crossfire*, *Hardball*, *Capital Gang*, and *The O'Reilly Factor* that promote entertainment value rather than political enlightenment. As Gephardt told his colleagues in 1998, "We are now rapidly descending into a politics where life imitates farce, fratricide dominates our public debate, and America is held hostage to tactics of smear and fear." While these words were uttered in the passions swirling around Clinton's impeachment, . . . the polarization created by values-minded activists, means that governing in the morally free twenty-first century is more difficult than ever before. Reflecting on "the politics of personal destruction" that characterized the Clinton era, Gephardt observed that it caused citizens to hate their leaders and their government: "In time, they drop out and begin treating politics as just another form of gladiatorial entertainment; they start electing professional wrestlers as governors."

Thus, we are likely to muddle along with a small-minded politics that

avoids answering the most important questions of our time. To the extent
these values questions are resolved, it is likely to be outside the realm of
the very partisan . . . politics that characterizes the present era. Values will
continue to matter more than ever before, but it is our politics that remains
unable to cope.

78

MARK MONMONIER

From *Bushmanders and Bullwinkles*

*Why is a geography professor's book included in a reader on American
government? First, learn the vocabulary of professor Mark Monmonier:
remapping, redistricting, reapportionment, gerrymandering. Every decade a
census is taken of the U.S. population. While many citizens are aware of
the importance of the census's demographic statistics in determining how
many people live where and how well in the U.S., few realize the political
consequences of the census. It decides how the 435 House of Representatives
districts will be reapportioned so that they are equal in population, ensuring
"one person, one vote" in the House. The electoral college is affected too,
as are state legislative districts. Monmonier looks at the case study of New
York City's so-called Bullwinkle District, drawn in 1992 to encompass a
majority of one minority group—Hispanics. He explains why various disparate groups favor such gerrymanders. Monmonier gives political scientists a
special reason to study with care the results of the 2000 and forthcoming
2010 censuses.*

"REMAP" IS NOT IN THE dictionary, but it should be, as both
verb and noun. Every ten years America counts heads, reallocates seats
in the House of Representatives, and raises the blood pressure of elected
officials and wannabe lawmakers by remapping election districts for Congress and state legislatures. And many jurisdictions also reconfigure city
councils, town boards, or school districts. Because the way political cartographers relocate district boundaries affects who runs as well as who wins,
a remap can strongly influence, if not determine, what a government does
or doesn't do, what activities it bans or encourages, and which citizens
absorb the costs or reap the benefits. Although "redistricting" refers to
the process of drawing lines while "reapportionment" more narrowly

connotes the reallocation of House seats among the states, neither term adequately alludes to the map itself as an object of debate and manipulation, if not litigation and ridicule.

Equally important is "gerrymander," a dictionary term with two shades of meaning. For many political scientists, gerrymandering is nothing more than deliberately increasing the number of districts in which a particular party or group is in the majority. They see this kind of manipulation as neither unfair nor illegal: if a state's constitution lets the party in power enhance its control, so be it. But for the media, the general public, and some judges, the term suggests sinister shapes that signify unfair if not illegal manipulation and undermine confidence in our electoral system. Although legal scholars differ on whether irregularly shaped districts are "expressive harms" that warrant judicial intervention, the post-1990 remap made unprecedented use of electronic cartography to craft cleverly contorted, racially motivated gerrymanders.

I wrote *Bushmanders and Bullwinkles* to promote an informed appreciation of redistricting, including the variety of plausible remaps and their diverse effects. In showing how boundaries can serve or disadvantage political parties, incumbents, and racial or ethnic groups, I want to make readers aware of how legislators, judges, and other elected officials use the decennial remap to promote personal or ideological agendas. Although the discussion frequently raises questions of fairness, my goal is not a cynical deconstruction of a fundamental political process but a skeptical, and I hope insightful, look at the complex relationships among geography, demography, and power. . . .

George Herbert Walker Bush, forty-first president of the United States, shares a unique political legacy with Elbridge Gerry, our fifth vice president, under James Madison. In 1812, while Gerry was governor of Massachusetts, his party, Thomas Jefferson's Democratic-Republicans, controlled the state legislature. In redrawing senatorial district boundaries after the census of 1810, the Jeffersonians hoped to win more seats by packing Federalist voters into a few strongholds while carving out a long, thin Republican district along the northern, western, and southwestern edges of Essex County. Gerry disliked the plan but signed the remap into law anyway—a veto, he thought, would be improper. The Federalist press was not amused. When a reporter pointed out the new district's lizardlike appearance, his editor exclaimed, "Salamander! Call it a Gerrymander!" Artist-cartoonist Elkanah Tisdale added the wings, teeth, and claws (FIG. 1.1) that enshrined Gerry's name in the language as a political pejorative, with its hard *g* mispronounced like the *j* in Jerry. Ironically, the sinuous district crafted by the governor's cronies is far less troublesome in form,

FIGURE 1.1. The newly configured Essex County, Massachusetts, senatorial district, as embellished by Elkanah Tisdale. Originally published in the Boston *Gazette* for March 26, 1812. From James Parton, *Caricature and Other Comic Art* (New York: Harper and Brothers, 1877), 316.

if not intent, than the cartographic manipulations encouraged by the Department of Justice under the Bush administration. I call them "bushmanders."

This new species is also more ragged around the edge than its nineteenth-century ancestors. In figure 1.2, for instance, New York State's Twelfth Congressional District, crafted as a Hispanic-majority district in 1992, looks more intricate and fragile than the famed Essex County senatorial district of 1812. Although the unadorned Massachusetts prototype provoked cynical slurs, Tisdale's sinister enhancements probably account for its longevity as a political icon: widely reproduced in books and articles on electoral manipulation, the classic gerrymander is rarely rendered as an unembellished contour. By contrast, New York's Twelfth District needs no adornments to explain journalists' delight in labeling it the "Bullwinkle District," after the loquacious moose who shared a Saturday morning spotlight with his cartoon-show sidekick Rocky the flying squirrel. Although the narrow rows of comblike prongs and wider blobs awkwardly connected by thin corridors only faintly resemble antlers, once some clever wag linked the district's contour to the beloved talking moose,

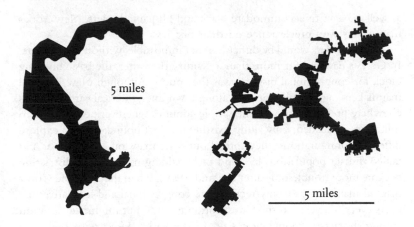

FIGURE 1.2. Silhouettes of the classic 1812 gerrymander of Essex County (left) and New York's Twelfth Congressional District as configured in 1992 (right). Left-hand map redrawn from map in the Boston *Weekly Messenger*, March 6, 1812, as reproduced in Elmer C. Griffith, *The Rise and Development of the Gerrymander* (Chicago: Scott, Foresman, 1907), 69. Right-hand map compiled from U.S. Bureau of the Census, *Congressional District Atlas: 103rd Congress of the United States* (Washington, D.C., 1993).

the name stuck. Nicknames are rare, though: most bushmanders inspire descriptions like "the 'Z' with drips" (Louisiana's Fourth District), a "spitting amoeba" (Maryland's Third District), and "a pair of earmuffs" (Illinois's Fourth District).

The emergence of these new political critters in the early 1990s is partly a consequence of the Voting Rights Act, passed in 1965 and modified several times. In addition to banning racial discrimination in voter registration, the law defends the right of minority voters to elect candidates of their choice and demands federal scrutiny where past abuse has been especially flagrant. Among other provisions, the Department of Justice must approve the postcensus remap in several states, mostly in the South, as well as the three New York City boroughs containing parts of the Bullwinkle District. Interpreted broadly, the Voting Rights Act also prohibits political cartographers from splitting a district in which members of a minority group constitute a majority. This stricture raises a thorny question: Can the Justice Department deny preclearance when a state chooses not to form a thinly stretched minority-majority district? In rejecting plans submitted by Georgia and North Carolina, George Bush's map editors answered with an assertive "Yes!" Intimidated by earlier rulings as well as eager to accommodate black and Hispanic leaders, New York's mapmakers won preclearance on their first try.

Bushmanders would be difficult, if not impossible, without computers. In Gerry's day, and for more than a century thereafter, the basic building block for congressional districts was the county. Although New England mapmakers eagerly split counties along town lines, political cartographers elsewhere preferred to combine whole counties wherever possible and to split cities, if needed, only along existing precinct boundaries. To explore different configurations, they spread out their maps on a large floor and tallied district populations by hand or by adding machine. Redistricting became more troublesome after the mid-1960s, when the Supreme Court insisted that states not only reconfigure congressional and legislative districts every ten years, as the Constitution intends, but minimize variation among districts in population size. In the early 1990s, with the Civil Rights Division of the Justice Department poised to reject plans that ignored possible minority-majority districts, states turned to interactive computers, electronic maps, and detailed census data, which made it easy to accumulate blocks inhabited by African Americans or Spanish-speaking Americans and link dispersed minority neighborhoods with thin corridors inhabited by few, if any, nonminority "filler people." To ignore this technology was to invite federal judges to draw the lines themselves. After all, Justice officials in Washington had similar tools, as did African American and Hispanic interest groups eager to sue for apparent violations of the Voting Rights Act.

The result typically was a district difficult to describe with maps or words. New York City's Bullwinkle District, for instance, is a polygon with no fewer than 813 sides. In a bill approved by the state legislature and signed into law by the governor in June 1992, District 12's perimeter requires 217 lines of verbal description, which read like the itinerary of a taxi driver trying desperately to run up the meter. Figure 1.3 shows how part of the boundary twisting across Brooklyn helped elect a Hispanic to the House of Representatives by capturing blocks rich in Spanish surnames while avoiding blocks where Hispanics are a minority. The line became law as

to Linwood street, to Glenmore avenue, to Cleveland street, to Pitkin avenue, to Warwick street, to Glenmore avenue, to Jerome street, to Pitkin avenue, to Warwick street, to Glenmore avenue, to Jerome street, to Pitkin avenue, to Barbey street, to Glenmore avenue, to Schenck avenue, to Liberty avenue, to Barbey street, to Atlantic avenue, to Van Siclen avenue, to Liberty avenue, to Miller avenue, to Glenmore avenue, to Bradford street, to Liberty avenue, to Wyona street, to Glenmore avenue, to Pennsylvania avenue, to Liberty avenue, to Vermont avenue,

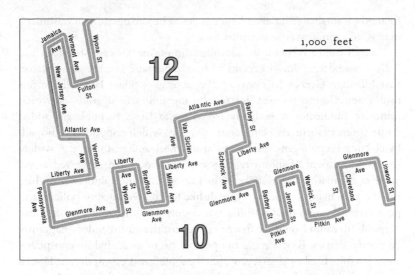

FIGURE 1.3. Excerpt from U.S. Bureau of the Census, *Congressional District Atlas: 103rd Congress of the United States* (Washington, D.C., 1993), NEW YORK-16.

to Atlantic avenue, to New Jersey avenue, to Jamaica avenue, to Vermont avenue, to Fulton street, to Wyona street. . . .

Lawmakers are word people, and before they vote on a redistricting bill, boundaries composed on a computer screen are converted to verbose lists of street segments, watercourses, and other fixed features.

Because politicians and election officials need to see where voters live, redistricting officials convert the lists back into maps. To supplement the electoral maps of individual states, the Bureau of the Census publishes the *Congressional District Atlas*, a standardized cartographic reference for the fifty states. Because the *Atlas's* letter-size pages are too small to show on one map the intricate details of computer-crafted gerrymanders, a single district can extend across a dozen pages or more. In the edition for the 103rd Congress, published in 1993, fragments of New York City's Bullwinkle District appear on twenty-two pages. Identified vaguely on the separate, single-page county maps for Brooklyn, Manhattan, and Queens, District 12 crops up in greater detail on eighteen partial-county inset maps, mostly printed one to a page, at various scales. Figure 1.3, extracted from one of the Brooklyn (Kings County) insets, illustrates the symbols and level of detail. Especially complex portions of the boundary in parts of Queens required eight additional subinset maps—insets of insets—

focused on small areas at even larger scales. The cartography of bushmanders is, to coin a word, insetuous. . . .

Why would a Republican administration favor African American and
Latino candidates, almost certain to be Democrats? For the same reason
that Elbridge Gerry's Jeffersonian Republicans packed Federalist voters
into Essex County's inner district: by creating safe districts in which
minority candidates were likely to win, the Bush Republicans added
white voters to formerly Democratic districts, which responded, as hoped,
by electing Republicans. There was another advantage, though. A widely
shared resentment of minority-majority districts, often perceived as yet
another affirmative action strike at the prerogatives and values of the white
middle-class majority, fueled white dislike for the Democrats' policies and
politicians. Because the GOP did not openly advocate minority districts,
Republican candidates were free to rail against the bushmanders' flagrantly
contorted shapes. Reinforcing the perception of an antiwhite conspiracy
were lawsuits filed by aggrieved "filler people" and promptly challenged
by pro-civil rights Democrats. Adding to the irony, federal judges appointed by Presidents Reagan and Bush won the public approval of white
Republicans by condemning the racial gerrymanders that helped their
party take over the House in 1994. . . .

Our examination of the American way of redistricting raises three
issues: Should race matter, should shape matter, and should geography
matter. The post-2000 remap and the prospect of ever more outrageous
congressional districts—but with less overt concern for ethnicity—raises
a fourth, perhaps more fundamental question: What next?

The answer to the race question is so obviously affirmative (Who can
deny the salient divisiveness of race in American society?) that the query
needs rephrasing, with emphasis on *how* rather than *whether*. Indeed, since
the early 1950s Congress and the courts have repeatedly wrestled with
how race should matter. In the process we buried Jim Crow,* as a century
earlier we dismantled slavery, and during the 1990s we demonstrated that
a remap designed to encourage minority candidates need not injure white
voters. Given most incumbents' irresistible urge to curry favor with all
constituents, regardless of color, was anyone truly surprised when political
scientist David Canon found that black-majority districts work quite well

---

*Jim Crow laws were common throughout the South, beginning in the 1890s, as a way
of enforcing legal segregation of the races in the post–Civil War period. Such laws mandated
racial segregation in all public facilities, such as schools, trains, playgrounds, and even drinking
fountains. Along with Jim Crow laws, black Americans were often prevented from registering
to vote by poll taxes, literacy tests, and "grandfather" clauses. These forms of legal discrimination in the United States lasted until the 1950s and 1960s. —EDS.

in representing whites? But in increasing the electability of minority candidates we have produced weird silhouettes that invoke public ridicule and judicial reprimand—shapes like the North Carolina district that white plaintiffs denounced as "harmful" and Justice Sandra Day O'Connor labeled "bizarre."

If minority-majority districts are at all harmful, the more likely victims are African Americans and Hispanics. That's the verdict of social scientists who question the effects of minority-majority districts on the "substantive representation" of minority groups, which refers to the groups' clout in getting laws passed and funding approved. Using the remap to increase "descriptive representation"—getting more people of color into House seats—concentrates minority voters into comparatively few black-majority or Hispanic-majority districts, thereby undermining minority support for white Democrats, their traditional allies. And a Congress with an increased number of minority representatives might well be a Congress dominated by Republicans, who are less likely to promote policies favored by minority-group leaders. At least that's the apparent result of the Republican takeover of the House in the 1994 elections and Congress's subsequent retreat from affirmative action into welfare reform and other tenets of the GOP's Contract with America. With time, though, stronger black and Hispanic caucuses and more experienced minority incumbents might prove a worthwhile investment.

Should shape matter? Not really, argue legal scholars like Pamela Karlan, who defends bizarre districts by noting the courts' inability "to identify a concrete harm to any identifiable individual." In a similar vein, political scientist Micah Altman, who examined the effects of geometrically irregular minority-majority districts on public confidence, found "no support for the hypothesis that 'ugly' districts send pernicious messages to voters that affect their attitudes toward government or Congress." Quoting a phrase rampant in recent redistricting lawsuits, Altman notes, "The only detectable effect of shape was on turnout. Moreover, I could find no evidence that bizarre districts cause 'expressive harms.'" And who can argue that the weirdly shaped or questionably contiguous districts drawn to promote minority representation are more difficult to represent than the far larger districts stretched across sparsely populated reaches of the American West? After all, dispersed minorities in parts of Chicago, New York City, or the rural South share common concerns much like the coastal issues that unite island residents with their mainland neighbors. Both kinds of districts constitute communities of interest in which compactness and contiguity have little relevance.

Shape will continue to matter, though, because highly irregular districts, at odds with how most Americans think elections districts should look, are a form of cartographic mischief. For this reason, tiny silhouette maps, with little relevance to how well a district can be represented, are enormously effective as propaganda against graphically flagrant gerrymanders of any sort, partisan as well as racial. And when the judiciary targets only racial gerrymanders, as in the 1990s, Rorschach-like silhouettes even provided a clever Why me? defense of deposed bushmanders: one of the most effective arguments supporting the Texas minority-majority districts struck down in Bush v. Vera* was a poster that juxtaposed four anonymous silhouettes and dared the viewer to separate two districts overturned by the Court from two equally irregular white-majority districts allowed to stand. Most viewers, I suspect, wondered why the Supreme Court didn't reject them all. . . .

If the Constitution mandates neither compactness nor contiguity, should geography matter? Absolutely, as long as we understand that geography means more than a simplistic sense of shape and distance. Because of vastly improved transport and communication, the geography that's relevant for the twenty-first century is very different from the geography of 1790, 1920, or even 1960. And though the slogan "all politics is local" remains valid, proximity plays a very different role today than in the heyday of ward politics and strong party loyalty. Demographic affinity— nothing new, really—is more germane to most concerns than neighborhoods are, and even neighborhood issues like crime and zoning frequently precipitate local alliances among geographically dispersed groups like elderly residents and upper-middle-class homeowners. Although African Americans, Hispanics, born-again Christians, young urban professionals, and other demographic clusters might have much in common with their neighbors, communities of interest are almost always larger and more fragmented than one's immediate neighborhood. As a result, traditional district boundaries, whether for congressional, state legislative, or city council districts, do not work as well as they once did.

Can the contorted boundaries drafted in the early 1990s to equalize district populations and protect coherent minority voting rights really work better than more traditional borders? Maybe, maybe not. But they're clearly less dysfunctional than silhouette maps and caustic critics suggest.

*Bush v. Vera (1996) was a Supreme Court case challenging the constitutionality of three Texas congressional districts that had been deliberately drawn up—gerrymandered—to create a majority of minority group voters; two districts were comprised of a majority of black Texans, one of Hispanic Texans. The unusual shape of the districts and their lack of a compact design led the Court to declare them invalid. Texas had to redraw the district lines. Again in 2006, the Court heard cases on certain Texas district boundaries that had already been redrawn in 2000 and 2003.—EDS

North Carolina's I-85 District, for instance, strongly reflects in both its name and its shape the radical reduction of functional distance between its seemingly dispersed nodes. And intricate inner city districts like New York's Bullwinkle District or Chicago's "pair of earmuffs" are comparatively compact in a social-geographic space based on personal interaction rather than surveyor's instruments. . . .

What's certain is a shift of approximately eleven House seats after the 2000 census. Although "equal proportions" reapportionment might well produce a few cliff-hangers, as it did in 1990, demographers expect Arizona, Georgia, and Texas to gain two seats each, while redistricting officials in New York and Pennsylvania face a remap with two fewer districts. Completing the exchange, Colorado, Florida, Montana, Nevada, Utah, and perhaps California should each pick up a seat, while Connecticut, Illinois, Michigan, Mississippi, Ohio, Oklahoma, and Wisconsin will each redistrict with one representative fewer.

What's not clear is whether redistricting committees will push partisan gerrymandering well beyond the public's begrudging tolerance of 1990s-style bushmanders and Bullwinkles.

PART FOURTEEN

The Media

79

KATHARINE GRAHAM

From *Personal History*

The Watergate story has been told from many sides: the Watergate burglars, President Nixon's aides, reporters Bob Woodward and Carl Bernstein, to name only a few who have added to the scandal's record. In this excerpt from her acclaimed book recounting a life filled with both joy and tragedy, Katharine Graham adds an indispensable account to the Watergate legacy. Graham was the owner and publisher of the Washington Post, *and thereby gave Woodward and Bernstein the backing they needed to pursue the Watergate story. She describes the requirement that "two sources" be used to confirm each facet of the story as it unfolded. She relates the pressure put on the* Post *as Watergate-related issues moved into the court system. The revelation of White House tapes, Graham feels, was the key to the whole story coming to light. Interestingly, Graham was never let in on nor ever requested to be let in on the hidden identity of Deep Throat, Woodward's and Bernstein's inside source. Graham died just a few years after her memoir was published. In 2005, Deep Throat was revealed to be FBI official Mark Felt.*

———

ON SATURDAY MORNING, June 17, 1972, Howard Simons called to say, "You won't believe what happened last night." He was right. I barely believed him, and listened with equal amounts of amusement and interest as he told me of a car that crashed into a house where two people had been making love on a sofa and went right out the other side. To top that, he related the fantastic story that five men wearing surgical gloves had been caught breaking into the headquarters of the Democratic National Committee.

President Nixon was in Key Biscayne, Florida, at the time. His press secretary, Ron Ziegler, dismissed the incident as "a third-rate burglary attempt," adding, "Certain elements may try to stretch this beyond what it is." None of us, of course, had any idea how far the story would stretch; the beginning—once the laughter died down—all seemed so farcical. . . .

The story of the break-in appeared on the front page of Sunday's paper, "5 Held in Plot to Bug Democrats' Office Here," with [veteran *Post* police reporter Al] Lewis's byline. Contributing to the story were several staff writers, including Bob Woodward and Carl Bernstein, who also did a separate report with background information on the suspects, four of whom, Carl discovered, were from Miami, where they had been involved in anti-Castro activities. Phil Geyelin's editorial appearing the next day in the *Post* was titled "Mission Incredible," and began with a quote from the CBS television show "Mission Impossible": "As always, should you or any of your force be caught or killed, the Secretary will disavow any knowledge of your actions. . . . "

What we were seeing, of course, was the legendary tip of the iceberg. And we might never have known the size of the iceberg had it not been for the extraordinary investigative and reporting efforts of Woodward and Bernstein, famous names now but then two young men who had never worked together, one of whom (Woodward) had not even been long at the paper. In some ways it was a natural pairing, since their qualities and skills complemented each other. Both are bright, but Woodward was conscientious, hardworking, and driven, and Bernstein messy and undisciplined. He was, however, the better writer, more imaginative and creative. In other ways the relationship was oil and water, but the end product came out right, despite—or perhaps because of—the strange mix. . . .

From the beginning, Bob distinguished himself, and there was no question in the editors' minds whom they were going to send to court to cover the break-in. Carl Bernstein, on the other hand, had been at the *Post* since the fall of 1966 but had *not* distinguished himself. He was a good writer, but his poor work-habits were well known throughout the city room even then, as was his famous roving eye. In fact, one thing that stood in the way of Carl's being put on the story was that Ben Bradlee was about to fire him. Carl was notorious for an irresponsible expense account and numerous other delinquencies—including having rented a car and abandoned it in a parking lot, presenting the company with an enormous bill. But Carl, looking over Bob's shoulder while he reworked Al Lewis's notes, immediately got hooked on this strange story and was off and running. It was Harry who saved him when both Ben and Howard wanted to fire him, saying that he was pursuing the Watergate story with verve, working hard, and contributing a great deal. And it was Carl who made the first connection of the crisp new $100 bills in the pockets of the burglars to money raised for the Nixon campaign.

Woodward and Bernstein clearly were the key reporters on the story—so much so that we began to refer to them collectively as Woodstein—but the cast of characters at the *Post* who contributed to the story from its inception was considerable. As executive editor, Ben was the classic leader at whose desk the buck of responsibility stopped. He set the ground rules—pushing, pushing, pushing, not so subtly asking everyone to take one more step, relentlessly pursuing the story in the face of persistent accusations against us and a concerted campaign of intimidation.

Howard Simons, with his semi-independent pocket of authority on the paper, helped move the story along enormously, particularly with his attitude, as Woodward later described it, of "inquisitiveness and 'Let's find out what's going on.'" Harry Rosenfeld said of Howard, "When the kids were running one way or the other, he would—if it was called for—stand up and screw the tide." It was Howard who carried the story in its early days. . . .

From the start, Woodward and Bernstein followed the trail of the Watergate burglars with alacrity and skill, and a lot of elbow grease. From the time Bob went to court and heard James McCord say "CIA," he was hooked on the story. When Carl came up with Howard Hunt's address book, and the two found in it the name "Colson" and the phrase "W. House," they, like Herblock, decided there was a connection to the White House. When it was discovered that numerous calls had been made from the phone of Bernard Barker, one of the burglars, to an office shared by Gordon Liddy and another lawyer at the Committee to Re-elect the President, whose acronym, CRP, quickly turned into the unfortunate CREEP, Woodward and Bernstein were off and running.

On August 1, over a month after the break-in, the first big story appeared under the joint byline of Bernstein and Woodward, reporting on the connection of the burglars to CRP. Three weeks later, on August 22, President Nixon was renominated with great fanfare at the Republican National Convention in Miami. The next week, apparently trying to declare the Watergate affair finished, Nixon announced that John Dean, counsel to the president, had thoroughly investigated the break-in and said, "I can state categorically that his investigation indicates that no one in the White House staff, no one in this administration, presently employed, was involved in this very bizarre incident. What really hurts is if you try to cover it up." Again, we learned only later, from John Dean's testimony, that he had never heard of "his" investigation until the president made that statement. Strange, indeed.

On September 15, a federal grand jury indicted the original five burglars as well as two former White House aides, E. Howard Hunt and G. Gordon Liddy. It was on that same day—but this came to light only two years later—that Nixon spoke to two of his aides, the White House chief of staff, Bob Haldeman, and John Dean, making threats of economic retaliation against the *Post*: "[I]t's going to have its problems. . . . The main thing is the *Post* is going to have damnable, damnable problems out of this one. They have a television station . . . and they're going to have to get it renewed. . . . And it's going to be God damn active here. . . . [T]he game has to be played awfully rough." Of our lawyer, Nixon said, "I wouldn't want to be in Edward Bennett Williams's position after this election. We are going to fix the son of a bitch, believe me. We are going to. We've got to, because he is a bad man."

Two weeks later, a seminal Bernstein and Woodward article appeared on page one of the *Post*. They had dug up information that there was a secret fund in the safe of Maurice Stans—former secretary of commerce, but finance chairman for CRP at the time—which was controlled by five people, one of whom was [Attorney General] John Mitchell, and which was to be used to gather intelligence on the Democrats. Thus the story reached a new level, involving Mitchell himself, not only in his new role in the campaign, but when he was still attorney general, since Woodward and Bernstein had unearthed Mitchell-authorized expenditures from the fund from the previous year.

CRP denied the story artfully—and graphically. In an effort to check it out, Bernstein, having been told by a press aide at CRP that there was "absolutely no truth to the charges," called Mitchell directly, reaching him at a hotel in New York, where Mitchell answered the phone himself. When Carl told him about the story, Mitchell exploded with exclamations of "JEEEEEEESUS," so violent that Carl felt it was "some sort of primal scream" and thought Mitchell might die on the telephone. After he'd read him the first two paragraphs, Mitchell interrupted, still screaming, "All that crap, you're putting it in the paper? It's all been denied. Katie Graham's gonna get her tit caught in a big fat wringer if that's published. Good Christ! That's the most sickening thing I ever heard."

Bernstein was stunned and called Ben at home to read him Mitchell's quotes and discuss adding them to the already prepared article. Ben told Carl to use it all except the specific reference to my "tit." The quote was changed to read that I was "gonna get caught in a big fat wringer." Ben decided he didn't have to forewarn me. (Later he told me, "That was too good to check with you, Katharine." I would have agreed with Ben's decision.) As it was, I was shocked to read what I did in the paper, but even more so to hear what Mitchell had actually said, so personal and offensive were the threat and the message. I ran into Carl by accident the next day and asked him if he had any other messages for me.

It was quite a temper tantrum on Mitchell's part—and especially strange of him to call me Katie, which no one has ever called me. Bob later observed that the interesting thing for him was that Mitchell's remark was an example of the misperception on the part of the Nixon people that I was calling all the shots and that I was the one who was printing everything on Watergate. In any case, the remark lived on in the annals of Watergate and was one of the principal public links of me with the affair. Later, though before Watergate had ended, I received a wonderful present from a California dentist who, using the kind of gold normally used to fill teeth, had crafted a little wringer complete with a tiny handle and gears that turned just like a regular old washing-machine wringer. And some time after that, Art Buchwald presented me with a tiny gold breast, which he had had made to go with the wringer. I occasionally wore the two of them together on a chain around my neck, and stopped only when a reporter threatened to tell Maxine Cheshire. . . .

. . . We always did our best to be careful and responsible, especially when we were carrying the burden of the Watergate reporting. From the outset, the editors had resolved to handle the story with more than the usual scrupulous attention to fairness and detail. They laid down certain rules, which were followed by everyone. First, every bit of information attributed to an unnamed source had to be supported by at least one other, independent source. Particularly at the start of Watergate, we had to rely heavily on confidential sources, but at every step we double-checked every bit of material before printing it; where possible, we had three or even more sources for each story. Second, we ran nothing that was reported by any other newspaper, television, radio station, or other media outlet unless it was independently verified and confirmed by our own reporters. Third, every word of every story was read by at least one of the senior editors before it went into print, with a top editor vetting each story before it ran. As any journalist knows, these are rigorous tests.

Yet, despite the care I knew everyone was taking, I was still worried. No matter how careful we were, there was always the nagging possibility that we were wrong, being set up, being misled. Ben would repeatedly reassure me — possibly to a greater extent than he may have actually felt — by saying that some of our sources were Republicans, Sloan especially, and that having the story almost exclusively gave us the luxury of not having to rush into print, so that we could be obsessive about checking everything. There were many times when we delayed publishing something until the "tests" had been met. There were times when something just didn't seem to hold up and, accordingly, was not published, and there were a number of instances where we withheld something not sufficiently confirmable that turned out later to be true.

At the time, I took comfort in our "two-sources" policy. Ben further assured me that Woodward had a secret source he would go to when he wasn't sure about something—a source that had never misled us. That was the first I heard of Deep Throat, even before he was so named by Howard Simons, after the pornographic movie that was popular in certain circles at the time. It's why I remain convinced that there was such a person and that he—and it had to be a he—was neither made up nor an amalgam or a composite of a number of people, as has often been hypothesized. The identity of Deep Throat is the only secret I'm aware of that Ben has kept, and, of course, Bob and Carl have, too. I never asked to be let in on the secret, except once, facetiously, and I still don't know who he is.

This attention to detail and playing by our own strict rules allowed us to produce, as Harry Rosenfeld later said, "the longest-running newspaper stories with the least amount of errors that I have ever experienced or will ever experience." . . .

The Washington Post Company had been in the public eye for several months—certainly more than I was comfortable with, and in ways we might not have wished. We didn't seek out the celebrity; it was thrust on us. During a *Newsweek* sales meeting at the time, I said it reminded me somewhat of the old story about the man who'd been tarred and feathered and ridden out of town on a rail. When asked how he felt, he said, "Except for the honor of the thing, I would rather have walked."

By early 1973, I was growing increasingly anxious and thought I ought to meet with Woodward and Bernstein in addition to the editors. Surprisingly, to this point—seven months into the story—I had had hardly any contact with the reporters. So, on January 15, Bob and Howard and I sat down to lunch together (Carl was out of town). Characteristically, Bob went right downstairs to the newsroom afterwards and made extensive notes about what we'd said—even going so far as to write down what we ate, the main course being eggs Benedict, which led to our future reference to this gathering as the "eggs-Benedict lunch."

My apprehensions about the whole Watergate affair were evident. "Is it all going to come out?" Woodward reported that I asked anxiously. "I mean, are we ever going to know about all of this?" As Bob later wrote, he thought it was the nicest way possible of asking, "What have you boys been doing with my newspaper?" He told me then that they weren't sure all of it ever *would* come out: "Depression seemed to register on her face. 'Never?' she asked. 'Don't tell me never.'"

It was also at this lunch that Woodward told me he had told no one the name of Deep Throat. "Tell me," I said quickly, and then, as he froze, I laughed, touched his arm, and said that I was only kidding—I didn't want to carry that burden around. He admitted that he was prepared to give me the name if I really wanted it, but he was praying I wouldn't press him. This luncheon was reassuring for me—or at least I gave the appearance of being reassured—but I remained nervous. Looking back, I'm surprised I wasn't even more frightened.

The period leading up to the trial of the "Watergate Seven," which began on January 8, 1973, had been extremely tense. Colson was talking around Washington about going to our national advertisers or our investors. A Wall Street friend of mine, André Meyer, a man with administration contacts, called me and asked me to come to see him. When I did, he advised me to be very careful of everything I did or said and—just like in the movies—he warned me "not to be alone." "Oh, André," I said, "that's really absurdly melodramatic. Nothing will happen to me."

"I'm serious," he said. "I've talked to them, and I'm telling you not to be alone." André never explained what his fears were based on, and I still have no idea what he had heard or even meant, but I certainly got the point about how serious he was. I lay awake many nights worrying, though not about my personal safety. Beyond its reputation, the very existence of the *Post* was at stake. I'd lived with White House anger before, but I had never seen anything remotely like the kind of fury and heat I was feeling targeted at us now. It seemed at times that we should really be worrying about some bizarre Kafkaesque plot—that maybe we were being led down a road to discredit the paper.

The moments of anxiety increased in quantity and intensity. Naturally, we were worried when our stories were denied repeatedly and vehemently. Even we, it seems, underestimated for a long time the capacity of government to hide and distort the truth. Finally, a series of events began to unfold in our favor. Three days after the beginning of the trial, Howard Hunt pleaded guilty to six of the charges against him. Four days later, the other burglars followed suit. On January 30, Liddy and McCord were convicted, continuing to claim that no higher-ups were involved and that they had not received any money. In fact, Hunt had urged the burglars to plead guilty and go to jail, assuring them he would take care of them.

Toward the end of February, a civil subpoena was served on five of us from the *Post*, and we were ordered to appear in the U.S. District Court to testify on our sources in the Democratic Party's civil suit against the Committee to Re-elect the President. The subpoena required that we produce a whole host of material, including documents, papers, letters, photographs, tapes, manuscripts, notes, copies, and final drafts of stories about Watergate. As Ben Bradlee put it, they asked us to bring "everything except the lint in our pockets." My name was misspelled, but I was subpoenaed, along with Woodward and Bernstein, Howard Simons, and another reporter, Jim Mann, who had worked on a few of the early

Watergate stories. Our lawyers decided to give me some of the reporters' notes. Bradlee had reassured Bernstein and Woodward that we would fight this case for as long as it took, adding:

> . . . and if the Judge wants to send anyone to jail, he's going to have to send Mrs. Graham. And, my God, the lady says she'll go! Then the Judge can have that on his conscience. Can't you see the pictures of her limousine pulling up to the Women's Detention Center and out gets our gal, going to jail to uphold the First Amendment? That's a picture that would run in every newspaper in the world. There might be a revolution.

At some point, Woodward had met with Deep Throat, who told him that the subpoenas were part of a response induced by Nixon's rampage against the *Post*, and that he, Nixon, would use the $5 million left over from his campaign "to take the *Post* down a notch." "It will be wearing on you but the end is in sight," Deep Throat told Woodward.

In the end, the subpoenas were quashed, but not before we had spent a great deal of energy and money. The intervening drama was intense. I wrote a friend, "The outrage of it is lost in the absurdity," also noting that one of the editors on the *Post*, who was not served, was said to be suffering from a case of "subpoena envy." . . .

The continuing efforts of the *Post*, and, *finally*, other newspapers and other media as well, and the Congress and the courts helped expose the size of the iceberg. There began a steady stream of revelations, with more and more evidence of scheming and political chicanery coming to light. Wiretaps of several journalists were revealed. We were told by many people that the *Post*'s building was bugged and even that I was being followed. Some of this was clearly an overreaction in an environment rife with paranoia. We did a sweep of our phones throughout the building and in my office and the offices of key editors, but turned up nothing. I'm fairly sure that my phones were never tapped, nor do I believe I was ever followed, but the atmosphere was so infected that this kind of suspicion didn't seem irrational at all.

In June 1973, Woodward and Bernstein wrote that the White House had maintained a list of "political enemies" in 1971 and 1972, and the disclosure surprised few of us. By that time, many people—several of my friends among them—regarded it as an honor to be on it. The list was yet another sign of the peculiar mentality of the small group of men running the country. I can't remember whether my name actually appeared on it, but it was clear to me that I was on it whether my name was written down or not.

A month later, a seismic Watergate event occurred—the turning point, the pivotal moment. In the course of his testimony before the Senate investigating committee, Alexander Butterfield, another Haldeman aide, revealed that there was a voice-activated recording system in the White House. Consequently, the vast majority of conversations the president had had in the Oval Office were on tape, a fact the president himself had clearly lost sight of; or perhaps he assumed that no one knew and that therefore the existence of the system would never become public knowledge. However, someone had to have installed this thing as well as run it, and that someone was Alexander Butterfield. As Woodward later said, it was yet another "incredible sequence of events, and luck for us and bad luck for Nixon. Wrong decisions, wrong turns. But full disclosure of it hung by that fragile thread that could have been cut hundreds of times."

Without the tapes, the true story would never have emerged. In fact, I believe that we at the *Post* were really saved in the end by the tapes and the lucky chance that they weren't destroyed. After the discovery of the tapes, people actually began waiting in the alley outside our building for the first edition of the paper, giving additional meaning to the phrase "hot off the presses." Everyone was now following the story.

Who knows why Nixon didn't destroy the tapes? He seemed to think that they were valuable and that he could defend their privacy, which for a long time he tried to do. . . .

. . . On March 1, 1974, indictments were handed down by a grand jury for seven former Nixon-administration and campaign officials for allegedly conspiring to cover up the Watergate burglary.

What next? On May 9, the House Judiciary Committee began formal hearings on the possible impeachment of Nixon. Though some of my friends, including André Meyer, suggested that the *Post* was trying to "extract every last drop of blood" from the president, I believed that we were following and reporting the impeachment process in a reasoned and dispassionate way, and replied to André, "I hardly see how anyone, no matter how ill-intentioned, could pervert this . . . to 'extracting every last drop of blood.' . . . It really has more to do with what is best for the country now and in the future, than it has to do with this president— who no longer matters, whereas the country does." Privately, I felt that impeachment was right, but my personal opinion didn't get mixed up in the paper's ongoing reporting. . . .

Watergate continued on its way toward an ending none of us could have imagined two years earlier. Even as late as the summer of 1974, amazing as it may seem after all that had been revealed and all the constitutional processes that had taken place—the grand juries, the courts, the

congressional committees—Nixon was still blaming the press for his predicament, saying at one point that, if he had been a liberal and "bugged
out of Vietnam," the press would never have played up Watergate. Despite
Nixon's protestations to his supporter Rabbi Baruch Korff that Watergate
would be remembered as "the broadest but thinnest scandal in American
history," it went on being revealed as anything but.

On July 8, the United States Supreme Court heard arguments in a
historic special session in the case of the *United States* v. *Richard M. Nixon*.
What was at stake was whether the Court would order the release of the
White House tapes. The next day, House Judiciary Committee Chairman
Peter Rodino divulged many of the differences between what the White
House had released and what the committee had found on certain tapes,
indicating that Nixon had played an active role in the cover-up, which
was still going on.

On July 24, 1974, events moved inexorably forward as the Supreme
Court ruled unanimously that Nixon had no right to withhold evidence
in criminal proceedings and ordered him to turn over the additional White
House tapes that had been subpoenaed by Jaworski. On July 27, 29, and
30, respectively, the House Judiciary Committee adopted three articles
of impeachment, charging President Nixon with obstruction of justice,
failure to uphold laws, and refusal to produce material subpoenaed by the
committee.

Editorially, the *Post* did not come out for resignation, as many other
papers did. We believed, as an independent paper, that people would
behave wisely and judiciously if given the information necessary to make
their decisions, and that the process should be allowed to work.

Finally, on August 5, the long-anticipated "smoking gun" turned up.
Three new transcripts were released by the White House, recounting
conversations between Nixon and Haldeman on June 23, 1972, six days
after the original break-in. The tapes showed that the president had
personally ordered a cover-up and that he had directed efforts to hide
the involvement of his aides in the break-in through a series of orders to
conceal details about it known to himself but not to the FBI. This was
such a dramatic and obviously final development that I left Martha's
Vineyard, where I had gone for my August vacation, and flew immediately
to Washington.

Nixon initially said that he would not resign, that he believed the
constitutional process should be allowed to run its course. All ten Republicans on the House Judiciary Committee who had voted against impeachment then announced they would vote in favor of at least the obstruction-

of-justice article. We led the paper with the possibility of Nixon's resignation, but made no predictions, despite speculation on every side.

On August 8, President Nixon announced that he would resign the next day. I stayed at the paper all that day. Together, many of us watched Nixon's television appearance about his decision to resign. . . .

As a story, Watergate was in many ways a journalist's dream—although it didn't seem that way in those first months when we were so alone. But the story had all the ingredients for major drama: suspense, embattled people on both sides, right and wrong, law and order, good and bad.

Watergate—that is, all of the many illegal and improper acts that were included under that rubric—was a political scandal unlike any other. Its sheer magnitude and reach put it on a scale altogether different from past political scandals, in part because of the unparalleled involvement of so many men so close to the president and because of the large amounts of money raised, stashed, and spent in covert and illegal ways. This was indeed a new kind of corruption in government.

Even today, some people think the whole thing was a minor peccadillo, the sort of thing engaged in by lots of politicians. I believe Watergate was an unprecedented effort to subvert the political process. It was a pervasive, indiscriminate use of power and authority from an administration with a passion for secrecy and deception and an astounding lack of regard for the normal constraints of democratic politics. To my mind, the whole thing was a very real perversion of the democratic system—from firing people who were good Republicans but who might have disagreed with Nixon in the slightest, to the wiretappings, to the breaking and entering of Ellsberg's psychiatrist's office, to the myriad dirty tricks, to the attempts to discredit and curb the media. As I said in a speech at the time, "It was a conspiracy not of greed but of arrogance and fear by men who came to equate their own political well-being with the nation's very survival and security."

The role of the *Post* in all of this was simply to report the news. We set out to pursue a story that unfolded before our eyes in ways that made us as incredulous as the rest of the public. The *Post* was never out to "get" Nixon, or, as was often alleged, to "bring down the president." It always seemed to me outrageous to accuse the *Post* of pursuing the Watergate story because of the Democratic bias of the paper. A highly unusual burglary at the headquarters of a national political party is an important story, and we would have given it the same treatment regardless of which party was in power or who was running for election. I was often asked why we didn't cover Ted Kennedy's debacle at Chappaquiddick* as fully as we were covering Watergate. The point is, we did, and the further point is that the Kennedys were probably as angry at us then as the Nixon administration was. Throughout Watergate, I was amazed at the regular allegations that somehow we had created the agony of Watergate by recklessly pursuing certain stories and thereby causing the turmoil that the president was in. How could anyone make this argument in light of the fact that the stories we reported turned out to be true?

In the end, Nixon was his own worst enemy. The *Post* had no enemies list; the president did. Nixon seemed to regard the *Post* as incurably liberal and ceaselessly anti-administration. In fact, the *Post* supported a great many of his policies and programs, but his paranoia, his hatred of the press, his scheming, all contributed to bringing him down—helped along by the appropriate constitutional processes, including the grand juries, courts, and Congress. Woodward and Bernstein were critical figures in seeing that the truth was eventually told, but others were at least as important: Judge Sirica; Senator Sam Ervin and the Senate Watergate Committee; Special Prosecutors Cox and Jaworski; the House Impeachment Committee under Representative Peter Rodino. The *Post* was an important part—but only a part—of the Watergate story.

My own role throughout Watergate is both easy and hard to define. Watergate no doubt was the most important occurrence in my working life, but my involvement was basically peripheral, rarely direct. For the most part I was behind-the-scenes. I was a kind of devil's advocate, asking questions all along the way—questions about whether we were being fair, factual, and accurate. I had a constant conversation with Ben and Howard, as I did with the top two editorial writers, Phil and Meg, so I was informed in general. As was my habit before Watergate, I often attended the daily morning editorial meetings, where the issues were regularly discussed and where editorial policy was formed.

What I did primarily was stand behind the editors and reporters, in whom I believed. As time went on, I did this more publicly, defending us in speeches and remarks to groups around the country—indeed, internationally as well. My larger responsibility was to the company as a whole—beyond the paper—and to our shareholders.

---

*In 1969, Senator Ted Kennedy was involved in a car accident on the summer resort island of Martha's Vineyard. A young woman, Mary Jo Kopechne, was in the car with the senator; she drowned when the car plunged off a bridge into the water. Kennedy swam away from the scene and did not tell authorities about the accident for many hours, but he was never officially charged with wrong-doing in the incident.—EDS.

I have often been credited with courage for backing our editors in Watergate. The truth is that I never felt there was much choice. Courage applies when one has a choice. With Watergate, there was never *one* major decisive moment when I, or anyone, could have suggested that we stop reporting the story. Watergate unfolded gradually. By the time the story had grown to the point where the size of it dawned on us, we had already waded deeply into its stream. Once I found myself in the deepest water in the middle of the current, there was no going back.

It was an unbelievable two years of pressured existence, which diminished only a little as other publications joined us and as the separate investigations and the court cases spawned by Watergate began to confirm and amplify our reporting. When it was perfectly obvious that our existence as a company was at stake, we of course became embattled. Watergate threatened to ruin the paper. The *Post* and The Washington Post Company survived partly because of the great skill and tenacity that our reporters and editors and executives brought to bear throughout the crisis, and partly because of luck.

In fact, the role of luck was essential in Watergate—and luck was on our side. One has to recognize it and use it, but without luck the end result for us could have been very different. From the first incident of the guard finding the taped door at the Watergate building, to the police sending to the scene of the crime a beat-up-looking undercover car that was cruising in the area rather than a squad car that might have tipped off the burglars, to the sources willing—some even eager—to talk and help, we were lucky. We were lucky that the original burglary took place in Washington and was a local story. We were lucky that those under investigation compounded their own situation by further mistakes and misassessments. We were lucky we had the resources to pursue the story. We were lucky that both Woodward and Bernstein were young and single and therefore willing and able to work sixteen- and eighteen-hour days, seven days a week for months on end, at least with fewer repercussions than married men might have had. We were lucky Nixon was eccentric enough to set up a taping system in the White House, without which he might have completed his term. . . .

As astounding as Watergate was to the country and the government, it underscored the crucial role of a free, able, and energetic press. We saw how much power the government has to reveal what it wants when it wants, to give the people only the authorized version of events. We relearned the lessons of the importance of the right of a newspaper to keep its sources confidential.

The credibility of the press stood the test of time against the credibility of those who spent so much time self-righteously denying their own wrong-doing and assaulting us by assailing our performance and our motives. In a speech I made in 1970—before the Pentagon Papers and before Watergate—I said: "[T]he cheap solutions being sought by the administration will, in the long run, turn out to be very costly." Indeed, they did.

80

LARRY SABATO

From *Feeding Frenzy*

When political scientist Larry Sabato published his 1991 book on the media's role in campaigning, he gave a term to a phenomenon others had already seen: a feeding frenzy. The press en masse attacks a wounded politician whose record—or more accurately, his or her character—has been questioned. Every network and cable station participates, often without any real evidence to back up the rumor. Sabato's list of thirty-six examples ends in 1990; knowledgeable readers will be able to update the list. Paradoxically, the spectacular success of the Washington Post's Bob Woodward and Carl Bernstein in investigating Watergate set the stage for recent feeding frenzies. Today, just the fear of being a media target may deter many qualified people from entering public service, Sabato notes.

IT HAS BECOME a spectacle without equal in modern American politics: the news media, print and broadcast, go after a wounded politician like sharks in a feeding frenzy. The wounds may have been self-inflicted, and the politician may richly deserve his or her fate, but the journalists now take center stage in the process, creating the news as much as reporting it, changing both the shape of election-year politics and the contours of government. Having replaced the political parties as the screening committee for candidates and officeholders, the media propel some politicians toward power and unceremoniously eliminate others. Unavoidably, this enormously influential role—and the news practices employed in exercising it—has provided rich fodder for a multitude of press critics.

These critics' charges against the press cascade down with the fury of rain in a summer squall. Public officials and many other observers see journalists as rude, arrogant, and cynical, given to exaggeration, harassment, sensationalism, and gross insensitivity. . . .

Press invasion of privacy is leading to the gradual erasure of the line protecting a public person's purely private life. This makes the price of public life enormously higher, serving as an even greater deterrent for those not absolutely obsessed with holding power—the kind of people we ought least to want in office. Rather than recognizing this unfortunate consequence, many in journalism prefer to relish their newly assumed role of "gatekeeper," which, as mentioned earlier, enables them to substitute for party leaders in deciding which characters are virtuous enough to merit consideration for high office. As ABC News correspondent Brit Hume self-critically suggests:

> We don't see ourselves institutionally, collectively anymore as a bunch of journalists out there faithfully reporting what's happening day by day. . . . We have a much grander view of ourselves: we are the Horatio at the national bridge. We are the people who want to prevent the bad characters from crossing over into public office.

Hume's veteran ABC colleague Sander Vanocur agrees, detecting "among some young reporters a quality of the avenging angel: they are going to sanitize American politics." More and more, the news media seem determined to show that would-be emperors have no clothes, and if necessary to prove the point, they personally will strip the candidates naked on the campaign trail. The sheer number of journalists participating in these public denudings guarantees riotous behavior, and the "full-court press" almost always presents itself as a snarling, unruly mob more bent on killing kings than making them. Not surprisingly potential candidates deeply fear the power of an inquisitorial press, and in deciding whether to seek office, they often consult journalists as much as party leaders, even sharing private vulnerabilities with newsmen to gauge reaction. The *Los Angeles Times's* Washington bureau chief, Jack Nelson, had such an encounter before the 1988 campaign season, when a prospective presidential candidate "literally asked me how long I thought the statute of limitations was" for marital infidelity. "I told him I didn't know, but I didn't think [the limit] had been reached in his case!" For whatever reasons, the individual chose not to run.

As the reader will see later in this volume, able members of the news corps offer impressive defenses for all the practices mentioned thus far, not the least of which is that the press has become more aggressive to combat the legions of image makers, political consultants, spin doctors, and handlers who surround modern candidates like a nearly impenetrable shield. Yet upon reflection, most news veterans recognize that press excesses are not an acceptable antidote for consultant or candidate evils. In fact, not one of the interviewed journalists even attempted to justify an increasingly frequent occurrence in news organizations: the publication of gossip and rumor *without convincing proof*. Gossip has always been the drug of choice for journalists as well as the rest of the political community, but as the threshold for publication of information about private lives has been lowered, journalists sometimes cover politics as "Entertainment Tonight" reporters cover Hollywood. A bitter Gary Hart* observed: "Rumor and gossip have become the coins of the political realm," and the *New York Times's* Michael Oreskes seemed to agree: "1988 was a pretty sorry year when the *National Enquirer* was the most important publication in American journalism." With all the stories and innuendo about personal vice, campaigns appear to be little more than a stream of talegates (or in the case of sexual misadventures, tailgates).

The sorry standard set on the campaign trail is spilling over into coverage of governmental battles. Ever since Watergate,† government scandals have paraded across the television set in a roll call so lengthy and numbing that they are inseparable in the public consciousness, all joined at the Achilles' heel. Some recent lynchings such as John Tower's failure to be confirmed as secretary of defense,‡ rival any spectacle produced by colonial Salem. At the same time more vital and revealing information is ignored or crowded off the agenda. *Real* scandals, such as the savings-and-loan heist or the influence peddling at the Department of Housing and Urban Development in the 1980s, go undetected for years. The sad conclusion is inescapable: The press has become obsessed with gossip rather than governance; it prefers to employ titillation rather than scrutiny; as a result, its political coverage produces trivialization rather than enlightenment. And the dynamic mechanism propelling and demonstrating this decline in news standards is the "feeding frenzy." . . .

The term *frenzy* suggests some kind of disorderly, compulsive, or agitated activity that is muscular and instinctive, not cerebral and thoughtful. In the animal world, no activity is more classically frenzied than the

---

*Former Senator (D-Col.) Gary Hart's 1988 presidential candidacy ended after media revelations about his extramarital relations with Donna Rice.—EDS.

†Watergate began with the 1972 break-in at the Democratic National headquarters by several men associated with President Nixon's re-election committee. Watergate ended two years later with the resignation of President Nixon. Nixon and his closest aides were implicated in the coverup of the Watergate burglary. Tapes made by President Nixon of his Oval Office conversations revealed lying and obstruction of justice at the highest levels of government.—EDS.

‡In 1989, the Senate rejected President Bush's nominee for secretary of defense, former Texas Senator John Tower. Senate hearings produced allegations that Tower was an excessive drinker and a womanizer.—EDS.

feeding of sharks, piranhas, or bluefish when they encounter a wounded prey. These attack-fish with extraordinarily acute senses first search out weak, ill, or injured targets. On locating them, each hunter moves in quickly to gain a share of the kill, feeding not just off the victim but also off its fellow hunters' agitation. The excitement and drama of the violent encounter builds to a crescendo, sometimes overwhelming the creatures' usual inhibitions. The frenzy can spread, with the delirious attackers wildly striking any object that moves in the water, even each other. Veteran reporters will recognize more press behavior in this passage than they might wish to acknowledge. This reverse anthropomorphism can be carried too far, but the similarity of piranha in the water and press on the campaign trail can be summed up in a shared goal: If it bleeds, try to kill it.

The kingdom of politics and not of nature is the subject of this volume, so for our purposes, a feeding frenzy is defined as the press coverage attending any political event or circumstance where a critical mass of journalists leap to cover the same embarrassing or scandalous subject and pursue it intensely, often excessively, and sometimes uncontrollably. No precise number of journalists can be attached to the term *critical mass*, but in the video age, we truly know it when we see it; the forest of cameras, lights, microphones, and adrenaline-choked reporters surrounding a Gary Hart, Dan Quayle, or Geraldine Ferraro is unmistakable. [The following table] contains a list of thirty-six events that surely qualify as frenzies. They are occasions of sin for the press as well as the politicians, and thus ideal research sites that will serve as case studies for this book. A majority (twenty-one) are drawn from presidential politics, while seven examples come from the state and local levels, with the remaining eight focused on government scandals or personal peccadilloes of nationally recognized political figures. . . .

Conditions are always ripe for the spawning of a frenzy in the brave new world of omnipresent journalism. Advances in media technology have revolutionized campaign coverage. Handheld miniature cameras (minicams) and satellite broadcasting have enabled television to go live anywhere, anytime with ease. Instantaneous transmission (by broadcast and fax) to all corners of the country has dramatically increased the velocity of campaign developments today, accelerating events to their conclusion at breakneck speed. Gary Hart, for example, went from front-runner to ex-candidate in less than a week in May 1987. Continuous public-affairs programming, such as C-SPAN and CNN, helps put more of a politician's utterances on the record, as Senator Joseph Biden discovered to his chagrin when C-SPAN unobtrusively taped Biden's exaggeration of his résumé at a New Hampshire kaffeeklatsch in 1987. (This

FEEDING FRENZIES: CASE STUDIES USED FOR THIS BOOK

From Presidential Politics
1952   Richard Nixon's "secret fund"
1968   George Romney's "brainwashing" about Vietnam
1968   Spiro Agnew's "fat Jap" flap
1969   Ted Kennedy's Chappaquiddick
1972   Edmund Muskie's New Hampshire cry
1972   Thomas Eagleton's mental health
1976   Jimmy Carter's "lust in the heart" *Playboy* interview
1976   Gerald Ford's "free Poland" gaffe
1979   Jimmy Carter's "killer rabbit"
1980   Billygate (Billy Carter and Libya)
1983   Debategate (Reagan's use of Carter's debate briefing books)
1984   Gary Hart's age, name, and signature changes
1984   Jesse Jackson's "Hymietown" remark
1984   Geraldine Ferraro's family finances
1985/86   Jack Kemp's purported homosexuality
1987   Gary Hart and Donna Rice
1987   Joseph Biden's plagiarism and Michael Dukakis's "attack video"
1987   Pat Robertson's exaggerated résumé and shotgun marriage
1988   Dukakis's mental health
1988   Dan Quayle (National Guard service, Paula Parkinson, academic
              record, rumors such as plagiarism and drugs)
1988   George Bush's alleged mistress

From the State and Local Levels
1987/88   Governor Evan Mecham on the impeachment trail (Arizona)
1987/88   Chuck Robb and the cocaine parties (Virginia)
1983/90   Mayor Marion Barry's escapades (District of Columbia)
1987   Governor Dick Celeste's womanizing (Ohio)
1988   Mayor Henry Cisneros's extramarital affair (San Antonio, Texas)
1989/90   Governor Gaston Caperton's "soap opera" divorce (West Virginia)
1990   Texas governor's election: drugs, rape, and "honey hunts"

Noncampaign Examples
1973/74   The Watergate scandals
1974   Congressman Wilbur Mills and stripper Fanne Foxe
1986/87   The Iran-Contra affair
1987   Supreme Court nominee Douglas Ginsburg's marijuana use (and
              campaign repercussions)
1989   John Tower's losing fight to become secretary of defense
1989   Speaker Jim Wright's fall from power
1989   Tom Foley's rocky rise to the Speakership
1989/90   Barney Frank and the male prostitute

became a contributing piece of the frenzy that brought Biden down.) C-SPAN, CNN, and satellite broadcasting capability also contribute to the phenomenon called "the news cycle without end," which creates a voracious news appetite demanding to be fed constantly, increasing the pressure to include marginal bits of information and gossip and producing novel if distorting "angles" on the same news to differentiate one report from another. The extraordinary number of local stations covering national politics today—up to several hundred at major political events—creates an echo chamber producing seemingly endless repetitions of essentially the same news stories. This local contingent also swells the corps traveling the campaign trail. In 1988 an estimated two thousand journalists of all stripes flooded the Iowa caucuses, for instance. Reporters not infrequently outnumber participants at meetings and whistlestops. . . .

Whether on the rise or not, the unfortunate effects of pack journalism are apparent to both news reporters and news consumers: conformity, homogeneity, and formulaic reporting. Innovation is discouraged, and the checks and balances supposedly provided by competition evaporate. Press energies are devoted to finding mere variations on a theme (new angles and wiggle disclosures), while a mob psychology catches hold that allows little mercy for the frenzy victim. CNN's Frank Sesno captures the pack mood perfectly:

I've been in that group psychology; I know what it's like. You think you're on to something, you've got somebody on the run. How dare they not come clean? How dare they not tell the full story? What are they trying to hide? Why are they hiding it? And you become a crusader for the truth. Goddammit, you're going to get the truth! . . .

Sesno's crusader spirit can be traced directly to the lingering effects of the Watergate scandal, which had the most profound impact of any modern event on the manner and substance of the press's conduct. In many respects Watergate began the press's open season on politicians in a chain reaction that today allows for scrutiny of even the most private sanctums of public officials' lives. Moreover, coupled with Vietnam and the civil rights movement, Watergate shifted the orientation of journalism away from mere description—providing an accurate account of happenings—and toward prescription—helping to set the campaign's (and society's) agendas by focusing attention on the candidates' shortcomings as well as certain social problems.

A new breed and a new generation of reporters were attracted to journalism, and particularly its investigative arm. As a group they were idealistic, though aggressively mistrustful of all authority, and they shared a contempt for "politics as usual." Critics called them do-gooders and purists who wanted the world to stand at moral attention for them. Twenty years later the Vietnam and Watergate generation dominates journalism: They and their younger cohorts hold sway over most newsrooms, with two-thirds of all reporters now under the age of thirty-six and an ever-increasing share of editors and executives drawn from the Watergate-era class. Of course, many of those who found journalism newly attractive in the wake of Watergate were not completely altruistic. The ambitious saw the happy fate of the *Washington Post's* young Watergate sleuths Bob Woodward and Carl Bernstein, who gained fame and fortune, not to mention big-screen portrayals by Robert Redford and Dustin Hoffman in the movie *All the President's Men. As U.S. News & World Report's* Steven Roberts sees it:

A lot of reporters run around this town dreaming of the day that Dustin Hoffman and Robert Redford are going to play them in the movies. That movie had more effect on the self-image of young journalists than anything else. Christ! Robert Redford playing a journalist? It lends an air of glamour and excitement that acts as a magnet drawing young reporters to investigative reporting.

The young were attracted not just to journalism but to a particular *kind* of journalism. The role models were not respected, established reporters but two unknowns who refused to play by the rules their seniors had accepted. "Youngsters learned that deductive techniques, all guesswork, and lots of unattributed information [were] the royal road to fame, even if it wasn't being terribly responsible," says Robert Novak. After all, adds columnist Mark Shields, "Robert Redford didn't play Walter Lippmann and Dustin Hoffman didn't play Joseph Kraft." (Kraft, like Lippmann, had a long and distinguished career in journalism.) . . .

A clear consequence of Watergate and other recent historical events was the increasing emphasis placed by the press on the character of candidates. As journalists reviewed the three tragic but exceptionally capable figures who had held the presidency since 1960, they saw that the failures of Kennedy, Johnson, and Nixon were not those of intellect but of ethos. Chappaquiddick, Spiro Agnew, and the Eagleton affair reinforced that view. The party affiliations and ideology of these disappointing leaders varied, but in common they possessed defects of personality, constitution, and disposition. In the world of journalism (or academe), as few as two data points can constitute a trend; these six together constituted an irrefutable mother lode of proof. "We in the press learned from experience that character flaws could have very large costs," says David Broder, "and we couldn't afford to ignore them if we were going to meet our responsibility." . . .

[A] troubling consequence of modern media coverage for the political system has to do with the recruitment of candidates and public servants. Simply put, the price of power has been raised dramatically, far too high for many outstanding potential officeholders. An individual contemplating a run for office must now accept the possibility of almost unlimited intrusion into his or her financial and personal life. Every investment made, every affair conducted, every private sin committed from college years to the present may one day wind up in a headline or on television. For a reasonably sane and moderately sensitive person, this is a daunting realization, with potentially hurtful results not just for the candidate but for his or her immediate family and friends. To have achieved a nongovernmental position of respect and honor in one's community is a source of pride and security, and the risk that it could all be destroyed by an unremitting and distorted assault on one's faults and foibles cannot be taken lightly. American society today is losing the services of many exceptionally talented individuals who could make outstanding contributions to the commonweal, but who understandably will not subject themselves and their loved ones to abusive, intrusive press coverage. Of course, this problem stems as much from the attitudes of the public as from those of the press; the strain of moral absolutism in portions of the American people merely finds expression in the relentless press frenzies and ethicsgate hunts. . . . *New York Times* columnist Anthony Lewis is surely correct when he suggests, "If we tell people there's to be absolutely nothing private left to them, then we will tend to attract to public office only those most brazen, least sensitive personalities. Is that what we want to do?"

81

BRADLEY PATTERSON

From *The White House Staff: The Advance Office*

Never on screen, not even allowed to snack from the "reporters' buffet," the White House advance team is charged with planning every presidential visit down to the last detail. After reading this account of the painstaking attention to detail required to make a trip successful and memorable, the two minutes of footage of a presidential visit on the nightly news will never seem the same again. In this excerpt, Bradley Patterson describes the many ele-

ments that go into presidential travel, from security to transportation to celebration: "three thousand balloons are recommended," notes the author. And don't forget the president's plane. Some people, Patterson discovers, will show up at the airport only to see Air Force One. *The advance team must make sure everything goes exactly as planned, including "The Moment" that sticks forever in the minds of the crowd and, the team hopes, that appears on page one of every newspaper.*

━━━

PRESIDENTS NEVER stay home. From Shawnee Mission High School to the emperor's palace, from the Kentucky State Fair to the Kremlin, the president of the United States is visitor in chief, representing now his government, now his party, now all the people of the nation. As chief of state, he has words of encouragement for the National Association of Student Councils; as chief partisan, he addresses a Senate candidate's closing rally; as national spokesman, he stands on the cliff above Normandy Beach; and as chief diplomat, he spends weary hours at the Wye Retreat Center, extracting tenuous Middle East peace agreements from skeptical antagonists. The lines between his roles are of course never quite that distinct: in each place he travels, the president is all these "chiefs" at once.

His national and political roles are public and he wants them to be so: cameras and the press are invited to witness every handshake, film each ceremony, record all the ringing words. A presidential trip is often substantive, but it is also always theater: each city an act, every stop a scene. As the Secret Service recognizes, however, in any balcony can lurk a John Wilkes Booth, at any window a Lee Harvey Oswald; a Sara Jane Moore or a John Hinckley may emerge from any crowd.* One other presidential role is quintessential but usually more concealed: as commander in chief, the American president must always—no matter where he is in the world—be able to reach his national security command centers.

A presidential trip, therefore, is not a casual sojourn: it is a massive expedition, its every mile planned ahead, its every minute preprogrammed. The surge of cheering thousands must stop just short of a moving cocoon of security; curtained behind each VIP receiving line is the military aide with the "doomsday briefcase." Except for the military aide with the "satchel," all of the first lady's travel presents similar requirements for minute care and advance attention.

---

*Booth assassinated President Abraham Lincoln. Oswald, at least according to official findings, was the assassin of President John Kennedy. Moore and Hinckley made assassination attempts on Presidents Gerald Ford and Ronald Reagan, respectively.—EDS.

These massive expeditions are the responsibility of the White House Advance Office. How large a job is this? In seven years in office, President Clinton made some 2,500 appearances in over 800 foreign or domestic cities or destinations, plus some 450 appearances at public events in the Washington area. The pace of the work in the Advance Office was nothing short of breathtaking.

While each chief executive's travel style is different, trip preparations are similar; the art of "advancing" is common to presidency after presidency, although new technological gadgetry has made the whole trip-preparation process swifter and more efficient.

Within any White House staff, trip planning calls for intricate choreography among more than a dozen separate offices: cabinet affairs, communications, domestic policy, intergovernmental, legislative, medical, military, national security (if the trip is overseas), scheduling, political, public liaison, press, Secret Service, social, speechwriting, transportation, the vice president's office, and the first lady's staff. The Advance Office is the orchestrator of this cluster and the manager of all the forthcoming on-scene arrangements.

How does the Advance Office organize a presidential trip? . . .

A domestic presidential visit can get its start from any one of the hundreds of invitations that pour into the White House, but more likely it originates from within, as a homegrown idea. What policy themes is the president emphasizing? To which areas of American life does he wish to draw attention? Educational excellence, industrial competitiveness, athletic prowess, racial harmony, minority achievement, environmental improvement . . . ? At campaign time, of course, electoral issues are foremost: What voters are targeted, which senators need help?

Like the daily schedule . . . , a trip is not a casual event but a calculated piece of a larger theme—and, as such, is designed to convey a message. A presidential trip, in other words, is an instrument of persuasion.

Forward planning for domestic presidential trips may be done from four to eight weeks in advance but is more likely compressed into an even shorter lead time. As soon as the desired message is framed and agreed to, through discussions within the White House, the Advance Office reviews the choices for domestic travel: Where in the country can the presidential theme best be dramatized? Which groups, which sponsors, which cities or towns? What already-scheduled local event could the president join, transforming it into an illustration of his own policy initiative? Local and state calendars are scanned, the *Farmer's Almanac* is studied. Invitations are searched, private suggestions reviewed. Long lists are discussed with the Scheduling Office and vetted into short lists; tentative alternatives are identified. If the president is campaigning, all the processes mentioned here are melded together: the president may do twelve to eighteen events in a week.

For domestic trips, in previous years, "site surveys" would be undertaken perhaps six weeks ahead of time, and "pre-advance" teams would be sent out weeks beforehand. Money then became tighter and staffs smaller. The Bush Advance Office staff totaled eighteen; the Clinton White House had only twelve, four of whom were interns. Communications have speeded up as well. "Reactivity time"—that is, the period needed to respond to changes in circumstances—has dwindled, with the consequence that lead time for decisions may be greatly shortened, alterations more easily tolerated, last-minute revisions accepted. All arrangements can be more flexible; some can be consummated with only hours to spare. The final "go" decision, therefore, has sometimes been made as little as two weeks before the event—or less, as Clinton Advance Office director Paige Reffe described:

I was walking into an afternoon meeting in the deputy chief of staff's office that I thought was supposed to be about the first family's vacation . . . and the deputy turns to me and says, "By the way, we are thinking of the president going to New York at nine o'clock to meet with the TWA Flight 800 families." I said, "Nine o'clock when?" And she said, "Nine o'clock tomorrow morning," about eighteen hours from now. I said, "I didn't bring my top hat, I didn't bring my cane, and I don't have any rabbits to pull out today. . . . Let's stop *thinking* about this; there is a 5:30 P.M. flight to Kennedy; I can get people on that flight. I can actually get something set up if the decision is made in the next hour." In the end, sometimes those things are easier than normal events, because there isn't time for people to start picking them apart and making changes.

Floods, disasters, hurricane damage, funerals: a presidential presence is often required. But then the advance office looks less like a long-range-planning unit and more like a firehouse.

The White House counsel makes a key determination: Is any part of the trip for a clearly political purpose? Is the president going to be partisan in speech and act, or will he be entirely "presidential"? In scrupulous detail, all the proposed meetings, site events, rallies, and addresses are divided into rigid categories so that mathematically precise formulas can be used to allocate expenses between the political sponsors and the government: "21.7 percent of the trip is political, 78.3 percent is official," explains one illustrative memorandum. The counsel and the political affairs director sign off on the allocation. If the White House asks any federal political appointees to serve as volunteers on the advance team (which it often does), they must take annual leave if they work on any part of the trip that is political—and any expenses they incur must be paid for by the host political group or by party national headquarters.

Funding is a sensitive issue. There is a four-way division: (1) Assuming the trip is nonpolitical, the White House budget itself supports only the travel expenses of the advance teams and the presidential party (and its VIP guests), including the staff of the White House Press Office. (2) For any trip, political or not, the government covers those costs that relate to the president's security. In this category are the costs incurred by the White House Military Office (financed by the Department of Defense); this office covers the expenses of its medical personnel, military aides, and the White House Communications Agency (WHCA), which supplies lights and amplification equipment as well as its own ample communications gear. Also in this category are the costs incurred by the Secret Service (actually part of the Treasury Department), which has its own budget for travel and equipment (including the presidential limousine and other special cars). The Military Office's *Air Force One* will be supplied, but its costs must be reimbursed if the trip is political. (3) Members of the White House press corps pay for their own travel expenses (via reimbursement to the White House Travel Office). (4) All local "event" expenses must be borne by host groups: for example, the costs of renting a hall, constructing risers for the press, furnishing the stage backdrops, providing banners and hand-held signs, printing and sending out flyers, printing tickets, arranging for advertising, and providing motorcade vehicles for nonfederal dignitaries. A letter spelling out these financial obligations is sent to the host, who must send back a signed formal agreement.

The government's actual total cost for a domestic presidential trip is almost impossible to pin down, but it is high. No host group, political or otherwise, could afford all the charges, including those relating to security. Therefore, no matter what reimbursement is obtained, there is a significant publicly financed subsidy for any presidential expedition. It is simply the cost of having a president who travels.

Within the White House, an Advance Office "staff lead' is named who will head up all the advance work. In addition, a trip coordinator is designated—a stay-on-home-base "ringmaster" to whom the advance team's queries are directed and on whose desk all plans and all logistical details are centralized. "She is the lifeline for the advance people," explained Bush advance director John Keller. "Whenever the advance people call back to the office, that's the one they talk to."

Once the two lead people are designated, internal assignments are specified. It is a broad "ring": the Intergovernmental Affairs and Political Affairs Offices will recommend governors, mayors, or local officials to be asked to sit on the dais; the legislative affairs staff will identify the senators and representatives who would be affronted if they were not invited to accompany the president. If the trip is political, the political affairs director will compose a detailed list of themes that will gain a warm local reception, and of issues to avoid. The event will usually be designated as "open press"—but if not, the Press Office will organize a pool of the White House press corps, and the media relations unit will prepare credentials for the local press.

Speechwriters are at work, the medical staff makes its preparations, the Secret Service will ask its local field agents to supplement its regular presidential protective detail. WHCA will box up a mobile satellite sending and receiving station along with the president's armored "Blue Goose" podium. The Air Force will make sure that the local airport can handle the "footprint" of the huge 747 *Air Force One* and will stash two presidential limousines, the necessary Secret Service vehicles, and WHCA's "Road-runner" communications van into a C-141 transport. If it is called for, the Marine Corps will add in HMX-1, one of the presidential helicopters.

The White House advance team itself is assembled. Headed by the staff lead, the team includes representatives from many of the offices just mentioned. Unless the occasion is unusually complicated, current practice is for the advance team for a domestic trip to leave the White House only six days before the president is scheduled to arrive (seven for a RON—"remain overnight"—visit). In what is likely to be a rather frantic final five days, the advance team must complete an unbelievably compli-cated checklist: one such list was twenty-six pages long and included 485 items.

The team visits the airport, draws (and faxes to Washington) rough site diagrams—showing where planes, helicopters, and cars will park—and reviews the planned arrival ceremonies. Who will the greeters be? (Each hand-shaker must be approved in Washington.) Are the toe strips in place to show the greeters where to stand? Where is the rope line? The team is admonished: "Inconvenience as few commercial airline pas-sengers as possible." Not even a wheeled set of stairs needs to be comman-deered; *Air Force One* has its own mobile stairs.

The motorcade is organized with minute precision. The advance team is reminded that "all the substantive success in the world can be overshadowed if those involved cannot get where they need to be." The motorcade may be the standard minimum of twenty-four vehicles or it may be a hundred cars long. Each car is labeled and spotted on the diagram; every driver must be approved by the Secret Service. The last two cars, which are called "stragglers," will pick up staff members who may have missed the departure; the stragglers can also be used as alternates in case of breakdowns. Motorcades used to be important for generating crowds of sidewalk spectators—but no longer. Primarily for security reasons, the line of cars speeds by: the onlookers not only don't see the president, they can't even figure out which limo he is in.

Each event site must be examined in detail: What will be the backdrop, the "storyboard"—that is, the picture that television will capture? "Distill the message into a brief and catchy phrase," advises the detail-conscious Advance Manual, but "you *do not* want shiny white letters on shiny yellow vinyl." This is not some "pizza-parlor's grand opening." Walking routes are plotted: for the president, the guests, the press, the staff, and the public (more diagrams). There must be a presidential "holding room" where he meets sponsors and guests. What will be the program? What kind of audience is expected—students? senior citizens? friendly? skeptical? How long will it take for them to go through the magnetometers? If hotel overnights are planned, floor plans are needed.

No team is without its conflicts. The press advance staffers want to have an airport arrival at high noon, big crowds, remarks, greetings, bands, balloons ascending, people pressing against the ropes. The Secret Service looks through different eyes. "If they had their way," commented one advance veteran, "they would have the president arrive after dark, in an out-of-the-way corner of the airport, put him into a Sherman tank, lead him to a bank, and have him spend the night in a vault." He added: "They would say, 'You cannot choose that route,' and we would counter, 'No, he *will* drive that avenue, you go ahead and protect him.'" Since the assassination attempt on Reagan, the Secret Service wins more of these battles.

There are conflicts with the local hosts as well: Who will sit on the dais? Will spaces be saved for the local as well as the national press? One sponsoring group for a fund-raiser had sold every seat on the floor of a gymnasium: the advance team had to insist that the tables and seats be squeezed together to make room for the camera platforms. There must be two sets of such risers: one facing the speaker and one at an angle in the rear, for over-the-shoulder "cutaway" shots of the president together with the audience he is addressing. With luck, the risers can be borrowed; the advance team is instructed: "Don't go cutting down virgin forest to build press risers for one-time-only use."

The White House advance person, the instructions make clear, is a diplomat-in-temporary-residence, "the mover and the shaker, the stroker and the cajoler, the smoother of ruffled feathers and the soother of hard feelings. The staff lead is the captain of a great team." But the captain is forewarned: shun all media interviews. "*Never* be a spokesman or go on the record with the press. . . . You are invisible to the camera. Your work is done just outside the four corners of the picture frame. You do not eat up an inch of the screen that is the canvas that you and your colleagues have designed to be a 'picture of the day.' You and your advance team colleagues are not the story, the *president's visit* is. . . . And don't snack on the buffet food which the working press has paid for. . . . But get the job done."

A former advance chief slyly recalls:

> To be a successful advance person . . . you have to have that minor crooked side to you, and you have to be willing to do whatever you have to do. That doesn't necessarily mean breaking the law, but it means that you can't be shy and you have to be assertive. If I tell you to go find a podium, I know you're going to come back and you're going to find a podium. You may have just happened to have gotten it from that event three doors down, and they're wondering where their podium is right now, but the fallout had there not been a podium would be a hell of a lot bigger than somebody asking where the podium came from!

The advance team may include nongovernmental companions: technical experts from the news networks, news photographers, and representatives from the White House Correspondents Association. Satellite time must be reserved, transmitting "dishes" placed, camera angles planned. What will be the dramatic scenes? Where will the sun be?

The advance team's instructions leave no doubt as to the purpose of a presidential trip: "The President has a point to make and that's the message. The message of a trip . . . is the *mission* of a trip . . . The public events of a trip are the expression of the message. It is central to advance work and deserves a lot of time and energy. Every event or site must capture or reinforce the reason the President is there. . . . The trip's message has already been through a wringer of careful deliberation at the White House."

The government team and the news planning team represent institutions that are different and often at odds. In this mini-universe, however, they have a common purpose: to get the fullest stories and the best pictures to the most people the fastest. "All of them know that, visually and technically, there are right and wrong ways to do things," explained one former participant, "and this is true whoever is president; it's a professional business." Such symbiosis disturbed newsman Martin Schram, however. He quoted a colleague: "In a funny way, the . . . advance men and I have the same thing at heart—we want the piece to look as good as it possibly can. . . . That's their job and that's my job. . . . I'm looking for the best pictures, but I can't help it if the audiences that show up, or that are grouped together by the . . . [White House] look so good. . . . I can't help it if it looks like a commercial." Schram then adds, "That is what White House video experts . . . are counting on. Offering television's professionals pictures they could not refuse was at the core of the . . . officials' efforts to shape and even control the content of the network newscasts."

A Clinton advance officer described this duality from another angle:

> The most frustrating part of my job: . . . the advance team will make sure that [the press] are supplied with very nice visuals, with a great venue for the speech, and then you will see the most unbelievable choice of pictures that the producer or editor or newspaper . . . will actually decide to run. . . . We put all that blood, sweat, and tears into creating this beautiful visual backdrop and instead they will wind up with pictures of the president talking with some aide backstage. . . . The picture that we actually got out of all this hard work was completely disconnected from the story we were trying to achieve. So I think that coziness may not be as prevalent as it used to be . . . not with the people who are deciding what goes on the evening news or the front page. . . . It is also a function of volume: President Clinton travels exponentially more than President Reagan; editors probably tire of running the pictures that we "give" them.

There are still other items on the final checklist: "Effect of the motorcade on normal commuting patterns," "Lighting: 320 foot-candles on the speaker and 200 foot-candles on the crowd," "Overtime cost estimate," "Other appropriate music—can the band play it?" "Empty seats filled or draped," "List of gifts accepted for the President," "Bad weather alternative."

The advance team has a daily "countdown" meeting, where the team members make sure that they are all on the same page. "Never miss it!" warns the manual. There is also a daily conference call to home base, with the trip coordinator and all the affected White House offices. "Datetime stamp and file every piece of paper," the team is instructed, and "Keep Everybody Informed."

If the trip is political and a big rally is scheduled, the advance team will include another specialist, a "crowd-builder," who comes with the attitude that this "is a historic occasion, a great party, the biggest thing to ever happen to this town. If Joe Public misses it, Joe Public will regret it for the rest of his/her life. So, Joe Public better pack up the kids and bring Grandma and Grandpa or they will have missed one of the biggest days in their town's history!"

The local hosts must do the actual work, mobilizing hundreds of enthusiastic volunteers. A vast menu of techniques is systematically used, but all are on the advance team's checklist: not a single step is left to chance. For illustration:

— Event sites should be "expandable" or "collapsible," so that new seats can be added or empty chairs removed.
— Ten times as many handbills should be printed as there are places to be filled: enough for every shopping-center grocery bag, for door handles in parking lots, to tape to mirrors in public rest rooms, even to lay (right side up) on busy sidewalks. One last idea is suggested: "Stand on top of the highest building in town and throw the handbills into the wind." Leaflets must list the event as beginning at least one half hour before it will actually start: a president on the platform with a crowd still at the gates is chaos.
— *Air Force One* should be mentioned in leaflets for an airport rally; some folks will come just to see the plane. News stories about the history of presidential aircraft should be used to spark the interest of the crowd (but mention of their cost should be avoided).
— Bands, cheerleaders, pom-pom girls, and drill teams are to be mobilized (but the Secret Service has to check every make-believe rifle).
— Banner-painting parties are suggested, with supplies of butcher paper and tempera paint; a "hand-held sign committee" should be organized.
— Three thousand balloons are recommended, with balloon rises preferred over balloon drops. The truly experienced may try to do both simultaneously in the same auditorium: helium in the ones to go up, air in the ones to come down. The hall manager must be consulted first, however: the risen balloons will cling to the ceiling for two days afterwards.

No matter how rah-rah some aspects of a trip may be, White House advance staffers are forever conscious that it is the president of the United States who is there. They strive for a "colorful and mediagenic setting"— but never at the expense of the dignity of the person or the office. Their instructions state: "The President must never be allowed into a potentially awkward or embarrassing situation, and the advance person is sometimes the only one who can keep that from happening. . . . For example, an oversized cowboy hat, a live farm animal, an Indian headdress, or a Shriner's 'Fez' could produce a decidedly un-presidential photograph. Common sense must be used to make sure that the dignity of the office of the President is never compromised by the well-intentioned generosity of local partisans."

And no thank you to sound trucks, bands on flatbed trailers, elephants, clowns, and parachutists.

Like crowd-raising, press-advancing is a special skill of the advance team. At a major event site, a press area must be set apart. Camera platforms and radio tables must be of the required size and height, and press-only magnetometers must be installed. Each event site must be equipped with a half-dozen long-distance telephones, and each desk needs an electric outlet for plugging in a laptop. Four nearby rooms are reserved (at their cost) for the three television networks to edit their tapes. A filing center is set up with tables and chairs for a hundred people; the press secretary and his staff need a large adjoining office area with six tables to hold their equipment. "We duplicate the White House Press Office on the scene of a presidential visit," one expert explained. "The White House press staff can do their work just as if they were at 1600 Pennsylvania Avenue."

The advance team stays on site, completing its prodigious checklist, until the very moment the president is to arrive.

Back at the White House, the formal press announcement is made, with the local sponsors tipped off ahead of time and the necessary representatives, senators, governors, and mayors likewise alerted just before the White House release. The speechwriters have prepared their drafts, idea notes, or complete remarks ahead of time for arrivals, departures, and each stop in between (but word processors and copiers are aboard *Air Force One* if last-minute changes are ordered). The earlier sketches of airports, motorcade arrival and departure points, corridors, rooms, and walkways are transformed into minute diagrams, with arrows drawn in showing each presidential footstep.

When its own thousand details are done, the White House Press Office compiles a "Press Schedule Bible," which is given out to the national press representatives.

On the morning before the day of departure, the Advance Office holds a final trip briefing for the chief of staff; it will be the chief of staff who gives the final imprimatur for the *Air Force One* manifest. The advance team staff lead composes the president's and first lady's personal schedule sheets. Even when airborne, *Air Force One*'s communications desk buzzes with last-minute advice from the advance team waiting at the arrival site.

As the presidential party approaches the runway, what goes through an advance person's mind? One veteran remembers: "There are a hundred bad variables when you look at a situation and go down your list. What you try to do is to reduce those down to zero. You never get them to zero, but if you get them down to six or five or four when the event occurs, then the odds are with you, and if they do go wrong they are at least in the manageable range."

The Advance Manual emphasizes: Pictures of the president standing behind the podium are dull stuff, and could just as well be snapped in the Rose Garden. Plan to have the cameras catch the president doing something unique and special, of exciting human-interest quality:

The high point . . . is "The Moment," the one snippet of action that visually tells the story of why the trip was undertaken in the first place. Media organizations need this moment to encapsulate the event. It will be rare that a newspaper will carry the complete transcript and equally rare that a local affiliate will broadcast the event "live" on television. . . . So we strive to create a moment: that ten-second slice of uplifting video . . . or that full-color, top-of-the-fold newspaper photo. . . . As the cliche goes, a picture is worth a thousand words. . . . "The Moment" is what you make of it. Don't let a visit go by without creating one.

82

MARTIN WATTENBERG

From *Where Have All the Voters Gone?*

Young voters—or more accurately, young non-voters—are the subject of this excerpt from Martin Wattenberg. Yes, it's true that more young people turned out to vote in 2004, but more people of all age groups turned out to vote, so young voters still voted in low numbers relative to their percentage in the American population. Where have all the young voters gone? Wattenberg notes some surprising paradoxes based on the many young people who volunteer for community activities and the high educational levels of the young. Wattenberg offers readers some statistics on interest in political affairs among different age groups. To explain youths' lower levels of interest, he examines the changing nature of the mass media. Likewise, lower levels of actual knowledge about politics can be traced to media exposure, Wattenberg argues. Beware of this situation, the author warns: those who vote set the agenda, and those who don't vote are ignored.

━━◆━━

. . . TODAY THE STEREOTYPE OF politically apathetic youth is so widespread that politicians are even discussing it openly. For example, before his historic return to space, Senator John Glenn remarked that he worried "about the future when we have so many young people who feel apathetic and critical and cynical about anything having to do with politics. They don't want to touch it. And yet politics is literally the personnel system for democracy." Similarly, when Al Gore appeared on

MTV during the 2000 presidential campaign, he said, "There are a lot of young people who have kind of stayed away from the political process. There is a lot of disillusionment. Try to fight through that."

Stereotypes can be found to be mistaken; unfortunately this is one case where widely held impressions are overwhelmingly supported by solid evidence, which will be reviewed briefly here. It is important to note that this is not to say that young people are inactive in American society. Nearly three of four college freshmen surveyed in 1998 reported volunteering for a community group during their senior year in high school. It is only when it comes to politics that young people seem to express indifference about getting involved. Whether because they feel they can't make a difference, believe the political system to be corrupt, or just have not received any exposure to politics, young Americans are clearly apathetic about public affairs. And while political apathy isn't restricted to young people, a tremendous gap has opened up between the young and the elderly on measures of political interest, media consumption about politics, political knowledge, and, of course, turnout.

The high level of political apathy among young people today is unexpected given that their educational achievement levels are so high. Even those who have made it into college are expressing remarkably little concern for politics. A yearly nationwide study of college freshmen recently found that among the class of 2002 only 26 percent said that "keeping up with politics" was an important priority for them, compared with 58 percent among the class of 1970—their parents' generation. If one looks more broadly at all people under the age of thirty, the NES data on "following what's going on in government and public affairs" display a striking decline in political attentiveness among young people since 1964 [The] table shows that from 1964 through 1976 there was little difference between those under thirty and those over sixty-five in terms of this measure of general political interest, with young people actually showing a bit more interest in 1968 and 1972. Since 1980, however, the youngest voting-age citizens have consistently expressed the least interest in public affairs by a substantial margin. The 2000 survey findings, in particular, mark a new low in political interest among young people. Only 33 percent of respondents under thirty said they followed government and public affairs most or some of the time; among senior citizens, the figure was 73 percent. As expected, campaign interest was also at a new low for young people in 2000—only 11 percent said they were very interested in the campaign as opposed to 39 percent among the elderly.

Why young people today are not interested in public affairs is a difficult

GENERAL INTEREST IN PUBLIC AFFAIRS IN THE UNITED STATES
BY AGE, 1964–2000

	18–29	30–44	45–64	65+	Difference between under 30 and over 65
1964	56	67	64	63	−7
1968	58	60	63	53	+5
1972	65	68	67	62	+3
1976	58	67	70	65	−7
1980	48	56	62	64	−16
1984	50	57	62	64	−14
1988	46	54	58	63	−17
1992	53	60	65	65	−12
1996	45	51	64	64	−19
2000	38	50	60	64	−26

Source: National Election Studies.
Note: The four response categories have been recoded as follows: hardly at all = 0; only now and then = 33; some of the time = 66; most of the time = 100.

question to answer. Since I started asking my students for their opinion on this nearly a decade ago, I have gotten more possible answers than I ever could have dreamed of. Typically, the first response I get is something to the effect that politics just hasn't affected their generation the way it did previous generations. Certainly, today's youth have not had any policy touch their lives the way the draft and the Vietnam War affected their parents, or the way Medicare has benefited their grandparents. Mark Gray and I asked a question regarding people's perceptions of this in our post-2000 election survey of four southern California counties. The question went as follows: "Some of the issues discussed during the campaigns for the November election directly related to policies affecting people of your generation. Do you think that politicians pay too much attention to these issues, about the right amount or too little?" Sixty-two percent of respondents under the age of thirty said "too little," 21 percent said "about the right amount," and 9 percent said "too much." The percentages for those sixty-five and over were 33, 41, and 11 percent, respectively.

However, I believe that the cause of young people's apathy runs much deeper than a sense that the issues aren't relevant to them and that the politicians ignore them. Central to any generational hypothesis are changes in socialization experiences. For the last two decades, young people have been socialized in a rapidly changing media environment that has been radically different from that experienced by the past couple of generations. Political scientists were slow to realize the impact of television—as late as 1980 there was surprisingly little literature on this subject. Today a similar shortcoming is the lack of research concerning how the shift from broadcasting to narrowcasting has dramatically altered how much exposure a young adult has received to politics while growing up. The first major networks—ABC, NBC, and CBS—chose to use the term "broadcasting" in the names of their companies because their signal was being sent out to a broad audience. As long as these networks dominated the industry, each would have to deal with general topics that the public as a whole was concerned with, such as politics and government. But with the development of cable television, market segmentation has taken hold. Sports buffs can watch ESPN all day, music buffs can tune to MTV or VH1, history buffs can go to the History Channel, and so forth. Rather than appealing to a general audience, channels such as ESPN, MTV, and C-SPAN focus on a narrow particular interest. Hence their mission has often been termed "narrowcasting," rather than the traditional "broadcasting." This is even more true for Web sites, which require far less in start-up costs than a television channel and hence can be successful with a very small and specific audience.

Because of the narrowcasting revolution, today's youth have grown up in an environment in which public affairs news has not been as readily visible as it has been in the past. It has become particularly difficult to convince members of a generation that has channel surfed all their lives that politics really does matter. Major political events were once shared national experiences. The current generation of young adults is the first to grow up in a media environment in which there are few such shared experiences. When CBS, NBC, and ABC dominated the airwaves, their blanket coverage of presidential speeches, political conventions, and presidential debates sometimes left little else to watch on television. As channels have proliferated over the last two decades, though, it has become much easier to avoid exposure to politics altogether by simply grabbing the remote control. Whereas President Nixon got an average rating of 50 for his televised addresses to the nation (meaning that half the population was watching), President Clinton averaged only about 30 in his first term. Political conventions, which once received more television coverage than the Summer Olympics, have been relegated to an hour per night, and even this highly condensed coverage gets poor ratings. The presidential debates of 1996 and 2000 drew respectable average ratings of 28, but this was only half the typical level of viewers drawn by debates held between 1960 and 1980. In sum, young people today have never known a time when most citizens paid attention to major political events. This is one

of the key reasons why so many of them have yet to get into the habit
of following and participating in politics. . . .

Because of the media environment that young people have been
socialized in, they have learned much less about politics than their elders.
The current pattern of political knowledge increasing with age has become
well known in recent years. But it was not always that way. The 1964
and 2000 National Election Studies each contain a substantial battery of
political knowledge questions that enable this point to be demonstrated.
[The] figure shows the percentage of correct answers to eight questions
in 1964 and nine questions in 2000 by age category. In 1964 there was
virtually no pattern by age, with those under thirty actually scoring 5
percent higher on this test than senior citizens. By contrast, in 2000
young people provided the correct answer to only one out of every three

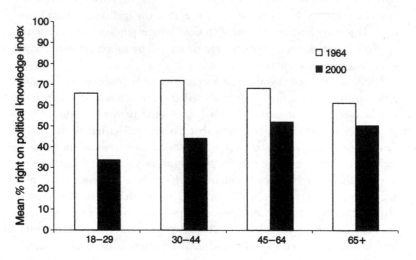

AGE AND POLITICAL KNOWLEDGE:
1964 AND 2000 COMPARED

Entries are based on the percentage of accurate responses to a series of eight
questions in 1964 and nine questions in 2000. In 1964, respondents were
given credit for knowing that Goldwater was from Arizona, Johnson was
from Texas, Goldwater and Johnson were protestants, Democrats had the
majority in Congress both before and after the election, Johnson had supported civil rights legislation, and Goldwater had opposed it. In 2000, respondents were given credit for knowing that Bush was from Texas, Gore was
from Tennessee, Republicans had the majority in the House and Senate
before the election, Lieberman was Jewish, and for identifying William
Rehnquist, Tony Blair, Janet Reno, and Trent Lott. (Data from National
Election Studies, 1964 and 2000.)

questions, whereas people over sixty-five were correct half the time. Regardless of whether the question concerned identifying current political leaders, information about the presidential candidates, or partisan control of the Congress, the result was the same: young people were less knowledgeable than the elderly.

Given that today's youth has not been exposed to politics through the broadcasting of national shared experiences, the label of the "know-nothing generation" ought to be considered descriptive, not pejorative. It is not their fault. But nevertheless the consequences are real and important. Thomas Jefferson once said that there has never been, nor ever will be, a people who are politically ignorant and free. If this is indeed the case, write Stephen Bennett and Eric Rademacher, then "we can legitimately wonder what the future holds if Xers remain as uninformed as they are about government and public affairs." . . .

Although many young people seem to think it doesn't matter if they don't vote, it does. Harold Lasswell wrote many years ago that "politics is who gets what, when, and how." As long as young people have low rates of participation in the electoral process, then they should expect to be getting relatively little of whatever there is to get from government. Yet until they start showing up in greater numbers at the polls, there will be little incentive for politicians to focus on programs that will help them. Politicians are not fools; they know who their customers are. Why should they worry about young nonvoters any more than the makers of denture cream worry about people with healthy teeth? . . .

It is not young people's fault that they have not been exposed much to politics while growing up and hence are less informed about politics than previous generations. Their low turnout rates are understandable in light of their unique socialization experience.

American politicians are not really to blame for this inequitable pattern of generational representation, either. They didn't consciously try to create a situation that would greatly benefit older people. It is only natural for them to study who has voted in the past and to focus on these people, thereby leaving most young adults out of the picture. But if politicians were to ponder the principles universally valued in any democracy they might be moved to address this problem. If official election observers in a third world country noticed that older people were three times as likely as younger people to vote, they would no doubt call this fact to the attention of local authorities and suggest there was an imbalance that ought to be looked into. As former president Jimmy Carter remarked at a hearing of the 2001 National Commission on Federal Election Reform,

"This [issue of young people not voting] is something that is just as bad as the difference in ethnic groups or minorities not voting." . . .

Although the solution to the new generation gap in voting participation in the United States is going to be difficult to find, the consequences for the present are readily apparent. Major issues that affect young adults are not even making it onto the public agenda, and young people's opinions on the issues are not being faithfully represented through the political process. Who votes does matter. . . .

83

BRIAN ANDERSON

From *South Park Conservatives*

Readers do not have to be fans of South Park to understand Brian Anderson's commentary on the influence of "new media" on politics today. As Anderson explains in his introduction, "The new media have nourished a fiercely anti-liberal comedic spirit, whose anarchic, vulgar archetype is Comedy Central's brilliant cartoon series South Park, depicting the adventures of four foulmouthed fourth-graders." Nowhere is this spirit more evident, notes Anderson, than in the "blogosphere" where bloggers of every political persuasion—but especially conservative ones—say what's on their minds. Anderson discusses the Drudge Report and RealClearPolitics as examples of blogs that offer strong opinions along with links to other more obscure web sites. The blogosphere has challenged the old traditional media establishment, Anderson observes, and its audience is young. Far from reinforcing extreme views without challenge, the blogosphere offers a sometimes humorous, sometimes irreverent, but always genuine exchange of opinion.

———————

As CBS NEWS CAN TELL YOU, the rise of the Internet—something that really took off only twelve years ago, with the invention of the Netscape web browser—is the latest and perhaps most explosive change that is shaking liberal media dominance. It's hard to overstate the impact that news and opinion websites like the Drudge Report, FrontPage, NewsMax, and Dow Jones's OpinionJournal are having on politics and culture, as are current-event weblogs, or blogs—individual or group web diaries—like andrewsullivan.com, InstaPundit, Kausfiles, Power Line . . . , PoliPundit, and "The Corner" department of National Review Online, where the editors and writers argue, joke around, and call attention to articles elsewhere on the web. For simplicity's sake, let's refer to this whole universe of web-based discussion as the "blogosphere," though some apply that recently minted (post-September 11) term only to blogs proper.

While there are influential left-of-center sites—Joshua Micah Marshall's lively Talking Points Memo and liberal webzines Slate and Salon (both featuring blogs) come quickly to mind—the blogosphere currently leans right, albeit idiosyncratically, reflecting in part the hard-to-pigeon-hole politics of some leading bloggers. Like talk radio and FOX News, the right-leaning sites fill a market void. "Many bloggers felt shut out by institutions that have adopted—explicitly or implicitly—a left-wing orthodoxy," says Erin O'Connor, whose blog, Critical Mass, exposes campus PC gobbledygook.

The orthodox Left's blame-America-first response to September 11 gave a powerful rightward tilt to the blogosphere. "There were damned few noble responses to that cursed day from the 'progressive' part of the political spectrum," avers Los Angeles-based blogger and journalist Matt Welch, "so untold thousands of people just started blogs, in anger." Welch, who considers himself an "*Economist*-style" conservative liberal, was among them. "I was pushed into blogging on September 16, 2001, in direct response to reading five days' worth of outrageous bullshit in the media from people like Noam Chomsky and Robert Jensen."

It's easy for frustrated citizens like Welch to get their ideas circulating on the Internet. Start-up and maintenance costs for a blog are small—less than $200 a year, thanks to easy-to-use technology invented by Pyra Labs in the late 1990s—and printing and mailing costs are of course nonexistent. Few blogs make a lot of money, though—or any—since some advertisers remain leery of the web, and no one seems willing to pay to read anything on it. Advertisers are starting to wake up to the web's power, however. The top sites can now charge anywhere from $300 to a couple of thousand bucks for a weeklong ad.

The absence of remuneration hasn't dampened the medium's scorching rate of growth. In 1999, there were fewer than one hundred blogs proper (web diaries, that is). Five years later, the number has rocketed to more than four million and, according to some estimates, will soon reach ten million. "There are more bloggers *writing* . . . than people reading *USA Today* (whose circulation is 2.6 million)," web journalist Ed Driscoll points out. Observes the *Dallas News*'s Rod Dreher, "It makes every man and woman a publisher and is the most democratic form of journalism yet devised." Many call the bloggers "citizen journalists."

Most blogs are indulgences, of zero interest to the general public and read only by family members and friends; most aren't political. But add the leading political blogs to the news and opinion websites that have proliferated since the late 1990s, and you really do have a brand-new media sphere—one that already is rivaling print, radio, and television for "mindshare," as *Wired* magazine calls it.

The Internet's most powerful effect has been to expand vastly the range of opinion—especially right-of-center opinion—at everyone's fingertips. "The Internet helps break up the traditional cultural gatekeepers' power to determine (a) what's important and (b) the range of acceptable opinion," says former *Reason* editor and libertarian blogger Virginia Postrel. Insta-Pundit's Glenn Reynolds, a hawkish law professor at the University of Tennessee, agrees: "The main role of the Internet and blogosphere is to call the judgment of elites about what is news into question."

The Drudge Report is a perfect case in point. Six years after the fedora-wearing, latter-day Walter Winchell Matt Drudge broke the Monica Lewinsky story, his news and gossip site has become an essential daily visit for political junkies, journalists, media types, and—with more than three *billion* visits to the site a year—seemingly anyone with an Internet connection. The site features newsworthy items investigated and written by Drudge, but it's primarily an editorial filter, linking to stories on other small and large news and opinion sites—a filter that crucially exhibits no bias against the Right. (Drudge, a registered Republican, calls himself "a pro-life conservative who doesn't want the government to tax me.")

Drudge enthusiast and cultural critic Camille Paglia observes that the site's constantly updated cornucopia of information, culled from a vast number of global sources and e-mailed tips from across the political spectrum, points up by contrast "the process of censorship that's going on, the filtering of the news by established news organizations." Basically a two-man operation, Drudge now nets an estimated $70,000 a month, according to *Business 2.0*.

RealClearPolitics, founded in 2000 by former Chicago options trader John McIntyre and friend Tom Bevan, a onetime ad executive, is an equally useful site for cutting through the liberal news fog. Every morning, RealClearPolitics links to the leading political editorials and news articles of the day, wherever they originate and whatever their political perspective. With your first few cups of coffee, you can read in one place—to take one typical day's samplings—a William Safire *New York Times* column, an Australian journalist eviscerating the United Nations for corruption, editorials from smaller-market daily papers like the *Rocky Mountain News* and the *Seattle Times*, top blogger commentaries, *U.S. News & World Report* wiseman Michael Barone analyzing America's voting dynamics, articles from the *Nation,* the *New Republic,* and the *Weekly Standard,* and McIntyre and Bevan's own informed musings.

And that's before you even get to the eye-poppingly comprehensive national and state polling data, transcripts of speeches, special interviews, think-tank reports, video feeds, and other raw information that the site gathers and organizes with luminous rationality. "The real value of what we do," Bevan says, "is to provide a daily political crib sheet—if you only have five minutes, you can still check in and get a quick snapshot of what is happening—as well as a kind of political almanac, in which you can spend as much time as you want reading and investigating issues and data." RealClearPolitics was *the* place to go to keep abreast of the 2004 election, a fact to which several of the nation's leading political analysts attested. "It's one of the first things I get to every morning," said Barone. Similarly, Charlie Cook of the *National Journal* said: "Not a day goes by that I don't click on RealClearPolitics at least once, the presidential poll charts, graphs and moving averages are great." "RealClearPolitics is the first website I check every morning," declared *New York Times* columnist David Brooks. "It's an invaluable tool for anybody interested in politics or public affairs." . . .

The web's interconnectivity—the fact that bloggers and news/opinion sites readily link to one another and comment on one another's postings, forming a kind of twenty-first-century electronic agora—amplifies and extends the influence of any site that catches the heavy hitters' attention. I can attest to this effect firsthand. On several occasions, online versions of magazine essays I've written have been linked on a bunch of heavily trafficked sites. The number of readers reached easily quintupled the twenty thousand or so subscribers to the print publications. Small wonder conservative print magazines like the *American Spectator* and the *New Criterion* are using the web so extensively these days.

The large numbers of readers these sites attract isn't the only significant boost for the conservative cause; it's also *who* those readers are. Just as FOX News is pulling in a younger viewership who will reshape the politics of the future, so these conservative sites are proving particularly popular with younger people, 72 percent of whom are now online in the United States, according to an Online Publishers Association survey. "They think, 'If it's not on the web, it doesn't exist,' " says Goldberg. FrontPage's web traffic shoots up dramatically during the school year, as lots of college students log on. "Half of our online audience is under forty-five," says NewsMax chief and 1990s Clinton foe Chris Ruddy. "Younger readers are coming in." *City Journal's* web readership skews significantly younger than its print subscribers, our in-house survey found.

A Pew poll found that 20 percent of young adults now use the Internet as a top source for political information—and the percentage is rising every year.

Equally important, the blogosphere's citizen journalists draw the attention of many who work in the broader mediasphere (as we've already noted with regard to RealClearPolitics). Prominent political journalists and editors at ABC News (which has started its own inside-baseball political blog, The Note), CNN, the *Los Angeles Times*, *Newsweek*, the *New Yorker*, the *New York Times*, *Time*, *U.S. News & World Report*, and other major press and broadcast outlets have publicly stated that consulting political blogs and Internet sites has become a normal part of their workday. For CNN political analyst Jeff Greenfield, the blogosphere provides "access to a whole bunch of things that if you just read the *New York Times* and the *Washington Post* and watched broadcast networks and CNN you're not going to get." . . .

Despite Al Gore's much-derided claim that he fathered the Internet, liberals have tended to distrust the wild and unregulated blogosphere. The *Boston Globe*'s Alex Beam gives an oft-heard liberal response: "Welcome to Blogistan, the Internet-based journalistic medium where no thought goes unpublished, no long-out-of-print book goes unhawked, and no fellow 'blogger,' no matter how outré, goes unpraised." Veteran *Washington Post* reporter David Broder even blames the shoddy journalistic ethics evident in the mainstream media of late on the bloggers! "When the Internet opened the door to scores of 'journalists' who had no allegiance at all to the skeptical and self-disciplined ethic of professional news gathering, the bars were already down in many old-line media organizations," he wrote with disgust. "This is how it happened that old pros such as Dan Rather and former *New York Times* editor Howell Raines got caught up in this fevered atmosphere and let their standards slip." And of course, as we saw in our introduction, you had the former executive vice president of CBS News (and now head of CNN's news group), Jonathan Klein, dismissing the blogger "sitting in his living room in his pajamas writing." The pajama people get the editor of the *Argus Leader* spitting bile: "True believers of one stripe or another, no longer content to merely bore spouses and neighbors with their nutty opinions, can now spew forth on their own blogs. . . . If Hitler were alive today, he'd have his own blog." In other words: How dare the peasants!

Such elitist contempt toward Internet publishing is diminishing on the Left these days, though, especially after Howard Dean (or better, his tech-savvy campaign boss Joe Trippi) showed during the Democratic presidential primaries just how much money and interest a left-wing candidate could raise via the web. Bloggers also received press passes to the 2004 Democratic and Republican conventions—a historic first.

Nonetheless, liberal unease about the Internet remains. In his 2001 book *Republic.com*, legal theorist Cass Sunstein argued that the increasing influence of the web's political sites could lead to a kind of cyber-balkanization (I'm indebted here to Drezner and Farrell's excellent discussion of this problem). "New technologies, emphatically including the Internet, are dramatically increasing people's ability to hear echoes of their own voices and to wall themselves off from others," Sunstein noted. "In a system in which each person can 'customize' his own communications universe, there is a risk that people will make choices that generate too little information, at least to the extent that individual choices are not made with reference to their social benefits." In an article headlined "People Getting News They Want—Not the News They Need," the *Los Angeles Times*'s David Shaw struck a similar note, complaining about the "intellectually lazy" people who now get their news from the Internet, where their views find "reinforcement and validation," instead of seeking out the unbiased reporting of the traditional news media. "[W]hat Matt Drudge calls news is very different from what, say, Walter Cronkite called news," Shaw opined sourly.

Worries about such virtual cocooning may be exactly contrary to the truth. Blogger and Yale law prof Jack Balkin gives one explanation why. "[Most] bloggers who write about political subjects cannot avoid addressing (and, more importantly, linking to) arguments made by people with different views," he points out. "The reason is that much of the blogosphere is devoted to criticizing what other people have to say. It's hard to argue with what the folks at National Review Online or Salon are saying unless you go read their articles, and, in writing a post about them, you will almost always either quote or link to the article or both." NRO and the New Republic website have occasionally run an "Opinion Dual" in which writers from each camp debate major issues, with their back-and-forth appearing simultaneously on both sites.

At *City Journal*, the Internet has brought us numerous new readers who don't share our politics. Before we started posting our articles on the web, we'd get the occasional letter from an angry liberal who'd come across us in a library or from a newspaper mention or excerpt. Now that we've entered the blogosphere era, we get bombarded with e-letters from the Left, especially when an ecumenical site like Arts & Letters Daily or RealClearPolitics links to us. Most of the left-wing letter writers curse us out. Others make thoughtful criticisms. And a few say, "Wow, you've changed my mind." How is that cyber-balkanization? Isn't it just democratic debate in action?

PART FIFTEEN

Political Economy and Public Welfare

84

MICHAEL HARRINGTON

From *The Other America*

Poverty in the United States is not new, but it took social critic Michael Harrington's acclaimed book, published in 1962, to bring the reality of "the other America" in the midst of the "affluent society" to the nation's attention. Harrington's study of the middle class's withdrawal from the problems of poor city-dwellers marked the philosophical start of the "war on poverty," which was to begin later in the 1960s. Harrington explored the situation of people who were poor within a society of plenty. His characterization of the poor as "socially invisible" and "politically invisible" led to wide public recognition of the problem of poverty in America. President Lyndon B. Johnson's "war on poverty" legislation has faded, but the "invisible" poor do, from time to time, reappear, never more poignantly than in the film footage of New Orleans's residents, many of them poor, calling out for help from the Superdome, from the Convention Center, and from city rooftops day after day while waiting in vain for a response from the Federal Emergency Management Agency (FEMA) following the disastrous 2005 Hurricane Katrina.

THERE IS a familiar America. It is celebrated in speeches and advertised on television and in the magazines. It has the highest mass standard of living the world has ever known.

In the 1950s this America worried about itself, yet even its anxieties were products of abundance. The title of a brilliant book was widely misinterpreted, and the familiar America began to call itself "the affluent society." There was introspection about Madison Avenue and tail fins*; there was discussion of the emotional suffering taking place in the suburbs. In all this, there was an implicit assumption that the basic grinding economic problems had been solved in the United States. In this theory the nation's problems were no longer a matter of basic human needs, of food, shelter, and clothing. Now they were seen as qualitative, a question of learning to live decently amid luxury.

While this discussion was carried on, there existed another America.

---

*Madison Avenue, in New York City, is the traditional home of the advertising industry. It is there that plans have been hatched for selling Americans products that they may not yet really know they want—like, in the 1950s, cars with tail fins. —EDS.

In it dwelt somewhere between 40,000,000 and 50,000,000 citizens of this land. They were poor. They still are.

To be sure, the other America is not impoverished in the same sense as those poor nations where millions cling to hunger as a defense against starvation. This country has escaped such extremes. That does not change the fact that tens of millions of Americans are, at this very moment, maimed in body and spirit, existing at levels beneath those necessary for human decency. If these people are not starving, they are hungry, and sometimes fat with hunger, for that is what cheap foods do. They are without adequate housing and education and medical care.

The Government has documented what this means to the bodies of the poor, and the figures will be cited throughout this book. But even more basic, this poverty twists and deforms the spirit. The American poor are pessimistic and defeated, and they are victimized by mental suffering to a degree unknown in Suburbia.

This book is a description of the world in which these people live; it is about the other America. Here are the unskilled workers, the migrant farm workers, the aged, the minorities, and all the others who live in the economic underworld of American life. . . .

The millions who are poor in the United States tend to become increasingly invisible. Here is a great mass of people, yet it takes an effort of the intellect and will even to see them. . . .

. . . The other America, the America of poverty, is hidden today in a way that it never was before. Its millions are socially invisible to the rest of us. No wonder that so many misinterpreted [economist John Kenneth] Galbraith's title and assumed that "the affluent society" meant that everyone had a decent standard of life. The misinterpretation was true as far as the actual day-to-day lives of two-thirds of the nation were concerned. Thus, one must begin a description of the other America by understanding why we do not see it.

There are perennial reasons that make the other America an invisible land.

Poverty is often off the beaten track. It always has been. . . .

. . . The American city has been transformed. The poor still inhabit the miserable housing in the central area, but they are increasingly isolated from contact with, or sight of, anybody else. Middle-class women coming in from Suburbia on a rare trip may catch the merest glimpse of the other America on the way to an evening at the theater, but their children are segregated in suburban schools. The business or professional man may drive along the fringes of slums in a car or bus, but it is not an important experience to him. The failures, the unskilled, the disabled, the aged, and the minorities are right there, across the tracks, where they have always been. But hardly anyone else is.

In short, the very development of the American city has removed poverty from the living, emotional experience of millions upon millions of middle-class Americans. Living out in the suburbs, it is easy to assume that ours is, indeed, an affluent society.

This new segregation of poverty is compounded by a well-meaning ignorance. A good many concerned and sympathetic Americans are aware that there is much discussion of urban renewal. Suddenly, driving through the city, they notice that a familiar slum has been torn down and that there are towering, modern buildings where once there had been tenements or hovels. There is a warm feeling of satisfaction, of pride in the way things are working out: the poor, it is obvious, are being taken care of. . . .

And finally, the poor are politically invisible. It is one of the cruelest ironies of social life in advanced countries that the dispossessed at the bottom of society are unable to speak for themselves. The people of the other America do not, by far and large, belong to unions, to fraternal organizations, or to political parties. They are without lobbies of their own; they put forward no legislative program. As a group, they are atomized. They have no face; they have no voice.

Thus, there is not even a cynical political motive for caring about the poor, as in the old days. Because the slums are no longer centers of powerful political organizations, the politicians need not really care about their inhabitants. The slums are no longer visible to the middle class, so much of the idealistic urge to fight for those who need help is gone. Only the social agencies have a really direct involvement with the other America, and they are without any great political power. . . .

Indeed, the paradox that the welfare state benefits those least who need help most is but a single instance of a persistent irony in the other America. Even when the money finally trickles down, even when a school is built in a poor neighborhood, for instance, the poor are still deprived. Their entire environment, their life, their values, do not prepare them to take advantage of the new opportunity. The parents are anxious for the children to go to work; the pupils are pent up, waiting for the moment when their education has complied with the law.

Today's poor, in short, missed the political and social gains of the thirties. They are, as Galbraith rightly points out, the first minority poor in history, the first poor not to be seen, the first poor whom the politicians could leave alone. . . .

What shall we tell the American poor, once we have seen them? Shall we say to them that they are better off than the Indian poor, the Italian poor, the Russian poor? That is one answer, but it is heartless. I should put it another way. I want to tell every well-fed and optimistic American that it is intolerable that so many millions should be maimed in body and in spirit when it is not necessary that they should be. My standard of comparison is not how much worse things used to be. It is how much better they could be if only we were stirred. . . .

First and foremost, any attempt to abolish poverty in the United States must seek to destroy the pessimism and fatalism that flourish in the other America. In part, this can be done by offering real opportunities to these people, by changing the social reality that gives rise to their sense of hopelessness. But beyond that (these fears of the poor have a life of their own and are not simply rooted in analyses of employment chances), there should be a spirit, an élan, that communicates itself to the entire society.

If the nation comes into the other America grudgingly, with the mentality of an administrator, and says, "All right, we'll help you people," then there will be gains, but they will be kept to the minimum; a dollar spent will return a dollar. But if there is an attitude that society is gaining by eradicating poverty, if there is a positive attempt to bring these millions of the poor to the point where they can make their contribution to the United States, that will make a huge difference. The spirit of a campaign against poverty does not cost a single cent. It is a matter of vision, of sensitivity. . . .

Second, this book is based upon the proposition that poverty forms a culture, an interdependent system. In case after case, it has been documented that one cannot deal with the various components of poverty in isolation, changing this or that condition but leaving the basic structure intact. Consequently, a campaign against the misery of the poor should be comprehensive. It should think, not in terms of this or that aspect of poverty, but along the lines of establishing new communities, of substituting a human environment for the inhuman one that now exists. . . .

There is only one institution in the society capable of acting to abolish poverty. That is the Federal Government. In saying this, I do not rejoice, for centralization can lead to an impersonal and bureaucratic program, one that will be lacking in the very human quality so essential in an approach to the poor. In saying this, I am only recording the facts of political and social life in the United States. . . .

[However] it is not necessary to advocate complete central control of such a campaign. Far from it. Washington is essential in a double sense: as a source of the considerable funds needed to mount a campaign against the other America, and as a place for coordination, for planning, and the establishment of national standards. The actual implementation of a program to abolish poverty can be carried out through myriad institutions, and the closer they are to the specific local area, the better the results. There are, as has been pointed out already, housing administrators, welfare workers, and city planners with dedication and vision. They are working on the local level, and their main frustration is the lack of funds. They could be trusted actually to carry through on a national program. What they lack now is money and the support of the American people. . . .

There is no point in attempting to blueprint or detail the mechanisms and institutions of a war on poverty in the United States. There is information enough for action. All that is lacking is political will. . . .

These, then, are the strangest poor in the history of mankind.

They exist within the most powerful and rich society the world has ever known. Their misery has continued while the majority of the nation talked of itself as being "affluent" and worried about neuroses in the suburbs. In this way tens of millions of human beings became invisible. They dropped out of sight and out of mind; they were without their own political voice.

Yet this need not be. The means are at hand to fulfill the age-old dream: poverty can now be abolished. How long shall we ignore this underdeveloped nation in our midst? How long shall we look the other way while our fellow human beings suffer? How long?

85

MILTON FRIEDMAN

From *Free to Choose*

Conservative economists are numerous today. But none can compete for style and consistency of viewpoint with Nobel Prize–winning Economics Professor Milton Friedman. Friedman has been the voice of conservative economics over the past half-century, during times when his ideas received little public acceptance. Free to Choose, written with his wife Rose Friedman, became the basis for an informative, entertaining—and controversial—TV series. Friedman's central theme is "freedom," both in economics and in politics. He advocates that the maximum amount of economic power be left to individual citizens, to make their own choices, with the least possible control placed in the central government's province. Big government is Friedman's target. In the excerpt, Friedman mentions his heroes, classical economists

Adam Smith and Friedrich Hayek. The name of Milton Friedman will join that list for future generations of conservatives.

⬥

THE STORY of the United States is the story of an economic miracle and a political miracle that was made possible by the translation into practice of two sets of ideas—both, by a curious coincidence, formulated in documents published in the same year, 1776.

One set of ideas was embodied in *The Wealth of Nations*, the masterpiece that established the Scotsman Adam Smith as the father of modern economics. It analyzed the way in which a market system could combine the freedom of individuals to pursue their own objectives with the extensive cooperation and collaboration needed in the economic field to produce our food, our clothing, our housing. Adam Smith's key insight was that both parties to an exchange can benefit and that, *so long as cooperation is strictly voluntary*, no exchange will take place unless both parties do benefit. No external force, no coercion, no violation of freedom is necessary to produce cooperation among individuals all of whom can benefit. That is why, as Adam Smith put it, an individual who "intends only his own gain" is "led by an invisible hand to promote an end which was no part of his intention. Nor is it always the worse for the society that it was no part of it. By pursuing his own interest he frequently promotes that of the society more effectually than when he really intends to promote it. I have never known much good done by those who affected to trade for the public good."

The second set of ideas was embodied in the Declaration of Independence, drafted by Thomas Jefferson to express the general sense of his fellow countrymen. It proclaimed a new nation, the first in history established on the principle that every person is entitled to pursue his own values: "We hold these truths to be self-evident, that all men are created equal, that they are endowed by their Creator with certain unalienable Rights; that among these are Life, Liberty, and the pursuit of Happiness." . . .

Economic freedom is an essential requisite for political freedom. By enabling people to cooperate with one another without coercion or central direction, it reduces the area over which political power is exercised. In addition, by dispersing power, the free market provides an offset to whatever concentration of political power may arise. The combination of economic and political *power* in the same hands is a sure recipe for tyranny. . . .

Ironically, the very success of economic and political freedom reduced its appeal to later thinkers. The narrowly limited government of the late nineteenth century possessed little concentrated power that endangered the ordinary man. The other side of that coin was that it possessed little power that would enable good people to do good. And in an imperfect world there were still many evils. Indeed, the very progress of society made the residual evils seem all the more objectionable. As always, people took the favorable developments for granted. They forgot the danger to freedom from a strong government. Instead, they were attracted by the good that a stronger government could achieve—if only government power were in the "right" hands. . . .

These views have dominated developments in the United States during the past half-century. They have led to a growth in government at all levels, as well as to a transfer of power from local government and local control to central government and central control. The government has increasingly undertaken the task of taking from some to give to others in the name of security and equality. . . .

These developments have been produced by good intentions with a major assist from self-interest. [Yet] even the strongest supporters of the welfare and paternal state agree that the results have been disappointing. . . .

The experience of recent years—slowing growth and declining productivity—raises a doubt whether private ingenuity can continue to overcome the deadening effects of government control if we continue to grant ever more power to government, to authorize a "new class" of civil servants to spend ever larger fractions of our income supposedly on our behalf. Sooner or later—and perhaps sooner than many of us expect—an ever bigger government would destroy both the prosperity that we owe to the free market and the human freedom proclaimed so eloquently in the Declaration of Independence.

We have not yet reached the point of no return. We are still free as a people to choose whether we shall continue speeding down the "road to serfdom," as Friedrich Hayek entitled his profound and influential book, or whether we shall set tighter limits on government and rely more heavily on voluntary cooperation among free individuals to achieve our several objectives. Will our golden age come to an end in a relapse into the tyranny and misery that has always been, and remains today, the state of most of mankind? Or shall we have the wisdom, the foresight, and the courage to change our course, to learn from experience, and to benefit from a "rebirth of freedom"? . . . If the cresting of the tide . . . is to be followed by a move toward a freer society and a more limited government

rather than toward a totalitarian society, the public must not only recognize
the defects of the present situation but also how it has come about and
what we can do about it. Why are the results of policies so often the
opposite of their ostensible objectives? Why do special interests prevail
over the general interest? What devices can we use to stop and reverse
the process? . . .

. . . Whenever we visit Washington, D.C., we are impressed all over
again with how much power is concentrated in that city. Walk the halls
of Congress, and the 435 members of the House plus the 100 senators
are hard to find among their 18,000 employees—about 65 for each senator
and 27 for each member of the House. In addition, the more than 15,000
registered lobbyists—often accompanied by secretaries, typists, researchers,
or representatives of the special interest they represent—walk the same
halls seeking to exercise influence.

And this is but the tip of the iceberg. The federal government employs
close to 3 million civilians (excluding the uniformed military forces).
Over 350,000 are in Washington and the surrounding metropolitan area.
Countless others are indirectly employed through government contracts
with nominally private organizations, or are employed by labor or business
organizations or other special interest groups that maintain their headquarters, or at least an office, in Washington because it is the seat of
government. . . .

. . . Both the fragmentation of power and the conflicting government
policies are rooted in the political realities of a democratic system that
operates by enacting detailed and specific legislation. Such a system tends
to give undue political power to small groups that have highly concentrated
interests, to give greater weight to obvious, direct, and immediate effects
of government action than to possibly more important but concealed,
indirect, and delayed effects, to set in motion a process that sacrifices the
general interest to serve special interests, rather than the other way around.
There is, as it were, an invisible hand in politics that operates in precisely the opposite direction to Adam Smith's invisible hand. Individuals
who intend only to promote the *general interest* are led by the invisible
political hand to promote a *special interest* that they had no intention to
promote. . . .

The benefit an individual gets from any one program that he has a
special interest in may be more than canceled by the costs to him of many
programs that affect him lightly. Yet it pays him to favor the one program,
and not oppose the others. He can readily recognize that he and the small
group with the same special interest can afford to spend enough money

and time to make a difference in respect of the one program. Not promoting that program will not prevent the others, which do him harm, from being adopted. To achieve that, he would have to be willing and able to devote as much effort to opposing each of them as he does to favoring his own. That is clearly a losing proposition. . . .

Currently in the United States, anything like effective detailed control of government by the public is limited to villages, towns, smaller cities, and suburban areas—and even there only to those matters not mandated by the state or federal government. In large cities, states, Washington, we have government of the people not by the people but by a largely faceless group of bureaucrats.

No federal legislator could conceivably even read, let alone analyze and study, all the laws on which he must vote. He must depend on his numerous aides and assistants, or outside lobbyists, or fellow legislators, or some other source for most of his decisions on how to vote. The unelected congressional bureaucracy almost surely has far more influence today in shaping the detailed laws that are passed than do our elected representatives.

The situation is even more extreme in the administration of government programs. The vast federal bureaucracy spread through the many government departments and independent agencies is literally out of control of the elected representatives of the public. Elected Presidents and senators and representatives come and go but the civil service remains. Higher-level bureaucrats are past masters at the art of using red tape to delay and defeat proposals they do not favor; of issuing rules and regulations as "interpretations" of laws that in fact subtly, or sometimes crudely, alter their thrust; of dragging their feet in administering those parts of laws of which they disapprove, while pressing on with those they favor. . . .

Bureaucrats have not usurped power They have not deliberately engaged in any kind of conspiracy to subvert the democratic process. Power has been thrust on them. . . .

The growth of the bureaucracy in size and power affects every detail of the relation between a citizen and his government. . . . Needless to say, those of us who want to halt and reverse the recent trend should oppose additional specific measures to expand further the power and scope of government, urge repeal and reform of existing measures, and try to elect legislators and executives who share that view. But that is not an effective way to reverse the growth of government. It is doomed to failure. Each of us would defend our own special privileges and try to limit government at someone else's expense. We would be fighting a many-headed hydra that would grow new heads faster than we could cut old ones off.*

Our founding fathers have shown us a more promising way to proceed: by package deals, as it were. We should adopt self-denying ordinances that limit the objectives we try to pursue through political channels. We should not consider each case on its merits, but lay down broad rules limiting what government may do. . . .

We need, in our opinion, the equivalent of the First Amendment to limit government power in the economic and social area—an economic Bill of Rights to complement and reinforce the original Bill of Rights. . . .

The proposed amendments would alter the conditions under which legislators—state or federal, as the case may be—operate by limiting the total amount they are authorized to appropriate. The amendments would give the government a limited budget, specified in advance, the way each of us has a limited budget. Much special interest legislation is undesirable, but it is never clearly and unmistakably bad. On the contrary, every measure will be represented as serving a good cause. The problem is that there are an infinite number of good causes. Currently, a legislator is in a weak position to oppose a "good" cause. If he objects that it will raise taxes, he will be labeled a reactionary who is willing to sacrifice human need for base mercenary reasons—after all, this good cause will only require raising taxes by a few cents or dollars per person. The legislator is in a far better position if he can say, "Yes, yours is a good cause, but we have a fixed budget. More money for your cause means less for others. Which of these others should be cut?" The effect would be to require the special interests to compete with one another for a bigger share of a fixed pie, instead of their being able to collude with one another to make the pie bigger at the expense of the taxpayer. . . .

. . . The two ideas of human freedom and economic freedom working together came to their greatest fruition in the United States. Those ideas are still very much with us. We are all of us imbued with them. They are part of the very fabric of our being. But we have been straying from them. We have been forgetting the basic truth that the greatest threat to human freedom is the concentration of power, whether in the hands of government or anyone else. We have persuaded ourselves that it is safe to grant power, provided it is for good purposes.

Fortunately, we are waking up. . . .

*The Hydra was a mythical Greek monster that grew two heads for each one that was chopped off. It was killed by the hero Hercules.—EDS.

Fortunately, also, we are as a people still free to choose which way we should go—whether to continue along the road we have been following to ever bigger government, or to call a halt and change direction.

86

SHARON HAYS

From *Flat Broke with Children*

When the welfare program in the United States was drastically changed in 1996, the impact was multifaceted. States gained much more power to tailor their welfare plans to fit their needs. The emphasis shifted from giving needy people money for an indefinite period of time to offering job training and childcare for a short time, with a job and independence as the ultimate goals. Sharon Hays assesses the decade-old welfare reform from several points of view. She talks to caseworkers in several cities about how well they think the new approach is working. She follows several welfare recipients through the system; their experiences suggest a mixed result. Yes, the bureaucratic rules remain and the hope of getting a decent job quickly is sometimes unrealistic. However, Hays finds that the changes to the welfare program have benefited many recipients. Beyond just a job, a sense of accomplishment and a future with real possibilities have opened up for some of those she studied.

━━━◆━━━

A NATION'S LAWS REFLECT a nation's values. The 1996 federal law reforming welfare offered not just a statement of values to the thousands of local welfare offices across the nation, it also backed this up with something much more tangible. Welfare reform came with money. Lots of it. Every client and caseworker in the welfare office experienced this. New social workers and employment counselors were hired. New signs were posted. New workshops were set up. In Arbordale and Sunbelt City, the two welfare offices I studied to write this book, every caseworker found a new computer on her desk.* In small-town Arbordale, the whole office got a facelift: new carpets, new paint, a new conference room, new office chairs, and plush new office dividers. The reception area, completely

*Arbordale and Sunbelt City are pseudonyms for the two towns where I studied the effects of welfare reform. I gave them these fictitious names to protect all the clients and caseworkers who shared with me their experiences of reform.

remodeled with plants and posters and a children's play area, came to resemble the waiting room of an elite pediatrician's office more than the entrance to a state bureaucracy. Sunbelt City acquired new carpets, a new paint job, and new furniture as well. And all the public areas in that welfare office were newly decorated with images of nature's magnificence—glistening raindrops, majestic mountains, crashing waves, setting sun—captioned with inspirational phrases like "perseverance," "seizing opportunities," "determination," "success."

As I walked the halls of the Sunbelt City welfare office back in 1998, situated in one of the poorest and most dangerous neighborhoods of a western boom town, those scenes of nature's magnificence struck me as clearly out of place. But the inspirational messages they carried nonetheless seemed an apt symbolic representation of the new legislative strategy to train poor families in "mainstream" American values. Welfare reform, Congress had decreed, would "end the dependence of needy parents on government benefits by promoting job preparation, work, and marriage." Welfare mothers, those Sunbelt signs implied, simply needed a *push*—to get them out to work, to keep them from having children they couldn't afford to raise, to get them married and safely embedded in family life. Seizing opportunities.

States were awash in federal funds. And the economy was booming in those early years of reform. Everyone was feeling it. There was change in the air. A sense of possibilities—with just a tinge of foreboding.

The Personal Responsibility and Work Opportunity Reconciliation Act of 1996, the law that ended 61 years of poor families' entitlement to federal welfare benefits—the law that asserted and enforced a newly reformulated vision of the appropriate values of work and family life— provided all that additional funding as a way of demonstrating the depth of the nation's commitment to change in the welfare system. It provided state welfare programs with federal grants in amounts matching the peak years of national welfare caseloads (1992 to 1995)—even though those caseloads had everywhere since declined. This meant an average budget increase of 10 percent, before counting the tremendous amount of additional federal funding coming in for new childcare and welfare-to-work programs. Even though there was lots more money, most states did not pass it on to poor mothers in the form of larger welfare checks. In fact, only two states raised their benefit amounts, while two others lowered theirs at the inception of reform.

Most of the welfare caseworkers I met were optimistic about the new law, at least in the first year of its enactment. "Welfare reform is the best thing that ever happened," was a phrase I heard frequently. A number of

caseworkers, echoing popular sentiment, told me that "welfare had become a trap" and the clients had become "dependent." Some focused on
the tax money that would be saved. Others pointed out that lots of
caseworkers are mothers too, and economic necessity forces them to come
to work every day and leave their children in day care, so it seemed only
fair that welfare mothers should be required to do the same. Still others
emphasized that welfare reform provided caseworkers the opportunity to
do what they were meant to do all along—it allowed them to "help
people." Eligibility workers in particular, who had long had the job of
simply processing applications and pushing papers, told me that they had
grown tired of just "passing out the checks." Welfare reform, one such
worker enthusiastically noted, offered the training and services necessary
"to make our clients' lives better, to make them better mothers, to make
them more productive." At the same time, some welfare workers, especially
the social workers and employment counselors, worried about the long-
term consequences of reform and wondered about how some of their
clients would survive. But almost all caseworkers agreed that the old
system was a problem and that the "self-sufficiency" and familial responsibility required by welfare reform were (at minimum) good ideas. . . .

The Personal Responsibility Act offered wide discretion to states in
the enactment of welfare reform and in the use of welfare money. There
are, therefore, notable differences in the policies of Arbordale and Sunbelt
City. Arbordale's home state, for instance, has a "family cap" provision
that disallows welfare benefits to children born when their mothers are
already receiving aid; Sunbelt City's state does not. Sunbelt's state has a
provision to identify (and potentially protect) welfare mothers who are
the victims of domestic violence; Arbordale's state does not. Like most
states, both of these permit mothers with infants to be temporarily exempt
from the work requirements: Arbordale allows mothers to stay at home
when their children are younger than 18 months old (a very generous
provision relative to most states); Sunbelt City offers new mothers a
lifetime maximum of 12 months of work exemption. Also mimicking
wide variations among states, Arbordale and Sunbelt differ in the extent
to which they are willing to use the federal "hardship exemption" that
allows them to spare 20 percent of their cases from welfare time limits:
Sunbelt City maximizes its use of these exemptions; Arbordale exempts
almost no one.

Both Arbordale's and Sunbelt's home states have, as noted, instituted
two-year time limits on welfare, placing them among the 22 states that
have similarly chosen shortened time limits. Although some states are
allowing welfare clients the federal maximum of one year of training

toward work and some states are relatively flexible in the speed with which they require their clients to get jobs, both Arbordale and Sunbelt City have instituted "work first" policies that emphasize the expedient placement of recipients in whatever jobs are available. Relative to other states in the nation, neither Arbordale nor Sunbelt is particularly generous or particularly miserly in its welfare benefit amounts or in the number of programs they have instituted to aid welfare families. . . .

The first thing you see on entering the Arbordale welfare office is a large red banner, 12 feet long, 2 feet high, reading, "HOW MANY MONTHS DO YOU HAVE LEFT?" Underneath that banner is a listing of jobs available in the area—receptionist, night clerk, fast-food server, cashier, waitress, data entry personnel, beautician, forklift operator. In most cases, the hours, benefits, and pay rates are not listed. The message is unmistakable: you must find a job, find it soon (before your months run out), and accept whatever wages or hours you can get. . . .

Welfare recipients, of course, are not merely being encouraged to work. In Arbordale and Sunbelt City, they were reminded repeatedly that work requirements are backed up by strictly enforced time limits—two years at the state level, five years overall—and they were continuously admonished to "save their months." Welfare caseworkers and supervisors, for their part, were painfully aware of the time limits, and they were also aware that the work requirements are enforced through federal "participation rates" requiring states to place increasing percentages of their welfare clientele in jobs. Should a state fail in this task, its federal financial allotment will be decreased. If a caseworker failed in her piece of this task, she could lose her job. For welfare mothers, this translated into constant and intense pressure to find work. The symbolic device of the "ticking clock" measuring one's time on welfare was used incessantly by Arbordale and Sunbelt caseworkers and quickly found its way into the vocabulary of the welfare mothers I met.

Just as most of the public and the popular media have assumed all along, welfare reform's Work Plan thus takes center stage in the welfare office. According to the logic of this plan, if the welfare office can train mothers to value work and self-sufficiency, the need for welfare receipt will be eliminated, and former recipients will become respectable, "mainstream" American workers. In this model, the ideal of independence—long associated with values of citizenship, self-governance, and full social membership in Western culture—is thereby transformed into a simple demand for paid work.

There are a number of problems with that logic, as this chapter will demonstrate. A foundational problem is the false assumption that most welfare recipients were previously lacking the motivation to work. Another problem, apparent to anyone who has ever tried to survive on a minimum wage job, is that the low-wage work typically available to welfare recipients offers neither financial independence nor the independence associated with the higher ideals of American citizenship. These difficulties, I soon discovered, are made worse by the procedural enactment of reform. Immersed in a bureaucratic machine, the rigid rules and demanding regulations of reform not only diminish the dignity of the people being served, they also degrade the values that the Personal Responsibility Act purports to champion. . . .

As a start, consider Carolyn. A once-married, black Sunbelt City welfare mother with a high school diploma, her story contained a number of the patterns I saw in the lives of welfare recipients. She had worked for most of her adult life, and she had also spent nearly all her life hovering somewhere close to the poverty line. She had been employed as a waitress, a clerk at the District Attorney's office, a telephone operator, a nurse's aide, a receptionist at the power company, a childcare worker, and a discount-store cashier. She initially went on welfare when she had her first and only child with a man she planned to marry. Carolyn cried when she told me the story of how that man began to physically abuse her and ultimately raped her during her pregnancy: "When I first met him, he was a really good man," she said. "But then he started taking drugs. It was terrible. I was afraid all the time." Shortly after the rape, she escaped that situation and moved in with her sister, but lost her job. By the time she gave birth, she was suffering from a nervous breakdown. ("He had drove me insane: that's what they said, in the letter from the psychiatrist.") It was following her hospitalization for that breakdown, ten years before I met her, that she first went on welfare with her then two-month-old baby girl.

By the time her daughter was two years old, Carolyn went back to work. Three years after that she took on the full-time care of her three nieces (aged 3, 9, and 12) when their mother was imprisoned for selling drugs and Carolyn learned that those children were otherwise bound for the foster care system. At that point, she took a second job to care for those four kids, and tried hard to avoid returning to welfare. But after a few years her carefully organized (though always precarious and stressful) work/family balance was thrown into disarray. Her brother and sister-in-law who had been helping with childcare and transportation moved out of town. This left Carolyn trying to manage with the public bus system, paid caregivers, and after-school programs for her daily round of transportation to two jobs, the childcare provider, the older kids' schools, and

back home again—along with all the added expenses that went with this
new strategy.

Then came the final straw. Carolyn was laid off one of her jobs. By
this time, she was deeply in debt and ill: the stress of her situation had
contributed to serious heart problems, and her doctor was urging her to
"take it easy." All these difficulties—transportation, relationships, low
wages, precarious jobs, ill health, and the care of children—came together
and landed her in the welfare office where I met her. It was clear to me
that, at that point in her life, Carolyn was hoping for a little rest and
recuperation. But the terms of the newly reformed welfare office, as you'll
soon see, required just the opposite.

Although the poor mothers I met in Arbordale and Sunbelt City all
came from different circumstances, many of them shared at least some of
the troubles from which Carolyn had suffered. The primary point is that,
in the vast majority of cases, when women end up on welfare it is not
because they have lost (or never found) the work ethic. It is only because
a moral commitment to work is, by itself, not always sufficient for the
practical achievement of financial and familial stability. . . .

Overall, the rules designed to enforce work emerge as a relatively
confusing mix of commands, backed up by some welcome gifts, and
many, many, less welcome requirements. In pondering this system of rules,
rewards, and punishments, the observer might consider to what extent it
adds up to a model of the values of "mainstream" America.

The welfare clients I met heard two pieces of this message loud and
clear: they knew they were expected to find jobs, and they knew they
were expected to obey the rules. Many of them also heard, more faintly
perhaps, the enthusiasm that was often conveyed by the caseworkers who
enforced those rules, an enthusiasm for genuinely improving the lives of
welfare families. Yet, just as the behaviorist model of welfare mixes rewards
with punishments, that enthusiasm was also mirrored by another implicit
message, one that emerged from the constant pressure, echoed persistently
in the background, and was assimilated by most of the welfare mothers
I encountered: "You are not wanted here. Americans are tired of helping
you out, and we will not let you rest, not even for an instant, until you
find a way to get off welfare."

The message of the importance of paid work is a very powerful
message indeed. . . .

The welfare office is, first and foremost, a bureaucracy. It is a world
of rigid rules and formal procedures. It is a world where every new welfare
client can be represented as a series of numbers: a case number, a number
of children, a number of fathers of those children, a number of dollars

in cash income, a number of months on welfare, a number of required forms, oaths, and verifications. It is also a world where every welfare client has come to symbolize a potential case of fraud and a potential "error" in the calculation of appropriate benefits. It is no surprise, therefore, that the congressional Work Plan was simply translated into a complex system of bureaucratic rules and regulations. . . .

For all the hardships and discontent, for all those clients whose experiences with reform were unequivocally negative, most welfare mothers, most of the time, remained positive, chin up, eyes to the future. As much as almost no one was happy with *all* the rules and regulations, and although almost everyone recognized some problems, the largest proportion of the poor mothers I talked to were genuinely hopeful about reform and tried hard to make the best of it. They knew what the welfare office and the nation were asking of them, and they did whatever they could to get training, seek out work, find good childcare, manage their budgets, and get off the welfare rolls.

For those who clearly benefited from the programs instituted by reform their positive attitude was easy to understand. If they found both suitable childcare and decent jobs with regular hours that paid above the minimum wage, it made sense that they were grateful for the increased benefits offered as "transitional" (time-limited) assistance with childcare, transportation, medical insurance, and clothing. They were even more appreciative of the welfare checks they continued to receive if their wages were low in relation to their family size. Those benefits meant that this group of clients was, temporarily at least, clearly better off than they would have been prior to welfare reform. And, for some, this was just the boost they needed to achieve familial financial stability.

More surprising was the sense of hope that I regularly encountered among those who were having a harder time. This included mothers who ran through one training program after another, hoping that the next one would prove the "right" one—the one that would help them to get a good job, the kind that offered some flexibility and paid wages sufficient to support their family. It included all those women who took jobs paying minimum wage, jobs with irregular schedules, and jobs that were less than full time. It even included many of those who were forced to take unpaid workfare placements and who interpreted these placements as a chance to get much needed work experience.

Overall, for every client who complained to me of ill treatment and of the inappropriate logic of reform, there were at least two others who responded to my questions about their experiences by recounting positive encounters and emphasizing the helpful services. Shannon, a Sunbelt mother with two kids, was particularly enthusiastic. She'd been out of work for over a year before reform and, when I met her, she'd just started a three-month temporary job as a bill collector:

> I think welfare reform is great! It helps with the transportation and the day care, so it helps out a lot. And my caseworker is so nice—she takes care of me, and she tells me stuff. The classes teach you how to prepare yourself to go out for a job and have the right attitude. They taught me how to do my resume and things like that. And you learn how to feel good about yourself too. And, you know, things get tough sometimes, so the welfare office has helped me. I thank God for that.

Julia, pregnant with her second child, was equally positive. Even though she had not yet found work, she was still feeling hopeful, and grateful for the help that came with reform:

> They've been very good to me; I've never really had a problem with anything. I mean, the only thing that holds you back is you. My caseworker got me into classes for computer skills. I was looking at the lists and it's like $1,000 for a course like that! So welfare is really forking out the bucks. You know, people are saying, "This is our tax dollars!" and I think they're being put to good use.

Despite the rigmarole, the bureaucratic maze, the intrusions, the sanctions, and the massive number of strict requirements, many of the women I encountered expressed similar sentiments. Although I had read the statistics reporting that welfare recipients are nearly as likely as other Americans to support reform, in the context of the welfare office, I was more surprised by this fact than any other.

This ability to retain hope surely speaks to a resilience of the human spirit. And part of that hope, as I've suggested, clearly arose from practical calculations—no matter what one's circumstances, the supportive services and income disregards could make it feel like Christmastime, with gifts and pennies falling from heaven. Similarly, although the content of the training programs in computers, food service, and general office skills often bore little relation to what is actually required to achieve financial stability, and as often as I heard clients complain about bad teachers or demanding schedules, I also witnessed, firsthand, the way some of those programs offered some participants a sense of collective purpose and a feeling that they might actually have a better shot at the brass ring. Along the same lines, the new discretion and maternalism that entered the welfare office with reform meant that a number of clients established warm ties with their caseworkers and came to understand them as important life mentors. Those welfare mothers who made their way to the protection of Sunbelt's social workers often felt especially grateful for the help they received. In all this, there was no question that this welfare office was indeed different from the one where eligibility workers used to just "pass out the checks."

Practical considerations and warm ties, however, were not the only source of welfare mothers' positive assessment of reform. As you can begin to hear in the words of Shannon and Julia, the supportive programs offered by reform were also important because, for some welfare mothers, they seemed to indicate that not just the welfare office but also the nation as a whole wanted to help low-income families to achieve a *better* future. When Julia commented on those $1,000 training courses, even though she knew that Americans were primarily interested in getting her off the welfare rolls, she was also feeling that those Americans were standing with her, rather than against her.

Nonetheless, to maintain this positive attitude, this "ideal" vision of reform, often required welfare mothers to sustain a protective mental and emotional barrier between their hopes and their circumstances. The $6.00-an-hour jobs, the troubles in caring for one's children, the bureaucratic regulations, after all, didn't offer a perfect image of financial stability, happy family life, and a nation dedicated to the common good. But maybe, just maybe, many welfare mothers seemed to say, such a world was possible. . . .

The number of families that have been genuinely helped by reform is neither insignificant nor superfluous. At a practical as well as moral level, the services and income supports offered by the Personal Responsibility Act have clearly been positive. Yet in the long run and in the aggregate, poor mothers and children are worse off now than they were prior to reform. Among those who are working and still poor, among those without work or welfare, and among those who are still facing constant and intense pressure to find work and figure out some way to care for their children, we can only guess what impact this law will have on their ability to retain hope over the long term. Even the U.S. Census Bureau (not anyone's idea of a bleeding heart organization) has found itself answering the question, "Is work better than welfare?" in the negative, at least for those without substantial prior education and work experience. With a slower economy and increasing numbers of poor families due to hit their time limits in coming years, there are reasons to expect that conditions will become increasingly difficult.

Empathy for the downtrodden is one reason to worry about these results. As the following sections will emphasize, enlightened self-interest, a concern with financial costs, and a commitment to our collective future are also very good reasons to be troubled by the consequences of welfare reform. . . .

The extent to which the facts about the declining welfare rolls are read as a success ultimately depends on one's primary goals. If the goal of reform was solely to trim the rolls, then it has surely succeeded. If the goal was to place more single mothers in jobs regardless of wages, that goal has been met. If we sought to ensure that more welfare mothers would face a double shift of paid work and childcare, placing them on an "equal" footing with their middle-class counterparts, then some celebrations are in order. If the aim was to ensure that poor men are prosecuted for failure to pay child support, then welfare reform has been relatively effective. If the goal was to make low-income single mothers more likely to seek out the help of men, no matter what the costs, there is some (inconclusive) evidence that this strategy may be working. If the goal was to decrease poverty overall, there is no indication that anything but the cycle of the economy has had an impact. Beyond this, the answers are more complicated.

Thinking about losers, one can start with the families who have left welfare. One-half are sometimes without enough money to buy food. One-third have to cut the size of meals. Almost half find themselves unable to pay their rent or utility bills. Many more families are turning to locally funded services, food banks, churches, and other charities for aid. Many of those charities are already overburdened. In some locales, homeless shelters and housing assistance programs are closing their doors to new customers, food banks are running out of food, and other charities are being forced to tighten their eligibility requirements. . . .

Although the results of welfare reform may creep up on us slowly and almost imperceptibly, to proclaim this experiment in family values and the work ethic a "success" would be, at minimum, short-sighted. If we care only about our pocketbooks, the results of this reform will ultimately be more costly than the system that preceded it. If we care only about the nation's productivity, then the principles of enlightened self-interest would suggest that malnourished future laborers and caregivers stressed to the breaking point are not going to further that goal. If we care about the family, then tortured gender relations, double-shifts, family unfriendly employers, latch key kids, inadequately funded childcare centers, and high rates of domestic violence are nothing to celebrate. And if we care about the principles of independent citizenship and commitment to others, then it must be recognized that welfare reform represents little more than a weak-kneed retreat and a cowardly response to massive social change.

To confront the social problems that welfare reform was purported to solve requires public support for the work of care and directly addressing unjust social inequalities that leave so many Americans excluded from full citizenship. This is no small order. But this examination of welfare reform, I hope, can serve as a reminder that the effort required is important not only for those at the bottom of the social hierarchy, but for all of us.

PART SIXTEEN

America in a Changed World

87

BENJAMIN BARBER

From *Jihad vs. McWorld*

In this selection political scientist Benjamin Barber writes from the perspective of an advocate of democracy—the right of the people to be a voice in a genuine citizen-led society. In his important 1995 book, that takes on additional meaning after September 11, 2001, Barber contrasts two visions of the world, neither one of which is compatible with the kind of democracy he believes in. One vision is the world engaged in Jihad, "in which culture is pitted against culture, people against people, tribe against tribe"; if students had trouble understanding what Barber meant when he wrote in 1995, they have no trouble understanding it today. The contrary vision is McWorld, "onrushing economic, technological, and ecological forces that demand integration and uniformity and mesmerize peoples everywhere with fast music, fast computers, and fast food." This, too, is easily understood. Jihad and McWorld feed off one another—but in opposition. Neither one has any place for a citizen-based democracy where all participate. Barber's analysis is incisive, original, and scary.

———◆———

HISTORY IS NOT OVER. Nor are we arrived in the wondrous land of techné promised by the futurologists. The collapse of state communism has not delivered people to a safe democratic haven, and the past, fratricide and civil discord perduring, still clouds the horizon just behind us. Those who look back see all of the horrors of the ancient slaughterbench reenacted in disintegral nations like Bosnia, Sri Lanka, Ossetia, and Rwanda and they declare that nothing has changed. Those who look forward prophesize commercial and technological interdependence—a virtual paradise made possible by spreading markets and global technology—and they proclaim that everything is or soon will be different. The rival observers seem to consult different almanacs drawn from the libraries of contrarian planets.

Yet anyone who reads the daily papers carefully, taking in the front page accounts of civil carnage as well as the business page stories on the mechanics of the information superhighway and the economics of communication mergers, anyone who turns deliberately to take in the whole 360-degree horizon, knows that our world and our lives are caught between what William Butler Yeats called the two eternities of race and soul: that of race reflecting the tribal past, that of soul anticipating the cosmopolitan future. Our secular eternities are corrupted, however, race reduced to an insignia of resentment, and soul sized down to fit the demanding body by which it now measures its needs. Neither race nor soul offers us a future that is other than bleak, neither promises a polity that is remotely democratic.

The first scenario rooted in race holds out the grim prospect of a retribalization of large swaths of humankind by war and bloodshed: a threatened balkanization of nation-states in which culture is pitted against culture, people against people, tribe against tribe, a Jihad in the name of a hundred narrowly conceived faiths against every kind of interdependence, every kind of artificial social cooperation and mutuality: against technology, against pop culture, and against integrated markets; against modernity itself as well as the future in which modernity issues. The second paints that future in shimmering pastels, a busy portrait of onrushing economic, technological, and ecological forces that demand integration and uniformity and that mesmerize peoples everywhere with fast music, fast computers, and fast food—MTV, Macintosh, and McDonald's—pressing nations into one homogenous global theme park, one McWorld tied together by communications, information, entertainment, and commerce. Caught between Babel and Disneyland, the planet is falling precipitously apart and coming reluctantly together at the very same moment.

Some stunned observers notice only Babel, complaining about the thousand newly sundered "peoples" who prefer to address their neighbors with sniper rifles and mortars; others—zealots in Disneyland—seize on futurological platitudes and the promise of virtuality, exclaiming "It's a small world after all!" Both are right, but how can that be?

We are compelled to choose between what passes as "the twilight of sovereignty" and an entropic end of all history; or a return to the past's most fractious and demoralizing discord; to "the menace of global anarchy," to Milton's capital of hell, Pandaemonium; to a world totally "out of control."

The apparent truth, which speaks to the paradox at the core of this book, is that the tendencies of both Jihad *and* McWorld are at work, both visible sometimes in the same country at the very same instant. Iranian zealots keep one ear tuned to the mullahs urging holy war and the other cocked to Rupert Murdoch's Star television beaming in *Dynasty, Donahue*, and *The Simpsons* from hovering satellites. Chinese entrepreneurs vie for the attention of party cadres in Beijing and simultaneously pursue KFC franchises in cities like Nanjing, Hangzhou, and Xian where twenty-eight outlets serve over 100,000 customers a day. The Russian Orthodox church, even as it struggles to renew the ancient faith, has entered a joint venture with California businessmen to bottle and sell natural waters under the rubric Saint Springs Water Company. Serbian assassins wear Adidas sneakers and listen to Madonna on Walkman headphones as they take aim through their gunscopes at scurrying Sarajevo civilians looking to fill family watercans. Orthodox Hasids and brooding neo-Nazis have both turned to rock music to get their traditional messages out to the new generation, while fundamentalists plot virtual conspiracies on the Internet.

Now neither Jihad nor McWorld is in itself novel. History ending in the triumph of science and reason or some monstrous perversion thereof (Mary Shelley's Doctor Frankenstein) has been the leitmotiv of every philosopher and poet who has regretted the Age of Reason since the Enlightenment. Yeats lamented "the center will not hold, mere anarchy is loosed upon the world," and observers of Jihad today have little but historical detail to add. The Christian parable of the Fall and of the possibilities of redemption that it makes possible captures the eighteenth-century ambivalence—and our own—about past and future. I want, however, to do more than dress up the central paradox of human history in modern clothes. It is not Jihad and McWorld but the relationship between them that most interests me. For, squeezed between their opposing forces, the world has been sent spinning out of control. Can it be that what Jihad and McWorld have in common is anarchy: the absence of common will and that conscious and collective human control under the guidance of law we call democracy?

Progress moves in steps that sometimes lurch backwards; in history's twisting maze, Jihad not only revolts against but abets McWorld, while McWorld not only imperils but re-creates and reinforces Jihad. They produce their contraries and need one another. My object here then is not simply to offer sequential portraits of McWorld and Jihad, but while examining McWorld, to keep Jihad in my field of vision, and while dissecting Jihad, never to forget the context of McWorld. Call it a dialectic of McWorld: a study in the cunning of reason that does honor to the radical differences that distinguish Jihad and McWorld yet that acknowledges their powerful and paradoxical interdependence.

There is a crucial difference, however, between my modest attempt at dialectic and that of the masters of the nineteenth century. Still seduced by the Enlightenment's faith in progress, both Hegel and Marx believed reason's cunning was on the side of progress. But it is harder to believe that the clash of Jihad and McWorld will issue in some overriding good. The outcome seems more likely to pervert than to nurture human liberty. The two may, in opposing each other, work to the same ends, work in apparent tension yet in covert harmony, but democracy is not their beneficiary. In East Berlin, tribal communism has yielded to capitalism. In Marx-Engelsplatz, the stolid, overbearing statues of Marx and Engels face east, as if seeking distant solace from Moscow: but now, circling them along the streets that surround the park that is their prison are chain eateries like T.G.I. Friday's, international hotels like the Radisson, and a circle of neon billboards mocking them with brand names like Panasonic, Coke, and GoldStar. New gods, yes, but more liberty?

What then does it mean in concrete terms to view Jihad and McWorld dialectically when the tendencies of the two sets of forces initially appear so intractably antithetical? After all, Jihad and McWorld operate with equal strength in opposite directions, the one driven by parochial hatreds, the other by universalizing markets, the one re-creating ancient subnational and ethnic borders from within, the other making national borders porous from without. Yet Jihad and McWorld have this in common: they both make war on the sovereign nation-state and thus undermine the nation-state's democratic institutions. Each eschews civil society and belittles democratic citizenship, neither seeks alternative democratic institutions. Their common thread is indifference to civil liberty. Jihad forges communities of blood rooted in exclusion and hatred, communities that slight democracy in favor of tyrannical paternalism or consensual tribalism. McWorld forges global markets rooted in consumption and profit, leaving to an untrustworthy, if not altogether fictitious, invisible hand issues of public interest and common good that once might have been nurtured by democratic citizenries and their watchful governments. Such governments, intimidated by market ideology, are actually pulling back at the very moment they ought to be aggressively intervening. What was once understood as protecting the public interest is now excoriated as heavy-handed regulatory browbeating. Justice yields to markets, even though, as Felix Rohatyn has bluntly confessed, "there is a brutal Darwinian logic to these markets. They are nervous and greedy. They look for stability and transparency, but what they reward is not always our preferred form of democracy." If the traditional conservators of freedom were democratic constitutions and Bills of Rights, "the new temples to liberty," George Steiner suggests, "will be McDonald's and Kentucky Fried Chicken."

In being reduced to a choice between the market's universal church and a retribalizing politics of particularist identities, peoples around the globe are threatened with an atavistic return to medieval politics where local tribes and ambitious emperors together ruled the world entire, women and men united by the universal abstraction of Christianity even as they lived out isolated lives in warring fiefdoms defined by involuntary (ascriptive) forms of identity. This was a world in which princes and kings had little real power until they conceived the ideology of nationalism. Nationalism established government on a scale greater than the tribe yet less cosmopolitan than the universal church and in time gave birth to those intermediate, gradually more democratic institutions that would come to constitute the nation-state. Today, at the far end of this history, we seem intent on re-creating a world in which our only choices are the secular universalism of the cosmopolitan market and the everyday particularism of the fractious tribe.

In the tumult of the confrontation between global commerce and parochial ethnicity, the virtues of the democratic nation are lost and the instrumentalities by which it permitted peoples to transform themselves into nations and seize sovereign power in the name of liberty and the commonweal are put at risk. Neither Jihad nor McWorld aspires to rese-cure the civic virtues undermined by its denationalizing practices; neither global markets nor blood communities service public goods or pursue equality and justice. Impartial judiciaries and deliberative assemblies play no role in the roving killer bands that speak on behalf of newly liberated "peoples," and such democratic institutions have at best only marginal influence on the roving multinational corporations that speak on behalf of newly liberated markets. Jihad pursues a bloody politics of iden-tity, McWorld a bloodless economics of profit. Belonging by default to McWorld, everyone is a consumer; seeking a repository for identity, everyone belongs to some tribe. But no one is a citizen. Without citizens, how can there be democracy? . . .

Jihad is, I recognize, a strong term. In its mildest form, it betokens religious struggle on behalf of faith, a kind of Islamic zeal. In its strongest political manifestation, it means bloody holy war on behalf of partisan identity that is metaphysically defined and fanatically defended. Thus, while for many Muslims it may signify only ardor in the name of a religion that can properly be regarded as universalizing (if not quite ecumenical), I borrow its meaning from those militants who make the slaughter of the "other" a higher duty. I use the term in its militant construction to suggest dogmatic and violent particularism of a kind known to Christians no less than Muslims, to Germans and Hindis as well as to Arabs. The phenomena to which I apply the phrase have innocent enough beginnings: identity politics and multicultural diversity can represent strategies of a free society trying to give expression to its diversity. What ends as Jihad may begin as a simple search for a local identity, some set of common personal attributes to hold out against the numbing and neutering uniformities of industrial modernization and the colonizing culture of McWorld. . . .

McWorld is a product of popular culture driven by expansionist commerce. Its template is American, its form style. Its goods are as much images as matériel, an aesthetic as well as a product line. It is about culture as commodity, apparel as ideology. Its symbols are Harley-Davidson motorcycles and Cadillac motorcars hoisted from the roadways, where they once represented a mode of transportation, to the marquees of global market cafés like Harley-Davidson's and the Hard Rock where they become icons of lifestyle. You don't drive them, you feel their vibes and rock to the images they conjure up from old movies and new celebrities, whose personal appearances are the key to the wildly popular international café chain Planet Hollywood. Music, video, theater, books, and theme parks—the new churches of a commercial civilization in which malls are the public squares and suburbs the neighborless neighborhoods—are all constructed as image exports creating a common world taste around common logos, advertising slogans, stars, songs, brand names, jingles, and trademarks. Hard power yields to soft, while ideology is transmuted into a kind of videology that works through sound bites and film clips. Videology is fuzzier and less dogmatic than traditional political ideology: it may as a consequence be far more successful in instilling the novel values required for global markets to succeed. . . .

Nowhere is the tension between democracy and Jihad more evident than in the Islamic world, where the idea of Jihad has a home of birth but certainly not an exclusive patent. For, although it is clear that Islam is a complex religion that by no means is synonymous with Jihad, it is relatively inhospitable to democracy and that inhospitality in turn nurtures conditions favorable to parochialism, antimodernism, exclusiveness, and hostility to "others"—the characteristics that constitute what I have called Jihad.

While *Jihad* is a term associated with the moral (and sometimes armed) struggle of believers against faithlessness and the faithless, I have used it here to speak to a generic form of fundamentalist opposition to modernity that can be found in most world religions. In their massive five-volume study of fundamentalisms, Martin E. Marty and R. Scott Appleby treat Sunni and Shiite Islam but pay equal attention to Protestantism and Catholicism in a variety of European, and North and South American forms, to Hinduism, to the Sikhs, to Theravada Buddhism, to Confucianist Revivalism, and to Zionism. Marty and Appleby take fundamentalist religions to be engaged in militancy, in a kind of permanent *fighting*: they are "militant, whether in the use of words and ideas or ballots or, in extreme cases, bullets." They fight back, struggling reactively against the present in the name of the past; they fight for their religious conception of the world against secularism and relativism; they fight with weapons of every kind, sometimes borrowed from the enemy, carefully chosen to secure their identity; they fight against others who are agents of corruption; and they fight under God for a cause that, because it is holy, cannot be lost even when it is not yet won. The struggle that is Jihad is not then just a feature of Islam but a characteristic of all fundamentalisms. Nevertheless, *Jihad* is an Islamic term and is given its animating power by its association not just with fundamentalism in general but with Islamic fundamentalism in particular and with the armed struggles groups like Hamas and Islamic Jihad have engaged in. There are moderate and liberal strands in Islam, but they are less prominent at present than the militant strand. . . .

If McWorld in its most elemental negative form is a kind of animal greed—one that is achieved by an aggressive and irresistible energy, Jihad in its most elemental negative form is a kind of animal fear propelled by anxiety in the face of uncertainty and relieved by self-sacrificing zealotry—an escape out of history. Because history has been a history of individuation, acquisitiveness, secularization, aggressiveness, atomization, and immoralism it becomes in the eyes of Jihad's disciples the temporal chariot of wickedness, a carrier of corruption that, along with time itself, must be rejected. Moral preservationists, whether in America, Israel, Iran, or India, have no choice but to make war on the present to secure a future more like the past: depluralized, monocultured, unskepticized, reenchanted. Homogenous values by which women and men live orderly and simple lives were once nurtured under such conditions. Today, our lives have become pulp fiction and *Pulp Fiction* as novel, as movie, or as life promises no miracles. McWorld is meager fare for hungry moralists and shows only passing interest in the spirit. However outrageous the deeds associated with Jihad, the revolt the deeds manifest is reactive to changes that are themselves outrageous.

This survey of the moral topography of Jihad suggests that McWorld—the spiritual poverty of markets—may bear a portion of the blame for the excesses of the holy war against the modern; and that Jihad as a form of negation reveals Jihad as a form of affirmation. Jihad tends the soul that McWorld abjures and strives for the moral well-being that McWorld, busy with the consumer choices it mistakes for freedom, disdains. Jihad thus goes to war with McWorld and, because each worries the other will obstruct and ultimately thwart the realization of its ends, the war between them becomes a holy war. The lines here are drawn not in sand but in stone. The language of hate is not easily subjected to compromise: the "other" as enemy cannot easily be turned into an interlocutor. But as McWorld is "other" to Jihad, so Jihad is "other" to McWorld. Reasoned communication between the two is problematic when for the partisans of Jihad both reason and communication appear as seductive instrumentalities of the devil, while for the partisans of McWorld both are seductive instrumentalities of consumerism. For all their dialectical interplay with respect to democracy, Jihad and McWorld are moral antinomies. There is no room in the mosque for Nintendo, no place on the Internet for Jesus—however rapidly "religious" channels are multiplying. Life cannot be both play and in earnest, cannot stand for the lesser gratification of a needy body and simultaneously for the greater glory of a selfless soul. Either the Qur'an speaks the Truth, or Truth is a television quiz show. History has given us Jihad as a counterpoint to McWorld and made them inextricable; but individuals cannot live in both domains at once and are compelled to choose. Sadly, it is not obvious that the choice, whatever it is, holds out much promise to democrats in search of a free civil society.

Should would-be democrats take their chances then with McWorld, with which they have shared the road to modernity but that has shown so little interest in them? Or try to reach an accommodation with Jihad, whose high moral purpose serves democracy's seriousness yet leaves but precious little space for its liberties? As it turns out, neither Jihad nor McWorld—and certainly not the quarrel between them—allows democracy much room. . . .

If my fundamental analysis of the dialectics that bind Jihad and McWorld together continues to be validated by current events, there are, nonetheless, issues raised by critics that merit some reply. . . .

My discussion of Jihad—indeed the very use of the word in the title— has drawn . . . criticism. . . . For although I made clear that I deployed Jihad as a generic term quite independently from its Islamic theological origins, and although I insisted that Islam has itself both democratic and nondemocratic manifestations and potentials, some readers felt the term singled out Islam and used it in pejorative ways to criticize non-Islamic phenomena. While extremist groups like Islamic Jihad have themselves associated the word with armed struggle against modernizing, secular infidels, I can appreciate that the great majority of devout Muslims who harbor no more sympathy for Islamic Jihad than devout Christians feel for the Ku Klux Klan or for the Montana Militia might feel unfairly burdened by my title. I owe them an apology, and hope they will find their way past the book's cover to the substantive reasoning that makes clear how little my argument has to do with Islam as a religion or with resistance to McWorld as a singular property of radical Muslims.

I have much less sympathy for those who read only one or another section of the book and concluded, lazily, that I must be writing either about McWorld alone or Jihad alone. Some critics have simply lumped *Jihad vs. McWorld* in together with Pandemonium prophets like Robert D. Kaplan (*The Ends of the Earth*) and Samuel P. Huntington ("The Clash of Civilizations"), dismissing us all as Pandoric pessimists. But as must be clear to anyone who reads the book cover to cover, it is finally about neither Jihad nor McWorld but about democracy—and the dangers democracy faces in a world where the forces of commerce and the forces reacting to commerce are locked in struggle. . . .

88

SAMUEL HUNTINGTON

From *The Clash of Civilizations*

Renowned scholar Samuel Huntington's 1996 book has received much attention since the terrorist attacks against the United States in 2001. Writing several years earlier, Huntington anticipates the vastly changed landscape of world conflict after the collapse of Soviet communism and after the end of the U.S.-Soviet Cold War. "Power is shifting from the long predominant West to non-western civilizations," Huntington writes. He explores the reasons why he believes this is happening, emphasizing the renewal of religion as central to the changes in power. Religious conflicts, especially between Islam and Christianity, are inevitable, the author feels. Not all Americans will agree with Huntington's grim thesis, but his ideas are important reading for people who have been brought up in the United States. Modernism, reason, progress, and prosperity are key American values, but not necessarily those of much of the rest of the world.

———

IN THE POST-COLD WAR WORLD, for the first time in history, global politics has become multipolar *and* multicivilizational. During most of human existence, contacts between civilizations were intermittent or nonexistent. Then, with the beginning of the modern era, about A.D. 1500, global politics assumed two dimensions. For over four hundred years, the nation states of the West—Britain, France, Spain, Austria, Prussia, Germany, the United States, and others—constituted a multipolar international system within Western civilization and interacted, competed, and fought wars with each other. At the same time, Western nations also expanded, conquered, colonized, or decisively influenced every other civilization. During the Cold War global politics became bipolar and the world was divided into three parts. A group of mostly wealthy and democratic societies, led by the United States, was engaged in a pervasive ideological, political, economic, and, at times, military competition with a group of somewhat poorer communist societies associated with and led by the Soviet Union. Much of this conflict occurred in the Third World outside these two camps, composed of countries which often were poor, lacked political stability, were recently independent, and claimed to be nonaligned.

In the late 1980s the communist world collapsed, and the Cold War international system became history. In the post-Cold War world, the most important distinctions among peoples are not ideological, political, or economic. They are cultural. Peoples and nations are attempting to answer the most basic question humans can face: Who are we? And they are answering that question in the traditional way human beings have answered it, by reference to the things that mean most to them. People define themselves in terms of ancestry, religion, language, history, values, customs, and institutions. They identify with cultural groups: tribes, ethnic groups, religious communities, nations, and, at the broadest level, civilizations. People use politics not just to advance their interests but also to define their identity. We know who we are only when we know who we are not and often only when we know whom we are against.

Nation states remain the principal actors in world affairs. Their behavior is shaped as in the past by the pursuit of power and wealth, but it is also shaped by cultural preferences, commonalities, and differences. The most important groupings of states are no longer the three blocs of the Cold War but rather the world's seven or eight major civilizations. Non-Western societies, particularly in East Asia, are developing their economic wealth and creating the basis for enhanced military power and political influence. As their power and self-confidence increase, non-Western societies increasingly assert their own cultural values and reject those "imposed" on them by the West. The "international system of the twenty-first century," Henry Kissinger has noted," . . . will contain at least six major powers—the United States, Europe, China, Japan, Russia, and probably India—as well as a multiplicity of medium-sized and smaller countries." Kissinger's six major powers belong to five very different civilizations, and in addition there are important Islamic states whose strategic locations, large populations, and/or oil resources make them influential in world affairs. In this new world, local politics is the politics of ethnicity; global politics is the politics of civilizations. The rivalry of the superpowers is replaced by the clash of civilizations. . . .

The philosophical assumptions, underlying values, social relations, customs, and overall outlooks on life differ significantly among civilizations. The revitalization of religion throughout much of the world is reinforcing these cultural differences. Cultures can change, and the nature of their impact on politics and economics can vary from one period to another. Yet the major differences in political and economic development among civilizations are clearly rooted in their different cultures. East Asian economic success has its source in East Asian culture, as do the difficulties East Asian societies have had in achieving stable democratic political systems. Islamic culture explains in large part the failure of democracy to emerge in much of the Muslim world. Developments in the postcommunist societies of Eastern Europe and the former Soviet Union are shaped by their civilizational identities. Those with Western Christian heritages are making progress toward economic development and democratic politics; the prospects for economic and political development in the Orthodox countries are uncertain; the prospects in the Muslim republics are bleak.

The West is and will remain for years to come the most powerful civilization. Yet its power relative to that of other civilizations is declining. As the West attempts to assert its values and to protect its interests, non-Western societies confront a choice. Some attempt to emulate the West and to join or to "bandwagon" with the West. Other Confucian and Islamic societies attempt to expand their own economic and military power to resist and to "balance" against the West. A central axis of post-Cold War world politics is thus the interaction of Western power and culture with the power and culture of non-Western civilizations.

In sum, the post-Cold War world is a world of seven or eight major civilizations. Cultural commonalities and differences shape the interests, antagonisms, and associations of states. The most important countries in the world come overwhelmingly from different civilizations. The local conflicts most likely to escalate into broader wars are those between groups and states from different civilizations. The predominant patterns of political and economic development differ from civilization to civilization. The key issues on the international agenda involve differences among civilizations. Power is shifting from the long predominant West to non-Western civilizations. Global politics has become multipolar and multicivilizational. . . .

The distribution of cultures in the world reflects the distribution of power. Trade may or may not follow the flag, but culture almost always follows power. Throughout history the expansion of the power of a civilization has usually occurred simultaneously with the flowering of its culture and has almost always involved its using that power to extend its values, practices, and institutions to other societies. A universal civilization requires universal power. Roman power created a near-universal civilization within the limited confines of the Classical world. Western power in the form of European colonialism in the nineteenth century and American hegemony in the twentieth century extended Western culture throughout much of the contemporary world. European colonialism is over; American hegemony is receding. The erosion of Western culture follows, as indigenous, historically rooted mores, languages, beliefs, and institutions reassert themselves. The growing power of non-Western societies produced by modernization is generating the revival of non-Western cultures throughout the world.

A distinction exists, Joseph Nye has argued, between "hard power," which is the power to command resting on economic and military strength, and "soft power," which is the ability of a state to get "other countries to *want* what it wants" through the appeal of its culture and ideology. As Nye recognizes, a broad diffusion of hard power is occurring in the world and the major nations "are less able to use their traditional power resources to achieve their purposes than in the past." Nye goes on to say that if a state's "culture and ideology are attractive, others will be more willing to follow" its leadership, and hence soft power is "just as important as hard command power." What, however, makes culture and ideology attractive? They become attractive when they are seen as rooted in material success and influence. Soft power is power only when it rests on a foundation of hard power. Increases in hard economic and military power produce enhanced self-confidence, arrogance, and belief in the superiority of one's own culture or soft power compared to those of other peoples and greatly increase its attractiveness to other peoples. Decreases in economic and military power lead to self-doubt, crises of identity, and efforts to find in other cultures the keys to economic, military, and political success. As non-Western societies enhance their economic, military, and political capacity, they increasingly trumpet the virtues of their own values, institutions, and culture.

Communist ideology appealed to people throughout the world in the 1950s and 1960s when it was associated with the economic success and military force of the Soviet Union. That appeal evaporated when the Soviet economy stagnated and was unable to maintain Soviet military strength. Western values and institutions have appealed to people from other cultures because they were seen as the source of Western power and wealth. This process has been going on for centuries. Between 1000 and 1300, as William McNeill points out, Christianity, Roman law, and other elements of Western culture were adopted by Hungarians, Poles, and Lithuanians, and this "acceptance of Western civilization was stimulated by mingled fear and admiration of the military prowess of Western princes." As Western power declines, the ability of the West to impose Western concepts of human rights, liberalism, and democracy on other civilizations also declines and so does the attractiveness of those values to other civilizations.

It already has. For several centuries non-Western peoples envied the economic prosperity, technological sophistication, military power, and political cohesion of Western societies. They sought the secret of this success in Western values and institutions, and when they identified what they thought might be the key they attempted to apply it in their own societies. To become rich and powerful, they would have to become like the West. Now, however, these Kemalist attitudes have disappeared in East Asia. East Asians attribute their dramatic economic development not to their import of Western culture but rather to their adherence to their own culture. They are succeeding, they argue, because they are different from the West. Similarly, when non-Western societies felt weak in relation to the West, they invoked Western values of self-determination, liberalism, democracy, and independence to justify their opposition to Western domination. Now that they are no longer weak but increasingly powerful, they do not hesitate to attack those same values which they previously used to promote their interests. The revolt against the West was originally legitimated by asserting the universality of Western values; it is now legitimated by asserting the superiority of non-Western values.

The rise of these attitudes is a manifestation of what Ronald Dore has termed the "second-generation indigenization phenomenon." In both former Western colonies and independent countries like China and Japan, "The first 'modernizer' or 'post-independence' generation has often received its training in foreign (Western) universities in a Western cosmopolitan language. Partly because they first go abroad as impressionable teenagers, their absorption of Western values and life-styles may well be profound." Most of the much larger second generation, in contrast, gets its education at home in universities created by the first generation, and the local rather than the colonial language is increasingly used for instruction. These universities "provide a much more diluted contact with metropolitan world culture" and "knowledge is indigenized by means of translations—usually of limited range and of poor quality." The graduates of these universities resent the dominance of the earlier Western-trained generation and hence often "succumb to the appeals of nativist opposition movements." As Western influence recedes, young aspiring leaders cannot look to the West to provide them with power and wealth. They have to find the means of success within their own society, and hence they have to accommodate to the values and culture of that society. . . .

In the first half of the twentieth century intellectual elites generally assumed that economic and social modernization was leading to the withering away of religion as a significant element in human existence. This assumption was shared by both those who welcomed and those who deplored this trend. Modernizing secularists hailed the extent to which science, rationalism, and pragmatism were eliminating the superstitions, myths, irrationalities, and rituals that formed the core of existing religions. The emerging society would be tolerant, rational, pragmatic, progressive, humanistic, and secular. Worried conservatives, on the other hand, warned of the dire consequences of the disappearance of religious beliefs, religious institutions, and the moral guidance religion provided for individual and collective human behavior. The end result would be anarchy, depravity, the undermining of civilized life. "If you will not have God (and He is a jealous God)," T. S. Eliot said, "you should pay your respects to Hitler or Stalin."

The second half of the twentieth century proved these hopes and fears unfounded. Economic and social modernization became global in scope, and at the same time a global revival of religion occurred. This revival, *la revanche de Dieu*, Gilles Kepel termed it, has pervaded every continent, every civilization, and virtually every country. In the mid-1970s, as Kepel observes, the trend to secularization and toward the accommodation of religion with secularism "went into reverse. A new religious approach took shape, aimed no longer at adapting to secular values but at recovering a sacred foundation for the organization of society—by changing society if necessary. Expressed in a multitude of ways, this approach advocated moving on from a modernism that had failed, attributing its setbacks and dead ends to separation from God. The theme was no longer *aggiornamento* but a 'second evangelization of Europe,' the aim was no longer to modernize Islam but to 'Islamize modernity.' "

This religious revival has in part involved expansion by some religions, which gained new recruits in societies where they had previously not had them. To a much larger extent, however, the religious resurgence involved people returning to, reinvigorating, and giving new meaning to the traditional religions of their communities. Christianity, Islam, Judaism, Hinduism, Buddhism, Orthodoxy, all experienced new surges in commitment, relevance, and practice by erstwhile casual believers. In all of them fundamentalist movements arose committed to the militant purification of religious doctrines and institutions and the reshaping of personal, social, and public behavior in accordance with religious tenets. The fundamentalist movements are dramatic and can have significant political impact. They are, however, only the surface waves of the much broader and more fundamental religious tide that is giving a different cast to human life at the end of the twentieth century. The renewal of religion throughout the world far transcends the activities of fundamentalist extremists. In society after society it manifests itself in the daily lives and work of people and the concerns and projects of governments. The cultural resurgence in the secular Confucian culture takes the form of the affirmation of Asian values but in the rest of the world manifests itself in the affirmation of religious values. The "unsecularization of the world," as George Weigel remarked "is one of the dominant social facts in the late twentieth century." . . .

How can this global religious resurgence be explained? Particular causes obviously operated in individual countries and civilizations. Yet it is too much to expect that a large number of different causes would have produced simultaneous and similar developments in most parts of the world. A global phenomenon demands a global explanation. However much events in particular countries may have been influenced by unique factors, some general causes must have been at work. What were they?

The most obvious, most salient, and most powerful cause of the global religious resurgence is precisely what was supposed to cause the death of religion: the processes of social, economic, and cultural modernization that swept across the world in the second half of the twentieth century. Long-standing sources of identity and systems of authority are disrupted. People move from the countryside into the city, become separated from their roots, and take new jobs or no job. They interact with large numbers of strangers and are exposed to new sets of relationships. They need new sources of identity, new forms of stable community, and new sets of moral precepts to provide them with a sense of meaning and purpose. Religion, both mainstream and fundamentalist, meets these needs. As Lee Kuan Yew explained for East Asia:

We are agricultural societies that have industrialized within one or two generations. What happened in the West over 200 years or more is happening here in about 50 years or less. It is all crammed and crushed into a very tight time frame, so there are bound to be dislocations and malfunctions. If you look at the fast-growing countries—Korea, Thailand, Hong Kong, and Singapore—there's been one remarkable phenomenon: the rise of religion. . . . The old customs and religions—ancestor worship, shamanism—no longer completely satisfy. There is a quest for some higher explanations about man's purpose, about why we are here. This is associated with periods of great stress in society.

People do not live by reason alone. They cannot calculate and act rationally in pursuit of their self-interest until they define their self. Interest politics presupposes identity. In times of rapid social change established identities dissolve, the self must be redefined, and new identities created. For people facing the need to determine Who am I? Where do I belong? religion provides compelling answers, and religious groups provide small social communities to replace those lost through urbanization. All religions, as Hassan al-Turabi said, furnish "people with a sense of identity and a direction in life." In this process, people rediscover or create new historical identities. Whatever universalist goals they may have, religions give people identity by positing a basic distinction between believers and nonbelievers, between a superior in-group and a different and inferior out-group.

In the Muslim world, Bernard Lewis argues, there has been "a recurring tendency, in times of emergency, for Muslims to find their basic identity and loyalty in the religious community — that is to say, in an entity defined by Islam rather than by ethnic or territorial criteria." Gilles Kepel similarly highlights the centrality of the search for identity: "Re-Islamization 'from below' is first and foremost a way of rebuilding an identity in a world that has lost its meaning and become amorphous and alienating." In India, "a new Hindu identity is under construction" as a response to tensions and alienation generated by modernization. In Russia, the religious revival is the result "of a passionate desire for identity which only the Orthodox church, the sole unbroken link with the Russians' 1000-year past, can provide," while in the Islamic republics the revival similarly stems "from the Central Asians' most powerful aspiration: to assert the identities that Moscow suppressed for decades." Fundamentalist movements, in particular, are "a way of coping with the experience of chaos, the loss of identity, meaning and secure social structures created by the rapid introduction of modern social and political patterns, secularism, scientific culture and economic development." The fundamentalist "movements that matter," agrees William H. McNeill, " . . . are those that recruit from society at large and spread because they answer, or seem to answer, newly felt human needs. . . . It is no accident that these movements are all based in countries where population pressure on the land is making continuation of old village ways impossible for a majority of the population, and where urban-based mass communications, by penetrating the villages, have begun to erode an age-old framework of peasant life."

More broadly, the religious resurgence throughout the world is a reaction against secularism, moral relativism, and self-indulgence, and a reaffirmation of the values of order, discipline, work, mutual help, and human solidarity. Religious groups meet social needs left untended by state bureaucracies. These include the provision of medical and hospital services, kindergartens and schools, care for the elderly, prompt relief after natural and other catastrophes, and welfare and social support during periods of economic deprivation. The breakdown of order and of civil society creates vacuums which are filled by religious, often fundamentalist, groups. . . .

. . . "More than anything else," William McNeill observes, "reaffirmation of Islam, whatever its specific sectarian form, means the repudiation of European and American influence upon local society, politics, and morals." In this sense, the revival of non-Western religions is the most powerful manifestation of anti-Westernism in non-Western societies. That revival is not a rejection of modernity; it is a rejection of the West and of the secular, relativistic, degenerate culture associated with the West. It is a rejection of what has been termed the "Westoxification" of non-Western societies. It is a declaration of cultural independence from the West, a proud statement that: "We will be modern but we won't be you." . . .

Some Westerners, including [former] President Bill Clinton, have argued that the West does not have problems with Islam but only with violent Islamist extremists. Fourteen hundred years of history demonstrate otherwise. The relations between Islam and Christianity, both Orthodox and Western, have often been stormy. Each has been the other's Other. The twentieth-century conflict between liberal democracy and Marxist-Leninism is only a fleeting and superficial historical phenomenon compared to the continuing and deeply conflictual relation between Islam and Christianity. At times, peaceful coexistence has prevailed; more often the relation has been one of intense rivalry and of varying degrees of hot war. Their "historical dynamics," John Esposito comments, " . . . often found the two communities in competition, and locked at times in deadly combat, for power, land, and souls." Across the centuries the fortunes of the two religions have risen and fallen in a sequence of momentous surges, pauses, and countersurges. . . .

A . . . mix of factors has increased the conflict between Islam and the West in the late twentieth century. First, Muslim population growth has generated large numbers of unemployed and disaffected young people who become recruits to Islamist causes, exert pressure on neighboring societies, and migrate to the West. Second, the Islamic Resurgence has given Muslims renewed confidence in the distinctive character and worth of their civilization and values compared to those of the West. Third, the West's simultaneous efforts to universalize its values and institutions, to

maintain its military and economic superiority, and to intervene in con-
flicts in the Muslim world generate intense resentment among Muslims.
Fourth, the collapse of communism removed a common enemy of the
West and Islam and left each the perceived major threat to the other.
Fifth, the increasing contact between and intermingling of Muslims and
Westerners stimulate in each a new sense of their own identity and how it
differs from that of the other. Interaction and intermingling also exacerbate
differences over the rights of the members of one civilization in a country
dominated by members of the other civilization. Within both Muslim
and Christian societies, tolerance for the other declined sharply in the
1980s and 1990s.

The causes of the renewed conflict between Islam and the West thus
lie in fundamental questions of power and culture. *Kto? Kovo?* Who is to
rule? Who is to be ruled? The central issue of politics defined by Lenin
is the root of the contest between Islam and the West. There is, however,
the additional conflict, which Lenin would have considered meaningless,
between two different versions of what is right and what is wrong and,
as a consequence, who is right and who is wrong. So long as Islam remains
Islam (which it will) and the West remains the West (which is more
dubious), this fundamental conflict between two great civilizations and
ways of life will continue to define their relations in the future even as
it has defined them for the past fourteen centuries. . . .

The underlying problem for the West is not Islamic fundamentalism.
It is Islam, a different civilization whose people are convinced of the
superiority of their culture and are obsessed with the inferiority of their
power. The problem for Islam is not the CIA or the U.S. Department of
Defense. It is the West, a different civilization whose people are convinced
of the universality of their culture and believe that their superior, if
declining, power imposes on them the obligation to extend that culture
throughout the world. These are the basic ingredients that fuel conflict
between Islam and the West.

In the 1950s Lester Pearson warned that humans were moving into
"an age when different civilizations will have to learn to live side by side
in peaceful interchange, learning from each other, studying each other's
history and ideals and art and culture, mutually enriching each others'
lives. The alternative, in this overcrowded little world, is misunderstanding,
tension, clash, and catastrophe." The futures of both peace and Civilization
depend upon understanding and cooperation among the political, spiritual, and intellectual leaders of the world's major civilizations. In the clash
of civilizations, Europe and America will hang together or hang separately.
In the greater clash, the global "*real* clash," between Civilization and

barbarism, the world's great civilizations, with their rich accomplishments in religion, art, literature, philosophy, science, technology, morality, and compassion, will also hang together or hang separately. In the emerging era, clashes of civilizations are the greatest threat to world peace, and an international order based on civilizations is the surest safeguard against world war.

89

JOSEPH NYE

From *Soft Power*

When the United States flexes its military or economic muscle, it is using "hard power," a long used and much relied upon strategy for a superpower. Foreign policy specialist Joseph Nye introduces us here to "soft power," a littler known but no less important source of international influence. "Soft power," Nye explains, "rests on the ability to shape the preferences of others." Culture, values, and the legitimacy of foreign policy all contribute to a nation's soft power. In this selection, Nye gives a brief introduction to some of the competing views of foreign policy, including the Realists, the Wilsonians, the Neoconservatives, and the New Unilateralists. Nye believes that the ultimate success of the United States in protecting its interests in today's world lies in learning how to better utilize soft power along with the hard power we so quickly embrace. Whether you fully agree or not, Nye raises interesting points about the importance of soft power, the power that brought the United States into such prominence after World War II and won the Cold War.

MORE THAN FOUR CENTURIES AGO, Niccolo Machiavelli advised princes in Italy that it was more important to be feared than to be loved. But in today's world, it is best to be both. Winning hearts and minds has always been important, but it is even more so in a global information age. Information is power, and modern information technology is spreading information more widely than ever before in history. Yet political leaders have spent little time thinking about how the nature of power has changed and, more specifically, about how to incorporate the soft dimensions into their strategies for wielding power. . . .

Everyone is familiar with hard power. We know that military and economic might often get others to change their position. Hard power can rest on inducements ("carrots") or threats ("sticks"). But sometimes you can get the outcomes you want without tangible threats or payoffs. The indirect way to get what you want has sometimes been called "the second face of power." A country may obtain the outcomes it wants in world politics because other countries—admiring its values, emulating its example, aspiring to its level of prosperity and openness—want to follow it. In this sense, it is also important to set the agenda and attract others in world politics, and not only to force them to change by threatening military force or economic sanctions. This soft power—getting others to want the outcomes that you want—co-opts people rather than coerces them.

Soft power rests on the ability to shape the preferences of others. At the personal level, we are all familiar with the power of attraction and seduction. In a relationship or a marriage, power does not necessarily reside with the larger partner, but in the mysterious chemistry of attraction. And in the business world, smart executives know that leadership is not just a matter of issuing commands, but also involves leading by example and attracting others to do what you want. It is difficult to run a large organization by commands alone. You also need to get others to buy in to your values. Similarly, contemporary practices of community-based policing rely on making the police sufficiently friendly and attractive that a community wants to help them achieve shared objectives.

Political leaders have long understood the power that comes from attraction. If I can get you to want to do what I want, then I do not have to use carrots or sticks to make you do it. Whereas leaders in authoritarian countries can use coercion and issue commands, politicians in democracies have to rely more on a combination of inducement and attraction. Soft power is a staple of daily democratic politics. The ability to establish preferences tends to be associated with intangible assets such as an attractive personality, culture, political values and institutions, and policies that are seen as legitimate or having moral authority. If a leader represents values that others want to follow, it will cost less to lead. . . .

The soft power of a country rests primarily on three resources: its culture (in places where it is attractive to others), its political values (when it lives up to them at home and abroad), and its foreign policies (when they are seen as legitimate and having moral authority.)

Let's start with culture. Culture is the set of values and practices that create meaning for a society. It has many manifestations. It is common to distinguish between high culture such as literature, art, and education,

which appeals to elites, and popular culture, which focuses on mass entertainment.

When a country's culture includes universal values and its policies
promote values and interests that others share, it increases the probability
of obtaining its desired outcomes because of the relationships of attraction
and duty that it creates. Narrow values and parochial cultures are less
likely to produce soft power. The United States benefits from a universal-
istic culture. The German editor Josef Joffe once argued that America's
soft power was even larger than its economic and military assets. "U.S.
culture, low-brow or high, radiates outward with an intensity last seen in
the days of the Roman Empire—but with a novel twist. Rome's and
Soviet Russia's cultural sway stopped exactly at their military borders.
America's soft power, though, rules over an empire on which the sun
never sets."

Some analysts treat soft power simply as popular cultural power. They
make the mistake of equating soft power behavior with the cultural resources that sometimes help produce it. They confuse the cultural resources
with the behavior of attraction. For example, the historian Niall Ferguson
describes soft power as "nontraditional forces such as cultural and commercial goods" and then dismisses it on the grounds "that it's, well, soft." Of
course, Coke and Big Macs do not necessarily attract people in the Islamic
world to love the United States. The North Korean dictator Kim Jong-
il is alleged to like pizza and American videos, but that does not affect
his nuclear programs. Excellent wines and cheeses do not guarantee attraction to France, nor does the popularity of Pokémon games assure that
Japan will get the policy outcomes it wishes. . . .

The values a government champions in its behavior at home (for
example, democracy), in international institutions (working with others),
and in foreign policy (promoting peace and human rights) strongly affect
the preferences of others. Governments can attract or repel others by
the influence of their example. But soft power does not belong to the
government in the same degree that hard power does. Some hard-power
assets such as armed forces are strictly governmental; others are inherently
national, such as oil and mineral reserves, and many can be transferred
to collective control, such as the civilian air fleet that can be mobilized
in an emergency. In contrast, many soft-power resources are separate from
the American government and are only partly responsive to its purposes.
In the Vietnam era, for example, American popular culture often worked
at cross purposes to official government policy. Today, Hollywood movies
that show scantily clad women with libertine attitudes or fundamentalist
Christian groups that castigate Islam as an evil religion are both (properly)

outside the control of government in a liberal society, but they undercut government efforts to improve relations with Islamic nations. . . .

Hard and soft power sometimes reinforce and sometimes interfere with each other. A country that courts popularity may be loath to exercise its hard power when it should, but a country that throws its weight around without regard to the effects on its soft power may find others placing obstacles in the way of its hard power. No country likes to feel manipulated, even by soft power. . . .

. . . Moreover, as we saw earlier, hard power can sometimes have an attractive or soft side. As Osama bin Laden put it in one of his videos, "When people see a strong horse and a weak horse, by nature, they will like the strong horse." And to deliberately mix the metaphor, people are more likely to be sympathetic to underdogs than to bet on them.

The 2003 Iraq War provides an interesting example of the interplay of the two forms of power. Some of the motives for war were based on the deterrent effect of hard power. Donald Rumsfeld is reported to have entered office believing that the United States "was seen around the world as a paper tiger, a weak giant that couldn't take a punch" and determined to reverse that reputation. America's military victory in the first Gulf War had helped to produce the Oslo process on Middle East peace, and its 2003 victory in Iraq might eventually have a similar effect. Moreover, states like Syria and Iran might be deterred in their future support of terrorists. These were all hard power reasons to go to war. But another set of motives related to soft power. The neoconservatives believed that American power could be used to export democracy to Iraq and transform the politics of the Middle East. If successful, the war would become self-legitimizing. As William Kristol and Lawrence Kaplan put it, "What is wrong with dominance in the service of sound principles and high ideals?" . . .

Foreign policies also produce soft power when they promote broadly shared values such as democracy and human rights. Americans have wrestled with how to integrate our values with other interests since the early days of the republic, and the main views cut across party lines. Realists like John Quincy Adams warned that the United States "goes not abroad in search of monsters to destroy," and we should not involve ourselves "beyond the power of extrication in all the wars of interest and intrigue." Others follow the tradition of Woodrow Wilson and emphasize democracy and human rights as foreign policy objectives. As we shall see . . . , today's neoconservatives are, in effect, right-wing Wilsonians, and they are interested in the soft power that can be generated by the promotion of democracy.

During the 2000 election campaign, when George W. Bush frequently expressed traditional realist warnings that the United States should not become overextended, leading neoconservatives urged him to make human rights, religious freedom, and democracy priorities for American foreign policy and "not to adopt a narrow view of U.S. national interests." After 9/11, Bush's policy changed and he spoke of the need to use American power to bring democracy to the Middle East. As Lawrence Kaplan and William Kristol put it, "When it comes to dealing with tyrannical regimes like Iraq, Iran and, yes, North Korea, the U.S. should seek transformation, not coexistence, as a primary aim of U.S. foreign policy. As such, it commits the U.S. to the task of maintaining and enforcing a decent world order."

The neoconservatives are correct that such a world order could be a global public good, but they are mistaken to assume that their vision will be shared by all those affected by it. Whether the neoconservative approach creates rather than consumes American soft power depends not only on the results but also on who is consulted and who decides. The neoconservatives pay less heed than traditional Wilsonians to consultation through international institutions. But because the currency of soft power is attraction, it is often easier to generate and wield in a multilateral context.

In recent years, other countries have increasingly complained about the unilateralism of American foreign policy. Of course such differences are a matter of degree, and there are few countries that are pure unilateralists or multilateralists. International concerns about unilateralism began well before George W. Bush became president, and involved Congress as well as the executive branch. The president has disclaimed the label but most observers describe his administration as divided between traditional pragmatists and a more ideological school that the columnist Charles Krauthammer celebrated as "the new unilateralism."

The "new unilateralists" advocate an assertive approach to promoting American values. They worry about a flagging of internal will and a reluctance to turn a unipolar moment into a unipolar era. American intentions are good, American hegemony is benevolent, and that should end the discussion. To them, multilateralism means "submerging American will in a mush of collective decision-making—you have sentenced yourself to reacting to events or passing the buck to multilingual committees with fancy acronyms." They deny that American "arrogance" is a problem. Rather, the problem is "the inescapable reality of American power in its many forms." Policy is legitimized by its origins in a democracy and by the outcome—whether it results in an advance of freedom and democracy. That post hoc legitimization will more than compensate for any loss of legitimacy through unilateralism.

Unfortunately, the approach of the new unilateralists is not very convincing to other countries whose citizens observe that Americans are not immune from hubris and self-interest. Americans do not always have all the answers. As one realist put it, "If we were truly acting in the interests of others as well as our own, we would presumably accord to others a substantive role and, by doing so, end up embracing some form of multilateralism. Others, after all, must be supposed to know their interests better than we can know them." Since the currency of soft power is attraction based on shared values and the justness and duty of others to contribute to policies consistent with those shared values, multilateral consultations are more likely to generate soft power than mere unilateral assertion of the values. . . .

Anti-Americanism has increased in the past few years. Thomas Pickering, a seasoned diplomat, considered 2003 "as high a zenith of anti-Americanism as we've seen for a long time." Polls show that our soft-power losses can be traced largely to our foreign policy. "A widespread and fashionable view is that the United States is a classically imperialist power. . . . That mood has been expressed in different ways by different people, from the hockey fans in Montreal who boo the American national anthem to the high school students in Switzerland who do not want to go to the United States as exchange students." An Australian observer concluded that "the lesson of Iraq is that the US's soft power is in decline. Bush went to war having failed to win a broader military coalition or UN authorization. This had two direct consequences: a rise in anti-American sentiment, lifting terrorist recruitment; and a higher cost to the US for the war and reconstruction effort." Pluralities in 15 out of 24 countries responding to a Gallup International poll said that American foreign policies had a negative effect on their attitudes toward the United States. . . .

Skeptics about soft power say not to worry. Popularity is ephemeral and should not be a guide for foreign policy in any case. The United States can act without the world's applause. We are so strong we can do as we wish. We are the world's only superpower, and that fact is bound to engender envy and resentment. Fouad Ajami has stated recently, "The United States need not worry about hearts and minds in foreign lands." Columnist Cal Thomas refers to "the fiction that our enemies can be made less threatening by what America says and does." Moreover, the United States has been unpopular in the past yet managed to recover. We do not need permanent allies and institutions. We can always pick up a coalition of the willing when we need to. Donald Rumsfeld is wont to say that the issues should determine the coalitions, not vice versa.

But it would be a mistake to dismiss the recent decline in our attractiveness so lightly. It is true that the United States has recovered from unpopular policies in the past, but that was against the backdrop of the Cold War, in which other countries still feared the Soviet Union as the greater evil. Moreover, . . . while the United States' size and association with disruptive modernity is real and unavoidable, smart policies can soften the sharp edges of that reality and reduce the resentments they engender. That is what the U.S. did after World War II. We used our soft-power resources and co-opted others into a set of alliances and institutions that lasted for 60 years. We won the Cold War against the Soviet Union with a strategy of containment that used our soft power as well as our hard power.

It is true that the new threat of transnational terrorism increased American vulnerability, and some of our unilateralism after September 11 was driven by fear. But the United States cannot meet the new threat identified in the national security strategy without the cooperation of other countries. They will cooperate up to a point out of mere self-interest, but their degree of cooperation is also affected by the attractiveness of the United States. Take Pakistan for example. President Pervez Musharraf faces a complex game of cooperating with the United States in the war on terrorism while managing a large anti-American constituency at home. He winds up balancing concessions and retractions. If the United States were more attractive to the Pakistani populace, we would see more concessions in the mix.

It is not smart to discount soft power as just a question of image, public relations, and ephemeral popularity. As we argued earlier, it is a form of power—a means of obtaining desired outcomes. When we discount the importance of our attractiveness to other countries, we pay a price. Most important, if the United States is so unpopular in a country that being pro-American is a kiss of death in that country's domestic politics, political leaders are unlikely to make concessions to help us. Turkey, Mexico, and Chile were prime examples in the run-up to the Iraq War in March 2003. When American policies lose their legitimacy and credibility in the eyes of others, attitudes of distrust tend to fester and further reduce our leverage. For example, after 9/11 there was an outpouring of sympathy from Germans for the United States, and Germany joined a military campaign against the Al Qaeda network. But as the United States geared up for the unpopular Iraq War, Germans expressed widespread disbelief about the reasons the U.S. gave for going to war such as the alleged connection of Iraq to 9/11 and the imminence of the threat of weapons of mass destruction.

German suspicions were reinforced by what they saw as biased American media coverage during the war, and by the failure to find weapons of mass destruction or prove the connection to 9/11 in the aftermath of the war. The combination fostered a climate in which conspiracy theories flourished. By July 2003, according to a Reuters poll, one-third of Germans under the age of 30 said that they thought the American government might even have staged the original September 11 attacks.

Absurd views feed upon each other, and paranoia can be contagious. American attitudes toward foreigners harden, and we begin to believe that the rest of the world really does hate us. Some Americans begin to hold grudges, to mistrust all Muslims, to boycott French wines and rename French fries, to spread and believe false rumors. In turn, foreigners see Americans as uninformed and insensitive to anyone's interests but their own. They see our media wrapped in the American flag. Some Americans in turn succumb to residual strands of isolationism, and say that if others choose to see us that way, "To hell with 'em." If foreigners are going to be like that, who cares whether we are popular or not. But to the extent that Americans allow ourselves to become isolated, we embolden our enemies such as Al Qaeda. Such reactions undercut our soft power and are self-defeating in terms of the outcomes we want.

Some hard-line skeptics might say that whatever the merits of soft power, it has little role to play in the current war on terrorism. Osama bin Laden and his followers are repelled, not attracted, by American culture, values, and policies. Military power was essential in defeating the Taliban government in Afghanistan, and soft power will never convert fanatics. Charles Krauthammer, for example, argued soon after our swift military victory in Afghanistan that it proved that "the new unilateralism" worked. That is true up to a point, but the skeptics mistake half the answer for the whole solution.

Look again at Afghanistan. Precision bombing and Special Forces defeated the Taliban government, but U.S. forces in Afghanistan wrapped up less than a quarter of Al Qaeda, a transnational network with cells in 60 countries. The United States cannot bomb Al Qaeda cells in Hamburg, Kuala Lumpur, or Detroit. Success against them depends on close civilian cooperation, whether sharing intelligence, coordinating police work across borders, or tracing global financial flows. America's partners work with us partly out of self-interest, but the inherent attractiveness of U.S. policies can and does influence their degree of cooperation.

Equally important, the current struggle against Islamist terrorism is not a clash of civilizations but a contest whose outcome is closely tied to a civil war between moderates and extremists within Islamic civilization.

The United States and other advanced democracies will win only if moderate Muslims win, and the ability to attract the moderates is critical to victory. We need to adopt policies that appeal to moderates, and to use public diplomacy more effectively to explain our common interests. We need a better strategy for wielding our soft power. We will have to learn better to combine hard and soft power if we wish to meet the new challenges. . . .

Americans are still working their way through the aftermath of September 11. We are groping for a path through the strange new landscape created by technology and globalization whose dark aspects were vividly illuminated on that traumatic occasion. The Bush administration has correctly identified the nature of the new challenges that the nation faces and has reoriented American strategy accordingly. But the administration, like the Congress and the public, has been torn between different approaches to the implementation of the new strategy. The result has been a mixture of successes and failures. We have been more successful in the domain of hard power, where we have invested more, trained more, and have a clearer idea of what we are doing. We have been less successful in the areas of soft power, where our public diplomacy has been woefully inadequate and our neglect of allies and institutions has created a sense of illegitimacy that has squandered our attractiveness.

Yet this is ironic, because the United States is the country that is at the forefront of the information revolution as well as the country that built some of the longest-lasting alliances and institutions that the modern world has seen. We should know how to adapt and work with such institutions since they have been central to our power for more than half a century. And the United States is a country with a vibrant social and cultural life that provides an almost infinite number of points of contact with other societies. What's more, during the Cold War, we demonstrated that we know how to use the soft-power resources that our society produces. . . .

. . . In short, America's success will depend upon our developing a deeper understanding of the role of soft power and developing a better balance of hard and soft power in our foreign policy. That will be smart power. We have done it before; we can do it again.

90

CHALMERS JOHNSON

From *Blowback*

A scholar on American foreign affairs, Chalmers Johnson applies the CIA term "blowback" to the dilemma of this nation's military and diplomatic actions: many problems we grapple with currently are "unintended consequences of policies that were kept secret from the American people." Johnson discusses drug trafficking, terrorist acts, and economic retaliation as examples of other nations reacting to American policies, no matter how unintentional the negative results of those policies were. In the United States, Johnson argues, the military is becoming an ever stronger and less politically accountable arm of government. The military's actions may well produce more future blowback without citizens realizing what's ahead. Johnson's warning about American foreign policy is harsh: " . . . a nation reaps what it sows, even if it does not fully know or understand what it has sown."

———

NORTHERN ITALIAN COMMUNITIES HAD, for years, complained about low-flying American military aircraft. In February 1998, the inevitable happened. A Marine Corps EA-6B Prowler with a crew of four, one of scores of advanced American jet fighters and bombers stationed at places like Aviano, Cervia, Brindisi, and Sigonella, sliced through a ski-lift cable near the resort town of Cavalese and plunged twenty people riding in a single gondola to their deaths on the snowy slopes several hundred feet below. Although marine pilots are required to maintain an altitude of at least one thousand feet (two thousand, according to the Italian government), the plane had cut the cable at a height of 360 feet. It was traveling at 621 miles per hour when 517 miles per hour was considered the upper limit. The pilot had been performing low-level acrobatics while his copilot took pictures on videotape (which he later destroyed).

In response to outrage in Italy and calls for vigorous prosecution of those responsible, the marine pilots argued that their charts were inaccurate, that their altimeter had not worked, and that they had not consulted U.S. Air Force units permanently based in the area about local hazards. A court-martial held not in Italy but in Camp Lejeune, North Carolina, exonerated everyone involved, calling it a "training accident." Soon after,

President Bill Clinton apologized and promised financial compensation to the victims, but on May 14, 1999, Congress dropped the provision for aid to the families because of opposition in the House of Representatives and from the Pentagon. . . .

I believe it is past time for such a discussion to begin, for Americans to consider why we have created an empire—a word from which we shy away—and what the consequences of our imperial stance may be for the rest of the world and for ourselves. Not so long ago, the way we garrisoned the world could be discussed far more openly and comfortably because the explanation seemed to lie at hand—in the very existence of the Soviet Union and of communism. Had the Italian disaster occurred two decades earlier, it would have seemed no less a tragedy, but many Americans would have argued that, given the Cold War, such incidents were an unavoidable cost of protecting democracies like Italy against the menace of Soviet totalitarianism. With the disappearance of any military threat faintly comparable to that posed by the former Soviet Union, such "costs" have become easily avoidable. American military forces could have been withdrawn from Italy, as well as from other foreign bases, long ago. That they were not and that Washington instead is doing everything in its considerable powers to perpetuate Cold War structures, even without the Cold War's justification, places such overseas deployments in a new light. They have become striking evidence, for those who care to look, of an imperial project that the Cold War obscured. The by-products of this project are likely to build up reservoirs of resentment against all Americans—tourists, students, and businessmen, as well as members of the armed forces—that can have lethal results.

For any empire, including an unacknowledged one, there is a kind of balance sheet that builds up over time. Military crimes, accidents, and atrocities make up only one category on the debit side of the balance sheet that the United States has been accumulating, especially since the Cold War ended. To take an example of quite a different kind of debit, consider South Korea, a longtime ally. On Christmas Eve 1997, it declared itself financially bankrupt and put its economy under the guidance of the International Monetary Fund, which is basically an institutional surrogate of the United States government. Most Americans were surprised by the economic disasters that overtook Thailand, South Korea, Malaysia, and Indonesia in 1997 and that then spread around the world, crippling the Russian and Brazilian economies. They could hardly imagine that the U.S. government might have had a hand in causing them, even though various American pundits and economists expressed open delight in these disasters, which threw millions of people, who had previously had hopes of achieving economic prosperity and security, into the most abysmal poverty. At worst, Americans took the economic meltdown of places like Indonesia and Brazil to mean that beneficial American-supported policies of "globalization" were working—that we were effectively helping re-structure various economies around the world so that they would look and work more like ours. . . .

If Washington is the headquarters of a global military-economic do-minion, the answers will be very different than if we think of the United States as simply one among many sovereign nations. There is a logic to empire that differs from the logic of a nation, and acts committed in service to an empire but never acknowledged as such have a tendency to haunt the future.

The term "blowback," which officials of the Central Intelligence Agency first invented for their own internal use, is starting to circulate among students of international relations. It refers to the unintended consequences of policies that were kept secret from the American people. What the daily press reports as the malign acts of "terrorists" or "drug lords" or "rogue states" or "illegal arms merchants" often turn out to be blowback from earlier American operations.

It is now widely recognized, for example, that the 1988 bombing of Pan Am flight 103 over Lockerbie, Scotland, which resulted in the deaths of 259 passengers and 11 people on the ground, was retaliation for a 1986 Reagan administration aerial raid on Libya that killed President Muammar Khadaffi's stepdaughter. Some in the United States have suspected that other events can also be explained as blowback from imperial acts. For example, the epidemic of cocaine and heroin use that has afflicted Ameri-can cities during the past two decades was probably fueled in part by Central and South American military officers or corrupt politicians whom the CIA or the Pentagon once trained or supported and then installed in key government positions. For example, in Nicaragua in the 1980s, the U.S. government organized a massive campaign against the socialist-oriented Sandinista government. American agents then looked the other way when the Contras, the military insurgents they had trained, made deals to sell cocaine in American cities in order to buy arms and supplies.

If drug blowback is hard to trace to its source, bomb attacks, whether on U.S. embassies in Africa, the World Trade Center in New York City, or an apartment complex in Saudi Arabia that housed U.S. servicemen, are another matter. One man's terrorist is, of course, another man's freedom fighter, and what U.S. officials denounce as unprovoked terrorist attacks on its innocent citizens are often meant as retaliation for previous American imperial actions. Terrorists attack innocent and undefended American targets precisely because American soldiers and sailors firing cruise missiles from ships at sea or sitting in B-52 bombers at extremely high altitudes or supporting brutal and repressive regimes from Washington seem invulnerable. As members of the Defense Science Board wrote in a 1997 report to the undersecretary of defense for acquisition and technology, "Historical data show a strong correlation between U.S. involvement in international situations and an increase in terrorist attacks against the United States. In addition, the military asymmetry that denies nation states the ability to engage in overt attacks against the United States drives the use of transnational actors [that is, terrorists from one country attacking in another]." . . .

Blowback itself can lead to more blowback, in a spiral of destructive behavior. A good illustration of this lies in the government's reaction to the August 7, 1998, bombings of American embassy buildings in Nairobi and Dar es Salaam, with the loss of 12 American and 212 Kenyan and Tanzanian lives and some 4,500 injured. The U.S. government promptly placed the blame on Osama bin Laden, a Saudi who had long denounced his country's rulers and their American allies. On August 20, the United States retaliated by firing nearly eighty cruise missiles (at a cost of $750,000 each) into a pharmaceutical plant in Khartoum, Sudan, and an old mujahideen camp site in Afghanistan. (One missile went four hundred miles off course and landed in Pakistan.) Both missile targets had been identified by American intelligence as enterprises or training areas associated with bin Laden or his followers. It was soon revealed, however, that the intelligence on both places had been faulty and that neither target could be connected with those who were suspected of attacking the embassies. On September 2, 1998, the U.S. secretary of defense said that he had been unaware that the plant in Khartoum made medicines, not nerve gas, when he recommended that it be attacked. He also admitted that the plant's connection to bin Laden was, at best, "indirect." Nonetheless, President Clinton continued to insist that he had repelled an "imminent threat to our national security," and Secretary of State Madeleine Albright called Sudan a "viper's nest of terrorists."

Government spokesmen continue to justify these attacks as "deterring" terrorism, even if the targets proved to be irrelevant to any damage done to facilities of the United States. In this way, future blowback possibilities are seeded into the world. The same spokesmen ignore the fact that the alleged mastermind of the embassy bombings, bin Laden, is a former protégé of the United States. When America was organizing Afghan rebels against the USSR in the 1980s, he played an important role in driving the Soviet Union from Afghanistan and only turned against the

United States in 1991 because he regarded the stationing of American troops in his native Saudi Arabia during and after the Persian Gulf War as a violation of his religious beliefs. Thus, the attacks on our embassies in Africa, if they were indeed his work, are an instance of blowback rather than unprovoked terrorism. Instead of bombing sites in Sudan and Afghanistan in response, the United States might better have considered reducing or removing our large-scale and provocative military presence in Saudi Arabia. . . .

In a sense, blowback is simply another way of saying that a nation reaps what it sows. Although people usually know what they have sown, our national experience of blowback is seldom imagined in such terms because so much of what the managers of the American empire have sown has been kept secret. As a concept, blowback is obviously most easy to grasp in its most straightforward manifestation. The unintended consequences of American policies and acts in country X are a bomb at an American embassy in country Y or a dead American in country Z. Certainly any number of Americans have been killed in that fashion, from Catholic nuns in El Salvador to tourists in Uganda who just happened to wander into hidden imperial scenarios about which they knew nothing. But blowback, as demonstrated in this book, is hardly restricted to such reasonably straightforward examples. . . .

I do not believe that America's "vast array of strategical commitments" were made in past decades largely as the result of attempts to exploit other nations for economic gain or simply to dominate them politically and militarily. Although the United States has in the past engaged in imperialist exploitation of other nations, particularly in Latin America, it has also tried in various ways to liquidate many such commitments. The roots of American "imperial overstretch" today are not the same as those of past empires. Instead they more closely resemble those that brought down the Soviet Union.

Many Americans do not care to see their country's acts, policies, or situations compared with the Soviet Union's; some condemn such a comparison because it commits the alleged fallacy of "moral equivalence." They insist that America's values and institutions are vastly more humane than those of Stalin's Russia. I agree. Throughout the years of the Cold War, the United States remained a functioning democracy, with rights for its citizens unimaginable in the Soviet context (even if its more recent maintenance of the world's largest prison population suggests that it should be cautious in criticizing other nations' systems of criminal justice). Comparisons between the United States and the former Soviet Union are useful, however, because those two hegemons developed in tandem, challenging each other militarily, economically, and ideologically. In the long run, it may turn out that, like two scorpions in a bottle, they succeeded in stinging each other to death. The roots of both modern empires lay in World War II and in their subsequent contest to control the forces that the war unleashed. A stress on the costs of the Cold War to the United States also draws attention to the legacies of that struggle. America's role as the planet's "lone superpower"—as leader of the peace-loving nations and patron of such institutions as the United Nations, the World Bank, and the World Trade Organization—is made much more difficult by the nature of the harvest we continue to reap for imprudent, often secret operations undertaken in the past. . . .

Terrorism by definition strikes at the innocent in order to draw attention to the sins of the invulnerable. The innocent of the twenty-first century are going to harvest unexpected blowback disasters from the imperialist escapades of recent decades. Although most Americans may be largely ignorant of what was, and still is, being done in their names, all are likely to pay a steep price—individually and collectively—for their nation's continued efforts to dominate the global scene. Before the damage of heedless triumphalist acts and the triumphalist rhetoric and propaganda that goes with them becomes irreversible, it is important to open a new discussion of our global role during and after the Cold War. . . .

The American military at the end of the century is becoming an autonomous system. We no longer have a draft army based on the obligation of citizens to serve their nation. When the Vietnam War exposed the inequities of the draft—for example, the ease with which college students could gain deferments—Congress decided to abolish conscription rather than enforce it in an equitable manner. Today, the military is an entirely mercenary force, made up of volunteers paid salaries by the Pentagon. Although the military still tries to invoke the public's support for a force made up of fellow citizens, this force is increasingly separated from civilian interests and devoted to military ones.

Equipped with the most advanced precision-guided munitions, high-performance aircraft, and intercontinental-range missiles, the American armed forces can unquestionably deliver death and destruction to any target on earth and expect little in the way of retaliation. Even so, these forces voraciously demand more and newer equipment, while the Pentagon now more or less sets its own agenda. Accustomed to life in a half-century-old, well-established empire, the corporate interests of the armed forces have begun to take precedence over the older idea that the military is only one of several means that a democratic government might employ to implement its policies. As their size and prominence grow over time, the armed forces of an empire tend to displace other instruments of foreign policy implementation. What also grows is militarism, "a vast array of customs, interests, prestige, actions, and thought associated with armies and wars and yet transcending true military purpose"—and certainly a reasonable description of the American military ethos today.

"Blowback" is shorthand for saying that a nation reaps what it sows, even if it does not fully know or understand what it has sown. Given its wealth and power, the United States will be a prime recipient in the foreseeable future of all of the more expectable forms of blowback, particularly terrorist attacks against Americans in and out of the armed forces anywhere on earth, including within the United States. But it is blowback in its larger aspect—the tangible costs of empire—that truly threatens it. Empires are costly operations, and they become more costly by the year. The hollowing out of American industry, for instance, is a form of blowback—an unintended negative consequence of American policy—even though it is seldom recognized as such. The growth of militarism in a once democratic society is another example of blowback. Empire is the problem. Even though the United States has a strong sense of invulnerability and substantial military and economic tools to make such a feeling credible, the fact of its imperial pretensions means that a crisis is inevitable. More imperialist projects simply generate more blowback. If we do not begin to solve problems in more prudent and modest ways, blowback will only become more intense.

PERMISSIONS ACKNOWLEDGMENTS

1. From *Democracy in America* by Alexis de Tocqueville, translated by Henry Reeve, published by Schoeken Books, 1961. Originally published in 1835.
2. From *The American Commonwealth* by James Bryce. Published by Macmillan, 1888.
3. Excerpts from *The Liberal Tradition in America: An Interpretation of American Political Thought Since the Revolution*, copyright © 1955 and renewed 1983 by Louis Hartz, reprinted by permission of Harcourt, Inc.
4. From *Diminished Democracy: From Membership to Management in American Civic Life*, by Theda Skocpol. Copyright © 2003 by the University of Oklahoma Press, Norman, Publishing Division of the University. Reprinted by permission of the University of Oklahoma Press.
5. From *Race Matters*, by Cornel West. Copyright © 1993, 2001 by Cornel West. Reprinted by permission of Beacon Press, Boston.
6. From *People of Paradox* by Michael Kammen. Copyright © 1972 by Michael Kammen. Reprinted by permission of Alfred A. Knopf, a Division of Random House, Inc.
7. From *Habits of the Heart: Individualism and Commitment in American Life* by Robert Bellah, et al. Copyright © 1985, 1996 The Regents of the University of California. Reprinted by permission of The University of California Press.
8. From *The American Political Tradition* by Richard Hofstadter. Copyright © 1948 by Alfred A. Knopf, Inc. and renewed 1976 by Beatrice Hofstadter. Reprinted by permission of Alfred A. Knopf, a Division of Random House, Inc.
9. *The Federalist* 10, by James Madison, 1787.
10. From *A Machine That Would Go of Itself* by Michael Kammen (Knopf, 1986). Copyright © 1986 by Michael Kammen. Reprinted by permission of the author.
11. Reprinted with the permission of The Free Press, a division of Simon & Schuster Adult Publishing Group, from *The Tyranny of the Majority: Fundamental Fairness in Representative Democracy*, by Lani Guinier. Copyright © 1994 by Lani Guinier. All rights reserved.
12. From *The Power Elite, New Edition* by C. Wright Mills. Copyright © 1956, 2000 by Oxford University Press, Inc. Used by permission of Oxford University Press, Inc.
13. From Richard Zweigenhaft and G. William Domhoff, *Diversity in the Power*

48. Excerpts from *Miranda v. Arizona*, 384 U.S. 436, 86 S.Ct. 1602 (1966).
49. From *System Under Stress: Homeland Security and American Politics*, by Donald F. Kettl. Copyright © 2004 by CQ Press, a division of Congressional Quarterly, Inc. Reprinted by permission of Congressional Quarterly, Inc.
50. From *Simple Justice* by Richard Kluger. Copyright © 1975 by Richard Kluger. Reprinted by permission of Alfred A. Knopf, a division of Random House Inc.
51. From *All Deliberate Speed: Reflections on the First Half Century of Brown v. Board of Education*, by Charles J. Ogletree, Jr. Copyright © 2004 by Charles J. Ogletree, Jr. Used by permission of W. W. Norton & Company, Inc.
52. From pages 1–2, 82–83, 104–106, 112–115 from *From Identity to Politics: The Lesbian and Gay Movements in the United States*, by Craig A. Rimmerman. Used by permission of Temple University Press. Copyright © 2002 by Temple University. All Rights Reserved.
53. Eight pages from *In Our Defense* by Ellen Alderman and Caroline Kennedy. Copyright © 1991 by Ellen Alderman and Caroline Kennedy. Published by William Morrow & Company, Inc. Reprinted by permission of HarperCollins Publishers.
54. Reprinted with the permission of The Free Press, a Division of Simon & Schuster Adult Publishing Group, from *Rights Talk: The Impoverishment of Political Discourse* by Mary Ann Glendon. Copyright © 1991 by Mary Ann Glendon. All rights reserved.
55. Reprinted with the permission of Scribner, a Division of Simon & Schuster Adult Publishing Group, from *The Phantom Public* by Walter Lippmann. Copyright © 1925 by Walter Lippmann. Copyright © renewed 1953 by Walter Lippmann. All rights reserved.
56. From *Public Opinion and American Democracy* by V. O. Key, published by Alfred Knopf, 1961. Permission granted by the executors of the Key Estate.
57. From *Direct Democracy: The Politics of Initiative, Reform, and Recall*, by Thomas Cronin, pp. 1–3, 5, 6, 10–12, 196–199, 222, Cambridge, Mass.: Harvard University Press, Copyright © 1989 by the Twentieth Century Fund, Inc. Reprinted by permission of Harvard University Press.
58. From *Politicians Don't Pander: Political Manipulation and the Loss of Democratic Responsiveness* by Lawrence R. Jacobs and Robert Y. Shapiro. Copyright © 2000 by The University of Chicago. Used by permission of the University of Chicago Press.
59. From *Democracy in America* by Alexis de Tocqueville, translated by Henry Reeve, published by Schoeken Books, 1961. Originally published 1835.
60. Excerpts from *The Semisovereign People: A Realist's View of Democracy in America, 1st Edition*, by E. E. Schattschneider. Copyright © 1961. Reprinted by permission of Wadsworth, a division of Thompson Learning: www.thompsonrights.com. FAX 800 730-2215.
61. From *The End of Liberalism: The Second Republic of the United States*, Second Edition, by Theodore J. Lowi. Copyright © 1979, 1969 by W. W. Norton & Company, Inc. Used by permission of W. W. Norton & Company, Inc.
62. From *The Lobbyists*, by Jeffrey Birnbaum. Copyright © 1992 by Jeffrey Birnbaum. Used by permission of Times Books, a division of Random House, Inc.
63. Reprinted with the permission of Simon & Schuster Adult Publishing Group